Crime and Justice in America, 1975–2025

Associate Editors
Philip J. Cook
Francis T. Cullen
Anthony N. Doob
Jeffrey A. Fagan
Daniel S. Nagin

Crime and Justice in America, 1975–2025

Edited by Michael Tonry

Crime and Justice
A Review of Research
Edited by Michael Tonry

VOLUME 42

The University of Chicago Press, Chicago and London

The University of Chicago Press, Chicago 60637
The University of Chicago Press, Ltd., London

© 2013 by The University of Chicago
All rights reserved.
Printed in the United States of America

ISSN: 0192-3234

ISBN: 978-0-226-09751-0

LCN: 80-642217

Library of Congress Cataloging-in-Publication Data

Crime and justice in America: 1975–2025 / edited by Michael Tonry.
    pages cm — (Crime and justice , ISSN 0192-3234 ; volume 42)
  "Initial drafts of the essays in this book were presented as public lectures at the Robina
Institute Annual Conference at the University of Minnesota Law School in Minneapolis
in April 2012 and were discussed at a seminar, also in Minneapolis, the following two
days."—Preface.
    Includes bibliographical references and index.
    ISBN 978-0-226-09751-0 (cloth) — ISBN 978-0-226-10592-5 (paperback) 1. Criminal
justice, Administration of—United States—History. 2. Criminology—United States—
History. I. Tonry, Michael H., editor. II. Series: Crime and justice (Chicago, Ill.) ; v. 42.
HV6001.C672 vol. 42
364.973—dc23

                                                                                    2013024648

The paper used in this publication meets the minimum requirements of American
National Standard for Information Sciences—Permanence of Paper for Printed
Library Materials, ANSI Z39.48-1984. ∞

Contents

Preface

The development of a large and productive community of criminal justice programs, scholars, and researchers in the United States since the 1970s has not led to the emergence of a general norm of evidence-based policy making. Nor on many subjects have accumulations of improved knowledge had much influence. On a few they have. The two best examples of influence are policing and early childhood prevention programs. Concerning policing, a plausible story can be told of an iterative process of research showing that police practices and methods do and do not achieve sought-after results, followed by successive changes in how policing is done. Concerning early childhood programs, a conventional scientific process of hypothesis testing and repeated pilot projects with strong evaluations led to widespread adoption of improved programs and techniques. Concerning sentencing, sanctioning policies, firearms and violence, and drug policy, by contrast, strong bodies of accumulating evidence have consistently been ignored. Correctional rehabilitation research is a hybrid. Eclipsed in the 1970s by a gloomy view that "nothing works," research on correctional treatment in the 1980s and 1990s demonstrated that a wide variety of programs can improve offenders' lives and reduce reoffending. The findings have influenced the development of reentry and other programs that focus primarily on risk classification and reduction of recidivism rates, but only incidentally on addressing offenders' social welfare needs.

The essays in this volume tell those research-and-policy stories. The writers are *Crime and Justice* recidivists who have previously several times written essays summarizing what was then known about their subjects. This time they were asked to write intellectual histories, telling how research and policy have evolved over time, and why, where things now stand, and what they expect to happen in coming years.

No one expects that research findings will automatically and inevitably influence policy decisions. The policy process is too complex for that. It is nonetheless striking how little influence research findings have had. There are two principal reasons.

The first is that most people, including politicians, have strong intuitions about the calculations of offenders and the preventive effects of sanctions. The National Commission on Law Observance and Enforcement, better known as the Wickersham Commission after its chairman US Attorney General George Wickersham, in 1931 noted, "Most of those . . . who speak on American criminal justice assume certain things to be well known or incontrovertible." Harvard Law School professor and later Supreme Court Justice Felix Frankfurter averred that crime and crime control are subjects "overlaid with shibboleths and clichés." University of Chicago Law School professor Norval Morris observed that "people are born experts on the causes and control of crime; they sense the solutions in their bones. Those solutions differ dramatically from person to person, but each one knows, and knows deeply and emotionally, that his perspective is the way of truth."

The strength of those intuitions is one reason why scientific evidence in recent years has not had much influence in shaping the American criminal justice system. Another, more powerful reason is political. Ideological conservatives, mostly Republicans, long ago recognized that "tough on crime" policies, whatever their effectiveness or injustice, could be used as "wedge issues" to separate white and working class Americans from their traditional support of liberal politicians. That strategy worked. For nearly 40 years, conservative political values have dominated criminal justice policy making. That minority and disadvantaged people, who typically vote Democratic, have disproportionately borne the brunt of harsh drug and crime control policies, rather than white conservative voters, who typically vote Republican, has not been coincidental.

Conservative politicians also often have a moralistic outlook on crime and drug use, seeing them only as the products of bad choices of individuals, regardless of what is known about the complicated causes of crime and drug dependence and the troubled lives of most offenders. As Alfred Blumstein and Joan Petersilia put it, "It may be that the policies intended to address crime and criminal justice are so strongly driven by fundamental ideological convictions" that policy makers do not want "to confront empirical reality because that might undermine their deeply held beliefs."

The best available evidence about the likely effects of alternate policy choices ought to matter. In the end, policy makers might find evidence incomplete, ambiguous, or unconvincing. They might conclude that political considerations, ideology, or self-interest outweighs it. Nonetheless, it is hardly a radical proposal that evidence should at least be aired and considered.

Contemporary politicians may prefer to set policy in evidence-free zones, but that has not always been true. For much of the twentieth century until the 1970s, criminal justice policy was not a field of ideological combat or a captive of partisan politics. It is not inevitable that politicians will continue to be oblivious to scientific evidence about the effects of the policies they choose. When the change comes, books like this one will be of use.

Initial drafts of the essays in this book were presented as public lectures at the Robina Institute annual conference at the University of Minnesota Law School in Minneapolis in April 2012 and were discussed at a seminar, also in Minneapolis, the following two days. That conference and seminar were attended by the writers and also by Wim Bernasco (Netherlands Institute for the Study of Crime and Law Enforcement), Gerben Bruinsma (Netherlands Institute for the Study of Crime and Law Enforcement), Anthony Doob (University of Toronto), Antony Duff (University of Minnesota), John Eck (University of Cincinnati), Barry Feld (University of Minnesota), Thomas Feucht (National Institute of Justice), Jeffrey Fagan (Columbia University), Richard Frase (University of Minnesota), Rosemary Gartner (University of Toronto), Ted Gest (Jerry Lee Center of Criminology, University of Pennsylvania), David Hemenway (Harvard), Zach Hoskins (University of Minnesota), Candace Kruttschnitt (University of Toronto), Sandra Marshall (University of Minnesota), Perry Moriearty (University of Minnesota), Joshua Page (University of Minnesota), Alex Piquero (University of Texas at Dallas), Kevin Reitz (University of Minnesota), Richard Rosenfeld (University of Missouri–St. Louis), Francis Shen (University of Minnesota), Michael Smith (University of Minnesota), Cassia Spohn (Arizona State University), and Chris Uggen (University of Minnesota). Sixteen people served as anonymous reviewers of the initial drafts. David Hanbury and Robbi Strandemo, with help from University of Minnesota law students Amanda Ruiz and Reece Almond, organized the conference and seminar. Su Smallen and Robbi Strandemo prepared the manuscripts for publication and coordinated the handling of edited copy and proofs. Support for the conference and seminar was provided by the National Institute of Justice, US Department of Justice, under grant CON000000033717. Additional support for the seminar and for preparation of this volume was provided by the Robina Foundation as part of its award to the University of Minnesota Law School to establish the Robina Institute of Criminal Law and Criminal Justice. I am grateful to them all.

Michael Tonry
Bologna, Italy, August 2013

Michael Tonry

Evidence, Ideology, and Politics in the Making of American Criminal Justice Policy

Criminal justice policy and research in the United States have mostly marched in different directions since the mid-1970s. Sizable bodies of high-quality research have accumulated on many subjects on which policy making in a rational world would be evidence based, but only on a few have they had substantial influence. Policy making on some subjects has occurred mostly in an evidence-free zone. The comparatively slight influence of scientific research findings is a modest payoff from 50 years of public investment. The report of the President's Commission on Law Enforcement and Administration of Justice, *The Challenge of Crime in a Free Society*, observed that "what has been found to be the greatest need is the need to know" (1967, p. 273) and that "we need to know much more about crime. A national strategy against crime must be in large part a strategy of research" (p. 270). "Accurate data are the beginning of wisdom," likewise observed America's first national crime commission, the Wickersham Commission (National Commission on Law Observance and Enforcement 1931, p. 3), in recommending a plan for creating a body of knowledge "covering crime, criminals, criminal justice, and penal treatment" at federal, state, and local levels and proposing to entrust this task to a single federal agency.

The 1967 President's Commission proposed the establishment of an independent national institute on criminal justice research equivalent to the National Science Foundation or the National Institutes of Health. The US Congress in the Omnibus Crime Control and Safe Streets Act of 1968 established the Law Enforcement Assistance Administration (LEAA), with an embedded research institute, inside the US Department of Justice. Within a few years, billions of dollars were appropriated to fund justice system improvements and research.

LEAA funding for police education in the 1970s catalyzed the establishment of criminal justice and criminology programs throughout the United States.[1] They proliferated, and some matured into world-class institutions. In 1970, there were but a handful of criminology programs, mostly within sociology departments. Most awarded degrees in traditional social science disciplines. Today there are hundreds of undergraduate criminal justice and criminology departments. In many universities, they are among the largest, fastest-growing, and most popular degree programs. Forty or more universities offer criminal justice and criminology doctorates,[2] and many more are granted on related topics in other social science disciplines.

Criminal justice and criminological research blossomed. By fostering cadres of research professionals, the new university departments created a mass of intellectual capital that had never before existed in the United States or any other country. Large high-quality literatures accumulated, specialist research journals thrived, and research-based understanding of the causes of crime and the operation of criminal justice institutions and processes advanced substantially. Subjects in which notable progress was made include policing, sentencing, the effects of sanctions, rehabilitation of offenders, firearms and violence, drug policy, and developmental criminology.

Despite those advances, however, the members of the President's Commission—assuming that some are still paying attention—would have little cause for delight about the influence of research on policy making. Their aim was not to motivate expansion and improvement of education and research as ends in themselves but as means to facilitate the development of evidenced-based methods for preventing crime and

---

[1] LEAA itself survived for less than a decade. Stories of its problems and its demise are told in Cronin, Cronin, and Milakovich (1981) and Feeley and Sarat (1981).

[2] In 2012, the Association of Doctoral Programs in Criminology and Criminal Justice (ADPCJ) had 35 US members. The ADPCJ is a membership association of which in 2012 half were in the Southeast and only two on the West Coast, suggesting that the total number of PhD-granting programs is significantly larger (Huebner et al. 2012). Chris Eskridge, executive director of the American Society of Criminology, reports that Google searches identify more than 1,700 undergraduate degree programs of which, discounting for low-quality online programs and diploma mills, he estimates 700–800 are "relatively valid undergraduate criminology/criminal justice programs in the United States" (personal communication, May 2, 2013).

creating more just, effective, and economical criminal justice systems. From that perspective, the policy payoffs on the national investment in a research infrastructure have been much less than the commission's members must have hoped for.

No one would expect well-vetted, reliable research findings inexorably, automatically, or easily to shape or influence policy decisions. Vested interests, politics, competing priorities, and personalities all have roles to play. The limited influence of scientific knowledge on criminal justice policy in the United States since the early 1980s nonetheless remains conspicuous. In the pages that follow, I discuss influences and processes that have limited the role of evidence. Section I discusses illustrative realms in which evidence has and has not mattered. Section II steps back to discuss the unfortunately named "research utilization" literature, which provides frameworks for understanding and vocabulary for discussing the influence of scientific findings on policy. Section III steps to the side to discuss the development of specialized government research institutes and university departments and the comparative failure of the National Institute of Justice to serve as a federal engine for developing scientific knowledge and motivating the development of evidence-based policies. The President's Commission members cannot have expected a single federal agency to shape a nation's policy processes, but they could reasonably have hoped that it would provide leadership and a model for the states. Section IV considers why the initiatives the President's Commission set in motion did not generate the evidence-based, or at least evidence-informed, policy processes they imagined.

I. When Evidence Has and Has Not Mattered

Research-derived evidence influences policy and practice in some places, at some times, and on some subjects. Sometimes research matters, sometimes not. The time, the place, and the subject are important. The salience of research to developments in policing and sentencing provides a stark contrast of success and failure.

The world of policing has been permeable to and influenced by research since the mid-1970s. Policing scholars—notably including John Eck, Herman Goldstein, George Kelling, Stephen Mastrofsky, Mark H. Moore, Lawrence W. Sherman, Wesley G. Skogan, Michael E. Smith, David Weisburd, and James Q. Wilson—have been in the middle of successive transformations of American policing. Research in the 1970s concluded that some traditional practices—rapid response to calls, street patrol, and motorized patrol—were less effective than police had long believed and undermined support for top-down professional policing. Work by Herman Goldstein and others importantly influenced the development and dispersion of community and problem-oriented policing. Work by Lawrence Sherman and others on "hot spots," crackdowns, and geographic information systems led to major changes in police practice. Major research programs carried out or funded by the Police Foundation, the Police Executive Research Forum, and the National Institute of Justice tested and evaluated the effects of new initiatives and contributed to their refinement. Research and evidence have not been the only or the deciding influences on policy changes, but they have had influence and made a difference.[3]

Research on sentencing topics paralleled police research in the 1970s in undermining traditional ways of doing criminal justice business, for example, correctional treatment programs, discretionary parole release, and voluntary sentencing guidelines. After 1980, however, neither positive nor negative research findings were influential. Evaluations showed that parole guidelines and presumptive sentencing guidelines sometimes achieved their goals of reducing disparities, increasing consistency, and facilitating correctional planning and budgeting, but few states adopted either. Conversely, evaluations showed that voluntary sentencing guidelines seldom if ever reduced disparities, but states continued to establish them. Research in the 1970s and 1980s showed that mandatory minimum sentences had few or no deterrent effects, were often circumvented, and often resulted in unjustly severe punishments, but every state and the federal government enacted new ones in the 1980s and 1990s. The national American decline in crime rates since 1991, unprecedented imprisonment rates and costs, and the great recession of recent years have not resulted in major changes in sentencing laws.[4] Evidence of the effectiveness of the signature laws of the tough on crime period—mandatory minimums, truth-in-sentencing, three-strikes, life without possibility of parole—remains as exiguous as it has been for 30 years, but so far states and the federal government have made few significant changes to them (Austin et al. 2013).

[3] Sherman (in this volume) cites and discusses the relevant literature.
[4] Tonry (in this volume) cites and discusses the relevant literature.

Evidence on other subjects has been as influential as concerning policing and as little heeded as concerning sentencing. Large, sophisticated literatures have developed on drug law enforcement,[5] firearms and violence,[6] and deterrent effects of sanctions.[7] There is strong evidence that mass arrests of street-level drug dealers had little or no effect on drug sales, use, or availability but filled prisons with young, disadvantaged, minority inmates; that firearms make violent crimes more dangerous, elevate American homicide rates, and result in high rates of suicidal and accidental deaths and injuries; and that making sanctions more severe has either no discernible crime-preventive effects or effects that are so highly context specific as not to be salient to setting general policies. In each case, the evidence documents failures of current policies and massive undesirable consequences. The evidence has almost entirely been ignored.

Large, sophisticated literatures have likewise accumulated on correctional treatment programs[8] and developmental interventions targeting factors in early childhood associated with high rates of delinquency and antisocial behavior.[9] Well-designed, managed, and targeted rehabilitative programs of many kinds have been shown to have positive effects on offenders' personal deficits and problems and on subsequent offending. Developmental researchers have identified a wide range of risk and protective factors related to problem behaviors and have developed, tested, and implemented interventions that change young people's lives for the better. Policy makers have leapt on both sets of findings. Public and private investments in correctional treatments and early childhood interventions have increased substantially.

II. When and Whether Evidence Matters

Social science evidence has influenced policy making on some subjects at some times but not on others. Since the 1970s, writers on "research utilization" have been trying to figure out when and why evidence matters (e.g., Lindblom and Cohen 1979). An early National Research Council report, *Knowledge and Policy: The Uncertain Connection*, noted

---

[5] Reuter (in this volume) cites and discusses the relevant literature.

[6] Cook (in this volume) cites and discusses the relevant literature.

[7] Nagin (in this volume) cites and discusses the relevant literature.

[8] Cullen (in this volume) cites and discusses the relevant literature.

[9] Farrington (in this volume) cites and discusses the relevant literature.

that numerous social science studies of policy interventions by then had accumulated and numerous efforts had been made to increase their relevance to policy making, but it observed that "we lack systematic evidence as to whether these steps are having the results their sponsors hope for" (Lynn 1978, p. 5). In 2012, another National Research Council report, *Using Science as Evidence in Public Policy*, concluded that the connection between social science knowledge and policy remained "uncertain" and that "despite their considerable value in other respects, studies of knowledge utilization have not advanced understanding of the use of evidence in the policy process much beyond the decades-old National Research Council (1977) report" (Prewitt, Schwandt, and Straf 2012, p. 51).

Scholarship on research utilization has long been skeptical of bu-reaucratic rationality models and of the idea that policy decisions do or should flow more or less directly from scientific evidence. The 2012 National Research Council report observed that "some mixture of pol-itics, values, and science will be present in any but the most trivial of policy choices. It follows that use of science as evidence can never be a purely 'scientific' matter; and necessarily be used just because it is available. . . . Re-election concerns, interest group pressure, and polit-ical or moral values may be given more weight and may draw on rea-sons outside the sphere of what science has to say about likely conse-quences" (Prewitt, Schwandt, and Straf 2012, pp. 15, 17).

The literature on research utilization is simultaneously mundane and creative.[10] It is mundane in the sense that experienced policy makers, and others familiar with policy processes, will find little in it that is surprising. Few in either category will be surprised to learn that evi-dence seldom influences policy or practice directly. For evidence to matter, officials must be aware of it; they must consider it credible; they must think its implications important; they must believe the effort required to change policies is worth the hassle involved; and they must be prepared to work to overcome a series of political, ideological, and bureaucratic obstacles. Nothing surprising there.

The literature is creative in that it provides frameworks and vocab-ularies that illuminate issues and aid in understanding why some at-tempts at change succeed and others fail. Charles Lindblom and David

---

[10] More detailed discussion, including citations to major sources, can be found in Tonry (1998) and Tonry and Green (2003).

Cohen (1979), in the classic work on this subject, explored ways in which learning generated by systematic research, which they called "professional social inquiry" (PSI), influences policy. PSI can influence policy, they say, only when "social learning" has occurred that can overcome the influence of "ordinary knowledge." On important issues, change is difficult until social learning has produced new attitudes and political dispositions.

David Green and I have shown the importance of "windows of opportunity" (Tonry and Green 2003). Some policy options are politically or bureaucratically imaginable at some times but not at others. The assassinations of Robert F. Kennedy and Martin Luther King in 1968, for example, created windows of opportunity through which evidence about the negative public health effects of handguns could pass and lead to the enactment of federal gun control legislation. Windows of opportunity in some ways exist in the eyes of their beholders. National Rifle Association members might describe the 1968 assassinations that catalyzed major federal gun control legislation as a "moral panic" (Cohen 1972), in the same way I would use the term to refer to the deaths of Len Bias, Megan Kanka, and Polly Klass that precipitated enactment of the federal 100-to-1 crack cocaine sentencing law, "Megan's laws" throughout the United States, and California's three-strikes law. The late 1980s rise in youth violence that led to the short-lived invention of "superpredators" likewise fueled unprecedentedly harsh policies toward juveniles in the early 1990s.[11]

Carole Weiss (1986) showed that in any place and time, boundaries exist beyond which change is not possible or even politically imaginable. Public opinion pollster Daniel Yankelovich (1991) extended the notion to explore the "boundaries of public permission" outside of which policy changes are unlikely, but within which change is possible if advocates and public officials are prepared to invest the necessary effort. Windows of opportunity open in particular places at particular times; policy prescriptions that attempt to push social learning too far are not taken seriously (Stolz 2001).[12]

Finally, the influence of systematic evidence on policy depends on

[11] Zimring (in this volume) cites and discusses the relevant literature.

[12] Distinct literatures on research utilization focus on policy (e.g., Lindblom and Cohen 1979; Weiss, Murphy-Graham, and Birkeland 2005) and practice (e.g., Walter, Nutley, and Davies 2005) settings. Education, medicine, and public health are much more often the focus of the literature than criminal justice.

the permeability of a series of filters through which the evidence must pass (Tonry and Green 2003, pp. 486–89). One is the filter of prevailing paradigms and ways of thinking. Others are prevailing ideology, short-term political considerations, and short-term bureaucratic consider-ations (and inertia).

The obstacles to the adoption of policies based on systematic evi-dence, alas, are far easier to describe than to overcome.[13] Whether policy makers in particular places and times pay attention to research evidence depends on the subject. An extreme instance of obliviousness to evidence can be seen in the English Labour government's handling of its Crime Reduction Programme. Created in 1999 and promoted as an exercise in the development of evidence-based policies and practices, it was budgeted at £400 million over 10 years. Ten percent of the initial funding was set aside for independent evaluations of pilot and dem-onstration projects. The program was abandoned within 3 years for a variety of reasons, the most important of which was that the govern-ment knew what it wanted to do and in the end was not much inter-ested in receiving independent assessments of whether what it wanted to do actually worked (Maguire 2004; Nutley and Homel 2006).

Sometimes, governments are so committed to policies that they do not want to know whether they are effective. The American "war on drugs" is one classic example. Political scientist James Q. Wilson more than two decades ago, for example, observed that "significant reduc-tions in drug abuse will come only from reducing demand for those drugs. . . . [The] marginal product of further investment in supply reduction is likely to be small." He reported "that I know of no serious law-enforcement official who disagrees with this conclusion. Typically, police officials tell interviewers that they are fighting a losing war or, at best, a holding action" (1990, p. 534). At about the same time, New York Senator Daniel Patrick Moynihan observed, "Interdiction and 'drug busts' are probably necessary symbolic acts, but nothing more" (1993, p. 362).

A classic example of not wanting to know is California Governor Pete Wilson's statement, when vetoing legislation creating a commis-sion to study the effects of California three-strikes law, that the legis-lation's aim was to "disprove the obvious positive impact of the Three-

---

[13] Joan Petersilia has written several important articles on the influence of knowledge on policy that sketch out all the problems (e.g., Petersilia 1991, 2008; Blumstein and Petersilia 1995).

Strikes law. . . . There are many mysteries in life, but the efficiency of 'Three-Strikes' . . . is not one of them" (California District Attorneys Association 2004, p. 32). Another is provided by the unwillingness of Tony Blair's English Labour government to evaluate the preventive effects of its trademark Antisocial Behaviour Orders initiative (National Audit Office 2006).[14]

On some subjects, especially those that implicate contested normative and ideological concerns in particular times and places, such as capital punishment or severity of sentences, or strong emotional support such as drug courts or Megan's laws, evidence seldom makes much difference. On other subjects, especially concerning the police or policies that can be characterized as primarily technological (e.g., the crime-preventive effects of ignition locks or changes in credit card security), evidence has often been influential. For subjects falling in the great middle, evidence might or might not matter depending on the political and policy weight of considerations that point in other directions.

III. Institutional Infrastructures for Developing Evidence- Based Policies

What we now think of as the established social sciences began in the late nineteenth and early twentieth centuries. Social scientists of crime from the early days sought to develop evidence for informing policy making. In midcentury in the United States and other English-speaking countries, government officials invested in infrastructure for developing evidentiary bases for policy.

In the nineteenth and early twentieth centuries, the leading European criminologists were based in universities but were engaged deeply with the world. Gabriel Tarde in France; Franz von Liszt in Germany; Cesare Lombroso, Rafaele Garofalo, and Enrico Ferri in Italy; and Willem Bonger and Willem Pompe in the Netherlands all were con-

---

[14] Antisocial Behaviour Orders targeted noncriminal nuisance behaviors including littering, "noisy neighbors," street begging, prostitution (not criminal in England), and, famously in policy debates, children playing ball in the street. The orders were issued in civil legal proceedings, but violating an order was a criminal offense punishable by a prison term up to 5 years (Tonry 2010). The National Audit Office of England and Wales observed of Antisocial Behaviour Orders: "The absence of formal evaluation by the Home Office of the success of different interventions . . . prevents local areas targeting interventions in the most efficient way to achieve the best outcome" (2006, p. 5).

cerned centrally with the criminal justice policies of their times. Ferri (1921) drafted a complete proposed criminal code for Italy predicated on then-current knowledge about risk prediction (Tonry 2004).

Criminology in the United States dates from the early twentieth century. Early American criminologists, like the Europeans, were focused on the policy relevance of their work. Thorsten Sellin, the distinguished professor of sociology at the University of Pennsylvania, was actively and influentially engaged in the 1930s and 1940s in policy debates concerning capital punishment and racial disparities in the justice system. The major figures in the "Chicago School of Criminology" were doing equivalent things. Ernest W. Burgess in the 1920s laid a foundation for 50 years of quantitative research on parole decision making and recidivism prediction that provided PhD topics for three generations of celebrated sociologists including Lloyd Ohlin, Daniel Glaser, Dudley Duncan, and Albert J. Reiss Jr. (Harcourt 2006). Robert E. Park, Frederick Thrasher, Clifford Shaw, and William F. Whyte wrote classic works on gangs and on individual offenders in connection with the Chicago Area Project's street work projects (Schlossman and Sedlak 1983; Schlossman 1985). Sheldon and Eleanor Glueck's path-breaking delinquency studies were undertaken to provide a knowledge base for his detailed proposals for the reform of sentencing (Glueck 1928).

In the English-speaking countries, the earliest specialist criminology programs in universities were created with the purpose of aiding in the formulation of evidence-based criminal justice policies. The first, the School of Criminology at the University of California, Berkeley, was founded in 1950 with a "commitment to the extension and improvement of police training," under the leadership of August Vollmer, who combined a scholarly career with a professional career as a police executive (Morris 1975, p. 127). The aim of the first Australian criminology department, established in Melbourne in 1951, was the "development of a research base on crime and punishment which might then inform more effective and just policy" (Finnane 1998, p. 73). Richard A. Butler, the English Home Secretary who precipitated and provided funding to support the establishment in 1959 of the Cambridge Institute of Criminology, the first British university-based program, often spoke of his belief that research findings would show the way to the prevention of crime and the treatment of offenders (Radzinowicz 1999; Hood 2002). Butler later observed that "the money spent on research . . . could be expected to earn 'enormous dividends,' not least by reducing crime" (1974, p. 2). He also established the Home Office Research Unit, the first serious government-based criminal justice research program.

In the United States, the President's Commission on Law Enforcement and Administration of Justice (1967) proposed establishment of a National Foundation for Criminal Research as an independent agency patterned on the National Science Foundation. The Omnibus Crime Control and Safe Streets Act of 1968 created LEAA, which contained the National Institute of Law Enforcement and Criminal Justice (NILECJ). This arrangement proved unstable. *Understanding Crime*, a National Research Council report on NILECJ's early years, described a deeply troubled agency (White and Krislov 1977).

The National Institute of Justice survived the elimination of LEAA, emerging in the Justice Systems Improvement Act of 1979 as an incorporated agency under the umbrella of the US Department of Justice's Office of Justice Assistance, Research, and Statistics (now the Office of Justice Programs). Arguments again were made concerning the need for independence of the research agency, on the National Science Foundation model, but were unsuccessful. Attorney General Griffin Bell, for example, in a memo to the president noted that "a major cause of weakness in LEAA's research programs has been the failure to insulate research activities from the demands of policy makers and program managers for immediate results" (quoted in Early 1979, p. 357). Bert Early, executive director of the American Bar Association, testifying in favor of creation of an independent National Institute of Justice outside the Department of Justice, noted, "A research institute which is part of an 'action agency' such as the Department of Justice will inevitably be influenced and shaped by the Department's policy decisions and operational needs. Numerous studies of the current National Institute of Law Enforcement and Criminal Justice have cited such pressures as primary causes of the Institute's disappointing record in performing justice research" (1979, p. 357). Another National Research Panel examined the research programs of the National Institute of Justice in 2010 and reached conclusions unhappily similar to those of its third of a century earlier predecessor (White and Krislov 1977; Wellford, Chemers, and Schuck 2010).

The creation of governmental institutions that sponsor and fund research, the development of university departments in criminal justice and criminology, and the accumulation of large sophisticated scientific literatures have not resulted in the development of evidence-based policies as a norm in American criminal justice systems. The next section considers reasons why.

IV. Why Does Evidence So Often Fail to Influence Policy?

The development of a large and productive community of criminal justice programs, scholars, and researchers has not led to the emergence of evidence-based policies. Improved knowledge has had little demonstrable influence on many subjects. On a few it has. The two best examples are policing and early childhood prevention programs. Concerning policing, a plausible story can be told of an iterative process of research showing that police practices and methods did and did not achieve sought-after results and successive changes in police practices. Concerning early childhood programs, knowledge has slowly accumulated as part of a conventional process of hypothesis testing and pilot projects with strong evaluations. Concerning sentencing, firearms and violence, drug policy, and sanctioning policies, strong bodies of accumulating evidence have been consistently ignored.

Correctional rehabilitation programs are a hybrid case. Research findings in the 1970s that purported to show that "nothing works" led to major reductions in funding and programming. New work by Canadian researchers in the 1980s and 1990s showed that well-designed, implemented, managed, and targeted programs can reduce reoffending and sparked revived interest in rehabilitation programs.

Any effort to explain why evidence on most policy subjects has not mattered must be speculative. Simple allusion to the cautions contained in the research utilization literature by itself is not an explanation since in policing and early childhood prevention it has long been reasonable to speak of evidence-based policies. The same thing can more recently be said of rehabilitation programs. The early childhood programs may be *sui generis*, in large part because research funding has mostly come from human services agencies, federal science agencies such as the National Institutes of Health, and private foundations, and programs generally do not require legislation to be established (Farrington and Welsh 2007). It may also be that children who may or may not become criminals elicit much more sympathy than do adult offenders whose lives were shaped by the risk factors that early childhood programs attempt to ameliorate.

Policing changes also can usually be adopted and implemented without need for authorizing legislation, but that cannot be the whole story. Policing research has often been funded by the National Institute of Justice, and federal legislation has often enabled changes. The US Congress has regularly authorized funding for police innovation. The most likely explanation is that politicians "trust" police more than they trust other criminal justice officials. David Boerner (1995) long ago persuasively offered a similar explanation for why legislators in the 1980s and 1990s enacted laws that took discretion away from parole boards and judges and gave it instead to prosecutors. Elected and politically vetted prosecutors could be relied on to be "tough on crime." Judges and parole boards, who worry about making just and sensible decisions in individual cases, could not.

That may explain both why evidence-based policing has emerged and why evidence-based sentencing, sanctioning, drug policy, and gun policy have not. Conservatives, mostly Republicans, long ago recognized that "tough on crime" policies, whatever their effectiveness or injustice, could be used as "wedge issues" to separate white and working class Americans from their traditional support of liberal politicians (Edsall and Edsall 1991). That strategy has worked. For nearly 40 years, conservative political values have dominated criminal justice policy making. That minority and disadvantaged people, who typically vote Democratic if they vote at all, have disproportionately borne the brunt of harsh drug and crime control policies, rather than white conservative voters, has not been coincidental (Massey 2007; Alexander 2010; Tonry 2011).

Conservative politicians also often have a moralistic outlook on crime and drug use, seeing them only as the products of bad choices of individuals, regardless of what is known about the complicated causes of crime and drug dependence and the troubled backgrounds of most offenders. As Alfred Blumstein and Joan Petersilia put it, "It may be that the policies intended to address crime and criminal justice are so strongly driven by fundamental ideological convictions" that policy makers do not want "to confront empirical reality because that might undermine their deeply held beliefs" (1995, p. 468). It should not be surprising if many policy makers, already possessed of what they see as truth, are not easy to persuade about the merits of substantial, long-term public investment in the acquisition of knowledge about crime and its control.

The best available evidence about the likely effects of alternative policy choices ought to make a difference. In the end, policy makers might find evidence incomplete, ambiguous, or unconvincing. They might conclude that political considerations, ideology, or self-interest outweighs it. Nonetheless, it is hardly a radical proposal that evidence should at least be aired and considered. That is why the term "evidence-based policy" is in vogue and why the word "rational" has long appeared in the titles of scholarly books and articles on policy subjects. Examples include Sheldon Glueck's "Principles of a Rational Penal Code" (1928), Nigel Walker's *Sentencing in a Rational Society* (1969), and Norval Morris's and my *Between Prison and Probation: Intermediate Punishments in a Rational Sentencing System* (1990).

Evidence is intellectually and socially important on all the subjects discussed in this essay. Even concerning the relatively impervious issues such as capital punishment and sentencing severity, evidence sharpens the debates and clarifies what the issues really are. It is important to show and know, for example, that no credible empirical evidence suggests that capital punishment is an effective deterrent of homicide (Nagin and Pepper 2012). If the evidence is absent or unclear, then people who support the death penalty for ideological reasons, but feel uncomfortable saying so, can hide behind claims that they support capital punishment as a means to saving innocent victims' lives. If the evidence does not show that the threat of death deters homicide, then the debate must be made in the moral terms that really motivate opponents and supporters. Likewise, if the evidence shows that California's three-strikes law had no discernible effects on crime patterns or trends, its defenders should be required to defend the savage sentences it requires in moral terms. That is a good thing.

REFERENCES

Alexander, Michelle. 2010. *The New Jim Crow: Mass Incarceration in the Age of Colorblindedness*. New York: New Press.
Austin, James, Eric Cadora, Todd R. Clear, Kara Dansky, Judith Greene, Vanita Gupta, Marc Mauer, Nicole Porter, Susan Tucker, and Malcolm C. Young.

2013. *Ending Mass Incarceration: Charting a New Justice Reinvestment.* Washington, DC: Sentencing Project.

Blumstein, Alfred, and Joan Petersilia. 1995. "Investing in Criminal Justice Research." In *Crime*, edited by James Q. Wilson and Joan Petersilia. San Francisco: ICS Press.

Boerner, David. 1995. "Sentencing Guidelines and Prosecutorial Discretion." *Judicature* 78:196–200.

Butler, Richard Austen. 1974. "The Foundation of the Institute of Criminology in Cambridge." In *Crime, Criminology, and Public Policy*, edited by Roger Hood. London: Heinemann.

California District Attorneys Association. 2004. *Prosecutors' Perspectives on California's Three Strikes Law: A 10-Year Retrospective.* Sacramento: California District Attorneys Association.

Cohen, Stanley. 1972. *Folk Devils and Moral Panics.* New York: St. Martin's.

Cook, Philip J. In this volume. "The Great American Gun War: Notes from Four Decades in the Trenches."

Cronin, Thomas E., Tania Z. Cronin, and Michael E. Milakovich. 1981. *U.S. v. Crime in the Streets.* Bloomington: University of Indiana Press.

Cullen, Francis T. In this volume. "Rehabilitation: Beyond Nothing Works."

Early, Bert. 1979. "Testimony before the Senate Committee on the Judiciary, Tuesday, March 13, 1979." In *Hearings before the Committee of the Judiciary, United States Senate. 96th Congress, 1st Session, on S. 241.* February 9, 15, 28, and March 7, 13. Washington, DC: US Government Printing Office.

Edsall, Thomas, and Mary Edsall. 1991. *Chain Reaction: The Impact of Race, Rights, and Taxes on American Politics.* New York: Norton.

Farrington, David P. In this volume. "Longitudinal and Experimental Research in Criminology."

Farrington, David P., and Brandon C. Welsh. 2007. *Saving Children from a Life of Crime: Early Risk Factors and Effective Interventions.* New York: Oxford University Press.

Feeley, Malcolm M., and Austin D. Sarat. 1981. *The Policy Dilemma: Federal Crime Policy and the Law Enforcement Assistance Administration, 1968–1978.* Minneapolis: University of Minnesota Press.

Ferri, Enrico. 1921. *Relazione sul progetto preliminare di Codice Penale Italiano.* Rome: L'Universelle.

Finnane, Mark. 1998. "Sir John Barrie and the Melbourne Institute of Criminology." *Australian and New Zealand Journal of Criminology* 31:69–82.

Glueck, Sheldon. 1928. "Principles of a Rational Penal Code." *Harvard Law Review* 41(4):453–82.

Harcourt, Bernard E. 2006. *Against Prediction: Profiling, Policing, and Punishing in an Actuarial Age.* Chicago: University of Chicago Press.

Hood, Roger. 2002. "Criminology and Public Policy: The Vital Role of Empirical Research." In *Ideology, Crime, and Criminal Justice*, edited by Anthony Bottoms and Michael Tonry. Devon, UK: Willan.

Huebner, Beth, Pauline Brennan, Jennifer Roberts, and Scott Decker. 2012.

Association of Doctoral Programs in Criminology and Criminal Justice 2012 Survey Report. http://www.adpccj.com/documents/2012survey.pdf.

Lindblom, Charles E., and David Cohen. 1979. *Usable Knowledge.* New Haven, CT: Yale University Press.

Lynn, Laurence E. 1978. *Knowledge and Policy: The Uncertain Connection.* Study Project on Social Research and Development. Washington, DC: National Research Council, National Academy Press.

Maguire, Mike. 2004. "The Crime Reduction Programme in England and Wales: Reflections on the Vision and the Reality." *Criminal Justice* 4:213–37.

Massey, Douglas S. 2007. *Categorically Unequal.* New York: Russell Sage Foundation.

Morris, Albert. 1975. "A History of the American Society of Criminology: 1941–1974." *Criminology* 13:123–67.

Morris, Norval, and Michael Tonry. 1990. *Between Prison and Probation: Intermediate Punishments in a Rational Sentencing System.* Oxford: Oxford University Press.

Moynihan, Daniel Patrick. 1993. "Iatrogenic Government—Social Policy and Drug Research." *American Scholar* 62(3):351–62.

Nagin, Daniel S. In this volume. "Deterrence in the Twenty-First Century."

Nagin, Daniel S., and John V. Pepper, eds. 2012. *Deterrence and the Death Penalty.* Washington, DC: National Academies Press.

National Audit Office. 2006. *The Home Office: Tackling Anti-social Behaviour.* Report by the Comptroller and the Auditor General. London: Her Majesty's Stationery Office.

National Commission on Law Observance and Enforcement. Wickersham Commission. 1931. *Report.* Vol. 1. Washington, DC: US Government Printing Office.

Nutley, Sandra, and Peter Homel. 2006. "Delivering Evidence-Based Policy and Practice: Lessons from the Implementation of the UK Crime Reduction Programme." *Evidence and Policy* 2:5–26.

Petersilia, Joan. 1991. "Policy Relevance and the Future of Criminology." *Criminology* 29:1–15.

———. 2008. "Influencing Public Policy: An Embedded Criminologist Reflects on California Prison Reform." *Journal of Experimental Criminology* 4: 335–56.

President's Commission on Law Enforcement and Administration of Justice. 1967. *The Challenge of Crime in a Free Society.* Washington, DC: US Government Printing Office.

Prewitt, Kenneth, Thomas A. Schwandt, and Miron L. Straf, eds. 2012. *Using Science as Evidence in Public Policy.* Committee on the Use of Social Science Knowledge in Public Policy. Washington, DC: National Academy Press.

Radzinowicz, Leon. 1999. *Adventures in Criminology.* London: Routledge.

Reuter, Peter. In this volume. "Why Has US Drug Policy Changed So Little over 30 Years?"

Schlossman, Steven. 1985. *Delinquency Prevention in South Chicago: A Fifty-Year*

Assessment of the Chicago Area Project. Santa Monica, CA: RAND Corporation.

Schlossman, Steven, and Michael Sedlak. 1983. "The Chicago Area Project Revisited." *Crime and Delinquency* 29:398–462.

Sherman, Lawrence W. In this volume. "The Rise of Evidence-Based Policing: Targeting, Testing, and Tracking."

Stolz, Barbara. 2001. *Criminal Justice Policy Making: Federal Roles and Processes.* Westport, CT: Praeger.

Tonry, Michael. 1998. "Building Better Policies on Better Knowledge." In *The Challenge of Crime in a Free Society: Looking Back, Looking Forward.* Washington, DC: US Government Printing Office.

———. 2004. "Criminology and Criminal Justice Research in Europe." In *Developments in Criminology and Criminal Justice Research*, edited by Gerben Bruinsma, Henk Elffers, and Jan de Keijser. Cullompton, Devon, UK: Willan.

———. 2010. "The Costly Consequences of Populist Posturing: ASBOs, Victims, 'Rebalancing,' and Diminution of Support for Civil Liberties." *Punishment and Society* 12(4):387–413.

———. 2011. *Punishing Race: A Continuing American Dilemma.* New York: Oxford University Press.

———. In this volume. "Sentencing in America, 1975–2025."

Tonry, Michael, and David Green. 2003. "Criminology and Public Policy in the USA and UK." In *The Criminological Foundations of Penal Policy: Essays in Honour of Roger Hood*, edited by Lucian Zedner and Andrew Ashworth. Oxford: Oxford University Press.

Walker, Nigel. 1969. *Sentencing in a Rational Society.* London: Allen Lane.

Walter, Isabel, Sandra Nutley, and Huw Davies. 2005. "What Works to Promote Evidence-Based Practice? A Cross-Sector Review." *Evidence and Policy* 1:335–63.

Weiss, Carol H. 1986. "Research and Policy-Making: A Limited Partnership." In *The Use and Abuse of Social Science*, edited by Frank Heller. London: Sage.

Weiss, Carol H., Erin Murphy-Graham, and Sarah Birkeland. 2005. "An Alternate Route to Policy Influence: How Evaluations Affect D.A.R.E." *American Journal of Evaluation* 26:12–30.

Wellford, Charles F., Betty M. Chemers, and Julie A. Schuck, eds. 2010. *Strengthening the National Institute of Justice.* Committee on Assessing the Research Program of the National Institute of Justice. Washington, DC: National Academy Press.

White, Susan O., and Samuel Krislov, eds. 1977. *Understanding Crime: An Evaluation of the National Institute of Law Enforcement and Criminal Justice.* Committee on Research on Law Enforcement and Criminal Justice, Assembly of Behavioral and Social Sciences. Washington, DC: National Academy Press.

Wilson, James Q. 1990. "Drugs and Crime." In *Drugs and Crime*, edited by Michael Tonry and James Q. Wilson. Vol. 13 of *Crime and Justice: A Review of Research*, edited by Michael Tonry and Norval Morris. Chicago: University of Chicago Press.

Yankelovich, Daniel. 1991. *Coming to Public Judgment: Making Democracy Work in a Complex World.* Syracuse, NY: Syracuse University Press.

Zimring, Franklin E. In this volume. "American Youth Violence: A Cautionary Tale."

Philip J. Cook

The Great American Gun War: Notes from Four Decades in the Trenches

ABSTRACT

In this essay I provide an account of how research on gun violence has evolved over the last four decades, intertwined with personal observations and commentary on my contributions. It begins with a sketch of the twentieth century history of gun control in the United States. I then provide an account of why gun violence is worth studying, with a discussion of how and why the type of weapon used in crime matters, and assess the social costs of the widespread private ownership of firearms. I then detour into the methodological disputes over estimating basic facts relevant to understanding gun use and misuse. In Section IV, I focus on how gun availability influences the use of guns in crime and whether the incidence of misuse is influenced by the prevalence of gun ownership, regulations, and law enforcement. I go on to review evaluations of efforts to focus law enforcement directly at gun use in violent crime. Next I turn to the hottest topic of our day, the role of guns in self-defense and what might be deemed private deterrence. The conclusion summarizes the claims and counterclaims concerning gun regulation and asks, finally, if there is the possibility of an influential role for scientific research in the policy debate.

In 1976, the year I published my first research on gun violence, *The Public Interest* ran an article that should have served as a warning. Titled "The Great American Gun War," the author asserted that "no policy

Philip J. Cook is ITT/Terry Sanford Professor of Public Policy, Duke University. David Hemenway provided very helpful suggestions on an earlier draft, as did participants in the April 2012 Robina Institute conference "Crime and Justice in America, 1975–2025." I am indebted to Michael Tonry for his support and guidance along the way.

19

research worthy of the name has been done on the issue of gun control. The few attempts at serious work are of marginal competence at best, and tainted by obvious bias. Indeed, the gun control debate has been conducted at a level of propaganda more appropriate to social warfare than to democratic discourse" (Bruce-Briggs 1976, p. 37).

In the years since, the quality of the public debate has kept its "incredible virulence" and intensity, but the research drought has long since ended.[1] Criminologists, economists, public health scholars, and policy scientists have all made substantive contributions. Unfortunately, it is not clear that this research has improved the quality of the debate or of policy making. The research results that have obtained greatest visibility and public influence are not necessarily those that stand up well to scientific review and replication, but rather those that serve powerful ideological interests. In short, gun violence serves as a challenge to the very possibility of evidence-based policy making in a contentious arena. After nearly four decades in the academic trenches of this "war," I remain convinced that dispassionate research has much to offer in designing cost-effective policy. But it is all too rare that there is a quiet forum available for that discussion.

There have been two "fronts" in the gun war. The first is the primary domain of the social scientists who investigate the interconnections between guns and crime using available data and standard statistical methods. For example, the question of whether authorizing more people to carry guns in public will lead to a reduction or increase in crime is in principle a subject for scientific inquiry with a correct answer that may be discoverable from systematic analysis of data. The second front is the analysis of the "true" meaning of the Second Amendment to the US Constitution, to wit: "A well regulated militia, being necessary to the security of a free state, the right of the people to keep and bear arms, shall not be infringed." Arguments about the proper interpretation of this brief but obscure statement have engaged numerous legal scholars, historians, and grammarians, with little input from social science.

It is fair to say that these days the pro-gun side has the upper hand

---

[1] Actually, Bruce-Briggs was too negative about the state of research in 1976. By then Franklin Zimring had published a series of articles and a monograph that have stood up well to the test of time: see Zimring (1968, 1972, 1975) and Newton and Zimring (1971). But one can marvel that criminologists did not take a greater interest in gun violence in the 1960s and 1970s, a time in which the epidemic of violent crime that began in 1963 was eroding the quality of life in many American cities.

on both fronts. In 2008, in *District of Columbia v. Heller*, 554 US 570 (2008), the US Supreme Court asserted for the first time that there is a personal right to "keep and bear arms," a right that serves as a limit to gun regulation in the federal arena; in *McDonald v. City of Chicago*, 561 US 3025 (2010), the Court extended this right to the state and local arena. The situation is less clear on the first (empirical) front, but I believe that the pro-gun drift in public opinion and public discourse owes a great deal to research claiming that there are millions of instances each year in which guns are used in self-defense and that widespread gun carrying for self-defense purposes has a deterrent effect on all sorts of street crime. Whether these claims are correct or not, they are embraced and heavily promoted by pro-gun advocates. John Lott's (1998) book *More Guns, Less Crime* is the University of Chicago Press's best seller of all time. Contrary findings by reputable scholars have had less traction in the public arena (Ayres and Donohue 2009). Furthermore, research that would likely point to the hazards of gun ownership has been undercut by lack of funding; the pro-gun advocates were able to use their extraordinary influence with Congress to discourage federal research funding for investigation of the public health effects of private gun possession.[2]

Viewed in this political context, much of my research has had the effect of supporting the positions of the losing side. While it has not been my intent to promote one side or the other, my findings have helped to make the case for the importance of reducing gun use in violent crime while calling into question the value of private guns as a deterrent or effective tool of self-defense. Indeed, one clear conclusion supported by my research dating back to the 1970s could be summarized as "more guns, more homicide." Much of my career with gun research has been on the defensive, responding to far-fetched claims by legal scholars, criminologists, and economists. I consider the following examples far-fetched:

- The type of weapon used in criminal assault has little effect on the likelihood that the victim is killed.

[2] The Centers for Disease Control and Prevention (CDC) funded some extramural research on gun violence that helped establish that gun ownership had a detrimental effect on the public health and that private possession of guns increased the likelihood that a household member would be shot or killed. Congress responded by redirecting the funds used to fund this research program and barring the CDC from using federal funds to advocate or promote gun control (see Mair, Teret, and Frattaroli 2005; Goss 2006).

- Guns are so plentiful in the United States that they are as readily available to youths and criminals as hamburgers.
- There are millions of defensive gun uses each year, and defensive uses vastly outnumber criminal uses of guns.
- Increasing the number of guns on the street or in homes has a large deterrent effect on all sorts of crime.
- Only criminals misuse guns, and they are either readily identified or unaffected by gun regulations.

Of course scientists make mistaken claims all the time; the beauty of the scientific process is that when there is an open inquiry on important topics, mistakes are ultimately exposed and corrected, and a scientific consensus is achieved. The belief in that self-correcting scientific process underlies the hope for evidence-based policy. That hope may be misplaced when the scientific process is entwined with the process of political advocacy, where findings are in effect evaluated by whose purposes are served.

Of course, social scientists do not normally evaluate research by its influence on policy or public opinion, but rather by its contribution to scholarly knowledge as judged by academic peers. I have had the opportunity to work on a number of research projects that, while pertaining to gun violence, have broader methodological lessons. For example, my coauthors and I have helped uncover and document some previously unknown limitations of sample surveys. In particular, we found that even high-quality surveys have large biases in estimating the prevalence of gun ownership, the incidence of gunshot wounds in assaults, and the frequency with which guns are used in self-defense. The sources of bias appear to be different in each case, but the common element is unexpectedly large error that should encourage skepticism of a variety of survey results in other domains as well. In other methodological contributions, we created the first crime application of the contingent-valuation method, demonstrated that market frictions (in the underground gun market) can be investigated through a combination of ethnographic and econometric methods, and demonstrated the power of the "limited rationality" perspective in characterizing the choices made by robbers. All of this is to say that our research program in this particular applied area of social science is not just a consumer of social science methods but also a producer (or critic) and hence is of broader scientific interest. But the policy-advocacy context is inescapably important. It has had great influence on our research agenda and on the public reception of findings.

In this essay I have attempted to provide an account of how research on gun violence has evolved over the last four decades, intertwined with personal observations and more commentary on my own contributions than modesty would ordinarily permit. It is, to borrow a current phrase, a "hybrid vehicle." For anyone seeking a more straight-ahead review of the literature, I can suggest (having already given up on modesty) Cook and Ludwig (2006a, 2006b) or Cook, Braga, and Moore (2010).

The rather twisty road that I navigate with this hybrid vehicle can be briefly mapped. I begin with a sketch of the twentieth-century history of gun control in the United States, simply because gun policy and debates over gun policy form such an important context for research on gun violence. Section II then provides an account of why gun violence is worth studying, with a discussion of how and why the type of weapon used in crime matters, and assesses the social costs of the widespread private ownership of firearms. Section III is a bit of a detour into the methodological disputes over estimating basic facts relevant to understanding gun use and misuse. In Section IV, I focus on how gun availability influences the use of guns in crime and whether the incidence of misuse is influenced by the prevalence of gun ownership, regulations, and law enforcement. Section V looks at evaluations of efforts to focus law enforcement efforts directly at gun use in violent crime. Section VI then turns to the hottest topic of our day, the role of guns in self-defense and what might be deemed private deterrence. Section VII, unlike my research career in this area, concludes the essay.

I. Regulation of Firearms in the Twentieth Century

Compared to other developed nations, the United States is lax in regulating firearms. Nonetheless, there is some nontrivial regulation of the design, possession, transfer, and use of firearms. A teenager shooting squirrels with a sawed-off shotgun in New York's Central Park would be in violation of a number of local, state, and federal laws.

Table 1 summarizes the sequence of prominent federal laws and litigation, coupled with comments on the trends in criminal violence of the time. Congress first got into this arena during the Prohibition Era

TABLE 1

Time Line of Federal Gun Policy

Era	Crime Patterns	Federal Crime Policy Innovations
1920s	Prohibition-related gang violence Tommy gun era	1919: federal excise tax on handguns (10%) and long guns (11%) 1927: handgun shipments banned from the US mail
1930s	End of Prohibition in 1933	1934: National Firearms Act: requires registration and high transfer tax on fully automatic weapons and other gangster weapons
	Declining violence rates	1938: Federal Firearms Act: requires anyone in the business of shipping and selling guns to obtain a federal license and record names of purchasers
1960s	Crime begins steep climb in 1963 with Vietnam era and heroin epidemic	1968: Gun Control Act: bans mail-order shipments except between federally licensed dealers (FFLs); strengthens licensing and record-keeping requirements
	Assassinations	Limits purchases to in-state or neighboring-state residents
	Urban riots	Defines categories of people (felons, children, etc.) who are banned from possession Bans import of "Saturday night specials"
1970s	Violence rates peak in 1975 (heroin) and again in 1980 (powder cocaine era)	1972: Bureau of Alcohol, Tobacco and Firearms (ATF) created and located in the US Department of Treasury
1980s	Epidemic of youth violence begins in 1984 with introduction of crack	1986: Firearm Owners Protection Act: eases restrictions on in-person purchases of firearms by people from out of state Limits FFL inspections by ATF and bans the maintenance of some databases on gun transfers Ends manufacture of National Firearm Act weapons for civilian use
1990s	Violence rates peak in early 1990s, begin to subside	1994: Brady Handgun Violence Prevention Act: requires licensed dealers to perform a criminal background check on each customer before transferring a firearm
	School rampage shootings	1994: Partial ban on manufacture of "assault" weapons and large magazines for civilian use 1996: Congress bans the CDC from promoting gun control and effectively stops the CDC from funding research on gun violence

TABLE 1 (*Continued*)

Era	Crime Patterns	Federal Crime Policy Innovations
2000s	Crime and violence continue to decline	1996: Lautenberg Amendment bans possession by those convicted of misdemeanor domestic violence 2004: Assault weapons ban is allowed to sunset 2005: Congress immunizes firearms industry against civil suits in cases in which a gun was used in crime 2008: *District of Columbia v. Heller* for the first time establishes personal right under the Second Amendment

and its associated gang violence. The federal excise tax on guns was imposed in 1919 primarily for revenue purposes (although the sumptuary aspects were noted in the congressional debate). In 1927, well into the "Roaring Twenties," a ban was imposed on the use of the US mail to ship handguns. The focus on particular types of guns continued with the National Firearms Act of 1934, which required owners of fully automatic weapons (machine guns), sawed-off shotguns, and other weapons famously used by gangsters to register these weapons with the federal authorities. All transfers were subjected to a tax of $200, which at the time was confiscatory.[3] There is some indication that this law has been effective: the use of fully automatic weapons in crime appears to be quite rare in modern times.[4]

The most important federal legislation was not enacted until 1968, following a surge in crime, urban riots, and political assassinations (Zimring 1975). Building on the precedent of the Federal Firearms Act of 1938, the Gun Control Act (GCA) strengthened federal licensing of firearms dealers and limited interstate shipments of guns to licensees. The goal was to protect states that opted for tighter regulation against inflows of guns from states with lax regulations. In particular, the GCA banned mail-order shipments of the sort that supplied Lee Harvey Oswald with the gun he used to assassinate President Kennedy.

---

[3] It was not until 1986 that Congress banned the manufacture of National Firearms Act weapons for civilian use.

[4] Gary Kleck (1991) offers some evidence in *Point Blank* and notes that "although, oddly enough, gun control advocates rarely mention it, the *de facto* federal machine gun ban in place since 1934 may well be an example of a successful gun control effort" (p. 70).

The GCA also established a federal prohibition on possession by certain categories of people deemed dangerous because of their criminal record, drug abuse, mental illness, or youth. "Felon in possession" thus became a federal offense, which helped create the possibility of a partnership between local prosecutors and US attorneys in combating violent crime. The GCA's record-keeping requirements assisted law enforcement agencies in tracing guns to their first retail sale, which like felon in possession laws has proven quite useful in documenting interstate trafficking patterns and also in some murder investigations. Finally, the GCA banned the import of foreign-made handguns that were small or low quality and hence did not meet a "sporting purposes" test.

The agency created to do the regulatory enforcement and criminal investigation of gun trafficking is the Bureau of Alcohol, Tobacco, Firearms, and Explosives (ATF). It has been something of a political football since its creation. In 1986 the Firearm Owners Protection Act placed limits on ATF's ability to inspect dealers and keep records that would help identify suspicious purchasing patterns. But with the surge of violence during the 1980s associated with the introduction of crack cocaine and a shift in the political winds in favor of the Democrats, it became politically possible to strengthen the federal regulatory scheme in one important respect: the Brady Act was adopted in 1994, requiring that every purchase from a federally licensed dealer be preceded by a background check, helping establish a federal "instant check" system that dealers could access. Also in that year, Congress imposed a ban on the manufacture or import of "assault weapons" for civilian use as well as large-capacity magazines.[5] In 1996, the Lautenberg Amendment expanded the list of people proscribed from possessing a firearm to those who had been convicted of domestic violence, even at the misdemeanor level.

In recent years the federal "action" has shifted from Congress to the courts. Following the success of the state attorneys general in suing the tobacco industry (resulting in the Master Settlement Agreement of 1998),[6] a number of cities filed suit against the gun industry. These

[5] That ban was allowed to sunset 10 years later and survives in the laws of only a few states.

[6] The cause of action against the cigarette manufacturers focused on the costs to the states of paying for treatment of smoking-related illnesses through the Medicaid program. The Master Settlement Agreement was signed by the four largest manufacturers and 46 attorneys general. Among other things it obligated the manufacturers to make annual payments to the states in exchange for some exemption from subsequent liability.

suits employed various theories of mass tort, but with the common goal of using the courts to do what the legislatures would not when it came to regulating the design and marketing of firearms. In 2005, Congress intervened to stop this litigation by taking the extraordinary step of immunizing the gun industry from lawsuits in which the damages had resulted from misuse of a gun (the Protection of Lawful Commerce in Arms Act, PL 109-92). But the courts have nonetheless become an important arena for the fight over gun control; with the *District of Columbia v. Heller* decision in 2008, the US Supreme Court for the first time discovered in the Second Amendment a personal right to keep a handgun in the home for self-protection, with the suggestion that this personal right might also bar other sorts of regulations. Two years later in *McDonald v. City of Chicago*, the Court indicated that the constitutional restriction also applied to states and local governments. Gun-rights advocates have now brought a flood of litigation challenging every sort of restriction on gun design, possession, transactions, and use, with no clear indication of what content the courts will end up assigning to the newfound freedom (Cook, Ludwig, and Samaha 2009, 2011).

Of course much of the "action" in gun control has not been federal, but rather at the state and local levels. Going back to the days of Dodge City and the wild (heavily armed) nineteenth-century frontier, cities have regulated the place and manner of gun carrying and discharge. States have imposed a variety of requirements or bans on transfers, possession, and carrying, with a particular focus on handguns. For example, New York State's Sullivan Law of 1911 mandated a license for anyone wishing to possess or carry a handgun; in 1921 North Carolina required that anyone seeking to acquire a handgun obtain a pistol permit after satisfying the sheriff of the buyer's good moral character and need for a handgun for defense of home. In recent years the National Rifle Association has been highly effective in getting the great majority of states to relax their regulations. Most states have now adopted preemption laws (banning local governments from imposing regulations that go beyond the state law) and have eased or erased restrictions on carrying concealed firearms. On another front, about half the states have very recently adopted some version of the "stand your ground" law that allows people to use deadly force to defend themselves if they feel threatened, even if they are in a public place and have a realistic option to retreat.[7]

Thus the "gun rights" movement has made broad gains in erasing the modest level of control on gun carrying and use that had traditionally been applied by state and local governments. So far, however, federal regulations on gun design and transactions, and on who can legally be in possession, have remained in place. Data systems for background checks have been improved since the Brady Act was first put in place so that would-be buyers with a serious criminal record or a history of serious mental illness are more likely to be blocked from buying a gun from a dealer, although they may well be able to pick up a gun in the secondary market. In any event, it remains to be seen where the US Supreme Court will ultimately draw the line when it comes to protecting the personal right to keep and bear arms.

II. Why Gun Violence Is Worth Studying

I have not been inclined to second-guess my decision to spend so much of my career studying gun violence. Gun violence is an important detriment to our standard of living in the United States and for that reason alone deserves a place on the social science and public health research agendas. Gunshot injuries and deaths have a noticeable effect on life expectancy and contribute to health disparities across race and gender. Guns and gunfire terrorize some inner-city neighborhoods and degrade community life. The choice of weapons by offenders appears to have a profound effect on crime patterns and outcomes. Developing a better understanding of these matters is a worthy goal and may, despite the current political climate, someday prove helpful in redressing the problem.

A. Victimization

Approximately 1 million Americans have died from gunshot wounds in homicides, accidents, and suicides during the last three decades. In 2009, the most recent year for which the National Center for Health Statistics provides final tabulations on injury deaths, there were 31,347 firearms deaths, including 11,493 homicides, 18,735 suicides, and 554

[7] The resulting increase in homicide rates has been persuasively documented (Cheng and Hoekstra 2012; McClelland and Tekin 2012).

unintentional killings.[8] These counts are similar to those in other years during the last decade. As a point of reference, there were almost as many gun deaths as traffic deaths in 2009 (86 percent). Another point of reference is the years of potential life lost before age 65: guns account for 1 of every 15 years lost to early death from all causes.

Most homicides are committed with guns. Of the 18,361 criminal homicides in 2009, 68 percent were by gunshot. It is also true that half of all suicides are committed with firearms. Of course not all gunshot injuries are fatal. Emergency rooms treated 66,769 nonfatal gunshot injuries in 2009, including 44,466 nonfatal injuries from criminal assaults. And the police recorded over 300,000 assaults and robberies in that year in which the perpetrator used a gun, in most cases to threaten the victim (http://www2.fbi.gov/ucr/cius2009/data/table_19.html).

Gun violence contributes to racial and ethnic disparities in mortality. If one focuses just on males aged 15–34, homicide victimization rates in 2009 (consistent with earlier years) were 16 times as high for blacks as for non-Hispanic whites. Homicide is the leading cause of death for blacks in this age group and the second-leading cause of death for Hispanic males. For all men in this age range, most (84 percent) homicides are committed with guns.

Guns are the weapon of choice for assassins and cop killers. Fourteen of the 15 direct assaults against presidents, presidents-elect, and presidential candidates in US history were perpetrated with firearms, including the five resulting in death. (The one exception of the 15, a failed attack with a hand grenade against President George W. Bush, occurred overseas [Kaiser 2008].) Of the 541 law enforcement officers who were feloniously killed between 2001 and 2010, 490 (92 percent) died of gunshot wounds (http://www.fbi.gov/about-us/cjis/ucr/leoka/leoka-2010/tables/table27-leok-feloniously-type-of-weapon-01-10.xls).

Fortunately the homicide rate (both gun and nongun) has dropped in recent years, but from twentieth-century highs in 1980 and 1991 of over 10 per 100,000. The rate was just 5.5 in 2009. The persistent characteristic of American homicide through these ups and downs is the high involvement of guns, particularly handguns. Overall violence rates in the United States are also above average, though not to nearly

---

[8] The classification of gunshot deaths as "unintentional" in the Vital Statistics Registry is unreliable. Barber and Hemenway (2011) demonstrate that there are numerous false positives and false negatives in this classification and that to some extent they balance out.

the same extent: one comparison of the United States with other high-income countries found that the US firearm homicide rate was almost 20 times as high but that the nongun homicide rate was "just" 2.9 times as high as the average of the other countries (Richardson and Hemenway 2011).

B. How and Why the Type of Weapon Matters

Years ago a popular bumper sticker claimed that "Guns don't kill people, people kill people." The intent was no doubt to suggest that depriving "people" of guns would not remove the impulse to kill. What is missing from this "argument" is that without a gun, the capacity to kill may be greatly diminished. One wag suggested, "Guns don't kill people, they just make it real easy." Bumper stickers aside, the true causal role of guns in homicide is one of the fundamental issues in gun violence research and evidence-based policy making.

In some circumstances the claim that the type of weapon matters seems indisputable. There are very few drive-by knifings or people killed accidentally by stray fists. When well-protected people are murdered, it is almost always with a gun; as mentioned above, over 90 percent of lethal attacks on law enforcement officers are with firearms, and all assassinations of US presidents have been by firearm. When lone assailants set out to kill as many people as they can in a commuter train, business, or campus, the most readily available weapon that will do the job is a gun. But what about the more mundane attacks that make up the vast bulk of violent crime?

The first piece of evidence is that robberies and assaults committed with guns are more likely to result in the victim's death than are similar violent crimes committed with other weapons. In the public health jargon, the "case-fatality rates" differ by weapon type. Take the case of robbery, a crime that includes holdups, muggings, and other violent confrontations motivated by theft. The case-fatality rate for gun robbery is three times as high as for robberies with knives and 10 times as high as for robberies with other weapons (Cook 1987). For aggravated (serious) assault it is more difficult to come up with a meaningful case-fatality estimate since the crime itself is in part defined by the type of weapon used.[9] We do know that for assaults from which the

---

[9] In the FBI's Uniform Crime Reports, a threat delivered at gunpoint is likely to be classified as an aggravated assault, while the same threat delivered while shaking a fist would be classified as a simple assault.

victim sustains an injury, the case-fatality rate is closely linked to the type of weapon (Zimring 1968, 1972; Kleck and McElrath 1991), as is also the case for family and intimate assaults (Saltzman, Mercy, and Rhodes 1992).

Case-fatality rates do not by themselves prove that the type of weapon has an independent causal effect on the probability of death. It is possible that the type of weapon is simply an indicator of the seriousness of the assailant's intent and that it is the intent, rather than the weapon, that determines whether the victim lives or dies. This view was offered as a reasonable possibility by the revered criminologist Marvin Wolfgang, who in his seminal study of homicide in Philadelphia stated that "it is the contention of this observer that few homicides due to shooting could be avoided merely if a firearm were not immediately present, and that the offender would select some other weapon to achieve the same destructive goal" (1958, p. 83). Wolfgang eventually changed his mind, publishing a retraction in 1995. The same theme is offered by Wright, Rossi, and Daly (1983) and others: the gun makes the killing easier and is hence the obvious choice if the assailant's intent is indeed to kill; but if no gun were available, then, it is asserted, most would-be killers would still find a way. In this view, fatal and nonfatal attacks form two distinct sets of events with little overlap, at least in regard to the assailant's intent.

The speculation that the intent is all that matters always struck me as far-fetched. When a tool is available to make a difficult task (such as killing another person) much easier, then we expect that the task will be undertaken with greater frequency and likelihood of success. Perhaps the most telling empirical evidence on this matter came from Franklin Zimring (1968, 1972), who demonstrated that there is a good deal of overlap between fatal and nonfatal attacks; even in the case of earnest and potentially deadly attacks, assailants commonly lack a clear or sustained intent to kill. For evidence on this perspective, Zimring notes that in a high percentage of cases the assailant is drunk or enraged and is unlikely to be acting in a calculating fashion. Whether the victim lives or dies then depends importantly on the lethality of the weapon with which the assailant strikes the first blow or two.

Zimring's studies of wounds inflicted in gun and knife assaults suggest that the difference between life and death is often just a matter of chance, determined by whether the bullet or blade finds a vital organ. It is relatively rare for assailants to administer the coup de grace that would ensure their victim's demise. For every homicide inflicted with a single bullet wound to the chest, there are two survivors of a bullet wound to the chest that are indistinguishable with respect to intent. It is largely because guns are intrinsically more lethal than knives that gunshot injuries are more likely to result in death than sustained attacks with a knife to vital areas of the body (Zimring 1968). Zimring's second study provided still more compelling evidence by comparing case-fatality rates for gunshot wounds with different calibers: a wound inflicted by a larger-caliber gun was more likely to prove lethal than a wound inflicted by a smaller-caliber gun. Assuming that the caliber of a gun is not correlated with the intent of the assailant, the clear suggestion is that the type of weapon has a causal effect on outcome.

Zimring's argument in a nutshell is that robbery murder is a close relative of robbery, and assaultive homicide is a close relative to armed assault; death is in effect a probabilistic by-product of violent crime. Thus while the law determines the seriousness of the crime by whether the victim lives or dies, that outcome is not a reliable guide to the assailant's intent or state of mind.

One logical implication of this perspective is that there should be a close link between the overall volume of violent crimes and the number of murders, moderated by the types of weapons used. Where Zimring provided a detailed description of cases as the basis for his conclusion, tests based on aggregate data are also potentially informative. My contribution was to demonstrate that robbery murder trends in 43 large cities (those for which I could obtain data) behaved just as we would expect given the "probabilistic by-product" claim: a tight connection between variation in robbery and in robbery murder and a finding that an increase of, say, 1,000 gun robberies was associated with three times as many additional murders as an increase of 1,000 nongun robberies (Cook 1987). "Instrumentality" provides a natural explanation for these patterns.

Years later, Franklin Zimring and Gordon Hawkins (1997) published *Crime Is Not the Problem*, making the case that violent crime rates in American cities are not particularly high relative to their counterparts in other parts of the developed world except for homicide and gun-related crimes generally. American "exceptionalism" is the result of the unparalleled prevalence of firearms in assaults and robberies in the United States. In this view, American perpetrators are not more vicious than those in Canada, Western Europe, and Australia. Americans are just better armed.

As it turns out, my first entry in gun violence research was about instrumentality (Cook 1976). In 1975, criminologist Wesley Skogan was pioneering a research program based on the newly released federal crime survey data. He provided me with access to the data and encouragement to work on a detailed study of robbery. True to my economics training, my inquiry was guided by speculations based on the likely objectives of robbers (choose lucrative victims, control them, make good the escape). Use of a gun enhances the robber's power, making it possible successfully to rob hard-to-control but relatively lucrative victims (groups, businesses). On the basis of this reasoning, I predicted that gun robberies would be more likely to be successful than other robberies and involve more loot when they do succeed. Further, robbers with guns should be able to control the situation by use of the potent threat of the gun rather than by physical attack (as with a strong-arm robbery or mugging).

These predicted patterns were evident in the victim survey data. The success of this "strategic choice analysis" of robbery helped establish that robbers can be usefully viewed as making choices that are sensible given their goals. It also provided a basis for quantifying the value of a gun in this type of crime. I recently returned to this topic and found that, other things equal, robbers bearing guns are 12.5 percentage points more likely to succeed than are their knife-wielding counterparts, and when robberies by firearm do succeed, the average value of offenders' "take" almost doubles (Cook 2009).[10] Further, the likelihood of injury to the victim depends on the type of weapon, with gun robberies the least likely to involve injury. Of course when the robber does fire his gun, it is quite likely that the victim will die, making gun robberies by far the most lethal type of robbery (Cook 1980). In any event, that gun robberies are so much more lucrative than robberies with other weapons raises an interesting question: Why are most robberies committed without a gun? One likely answer is that many robbers lack ready access to a gun.

In sum, the type of weapon deployed in violent confrontations is not just an incidental detail; it matters in several ways. Because guns pro-

---

[10] Kleck and McElrath (1991) found similar patterns in aggravated assault, which, like robbery, is often motivated by the desire to coerce the victim to do something against his or her will.

vide the power to kill quickly, at a distance, and without much skill or strength, they also provide the power to intimidate other people and gain control of a violent situation without an actual attack. When there is a physical attack, then the type of weapon is an important determinant of whether the victim survives, with guns far more lethal than other commonly used weapons.

The most important implication of this "instrumentality" perspective is that policies that are effective in reducing gun use in violent crime would reduce the murder rate, even if the volume of violent crime were unaffected. As it turns out, about half of the states have incorporated sentencing enhancements for use of a gun in crime (Vernick and Hepburn 2003). These enhancements, most of which were adopted in the 1970s and 1980s, were intended to reduce gun use in violence; systematic evaluations offer some indication that they have been effective (Loftin and McDowell 1981, 1984; Abrams 2012).[11] In any event, the widespread adoption of gun enhancements by state legislatures is a clear indication of the commonsense appeal of the instrumentality effect.

C. The Social Costs of Gun Violence

Generating a comprehensive measure of the societal impact of gun violence requires imagining all the ways in which it affects the quality of life. The elevated rate of homicide, as important as it is, provides just the beginning in this calculation. I was given the opportunity to generate a broader estimate of social costs with a grant from the Joyce Foundation in 1997.[12] I had the good fortune to persuade Jens Ludwig to join me on this project. We had already begun a highly rewarding collaboration that continues to this day. Our ultimate goal was to establish a ballpark estimate of the magnitude of this problem in terms that could be compared with other problems of health, safety, and urban development.

[11] Cook and Nagin (1979) documented the influence of weapon use in a case on prosecutorial and judicial discretion. Defendants who used weapons were more likely to be convicted and sentenced to prison in the District of Columbia in 1974, but there was little distinction between guns and other types of weapons. Podkopacz and Feld (1996) document the importance of weapon use as an influence on the decision to waive juveniles to adult courts.

[12] In the 1990s the Joyce Foundation initiated a funding stream in the area of gun violence under the leadership of its president, Deborah Leff. Joyce remains the leading funder in this area.

The traditional approach for valuing disease and injury is the "cost-of-illness" method, a method that we rejected since it misses most of what is important about gun violence. In essence, the cost-of-illness approach values people the way a farmer would value his livestock, on the basis of their productivity and market value. Our alternative approach, which is generally favored by economists, values the reduction in risk of injury according to the effect on the subjective quality of life. In short, the difference is between whether we value safety on the basis of how the lives saved contribute to gross domestic product (the cost-of-illness approach) or rather by the value that people place on living in a safer environment.

In our perspective, violence, particularly gun violence, is a neighborhood disamenity like pollution, traffic, and poor schools. Anyone living in a neighborhood where gunshots are commonly heard is likely to be negatively affected. The possibility of being shot, or of a loved one's being shot, engenders fear and costly efforts at avoidance and self-protection, as when mothers keep their children from playing outside for fear of stray bullets. Property values suffer as people with sufficient means move to safer neighborhoods, and businesses suffer as customers gravitate to shopping areas where they feel comfortable. Tax revenues are diverted to cover the financial costs of medically treating gunshot victims (usually at public expense) and of law enforcement needs (Cook et al. 1999).

The costs of fear, suffering, and avoidance are largely subjective. The challenge is to place a monetary value on these subjective effects and, in particular, to estimate how much households would be willing to pay to reduce the perceived risks. One approach is to analyze property values, comparing neighborhoods that are differentially affected by gun violence while controlling for other factors that may be relevant in that market.[13] That approach is bound to be incomplete (since at best it can capture only the local place-related effects of gun violence) and poses an almost insurmountable statistical challenge (since other disamenities are highly correlated with gun violence). For those reasons we opted to use an entirely different approach, the contingent valuation method, to provide a comprehensive cost estimate in monetary terms. This method, widely used by economists in valuing different aspects of the environment, had not previously been used to value a reduction in

[13] One of the first studies of property values and crime was by Thaler (1978).

crime or violence, although it is appropriate for the task and was later used by Mark Cohen and his colleagues (2004) to estimate the social cost of several types of crime.

To perform the contingent valuation estimate, we included a series of questions on a national survey that asked whether respondents would be willing to vote for a measure that would reduce gun violence in their community by 30 percent, if it were going to cost them a specified amount (which we varied across respondents). The pattern of answers was interesting and quite reasonable; for example, respondents with children at home had a greater willingness to pay than those without. Our overall estimate was that such a reduction would be worth $24 billion (Cook and Ludwig 2000; Ludwig and Cook 2001). Multiplying up to a hypothetical 100 percent reduction, we could estimate that interpersonal gun violence at the time was an $80 billion problem and that the subjective costs were by no means confined to the people and communities that were at highest risk of injury; indeed, the willingness to pay for this reduction actually increased with income.

In sum, the threat of gun violence degrades the quality of life in affected communities. Reducing gun violence would have tangible societal value, which we measured by asking how much households would be willing to pay for a specified reduction in this disamenity. Our estimate is large enough to establish gun violence as a serious problem.[14]

D. The Opportunity to Inform Law and Policy

It could be argued that while gun violence is important in terms of its societal impact, research is unlikely to make a difference in the political arena and hence is of little practical value. While it is true that Congress seems unlikely to make large changes in the legal framework for regulating guns in the foreseeable future, it is not true that policy is static in this area. Local authorities continue to wrestle with the problem of gun violence and in many cases have adopted law enforcement tactics that are intended to deter gun use by gangs and

---

[14] We have been accused of focusing on the costs of gun violence while ignoring the benefits conferred to owners. But we do not claim to have presented a complete cost-benefit analysis of any particular intervention, let alone a ban on private gun ownership. Many of the available approaches to reducing gun violence have little effect on the enjoyment of guns by law-abiding owners, e.g., sentencing enhancements for use of guns in crime or improved record keeping of gun transactions. In colloquial terms, our estimate is relevant to judging whether gun violence is a big enough problem to deserve priority for policy makers. Any specific intervention should be evaluated in terms of both its benefits (reduced gun violence) and its costs.

criminals. There are numerous bills before state legislatures every year, in most cases seeking to relax legal restrictions on gun carrying, possession, and use. And perhaps most important, the federal courts are deluged with Second Amendment lawsuits seeking to tear down existing firearms regulations of all sorts.

The relevant Supreme Court opinions (in the *Heller* and *McDonald* cases) did not specify how the Court would ultimately decide the scope of the new personal right to keep and bear arms. The majority opinion in *Heller* stated that the door was left open to continued restrictions on the types of weapons allowed in private commerce and the kinds of people that would be allowed to acquire and keep firearms. It is possible that the court will consider arguments about the costs of doing away with particular regulations as part of what in effect would become a test that balances this new freedom against the legitimate concern of government for preserving public safety (Cook, Ludwig, and Samaha 2011). If so, then there is obvious scope for empirical social science, which offers the tools for estimating the relevant trade-offs.

III. Measurement Puzzles in the Quest for Evidence-Based Policy

The "evidence" base for the study of guns and violence begins with data on such fundamental issues as the number and distribution of guns, the number of people shot each year in criminal assaults, and the frequency of gun use in self-defense. These simple descriptive statistics should be readily available, and in fact the rhetoric of the Great American Gun War routinely includes reference to 300 million guns, or 100,000 people who are shot each year, or 2.5 million defensive gun uses. But it turns out that such statistics should be viewed with considerable skepticism. Developing reliable estimates of basic facts in this arena is surprisingly difficult, even with the best of intentions.

There exist administrative data compiled by government agencies on each of these topics, but those data are sometimes incomplete, difficult to access, unconnected with the context, or all of these. As a result, analysts have made extensive use of population surveys, which in principle can overcome the limitations of administrative data. For example, if you want to find out how many guns are in private hands, why not ask a representative sample of US households whether there is a gun on the premises and, if so, how many? However, it turns out that even state-of-the-art survey methods can generate heavily biased estimates. The existence and nature of these biases have been matters of heated debate in one of these areas, defensive gun uses, because of its political import. But it should be understood that the word "bias" in this context does not refer to political bias, but rather a predictable error characteristic of a particular estimation method. The surprise is that the survey methods used to generate such error-prone estimates are not obviously deficient but are widely accepted in social science. Hence there are methodological lessons that go well beyond the arena of gun violence. Here I recount three examples in domains in which I have been active.

A. How Many Guns in Private Hands?

Administrative data on manufacturing and net imports of guns since 1899 have been compiled by the federal government. These data provide only the roughest of guides to the total number of guns currently in private hands; the attrition rate of guns through breakage and confiscation is unknown, and administrative records have no information on off-the-books imports and exports (say, to Mexican drug gangs; Kleck 1991, app. 1). Administrative data on the prevalence of household gun ownership are almost entirely lacking. Data of that sort could be generated only through licensing or gun registration, which at the federal level is required only for owners of machine guns and other weapons of mass destruction. A few states require licensing or registration, but compliance with those requirements is likely to be far less than 100 percent.

Sample surveys appear to offer a good alternative to administrative data. For example, the General Social Survey (GSS), conducted by the National Opinion Research Center, has long included questions on gun ownership. In 1999 it estimated that just 36 percent of American households owned at least one firearm, down from nearly 50 percent in 1980 (Smith 2000, p. 55).[15] To determine the number of guns in private hands requires that a survey ask how many guns are in the household, and that question has been quite rare. In our first "gun" project together, Ludwig and I used the 1994 National Survey of Pri-

---

[15] The drop in household ownership may reflect the trend in household composition during this period; households are less likely to include a gun because they have become smaller and, in particular, are less likely to include a man (Wright, Jasinski, and Lanier 2012).

vate Ownership of Firearms (NSPOF) to generate detailed estimates. We found that 25 percent of adults (most of them men) owned at least one gun and that the average gun-owning adult owned 4.4; multiplying up, we estimated the total number of guns in private hands as 192 million (one-third of which were handguns; Cook and Ludwig 1996). The most detailed national survey on the subject since then (the National Firearms Survey) found that gun-owning households averaged 5.2 guns in 2004, up substantially from the 1970s (Hepburn et al. 2007).

As it turns out, however, survey-based estimates of gun ownership are subject to sizable bias. One piece of evidence comes from a comparison of responses by husbands and wives. In the GSS sampling procedure, whether the husband or wife is selected as the respondent for a household that is headed by a married couple is determined randomly, so we expect that about the same percentages should report a gun in the household. In fact husbands are consistently more likely than wives to report a gun, with the difference as high as 10 percentage points in some years (Ludwig, Cook, and Smith 1998). Using NSPOF data, we found that if husbands' answers were to be believed, the estimated national stock of handguns would be twice as high as if we believed the wives' answers (Cook and Ludwig 1996). It is tempting to believe that the husbands are more accurate since they are likely to be the primary owners and users of any guns and may be better informed and less reluctant to admit to owning a gun in a survey.[16] But that is not necessarily the case: some respondents may want to overstate their gun collection to impress the interviewer.

Analysis of a two-generation survey in California found that the same pattern appeared when teenagers were asked about guns in the home: the boys were much more likely to say yes than the girls (Cook and Sorenson 2006). In this survey there was enough information to determine that the difference in response was accounted for by the difference in participation in gun sports, suggesting that the response is influenced by whether the respondent has firsthand knowledge.

Thus we have no reliable way to estimate the number of guns in private hands, and survey-based estimates are problematic. The best

---

[16] NSPOF asks about how many guns the respondent personally owned and how many guns were in the household. We considered the answers to the personal ownership question more reliable and used them to generate the estimate of 192 million guns in private hands.

that can be hoped for is a ballpark estimate, something like 200–300 million. It should be noted that while survey responses provide an unreliable guide to the number of guns or prevalence of gun ownership in any one year, it is possible that the downward trend found in the GSS in the 1980s and 1990s reflects reality; that would be true, for example, if the extent of survey bias is more or less constant over time (like a scale that always weighs 5 percent light).

B. How Many Gun Injuries from Assaults?

The difficulty in estimating the number of assault victims who are shot in any one year follows somewhat the same story line, with one difference: the total of gunshot victims includes those who die, and that number is accurately recorded as part of the national Vital Statistics program. The count of nonfatal gunshot injuries is not compiled in any official record. Estimates based on a sample of emergency rooms (National Electronic Injury Surveillance System, or NEISS) may be reasonably accurate but are incomplete since some unknown fraction of gunshot victims do not seek treatment there.[17] The NEISS estimate that 44,000 assault victims were treated for gunshot wounds in 2009 thus understates the total number of gunshot victims in assaults. The police are likely to know about most of those cases (because medical staff are required to report in many states), and some of the cases not treated in emergency rooms will come to police attention as well (as a result of 911 calls).[18] Unfortunately, police records on gunshot victims are not separately compiled as part of the FBI's Uniform Crime Reporting system, but rather are submerged in the much larger category of "aggravated assault."

In principle, survey data could provide a comprehensive estimate of nonfatal injuries. The National Crime Victimization Survey (NCVS; conducted by the Census Bureau on behalf of the US Department of Justice) has asked the relevant questions of a nationally representative

---

[17] The gunshot injury data are based on a sample of emergency departments through the NEISS All Injury Program operated by the US Consumer Product Safety Commission with CDC's National Center for Injury Prevention and Control.

[18] Kellermann et al. (2001) report a systematic effort in the Atlanta area to compare gunshot cases from medical records with those known to the police through 911 calls. The overlap was far from complete, and it appears that in Atlanta and elsewhere the mandatory reporting requirement is not being enforced. The NEISS estimate, however, does not depend on reports by medical staff to the police, but rather is generated directly from medical records.

sample since 1973 and released annual estimates of the number of gun-shot victims in assaults. These estimates turn out to be highly biased, despite the fact that the NCVS is an exceptionally well-crafted survey. I first became aware that there might be a problem when I compared the estimated nonfatal injury rate with the known rate of fatal gunshot wounds in assaults (homicides). The ratio of nonfatal (from the NCVS) to fatal was 21, which implied that fully one in three gunshot victims die, which is not remotely true. I found a variety of sources of infor-mation on the case-fatality rate in assaults in which the victim was shot, and a consistent finding emerged: rather than a one in three death rate among victims of criminal shootings, the actual fatality rate is typically about one in seven (Cook 1985).[19]

The likely reason for the underestimate of nonfatal gunshot victims in the NCVS is that they are underrepresented in the sample. A large percentage of assault victims are drawn from the ranks of youthful men who are difficult to contact because they have no regular address and, in any event, may be reluctant to talk to an interviewer. In these re-spects there is a good deal of socioeconomic overlap between the shooters and the victims.

Fortunately the homicide fatality data are quite accurate, and we can get a pretty good estimate of the overall number of injuries by mul-tiplying by the inverse of the case-fatality rate. For example, using my one in seven case-fatality rate implies that the 11,493 gun homicide victims were among 80,000 shooting victims that year, of whom 68,500 survived. That estimate comports well with the 44,000 nonfatal crim-inal gunshot cases that NEISS estimates were treated in emergency departments.[20] What I have proposed, then, is to ignore the national survey estimates and generate estimates instead by using an evidence-based multiplier of the official count of gun homicides. That work-around appears to provide fairly accurate estimates.

Note that the large bias in the NCVS estimates that I discovered exists with respect to a narrow category of victimization (shot during a criminal assault) that is concentrated among a group that may in practice be underrepresented in the survey sample. For most types of criminal victimization the sampling procedure would be adequate for generating a good estimate.

[19] This estimate was subsequently confirmed and reported in a doctoral dissertation at the University of Maryland (Long-Onnen 2000).

[20] Note that suicides and attempted suicides are omitted from these calculations.

C. How Many Defensive Gun Uses?

While guns do enormous damage in crime, they also provide some crime victims with the means of escaping serious injury or property loss. The NCVS, despite its limitations, is generally considered the most reliable source of information on predatory crime since it has been in the field since 1973 and incorporates the best thinking of survey methodologists. From this source it would appear that use of guns in self-defense against criminal predation occurs approximately 100,000 times per year (Cook, Ludwig, and Hemenway 1997). Of particular interest is the likelihood that a gun will be used in self-defense against a residential intruder. Using the NCVS data for the mid-1980s, I found that only 3 percent of victims were able to deploy a gun against someone who broke in (or attempted to do so) while they were at home (Cook 1991). Since about 45 percent of all households possessed a gun during that period, I concluded that it is relatively unusual for victims to be able to deploy a gun against intruders even when they have one nearby.

In contrast are the results of several smaller, one-time telephone surveys, which provide a basis for asserting that there are millions of defensive gun uses per year (Kleck and Gertz 1995; Cook and Ludwig 1996). Why do these one-time surveys produce estimates that exceed the NCVS estimate by more than one order of magnitude? One explanation is that the NCVS asks questions about defensive actions only to those who report a victimization attempt, while the phone surveys ask such questions of every respondent. While as a logical matter it seems as if that should make little difference, it is quite possible that some NCVS respondents fail to report a defensive gun use (DGU) because they did not think to report to the interviewer the criminal threat that initiated it. In that case the NCVS will include false negatives in its estimate of DGUs. On the other hand, survey questionnaires that ask an open-ended question about self-defense uses greatly expand the scope for false positives (Cook, Ludwig, and Hemenway 1997; Hemenway 1997a, 1997b).[21] Moreover, as the National Research

---

[21] The possibility of false negatives is also increased. But given the rarity of gun use in self-defense, the effect of the two types of error is not symmetric. Even a small false positive rate will have a large proportional effect on self-defense uses. That insight is due to Hemenway (1997a, 1997b). For example, if 1 percent of responses are false positives, that by itself would be nearly enough to produce the Kleck and Gertz estimate of 2.5 million. Given that a representative sample of the US public would include many who are demented, are intoxicated, or have a political agenda around this issue,

Council's Committee to Improve Research Information and Data on Firearms notes, "fundamental problems in defining what is meant by defensive gun use may be a primary impediment to accurate measurement" (Wellford, Pepper, and Petrie 2005, p. 103; see also McDowall, Loftin, and Presser 2000). When respondents who report a defensive gun use are asked to describe the sequence of events, many of the cases turn out to have involved something other than an immediate threat, and a majority of such self-reported cases were thought by a panel of judges to be illegal (Hemenway, Miller, and Azrael 2000).

To my mind the most compelling challenge to the survey-based claim that there are millions of DGUs per year derives from a comparison with what we know about crime rates. The famous 2.5 million DGU estimate is well over twice the total number of gun crimes estimated at that time in the NCVS, which in turn is far more than the number of gun crimes known to the police.[22] Likewise, the number of shootings reported by those who claimed to be defending themselves vastly exceeds the total number of gunshot cases in the United States. The estimated number of DGUs from surveys is highly sensitive to the sequence of questions and to whether the respondent is given some help in placing events in time (so that when asked about the previous 12 months he or she does not bring in events that happened before that period).[23] When the same respondents in the same sort of one-time survey are asked about both DGUs and victimization by guns, they report many more victimizations than DGUs (Hemenway, Miller, and Azrael 2000).

There are lessons here for survey methodology and for gun policy. The methodological lesson is that survey-based estimates of what appears to be a well-defined construct (use of a gun in self-defense during the last year or last 5 years) are hypersensitive to survey design, to the extent that estimates may differ by a factor of 25 or more. Another

---

it would not be surprising to get that high of a false positive rate. It raises the larger question of when sample surveys can be trusted as the basis for estimating rare events.

[22] The NCVS for 1994 estimated that 10.9 percent of the nearly 10 million personal crimes of violence involved guns, for a total of 1.07 million gun crimes (http://bjs.ojp.usdoj.gov/content/pub/pdf/Cvius945.pdf, table 66).

[23] One of the great strengths of the NCVS, compared with these one-time surveys, is that its sample retains a household for seven interviews, one every 6 months. The previous interview is used as a way to provide the respondent with a bracket in placing events in time in answering the question of whether he or she had been victimized in the previous 6 months.

lesson for gun policy is that what some individuals consider to be a legitimate use of a gun in self-defense may be highly problematic in practice.

D. Thoughts on Methodology

Even surveys that meet the highest standards of current practice may produce heavily biased estimates. The results discussed here should encourage skepticism and engender what might be called "plausibility tests": commonsense comparisons of the resulting estimates with other sources of information. Too often the review of scientific contributions is like appellate review of a criminal conviction: the court focuses on just the process rather than on the outcome. For policy-relevant work it is important to test the conclusions against what else we know about the reality of the situation.

IV. Gun Availability and Use

My first project as a gun researcher, in 1976, focused on the "instrumentality effect." Convinced that the intrinsic lethality and power of an assault are influenced by the type of weapon, the next question was what determines the assailant's choice of weapon. The NCVS data indicate that the victim was confronted with a gun in only about one-quarter of robberies, a fact that has always struck me as surprising given my finding that gun robberies tend to be far more successful and lucrative than knife robberies. It is possible that the explanation for the low prevalence of gun use is that robbers consider it risky or uncomfortable to carry a gun or are concerned that a gun robbery would carry a heavier sentence if they are caught (Cook and Nagin 1979; Abrams 2012). Another possibility, of course, is that most robbers do not own or have ready access to a gun. Some evidence supports that view: in anonymous surveys a majority of arrestees and prisoners report that they do not own a gun. Some say that it would take them a day or more to obtain one or that guns are too expensive (Cook et al. 2007).

The notion that guns are scarce and that many youths and criminals would like to have one but do not is counterintuitive. After all, over one-third of households possess a gun, usually several, and the total number in private hands while uncertain is likely sufficient to provide one to every adult in the United States. New York University law professor James Jacobs (2002) observes in this regard, "Some criminals claim that it is as easy to buy a gun on the streets as it is to buy fast food. One Chicago gang member stated, 'It's like going through the drive-through window. Give me some fries, a Coke, and a 9-millimeter'" (quoted in Terry 1992, p. A1). Jacobs makes an extended argument that regulating gun markets is futile because underground markets will inevitably find ways around legal restrictions. This view of the power of the market and private incentives to surmount all obstacles is commonplace in economic rhetoric. Rightly or wrongly, that view, widely shared, has emboldened the gun rights movement (Goss 2006).

A. Do Youths and Criminals Have Trouble Obtaining Guns?

One approach to understanding whether the difficulty or expense of keeping a gun influences criminals' choice of weapons is to ask them. In one study, Stephanie Molliconi and I interviewed youths in a North Carolina reformatory and learned that most of them had some experience with guns, but possession for them was a fluid matter. They reported periods during their delinquent careers in which they were unarmed because they had sold their gun or traded it for other valued items—or had it stolen (Cook, Molliconi, and Cole 1995).

More recently the ethnographer Sudhir Venkatesh conducted a far more extensive inquiry into the underground gun market in two neighborhoods of South Side Chicago, interviewing hundreds of gang members, robbers, prostitutes, drug dealers, and people active in the gun trade (Cook et al. 2007). What he was able to document from these interviews is a widespread belief in the value of guns, coupled with surprising ignorance about how they work and how to go about obtaining one—or the appropriate ammunition. When there was a successful transaction, the prices tended to be substantially higher than in the legal market, despite the questionable quality of the guns that were changing hands. The drug-dealing gangs did not deal in guns because they were concerned that it would lead to a police crackdown (and would put their main source of income, drug dealing, at risk). Some criminals, wanting a gun but not knowing how to obtain one, hired a broker who for a substantial fee ($30–$50) attempted to find one. The overall impression from Venkatesh's ethnography, supplemented by more traditional evidence that we analyzed for this project, is that the underground market in guns does not work smoothly, as Jacobs and others had imagined. There were far fewer transactions than for the underground drug market and high transaction costs, since potential buyers and sellers had trouble finding each other or trusting each other. Inflated prices, long waits, and suspect quality were the norm.

It should be noted that Chicago at that time was exceptional in that it had a handgun prohibition (since found unconstitutional) and no retail gun dealers. While it is easy to imagine that active criminals might obtain guns by sending their girlfriends to a suburban dealer to make a straw purchase, that scenario was very rare, as we were able to demonstrate by analyzing the transaction history of guns confiscated by the Chicago Police Department (Cook et al. 2007). Do criminals have easier access to guns in jurisdictions where there is a legal market or where gun ownership is more prevalent than in Chicago? Based on survey data of arrestees collected through the Drug Use Forecasting program of the US Department of Justice, our tentative answer is yes; the fraction of arrestees who owned a gun increased with overall prevalence of household gun ownership across 22 cities (Cook et al. 2007, p. F605; see also Cook and Ludwig 2002).

The direct inquiries in the North Carolina reformatory and the Chicago streets both suggest that guns are desirable but scarce commodities to youths and criminals and that gun availability affects whether a particular criminal is armed at any one time. It appears that relative scarcity is one factor limiting the use of guns in crime.

B. *To What Extent Does the Prevalence of Gun Ownership Influence Gun Use in Crime?*

While the United States is an outlier among wealthy nations with its high prevalence of gun ownership, there are wide differences across jurisdictions within the United States. Rates range from something like 13 percent in Massachusetts to 60 percent in Mississippi (Azrael, Cook, and Miller 2004). It seemed plausible to me that the variation in gun ownership would influence the use of guns in crime, both in the obvious way (the household gun might be turned to criminal use, perhaps by a teenage son) and indirectly through theft, loans, and casual transactions—all of which would be easier to arrange in a gun-rich community than in one where guns were rare. The various channels by which criminals become armed can be documented up to a point from various data sources (Cook, Molliconi, and Cole 1995; Braga et al. 2002). For example, the 1997 Survey of Inmates in State Correctional Facilities asked inmates who had been in possession of a gun where they had obtained it. Of those serving their first prison sentence, less than 20 percent said they obtained their gun from a licensed dealer, while 40 percent got it from a friend or family member, 31 percent by theft or a transaction in the underground market, and 9 percent from other sources (Harlow 2001, table 9).

A test of the hypothesis that greater gun prevalence induces greater gun use in crime requires a measure of the prevalence of gun possession, a measure that is valid for comparing jurisdictions at a point in time and tracking movements over time. Given the lack of administrative data on ownership and of survey data for small areas on a consistent or reliable basis, I thought what was needed was an index that could be computed from reliable administrative data. My first effort (Cook 1979) was to average the percentages of suicides and homicides committed with guns. These percentages are available for states and large counties from the National Vital Statistics System and are highly correlated with each other, suggesting that they measured the same underlying construct. The geographic patterns in my index made sense from what was known or could be inferred from other sources. On the basis of this gun prevalence index, I was able to show, for example, that gun prevalence has a substantial effect on weapon choice in robbery and on the robbery murder rate but no effect on the overall robbery rate. Thus more guns meant more gun robberies, fewer nongun robberies, and more robbery murders (due to the instrumentality effect, presumably). Twenty years later, two scholars working at the Harvard Injury Control Research Center, Deborah Azrael and Matthew Miller, experimented with various indexes of gun prevalence and discovered that I had been half right in 1979: of all the indexes in use or that they could imagine, the best was simply the percentage of suicides with guns. We worked together to validate this new index (Azrael, Cook, and Miller 2004) and have since worked separately in using it to explore the effects of prevalence on injury and crime patterns. In a rare meeting of minds, Gary Kleck (2004) published an article that also endorsed the gun percentage in suicide as a valid index of cross-section variation in gun prevalence. He and I part ways on whether the index is also valid for tracking changes over time (Cook and Ludwig 2006a).

Several studies have investigated the effect of gun prevalence (measured by this proxy of firearm suicide divided by suicide) and homicide rates across counties (see, e.g., Cook and Ludwig 2002; Miller, Azrael, and Hemenway 2002). However, the interpretation of such results is in some doubt. It is difficult to isolate a causal mechanism from analysis of cross-section data. Gun-rich jurisdictions, such as Mississippi, are systematically different in various ways from jurisdictions with relatively few guns, such as Massachusetts. The usual approach for addressing this "apples and oranges" problem has been to control statistically for other characteristics, such as population density, poverty, and the age and racial composition of the population. But these variables never explain very much of the cross-sectional variation in crime rates (Glaeser, Sacerdote, and Scheinkman 1996), suggesting that the list of available control variables is inadequate to the task. Also unclear is whether widespread gun ownership is the cause or effect of an area's crime problem, since high crime rates may induce residents to buy guns for self-protection. These same concerns are arguably even more severe with cross-sectional comparisons across countries.

Some of the problems with cross-sectional studies can be overcome by using panel data—repeated cross sections of city, county, or state data measured at multiple points in time—to compare changes in gun ownership with changes in crime. Compared with Massachusetts, the state of Mississippi may have much higher homicide rates year after year for reasons that cannot be fully explained from existing data sources. But by comparing changes rather than levels, we implicitly control for any unmeasured differences across states that are relatively fixed over time, such as a "Southern culture of violence" (see Butterfield 1997; Loftin and McDowell 2003). The best available panel data evidence suggests that more guns lead to more homicides, a result that is driven entirely by a relationship between gun prevalence and homicides committed with firearms; there is little association of gun prevalence with nongun homicides or other types of crimes (Duggan 2001; Cook and Ludwig 2006a).

It is no surprise that not all scholars are on board with this finding. In his book *More Guns, Less Crime*, Lott (1998) reports an analysis that finds that an increase in gun prevalence is associated with a reduced murder rate. In that study Lott uses a measure of gun prevalence that has not been validated and is of dubious validity (see Cook and Ludwig 2006a).[24] His aberrant finding is an example of an important but un-

---

[24] Lott uses voter exit poll data to estimate state-level gun ownership. Voters are by no means a representative sample, and the voting "sample" changes from election to election. That may explain why Lott's data indicate that from 1988 to 1996 gun ownership rates increased for the United States as a whole from 27.4 to 37.0 percent (2000, p. 36). Yet the best source of national data on gun ownership trends, the GSS,

surprising lesson, that the analytical details, such as just what index of gun prevalence is used, can have a large effect on the results.

Finally, it is worth emphasizing that my conclusion is not "more guns, more crime." My research findings have been quite consistent in demonstrating that gun prevalence is unrelated to the rates of assault and robbery (Cook 1979; Cook and Ludwig 2006a; see also Kleck and Patterson 1993). The strong finding that emerges from this research is that gun use intensifies violence, making it more likely that the victim of an assault or robbery will die. The positive effect is on the murder rate, not on the overall violent-crime rate. More guns, more homicides.

C. What about Changes in Gun Market Regulation?

An alternative approach for learning about the effects of gun availability on public safety is to examine the effects of policy changes that are intended to influence overall gun ownership rates or gun availability to dangerous people. That approach has the advantage of being directly relevant to policy evaluation. But it has proven difficult in practice.

Since 1968, when the Gun Control Act was adopted, the biggest victory for those seeking stronger gun control was the Brady Handgun Violence Prevention Act (Pub. L. 103-59, 107 Stat. 1536). This act required that every state institute a system for checking the background of anyone seeking to purchase a firearm from a federally licensed dealer. Since some states already had background check systems in place, they were not affected by the law and hence served as a ready-made control group for determining the effect of the law in other states. Ludwig and I determined that the effects on homicide and overall suicide rates, if any, were not large enough to emerge from the statistical noise; that is, we accepted the null hypothesis (Ludwig and Cook 2000). Publication of this finding put us in the doghouse with gun control advocates and perhaps surprised pro-gun advocates who had long typecast me as "anti-gun." In fact there was no political agenda behind our research, except the judgment that the Brady Act was important enough to warrant evaluation.

So saying, it behooves us to be very careful about interpreting our

indicates that individual gun ownership trends were essentially flat during this period (Kleck 1997, pp. 98–99).

finding. Given our statistical results, we cannot rule out the possibility that the Brady Act reduced (or increased) the homicide rate by a small percentage. Our best estimate of its effect, which is near zero, is not that precise. Furthermore, the apparent lack of a strong effect may well be due to the weakness of the act itself rather than a flaw in the basic approach. Brady left unregulated the informal "secondary" market by which most youths and criminals actually obtain their guns. That is more than a loophole: it is a gaping barn door. Finally, our approach, which treats the "no-change" states as controls in a natural experiment, may underestimate the true effect if in fact there were spillovers from the "change" states. For example, Illinois was one of the states in the control group (states that were not required by the Brady Act to change the procedure for gun transactions), but there is very clear evidence that gun trafficking into Chicago was transformed by the Brady Act: licensed dealers in the deep South, which had been an important source of the guns that were ultimately used by criminals in Chicago, were almost eliminated as a source in 1994, apparently replaced by dealers in Illinois (Cook and Braga 2001). If the Brady Act reduced homicides in the control states, then our finding of "no difference between control states and treatment states" leaves open the possibility that the Brady Act was effective after all.

Other analysts have evaluated state and federal regulations on gun transactions and possession (e.g., Webster, Vernick, and Hepburn 2001, 2002; Webster, Vernick, and Bulzacchelli 2010).[25] It seems fair to say that a good deal of uncertainty remains about the efficacy of these measures on the ultimate outcomes of concern—most notably homicide rates. The National Firearms Act of 1934, which required national registration of weapons of mass destruction (such as submachine guns and hand grenades) and imposed a confiscatory transfer tax, appears to have been effective in curtailing the use of such weapons in crime. A variety of other regulations are sensible, are supported by some evidence, and may in fact have benefits that exceed costs. The statistical challenge is to persuasively document effects that are likely to be of modest size relative to the usual variability of violent crime rates.

Take for example the pending California "microstamp" requirement that semiautomatic pistols have the firing pin and breech plate en-

---

[25] For reviews, see Hemenway (2004), Wellford, Pepper, and Petrie (2005), and Cook, Braga, and Moore (2010).

graved with a registered serial number so that when the gun is fired the cartridge casing is traceable to the particular gun and its registered owner. This regulation is intended to assist law enforcement in solving crimes in which a pistol was fired by the perpetrator, and it is reasonable to believe that it will do so. It is true that savvy gunmen can avoid being caught if they remember to pick up any shell casings at the scene or use an older pistol or revolver. But fortunately not all shooters are that savvy. We can project a gradual increase in the rate of arrest for shootings (as new semiautomatics go into circulation) and a resulting deterrent effect on serious violent crime. A statistical test for these predicted effects requires isolating a proportionally small effect in a wilderness of natural variation over an extended time period.

Thus there is a considerable statistical challenge in establishing the effect of gun market regulations on the outcomes of ultimate concern—rates of homicide and criminal misuse of guns. The direct evidence on efficacy is likely to be imprecise (as in the evaluation of the Brady Act) or ambiguous. Given that reality, the best alternative is not to fall back on pure intuition, but rather to consider evidence on how regulations affect the relevant transactions. For example, Brady background checks have blocked the sale of about 2 million firearms since 1994, most commonly because the would-be purchaser had a felony record.[26] We do not know how many of those would-be buyers found another source or what they did with it, but it is at least plausible that some portion of those blocked sales saved lives.

D. Summing Up on Availability

My conclusions from my analysis in 1979 have been supported and contested in the years since. At this point I am confident in the following conclusions: the prevalence of gun ownership in a community has a direct effect on weapon choice by robbers and assailants—more guns, more gun use in crime. The prevalence of gun ownership has little or no effect on the overall volume of violent crime—more guns, same amount of violence. But the lethality of that violence depends on the mix of weapons—more guns, more murders.

The link between gun prevalence and gun use in crime suggests that criminals generally find it easier to obtain a gun in a gun-rich com-

---

[26] In 2006, 1.6 percent of the 8.6 million applications for firearm transfers or permits were denied by the FBI (69,930) or by state and local agencies (64,512; http://bjs .ojp.usdoj.gov/content/pub/pdf/bcft06st.pdf).

munity than in one where guns are scarcer. That speculation receives support from a variety of sources. What is not so clear is whether regulations on the gun market and gun possession can have any meaningful effect on the availability of guns. Even the prohibitions on handgun ownership in Chicago and the District of Columbia (both now deemed unconstitutional) do not appear to have had a large effect on the prevalence of gun ownership (Cook and Ludwig 2006*b*). In both cases, residents could readily purchase guns in neighboring jurisdictions. A national ban might well have greater effect.

V. Gun-Oriented Enforcement

The debate over gun control is typically focused on where to draw the line. What sorts of weapons should be banned in the civilian market? What categories of people should be banned from possession? What places should be designated gun-free? But since regulations, however defined, are not self-enforcing, the questions of implementation and enforcement are also crucial in determining their ultimate success in separating guns from crime.

Design and enforcement of gun regulations are large topics, but my discussion here will be limited to introducing two (overlapping) sets of issues that have received a good deal of attention in recent years: focused deterrence and gun-oriented police patrol.

A. Focused Deterrence

One noteworthy approach to deterring illicit carrying and use has been to threaten convicted felons with federal prosecution if they are arrested in possession of a gun. Since federal law specifies longer prison sentences for "felon in possession" convicts than do state laws, involving the "feds" in such cases might well have a deterrent effect on this high-risk group. A federal program called Project Safe Neighborhoods was implemented during the late 1990s with federal-local cooperation in prosecuting such cases as a key element.

The focus on felons is an example of "focused" or "targeted" deterrence. Those who have already been convicted of a felony most certainly constitute a relatively high-risk group, although they do not account for as much of the serious violence as is widely believed. Ludwig, Braga, and I analyzed murder defendants in Chicago and found that just 40 percent of the adult defendants had a felony conviction (Cook,

Ludwig, and Braga 2005)—far higher than the prevalence of felons in the general population (so collectively they are "high-risk"), but with the implication that well over half of murders are committed by people who lack a felony record.

The prominence of the federal prosecution strategy owed much to the publicity given Project Exile in Richmond, Virginia. This partnership between local prosecutors and the US Attorney was implemented in 1997; the subsequent drop in murder rates was widely credited to the deterrent effect of this program, although a careful look at the evidence suggests that that claim is dubious at best (Raphael and Ludwig 2003). However, a reputable evaluation of Project Safe Neighborhoods in Chicago found evidence of a remarkably large deterrent effect in a couple of high-violence neighborhoods. A key element of this project was the threat of long prison sentences for felons in possession. That threat was delivered in notification sessions with small groups of convicts (Papachristos, Meares, and Fagan 2007).

The best known of the focused-deterrence strategies to reduce illicit gun use is Boston's Operation Ceasefire. Beginning in 1995, an interagency working group composed of Harvard University researchers, members of the Boston Police Department, and other criminal justice agencies conducted research and analysis on Boston's youth violence problem, designed a problem-solving intervention to reduce youth violence, and implemented the intervention. The research showed that the problem of youth violence in Boston was concentrated among a small number of serially offending gang-involved youths (Kennedy, Piehl, and Braga 1996). The key problem-solving intervention that arose from the research diagnoses was to prevent gang violence by making gang members believe that gun use by any one member of the gang would result in legal problems for all members. The intent was to create an incentive for gang members to discourage each other from gunplay, thus reversing the usual group norm in support of violence. A key element of the strategy was the delivery of a direct and explicit "retail deterrence" message to a relatively small target audience regarding what kind of behavior would provoke a special response and what that response would be. The deterrence message was delivered by talking to gang members on the street, handing out fliers in the hot spot areas explaining the enforcement actions, and organizing forums between violent gang members and members of the interagency working group (Kennedy 2011). An evaluation of the Boston strategy to prevent youth violence found it to be associated with significant decreases in youth homicides, shots fired, and gun assaults (Braga et al. 2001; Piehl et al. 2003).[27] Several replications of this general approach have been evaluated, with generally positive results (Braga and Weisburd 2012).

B. Gun-Oriented Police Patrol

Police practice has been greatly influenced by recognition of the strategic implications of the geographic concentration of crime and violence within cities. Concentrating police activities in the high-crime areas ("hot spots") can be an efficient use of available police personnel, in part because displacement to other neighborhoods does not appear to be much of a problem (Clarke and Weisburd 1994; Weisburd and Telep 2012). Lawrence Sherman demonstrated the feasibility of directed patrol against gun violence hot spots in his well-known demonstration project in Kansas City (Sherman and Rogan 1995). Since then there have been positive evaluations of similar directed-patrol programs of short duration in Indianapolis and Pittsburgh, as well as two cities in Colombia (Koper and Mayo-Wilson 2006). While there have been no randomized controlled trials of this approach, the quasi-experimental evidence suggests that stepped-up police activity directed at illicit gun carrying can have a deterrent effect.

This approach has been adopted most visibly by New York City, where police officers conducted almost 700,000 stops in 2011 alone, mostly with youthful minority males. While the "yield" with respect to confiscated guns has been low, it is reasonable to believe that this tactic has had a deterrent effect on illicit carrying and gun use in crime—albeit at some cost in terms of police-community relations. We know that New York City enjoyed an extraordinary and sustained drop in violence since the early 1990s and that that drop was associated with a number of policing innovations (Zimring 2011). It is difficult to sort out the separate contribution of the stop-and-frisk policy.

---

[27] Other researchers, however, have observed that some of the decrease in homicide may have occurred without the Ceasefire intervention in place, as violence was decreasing in most major US cities (Fagan 2002; Rosenfeld, Fornango, and Baumer 2005). The National Research Council's Panel on Improving Information and Data on Firearms (Wellford, Pepper, and Petrie 2005) concluded that the Ceasefire evaluation was compelling in associating the intervention with the subsequent decline in youth homicide. However, the panel also suggested that many complex factors affect youth homicide trends, and it was difficult to specify the exact relationship between the Ceasefire intervention and subsequent changes in youth offending behaviors.

In any event, it should be noted that the potential effectiveness of targeted patrol against illicit carrying depends on the regulatory environment. If carrying a concealed gun does not require a permit (as in four states), then the goal of "getting guns off the street" is unattainable.

C. Other Enforcement Priorities

There is obviously much more to the "enforcement" question than efforts to deter dangerous people from carrying and using guns. As developed in my review with Ludwig (Cook and Ludwig 2006*b*), we can organize the larger discussion around two general approaches: making guns a liability to offenders or making guns more costly or less accessible. The enforcement strategies discussed above amplify the liability by increasing the perceived likelihood and severity of punishment to those who choose to misuse a gun (relative to some other weapon). There are other actions that could further penalize gun misuse, including a variety of measures that would improve record keeping so that police investigations could be more productive in associating a particular gun with a particular crime and individual. California is a leader in this regard with its handgun registration requirement and pending requirement that for new pistols the firing pin stamps the cartridge with a registered serial number. The other general approach, reducing gun availability, can be pursued through stronger regulatory enforcement of dealers, limitations on the number of guns sold per customer (such as the one handgun per month limit in several states), increased policing of the underground market in guns, and a number of other approaches.

This sort of strategic analysis is potentially useful even if direct estimates of the quantitative effects are lacking. For policy design purposes it is important to have a sense of what general mechanisms are likely to be effective since it is not possible to conduct gold-standard evaluations of the myriad possible interventions.

VI. Self-Defense and Private Deterrence

When I started my career-long research project on weapons and violence, there was little discussion of self-defense in the social science literature. Still, the fact was (and is) that most private citizens who acquired a handgun did so at least partly for self-defense purposes, and it was natural to ask whether guns were valuable in that regard. Researchers began looking into various aspects of this matter during the 1980s, and in subsequent years that issue has come to dominate the literature and much of the public rhetoric. The pro-gun groups have gone on the offensive, asserting that gun control measures that deprive private citizens of handguns perversely deprive them of an effective means of protecting their homes and communities. These advocates can now point to research findings that support this perspective. And in the *Heller* decision of 2008, the majority of the Supreme Court announced a Second Amendment right to keep a handgun in the home for protection.

Research on self-defense covers a number of issues: the frequency and success with which guns are used in self-defense, the hazards of keeping a gun in the home, and the deterrent effect of increasing the number of potential victims who are armed. It comes as no surprise that on each of these issues there is considerable disagreement in the social science literature.

A. How Many Defensive Gun Uses (Redux)?

While far from perfect, the NCVS is generally viewed as the best survey source for crime-related estimates. The NCVS questionnaire follows up on crime reports by asking respondents whether they acted to defend themselves. Using the NCVS data from the 1980s, I found that only about 1 percent of robbery victims attempted to use a gun in self-defense, as did 3 percent of victims of burglaries of occupied homes (Cook 1991). The overall NCVS estimate was on the order of 100,000 DGUs per year. As recounted in a previous section, Kleck reported the results of several smaller, one-time surveys to the effect that there were millions of DGUs per year (Kleck 1988; Kleck and Gertz 1995). And he is not alone: estimates in the millions are routine from this sort of unbounded survey.

We have learned from this literature that the wording of survey questions, the sequence in which they are presented, and other details of survey design can affect the estimate of DGUs by a factor of 20 or more. In my view the only way to anchor this discussion is to make commonsense comparisons with other statistics that are more reliable, such as the number of people who are shot each year and the volume of serious violent crime.

TABLE 2

The Likelihood of Victims Using a Gun in Self-Defense

Type of Personal-Contact Crime	DGUs/Crimes Reported in NCVS, 1992–2001	Unweighted %
All crimes with personal contact	247/27,595	.9
Robbery	32/2,640	1.2
Assault	166/21,570	.8
Confrontational burglaries	50/1,821	2.7
Sexual assaults	1/1,119	.1

SOURCE.—Computed from table 2 of Tark and Kleck (2004).

B. Are Victims Well Advised to Use a Gun in Self-Defense If They Have One Handy?

In an early analysis of this issue using NCVS data, I found that when a victim chooses to resist an assailant, using a gun is associated with a better outcome than resisting without a weapon.[28] That result could be considered as supporting the benefit of having a gun for self-defense, but as a logical matter, it provides little information on whether the gun itself was helpful. One problem is that the NCVS did not at that time provide the detailed information about the sequence of events that would be necessary to determine the meaning of the injury rates (Cook 1986).

Sequence information was incorporated in the NCVS following a revision of the questionnaire in 1992. Respondents who reported a crime against their person were asked about self-defense measures and injury; if they reported being injured, they were asked whether the injury occurred before, during, or after their self-defense effort. Jong-yeon Tark and Gary Kleck analyzed all personal-contact crime incidents reported in the NCVS between 1992 and 2001, distinguishing among 16 different types of self-defense, including "attacked with gun" and "threatened with gun." The sum of those two actions accounts for less than 1 percent of all personal-contact crimes. Table 2 reports the frequency of DGUs by crime category. The numbers of DGUs are far lower than suggested by Kleck's own surveys (leading, e.g., to the 2.5 million DGU estimate) and are in line with my earlier estimates. In this article, Tark and Kleck say that they think that "many cases of

---

[28] Those who resist with a knife do as well as those who use a gun.

armed resistance are probably not reported to the NCVS" (2004, p. 869).

There remains the question of whether resistance is associated with a greater chance of injury at the hands of the assailant. Tark and Kleck report the likelihood of injury to the victim-respondent following resistance by type of crime. They find that most injuries occur before any attempt at resistance, and injury following resistance is quite rare. On the basis of counts of self-reports in the 10 years of NCVS data, without applying sampling weights, those who used a gun to defend themselves had twice the rate of subsequent injury (3.6 percent) as those who used another type of weapon (1.8 percent) and about the same rate as those who fought back without a weapon (3.4 percent). For all three categories the percentage who were seriously injured was just 0.6 percent.

It appears, then, that injury following self-defense is unusual and that there is no advantage in that respect from using a gun in self-defense. (The authors also analyze these patterns using multiple regression analysis but find that the numbers are too small to find significant differences among type of defense.)

Somehow the authors conclude that "victim resistance appears to be generally a wise course of action" (Tark and Kleck 2004, p. 861). It is a strange conclusion for two reasons. First, they do not have a sound basis for comparing the causal effects of resisting versus not resisting. Assaults that engender resistance are systematically different from those that do not and in particular suggest a difference in victims' judgment concerning the best course of action given their assessment of the assailant's intent and strength. Second, the authors ignore a key fact about the NCVS, which is that it excludes cases in which the victim is killed. If resistance enhances the chance of getting killed, which it may, then this advice seems ill founded indeed.

In my view, then, there still is no basis from the NCVS statistics for judging whether resisting a robber, home intruder, or other assailant is generally a prudent course of action if the goal is to minimize the chance of serious injury or death.

C. Does Keeping a Gun in the Home Protect the Occupants?

The risks of keeping a firearm at home include accidental shootings, suicide, and use in intimidation and murder in battering relationships. In a particularly telling analysis, Hemenway (2011, table 2) compared the 15 states with the highest rates of gun ownership with the six states with the lowest rates. The two groups each had about 25 million people in 2004, but the high-gun states had 11 times as many unintentional firearm deaths and 12 times as many gun suicides. The nongun suicide rate was just 1.5 times as high in the high-gun states.

Guns are also perceived by many as reducing one risk to household members, injury at the hands of an intruder. A number of studies have compared the likelihood that a gun kept at home will be used to shoot an intruder with the likelihood that it will be used to shoot a household member (in suicide, assault, or accident). The latter is far more likely. Unfortunately, most studies do not measure the frequency with which guns kept at home are used to scare off an intruder without shooting him. The best national estimates of the frequency of defending against intruders come from the NCVS data. I found that in about 3 percent of home invasion crimes in the 1980s, a gun was used by a household member in self-defense, not always successfully (Cook 1991). That amounted to about 30,000 instances per year. Tark and Kleck (2004) report a very similar rate (2.7 percent) of DGU against home invasion for the period 1992–2001. Since the rate of gun ownership during those periods was over 35 percent, it appears that gun-owning households are unlikely to use their guns when there is a home invasion and very unlikely overall (about one in 1,000 in a year).

Keeping a gun at home has other benefits, including recreational benefits from hunting, target shooting, and collecting, and instrumental benefits such as shooting pesky woodchucks on the farm. All those uses are compatible with safe storage practices that will reduce the chance of accidental misuse. But those who keep a loaded handgun accessible to fend off intruders are buying their sense of security at a price in terms of the risks incurred, especially if there are children at home, or violence-prone adults, or anyone who abuses drugs or is suicidal. The *Heller* decision has given us the right to keep that loaded handgun at home, but that does not mean it is a good idea.

D. Does Private Gun Ownership Deter Crime?

The strongest claim in support of the public virtue of widespread gun possession (and the perversity of regulations that curtail guns) is that guns in private hands generate a general deterrent effect on crime. Early arguments along these lines speculated about the effect on residential burglary, and especially "hot" burglaries of occupied homes

(Kleck 1997; Kopel 2001). The first systematic analysis of this issue (Cook and Ludwig 2003) demonstrated by use of the geo-coded NCVS data that the individual likelihood of residential burglary or hot burglary is not reduced by living in a county with high gun prevalence.[29] To the contrary, we found that greater gun prevalence caused an increase in the residential burglary rate. One reason may be that more prevalent gun ownership increases the profitability of burglary because stolen guns are readily fenced for good prices. The fraction of burglaries that are hot is not affected by the prevalence of gun ownership.

By far the most prominent research findings on the "general deterrence" issue were based on an evaluation of changes in state laws governing concealed carrying of handguns. Over the 1980s and 1990s a number of states eased restrictions on concealed carry, adopting a regulation that required local authorities to issue permits to all applicants who met minimum conditions. These "shall issue" laws replaced "may issue" laws (which gave the authorities discretion) or outright bans. Economists John Lott and David Mustard published the first evaluation of these shall-issue laws, finding that they were associated with a reduction in homicide and some other types of crime (Lott and Mustard 1997). Lott went on to publish *More Guns, Less Crime* (1998), in which he reported these results and variations on them. He reached differing conclusions about the effect on property crime depending on how he specified his regression equations (Cook, Moore, and Braga 2002), but in every econometric specification he found that ending restrictive gun-carrying laws reduced homicide rates (Lott 1998, pp. 90, 100).

In the finest scientific tradition, a number of analysts have sought to replicate Lott's findings and confirm or disconfirm them. For example, economist John Donohue (2003) concluded that Lott's findings are unsupportable from the data he used. Donohue shows that Lott's estimates are sensitive to the correction of several coding errors and to reasonable changes in the model specification. More importantly, Donohue's reanalysis of the Lott data shows that states that eventually ended restrictive concealed carry laws had crime trends systematically different from those of the other states even before these law changes went into effect, suggesting that the adoption of these laws could not

---

[29] Note that this is the first and perhaps only use of geo-coded data, made possible by the Duke Census Data Research Center.

be considered exogenous to the process generating homicide rates. Donohue and his coauthors have published several additional evaluations of the shall-issue laws, taking advantage of additional years of data and exploring alternative specifications and data sets for the period 1977–2006 (Ayres and Donohue 2009; Aneja, Donohue, and Zhang 2012). One robust result from the most recent work is that the introduction of shall-issue laws is associated with an increase in aggravated assault rates.

The importance of this academic debate is indicated by the fact that a panel of 18 distinguished scholars was created by the National Research Council to review the conflicting research. Panelists were chosen because they had not been directly involved in research related to gun control. Among other things, this panel reanalyzed Lott's data and, with one dissent (by a political scientist who was not expert on the statistical methods used), judged his findings to be unreliable (Wellford, Pepper, and Petrie 2005).

In a sense, the claim of a large deterrent effect should have been challenged from the beginning as too good to be true. Whether the net effect of relaxing gun-carry laws is to increase or reduce the burden of crime, there is very good reason to believe that that effect is not large. One study found that in 12 of the 16 permissive concealed carry states studied, fewer than 2 percent of adults had obtained permits to carry concealed handguns (Hill 1997). The actual change in gun-carrying prevalence is smaller than the number of permits issued would suggest because many of those who obtained permits were already carrying guns in public (Robuck-Mangum 1997). Moreover, the permits issued were concentrated in rural and suburban areas where crime rates are already relatively low, among people who are at relatively low risk of victimization—white, middle-aged, middle-class males (Hill 1997). The available data about permit holders also imply that they are at fairly low risk of misusing guns, consistent with the relatively low arrest rates observed to date for permit holders (Lott 1998). In sum, changes to state laws governing legal gun carrying were unlikely to induce more than negligible change in the incentives facing criminals to go armed themselves or to avoid potentially armed victims.

What is the lesson? As in the case of Kleck's estimates of the number of DGUs, Lott's remarkable findings have received enormous attention simply because they provide academic support for pro-gun advocates. In both cases the authors have good credentials and are using methods that are quite standard in social science. That those methods in this case are producing results that are so at odds with what else we know is good reason to be skeptical. The case for skepticism is stronger yet given that those findings are not "robust": seemingly minor changes in survey methods or econometric analysis produce qualitatively different results. The scientific process has worked quite well in this case since replication has challenged dubious findings, just as in the case, say, of the "discovery" of a desktop cold-fusion process in 1989 by Utah chemists. That also seemed too good to be true and turned out to be so after many other labs attempted and failed to replicate the results. But the public debate over public safety and guns has been ill served by the selective attention to results that provide support for predetermined positions.

VII. Conclusion

When I was just 20 years into my career as a gun control researcher, already all too familiar with the quality of the public discourse on the subject, my colleague Jim Leitzel did me the great favor of introducing me to Albert Hirschman's (1991) book *The Rhetoric of Reaction* (Cook and Leitzel 1996). Hirschman observes that in a two-century history of debate over progressive reforms, there were three common themes used by conservative opponents: that the reform would have unintended negative consequences, would have no effect on the problem, and would come at the cost of fundamental rights or values. His subtitle, then, was *Perversity, Futility, Jeopardy*. That was a good overview of the arguments made by opponents of gun control then and is an even more apt summary today.

The "futility" argument was the primary basis for the critique of gun control by scholars in the 1980s, and it continues to be repeated; in this view, the "bad guys" will always have ready access to guns no matter what the regulatory structure because underground markets are so effective at circumventing whatever regulations are in place in the primary market. The belief in the power of markets, both licit and illicit, is coupled with a view of the criminal as a determined and resourceful person who "if he really wants to get a gun" will find a way to do so. An alternative version of the futility argument is that this self-same determined and resourceful criminal will find a way to commit his crimes and murders regardless of what weapons are available to him—that what matters is intent, not the instrument.

The "perversity" argument is somewhat newer among gun researchers but has become an important link between research and rhetoric. As recounted above, Kleck and Lott, among others, provided the empirical grist for the rhetorical mill. Kleck reported that guns were frequently and effectively used in self-defense and hence had great potential value to the individual. Lott reported that relaxing the regulations on concealed gun carrying created a powerful deterrent to all kinds of crime. One apparent implication, if these findings are believed, is that regulations that limit gun possession and use may have the perverse effect of depriving "law-abiding" citizens of an important means of fending off assailants while depriving communities of the deterrent effect of a heavily armed citizenry.

The "jeopardy" argument has of course been given zest by the Supreme Court's discovery of a personal right to keep a loaded handgun in the home. However the court ultimately defines the scope of this new freedom, the 2008 *Heller* decision has encouraged the popular belief in the armed citizen as the frontline defense against criminal predation and, in a more radical vision, against government tyranny (Horwitz and Anderson 2009).

Can we hope that the scientific process will ultimately succeed in sorting through conflicting claims and counterclaims, at least on those issues (futility and perversity) that are largely a matter of fact rather than personal values? For lawmakers, regulators, judges, and the public at large, it is hard to discern who has a better claim to the truth in the welter of technical arguments. But in the scientific forum, perhaps it is not unrealistic to aspire to a reality-based discourse in which scientific norms prevail. Those scientists who are conscientious objectors to the Great American Gun War are invited to join the Great American Gun Research Project. There is much to be learned, and perhaps the learning will ultimately have a constructive influence on policy making in this vital arena.

TABLE A1

Influential Contributions on Gun Policy

Year of Publication	Citation	Comments
1968	Franklin Zimring, *Journal of Legal Studies*	Criminology: the first systematic study of the "instrumentality" effect of weapon type; more generally, the first empirical scholarship on the harmful role of guns in criminal violence
1979	Philip Cook, *Policy Studies Review Annual*	Economics: demonstrates that the prevalence of gun ownership has a direct positive effect on weapon mix in robbery and the robbery murder rate
1980	Susan Baker, Stephen Teret, and Elliott Dietz, *Journal of Public Health Policy*	Public health: argues for the importance of regulating guns (rather than focusing only on criminal enforcement) to reduce injury and death
1983	James Wright, Peter Rossi, and Kathleen Daly, *Under the Gun*	Sociology: a skeptical review of evidence on the importance of guns in crime and the possibilities of gun control
1986	Arthur Kellermann and Don T. Reay, *New England Journal of Medicine*	Public health: presents evidence that keeping a gun in the home increases the chance of violent death for residents
1989	Sanford Levinson, *Yale Law Journal*	Law: an influential early contribution to the literature making the case for the Second Amendment as a source of a personal right to keep and bear arms
1991	Gary Kleck, *Point Blank: Guns and Violence in America*	Sociology: review of the evidence on guns and violence with a theme that weapon type makes little difference for crime rates and outcomes but does matter in self-defense

1994	Garen Wintemute, *Ring of Fire: The Handgun Makers of Southern California*	Public health: detailed inquiry into the design and marketing of cheap, low-quality handguns
1995	Gary Kleck and Marc Gertz, *Journal of Criminal Law and Criminology*	Sociology: reports often-repeated estimate that there are 2.5 million defensive gun uses per year
1996	David Kennedy, Anne Piehl, and Anthony Braga, *Law and Contemporary Problems*	Criminology: reports the development and effects of the Boston Gun Project, an innovative approach to reducing gun use by gangs through deterrence
1997	Franklin Zimring and Gordon Hawkins, *Crime Is Not the Problem*	Criminology: provides a variety of evidence indicating that the United States is not exceptionally violent compared with other developed nations but has a high murder rate due to widespread gun use
1998	John Lott, *More Guns, Less Crime*	Economics: reports econometric estimates suggesting that easing restrictions on gun carrying reduces all types of common crime
2000	Philip Cook and Jens Ludwig, *Gun Violence: The Real Costs*	Economics: reviews alternative conceptions of the social cost of gun violence and provides a new estimate based on a national contingent-valuation survey
2004	David Hemenway, *Private Guns, Public Health*	Public health: comprehensive account of the evidence concerning the effects of widespread gun ownership on injury rates and self-defense
2005	Charles Wellford, J. V. Pepper, and C. V. Petrie, *Firearms and Violence: A Critical Review*	National Research Council: review of the literature on gun violence by a scholarly panel that concludes that more research is needed to resolve disputes in the field
2009	David Hemenway et al., *American Journal of Preventive Medicine.*	Public health: a brief history of the Violent Death Reporting System, developed by the authors and implemented by CDC

TABLE A2

Additional Statistics from Tark and Kleck

Type of Self-Protection Action	Number of Reports in the NCVS Sample	Percentage Injured Following Self-Protection Action	Percentage Seriously Injured Following Self-Protection Action
Attacked or threatened with gun	166	3.6	.6
Attacked or threatened with other weapon	337	1.8	.6
Attacked without weapon	2,146	3.4	.6
Ran away, hid	3,179	1.6	.3
Argued, reasoned, pleaded	2,146	2.9	.2

SOURCE.—Computed from table 2 of Tark and Kleck (2004).

REFERENCES

Abrams, David S. 2012. "Estimating the Deterrent Effect of Incarceration Using Sentencing Enhancements." Unpublished manuscript. University of Pennsylvania Law School, Institute for Law and Economic Research.

Aneja, Abhay, John J. Donohue III, and Alexandria Zhang. 2012. "The Impact of Right to Carry Laws and the NRC Report: The Latest Lessons for the Empirical Evaluation of Law and Policy." NBER Working Paper no. 18294. Cambridge, MA: National Bureau of Economic Research.

Ayres, Ian, and John J. Donohue III. 2009. "More Guns, Less Crime Fails Again: The Latest Evidence from 1977–2006." *Econ Journal Watch* 6(2):218–38.

Azrael, Deborah, Philip J. Cook, and Matthew Miller. 2004. "State and Local Prevalence of Firearms Ownership: Measurement, Structure, and Trends." *Journal of Quantitative Criminology* 20(1):43–62.

Baker, Susan, Stephen Teret, and Elliott Dietz. 1980. "Firearms and the Public Health." *Journal of Public Health Policy* 1:224–29.

Barber, Catherine, and David Hemenway. 2011. "Too Many or Too Few Unintentional Firearm Deaths in Official US Mortality Data?" *Accident Analysis and Prevention* 43:724–31.

Braga, Anthony A., Philip J. Cook, David M. Kennedy, and Mark H. Moore. 2002. "The Illegal Supply of Firearms." In *Crime and Justice: A Review of Research*, vol. 29, edited by Michael Tonry. Chicago: University of Chicago Press.

Braga, Anthony A., David M. Kennedy, Elin J. Waring, and Anne M. Piehl. 2001. "Problem-Oriented Policing, Deterrence, and Youth Violence: An

Evaluation of Boston's Operation Ceasefire." *Journal of Research in Crime and Delinquency* 38(3):195–225.

Braga, Anthony A., and David L. Weisburd. 2012. "The Effects of Focused Deterrence Strategies on Crime: A Systematic Review and Meta-Analysis of the Empirical Evidence." *Journal of Research in Crime and Delinquency* 49(3): 323–58.

Bruce-Briggs, Barry. 1976. "The Great American Gun War." *Public Interest* 45: 33–62.

Butterfield, Fox. 1997. *All God's Children: The Bosket Family and the American Tradition of Violence.* New York: Knopf.

Cheng, Cheng, and Mark Hoekstra. 2012. "Does Strengthening Self-Defense Law Deter Crime or Escalate Violence? Evidence from Castle Doctrine." NBER Working Paper no. 18134. Cambridge, MA: National Bureau of Economic Research.

Clarke, Ronald V., and David Weisburd. 1994. "Diffusion of Crime Control Benefits: Observations on the Reverse of Displacement." In *Crime Prevention Studies*, vol. 2, edited by Ronald V. Clarke. Monsey, NY: Criminal Justice Press.

Cohen, Mark A., Roland T. Rust, Sara Steen, and Simon T. Tidd. 2004. "Willingness-to-Pay for Crime Control Programs." *Criminology* 42(1):89–109.

Cook, Philip J. 1976. "A Strategic Choice Analysis of Robbery." In *Sample Surveys of the Victims of Crimes*, edited by Wesley Skogan. Pensacola, FL: Ballinger.

———. 1979. "The Effect of Gun Availability on Robbery and Robbery Murder: A Cross Section Study of Fifty Cities." *Policy Studies Review Annual* 3: 743–81.

———. 1980. "Reducing Injury and Death Rates in Robbery." *Policy Analysis* 6(1):21.

———. 1985. "The Case of the Missing Victims: Gunshot Woundings in the National Crime Survey." *Journal of Quantitative Criminology* 1(1):91–102.

———. 1986. "The Relationship between Victim Resistance and Injury in Noncommercial Robbery." *Journal of Legal Studies* 15(1):405–16.

———. 1987. "Robbery Violence." *Journal of Criminal Law and Criminology* 78(2):357–76.

———. 1991. "The Technology of Personal Violence." In *Crime and Justice: A Review of Research*, vol. 14, edited by Michael Tonry. Chicago: University of Chicago Press.

———. 2009. "Robbery." In *Oxford Handbook on Crime and Public Policy*, edited by Michael Tonry. New York: Oxford University Press.

Cook, Philip J., and Anthony A. Braga. 2001. "Comprehensive Firearms Tracing: Strategic and Investigative Uses of New Data on Firearms Markets." *Arizona Law Review* 43(2):277–309.

Cook, Philip J., Anthony A. Braga, and Mark H. Moore. 2010. "Gun Control." In *Crime and Public Policy*, edited by James Q. Wilson and Joan Petersilia. New York: Oxford University Press.

Cook, Philip J., Bruce Lawrence, Jens Ludwig, and Ted Miller. 1999. "The

Medical Costs of Gunshot Wounds." *Journal of the American Medical Association* 282(5):447–54.

Cook, Philip J., and James A. Leitzel. 1996. "Perversity, Futility, Jeopardy: An Economic Analysis of the Attack on Gun Control." *Law and Contemporary Problems* 59(1):91–118.

Cook, Philip J., and Jens Ludwig. 1996. *Guns in America: Results of a Comprehensive National Survey on Firearms Ownership and Use.* Washington, DC: Police Foundation.

———. 2000. *Gun Violence: The Real Costs.* New York: Oxford University Press.

———. 2002. "Litigation as Regulation: Firearms." In *Regulation through Litigation*, edited by W. Kip Viscusi. Washington, DC: Brookings Institution Press.

———. 2003. "The Effects of Gun Prevalence on Burglary: Deterrence vs. Inducement." In *Evaluating Gun Policy*, edited by Jens Ludwig and Philip J. Cook. Washington, DC: Brookings Institution Press.

———. 2006a. "Aiming for Evidence-Based Gun Policy." *Journal of Policy Analysis and Management* 25(3):691–735.

———. 2006b. "The Social Costs of Gun Ownership." *Journal of Public Economics* 90(1–2):379–91.

Cook, Philip J., Jens Ludwig, and Anthony A. Braga. 2005. "Criminal Records of Homicide Offenders." *Journal of the American Medical Association* 294(5): 598–601.

Cook, Philip J., Jens Ludwig, and David Hemenway. 1997. "The Gun Debate's New Mythical Number: How Many Defensive Uses per Year?" *Journal of Policy Analysis and Management* 16(3):463–69.

Cook, Philip J., Jens Ludwig, and Adam M. Samaha. 2009. "Gun Control after Heller: Threats and Sideshows from a Social Welfare Perspective." *UCLA Law Review* 56(5):1041–93.

———. 2011. "Gun Control after Heller: Litigating against Regulation." In *Regulation versus Litigation*, edited by Daniel Kessler. Chicago: University of Chicago Press.

Cook, Philip J., Jens Ludwig, Sudhir A. Venkatesh, and Anthony A. Braga. 2007. "Underground Gun Markets." *Economic Journal* 117(524):588–618.

Cook, Philip J., Stephanie Molliconi, and Thomas Cole. 1995. "Regulating Gun Markets." *Journal of Criminal Law and Criminology* 86(1):59–92.

Cook, Philip J., Mark H. Moore, and Anthony A. Braga. 2002. "Gun Control." In *Crime: Public Policies for Crime Control*, edited by James Q. Wilson and Joan Petersilia. Oakland, CA: ICS Press.

Cook, Philip J., and Daniel Nagin. 1979. *Does the Weapon Matter? An Evaluation of a Weapons-Emphasis Policy in the Prosecution of Violent Offenders.* Washington, DC: Institute for Law and Social Research.

Cook, Philip J., and Susan B. Sorenson. 2006. "The Gender Gap among Teen Survey Respondents: Why Are Boys More Likely to Report a Gun in the Home than Girls?" *Journal of Quantitative Criminology* 22(1):61–76.

Donohue, John J., III. 2003. "The Impact of Concealed-Carry Laws." In *Eval-*

uating Gun Policy, edited by Jens Ludwig and Philip J. Cook. Washington, DC: Brookings Institution Press.

Duggan, Mark. 2001. "More Guns, More Crime." *Journal of Political Economy* 109(5):1086–1114.

Fagan, Jeffrey. 2002. "Policing Guns and Youth Violence." *Future of Children* 12(2):133–51.

Glaeser, Edward L., Bruce Sacerdote, and Jose A. Scheinkman. 1996. "Crime and Social Interactions." *Quarterly Journal of Economics* 111(2):507–48.

Goss, Kristin A. 2006. *Disarmed: The Missing Movement for Gun Control in America*. Princeton, NJ: Princeton University Press.

Harlow, Caroline Wolf. 2001. *Firearms Use by Offenders: 1997 Survey of Inmates in State and Federal Correctional Facilities*. Bureau of Justice Statistics Special Report, NCJ 189369. Washington, DC: Office of Justice Programs, US Department of Justice.

Hemenway, David. 1997*a*. "The Myth of Millions of Self-Defense Gun Uses: An Explanation of Extreme Overestimates." *Chance* 10(3):6–10.

———. 1997*b*. "Survey Research and Self-Defense Gun Use: An Explanation of Extreme Overestimates." *Journal of Criminal Law and Criminology* 87: 1430–45.

———. 2004. *Private Guns, Public Health*. Ann Arbor: University of Michigan Press.

———. 2011. "Risks and Benefits of a Gun in the Home." *American Journal of Lifestyle Medicine*, July 14. http://ajl.sagepub.com/content/5/6/502.

Hemenway, David, Catherine W. Barber, Susan S. Gallagher, and Deborah R. Azrael. 2009. "Creating a National Violent Death Reporting System: A Successful Beginning." *American Journal of Preventive Medicine* 37(1):68–71.

Hemenway, David, Matthew Miller, and Deborah Azrael. 2000. "Gun Use in the United States: Results from Two National Surveys." *Injury Prevention* 6: 263–67.

Hepburn, Lisa, Matthew Miller, Deborah Azrael, and David Hemenway. 2007. "The US Gun Stock: Results from the 2004 National Firearms Survey." *Injury Prevention* 13:15–19.

Hill, J. M. 1997. "The Impact of Liberalized Concealed Weapon Statutes on Rates of Violent Crime." Senior thesis, Duke University, Sanford School of Public Policy.

Hirschman, Albert O. 1991. *The Rhetoric of Reaction: Perversity, Futility, Jeopardy*. Cambridge, MA: Belknap Press of Harvard University Press.

Horwitz, Joshua, and Casey Anderson. 2009. *Guns, Democracy, and the Insurrectionist Idea*. Ann Arbor: University of Michigan Press.

Jacobs, James B. 2002. *Can Gun Control Work?* New York: Oxford University Press.

Kaiser, Frederick M. 2008. "Direct Assaults on Presidents, Presidents-Elect, and Candidates." *Congressional Research Service Report for Congress*, January 7. http://www.fas.org/sgp/crs/misc/RS20821.pdf.

Kellermann, Arthur L., Kidist Bartolomeos, Dawna Fuqua-Whitley, Tomoko Rie Sampson, and Constance S. Parramore. 2001. "Community-Level Firearm Injury Surveillance: Local Data for Local Action." *Annals of Emergency Medicine* 38(4):423–29.

Kellermann, Arthur L., and Don T. Reay. 1986. "Protection or Peril? An Analysis of Firearm-Related Death in the Home." *New England Journal of Medicine* 314(24):1557–60.

Kennedy, David M. 2011. *Don't Shoot: One Man, a Street Fellowship, and the End of Violence in Inner-City America.* New York: Bloomsbury USA.

Kennedy, David M., Anne M. Piehl, and Anthony A. Braga. 1996. "Youth Violence in Boston: Gun Markets, Serious Youth Offenders, and a Use-Reduction Strategy." *Law and Contemporary Problems* 59(1):147–98.

Kleck, Gary. 1988. "Crime Control through Private Use of Armed Force." *Social Problems* 35:1–21.

———. 1991. *Point Blank: Guns and Violence in America.* New York: Aldine de Gruyter.

———. 1997. *Targeting Guns: Firearms and Their Control.* Hawthorne, NY: Aldine de Gruyter.

———. 2004. "Measures of Gun Ownership Levels for Macrolevel Crime and Violence Research." *Journal of Research in Crime and Delinquency* 41(1):3–36.

Kleck, Gary, and Marc Gertz. 1995. "Armed Resistance to Crime: The Prevalence and Nature of Self-Defense with a Gun." *Journal of Criminal Law and Criminology* 86:150–87.

Kleck, Gary, and Karen McElrath. 1991. "The Effects of Weaponry on Human Violence." *Social Forces* 69:669–92.

Kleck, Gary, and E. Britt Patterson. 1993. "The Impact of Gun Control and Gun Ownership Levels on Violence Rates." *Journal of Quantitative Criminology* 9(3):249–87.

Kopel, David B. 2001. "Lawyers, Guns, and Burglars." *Arizona Law Review* 43(2):345–68.

Koper, Christopher S., and Evan Mayo-Wilson. 2006. "Police Crackdowns on Illegal Gun Carrying: A Systematic Review of Their Impact on Gun Crime." *Journal of Experimental Criminology* 2:227–61.

Levinson, Sanford. 1989. "The Embarrassing Second Amendment." *Yale Law Journal* 99:637–59.

Loftin, Colin, and David McDowall. 1981. "One with a Gun Gets You Two: Mandatory Sentencing and Firearms Violence in Detroit." *Annals of the American Academy of Political and Social Science* 455:150–67.

———. 1984. "The Deterrent Effects of the Florida Felony Firearm Law." *Journal of Criminal Law and Criminology* 75(1):250–59.

———. 2003. "Regional Culture and Patterns of Homicide." *Homicide Studies* 7(4):353–67.

Long-Onnen, Jamie Renee. 2000. "Measures of Lethality and Intent in the Geographic Concentration of Gun Homicides." PhD dissertation, University of Maryland, Department of Criminology and Criminal Justice.

Lott, John R. 1998. *More Guns, Less Crime.* Chicago: University of Chicago Press.

Lott, John R., and David B. Mustard. 1997. "Crime, Deterrence, and Right-to-Carry Concealed Handguns." *Journal of Legal Studies* 16(1):1–68.

Ludwig, Jens, and Philip J. Cook. 2000. "Homicide and Suicide Rates Associated with Implementation of the Brady Handgun Violence Prevention Act." *Journal of the American Medical Association* 284(5):585–91.

———. 2001. "The Benefits of Reducing Gun Violence: Evidence from Contingent-Valuation Survey Data." *Journal of Risk and Uncertainty* 22(3):207–26.

Ludwig, Jens, Philip J. Cook, and Tom Smith. 1998. "The Gender Gap in Reporting Household Gun Ownership." *American Journal of Public Health* 88(11):1715–18.

Mair, Julie Samia, Stephen Teret, and Shannon Frattaroli. 2005. "A Public Health Perspective on Gun Violence Prevention." In *Suing the Gun Industry: A Battle at the Crossroads of Gun Control and Mass Torts*, edited by Timothy D. Lytton. Ann Arbor: University of Michigan Press.

McClelland, Chandler, and Erdal Tekin. 2012. "Stand Your Ground Laws, Homicides, and Injuries." NBER Working Paper no. 18187. Cambridge, MA: National Bureau of Economic Research.

McDowall, David, Colin Loftin, and Stanley Presser. 2000. "Measuring Civilian Defensive Firearm Use: A Methodological Experiment." *Journal of Quantitative Criminology* 16(2):1–19.

Miller, Matthew, Deborah Azrael, and David Hemenway. 2002. "Household Firearm Ownership Levels and Homicide Rates across U.S. Regions and States, 1988–1997." *American Journal of Public Health* 92:1988–93.

Newton, George D., and Franklin E. Zimring. 1971. *Firearms and Violence in American Life*. Staff report to the National Commission on the Causes and Prevention of Violence. Washington, DC: US Government Printing Office.

Papachristos, Andrew, Tracey L. Meares, and Jeffrey Fagan. 2007. "Attention Felons: Evaluating Project Safe Neighborhoods in Chicago." *Journal of Empirical Legal Studies* 4(2):223–72.

Piehl, Anne M., S. J. Cooper, Anthony A. Braga, and David M. Kennedy. 2003. "Testing for Structural Breaks in the Evaluation of Programs." *Review of Economics and Statistics* 85(3):550–58.

Podkopacz, Marcy Rasmussen, and Barry C. Feld. 1996. "The End of the Line: An Empirical Study of Judicial Waiver." *Journal of Criminal Law and Criminology* 86(2):449–92.

Raphael, Stephen, and Jens Ludwig. 2003. "Prison Sentence Enhancements: The Case of Project Exile." In *Evaluating Gun Policy*, edited by Jens Ludwig and Philip J. Cook. Washington, DC: Brookings Institution Press.

Richardson, Erin G., and David Hemenway. 2011. "Homicide, Suicide, and Unintentional Firearm Fatality: Comparing the United States with Other High-Income Countries, 2003." *Journal of Trauma* 70(1):238–43.

Robuck-Mangum, Gail. 1997. "Concealed Weapon Permit Holders in North Carolina: A Descriptive Study of Handgun-Carrying Behavior." Master's thesis, University of North Carolina, School of Public Health.

Rosenfeld, Richard, Robert Fornango, and Eric Baumer. 2005. "Did Ceasefire,

Compstat, and Exile Reduce Homicide?" *Criminology and Public Policy* 4(3): 419–50.

Saltzman, Linda E., James A. Mercy, and Philip H. Rhodes. 1992. "Identification of Nonfatal Family and Intimate Assault Incidents in Police Data." *American Journal of Public Health* 82(7):1018–20.

Sherman, Lawrence W., and Dennis P. Rogan. 1995. "Effects of Gun Seizures on Gun Violence: 'Hot Spots' Patrol in Kansas City." *Justice Quarterly* 12(4): 673–93.

Smith, Tom W. 2000. "Public Opinion about Gun Policies." *Future of Children* 12(2):155–63.

Tark, Jongyeon, and Gary Kleck. 2004. "Resisting Crime: The Effects of Victim Action on the Outcomes of Crimes." *Criminology* 42(4):861–909.

Terry, Don. 1992. "How Criminals Get Their Guns: In Short, All Too Easily." *New York Times*, March 11.

Thaler, Richard. 1978. "A Note on the Value of Crime Control: Evidence from the Property Market." *Journal of Urban Economics* 5:137–45.

Vernick, Jon S., and Lisa M. Hepburn. 2003. "State and Federal Gun Laws: Trends for 1970–99." In *Evaluating Gun Policy: Effects on Crime and Violence*, edited by Jens Ludwig and Philip J. Cook. Washington, DC: Brookings Institution Press.

Webster, Daniel W., Jon S. Vernick, and M. T. Bulzacchelli. 2010. "Effects of State-Level Firearm Seller Accountability Policies on Firearms Trafficking." *Journal of Urban Health* 86:525–37.

Webster, Daniel W., Jon S. Vernick, and Lisa M. Hepburn. 2001. "Relationship between Licensing, Registration, and Other Gun Sale Laws and the Source State of Crime Guns." *Injury Prevention* 7:184–89.

———. 2002. "Effects of Maryland's Law Banning 'Saturday Night Special' Handguns on Homicides." *American Journal of Epidemiology* 155(5):406–12.

Weisburd, David, and Cody W. Telep. 2012. "Spatial Displacement and Diffusion of Crime Control Benefits Revisited: New Evidence on Why Crime Doesn't Just Move Around the Corner." In *The Reasoning Criminologist: Essays in Honour of Ronald V. Clarke*, edited by Nick Tilley and Graham Farrell. Florence, KY: Routledge.

Wellford, C. F., J. V. Pepper, and C. V. Petrie. 2005. *Firearms and Violence: A Critical Review*. Washington, DC: National Academies Press.

Wintemute, Garen J. 1994. *Ring of Fire: The Handgun Maker of Southern California*. Sacramento, CA: Violence Prevention Research Program.

Wolfgang, Marvin E. 1958. *Patterns of Criminal Homicide*. Philadelphia: University of Pennsylvania Press.

———. 1995. "A Tribute to a View I Have Opposed." *Journal of Criminal Law and Criminology* 86(1):188–92.

Wright, James D., Jana L. Jasinski, and Drew N. Lanier. 2012. "Crime, Punishment, and Social Disorder: Crime Rates and Trends in Public Opinion over More than Three Decades." In *Social Trends in American Life: Findings from the General Social Survey, 1972*, edited by Peter V. Marsden. Princeton, NJ: Princeton University Press.

Wright, James D., Peter H. Rossi, and Kathleen Daly. 1983. *Under the Gun: Weapons, Crime, and Violence in America.* New York: Aldine de Gruyter.

Zimring, Franklin E. 1968. "Is Gun Control Likely to Reduce Violent Killings?" *University of Chicago Law Review* 35:21–37.

———. 1972. "The Medium Is the Message: Firearm Caliber as a Determinant of Death from Assault." *Journal of Legal Studies* 1:97–123.

———. 1975. "Firearms and Federal Law: The Gun Control Act of 1968." *Journal of Legal Studies* 4:133–97.

———. 2011. *The City That Became Safe: New York's Lessons for Urban Crime and Its Control.* New York: Oxford University Press.

Zimring, Franklin E., and Gordon Hawkins. 1997. *Crime Is Not the Problem: Lethal Violence in America.* New York: Oxford University Press.

Peter Reuter

Why Has US Drug Policy Changed So Little over 30 Years?

ABSTRACT

Though almost universally criticized as overly punitive, expensive, racially disparate in impact, and ineffective, American drug policy remained largely unchanged from 1980 to 2010. Marijuana is an important exception: policy and law underwent many changes, with the strong likelihood of more, involving increased legal access to the drug, in the near future. For cocaine, heroin, and methamphetamine there has been an almost relentless increase in the numbers incarcerated for drug offenses, rising from about 50,000 in 1980 to 500,000 in 2010. The disparities in African American imprisonment rates are higher for drug offenses than for other types of crime; some of this disparity results from unjustifiably harsher sentences for crack than for powder cocaine offenses. The battles necessary to achieve even modest reductions in these disparities and other overly severe sentencing regimes at the state and federal levels demonstrate how difficult it is to achieve changes in drug policy. Recent reforms in health care at the federal level offer hope for increased access to treatment services, but otherwise only drug policy rhetoric has changed much.

No one is happy with American drug policy. The standard critique is liberal; the policy is overly punitive, racially unjust, extremely expen-

Peter Reuter is professor in the School of Public Policy and Department of Criminology, University of Maryland; a senior economist at the RAND Corporation; and a research fellow at the Institute for the Study of Labor (IZA), Bonn. This essay draws on long collaborations with Jonathan Caulkins and Robert MacCoun. Harold Pollack made helpful comments, and Steve Teles gave useful advice about the politics of reform. Holly Nguyen provided excellent research assistance. Three anonymous referees provided insightful comments.

sive, and, to boot, ineffective. The last charge is what distinguishes it from the critique of criminal justice trends generally. From the right, less articulate on this specific matter, the view is more complex. The US drug problem remains awful, but any change other than increasingly vigorous enforcement is a slippery slope to legalization, an anathema. Conservatives, other than libertarians, provide less a defense of the details of current policies than a vigorous critique of proposed reforms. Libertarians have an easy answer: legalize drugs and these problems will take care of themselves. This polarization is not a temporary state; with minor variation, it has been that way since Ronald Reagan's early years and arguably even since Richard Nixon's war on drugs in the early 1970s.

Marijuana is an important exception to these broad statements, and it receives a lengthy separate treatment in a later section of this essay. Much has changed in marijuana policy and in the intellectual framing of the relevant policy issues. Except where specifically stated in the rest of the introductory remarks, I refer to illegal drugs other than marijuana. I also do not refer here to nonmedical use of prescription drugs; a later section explains why it is appropriate to treat that as a distinct problem.

The stasis in policy and discontent is particularly puzzling since the extent and nature of the problem have changed substantially over the last 40 years. After rapid growth in the number of dependent users of various problematic drugs from about 1967 to 2000, drug use and dependence have been in decline; the same is true for associated violence and public disorder, in which downturns started as early as 1990. Yet there has been scarcely any serious policy change beyond a very recent increase in treatment funding and a period during the 1970s, mostly associated with the Nixon administration, when methadone maintenance was the central drug control program for the federal government. The attention to international drug policy has waxed and waned, reflecting more the nation's concerns with particular nations (Afghanistan, Colombia, and Mexico) than the belief that these interventions would affect US drug problems.

Policy makers' views about the nature of the drug problem have evolved, perhaps even matured, over time. There is now at least a dim understanding that attractive drugs have limited potential reach. None will engulf the nation's youth. The policy rhetoric is less overblown in recent years.[1] The idea that "addiction is a brain disease," promoted initially by the National Institute on Drug Abuse and now a part of federal government rhetoric generally, whatever its programmatic and conceptual weaknesses, at least has provided a basis for talking in a more therapeutic and less exclusively moralized frame about criminally active drug addicts.

One odd feature of the drug policy debate is the reluctance to acknowledge that the US drug problem, by some of the most significant measures, is declining. The White House Office of National Drug Control Policy (ONDCP), once any president has been in office for more than a year, will defensively point to signs of improvement,[2] but that is usually dismissed as political posturing, and the debate continues without any consideration of the decline and its causes.[3] The final section of the essay considers the significance of this observation.

In this essay, I make five major claims. First, marijuana must be treated separately as a social and criminal justice problem, as well as in terms of policy and research influences. Though it is used throughout American society and generates a huge number of arrests, it hardly touches the central problem of American criminal justice, namely, the high incarceration of minorities, nor does it cause great health and social harms. Perhaps the most serious harms relate to its trafficking and production in Mexico. There have been important changes in law over the 50 years to 2012, and there is promise of even greater change in the near future.

Second, for other illicit drugs the only major legal changes over much of that period have been steady increases in the severity of sentencing at both federal and state levels. The number of persons incarcerated for drug offenses rose from 50,000 in the early 1980s to about

---

[1] It is hard to object to the introduction of the 2012 *National Drug Control Strategy*: "Too many Americans need treatment for substance use disorders but do not receive it. Prescription drug abuse continues to claim American lives, and those who take drugs and drive threaten safety on our Nation's roadways. Young people's perceptions of the risks of drug use have declined over the past decade, and research suggests that this often predicts future increases in drug use. There is still much left to do to reform our justice system and break the cycle of drug use and crime" (ONDCP 2012*a*, p. iii).

[2] See, e.g., the Fact Sheet accompanying the release of the 2012 *National Drug Control Strategy*, which stated that "the rate of overall drug use in America *has dropped by roughly one-third over the past three decades. Since 2006, meth use in America has been cut by half and cocaine use has dropped by nearly 40 percent*" (ONDCP 2012*c*; emphasis in original).

[3] The public never sees the problem as getting better. See poll results in Gallup (2007).

500,000 in 2010. Efforts to find better ways to keep criminally active drug users out of prison (especially by use of drug courts) have achieved prominence in recent years but have had minimal success in keeping older and less violent addicts in the community. The criticism of sentencing for drug offenses has been well developed, with many claiming that the resulting racial disparities were not unintended; the disparities were both foreseeable and, at least for some policy makers, acceptable. The long battle to reduce 100-to-1 crack-powder disparities at the federal level to 18-to-1 in 2010 is another indicator of how deep is the sentiment in favor of tough penalties.

Third, harm reduction, the idea that governments should pay attention to the harmfulness of drug use, not just to the number of users of drugs, is a big idea that has importantly changed drug policy in much of the Western world, even in societies governed by otherwise conservative leaders and political parties. In the United States, among the core harm reduction programs, only methadone maintenance has been accepted. The federal government has so far rejected harm reduction both rhetorically and substantively; it refuses to consider efforts to directly reduce either the harms of drug use or the adverse consequences of programs aimed at lowering drug use. The slow uptake of needle exchange in the United States shows the strength of the drug war sentiment, even as the rhetoric has changed. The notion of addiction as a brain disease may be somewhat lessening the harshness of drug policies.

Fourth, legalization, the idea that drugs such as cocaine and heroin should be treated like alcohol and be made available legally under substantial regulatory restrictions, deserves separate discussion. Though it has no appeal to the general public, it continues to attract a great deal of interest from the educated elite and, very recently, from some Latin American presidents. The harms that make up the current drug problem are primarily the consequence of the policies used for control rather than the drugs. The gains from prohibition, if any, in terms of fewer users and addicts are hard to identify empirically. However, it is difficult to make a compelling empirical case for legalization.

Fifth, the prevalence of drug use, the most widely reported measure of drug problems, is not a good target for drug policy. Prevention and law enforcement are too ineffective, and treatment and harm reduction programs yield different benefits (such as lower crime and less transmission of blood-borne viruses). Nor does prevalence capture the heart of what disturbs American society about illicit drugs. Policy should be oriented toward reducing violence, dysfunction, and disease related to drug use and to reducing the use of incarceration and reducing racial disparities in that incarceration.

This essay is organized in six sections. Section I briefly summarizes the history of drug problems and drug policy, providing a setting for what follows. Section II discusses marijuana in some detail. Marijuana needs to be set aside since it is a distinct and separate problem and discussions that fail to distinguish it from the other drugs quickly become confused. Section III reviews policies toward other drugs, focusing on the goals of policies and briefly examining and assessing the array of programs that have aimed at reducing consumption of cocaine, heroin, and methamphetamine. Section IV then considers a number of important ideas that have played a role in recent debates about drug policy: harm reduction, addiction as a brain disease, legalization, and drug courts. New drug problems are the subject of Section V. Section VI justifies the claim of policy stasis and offers some speculations about the reasons for resistance to change.

I. The Long History

The prohibition of certain psychoactive substances on the basis of their harmfulness to users and others has a long history in the United States.[4] Tobacco and alcohol were the principal targets of prohibition in the nineteenth century (Aaron and Musto 1981; Troyer and Markle 1983). Only toward the end of that century and the beginning of the twentieth century did cocaine and heroin, recent and very powerful additions to the pharmacopoeia available to physicians, come into focus (Musto 1999; Spillane 2000). Until the early twentieth century, antidrug laws were mostly state and local measures. However, growing concern that lax state and municipal laws were failing to contain narcotics addiction, as well as the problems of a legal opium regime that the United States inherited with the conquest of the Philippines, prompted federal legislation, most importantly the Harrison Act in 1914. On its face, the Harrison Act appeared only to regulate the production and distribution of opium and coca derivatives, but in practice it was interpreted by the courts to preclude doctors from prescribing

---

[4] This section draws on Boyum and Reuter (2005).

drugs to maintain addiction, and it ushered in a half century of increasingly punitive antidrug laws. The act itself increased the maximum penalty specified in federal narcotics laws to 5 years from 2. But by the end of the 1950s, federal and some state antinarcotics laws included life imprisonment and the death penalty; they also prescribed mandatory minimum sentences for certain drug offenses. Still, the scale of enforcement was minor, as was drug use (Courtwright 1982). In assessing the success of prohibition of cocaine and heroin, it is useful to remember that there was a period, perhaps characterized by strong informal social controls, when prohibition largely achieved its goal of keeping drug use rare without intrusive enforcement.

Until 1969, federal government action regarding illicit drugs was rather limited. Although antidrug legislation, including the Marihuana Tax Act of 1937, the Boggs Act of 1951, and the Narcotics Control Act of 1956, had been enacted with much fanfare, neither federal funding nor programs were substantial.[5] Despite the international prominence of its long-time director, Harry Anslinger, the Federal Bureau of Narcotics remained a small agency with no more than 300 agents when he retired in 1962 (Epstein 1978). Drug treatment was provided in two federal facilities that were adjuncts to prisons in Lexington, Kentucky, and Fort Worth, Texas (Ball and Cottrell 1965).

But in 1971, faced with evidence of a growing heroin problem in many cities, President Nixon became the first president to declare a "war on drugs." The president focused initially on international controls, reflecting the belief that since the drugs originated overseas, so should the solution. As most heroin was thought to come from Turkey, Nixon pressured that nation to ban opium cultivation. The Turkish government enacted such a ban in 1971 in return for US provision of compensation payments to farmers, but Turkish electoral politics led to a rescinding of the ban and to a good deal of congressional rhetoric about faithless allies (Spain 1975). Even after the ban was lifted, however, tighter control by the Turkish government resulted in a sharp

---

[5] The Marihuana Tax Act of 1937 imposed a $1 tax on anyone selling marijuana; the bite was that paying the tax required declaration of participation in an illegal activity. The Supreme Court ruled the act unconstitutional in 1969, leading to the passage of the Controlled Substances Act in 1970. The Boggs Act of 1951 toughened sentences for federal drug offenses, including creation of mandatory minimums for second or subsequent offenses. The Narcotics Control Act of 1956 toughened sentences still further; the minimum sentence for a first offense of distribution was 5 years (National Commission on Marihuana and Drug Abuse 1972).

diminution in estimated heroin production in that country. Vietnam, neighboring the Golden Triangle, then the dominant source of heroin production globally, weighed in the mix. US troops were heavily involved in heroin use and, to a lesser extent, in trafficking back to the United States (Epstein 1978).

Under President Nixon, the Controlled Substances Act was passed in 1970; it remains the central statute for regulating psychoactive substances.[6] The other major initiative of the Nixon administration was the creation of a federally subsidized drug treatment system, built primarily around provision of methadone, which had been developed as a heroin agonist in the early 1960s. Treatment dominated federal antidrug spending from 1971 to 1975, although less because of a humane attitude toward drug users than because methadone seemed to offer a "silver bullet" for the heroin problem, and Nixon's aide Egil "Bud" Krogh had little faith in drug enforcement (Goldberg 1980; Massing 1998). Methadone maintenance was a centerpiece of the first modern presidential crackdown on crime (Massing 1998).

In the mid-1970s it became clear that the heroin epidemic had passed its peak, perhaps because of the success of overseas supply efforts, including the Turkish opium ban, the spraying of Mexican opium fields, and the breaking of the "French connection" trafficking route (Paoli, Greenfield, and Reuter 2009). As a result, interest in drug policy diminished at the federal level. Federal drug control expenditures declined in real terms,[7] and both presidents Ford and Carter distanced themselves from the drug issue. President Carter's one initiative, an endorsement of the removal of criminal penalties for possession of small amounts of marijuana for personal use, had no legislative consequence.[8] Carter's most memorable quote regarding the matter in a message to Congress on August 2, 1977, "Penalties against possession

[6] The act provides for the scheduling of psychoactive substances according to their abuse liability potential and their medicinal value. Schedule I drugs have high abuse potential and no approved medical use; heroin and marijuana are Schedule I drugs. Cocaine is Schedule II (high abuse potential and an approved medical use) since it has a minor niche in medical practice as a topical anesthetic for eye surgery and in dentistry.

[7] In 1974, the final year of the Nixon administration, the total drug control budget was $788 million; in 1978, during the Carter administration, the figure was $794 million (Carnevale and Murphy 1999). In real terms this was a decline of roughly 24 percent.

[8] Nor was President Carter's standing on this issue helped when his principal adviser on drug policy, Peter Bourne, was caught having written an unauthorized prescription for an opioid for a member of his staff. Bourne resigned over the incident (Meier 1994).

of a drug should not be more damaging to an individual than the use of the drug itself," did not remain in the collective memory for long. Even a substantial growth of marijuana use in high school popula- tions—in 1978, nearly one in nine high school seniors reported having used it on a daily basis during the previous month—did not trigger a strong response from the Carter administration, though it led to the emergence of a strong parents movement (Massing 1998; National In- stitute on Drug Abuse 2002).[9]

Federal interest grew rapidly again after the election of Ronald Rea- gan, who early in his first term gave major speeches announcing new initiatives against drugs. This time cocaine was the primary target, al- though marijuana also received increased attention, thanks in part to the growing influence of nonprofit antidrug organizations. For exam- ple, a Reagan speech at the Justice Department on October 14, 1982, announcing the creation of a new set of prosecutor-led units (the Or- ganized Crime Drug Enforcement Task Force program) was given great prominence. George H. W. Bush, then vice president, made much of his chairing of a border control committee and his leadership of the South Florida Initiative, aimed at closing down the major co- caine and marijuana smuggling routes into south Florida. Federal ex- penditures on drug control grew massively, from about $1.5 billion in fiscal year 1981 to $6.6 billion in fiscal year 1989. The bulk of that increase was for enforcement, especially interdiction, so that by 1989 less than 30 percent of federal expenditures went to prevention and treatment. The president's wife, Nancy Reagan, became famous for her "Just Say No" program.[10]

The growth of a visible cocaine problem, reflected in the deaths of two well-known young athletes 8 days apart in 1986, energized Con- gress.[11] In a series of broad-scope antidrug bills, the penalties for vi- olations of federal drug laws covering both possession and distribution

[9] For a lively discussion of what the parents movement represented in terms of class interests (i.e., whether it was primarily focused on protecting middle-class children), see the 1999 correspondence in the *New York Review of Books* (http://www.nybooks.com/ articles/archives/1999/apr/22/just-say-no-an-exchange/?pagination = false).

[10] There seems to be no relatively objective history of the Reagan era of drug policy. For a critical account from the reformers' side, see Bertram et al. (1996).

[11] Len Bias was a University of Maryland basketball star, recently drafted in the first round by the Boston Celtics, one of the glamor franchises of that era. Don Rogers was a young defensive player for the Cleveland Browns and the 1984 Defensive Player of the Year. See http://sportsillustrated.cnn.com/vault/article/magazine/MAG1064997/ index.htm.

were toughened significantly.[12] Nor was this just punitive rhetoric; by creating a commission to set guidelines for sentences in 1984 and later setting high mandatory minimums, Congress ensured that those convicted in federal courts would serve long sentences. By 1992 the average time served for drug offenses in federal prison had risen to more than 6 years, up from about 2 years in 1980. Combined with increasingly aggressive investigative and prosecutorial efforts, these measures resulted in an extraordinary increase in the number and length of federal prison sentences served for drug offenses, from the equivalent of 4,500 cell-years in 1980 to over 85,000 cell-years in 1992 and over 135,000 cell-years in 2001.[13] While many in Congress expressed dissatisfaction with the emphasis on enforcement over prevention and treatment, they were unable to affect the budget division for many years.

At about this time, a sharp spike in popular concern about the drug problem briefly made it the leading national issue in polls. President George H. W. Bush made drugs the subject of his first prime-time televised address in September 1989. The ONDCP's first director, William Bennett (appointed by President Bush), provided a clear rationale for the focus on criminal penalties. The problem, said Bennett, was drug use itself rather than its consequences; in this he departed from a number of earlier statements associated with the Carter and Ford administrations. Success was to be measured not by reductions in crime or disease associated with drugs but in the numbers of users (ONDCP 1989).

The Clinton administration efforts can readily be summarized: no change (Carnevale and Murphy 1999). There were some differences in rhetoric, with greater emphasis on the small number of offenders who were frequent drug users. However, that had no material impact on the allocation of the federal drug-control budget; two-thirds continued to go to enforcement activities, predominantly inside the United States. Sentencing policy did not change either: large numbers of federal de-

---

[12] For example, the Anti–Drug Abuse Act of 1986 imposed mandatory minimum sentences of 5 and 10 years for those convicted of trafficking in 500 grams of crack cocaine or 5,000 grams of powder cocaine. The Anti–Drug Abuse Act of 1988 extended these sentences to anyone involved in a criminal enterprise that handled such quantities, thus bringing in those with minimal active responsibility, such as a friend who lent an apartment for the trafficking. See Sullivan (1988) for a legal assessment of the act.

[13] Cell-years of sentences is the number of sentences multiplied by the average length of expected prison time per sentenced defendant.

fendants continued to receive and serve long prison sentences for drug offenses. Between 1992 and 2000, the number of federal prisoners serving time for drug offenses almost doubled, rising from 35,398 to 63,898 (Pastore and Maguire 2003).

The administration of George W. Bush made changes in both substance and rhetoric. Internationally, much less emphasis was placed on blaming Latin America for the inflow of drugs. Meeting with Mexican President Vicente Fox in February 2001, President Bush said, "The main reason why drugs are shipped through Mexico to the United States is because United States citizens use drugs. And our nation must do a better job of educating our citizenry about the dangers and evils of drug use. Secondly, I believe there is a movement in the country to review all the certification process" (Office of the Press Secretary 2001). As a consequence, an annual fight about certification of the drug control efforts by Mexico, often the source of great indignation there, subsided.

At the same time, the administration increased emphasis on the dangers of marijuana. Between 2001 and 2008, ONDCP published many documents making the case that marijuana was more dangerous than is generally perceived by adults, and certainly more dangerous than it was 20 years earlier, when it had a lower tetrahydrocannabinol (THC) content. Rhetoric emphasized both prevention and treatment, with President Bush making a number of statements about the importance of having an adequate number of treatment slots available; the allocation of the federal drug budget did not, however, shift much to prevention and treatment over that period.[14]

President Obama has personally been silent on the subject of drug policy, though the rhetoric of his administration has distinctly softened;[15] not only does the ONDCP director eschew the "war on drugs"

[14] The statement about the drug budget is deliberately vague since the Bush administration changed the way in which this was calculated. ONDCP dropped categories of expenditures that it viewed as passive rather than proactive. These included the costs of prosecution and incarceration since these were merely a response to investigation and arrest. The result was not simply a smaller budget but one that was less dominated by enforcement. For a criticism, see Walsh (2004). The budget estimation procedure was changed back to its original form in 2012.

[15] The fact that Obama in his autobiography *Dreams from My Father* (1995) admits to having used marijuana regularly at one stage of his youth and to having tried cocaine does not appear to have affected his image as a clean-living adult. However, as was true for President Clinton, it may hamper his ability to push for reforms that would reduce the severity of the regime.

terminology, he actively promotes more humane approaches to drug problems. The first African American president has not spoken out on the sentencing of drug offenders that has sent so many minority youths to jail or prison. The Obama administration did successfully battle with Congress to reduce the federal crack-cocaine powder sentencing disparity from 100-to-1 to 18-to-1. This is discussed below.

II. Marijuana

Marijuana needs to be separated from other illegal drugs for both substantive and rhetorical reasons.[16] It dominates many statistical series, such as drug arrests, numbers of users, and even dependent users and treatment episodes.[17] It is the only illegal drug whose use is a routine event of growing up in America, as it is in many other Western nations (Room et al. 2010). Simple possession of marijuana has accounted for about half of all drug arrests since the late 1990s.

Marijuana, however, probably contributes less than 5 percent to the numbers incarcerated for drug offenses, almost exclusively in local jails for pretrial detention.[18] The trade also generates little violence within the United States, though that is not true for Mexico.[19] To a larger extent than is true for cocaine and heroin, the harms of the drug under

[16] Prominent critiques of the drug war such as Michelle Alexander's *The New Jim Crow* (2010) or Doris Provine's *Unequal under Law: Race in the War on Drugs* (2007) give little attention to marijuana. In particular, they confound the interpretation of statistics by failing to separate out marijuana arrests from those for other drugs, for which arrestees face high risk of incarceration as a sentence. The same is true for Blumstein and Beck (2005). Tonry in his *Punishing Race* (2011) does separate it out at some points but not consistently.

[17] The number of dependent marijuana users, as estimated in the most recent National Survey on Drug Use and Health (2011), is 4.2 million. The Substance Abuse and Mental Health Services Administration (SAMHSA 2012) reports that according to the 2008 Treatment Episode Data Set, 321,000 of admission episodes are classified as having marijuana as the primary drug of abuse. This is the largest number for any single drug; the figure for cocaine is 213,000 and for heroin is 267,000.

[18] There has been considerable controversy around the extent and cost of incarceration of marijuana offenders. Legalization advocates have estimated the percentage of drug incarceration expenditures going to marijuana as high as 5.5 percent (e.g., Miron 2003, 2010). However, Miron's assumption that marijuana arrestees are as likely as other drug arrestees to end up incarcerated is implausible. For a painfully detailed analysis of California, generating much lower numbers, see Caulkins (2010).

[19] It is always difficult to document a negative, but there is little reference to homicides in the US marijuana trade. What share of Mexico's drug-related homicides can be attributed to marijuana is impossible to determine. It might be substantial, given that marijuana accounts, conservatively, for almost 25 percent of the revenues of Mexican drug-trafficking organizations (Kilmer et al. 2010).

prohibition are probably consequences of the drug itself, not of prohibition. Those harms come primarily from consuming an addicting intoxicant, with no acute deaths except through accidents. It is not clear whether, if legalized, marijuana would be consumed in a safer fashion than smoking or that high potency, prized by users now, would persist. There is indeed growing interest in other components of the drug, particularly CBD (cannabidiol), which has some positive effects that offset the harms of THC (McLaren et al. 2008). The marijuana trade generates substantial illegal earnings, about $30 billion according to the most recent estimates (ONDCP 2012*b*). In terms of the harms caused to US society by marijuana under current policies, it is much less important than cocaine or heroin, possibly even methamphetamine, notwithstanding its large user base, many dependent users, and many arrestees. It has caused great harm to Mexico, as a source of both homicides and corruption (Kleiman and Davenport 2012).

The politics of marijuana are much more contentious than those of the other drugs; it is the only currently illicit drug that might be made legal. Already medical marijuana initiatives have been passed in about one-third of states, generating growing conflict between the federal government and many states (e.g., Onishi 2012). Two states, Colorado and Washington, have recently passed initiatives that make it legal under state law to possess marijuana; they both also provide for a regulated system of production and distribution, the first such systems in modern times. All these activities remain illegal under federal law in those states, and as of this writing 6 months after the passage of the referendums in those two states, it remains unclear what the Department of Justice will do to support or thwart the will of the citizens of those states.

A. Use and Policies

Marijuana first became broadly popular in the 1960s, when it was also a symbol of generational clashes and a prominent weapon in the culture wars. Debate about policy became vigorous enough that President Nixon felt obliged to create a commission, led by former Pennsylvania governor Raymond Shaffer, to assess policy options for marijuana (National Commission on Marihuana and Drug Abuse 1972). The president was chagrined when the commission concluded that the existing prohibition might well be an error. He denounced the report even before it was delivered to him. At the time, this was thought to be a brief interruption in the march to sanity (e.g., Bonnie and White-bread 1974). A dozen states did in fact remove criminal penalties for the possession of small amounts of marijuana during the 1970s.

The prevalence of marijuana use among adolescents continued to rise through the 1970s, and public concern grew.[20] According to the annual Monitoring the Future high school student survey, about one in 10 high school seniors used marijuana daily in 1980 (Johnson, Bachman, and O'Malley 1981). What might be relatively harmless for adults seemed much more dangerous to the young, particularly in a period when many people believed in the "amotivational syndrome."[21] The "parents movement," focused on the problem, emerged.[22] The decriminalization movement came to a sudden halt; until a successful ballot initiative in Massachusetts in 2008, no state decriminalized for 30 years after 1978.

The 1980s saw two surprising changes. First was the plummeting of marijuana use among adolescents: by the end of the decade, the percentage of daily users among high school seniors had fallen by 80 percent; only one in 50 fell into that category by 1990. Second, the number of arrests for marijuana possession fell even faster than the number of past-12-month users so that the probability of arrest, conditional on use in the previous year, declined. A simple explanation for this sharp decline in arrests was that the war on other drugs had now started; cocaine and heroin arrest rates rose sharply as marijuana possession arrests declined. No other explanation appears in the literature.[23]

The standard explanation for the decline in marijuana use is that, as measured in Monitoring the Future, perceptions of its dangers increased (Pacula et al. 2000). However, that merely shifts the mystery;

[20] The annual Gallup Poll (2002) data show that in 1978, 66 percent of Americans said marijuana was a serious problem in high schools or middle schools. Moreover, there was little acceptance of marijuana: 21 percent said that they would welcome increased acceptance of marijuana, while 72 percent said that they would not.

[21] Amotivation syndrome is a psychological condition characterized by lack of desire to participate in social activities, diminished motivation, and apathy (Creason and Goldman 1981).

[22] The parents movement emerged in the late 1970s as a response to the rapid escalation in drug use by children and adolescents. It emphasized educating neighbors and friends about the harms of drugs, working with community groups, and closing stores that sold drug paraphernalia and local crack houses (Lune 2002).

[23] During the 1980s, cigarette use among high school seniors remained constant, while measures of drinking fell.

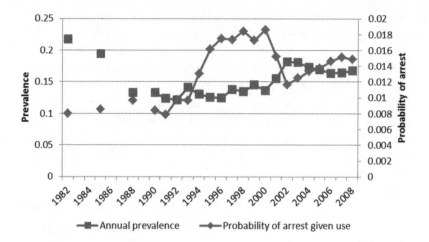

FIG. 1.—Probability of arrest for marijuana possession, conditional on use in past year and prevalence of past-year marijuana use, 1982–2008. Source: Nguyen and Reuter (2012).

why did perceptions of danger increase? Certainly no one claims that the decline was the result of effective prevention programs, which in that period took a particularly weak form, information only or fear tactics (Gottfredson 1997; Howell 2003). The list of possible factors is long and unexamined: economic events (e.g., the deep recession of 1981–83), growing conservatism generally, and the start of effective antismoking campaigns, to name just a few.

The decline in both use and arrests reversed sharply in the 1990s; again arrests and use were positively rather than negatively correlated. Prevalence of use among youths rose nearly one-third. Arrests rose even more rapidly, so that the probability of being arrested conditional on use had more than doubled (fig. 1). The unexpected positive correlation between arrest probabilities and youthful marijuana use is also unexamined.

It is worth noting the negative correlation of marijuana possession arrests with arrests for cocaine and heroin.[24] In 1991, when marijuana arrests bottomed out, arrests for heroin and cocaine (possession and sale) totaled 558,000, compared with a total for marijuana of 327,000. By 2010 the figures had reversed: the heroin and cocaine total had

[24] The Uniform Crime Reports combine cocaine and heroin arrests into one category.

fallen to 371,000 compared with a much higher total of 853,000 for marijuana.

By the late 1970s marijuana use had become normative in the sense that about half of each birth cohort had tried the drug at least once by age 21. Despite all the fluctuations in the rates for high school seniors, that statement continues to be true.

If the increase in the prevalence of marijuana use among youths in the early 1990s is hard to explain, the increase in arrests is downright mysterious. It is perilously hard to find any evidence that the rise in marijuana arrests of the last 20 years is the consequence of strategic policy decisions at the national level. The head of the ONDCP could be relied on in any administration to utter dire warnings about the dangers of marijuana.[25] There were also plenty of warnings about the menace of decriminalization, including some remarkably intemperate words in 2002 when Canada proposed to do what a dozen US states had done in the 1970s and remove penalties for possession of small amounts.[26] However, the Department of Justice as the principal enforcement agency did not elevate marijuana in its priorities; indeed, local prosecutors in border states were unhappy that US Attorneys' offices would generally prosecute marijuana smugglers only if the case involved at least 50 pounds of the drug.[27] Federal arrests for marijuana between 1996 and 2010 increased from 4,249 to 6,320.

Nor was there a rush of announcements of a crackdown on marijuana at the state or local level. New York City Mayor Rudy Giuliani proudly announced a large increase in marijuana arrests in 1998 at the beginning of his second term (Flynn 1998). This, however, seemed to

[25] Barry McCaffery in an interview at CNN in 1997 stated, "The most dangerous drug in America is a 12-year-old smoking pot because they put themselves in this enormous statistical probability of having a compulsive drug problem." John Walters authored an op-ed in the *Washington Post* entitled "The Myth of 'Harmless' Marijuana" (2002) and wrote, "marijuana is far from 'harmless'—it is pernicious. Parents are often unaware that today's marijuana is different from that of a generation ago, with potency levels 10 to 20 times stronger than the marijuana with which they were familiar."

[26] "After Canada introduced its initial marijuana bill in May 2003, Walters, the US Drug Control Policy Director, warned that if the bill passed, the result would be increased security and lengthy delays at the border" (*Detroit News* 2003). He was quoted as saying, "We don't want the border with Canada looking like the US-Mexico border" (*Boston Globe* 2003). "You expect your friends to stop the movement of poison toward your neighbourhood" (http://www.parl.gc.ca/content/LOP/ResearchPublications/prb 0433-e.htm).

[27] The argument of state and local officials is that the traffic serves national rather than local markets, and thus the federal government should take responsibility for prosecution as well as for arrests and seizures.

be claiming a victory for a war that had not previously been declared. Perhaps the rise in arrests was a consequence of "quality of life" policing that was a distinctive feature of the New York Policy Department strategy from 1993 onward, but large increases throughout the nation suggested that the source of the increase was something more fundamental than that. That arrests for marijuana distribution and cultivation rose so much less nationally from 1993 to 2010 also suggested that this increase nationally represented something less than a war on marijuana.[28]

There is little research on marijuana enforcement.[29] What empirical research has been done in recent years has mostly been about New York City, where marijuana possession arrest rates have been extraordinary. Before 1993 there had never been more than 2,500 arrests in a year for simple possession of marijuana. By 2000 the figure had reached about 50,000, a level at which it stayed through the next decade (and administration). Jeffrey Fagan, Andrew Golub, Harry Levine, and the late Bruce Johnson have all contributed empirical studies that document the extraordinarily high incidence of marijuana possession arrests in areas with high rates of poverty and proportions of minority residents (e.g., Johnson, Golub, and Dunlap 2006; Golub, Johnson, and Dunlap 2007; Levine and Small 2008). They have also documented practices that effectively mock the intent of the law criminalizing only public display of the drug;[30] this led in early 2012 to the long-term police commissioner, Raymond Kelly, reluctantly authorizing an inquiry into abusive arrest practices. In June 2012 Mayor Michael Bloomberg announced that he was backing legal changes that would decriminalize open possession of marijuana (Kaplan 2012). All this reinforces the sense that marijuana enforcement in New York City is not

---

[28] From 1991, the low point, to 2010, marijuana possession arrests more than tripled, whereas arrests for cultivation, distribution, and retailing increased by less than 50 percent. In 2010 the number of arrests for marijuana distribution was approximately 100,000, less than one-seventh the number of possession arrests.

[29] This lack of research is perhaps indicative of how lightly the criminological community has taken this drug, despite the ubiquity of its use and the large numbers of arrests in recent years.

[30] New York State has removed criminal penalties for the possession of less than 1 ounce of marijuana; this is subject only to a fine. However, public display of marijuana is an arrestable offense. An officer would ask an individual who had been stopped to empty his or her pockets; though this request can be refused, it rarely is. If the pocket contains marijuana, it is now in public view and an arrest can (and often will) be made (Levine and Siegel 2011).

about preventing drug use but is primarily another method of public order control, a correlate of the stop and frisk policies that have themselves generated so much anger because of their disparate impact on minority communities.

There are, as so often, few similar studies for other big cities, but the patterns of arrests in terms of race and age are similar across the country. Beckett, in a series of articles on marijuana enforcement in Seattle, has similar findings (e.g., Beckett 2004, 2008; Beckett et al. 2005): marijuana arrests have targeted minorities and youths. Nguyen and Reuter (2012) show that the probability of arrest for marijuana possession, conditional on use, rose much more for the young and for blacks than for other demographic groups. Whereas in 1990 the black arrest rates for marijuana possession were about twice those for whites (219 vs. 108 per 100,000), by 2010 the ratio was 3.5 to 1 (716 vs. 217), even though marijuana use is similar in the two groups, according to population surveys.

The total number of marijuana arrests nationally stopped rising in 2009. This may be related to a decline in the number of police officers, as state and local governments cut payrolls (Copeland 2009).

B. Decriminalization, Medical Marijuana, and Legalization

The issue of criminal penalties for possession of marijuana has been a hardy perennial of debates about the drug. Perhaps, many have argued, production and distribution of marijuana should be kept illegal, but surely criminal penalties for possession are overly severe. That was the argument that drove the reforms in 13 states in the 1970s and was reflected in President Carter's comments on marijuana. However, political attitudes change rapidly. Thirty years ago, with the Reagan administration still relatively new, a National Academy of Sciences (NAS) panel (National Research Council 1982) suggested that the existing policies merited reexamination and that decriminalization should be considered. Even that questioning of the status quo was enough to lead Frank Press, then head of the NAS, to disown the report in his introduction to it. "My own view is that the data available to the Committee were insufficient to justify on scientific or analytical grounds changes in current policies dealing with the use of marijuana" (National Research Council 1982, p. 2). It is almost unheard of for the president of the NAS to write such a letter, let alone require that it be included in the report itself. Moreover, Press insisted that only 300 copies of the report be printed. His statement may have simply reflected a concern that the report endangered funding for the NAS, at least with respect to drug policy and perhaps a bit more broadly. In any case, the report, issued near the beginning of the Reagan administration's launch of the war on drugs, attracted attention only briefly, perhaps reflecting the lack of copies in the pre-Internet era.

The removal of criminal penalties for possession of small quantities has turned out to be a less important change in the law than expected. There is no evidence that it has increased prevalence substantially in the United States; that finding appears in studies of similar legal changes in Australia (e.g., Donnelly, Hall, and Christie 1995) and Germany (Pacula et al. 2005).[31] There are many potential explanations for this phenomenon across all these countries, though a few are specific to the United States.

First, many individuals in the United States are poorly informed about the penalties for simple possession of marijuana in their state. MacCoun et al. (2009) find that "citizens in decriminalization states are only about 29 percent more likely to believe the maximum penalty for possessing an ounce of marijuana is a fine or probation rather than jail" (p. 366). Decriminalization states may not have much higher prevalence because so many individuals in those states think that they still face criminal penalties while substantial percentages of those in nondecriminalized states mistakenly believe that they face no criminal penalties.

One reason for being confused about this is that the law itself is confusing. Pacula, Chriqui, and King (2003) found that the standard classification of states into two groups, decriminalization and nondecriminalization, did not reflect the legal realities of states. Some states conventionally classified as having decriminalized marijuana possession had, by 2000, more severe penalties for marijuana offenses than other states that were not classified as decriminalization. Moreover, what had been decriminalized, simple possession, was not what users were typically arrested for; smoking in public was still a criminal offense, as discussed in relation to New York City's huge arrest numbers. Arrest

---

[31] Australia and Germany are federal countries, like the United States. The states have powers with respect to criminal laws, so it is possible to have variation across states that allows for quasi-experimental analysis. Canada is also a federal country, but the provinces do not have powers to create criminal offenses; only the Canadian Parliament can do that.

rates did not differ between the two groups of states, whether using the old definition of a decriminalized state or the one developed by Pacula, Chriqui, and King.

Moreover, it was not clear that decriminalization represented much change in the risks faced by marijuana users. Nguyen and Reuter (2012) estimate that the annual probability of arrest for a marijuana user is about one in 50 in recent years, even with the increased total number of arrests. A number of studies suggest that the average user consumes about 100 days per year. That would suggest a one in 5,000 risk of being arrested for lighting up a joint.[32] Moreover other research shows that penalties imposed on those convicted of marijuana possession rarely include incarceration. Reuter, Hirschfield, and Davies (2001) found that in Maryland, not a decriminalization state, not a single individual in a sample of about 1,000 arrestees received a jail or prison sentence for simple possession of marijuana, though about one-third stayed at least overnight in a jail before trial.

Ignorance of the law, confusion about what decriminalization means, and minimal penalties even without decriminalization: it is hardly surprising that decriminalization has affected few individuals' decision as to whether to use marijuana. Yet an enormous amount of political effort has been spent in the political fights over decriminalization.

Attitudes toward marijuana have changed substantially through the last 40 years as can be seen in Gallup Poll data. Figure 2 shows the percentage reporting support for removing penalties for consumption of marijuana from 1969 to 2011, along with changes in lifetime prevalence for high school seniors since 1975, the first year of Monitoring the Future. Since 1985 there has been an almost relentless increase in support for removing penalties, even as rates of use among youths have fluctuated.

What drives this increase in support for legalization? Medical marijuana initiatives may have played a role. The medical initiatives have always been presented by drug warriors as mere stalking horses for

---

[32] This is admittedly a very crude calculation. The one in 50 figure comes from dividing the total number of arrests by the total number of past-year users. Some users may be arrested more than once in a year; moreover, the vast majority of marijuana use sessions are accounted for by those who use frequently (weekly or more often). In addition, more frequent users may be more covert in their behavior, so that the risk per joint is unevenly spread among users, classified by frequency. If users mostly share joints, then the number of incidents in the denominator may be overstated. None of these qualifications should alter the order of magnitude.

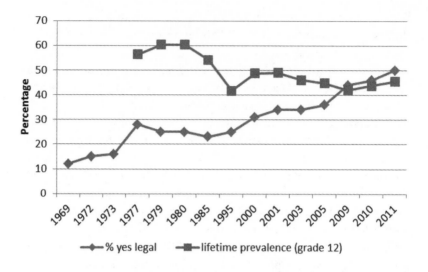

FIG. 2.—Support for making use of marijuana legal and lifetime prevalence, 1969–2011. Source: Gallup (2011) and Johnston et al. (2011).

legalization. They have probably been correct. The groups most aggressively pressing for medical marijuana are drug reform organizations, not patient advocacy groups, such as those representing the interests of AIDS patients. In California, medical marijuana has been implemented so loosely that it provides a legal protection for any user willing to perjure himself by claiming a medical problem for which the drug might be therapeutic; a good description of the anarchy at its worst is Samuels (2008). But other states have tried to create a tight access system, and the number of users with medical authorization in some states is quite small. For example, Vermont, 7 years after allowing the use of marijuana for medical purposes, had only 349 registered patients (Anderson and Rees 2011).

Recent years have seen more radical legislative initiatives. In 2010 a very poorly formulated initiative in California received 46.5 percent of the vote.[33] In 2012 better-constructed initiatives were presented to the

[33] Proposition 19 gave regulatory powers to county and municipal governments, not to the state. The specific formulation might well have triggered a "race to the bottom" for tax rates and regulatory controls. It was particularly troubling in light of the emphasis of the advocates for marijuana legalization generally that legalization might provide substantial revenues to the state.

voters in Colorado and Washington. Both passed with approximately 55 percent of the ballots cast.

Research on marijuana use and policy has consistently emphasized that the drug is indeed addictive and harmful and also that the effects on the prevalence of use, of criminalization, of possession, and of high arrest rates are slight; for a summary, see Room et al. (2010, chaps. 2–3). The experiences of Dutch coffee shops have been prominent in the American debate. It is generally, though not universally, accepted that these coffee shops have not led to a major increase in use of marijuana or any other drug (MacCoun and Reuter 2001; Korf 2002). That has provided support for the legalization movement, even though the Dutch policy is far from legalization; aggressive enforcement against cultivation and trafficking have kept prices in the Netherlands comparable to those in other European nations (MacCoun 2010) whereas legalization in the United States would substantially reduce marijuana prices.

The federal government has been relentless in its opposition to either medical marijuana or legalization. The rise in potency of marijuana, which has also occurred both in the United States and in many other Western countries (ONDCP 2010c; EMCDDA 2012), has given the federal government an additional tool in this campaign. The ONDCP and Drug Enforcement Administration (DEA) websites carry warnings to parents about extrapolating from their own benign experience with the drug because of the increase in potency and that parents should warn their children against experimentation as a consequence.[34] Not only does the federal government emphasize this but also some prominent public figures (e.g., Califano 2009). Whether higher potency has any consequences for either behavior or health is a matter of controversy; users may titrate their dose so as to maintain the same level of THC, but perhaps the titration is imperfect and the THC gets to the brain faster (Chait 1989; Justinova et al. 2005). There is no evidence on the health consequences of different potencies of marijuana.

The medical marijuana initiatives may well have prepared the way for the successful ballot initiatives for legalizing the drug by making the drug less of a fringe and suspect substance; if it is medicine, then

---

[34] See the DEA (http://www.justice.gov/dea/docs/marijuana_position_2011.pdf) and ONDCP (http://www.whitehouse.gov/ondcp/frequently-asked-questions-and-facts-about-marijuana).

just how dangerous can it be? Marijuana, like alcohol in the early 1930s and various forms of gambling from about 1970 to 2000, looms as an attractive source of tax revenues for state governments that have been in chronic fiscal trouble since 2008. Why should drug smugglers and retailers make money from what could be, it is claimed, an important source of state taxes?[35] All the usual arguments about the removal of criminal markets have been made and appear to have resonated with the public.

I return to cannabis in the concluding section.

III. Drugs Other than Marijuana

The story is very different for cocaine, heroin, and methamphetamine, the principal drugs of concern; I discuss prescription drug abuse separately in Section V. Each of these three drugs has occupied center stage for a period of time and then retreated from prominence but by no means disappeared. There has been a ritualized demonization of each drug as it appears, in which it is characterized as far worse than any of its predecessors, followed by a lengthening of the maximum sentences specified in federal and many state codes. Over time problematic users are gradually transformed in prevailing stereotypes from violent and predatory youngsters to ailing, disgusting, and pathetic middle-aged street bums. The criminal justice system does not adapt to the change in perceptions but keeps locking them up for increasingly long periods. The policy debate is generally restricted to critiques of sentencing and calls for increased emphasis on prevention and treatment.

A. Drug Policy Objectives

Drug policy is partly a heritage of historical efforts at drug control, but it is also a product of a particular conception of what control efforts should try to accomplish. The stated goals, although widely accepted, are problematic; some of the failures of current policies may be as much the consequence of inadequate or misguided goals as of approaches to achieving them.

At least from 1989, when the first National Drug Control Strategy was submitted to Congress by the George H. W. Bush administration,

---

[35] For an assessment of the uncertainties of these projections, see Kilmer et al. (2010).

until 2009 (the first Obama strategy), the principal (and sometimes sole) goal of federal drug policy was to reduce the number of users. "The highest priority of our drug policy," wrote ONDCP director Bennett, "must be a stubborn determination further to reduce the overall level of drug use nationwide—experimental first use, 'casual' use, regular use and addiction alike" (ONDCP 1989, p. 8). In other words, the principal goal was to reduce the percentage of Americans who used drugs, a measure commonly referred to as the prevalence of drug use. Although the National Drug Control Strategy documents produced by the Clinton administration placed less emphasis on reducing overall prevalence and called more attention to the problem of chronic drug abuse, there was, as noted earlier, little identifiable change in policy. The administration of George W. Bush returned to the emphasis on use reduction, particularly among youths. The Obama administration is the first explicitly and decisively to turn to a broader set of objectives, but the consequences are yet to be seen.[36]

Underlying the choice of prevalence indicators is the assumption that policy can indeed influence drug use, that is, that good prevention programs would lower initiation, particularly among youths. A better treatment system, with more addicts entering it, on this reasoning would reduce the extent of use in that population; treatment clients, at least while in treatment, would stop use of illicit drugs. Finally, it is assumed that effective enforcement can raise price, reduce availability, and thus lower the extent of use

Experience, in both the United States and other Western countries, raises questions about all those assumptions. Instead, drug use is driven mostly by broader social economic and cultural factors, as well as by

---

[36] The *2011 National Drug Control Strategy* (ONDCP 2011*b*, p. 7) lists its objectives as follows:

Goal 1: Curtail illicit drug consumption in America
    1a. Decrease the 30-day prevalence of drug use among 12- to 17-year-olds by 15 percent;
    1b. Decrease the lifetime prevalence of 8th graders who have used drugs, alcohol, or tobacco by 15 percent;
    1c. Decrease the 30-day prevalence of drug use among young adults aged 18–25 by 10 percent;
    1d. Reduce the number of chronic drug users by 15 percent.
    Goal 2: Improve the public health and public safety of the American people by reducing the consequences of drug abuse
    2a. Reduce drug-induced deaths by 15 percent;
    2b. Reduce drug-related morbidity by 15 percent;
    2c. Reduce the prevalence of drugged driving by 10 percent.

the internal dynamics of epidemics (Caulkins and Reuter 2010). All programs and laws, *within the context of prohibition*, have fairly minor effects on the prevalence of use. The major issue for drug epidemiology is the occurrence of epidemics, short periods of explosive growth in initiation, followed by comparably sharp declines in initiation and, for addictive drugs, slow declines in prevalence.[37] At present, evidence suggests that no practical policy measures can affect whether an epidemic of drug use starts, how severe that epidemic will be, or how rapidly it ends.

The basis for these broad statements can be found in the volume *Drug Policy and the Public Good* (Babor et al. 2010), which attempted to survey what was known about the effects of different kinds of programs. Prevention is focused largely on marijuana, the illegal drug of first use; few evaluations have long enough follow-up periods to detect the effects on use of more serious drugs, which typically comes after school completion. The program evaluations have been quite negative; effects are modest and not robust, particularly to the fidelity of implementation. Certainly there are no robust positive findings of substantial effects on drug use; Caulkins has pointed out that most of the benefits of prevention programs aimed at substance use derive from reductions in alcohol and cigarette use (Caulkins et al. 1999). To make matters worse, school systems systematically choose weak programs.[38] Given the choice between an effective program and a poor program with a nice label, they will choose the nice label. Hallfors and Godette (2002) studied prevention activities in schools in 11 states. The schools were formally required to adopt programs with a strong research base, but mostly they nonetheless adopted other programs; when they did adopt research-based programs, they typically implemented them poorly. Prevention science is improving, but at present drug prevention in

---

[37] Note again that marijuana is different. The rates of change over time, whether increases or decreases, are much smaller. Use is endemic in the United States and in many other Western nations.

[38] For many years by far the most popular school prevention program was DARE (Drug Abuse Resistance Education). Initiated by the Los Angeles Police Department in the 1970s, it brought uniformed police officers into the school room. Repeated evaluations found that DARE was ineffective (e.g., West and O'Neal 2004), but it remained popular until the program sponsors felt compelled to recognize the weaknesses of their venture and undertake a major redesign. Evaluations of the redesign have been generally negative (e.g., Vincus et al. 2010), but it still remains the most popular drug prevention program in American schools, albeit less popular than in the 1990s (Zilli Sloboda, personal communication).

schools is more a slogan than an effective program (e.g., Reuter and Timpane 2001).

Research on treatment has shown evidence of effectiveness and indeed even of cost effectiveness; see again Babor et al. (2010, p. 9). The evidence is strongest for opiate substitution treatment (OST), which involves regular provision of drugs such as methadone or buprenorphine, which are themselves opiates but provide lower and more extended psychoactive effects. Research over four decades has consistently, but not always, found that patients in OST use substantially less heroin, commit many fewer crimes, and engage in fewer HIV risk behaviors (e.g., Uchtenhagen et al. 2004).

Despite decades of research efforts, no similar substitute drug has been found for cocaine. The result is that the methods for treating dependence or abuse of cocaine, or indeed any stimulant, are less effective. Some of the methods used are therapeutic communities, contingency management, and self-help groups. For all of them there is some evidence that high-quality treatment can reduce drug use and associated problems somewhat but less substantially and reliably than OST.[39]

What is striking though is that most individuals under treatment continue to use drugs. They use less of them and the use causes less harm to themselves and others. Treatment tends to generate modest reductions in the measured prevalence of drug use. Most of those in treatment are still in fact users of illicit drugs. Switzerland, which set out to provide a large variety of accessible treatment options in the 1990s, was able to drive down the number of active heroin users by 25 percent over the period 1994–2002 (Maag 2003). That might reasonably be seen as an upper bound for what treatment can do to reduce the prevalence of drug use in the medium term.

Least effective from the perspective of prevalence reduction are harm reduction efforts that seek to reduce the damage caused by drug use rather than limit drug use itself. This may help explain why needle exchange was not supported by ONDCP before 2009. The overriding focus on prevalence also helps to explain why marijuana, the most widely used illicit drug, attracts so much attention from drug policy makers, even though its contribution to crime and violence, relative to

---

[39] For specific treatment modality reviews, see De Leon (2000) for therapeutic communities, Stitzer and Petry (2006) for contingency management, and Gould and Clum (1993) for self-help.

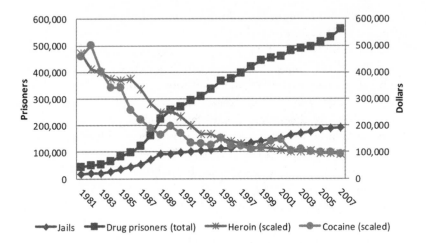

FIG. 3.—Incarceration and cocaine and heroin prices, 1981–2007. Source: For prices, Fries et al. (2008); for incarceration, Caulkins and Chandler (2006).

cocaine and heroin, is minor, as probably is its contribution to mortality and morbidity.[40]

There is very little evidence that enforcement can raise prices or reduce availability, the mechanisms through which it might reduce the prevalence of use. Figure 3 provides the most basic data. Over a nearly 30-year period (1980–2008) the number of persons incarcerated for drug offenses (i.e., for drug distribution, drug manufacturing, or drug use) in local jails and state and federal prisons increased about 10-fold, from about 50,000 to nearly 500,000; that does not include individuals incarcerated for "drug-related" crimes such as robbery to provide money for drug purchases. During that period of massively increased enforcement intensity, the retail prices of heroin and cocaine both fell about 70 percent;[41] it is interesting that price declines have been very parallel, even though the drugs are not good substitutes for each other.

It would be nice to have more sophisticated studies and not just rely on this very descriptive analysis. There is a dearth of studies at a more

[40] Marijuana may be causally related to premature death, e.g., through increased cancer risk or automobile accidents, but neither of these is included in the standard estimates of drug-related deaths, which focus only on those in which an illegal drug is the proximate cause of death.

[41] Incarceration imposes substantial costs on dealers, relative to arrests or convictions. Thus it seems a reasonable proxy for the extent of overall enforcement.

localized level. Kuziemko and Levitt (2004), using a variety of data sources and statistical modeling, found that during a period in which incarceration for cocaine offenses roughly tripled, the retail price of cocaine was 5–15 percent higher than it would otherwise have been.[42] Prohibition itself may have a profound effect on price, but tougher enforcement may not further increase it. This might reflect, for example, a very elastic supply of drug-selling labor; small increases in price could be enough to bring new players into the market, though there is no direct evidence for that proposition. A variety of other possible theoretical explanations are discussed in Reuter and Caulkins (2011); for none is there compelling evidence that can account for the decline.

If drug policy cannot affect prevalence, what can it do? We do know that bad policy choices can make drug use, drug distribution, and production more harmful. For example, if the police choose to use possession of prohibited syringes as the basis for targeting heroin injectors, they may accelerate the spread of HIV (Stimson 1988; Des Jarlais and Friedman 1992). Crackdowns on retail markets may lead to more youths becoming involved in drug selling; the unintended negative consequences of drug policy are numerous and serious (e.g., Costa 2009; Reuter 2009b).

B. International Policy

A feature that distinguishes drug policy from other crime control efforts is the importance of US efforts to suppress production or trafficking in other countries supplying the US market. These efforts are mostly programmatically separate and, more relevant for this essay, have their own political sources and analytic critiques.

For over 40 years the United States has been the principal bulwark of an international drug control regime that has emphasized the role of criminal law (e.g., Bruun, Pan, and Rexed 1975; McAllister 2000; Bewley-Taylor 2012). The original international treaty negotiations culminating in the Hague Convention of 1914 were initiated and dominated by the United States (Musto 1999). In recent decades, the United States has been willing to use a wide array of incentives and

---

[42] In an unpublished paper, Arkes et al. (2006), using more appropriate data and a model more grounded in economic theory, find no effect on cocaine prices from the increased enforcement over the same time period. The estimates have very large standard errors.

punishments to get its way in the formulation of policy at the annual meeting of the Commission on Narcotic Drugs, the United Nations body responsible for administration of the international treaties. For example, in 2004 the United States threatened to cut off funding for the UN Office on Drug Control if the executive director did not promise to end support for harm reduction programs (Bewley-Taylor 2012, p. 115).

The United States' own bilateral ventures in international drug control have been rhetorically and politically prominent. Relations with Mexico have occasionally been dominated by drug concerns, most prominently after the torture-killing of DEA agent Enrique Camarena in 1986.[43] That event led to the creation of an annual certification report (the International Narcotics Control Strategy Report [INCSR]) under the Foreign Assistance Act. Nations identified as major sources of drugs to the United States were certified as to whether they had cooperated fully with the United States in trying to reduce the flow of these drugs. Those not certified as such were at risk of losing US development assistance, US support for loans from multinational banks such as the Inter-American Development Bank, or both.

Until 2001 the assumption underlying US international drug control policy was that the United States was the victim of other nations' inability or unwillingness to control the production and export of dangerous drugs. The demonstrable corruption of so many of the source country governments gave this assumption a good deal of credibility. Thus the annual certification process involved the world's largest consumer of these drugs deciding who had done an adequate effort to stop the beast from being fed. The Mexican government and press were outraged by the process, but the government was helpless to do much about it (Cottam and Marenin 1999).[44]

Surprisingly, given his generally imperial approach to foreign policy, it was President George W. Bush who publicly conceded the obvious, namely, that suppliers can be replaced, but it was the demand that was

---

[43] The involvement of government officials in the crime was what generated the strong congressional reaction; see Shannon (1988).

[44] Storrs (1999), presenting arguments on congressional resolutions in support of, or in opposition to, President Clinton certifying Mexico, emphasized the fact that Mexico was, by its own calculations, spending a larger share of its budget on drug control than was the US government. This was emblematic of the reasons for the frustration that Latin American nations felt about the hypocrisy of the certification process.

essential. As noted earlier, in a meeting with President Fox of Mexico, President Bush said that Mexico would have a drug problem as long as US residents wanted to consume drugs. That transferred the sense of culpability and took the steam out of the certification program, which became even more ritualized than before and was seen in Latin America as no longer of consequence.[45] Secretary of State Hillary Clinton reiterated President Bush's statement in 2009, but by that time, with the extraordinary surge in drug-related homicides in Mexico, it was impossible to avoid the conclusion that the United States had the original responsibility for the problem.

President Felipe Calderon, after a narrow and highly contested victory in the 2006 Mexican presidential election, chose to launch an aggressive attack on the major drug trafficking organizations such as the Sinaloa cartel and the Zetas.[46] That led to a dramatic escalation in drug-related homicides. In the course of President Calderon's 6-year administration, it is estimated that there were approximately 50,000–60,000 homicides, some of a particularly horrific nature.[47] The mass killings and rising national death toll in Mexico became a prominent topic in the US media.

Though international programs have never taken much of the drug control budget, typically less than 5 percent, they have occupied a large share of the public attention to drug policy in the last decade at least. The US invasion of Afghanistan in late 2001 brought home to Americans the difficulties involved in controlling drug production in a developing country. In the early years of NATO occupation, there was much talk of eradicating poppy cultivation in the country that in most years supplied about 85 percent of the world's total heroin production (Schweich 2008; Blanchard 2009). This bravado quickly disappeared as the political economy realities confronted the occupying forces (Caulkins, Kleiman, and Kulick 2010). To take action against an agricultural product that accounted for one-quarter of gross domestic product and

[45] I can offer a small personal indicator of this. Until 2001, I routinely received press inquiries about the year's certification decisions when the INCSR was published around March 1. Since 2002 I have received no calls.

[46] For a history of the Mexican drug-trafficking problem, see Astorga and Shirk (2010). Efforts to explain the response to Calderon's crackdown continue to proliferate. See, e.g., Rios (2012).

[47] There are two sources of uncertainty. First, it is difficult to classify every homicide according to its relationship to drug trafficking. Second, the Mexican government has been secretive in its handling of these data; see Molzahn, Rios, and Shirk (2012).

was critical for the rural sector was to threaten the support of an already fragile government, America's ally in the fight against Al Quaida. By the time that Richard Holbrooke became director of President Obama's Afghanistan policies in 2009, all that remained of control efforts were a few ineffective alternative development schemes. Holbrooke, himself a skeptic on the effectiveness of eradication in Afghanistan, did nothing to expand them.

Plan Colombia, billed as a major drug control effort, has succeeded in some respects.[48] It has helped strengthen the central government, which had lost control of many areas of the country with the emergence of right-wing paramilitary groups on top of the long-standing left-wing Revolutionary Armed Forces of Colombia and the National Liberation Army. As a result of Plan Colombia, guerilla movements dependent on the drug trade became much weaker, and some of the cocaine trade moved back to Peru and Bolivia. The right-wing paramilitary agreed to surrender and was in principle integrated back into Colombian society; however, many of the paramilitary members joined the next generation of drug-trafficking organizations. The effects on flows to the United States appear to have been slight (Walsh 2004).

The critiques of these international programs have taken two forms: their lack of credibility in helping the United States and the damage that they do to the recipient countries. Despite three decades of active involvement in Bolivia, Colombia, and Peru, which account for all global production of cocaine for the illegal market, the volume of production has changed only modestly.[49] The location of production within the Andean region has been responsive to the US efforts. Tough enforcement against trafficking from Peru to Colombia in the mid-1990s helped push production to Colombia. Ten years later Plan Colombia has pushed some production back to Bolivia and Peru.[50] These shifts can hardly be claimed to represent gains for the United States.

The same shifts, and movements of production within an individual country, may, however, have serious consequences for those countries. For example, the environmental damage from coca planting, which

[48] For a micro evaluation of the interventions, focusing on cultivation and production of coca and opium poppies, as well as governmental strength, see Felbab-Brown et al. (2009). For a broader assessment, see Government Accountability Office (2008).

[49] For a recent analysis of the changes over time in production globally for cocaine and heroin, see Reuter and Trautmann (2009).

[50] For a history of the shifts in Andean coca production and the policy interventions, see Friesendorf (2007).

leaches soil and involves destruction of forest, is exacerbated when coca farmers are forced to plant more in order to replace what is destroyed by manual and aerial eradication. Aerial eradication, using powerful chemicals, is inevitably somewhat inaccurate (e.g., wind, poor information about plantings) and causes some damage to innocent neighbors. In addition, the movement to a new location requires corruption of new authorities while leaving behind weakened institutions in the previous cultivation area.

Though the balloon effect, the idea that pushing down on production or trafficking at one location will lead only to its popping up somewhere else, is a well-worn cliché in critiques of international drug policy (e.g., Nadelmann 1989), it is omitted from any government policy documents. Nor do the environmental issues get more than a defensive reference.

IV. The Big Ideas of Drug Policy

Notwithstanding the general stagnation of drug policy in this country, a few important ideas are part of the debate. Many believe that some or all have promise of reducing one or both of America's drug problem and its drug policy problem.

A. Harm Reduction

Needle exchange is the iconic program of the harm reduction movement. Originating in Europe, where the threat of HIV among needlesharing heroin addicts had become serious, the principle was straightforward. Policy could target the harmfulness of drug use, not just its extent. Given that drug use would occur, the state had an ethical obligation to minimize its adverse effects. AIDS, particularly in the early years before retrovirals were available, was horrifying enough that any concerns about making drug use more attractive seemed, at least to officials outside the United States, to be sufficiently remote and incomparably less threatening that resistance was slight. As a prominent report from the Advisory Commission on the Misuse of Drugs in the United Kingdom stated, "the spread of HIV is a greater danger to individual and public health than drug misuse" (1988, p. 17). In Australia, Canada, and most Western European nations, once the connection between HIV and needle sharing was established in the research literature, the government implemented syringe exchange programs

(SEPs) and aggressively promoted them to injecting drug users. Whether as a consequence or not, most of these countries were able to keep HIV rates among injectors (primarily heroin users but also including amphetamine users) to less than 2 percent, whereas in the United States the estimate was that the infection rate reached 18 percent in the 1990s (CDC 2012*a*).[51]

There is considerable empirical backing for claims that needle exchange programs can bring about significant reductions in HIV transmission. Favorable assessments of the evidence have been provided since the 1990s by a variety of expert groups, including Des Jarlais, Friedman, and Ward (1993), the Government Accounting Office (1993), and the Institute of Medicine/NAS (Normand, Vlahov, and Moses 1995). A comparison of 81 US cities estimated a 5.9 percent increase in HIV seroprevalence in 52 cities without needle exchange and a 5.8 percent decrease in 29 cities with needle exchange during the period 1988–93 (Hurley, Jolley, and Kaldor 1997). None of the studies is methodologically strong, and there is a small dissenting literature that claims that needle exchange made little difference in the HIV epidemic (e.g., Amundsen 2006). However, there is no claim that SEPs cause any additional harm.

Yet only 211 needle exchange programs were operating in the United States in 2011 (http://www.amfar.org/uploadedFiles/On_The _Hill/SEPS.pdf). Why? Because prescription laws, paraphernalia laws, and local "drug-free zone" ordinances banned or constrained needle exchange programs in most of the country. Almost half of the existing programs operated illicitly or quasi-legally for many years. Notwithstanding the endorsement of these programs by the Centers for Disease Control (CDC), the NAS, and various leading medical journals and health organizations, drug policy officials in the federal government and most state governments actively opposed needle exchange. Even in late 1997 Congress reaffirmed its hostility to needle exchange by including in the Department of Health and Human Services (DHHS) appropriations bill a total ban on federal funding of needle exchange. This strengthened previous language, which had allowed the secretary of DHHS to fund research on the topic.

In 1998, Secretary Donna Shalala publicly endorsed the scientific

---

[51] "Since the epidemic began, more than 182,000 injection drug users with an AIDS diagnosis have died" (http://www.cdc.gov/hiv/resources/factsheets/us.htm).

basis for the claim that needle exchange did not increase drug use; that announcement by the secretary of DHHS was a statutory preliminary to allowing federal funding. However, she announced that the administration had decided that such funding would be unwise. A *Washington Post* story reported that DHHS officials had already arranged a press conference in the belief that President Clinton would support funding needle exchange programs; Secretary Shalala's memo of talking points was reported to say "the evidence is airtight" and "from the beginning of this effort, it has been about science, science, science" (Harris and Goldstein 1998). General McCaffrey (the director of ONDCP) was the key figure in persuading President Clinton that funding SEPs would be a major blow to federal drug control efforts. The president instructed the secretary to change her recommendation.

During the 1998 debate, critics of needle exchange made much of two studies associating participation in needle exchanges with elevated HIV risk in Vancouver (Strathdee et al. 1997) and Montreal (Bruneau et al. 1997). These were just two studies from many that had been conducted in cities throughout the Western world. The authors of the two studies cautioned that this association might reflect features that distinguish these evaluations from others in the literature; for example, they were conducted at the peak of the HIV epidemic, their clients were heavily involved in cocaine injection, and the number of needles dispersed fell well short of the amount needed to prevent needle sharing (Bruneau and Schechter 1998). Later results and analyses (Schechter et al. 1999) indicate that the Vancouver result was spurious; the program simply attracted many of the city's highest-risk users—the young, the homeless, cocaine injectors, and sex trade workers. This is surely a desirable selection effect and brings those results back in line with the empirical literature.

Out of office, in 2002 President Clinton admitted regret that he had not ended the ban on SEPs.[52] The George W. Bush administration hardly discussed the issue, though there were occasional claims that needle exchange encouraged drug use. The National Institute on Drug Abuse, preserving its tradition of apolitical research, in 2002 published

[52] Nor was this the only hand-wringing of President Clinton on drug policy. In December 2000, on his way out of the White House, he also expressed regret that he had not done more to reduce penalties for marijuana use. He chose *Rolling Stone* as the outlet for that revelation, a symbolically important statement by our first baby boomer president, notorious for his line "but I didn't inhale." He also regretted his failure to tackle the 100 to 1 ratio in crack-powder sentencing (Tonry 2011, p. 79).

a research-based guide to preventing HIV in drug-using populations. Concerning needle exchange programs, the guide stated, "Evaluations of these programs indicate that they are an effective part of a comprehensive strategy to reduce the injection drug use-related spread of HIV and other blood-borne infections. In addition they do not encourage the use of illicit drugs" (National Institute on Drug Abuse 2002, p. 18). However, with Republicans in charge of both houses of Congress through most of the period, there was no effective congressional pressure for lifting the ban.

Candidate Obama pledged to reverse the policy but did not push hard for the reversal once in office. Finally, congressional actions led to a lifting of the ban in 2009, signed into law by the president in 2010. It had taken almost 25 years to accomplish this simple policy intervention. Given that the HIV epidemic had largely run its course, the change was more a recognition of the human rights of injecting drug users than an important policy intervention. In 2012, Congress eliminated all federal funding for needle exchange programs, indicative of continued political hostility to this intervention.

The other programs spawned by the harm reduction movement have barely registered in the American drug policy discussions. One is heroin maintenance, whereby heroin addicts who have failed in methadone maintenance programs are provided with their drug at government expense in medically supervised settings. This program has done well in every experimental evaluation; it has substantial benefits for some of the most methadone-resistant and criminally active users. There is no indication that it increases the extent of heroin use. It also has not turned out to be attractive to most heroin addicts; the enrollment in Switzerland is less than 10 percent of the current heroin-dependent population (Reuter 2009a). It is now a routine treatment option in Switzerland, the Netherlands, and some parts of Germany (Fischer et al. 2007); other countries are considering it. Drug consumption rooms, again aimed at reducing the risks of injecting drug use, this time by providing supervision and assistance at the time of injecting, have been established in 27 cities in eight countries including Canada, many European countries, and Australia (Dooling and Rachlis 2010). Neither is part of the debate in the United States.

Why has harm reduction fared so poorly here? A simple answer is that it rests on a pragmatic premise that is unacceptable in a nation that still prides itself on its idealism, no matter how soiled the historical record. Accepting that something as dangerous as injecting drug use will continue no matter what the government does is to admit limits that the national rhetoric, as in No Child Left Behind, will not permit.

It is also true that the programmatic implications are quite radical. After all, the state is not simply acknowledging that addicts will misbehave; the state is literally supplying them with the means to do so. No doubt there will be nonprofits that hand out the needles, without any sign that the government is helping them, but if the program is to take off, there will need to be government funding.

These are both relatively charitable interpretations of the resistance. A darker view is that the resistance does not pertain to this specific program but to the threat that harm reduction poses to the underpinnings of the drug war. Though there is now a consensus that the term "war on drugs" is inappropriate and misleading, there are clearly many former drug warriors who cling to the basic ideas that fueled the war. Harm reduction programs give the drug user a sympathetic face, undermining the fundamental message that "nicotine shortens life; cocaine debases it" (Wilson 1990).

The public health research community became substantially involved in drug policy debates through the fight over needle exchange, which it strongly supported. Prior to that there were small communities of researchers specialized in epidemiology, prevention, and treatment, but the emergence of AIDS as a major health problem in America brought attention to the draconian and inflexible nature of US drug policy. The public health community has, however, not taken up the issue of how to reduce the number of incarcerated drug users, though that is easily represented as a public health issue.

B. Drug Addiction as a Brain Disease

Alan Leshner, director of the National Institute on Drug Abuse (NIDA) from 1993 to 2002, was the first senior official to make this a key insight for policy purposes: "A core concept that has been evolving with scientific advances over the past decade is that drug addiction is a brain disease that develops over time as a result of the initially voluntary behavior of using drugs. The consequence is virtually uncontrollable compulsive drug craving, seeking, and use that interferes with, if not destroys, an individual's functioning in the family and in society. This medical condition demands formal treatment" (Leshner 2001). While the idea is compelling and the evidence from computer axial tomography and similar scans to back it up is vivid and persuasive, there is a vast amount of direct evidence that contradicts it; there has been a good deal of skepticism about its general validity (e.g., Satel and Goodwin 2003). Most dependent users of drugs, legal or illegal, quit without any formal treatment (Babor et al. 2010). Recent experiments in the criminal justice system in which incentives (frequent drug testing accompanied by immediate and modest sanctions for failure) have been enough to induce abstinence in populations with long histories of dependent use (Hawken and Kleiman 2009) also provide a challenge to the idea for many problem users. There may well be an important subgroup of addicted users for whom the brain disease model is valid, at least for specific drugs, and the large NIDA research program on these matters will probably eventually yield a qualified version of the statement that has a good empirical base.

Whatever its scientific merit, the idea appears now to provide an important platform for policy reform efforts, within the context of drug prohibition. In an increasingly therapeutically oriented society, this is a credible basis for sending criminally active addicts to treatment rather than to the criminal justice system. Enunciated first during the Bush administration, it has become a standard part of the rhetoric of Obama administration officials. For example, in releasing the 2012 National Drug Control Strategy (ONDCP 2012a), which emphasized shifts away from enforcement, ONDCP director Kerlikowske in a statement to the press said, "My colleagues—police and others—simply put often say that we can't arrest our way out of the drug problem. . . . Current thinking by health experts views drug addiction as a disease of the brain that can be prevented and treated." What is particularly striking about this emphasis on the brain disease model is the lack of new treatment methods that reflect the new neurological insights. The major treatment innovations of recent years are screening, brief intervention, and referral to treatment and cognitive behavioral therapy, which may refer to the brain disease concept but are certainly not dependent on it.[53] For patients it may be changes in the organizing and financing of treatment that have made the most difference in recent years.

---

[53] One reviewer of a draft of this essay noted that this model of addiction can also appeal to drug hawks. If adolescent use, whether from curiosity or peer pressure, has the power to throw a switch, leading to an irreversible, lifetime, relapsing condition, so much more important is it to have a zero tolerance policy.

C. Legalization

Hanging over all discussions of drug policy is the widespread belief among intellectuals that until these drugs are made legal, there cannot be sensible policies; we should regulate rather than prohibit. Having written extensively on the possible consequences (MacCoun and Reuter 2001, 2011), I here confine myself to how the idea has affected the policy debate.

The arguments for legalization are compelling. Almost all the costs associated with prohibited drugs in contemporary society (overdoses, blood-borne viruses, corruption, violence, and property crime) are a consequence of prohibition and its enforcement rather than the drugs themselves. Thus the elimination of prohibitions would greatly reduce these problems.

The difficult question is how much use and addiction would increase if drugs were legal and regulated. In *Drug War Heresies*, MacCoun and I argued that it is impossible to project even roughly how much prevalence of use or dependence would increase. Heroin addiction might increase only 50 percent or it might increase by as much as 500 percent; there is no compelling evidence that would allow one to choose a particular figure. Further, it is also impossible to know how to weigh the increased addiction against the gains in terms of reduced crime, disease, and so forth. Economists believe that crime and addiction itself can all be given dollar values; such calculations are more convincing to economists themselves than to others and in any case ignore the much subtler but comparably important factors such as the intrusiveness of the state or the apparently unavoidable racial disparities in sentencing. Finally, the change would have different consequences for specific population groups; some might benefit greatly (urban minority communities) while large groups would be somewhat worse off (perhaps the suburban middle class). MacCoun and I concluded that whether the United States would benefit from legalization would be difficult to show and that this inability to make more than a theoretical case was a major handicap.

The American population does not need such sophisticated arguments. Except concerning marijuana, support for drug legalization has been minimal; the Gallup Poll in 2010 found fewer than 10 percent of respondents favoring legalization of any of cocaine, ecstasy, heroin, or methamphetamine. This number has scarcely budged over the years.

Yet the voices of legalization advocates are very much heard by policy officials. Successive directors of ONDCP have devoted considerable time to rubbishing the arguments of legalizers. For example, the 2012 ONDCP website, in addition to a number of documents critiquing the legalization of marijuana, includes a two-page refutation of a study issued by the Cato Institute on decriminalization of drug use in Portugal (Greenwald 2009). Though decriminalization is far from legalization, the ONDCP (2010*b*) critique keeps referring to the weakness of the Cato study as evidence of the weakness of legalization arguments. One almost comes to suspect that officials are troubled by the very plausibility of the argument, that one day there will be enough dissatisfaction with the current system and its continuing failure for radical alternatives to be taken seriously.

Indeed that has, in a way, happened. The presidents of Colombia, Guatemala, and Mexico, all countries that have been severely harmed by drug-related violence fueled by the American drug market, have said that it is worth considering the legalization of drugs in their countries (Calmes 2012). They are less sure that drugs should be legalized than that the current situation is intolerable. For these countries, as well as for El Salvador and Honduras, drug-related violence has been the leading social problem of the last few years. It is hard to see any credible basis for optimism that US interventions are likely to help them substantially. President Obama tried to fend them off in the Summit of the Americas discussion in Cartagena in April 2012 but had at least to concede that the Organization of American States should be authorized to do a study of drug policy options for the region.[54]

The fear of legalization has probably made resistance to sensible reforms of US policies more difficult. Any softening of the system can be presented as a move along the path to the unacceptable, namely, availability of cocaine and other drugs comparable to current availability of alcohol.

D. Drug Courts

In a "drug court" a judge effectively acts as a probation officer, monitoring the behavior of a drug-involved offender who has pled guilty to a specific offense and receives a nonincarcerative sentence in return for entering a rehabilitation program, getting a job, and so forth.[55]

---

[54] Full disclosure: I am a coauthor of one draft chapter of this study.

[55] This section draws heavily on collaborative work with Harold Pollack and Eric Sevigny (Sevigny, Pollack, and Reuter 2013).

Drug courts emerged and proliferated because they had broad appeal across the range of stakeholders concerned with drug policy. Originated during the crack epidemic when the population of drug-involved offenders was expanding rapidly, they offered some promise to judges and policy makers as a strategy to conserve prison and jail bed space while retaining close monitoring of criminal offenders (Fluellen and Trone 2000). Implemented at the local level, drug courts vary greatly in their specific strategies, effectiveness, and populations served. The National Association of Drug Court Professionals has identified 10 core principles of effective drug court implementation, but the fidelity of the adhesion to these principles is unknown (King and Pasquarella 2009).

Drug courts hold considerable appeal to the treatment and public health communities because they offer the possibility of closer coordination between the criminal justice system and the treatment providers who serve the same offending populations. Finally, drug courts held considerable appeal to the defense bar and to advocates of less punitive drug policies who wished to support credible alternatives to incarceration. ONDCP identifies drug courts as a "smart approach to criminal justice" (ONDCP 2010a).

Drug court research conducted over the past two decades indicates that, on average, these programs are more effective than conventional correctional options at reducing the drug use and criminal activity of drug-involved offenders (e.g., Belenko 2001; Mitchell et al. 2012). The National Institute of Justice–sponsored Multi-site Adult Drug Court Evaluation, for example, found that drug court participants relapsed significantly less often and that those who did relapse reported significantly fewer days of drug consumption than a comparison group of offenders at the 18-month follow-up (Rossman et al. 2011). Likewise, meta-analyses confirm that drug courts reduce recidivism rates by 8–14 percent over other criminal justice interventions (e.g., Wilson, Mitchell, and MacKenzie 2006; Drake, Aos, and Miller 2009).

While drug courts may effectively reduce drug use and recidivism for individual offenders, there has been considerable debate over the ability of drug courts to reduce aggregate prison and jail populations, that is, to serve as an effective alternative to incarceration at the population level (Fluellen and Trone 2000; Drug Policy Alliance 2011). Some observers credit drug courts with helping to "bend the curve" of incarceration downward (Huddleston and Marlowe 2011, p. 16). Others suggest that drug courts and similar programs have a "low ceiling of possible impact on correctional populations" (Clear and Schrantz 2011, p. 14). Still others claim that drug courts "may ultimately serve not as an alternative but as an *adjunct* to incarceration" (Drug Policy Alliance 2011, p. 14; italics in original).

Even though the drug court movement is almost 20 years old and over 2,300 separate programs have been created (Bureau of Justice Assistance Drug Court Clearinghouse Project 2009), a 2008 study estimated that only 55,000 drug-involved defendants were processed in such courts around 2005. The same study estimated that over 1 million drug-abusing or dependent defendants entered the criminal justice system each year (Bhati, Roman, and Chalfin 2008).

Sevigny, Pollack, and Reuter (2013) show that many drug-involved offenders are precluded from participation in drug courts because of overriding sentencing laws, including sentencing guidelines, mandatory minimums, habitual offender laws, and other sentence enhancements. Eligibility rules also are often very tight. For example, most drug courts do not accept offenders with convictions for violent offenses, even if the conviction is long past. The result is that few of those who have been heavy users of cocaine and heroin over many years, a group that accounts for most cocaine and heroin users by now, can become drug court clients. Drug court advocates can reasonably be accused of cream skimming, avoiding clients at high risk of failure. While understandable as a strategy for a new program, it limits the value of the innovation.

As a consequence, it is unlikely that drug courts will have much impact on the number of drug users incarcerated. Prison and jail populations have grown rapidly through 2005, but they have aged at least since about 1990. Some of that aging is accounted for by inmates dependent on cocaine, heroin, or methamphetamine, many incarcerated for nondrug offenses (Pollack, Sevigny, and Reuter 2011). Unless drug courts are restructured to serve riskier clients, they will not have much impact on the number of drug users in American prisons and jails.[56]

---

[56] The federal courts have begun to experiment with drug courts for minor drug offenders facing long sentences, typically because they were caught in operations involving large quantities of drugs. According to the *New York Times*, as of March 2013, these efforts involved just 400 offenders nationwide (Secret 2013).

V. The Future

The drug problem changes in unforeseen ways with occasional epidemics that are unpredictable in their occurrence and magnitude. In this section, I describe first the emergence in the last decade of a new kind of drug problem, the use of diverted prescription drugs. Prescription drugs constitute a significant and disturbing public health problem; the appropriate policy response is almost certainly different from that for the wholly illegal drugs discussed so far. I then consider the ever-present fear of entirely new drugs, so called "legal highs," the expectation that some new psychoactive substance developed by "backyard chemists" will become a major new drug problem. It turns out surprisingly to be a very modest problem to date, but it is hard to understand why and this cannot be dismissed as a future threat.

A. Prescription Drug Misuse

Over the last decade there has been an important change in patterns of drug abuse in the United States and Canada (Babor et al. 2010).[57] Misuse of prescription drugs collectively has become more prevalent than use of any illegal drug except marijuana. For example, Monitoring the Future, the survey of high school seniors, reported that in 2011 the percentage of twelfth graders who had used a prescription drug in the previous 12 months was 21.7 percent, exceeded only by marijuana at 45.5 percent (Johnston et al. 2012). The drugs involved include opioid analgesics (e.g., hydrocodone and fentanyl) and benzodiazepines.

It is not just the use of these drugs that has increased; so have the harmful consequences. The CDC (2010) reports that emergency room visits "for nonmedical use of opioid analgesics increased 111 percent during 2004–2008 (from 144,600 to 305,900 visits), and increased 29 percent during 2007–2008" (p. 705). Further, deaths from poisonings from opiate pain killers alone now exceed the number of deaths from heroin and cocaine combined (as shown in fig. 4; CDC 2010). Interestingly, since 2002, more than twice as many people have died from methadone poisoning as from heroin poisoning (CDC 2012*b*). In some states deaths from prescription overdoses exceed automobile fatalities.

Part of the reason for the increase in use and harm is that more

---

[57] This subsection draws on work done collaboratively with Jonathan Caulkins, Beau Kilmer, and Rosalie Pacula. See Kilmer et al. (2012).

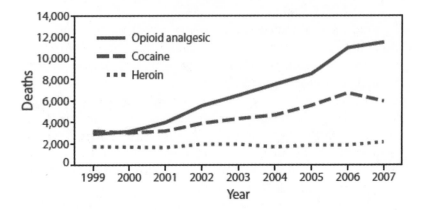

FIG. 4.—Unintentional drug overdose deaths involving opioid analgesics, cocaine, and heroin, United States, 1999–2007. Source: Reproduced from CDC (2012*b*).

people are being prescribed these substances. For example, methadone is increasingly prescribed as a painkiller as well as a substitute for heroin; in 2009, more than 4 million methadone prescriptions were written for pain even though the US Food and Drug Administration published warnings about the risks associated with methadone (Fareed et al. 2010). All these drugs are dangerous, even for the patient for whom they are prescribed. Some of the increase in deaths may then just represent the rise in total prescriptions. Compton and Volkow (2006) show that there is a close correlation for some major prescription drugs between the number of doses marketed and the number of emergency room cases.

Not much is known about how these prescription drugs reach the final users. A recent article by Coleman (2012) suggests that there is substantial leakage from the wholesale distribution system. Three corporations account for 90 percent of the distribution business, that is, the transfer from manufacturers to retailers such as CVS and Walgreens.[58] These firms are subject to extensive regulation and monitoring by the DEA. Occasionally they have been detected selling the drugs to retailers whose practices make clear that they do little to prevent leakage into nonprescribed use. For example, in 2008, Cardinal Health was fined $34 million for selling 8 million dosage units of hydrocodone

[58] The three corporations are McKesson, Cardinal Health, and AmerisourceBergen.

to pharmacies that were suspected of facilitating nonprescribed use. One of the minor distributors, KeySource Medical, reached a settlement with the DEA after the agency alleged that the company had filled suspicious orders for 48 million dosage units of oxycodone products.

Doctor shopping is a common practice, as publicized in a lengthy, front-page *New York Times* story (Schwarz 2013). An individual visits multiple doctors and obtains multiple prescriptions for the same ostensible problem. In an era when doctors are under time pressures, diagnoses of psychiatric problems are often casual, so that a student who wants prescriptions of Adderall, initially to improve concentration, will be able to obtain many, both for himself and for friends, through either gifts or purchases.

In addition to leakage from the distribution system, survey data indicate that many users acquire the drugs in other ways, including thefts from the family medicine cabinet, websites (domestic and international), and friends—all difficult outlets to control. The websites seem particularly unpromising as a policing target (Jena et al. 2011). A 2007 survey of 581 online pharmacies found that only two were registered with the appropriate national association and that none of the rest made a serious effort to establish the legitimacy of the claimed need (Jena et al. 2011). Given the ease with which websites can change their identities, federal legislation does not seem likely to make much difference.

Prescription drug misuse has not so far been associated much with illegal markets and violence. According to the 2011 National Survey on Drug Use and Health, 71 percent of those reporting nonprescribed use of a prescription drug gave the source as a gift, theft, or purchase from a friend. Only 3.9 percent acquired the drug from a dealer or stranger. Rogue pain clinics have received serious attention from law enforcement agencies, but they operate in a very different fashion than street drug markets. Davis and Johnson (2008) found that prescribed opiates are used by about one-third of street drug users in New York and are sold by a similar fraction of drug sellers.

These drugs have not as yet generated much treatment demand. The share of admissions for opiates other than heroin (most of which are prescription drugs such as Oxycontin and codeine) rose from 1.6 percent to 8.6 percent between 2000 and 2010; the share of admissions involving other prescription drugs (tranquilizers, sedatives, etc.) rose

only from 1.7 percent to 2.4 percent (SAMHSA 2012). This relatively modest flow into the treatment system, compared with marijuana-related admissions, could be explained by many factors, including (1) the relative recency of most initiates, since entry admission typically comes after some years of use; and (2) the low risk of arrest for possession or use, since arrest often motivates treatment seeking. Too little is yet known about the characteristics of the population using these drugs and their careers of use to make confident predictions about whether they will become an important source of treatment demand.

Thus, the methods for reducing the prescription drug problem will likely be different from those traditionally used when targeting wholly illegal drugs. For example, many states have developed online systems for recording prescriptions so as to detect patients who visit multiple doctors in order to acquire large and perhaps marketable quantities of abusable drugs (ONDCP 2011a). Because these drugs are primarily produced and distributed through legally regulated entities, there is the possibility of at least partly effective suppression without much enforcement against street markets, which generate so much of the incarceration and violence around distribution of the illegally produced drugs. Websites may be difficult to suppress, but as of 2011 less than 0.5 percent of users reported acquiring the drug through the Internet. The policy and political challenges for dealing with prescription drugs will be distinct.

B. "Legal Highs"

There has long been a concern about the development of new psychoactive substances, not covered by the existing system of drug-specific regulations and prohibitions.[59] Two recent prominent examples are mephedrone and Spice. Many, but not all, of these substances are the creation of entrepreneurial chemists operating clandestinely. Some are natural substances, for which new and more dangerous modes of ingestion have been developed or whose intoxicating properties have not previously been understood. Yet others are legally manufactured substances for which new uses as intoxicants have been found. Some examples include bath salts, poppers, and Salvia. A wide range of terms have been used to describe such substances, including legal highs, syn-

---

[59] This subsection draws on Reuter (2011).

thetics, research chemicals, designer drugs, and party drugs, all of which are within the scope of this brief subsection.

The problem is not an entirely new one. Late twentieth-century chemistry was advanced enough to produce a rapid flow of new psychoactive drugs that found their niches in recreational markets (e.g., ketamine and GHB). Alexander Shulgin, a prominent chemist in the development of new psychedelics in the United States, notes that there were only two such substances in 1900 (marijuana and mescalin, both naturally occurring), 20 by 1950, and over 200 by 2000 (quoted in Kau 2008, pp. 1079–80). Governments throughout the Western world struggled throughout the twentieth century with how to respond to these new entities whose effects were poorly understood, generally choosing to prohibit them for precautionary reasons. The number of drugs on the list banned by international conventions has risen sharply, very much as Shulgin sketched for psychedelics. When the Single Convention passed in 1961, there were 85 prohibited drugs; by 1995 there were 282 (Babor et al. 2010).

What is striking is how narrow or ephemeral are the niches that these new drugs have so far occupied in the recreational market. Even LSD, perhaps the most venerable of them, has almost disappeared in the United States, after 40 years, following a major enforcement success in the year 2000 (Grimm 2009).[60] Others simply lose popularity, either because that particular experience is unattractive to a new generation or because of fears about adverse effects, usually reflecting the experiences of recreational users rather than government announcements.[61]

Consider, for example, a very recent scare over some synthetic cathinones often marketed as "bath salts." These have been associated with some horrifying incidents (e.g., Kasic, McKnight, and Kilsovic 2011) and have attracted headlines in the media, including the *New York Times* (Goodnough and Zezima 2011). In early 2011 the director of the NIDA warned about the rising tide (pun intended) of bath salts; she noted that the number of emergency department admissions related to

[60] In 1999, 8.1 percent of high school seniors reported use of LSD in the previous month; that figure was 1.6 percent in 2009 (http://monitoringthefuture.org/data/09data/pr09t2.pdf).

[61] For example, in 1996, 4 percent of US high school students reported use of PCP (phencyclidine) in the previous 12 months. That figure fell steadily over the next 13 years; by 2009 it had fallen by almost 60 percent to just 1.7 percent. There have been no claims of enforcement success involving this particular drug.

these drugs in the first 2 months of 2011 exceeded the total number for 2010 (Volkow 2011).

These are dangerous drugs, and they provide only a moderately interesting experience; that can be seen in reports from users (Measham, Moore, and Newcombe 2010). By late 2012 the tide had mostly receded. The Monitoring the Future research group, in releasing its results for 2012, headlined that "use of bath salts is very low." It noted also that the number of calls to poison centers in the last 6 months of 2012 had fallen by half compared to the previous year.

It is puzzling that the wonders of modern chemistry have not yet turned up substances that can outcompete the long-standing sources of illicit altered states. One conjecture is that this is already occurring but through a different channel, namely, the misuse of prescription drugs. However, the prescription drugs that are causing the most problems are themselves remarkably close to substances that have long been used, in particular to heroin and morphine. It would be foolish to exclude the possibility that an entirely new drug might appear on the black market that provides a distinctive and attractive experience without posing too much risk to the user.

VI. The Resistance to Change

It is difficult to write about drug policy in the United States without becoming convinced that much of what is done in the name of reducing human suffering from drug addiction and its consequences is misguided and causes more harm than it alleviates, and also being convinced that the prospects of policy change continue to be slight. The nation's drug problem, at least if one restricts it to the wholly illegal as opposed to the relatively new and different phenomenon of misuse of prescription drugs, is falling. The populations dependent on cocaine, heroin, and methamphetamine are declining and aging; relatively few of those who experiment with these drugs go on to become dependent users, even though prices have fallen substantially. There is not much change in the numbers of related deaths and emergency department admissions, but this flatness may reflect (1) the aging of the dependent user populations; for example, longer exposure to adulterated heroin with dirty needles may increase vulnerability to fatal overdoses since it so negatively affects the user's health; and (2) the increasing number of heroin addicts released from prison each year.[62] One might have expected that the lower profile of drug problems would lead to a willingness to relax the ferocious grasp of the system that has been created. Alexander in *The New Jim Crow* (2010) makes a powerful case that the war on drugs has transformed the lives of African Americans in cities. There is growing consciousness of racial disparities. That has not been enough to trigger much reform.

Marijuana is a major exception to this statement. Two states have legalized the drug as a result of a ballot initiative; that is to say, they have eliminated all penalties under state law. The federal government has still not stated its position beyond a broad statement from President Obama that the federal government has better things to do with its resources than chase marijuana users (Dwyer 2012). The federal government has many tools to block a legal production and distribution system at the state level. Even if it never arrests another user, the Department of Justice can make it essentially impossible to sell the drug legally in Colorado and Washington. Indeed the department has turned out to be persistent and quite ingenious in its efforts to complicate the task of anything approaching legal production or distribution of medical marijuana in California, for example, threatening to seize property that a landlord has rented to a marijuana distributor (Eckholm 2011). The result of the Colorado and Washington initiatives may be a long and tangled series of court battles between state and federal authorities.

The explosion of drug-related violence in Mexico since 2006 may change American attitudes toward the drug problem. Colombia, Mexico, and Central America are now seen as victims of America's drug habit rather than as villains that profit from it. Optimistically, this will generate a reexamination of whether current policies that cause so much harm to other nations can be defended.

There is indeed one important change in process. The Affordable Care Act (ACA) provides access to treatment services for an important population of drug addicts who previously had no or very limited access. The individual exchanges that will provide insurance for many

---

[62] Another major source of overdose deaths is reduced tolerance, as may occur following release from prison. A small number of studies have found that heroin addicts have high rates of death following release from prison; this probably reflects their failure to realize that their tolerance has fallen as a result of a long period of abstinence (Merrell et al. 2010).

poor people are required to offer mental health services equivalent to what they offer for physical ailments (Buck 2011). Mental health services explicitly include substance abuse treatment. So males aged 18–64 without dependent children will, for the first time, be able to enter into drug treatment without being reliant on specific grant programs such as the Substance Abuse and Mental Health Block Grant, the size of which has varied from year to year and has never been large enough to provide decent quality services to all those who sought them.

There are important ACA details to be worked out. For example, reimbursement rates in these exchange insurance programs and in related Medicaid programs may be set too low for many providers; access may be limited on the supply side. It may turn out that few of those needing treatment will seek it. Many treatment facilities are poorly designed to participate in Medicaid as well; for example, they may lack required information technology systems or medical staff. Nonetheless, the ACA offers the prospect for major improvement for low-income male addicts who constitute a large part of the US drug problem.

A. Sentencing Reforms

More broadly, the forces of reform seem weak. The future expansion of treatment finance is a consequence of fundamental changes in health policy rather than a deliberate drug policy decision. The likely future is at best modest change in targeted drug policy.

The severity of sentencing for drug offenses is at the heart of the liberal critique of current drug policy. Though there seems to be considerable agreement that a less harsh sentencing regime is needed, it has proven exceptionally difficult to accomplish any meaningful change. This can be illustrated by consideration of the efforts to roll back two widely acknowledged excesses: the discrepancy between federal court sentences for crack cocaine and powder cocaine and the Rockefeller drug laws in New York State that imposed heavy sentences on minor drug offenders.

Federal Crack-Powder Disparity. Powder cocaine can be transformed into crack through a simple chemical process. In 1986 as part of the Anti–Drug Abuse Act, Congress specified a relationship between the penalties for crack and powder cocaine; for distributing 5 grams of crack the maximum sentence was 5 years, the same sentence that would be given for the distribution of 500 grams of powder. This represented the prevailing belief that crack was a much more dangerous drug than powder.

On its face, even if it were a mistake, it would be of only modest significance; some offenders would receive longer sentences than they should, which is known to happen anyway. What made this so significant was its racially disparate impact. In the federal system, an extraordinarily high percentage of those sentenced for crack offenses are African American: 79 percent in 2009 compared to 28 percent for cocaine powder offenses (US Sentencing Commission 2009, table 34). Moreover, this disparity was entirely predictable at time of passage in 1986, a point emphasized by Michael Tonry in his 1995 *Malign Neglect*.

Over time it became clear that crack, though indeed more harmful than cocaine powder, was certainly not 100 times worse (Hatsukami and Fishman 1996). It was impossible to justify the continued difference. Even the US Sentencing Commission, which has rarely pushed for reductions in mandatory minimum sentences, weighed in for a reduction in the crack penalties and the disparities. In 1996 Attorney General Janet Reno and the prominent head of ONDCP, Barry McCaffrey, also pushed for reductions in crack sentences. All to no avail. Congress was uninterested.

Only in 2010 did Congress finally agree to changes in sentencing rules, with the passage of the Fair Sentencing Act. The minimum amount of crack powder for a felony was raised from 5 grams to 28 grams (an ounce), so that the disparity between powder and crack cocaine was reduced to 18 to 1. Certainly that lowered the facial inequity of federal sentencing and should lead to fewer African Americans in federal prison at any one time as the result of convictions for crack offenses. It was far from the level appropriate to the harms of the substance. Moreover, the change was accomplished only after extensive and acrimonious hearings.

Indicative of how reluctant Congress was to make this change, it was done on a voice vote; no member of the House had to be on record declaring less vigor in his opposition to drugs. The battle then shifted to the question of retroactive application of the rule. Many members of Congress were opposed to allowing those sentenced under the old law from benefiting and having their sentences reduced. The Supreme Court ruled in favor of allowing that benefit (*Dorsey v. the United States*, US Court of Appeals for the Seventh Circuit, 11-5683 [2012]).

What is so striking is the depth of the opposition to a change in an indefensible law.

The Rockefeller Laws. In 1973, on the urging of Governor Nelson Rockefeller, who was responding to the sharp increase in heroin addiction, the New York State Legislature enacted draconian penalties for minor drug offenses. For example, possession of 4 ounces of heroin was subject to a mandatory sentence of 15 years to life. Weiman and Weiss (2009) found that there was little change in prison populations initially as prosecutors, who had opposed the rigidity of these laws, shifted their charging practices. Eventually, however, these provisions contributed to a dramatic rise in the New York State prison population, from 10,000 in 1975 to 70,000 in 2003, with nearly 20,000 of the 2003 prisoners being held for drug offenses (Mancuso 2010).

Despite decades of protest by a broad spectrum of law enforcement officials, including Chief Justice Judith Kaye of the state's highest court, in addition to the usual advocacy groups, the laws survived unchanged to 2005. Governor George Pataki, who was elected in 1994 with a promise of reforming these laws, was able to make only very modest changes, and those in 2005 near the end of his 12 years in office. For example, the new laws still required a sentence of incarceration for first-time offenders in possession of small amounts of cocaine or heroin (Mancuso 2010).

Only in 2009 were substantial changes made, and even those left behind a harsh set of penalties. For example, sentences for second-time B-class felony offenders were lowered only from 2 years to 1.5 years. Penalties for sales to an individual under age 17 were actually raised; determinate sentences went from 1 year to 2 years, with probation being increased to 25 years rather than 5 (Mancuso 2010).

Lofgren (2011) argues that the principal argument for the reforms in 2009 was the changed view of the addict. The 2009 reforms were focused on offenders who had a substance abuse problem; other offenders were in principle still subject to severe penalties.

As with the fight over federal sentencing disparities for crack and powder cocaine, a great deal of effort was expended on accomplishing modest changes. Those changes were certainly worthwhile, but they point to the difficulty of disassembling the machinery of excessive punishment that was created during specific drug scares, 1970s heroin in the case of the Rockefeller laws and the mid-1980s crack epidemic in the case of the federal laws.

B. Why?

The title of this essay promised more than a discussion of the past. It also promised an explanation for the long stasis in drug policy, during a period in which the problem has been through many phases if not full transformations. There are three possible forms of explanation.

One rests simply in popular attitudes. The American public became fearful of drugs in the 1970s and 1980s, with the heroin epidemic, two separate cocaine epidemics (powder and then crack), and the associated crime. The connection between drugs and crime was real, and violent crime was at its worst during the 1980s. It is not surprising that there is popular resistance to major changes in policy toward illegal drugs, a suspicion that anything other than tough enforcement of tough laws will be insufficient to protect society from a return to the horrible times of the 1980s, with their bloody battles between drug-selling gangs. In 2001, well after the worst of the drug problems had passed, the public still believed that the problem was worsening (74 percent agreed that the war on drugs was being lost) and was more supportive of interdiction and arresting sellers than of treatment or prevention, though they had little faith in any specific program (Pew Research Center for the People and the Press 2001).

Many observers expected that popular attitudes toward drugs as a class would become less harsh as the adult population became richer in experienced drug users. In 1982, the share of persons aged 26 or over who had used any illicit drug was only 37 percent; by 2010 that had risen to 48.1 percent, mostly reflecting individuals experienced with marijuana and no other illegal drug. Most of those who have used marijuana report no resulting problems; thus the increased support for marijuana decriminalization and legalization discussed earlier is hardly surprising. That has not led to comparable changes in policy attitudes with respect to other drugs.

A second factor that may help explain the stasis is general policy inertia. Big changes in any policy domain occur rarely and usually in response to a confluence of factors, a theory developed famously by John Kingdon (2010). Drug policy made major shifts in the mid- to late 1980s in response to a moral panic; readjusting after such panics have ended is notoriously a slow process. In this view, there will come a time, perhaps a response to fiscal strains and a series of scandals around overcrowded prisons, when the public will accept substantially less harsh policies.

There is one hopeful sign at this level, namely, a shift in conservative views about the desirability of continued growth of incarceration (Dagan and Teles 2012*a*, 2012*b*). In states as historically punitive as Mississippi and Texas, Republican leaders in the state legislatures have passed laws and funded programs that allow for early release and more intense supervision of parolees and probationers. Dagan and Teles suggest that this reflects a new view of criminal justice personnel; once seen as the defenders of society; they are now viewed as bureaucrats, yet another emanation of the modern state. Those fighting to shrink government no longer exempt correctional facilities.

The 2007–11 period certainly saw a straining of state and local budgets plus a great deal of hand-wringing about excessive federal deficits. The overcrowding and dangerousness of prisons, particularly those of California, have become a staple of the media and of federal judicial decrees. Actual incarceration has declined slightly, from 2,307,000 in 2008 (local jails, federal, and state prisons) to 2,239,000 in 2011.[63] Though with no particular focus on drugs, the decline in incarceration generally should help reduce the number of minor drug offenders incarcerated. Teles (personal communication) argues that the change is facilitated by the rapid turnover in state legislatures. The new conservative members, without a memory of when drugs were the nation's "scourge," as President George H. W. Bush put it, are more open to rational arguments about the undesirability of locking up minor offenders for long terms.

The third factor, and the most common explanation for the stasis, particularly at the federal level, is the timidity of politicians. It is routinely asserted that no politician wants to be seen to be soft on crime, and drugs are equated in the public mind with crime. It is easy rhetorically to claim that any softening of the severe sentences imposed on drug dealers, who account for the vast bulk of drug offenders in prison (Sevigny and Caulkins 2004), is a move toward undue leniency and would worsen the drug problem. The counter to that is a statement that actually there is no evidence that lighter sentences would make drugs more available or cheaper; that statement is not very convincing to the public. Having argued this often myself, I have a sense of how

[63] The per capita rate, a more appropriate measure for many purposes, has fallen further given the continued growth of the US population, from one per 100 in 2008 to one per 107 in 2011.

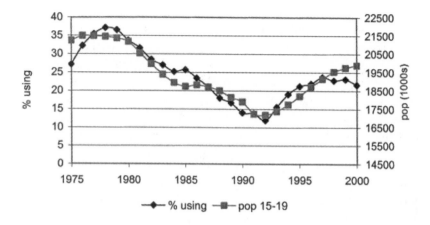

FIG. 5.—Prevalence of marijuana use and size of age cohorts, 1975–2000. Source: Jacobson (2004); Johnston et al. (2012).

hard it is to make a case that rests on a lack of evidence rather than on grand experimental results.

The argument that other countries have managed to avoid the seriousness of the US drug problem without high incarceration rates has no purchase. Except for Dutch coffee shops and, in recent years, the experience of Portugal with the decriminalization of drug possession generally, other countries' experiences hardly enter into the debate in the United States. Again, this parochialism is not confined to drug policy but is characteristic of many domains of policy discussion in the United States.

My own hypothesis is that the stasis is very much a consequence of the fact that the problem has been declining. Why risk change when existing policies are working? There are lots of good answers to that: the policies are expensive, divisive, and intrusive, to return to the starting point of this essay, and the problem is declining for reasons other than policy. Excessive punishment is itself offensive to Western sensibilities. These have not been persuasive arguments. The problem has declined, if you accept my argument about the distinct nature of the prescription drug misuse problem, and that may be enough to protect the status quo.

I conclude by again emphasizing the limited capacity of targeted drug policy to reduce use via prohibition. Consider figure 5, a graph from Jacobson (2004). It shows past-month marijuana use among high school seniors, a well-tracked figure, and the size of the age 15–19 cohort each year from 1975 to 2000. There is a remarkable positive correlation between cohort size and drug use in that age group. Jacobson concludes that the relationship reflects "strained monitoring resources" and scale economies in drug markets. "Strained monitoring resources" are the hypotheses "that efforts to prevent youth drug use are overwhelmed when cohorts are large, reducing the risk of punishment and increasing use. 'Scale economies' suggests that due to the fixed costs of illicit drug distribution, increases in cohort size lower the per-unit costs of drugs, reducing prices and increasing use" (Jacobson 2004, pp. 1482–83). This is consistent with the work of Easterlin (1987), which shows the influence of cohort size on many aspects of individual behavior. Jacobson conducted other subanalyses that further supported the notion that cohort size was a very important driver of prevalence.

The proposition that policy can do little to influence prevalence of use may seem nihilistic. Far from it. We know that bad policy choices can make drug use, drug distribution, and production more harmful. All that policy changes can in fact do is to reduce the harmfulness of these activities. I believe that this proposition has enormously liberating effects for policy. At present, many laws and interventions are justified because they might reduce drug use, even though we know with greater confidence that they cause harms. If prevalence of use is no longer seen as a plausible policy goal, then the harms can be avoided. Finding a way of making this persuasive to the public is the difficult task.

REFERENCES

Aaron, Paul, and David Musto. 1981. "Temperance and Prohibition in America: A Historical Overview." In *Alcohol and Public Policy: Beyond the Shadow of Prohibition*, edited by Mark H. Moore and Dean Gerstein. Washington, DC: National Academy Press.
Advisory Council on the Misuse of Drugs. 1988. *AIDS and Drug Misuse*. Pt. 1. London: HMSO.
Alexander, Michelle. 2010. *The New Jim Crow*. New York: New Press.
Amundsen, Ellen J. 2006. "Measuring Effectiveness of Needle and Syringe Exchange Programmes for Prevention of HIV among IDUs." *Addiction* 101: 161–63.

Anderson, D. Mark, and Daniel I. Rees. 2011. "Medical Marijuana Laws, Traffic Fatalities, and Alcohol Consumption." IZA Discussion Paper no. 6112. Bonn: Institute for the Study of Labor.

Arkes, Jeremy, Shawn Bushway, Jonathan P. Caulkins, and Peter Reuter. 2006. "Does State and Local Drug Enforcement Raise Retail Cocaine Prices?" Unpublished manuscript. University of Maryland, School of Public Policy and Department of Criminology. http://faculty.publicpolicy.umd.edu/reuter/publications.

Astorga, Luis, and David A. Shirk. 2010. "Drug Trafficking Organizations and Counter-drug Strategies in the US-Mexican Context." In *Shared Responsibility: US-Mexico Policy Options for Confronting Organized Crime*, edited by Eric Olson, Andrew Stelee, and David Shirk. San Diego: Woodrow Wilson International Center for Scholars; Trans-Border Institute, Joan B. Kroc School of Peace Studies, University of San Diego.

Babor, Thomas, et al. 2010. *Drug Policy and the Public Good.* Oxford: Oxford University Press.

Ball, John C., and Emily S. Cottrell. 1965. "Admissions of Narcotic Drug Addicts to Public Health Service Hospitals, 1935–63." *Public Health Reports* 80(6):471–75.

Beckett, Katherine. 2004. *Race and Drug Law Enforcement in Seattle.* Report prepared on behalf of the Defender Association's Racial Disparity Project. Seattle: Defender Association.

———. 2008. "Drugs, Data, Race, and Reaction: A Field Report." *Antipode* 40(3):442–47.

Beckett, Katherine, Kris Nyrop, Lori Pfingst, and Melissa Bowen. 2005. "Drug Use, Drug Possession Arrests and the Question of Race: Lessons from Seattle." *Social Problems* 52(3):419–41.

Belenko, Steven. 2001. *Research on Drug Courts: A Critical Review, 2001 Update.* New York: National Center on Addiction and Substance Abuse, Columbia University.

Bertram, E., M. Blachman, K. Sharpe, and P. Andreas. 1996. *Drug War Politics: The Price of Denial.* Berkeley: University of California Press.

Bewley-Taylor, David. 2012. *International Drug Control: Consensus Fractured.* Cambridge: Cambridge University Press.

Bhati, Avinash Singh, John K. Roman, and Aaron Chalfin. 2008. *To Treat or Not to Treat: Evidence on the Prospects of Expanding Treatment to Drug-Involved Offenders.* Washington, DC: Urban Institute.

Blanchard, Christopher M. 2009. *Afghanistan: Narcotics and US Policy.* Washington, DC: Diane Publishing.

Blumstein, Alfred, and Allen J. Beck. 2005. "Reentry as a Transient State between Liberty and Recommitment." In *Prisoner Reentry and Crime in America*, edited by Jeremy Travis and Christy Visher. New York: Cambridge University Press.

Bonnie, Richard J., and Charles H. Whitebread. 1974. *The Marihuana Conviction: A History of Marihuana Prohibition in the United States.* Charlottesville: University Press of Virginia.

Boston Globe. 2003. "Canada Offers Liberal Marijuana Bill: Decriminalization Would Hike US Use, White House Warns." May 28.

Boyum, David, and Peter Reuter. 2005. *An Analytic Assessment of US Drug Policy.* Washington, DC: American Enterprise Institute.

Bruneau, Julie, Francois Lamoth, Eduardo Franco, Nathalie Lachance, Marie Désy, Julio Soto, and JeanVincelette. 1997. "High Rates of HIV Infection among Injection Drug Users Participating in Needle Exchange Programs in Montreal: Results of a Cohort Study." *American Journal of Epidemiology* 146: 994–1002.

Bruneau, Julie, and M. T. Schechter. 1998. "The Politics of Needles and AIDS." *New York Times*, April 9.

Bruun, Kettil, Lynn Pan, and Ingemar Rexed. 1975. *The Gentlemen's Club: International Control of Drugs and Alcohol.* Chicago: University of Chicago Press.

Buck, J. A. 2011. "Looming Expansion and Transformation of Public Substance Abuse Treatment under the Affordable Care Act." *Health Affairs* 30(8):1402–10. http://www.ncbi.nlm.nih.gov/pubmed/21821557.

Bureau of Justice Assistance. Drug Court Clearinghouse Project. 2009. *Summary of Drug Court Activity by State and County, July 14, 2009.* Washington, DC: American University, Bureau of Justice Assistance Drug Court Clearinghouse Project.

Califano, Joe. 2009. "Not Your Father's Marijuana: Ideas Special Report." *Atlantic*, July 24.

Calmes, Jackie. 2012. "Obama Says Legalization Is Not the Answer on Drugs." *New York Times*, April 14.

Carnevale, John T., and Patrick J. Murphy. 1999. "Matching Rhetoric to Dollars: Twenty-Five Years of Federal Drug Strategies and Drug Budgets." *Journal of Drug Issues* 29(2):299–322.

Caulkins, Jonathan P. 2010. *The Cost of Marijuana Enforcement on the California Criminal Justice System.* Santa Monica, CA: RAND.

Caulkins, Jonathan P., and Sara Chandler. 2006. "Long-Run Trends in Incarceration of Drug Offenders in the US." *Crime and Delinquency* 52(4):619–41.

Caulkins, Jonathan P., Mark Kleiman, and Jonathan Kulick. 2010. *Drug Production and Trafficking, Counterdrug Policies, and Security and Governance in Afghanistan.* New York: New York University, Center on International Cooperation.

Caulkins, Jonathan, and Peter Reuter. 2010. "How Drug Enforcement Affects Drug Prices." In *Crime and Justice: A Review of Research*, vol. 39, edited by Michael Tonry. Chicago: University of Chicago Press.

Caulkins, Jonathan P., C. Peter Rydell, Susan S. Everingham, James Chiesa, and Shawn Bushway. 1999. *An Ounce of Prevention, a Pound of Uncertainty: The Cost-Effectiveness of School-Based Drug Prevention Programs.* Santa Monica, CA: RAND.

CDC (Centers for Disease Control and Prevention). 2010. *Emergency Depart-*

ment Visits Involving Nonmedical Use of Selected Prescription Drugs—United States, 2004–2008. Atlanta: CDC.

———. 2012*a*. "HIV Infection and HIV-Associated Behaviors among Injecting Drug Users—20 Cities, United States, 2009." *Morbidity and Mortality Weekly Report* 61(8):133–47.

———. 2012*b*. *National Vital Statistics System, Multiple Cause of Death Dataset*. Atlanta: CDC.

Chait, L. D. 1989. "Delta-9-Tetrahydrocannabinol Content and Human Marijuana Self-Administration." *Pyschopharmacology* 98:51–55.

Clear, Todd, and Dennis Schrantz. 2011. "Strategies for Reducing Prison Populations." *Prison Journal* 91(3):138–59.

Coleman, John J. 2012. "The Supply Chain of Medicinal Controlled Substances: Addressing the Achilles Heel of Drug Diversion." *Journal of Pain and Palliative Care Pharmacotherapy* 26:233–50.

Compton, Wilson, and Nora Volkow. 2006. "Major Increases in Opioid Analgesic Abuse in the United States: Concerns and Strategies." *Drug and Alcohol Dependence* 81:103–10.

Copeland, Larry. 2009. "State Police Forces Shrink." *USA Today*, November 15.

Costa, Antonio Maria. 2009. "How Many Lives Would Have Been Lost If We Didn't Have Controls on Drugs?" *Guardian*, September 19.

Cottam, Martha L., and Otwin Marenin. 1999. "International Cooperation in the War on Drugs: Mexico and the United States." *Policing and Society* 9(3): 209–40.

Courtwright, David T. 1982. *Dark Paradise: Opiate Addiction in America before 1940*. Cambridge, MA: Harvard University Press.

Creason, Christopher R., and Morton Goldman. 1981. "Varying Levels of Marijuana Use by Adolescents and the Amotivational Syndrome." *Psychological Reports* 48:447–54.

Dagan, David, and Steven Teles. 2012*a*. "The Conservative War on Prisons." *Washington Monthly*, November/December.

———. 2012*b*. "The Social Construction of Negative Feedback Incarceration, Conservatism, and Policy Change." Paper prepared for the American Political Science Association annual meeting, New Orleans, August 30.

Davis, W. Rees, and Bruce D. Johnson. 2008. "Prescription Opioid Use, Misuse, and Diversion among Street Drug Users in New York City." *Drug and Alcohol Dependence* 92(1–3):267–76.

De Leon, George. 2000. *The Therapeutic Community: Theory, Model, and Method*. New York: Springer.

Des Jarlais, Don C., and Samuel R. Friedman. 1992. "AIDS and Legal Access to Sterile Drug Injection Equipment." *Annals of the American Academy of Political and Social Science* 521(1):42–65.

Des Jarlais, Don C., Samuel R. Friedman, and Thomas P. Ward. 1993. "Harm Reduction: A Public Health Response to the AIDS Epidemic among Injecting Drug Users." *Annual Review of Public Health* 14:413–50.

Detroit News. 2003. "It's Time to Ease Nation's Laws on Marijuana." July 29.

Donnelly, Neil, Wayne Hall, and Paul Christie. 1995. "The Effects of Partial Decriminalisation on Cannabis Use in South Australia 1985–1993." *Australian Journal of Public Health* 19:281–87.

Dooling, Kathleen, and Michael Rachlis. 2010. "Vancouver's Supervised Injection Facility Challenges Canada's Drug Laws." *Canadian Medical Association Journal* 182(13):1440–44.

Drake, Elizabeth K., Steven Aos, and Marna G. Miller. 2009. "Evidence-Based Public Policy Options to Reduce Crime and Criminal Justice Costs: Implications in Washington State." *Victims and Offenders* 4:170–96.

Drug Policy Alliance. 2011. *Drug Courts Are Not the Answer: Toward a Health-Centered Approach to Drug Use*. New York: Drug Policy Alliance.

Dwyer, Devin. 2012. "Marijuana Not High Obama Priority." *ABC News*, December 14. http://abcnews.go.com/Politics/OTUS/president-obama-marijuana-users-high-priority-drug-war/story?id=17946783.

Easterlin, Richard. 1987. *Birth and Fortune*. Chicago: University of Chicago Press.

Eckholm, Erick. 2011. "Medical Marijuana Industry Is Unnerved by US Crackdown." *New York Times*, November 23. http://www.nytimes.com/2011/11/24/us/medical-marijuana-target-of-us-prosecutors.html.

EMCDDA (European Monitoring Center on Drugs and Drug Abuse). 2012. *Cannabis Production and Markets in Europe*. Lisbon: EMCDDA.

Epstein, Edward J. 1978. *Agency of Fear*. New York: Putnam.

Fareed, Ayman, Jennifer Casarella, Richard Amar, Sreedevi Vayalapalli, and Karen Drexler. 2010. "Methadone Maintenance Dosing Guideline for Opioid Dependence, a Literature Review." *Journal of Addictive Diseases* 29:1–14.

Felbab-Brown, Vanda, Joel M. Jutkowitz, Sergio Rivas, Ricardo Rocha, James T. Smith, Manuel Supervielle, and Cynthia Watson. 2009. *Assessment of the Implementation of the United States Government's Support for Plan Colombia's Illicit Crop Reduction Components*. Washington, DC: USAID from the American People. http://pdf.usaid.gov/pdf_docs/PDACN233.pdf.

Fischer, Benedikt, Eugenia Oviedo-Joekes, Peter Blanken, Christian Haasen, Jürgen Rehm, Martin T. Schechter, John Strang, and Wim van den Brink. 2007. "Heroin-Assisted Treatment (HAT) a Decade Later: A Brief Update on Science and Politics." *Journal of Urban Health* 84(4):552–62.

Fluellen, Reginald, and Jennifer Trone. 2000. *Do Drug Courts Save Jail and Prison Beds?* New York: Vera Institute of Justice.

Flynn, Kevin. 1998. "Arrests Soar in Crackdown on Marijuana." *New York Times*, November 17.

Fries, Arthur, Robert W. Anthony, Andrew Cseko Jr., Carl C. Gaither, and Eric Schullman. 2008. *Technical Report for the Price and Purity of Illicit Drugs: 1981–2007*. Alexandria, VA: Institute for Defense Analysis.

Friesendorf, Cornelius. 2007. *US Foreign Policy and the War on Drugs: Displacing the Cocaine and Heroin Industry*. New York: Routledge.

Gallup. 2002. "Decades of Drug Use: Data From the '60s and '70s." http://www.gallup.com/poll/6331/decades-drug-use-data-from-60s-70s.aspx.

———. 2007. "Little Change in Public's View of the US Drug Problem." http://www.gallup.com/poll/102061/little-change-publics-view-us-drug-problem.aspx.

———. 2011. "Record-High 50 percent of Americans Favor Legalizing Marijuana Use." http://www.gallup.com/poll/150149/record-high-americans-favor-legalizing-marijuana.aspx.

Government Accounting Office. 1993. *Needle Exchange Programs: Research Suggests Promise as an AIDS Prevention Strategy.* Washington, DC: US Government Printing Office.

Goldberg, Peter. 1980. "The Federal Government's Response to Illicit Drugs, 1969–1978." In *The Facts about Drug Abuse,* edited by the Drug Abuse Council. New York: Free Press.

Golub, Andrew, Bruce D. Johnson, and Eloise Dunlap. 2007. "The Race/Ethnicity Disparity in Misdemeanor Marijuana Arrests in New York City." *Criminology and Public Policy* 6(1):131–64.

Goodnough, Abby, and Katie Zezima. 2011. "An Alarming New Stimulant, Legal in Many States." *New York Times,* July 16.

Gottfredson, Denise. 1997. "School-Based Crime Prevention." In *Preventing Crime: What Works, What Doesn't, What's Promising,* edited by Lawrence W. Sherman, Denise C. Gottfredson, Doris MacKenzie, John Eck, Peter Reuter, and Shawn Bushway. Washington, DC: US Department of Justice, Office of Justice Programs.

Gould, Robert A., and George A. Clum. 1993. "A Meta-Analysis of Self-Help Treatment Approaches." *Clinical Psychology Review* 13:169–86.

Government Accountability Office. 2008. *Plan Colombia: Drug Reduction Goals Were Not Fully Met but Security Has Improved: US Agencies Need More Detailed Plan to Reduce Assistance.* Washington, DC: Government Accountability Office.

Greenwald, G. 2009. *Drug Decriminalization in Portugal: Lessons for Creating Fair and Effective Drug Policies.* Washington, DC: Cato Institute.

Grimm, Ryan. 2009. *This Is Your Country on Drugs.* Hoboken, NJ: Wiley.

Hallfors, Denise, and Dionne C. Godette. 2002. "Will the 'Principles of Effectiveness' Improve Prevention Practice? Early Findings from a Diffusion Study." *Health Education Review* 17:461–70.

Harris, John F., and Amy Goldstein. 1998. "Puncturing an AIDS Initiative." *Washington Post,* April 23.

Hatsukami, Dorthy K., and Marian W. Fishman. 1996. "Crack Cocaine and Cocaine Hydrochloride: Are the Differences Myth or Reality?" *Journal of the American Medical Association* 276:1580–88.

Hawken, Angela, and Mark Kleiman. 2009. *Managing Drug Involved Probationers with Swift and Certain Sanctions: Evaluating Hawaii's HOPE.* Washington, DC: National Institute of Justice.

Howell, James C. 2003. *Preventing and Reducing Juvenile Delinquency: A Comprehensive Framework.* Thousand Oaks, CA: Sage.

Huddleston, West, and Douglas B. Marlowe. 2011. *Painting the Current Picture:*

A National Report on Drug Courts and Other Problem-Solving Court Programs in the United States. Washington, DC: National Drug Court Institute.

Hurley, Susan F., Damein J. Jolley, and John M. Kaldor. 1997. "Effectiveness of Needle-Exchange Programmes for Prevention of HIV Infection." *Lancet* 349(9068):1797–1800.

Jacobson, Mireille. 2004. "Baby Booms and Drug Busts: Trends in Youth Drug Use in the United States, 1975–2000." *Quarterly Journal of Economics* 119(4): 1481–1512.

Jena, Anupam, Dana Goldman, Susan Foster, and Joseph Califano. 2011. "Prescription Medication Abuse and Illegitimate Internet-Based Pharmacies." *Annals of Internal Medicine* 155(12):848–51.

Johnson, Bruce D., Andrew Golub, and Eloise Dunlap. 2006. "The Rise and Decline of Drugs, Drug Markets, and Violence in New York City." In *The Crime Drop in America*, rev. ed., edited by Alfred Blumstein and Joel Wallman. New York: Cambridge University Press.

Johnston, Lloyd D., Jerald G. Bachman, and Patrick M. O'Malley. 1981. *Highlights from Student Drug Use in America, 1975–1981*. Washington, DC: National Institute on Drug Abuse, US Department of Health and Human Services.

Johnston, Lloyd D., Patrick M. O'Malley, Jerald G. Bachman, and Jennifer E. Schulenberg. 2011. *Monitoring the Future: National Survey Results on Drug Use, 1975–2010*. Vol. 1, *Secondary School Students*. Ann Arbor: Institute for Social Research, University of Michigan.

———. 2012. *Monitoring the Future: National Survey Results on Drug Use, 1975–2011*. Vol. 1, *Secondary School Students*. Ann Arbor: Institute for Social Research, University of Michigan.

Justinova, Zuzana, Steven R. Goldberg, Stephen J. Heishmban, and Gianluigi Tanda. 2005. "Self-Administration of Cannabinoids by Experimental Animals and Human Marijuana Smokers." *Pharmacology Biochemistry and Behavior* 81(2):285–99.

Kaplan, Tom. 2012. "Mayor Bloomberg Backs Plan to Limit Arrests for Marijuana." *New York Times*, June 4.

Kasick, D. P., C. A. McKnight, and E. Kilsovic. 2011. "Bath Salt Ingestion Leading to Severe Intoxication Delirium: Two Cases and a Brief Review of the Emergence of Mephedrone Use." *Amercan Journal of Substance Abuse* 38(2):176–80.

Kau, G. 2008. "Flashback to the Federal Analog Act of 1986: Mixing Rules and Standards in the Cauldron." *University of Pennsylvania Law Review* 156: 1077–1115.

Kilmer, Beau, Jonathan Caulkins, Rosalie Pacula, Robert MacCoun, and Peter Reuter. 2010. *Altered State? Assessing Marijuana Legalization Could Affect Marijuana Consumption and Public Budgets in California*. Santa Monica, CA: RAND.

Kilmer, Beau, Jonathan Caulkins, Rosalie Pacula, and Peter Reuter. 2012. *The US Drug Policy Landscape: Insights and Opportunities for Improving the View*. Occasional Paper. Santa Monica: RAND.

King, Ryan S., and Jill Pasquarella. 2009. *Drug Courts: A Review of the Evidence*. Washington, DC: Sentencing Project.

Kingdon, John W. 2010. *Agendas, Alternatives, and Public Policies*. 2nd ed. London: Pearson.

Kleiman, Mark A. R., and Steven Davenport. 2012. "Strategies to Control Mexican Drug-Trafficking Violence." *Journal of Drug Policy Analysis* 1:1–11.

Korf, Dirk. 2002. "Dutch Coffee Shops and Trends in Cannabis Use." *Addictive Behaviors* 27(6):851–66.

Kuziemko, Ilyana, and Steven D. Levitt. 2004. "An Empirical Analysis of Imprisoning Drug Offenders." *Journal of Public Economics* 88(9–10):2043–66.

Leshner, Alan. 2001. "Drug Addiction Is a Brain Disease." *Science and Technology* 17(3). http://www.freepatentsonline.com/article/Issues-in-Science-Technology/75286580.html.

Levine, Harry, and Loren Siegel. 2011. *$75 Million a Year the Cost of New York City's Marijuana Possession Arrests*. New York: Drug Policy Alliance.

Levine, Harry, and Deborah Peterson Small. 2008. *Marijuana Arrest Crusade: Racial Bias and Police Policy in New York City, 1997–2007*. New York: New York Civil Liberties Union.

Lofgren, Andrea. 2011. "A Sign of Things to Come? Drug Policy Reforms in Arizona, California, and New York." *New York University Journal of Legislation and Public Policy* 14(3):773–804.

Lune, Howard. 2002. "Reclamation Activism in Anti-drug Organizing in the USA." *Social Movement Studies* 1(2):147–68.

Maag, Verena. 2003. "Estimated Trends in the Prevalence of Heroin Addiction in Switzerland." *European Addiction Research* 9(4):176–81.

MacCoun, Robert J. 2010. *Estimating the Non-price Effects of Legalization on Cannabis Consumption*. Santa Monica, CA: RAND.

MacCoun, Robert J., Rosalie Pacula, Jamie Chiriqi, Katherine Harris, and Peter Reuter. 2009. "Do Citizens Know Whether Their State Has Decriminalized Marijuana? Assessing the Perceptual Component of Deterrence Theory." *Review of Law and Economics* 5(1):347–71.

MacCoun, Robert J., and Peter Reuter. 2001. *Drug War Heresies: Learning from Other Places, Times and Vices*. Cambridge: Cambridge University Press.

———. 2011. "Assessing Drug Prohibition and Its Alternatives: A Guide for Agnostics." *Annual Review of Law and Social Sciences* 7:61–78.

Mancuso, Peter. 2010. "Resentencing after the Fall of Rockefeller: The Failure of the Drug Law Reform Acts of 2004 and 2005 to Remedy the Injustices of New York's Rockefeller Drug Laws and the Compromise of 2009." *Albany Law Review* 73:1535–81.

Massing, Michael. 1998. *The Fix*. New York: Simon & Schuster.

McAllister, William B. 2000. *Drug Diplomacy in the Twentieth Century*. London: Routledge.

McLaren, Jennifer, Wendy Swift, Paul Dillon, and Steve Allsop. 2008. "Cannabis Potency and Contamination: A Review of the Literature." *Addiction* 103:1100–1109.

Measham, Fiona, Karena Moore, and Russell Newcombe. 2010. "Tweaking,

Bombing, Dabbing, and Stockpiling: The Emergence of Mephedrone and the Perversity of Prohibition." *Drugs and Alcohol Today* 10(1):14–21.

Meier, Kenneth J. 1994. *The Politics of Sin: Drugs, Alcohol, and Public Policy.* Washington, DC: Library of Congress.

Merrell, Elizabeth, Azar Kariminia, Ingrid A. Binswanger, Michael S. Hobbs, Michael Farrell, John Marsden, Sharon J. Hutchinson, and Sheila M. Bird. 2010. "Meta-Analysis of Drug-Related Deaths Soon after Release from Prison." *Addiction* 105(9):1545–54.

Miron, Jeffery A. 2003. *The Budgetary Implications of Marijuana Legalization in Massachusetts.* Greenfield, MA: Changing the Climate.

———. 2010. *The Budgetary Implications of Drug Prohibition.* Boston: Harvard University, Criminal Justice Policy Foundation.

Mitchell, Ojmarrh, David Wilson, Amy Eggers, and Doris MacKenzie. 2012. "Assessing the Effectiveness of Drug Courts on Recidivism: A Meta-Analytic Review of Traditional and Non-traditional Drug Courts." *Journal of Criminal Justice* 40(1):60–71.

Molzahn, Corey, Rios Viridano, and David Shirk. 2012. *Drug Violence in Mexico: Data and Analysis through 2012.* San Diego: Trans Border Institute.

Musto, David F. 1999. *The American Disease.* 3rd ed. New York: Oxford University Press.

Nadelmann, Ethan. 1989. "Drug Prohibition in the United States: Costs, Consequences, and Alternatives." *Science* 245(4921):939–47.

National Commission on Marihuana and Drug Abuse. 1972. *Marihuana: A Signal of Misunderstanding; the Official Report of the National Commission on Marihuana and Drug Abuse.* New York: Signet.

National Institute on Drug Abuse. 2002. *Principles of HIV Prevention in Drug-Using Populations: A Research-Based Guide.* Washington, DC: National Institutes of Health.

National Research Council. 1982. *An Analysis of Marijuana Policy.* Washington, DC: National Academies Press.

National Survey on Drug Use and Health. 2011. *Results from the 2011 National Survey on Drug Use and Health: Summary of National Findings.* Rockville, MD: Substance Abuse and Mental Health Services Administration.

Nguyen, Holly, and Peter Reuter. 2012. "How Risky Is Marijuana Possession? Considering the Role of Age, Race and Gender." *Crime and Delinquency* 58(6):879–910.

Normand, Jacques, David Vlahov, and Lincoln Moses. 1995. *Preventing HIV Transmission: The Role of Sterile Needles and Bleach.* Panel on Needle Exchange and Bleach Distribution Programs, Commission on Behavioral and Social Sciences and Education, National Research Council Institute of Medicine. Washington, DC: National Academy Press.

Obama, Barack. 1995. *Dreams from My Father.* New York: Times Books.

Office of the Press Secretary. 2001. "Remarks by President George W. Bush and President Vicente Fox of Mexico in Joint Press Conference." Washington, DC: Office of the Press Secretary, February 16. http://www.white house.gov/news/releases/2001/02/print/20010216-3.html.

ONDCP (Office of National Drug Control Policy). 1989. *National Drug Control Strategy, 1989*. Washington, DC: Executive Office of the President.

———. 2010a. *Drug Courts: A Smart Approach to Criminal Justice*. Washington, DC: Executive Office of the President. http://whitehouse.gov/sites/default/files/ondcp/Fact_Sheets/drug_courts_fact_sheet_5-31-11.pdf.

———. 2010b. *Drug Decriminalization in Portugal: Challenges and Limitations Fact Sheet*. Washington, DC: Executive Office of the President. http://www.whitehouse.gov/sites/default/files/ondcp/Fact_Sheets/portugal_fact_sheet_8-25-10.pdf.

———. 2010c. *Marijuana: Know the Facts; Fact Sheet*. Washington, DC: Executive Office of the President.

———. 2011a. *Epidemic: Responding to America's Prescription Drug Abuse Crisis*. Washington, DC: Office of the President.

———. 2011b. *National Drug Control Strategy, 2011*. Washington, DC: Executive Office of the President.

———. 2012a. *National Drug Control Strategy, 2012*. Washington, DC: Executive Office of the President.

———. 2012b. *What America's Users Spend on Illicit Drugs, 2000–2006*. Washington, DC: Executive Office of the President.

———. 2012c. *White House Fact Sheet on US Drug Policy*. Washington, DC: Executive Office of the President. http://iipdigital.usembassy.gov/st/english/texttrans/2012/04/201204174016.html#axzz20nMVRnEi.

Onishi, Norimitsu. 2012. "Cities Balk as Federal Law on Marijuana Is Enforced." *New York Times*, June 6.

Pacula, Rosalie L., Jamie F. Chriqui, and Joanna King. 2003. "Decriminalization in the United States: What Does It Mean?" NBER Working Paper no. 9690. Cambridge, MA: National Bureau of Economic Research.

Pacula, Rosalie L., Michael Grossman, Frank Chaloupka, Patrick O'Malley, Lloyd Johnson, and Matthew Farrelly. 2000. "Marijuana and Youth." NBER Working Paper no. 7703. Cambridge, MA: National Bureau of Economic Research. http://www.nber.org/papers/w7703.pdf.

Pacula, Rosalie L., Robert MacCoun, Peter Reuter, Jamie Chriqui, Beau Kilmer, Katherine Harris, Letizia Paoli, and Carsten Schäfer. 2005. "What Does It Mean to Decriminalize Cannabis? A Cross-National Empirical Examination." In *Substance Use: Individual Behavior, Social Interaction, Markets and Politics*, Advances in Health Economics and Health Services Research, vol. 16, edited by Björn Lindgren and Michael Grossman. Amsterdam: Elsevier.

Paoli, Letizia, Victoria A. Greenfield, and Peter Reuter. 2009. *The World Heroin Market: Can Supply Be Cut?* New York: Oxford University Press.

Pastore, Ann L., and Kathleen Maguire. 2003. *Sourcebook of Criminal Justice Statistics*. Washington, DC: US Department of Justice, Bureau of Justice Statistics. http://www.albany.edu/sourcebook/.

Pew Research Center for the People and the Press. 2001. *Interdiction and Incarceration Still Top Remedies: 74 Percent Say Drug War Being Lost*. Washington, DC: Pew Research Center for the People and the Press.

Pollack, H., E. Sevigny, and P. Reuter. 2011. "If Drug Treatment Works So Well, Why Are So Many Drug Users Incarcerated?" In *Controlling Crime: Strategies and Trade-offs*, edited by Phil Cook, Jens Ludwig, and Justin McCrary. Chicago: University of Chicago Press.

Provine, Doris M. 2007. *Unequal under Law: Race in the War on Drugs*. Chicago: University of Chicago Press.

Reuter, Peter. 2009a. *Can Heroin Maintenance Help Baltimore? What Baltimore Can Learn from the Experience of Other Countries*. Baltimore: Abell Foundation.

———. 2009b. "The Unintended Consequences of Drug Policies." In *A Report of Global Illicit Drug Markets, 1998–2007*, edited by Peter Reuter and Franz Trautmann. Utrecht: Trimbos Institute.

———. 2011. *Options for Regulating New Psychoactive Drugs: A Review of Recent Experiences*. London: UK Drug Policy Commission. http://www.ukdpc.org.uk/resources/Reuter_Legal_highs_report.pdf.

Reuter, Peter, and Jonathan Caulkins. 2011. "Purity, Price, and Production: Are Drug Markets Different?" In *Illicit Trade and Globalization*, edited by Paul De Grauwe and Cláudia Costa Storti. Cambridge, MA: MIT Press.

Reuter, Peter, Paul Hirschfield, and Kurt Davies. 2001. "Assessing the Crackdown on Marijuana in Maryland." Unpublished manuscript. University of Maryland. http://www.drugpolicy.org/doc/Uploads/md_mj_crackdown.pdf.

Reuter, Peter, and Mike Timpane. 2001. *Assessing Options for the Safe and Drug Free Schools and Communities Act*. Santa Monica, CA: RAND.

Reuter, Peter, and Franz Trautmann, eds. 2009. *Assessing the Operations of the Global Illicit Drug Markets, 1998–2007*. Report for the European Commission. Utrecht: Trimbos Institute. http://ec.europa.eu/justice_home/doc_centre/drugs/studies/doc_drugs_studies_en.htm.

Rios, Viridano. 2012. "Why Are Mexican Traffickers Killing Each Other? Government Co-ordination and Violence Deterrence in Mexico's Drug War." Unpublished manuscript. Harvard University, Department of Government.

Room, R., B. Fischer, W. Hall, S. Lenton, and P. Reuter. 2010. *Cannabis Policy: Moving beyond Stalemate*. Oxford: Oxford University Press.

Rossman, Shelli B., John K. Roman, Janine M. Zweig, Michael Rempel, Christine H. Lindquist, Mia Green, P. Mitchell-Downey, Jennifer Yahner, Avinash S. Bhati, and Donald J. Farole. 2011. *The Multi-site Adult Drug Court Evaluation: The Impact of Drug Courts*. Vol. 4. Washington, DC: Urban Institute, Justice Policy Center.

SAMHSA (Substance Abuse and Mental Health Services Administration). Center for Behavioral Health Statistics and Quality. 2012. *Treatment Episode Data Set (TEDS), 2000–2010: National Admissions to Substance Abuse Treatment Services*. Rockville, MD: SAMHSA.

Samuels, David. 2008. "Dr. Kush: How Medical Marijuana Is Transforming the Pot Industry." *New Yorker*, July 28.

Satel, Sally, and Frederick Goodwin. 2003. *Is Drug Addiction a Brain Disease?* Washington, DC: Ethics and Public Policy Center.

Schechter, Martin T., Steffanie A. Strathdee, Peter G. A. Cornelisse, Sue Currie, David M. Patrick, Michael L. Rekart, and Michael V. O'Shaughnessy. 1999. "Do Needle Exchange Programmes Increase the Spread of HIV among Injection Drug Users? An Investigation of the Vancouver Outbreak." *AIDS* 13(6):45–51.

Schwarz, Alan. 2013. "Drowned in a Stream of Prescriptions." *New York Times*, February 3. http://www.nytimes.com/2013/02/03/us/concerns-about-adhd-practices-and-amphetamine-addiction.html?ref=usand_r=0.

Schweich, Thomas. 2008. "Is Afghanistan a Narco-State?" *New York Times*, July 27.

Secret, Mosi. 2013. "Outside Box, Federal Judges Offer Addicts Free Chance." *New York Times*, March 2.

Sevigny, Eric, and Jonathan P. Caulkins. 2004. "Kingpins or Mules: An Analysis of Drug Offenders Incarcerated in Federal and State Prisons." *Criminology and Public Policy* 3(3):401–34.

Sevigny, Eric L., Harold A. Pollack, and Peter Reuter. 2013. "Can Drug Courts Help Reduce Prison and Jail Populations?" *Annals of the American Academy of Political and Social Science* 647:190–212.

Shannon, Elaine. 1988. *Desperados: Latin Druglords, US Lawmen, and the War America Can't Win*. New York: Viking.

Spain, James W. 1975. "The United States, Turkey, and the Poppy." *Middle East Journal* 29(3):295–309.

Spillane, Joseph F. 2000. *Cocaine: From Medical Marvel to Modern Menace in the United States, 1884–1920*. Baltimore: Johns Hopkins University Press.

Stimson, Gerry V. 1988. "Injecting Equipment Exchange Schemes in England and Scotland." In *Needle Sharing among Intravenous Drug Abusers: National and International Perspectives*, edited by Robert Battjes and Roy Pickens. Washington, DC: National Institute on Drug Abuse.

Stitzer, Maxine, and Nancy Petry. 2006. "Contingency Management for Treatment of Substance Abuse." *Annual Review of Clinical Psychology* 2:411–34.

Storrs, Larry. 1999. *Drug Certification for Mexico, 1999: Arguments For and Against Congressional Resolutions of Disapproval*. Washington, DC: Congressional Research Service.

Strathdee, Steffanie A., David M. Patrick, Sue L. Currie, Peter G. A. Cornelisse, Michael L. Rekart, Julio S. G. Montaner, Martin T. Schechter, and Michael V. O'Shaughnessy. 1997. "Needle Exchange Is Not Enough: Lessons from the Vancouver Injecting Drug Use Study." *AIDS* 11:59–65.

Sullivan, Christopher. 1988. "User-Accountability Provisions in the Anti–Drug Abuse Act of 1988: Assaulting Civil Liberties in the War on Drugs." *Hastings Law Journal* 40:1223–51.

Tonry, Michael. 1995. *Malign Neglect*. New York: Oxford University Press.

———. 2011. *Punishing Race: A Continuing American Dilemma*. New York: Oxford University Press.

Troyer, Ronald J., and Gerald Markle. 1983. *Cigarettes: The Battle over Smoking*. New Brunswick, NJ: Rutgers University Press.

Uchtenhagen, A., R. Ali, M. Berglund, C. Eap, M. Farrell, R. Mattick, T. McLellan, J. Rehm, and S. Simpson. 2004. *Methadone as a Medicine for the*

Management of Opioid Dependence and HIV/AIDS Prevention. Geneva: World Health Organization.

US Sentencing Commission. 2009. Datafile USSCFY09. http://www.ussc.gov/Data_and_Statistics/Annual_Reports_and_Sourcebooks/2009/Table34.pdf.

Vincus, Amy, Chris Ringwalt, Melissa S. Harris, and Stephen R. Shamblen. 2010. "A Short-Term, Quasi-Experimental Evaluation of D.A.R.E.'s Revised Elementary School Curriculum." *Journal of Drug Education* 40(1):37–49.

Volkow, Nora. 2011. "Bath Salts: Emerging and Dangerous Products." Bethesda, MD: National Institute on Drug Abuse. http://www.drugabuse.gov/about-nida/directors-page/messages-director/2011/02/bath-salts-emerging-dangerous-products.

Walsh, John. 2004. *Are We There Yet? Measuring Progress in the US War on Drugs in Latin America.* Drug War Monitor. Washington, DC: Washington Office on Latin America. http://www.wola.org/sites/default/files/downloadable/Drug%20Policy/past/Are%20we%20there%20yet.pdf.

Walters, John P. 2002. "The Myth of 'Harmless' Marijuana." *Washington Post*, May 1.

Weiman, David F., and Christopher C. Weiss. 2009. "The Origins of Mass Incarceration in New York State: The Rockefeller Drug Laws and the Local War on Drugs." In *Do Prisons Make Us Safer? The Benefits and Costs of the Prison Boom*, edited by Steven Raphael and Michael A. Stoll. Thousand Oaks, CA: Sage.

West, Steven L., and Keri K. O'Neal. 2004. "Project D.A.R.E. Outcome Effectiveness Revisited." *American Journal of Public Health* 94:1027–29.

Wilson, David B., Ojmarrh Mitchell, and Doris L. MacKenzie. 2006. "A Systematic Review of Drug Court Effects on Recidivism." *Journal of Experimental Criminology* 2(4):459–87.

Wilson, James Q. 1990. "Against the Legalization of Drugs." *Commentary* 89(2):21–28.

Michael Tonry

Sentencing in America, 1975–2025

ABSTRACT

American sentencing policy has gone through four stages in the past 50 years. Indeterminate sentencing was followed by a sentencing reform period in which policy initiatives sought to make sentencing fairer and more consistent, a tough on crime period in which initiatives sought to make sentences harsher and more certain, and the current period, which is hard to characterize. Most tough on crime initiatives remain in place, coexisting with rehabilitative and restorative programs that aim to individualize sentencing and programming. Social science evidence was influential in the second period and to a limited degree in the current period. Indeterminate sentencing was broadly compatible with prevailing utilitarian ideas about the purposes of punishment and the sentencing reform period was broadly compatible with retributive ideas. The initiatives of the tough on crime period are difficult to reconcile with any coherent set of normative ideas. Current sentencing policies are a crazy quilt, making it impossible to generalize about prevailing normative ideas or an "American system of sentencing."

Sentencing policies, practices, and patterns in the United States have changed radically since the early 1970s. Were it possible for a representative group of time-traveling federal and state judges, prosecutors, defense lawyers, and correctional officials from 1970 to attend a national conference on American sentencing in 2013, they would find the contemporary system unrecognizable. Most would probably find it unimaginable.

In 1970, every American state and the federal system since at least

Michael Tonry is professor of law and public policy at the University of Minnesota. He is grateful to Richard Frase and Kevin Reitz for comments on a draft of this essay.

141

the 1930s had operated an "indeterminate sentencing" system premised on rehabilitation as the primary aim of punishment and on the desirability of tailoring sentences in every case to the offender's circumstances and needs (e.g., Rothman 1971). Sentencing was seen as a professional matter requiring specialized expertise and best handled by knowledgeable officials behind closed doors. Details varied, but the broad picture was everywhere the same. Statutes defined crimes and set out broad ranges of authorized sentences. Few laws mandated minimum sentences, and when they did, it was typically for 1 or 2 years. Judges adjudicated cases; decided whether to impose prison, jail, probation, or monetary sentences; and set maximum and occasionally minimum prison terms. Sentence appeals were for all practical purposes unavailable. Since sentencing was supposed to be individualized and judges had broad discretion to do so, there were no standards for appellate judges to use in evaluating a challenged sentence. Parole boards decided who would be released and when and subject to what conditions. Prison systems operated extensive systems of time off for good behavior. Punishments were mostly moderate. In 1970, the incarceration rate for federal and state prisons had been fluctuating in a narrow band around 110 per 100,000 population since the 1920s. When jail inmates are added, the total rate was 150–60. Since 1961 the rate had been falling modestly but continuously (Blumstein and Cohen 1973).

Indeterminate sentencing was not controversial. The *Model Penal Code* (1962), under development by the American Law Institute for 13 years, endorsed it and contained numerous provisions meant to improve it. In 1972, the National Council on Crime and Delinquency's Advisory Council of Judges issued the second edition of its *Model Sentencing Act*; it too assumed the continuation of indeterminate sentencing. So did the National Commission on Reform of Federal Criminal Law (1971) in its *Proposed Federal Criminal Code*.

That is the tidy, familiar, and predictable world the time travelers would have left behind. It bears little resemblance to American sentencing systems in the second decade of the twenty-first century. In the intervening years, indeterminate sentencing imploded. All its premises and assumptions about rehabilitation, individualization, and broad discretion were challenged. Judge Marvin Frankel's *Criminal Sentences—Law without Order* (1973) referred to indeterminate sentencing as "lawless" because of the absence of standards for sentencing decisions and of opportunities for appeals. Criticisms piled up. Unwarranted sentencing disparities were said to be common, and risks of racial bias and arbitrariness were said to be high (e.g., American Friends Service Committee 1971). Legal academics criticized the system's lack of procedural fairness, transparency, and predictability (e.g., Davis 1969; Dershowitz 1976). Researchers argued that the system did not and could not keep its rehabilitative promises (e.g., Kassebaum, Ward, and Wilner 1971; Martinson 1974). Others argued that parole release procedures were unfair and decisions inconsistent (e.g., Morris 1974; von Hirsch and Hanrahan 1979).

The criminal justice system in 2013 bears little resemblance to the one the time travelers would have left behind. Sentencing ceased being something best handled by experts behind closed doors but instead became a central issue in partisan politics (Edsall and Edsall 1991; Anderson 1995). The combined incarceration rate for federal, state, and local facilities quintupled to more than 750 per 100,000 in 2007 before beginning to fall (Carson and Sabol 2012; Minton 2012). One-third of the states had abandoned parole release, the signature characteristic of indeterminate sentencing, and all had abandoned it for some categories of prisoners. About one-third of the states, the District of Columbia, and the federal system operated some form of sentencing guidelines. All states and the federal government had enacted mandatory minimum sentence laws for drug and violent crimes or for "repeat" or "career" criminals, many requiring 5-, 10-, or 20-year or longer prison terms.

Complicating things further, a diverse set of new programs and policies in operation in 2013 aimed at individualizing sanctions to fit offenders' problems and needs. Most have emerged since the mid-1990s. They include drug and other problem-solving courts, reentry programs aimed at reducing reoffending, increased investment and confidence in treatment programs, and in many places programs incorporating ideas about restorative justice.

In retrospect, four distinct periods of sentencing policy are discernible. Indeterminate sentencing reigned from 1930 to 1975. From 1975 to the mid-1980s, the second period, a primarily liberal reform movement sought to make sentencing procedures fairer and outcomes more predictable and consistent. The totemic target was "racial and other unwarranted disparities," and the mechanisms for addressing them were guidelines for judges and parole boards (Blumstein et al. 1983).

During the third period, from the mid-1980s through 1996, sentencing policy changes aimed primarily to make prison sentences longer and their imposition more certain. The principal mechanisms were mandatory minimum sentence, three-strikes, truth-in-sentencing, and life-without-possibility-of-parole laws (LWOPs). Three-strikes laws typically required minimum 25-year sentences for people convicted of a third felony. State truth-in-sentencing laws were enacted to obtain federal funds for prison construction under the Violent Crime Control and Law Enforcement Act of 1994, as amended in 1996; to qualify, states had to demonstrate that people sentenced to imprisonment for violent crimes would serve at least 85 percent of their nominal sentences.

Almost none of the initiatives characterizing the second and third periods would make sense to the time travelers. In 1970 it seemed obvious to most informed people that judges and parole boards needed broad discretion in order to individualize sentences. Lengthy prison terms were not in vogue: they violated a widely supported "least restrictive alternative" logic. Mandatory punishments were commonly seen as unwise and unjust. The US Congress, for example, in the Comprehensive Drug Abuse Prevention and Control Act of 1970 repealed most then-existing federal mandatory minimum sentence laws (US Sentencing Commission 1991). The *Model Penal Code* and the *Model Sentencing Act* disapproved of them.

Generalizing about the fourth, most recent, period is harder. It is not difficult to identify principal aims of the first three periods: rehabilitation for the first, greater fairness for the second, and greater severity for the third. The purposes of the initiatives of the fourth period cannot be encapsulated in any single term. Some aim at greater severity, some at greater fairness, some at reducing recidivism, some at reducing costs. New mandatory minimum sentence laws target firearms and immigration offenses, human trafficking, carjacking, and child pornography, but after 1996 few more of the severest laws that characterized the third period were enacted. Drug and other problem-solving courts, reentry programs, and diverse treatment programs sought in many states to tailor programs and dispositions to the circumstances of individual offenders. After 2000, many state legislatures, generally in search of cost savings, enacted laws limiting the scope of some harsh sentencing provisions, reducing the numbers of revocations of parole and probation, and authorizing earlier releases from prison for selected offenders.[1] With few exceptions the statutory changes made minor adjustments and nibbled at the edges of correctional budgets and imprisonment rates (Austin et al. 2013).

In this essay, in an effort to explain what happened and why, I explore interactions among ideas, research findings, and policy making. Section I surveys changes in sentencing laws and practices since 1975 and what we know about their effects.

Section II discusses the influence of normative ideas on those changes. It is common to link the decline of indeterminate sentencing in the 1970s to a shift away from utilitarian (or, as now would be said, consequentialist) ways of thinking and toward retributive ones. Through the mid-1980s there was some basis for believing that such a shift occurred and that newly enacted sentencing laws and guidelines reflected it. After the mid-1980s it is difficult to identify initiatives that are reconcilable with retributivist values. There are many slightly different retributivist theories of punishment, but all have at their core the idea that criminal punishments, to be just, must in some meaningful way be proportionate to the seriousness of the offender's crime. Many recent initiatives—three-strikes and other mandatory minimum sentence laws, LWOPs, drug courts, restorative justice programs—are flatly incompatible with retributive theories of punishment. None of them, whether aiming for harsher, more humane, or more crime-preventive handling of offenders, attaches significant importance to achievement of proportionality or to treating like cases alike.

Section III discusses the influence of research findings on policy making. Credible research findings had no role in the first period; it was simply assumed that correctional programs can rehabilitate offenders. Research influenced sentencing policy significantly in the second period and little or not at all in the third. Parole guidelines and presumptive sentencing guidelines were shown to be effective at achieving their goals, but parole guidelines were quickly abandoned and presumptive sentencing guidelines were seldom adopted after the

---

[1] Summaries such as this have to be hedged because no organization maintains a comprehensive database on sentencing law changes. The National Conference of State Legislatures for many years compiled annual summaries (of uncertain comprehensiveness) and maintains a searchable database beginning with developments in 2010 (http://www.ncsl.org/issues-research/justice/state-sentencing-and-corrections-legislation.aspx), and organizations such as The Sentencing Project (e.g., Porter 2013), the Vera Institute of Justice (e.g., Austin 2010), and the Public Safety Performance Project of the Pew Charitable Trusts issue occasional selective summaries of major legislative changes. None of these, however, is comprehensive or cumulative.

first burst of activity. Conversely, mandatory minimum sentence and three-strikes laws were repeatedly shown not to achieve their goals, but almost all those enacted remain in effect in 2013.

Section IV offers explanations for the divorces between sentencing policy and either evidence or normative theory. Conceivably, the recent flattening out of the American prison population, many nibbles at the edges of harsh laws, and the emergence of less punitive restorative and rehabilitative programs signal a change of direction. On the possibility that it does, I conclude with a laundry list of policy changes that would move the United States back into the mainstream of developed countries' approaches to addressing the perplexing problems of crime and punishment.

I. Changes in American Sentencing Laws and Policies since 1975

The explanations for the first and second periods of recent American sentencing policies are straightforward. Indeterminate sentencing originated in the mid-nineteenth century and reflected Progressive Era ideas about causes of crime that are well understood and expressed views that were widely held through the 1970s (Rothman 1971). The explanations for the sentencing reform period—principally the conjoint influence of the due process and civil rights movements of the 1960s and 1970s and the decline in support for the rehabilitative ideal—are likewise well documented (Blumstein et al. 1983). The most recent period, as Winston Churchill once said of puddings, lacks a theme and inevitably lacks a simple general explanation. Its components include inertia, reactions to the excesses of the tough on crime period, renewed belief in human malleability, and the emergence of new paradigms of restorative and community justice.

What needs explanation is the tough on crime period. What happened is clear enough. Crime became a central issue in partisan politics. From the 1964 presidential campaign of Barry Goldwater, "crime in the streets" as it was first called and "law and order" later on was emphasized by Republican politicians as an indirect appeal to white voters threatened by the civil rights movement and as a "wedge" issue meant to separate white working class and southern voters from their earlier support of the Democratic Party (Edsall and Edsall 1991). Both crime policy and drug policy became highly moralized, black-and-white subjects of right and wrong (Windlesham 1998; Musto 1999). Evidence about the effectiveness of policies was unimportant. Sentencing laws and policies of increasing severity were adopted. Minority defendants were the group most affected, and both the prison population and racial disparities grew to record highs (Tonry 2011*b*). Though we know what happened, we know much less about why it happened, a subject to which I return in Section IV.

What we know about the effects of sentencing policy changes during all these periods can, broadly brushed, be summarized in comparatively few words. Parole guidelines and presumptive sentencing guidelines, when well designed and implemented, reduce unwarranted racial and other disparities, make decisions more consistent and predictable, and facilitate improved programmatic and budgetary planning. Statutory determinate sentencing systems in which laws specify typical sentences and voluntary systems of sentencing guidelines have few if any discernible effects on sentencing patterns. Mandatory minimum and three-strikes laws have little or no effect on crime rates, shift sentencing power from judges to prosecutors, often result in imposition of sentences that practitioners believe to be unjustly severe, and for those reasons foster widespread circumvention. Mandatory minimum, three-strikes, and truth-in-sentencing laws have greatly increased the lengths of prison terms and for that reason are a major cause of the fivefold increase in America's imprisonment rate between 1972 and 2007 (Blumstein and Beck 1999; Blumstein and Wallman 2006; Spelman 2009).

A. A Bird's-Eye View of 40 Years of Sentencing Policy

Table 1 provides an overview of the four periods along four dimensions. For each it shows representative institutions, the policy goals each implicitly or explicitly sought to achieve, the normative values or purposes each implicitly or explicitly expressed, and a summary of such evidence as exists concerning whether it achieved its goals or purposes.

Indeterminate Sentencing. From 1950 through 1975, the states and the federal government had broadly similar sentencing systems in which judges decided who went to prison and sometimes set minimum or maximum sentences, parole boards decided who was released and when, and offenders had few opportunities to challenge or appeal decisions. Normative ideas lined up nicely with practice. Philosophers and practitioners described the system as utilitarian and believed that

TABLE 1
Periods of American Sentencing Reform

	Representative Institutions	Goals	Values	Evidence
Indeterminate sentencing (1930–75)	Broad judicial discretion Presentence investigations Parole release Large prison Good time	Rehabilitation (Incapacitation) Least restrictive alternative	REHABILITATION Compassion Restraint Reintegration Crime reduction Social welfare	Rehabilitation—little Prevention—little Social welfare—some Restraint—some

Sentencing reform (1975–84)	Parole:
	  1. Guidelines
	  2. Abolition
	Sentencing guideline:
	  1. Presumptive
	  2. Voluntary
	Determinate sentencing
	Sentence appeals
		Equality
		Consistency
		Transparency
		Proportionality
		Accountability
			JUSTICE AS FAIRNESS
			Fairness
			Equal treatment
			Proportionality
			Nondiscrimination
				Disparity—yes
				Parole guidelines
				Presumptive sentencing guidelines
				Disparity—no
				Determinate sentencing
				Voluntary guidelines
				Mandatory minimums
				Crime Prevention—no
				Mandatory minimums

Tough on crime (1984–96)	Mandatory minimums Three strikes LWOPs Juvenile transfers "Sexual predator" laws	Crime prevention Political support Public confidence Severity Reduce political risk	EXPULSION/OUTLAWS Severity Populist democracy Denunciation Ostracism	Disparity—no Mandatory minimums Three strikes Capital punishment Crime prevention—no Mandatory minimums Three strikes Capital punishment LWOPs
Equilibrium (1996–2013)	All tough on crime policies Sentencing guidelines Risk prediction Treatment programs Reentry programs Drug courts Nibbling at the severity edges	Cost containment Reduce reoffending Reduce political risks Crime prevention	AMBIVALENCE Severity Bifurcation Reintegration Compassion	Tough on crime, as above Sentencing reform, as above Reduce recidivism—yes Treatment programs Reduce recidivism—mixed Drug courts Reentry programs

retributive ideas were cruel and anachronistic.[2] The principal aim was to individualize treatment of offenders in order to rehabilitate most and incapacitate the rest. Policies sometimes referred to as "the least restrictive alternative" or parsimony created presumptions that punishments should be as unrestrictive as possible and that prisoners should ordinarily be released when first they became eligible. Underlying implicit values included compassion, reintegration, rationality, and social welfare. The evidence showing that rehabilitation programs were effective or that punishment regimes prevented crime better than other possible programs or policies was weak to nonexistent. The imprisonment rate, including jail inmates, for many years through the early 1970s fluctuated within a narrow range around 150–60 per 100,000 population.[3]

Sentencing Reform.   From 1975 through 1986, many jurisdictions in one way or another—parole guidelines, voluntary and presumptive sentencing guidelines, determinate sentencing statutes, appellate review of sentencing—attempted to make sentencing fairer, more consistent, and more transparent. As in the preceding period, the prevailing views of theorists and of practitioners lined up nicely. Utilitarian ideas and aims were not entirely excluded (e.g., Morris 1974), but the overall logic was retributive (e.g., Murphy 1973; von Hirsch 1976; Morris 1981). Crime prevention was seldom an explicit goal, or even an implicit one.[4]

---

[2] Herbert Wechsler, later the reporter for the *Model Penal Code*, and his Columbia Law School mentor Jerome Michael observed that retribution may represent "the unstudied belief of most men" but asserted that "no legal provision can be justified merely because it calls for the punishment of the morally guilty by penalties proportioned to their guilt, or criticized merely because it fails to do so" (Michael and Wechsler 1940, pp. 7, 11). Jerome Michael and University of Chicago philosophy professor Mortimer Adler earlier explained that there are two incompatible theories of punishment: the "punitive" (retributive) and the "non-punitive" (consequentialist) and that "it can be shown that the punitive theory is a fallacious analysis and that the non-punitive theory is correct. . . . The infliction of pain is never justified merely on the ground that it visits retributive punishment upon the offender. Punitive retribution is never justifiable in itself" (Michael and Adler 1933, pp. 341, 344).

[3] The text is imprecise because annual jail population data became available only in the 1980s. Jail populations typically average about half of combined federal and state prison populations. The 100–110 per 100,000 population rates for the latter in 1970–73 suggest a total incarceration rate of 150–60.

[4] Crime prevention was sometimes the goal of more narrowly focused sentencing law changes. During the 1970s and early 1980s, every state but Wisconsin enacted one or more mandatory minimum sentence laws. With the conspicuous exception of the Rockefeller Drug Laws in New York, which mandated lengthy prison sentences (Joint Committee on New York Drug Law Evaluation 1978), those laws were typically much less severe than the minimum sentence laws enacted in the 1980s and 1990s. Most

The focus was on the sentencing process and on individual sentences, but not on their effects. The underlying values were procedural fairness, proportionality, equal treatment, and rationality. Evaluations showed that some initiatives were successful and others were not. With the exception of a few studies of mandatory minimum sentence laws, evaluations did not attempt to measure crime prevention effects. The total incarceration rate rose rapidly, reaching 313 per 100,000 in 1986, principally because of increases in the number of cases being processed, the probability of imprisonment given a conviction, and the lengths of sentences imposed (Gilliard and Beck 1997; Blumstein and Beck 1999).

Tough on Crime. From 1984 through 1996, most jurisdictions enacted some or all of mandatory minimum sentence, truth-in-sentencing, "sexual predator," "career criminal," three-strikes, and LWOP laws (Sabol et al. 2002; Stemen, Rengifo, and Wilson 2006). These initiatives sought to make punishments more severe and express moral outrage. In contrast to the preceding two periods, prevailing normative ideas among philosophers and other theorists were not reconcilable with the logic of policy making (Tonry 2011*a*). Theorists remained mostly retributivist (e.g., Hampton 1984; von Hirsch 1985; Duff 1986; Robinson 1987; Moore 1993), but sentencing policies were hard to reconcile with ideas about proportionality in punishment. They also found little support in research findings. Research showed that severe punishments have little if any effect on crime rates (e.g., Nagin 1998; von Hirsch et al. 1999) and often resulted in circumvention by practitioners in some cases and in others in imposition of sentences everyone directly involved believed to be unjust (Tonry 2009*b*). The imprisonment rate continued to increase rapidly, reaching 615 per 100,000 in 1996, principally because of increases in sentence lengths and sharply increased arrest and imprisonment rates for drug offenders (Gilliard and Beck 1997; Blumstein and Beck 1999).

Equilibrium. A huge amount of state and federal sentencing legislation was enacted after 1996, but generalizations are difficult to offer. New mandatory minimum sentence laws were enacted for child pornography, carjacking, and human smuggling, but they typically lack the breadth and severity of the preceding generation of mandatories. Few

---

mandated short jail terms for driving while intoxicated or 1- or 2-year prison terms for offenses involving firearms (Shane-DuBow, Brown, and Olsen 1985).

of the laws characteristic of the tough on crime period were enacted.[5] No major ones have been repealed, but a few have been revised in minor ways. New York's Rockefeller Drug Law was moderated, and California voters in 2012 narrowed the scope of the three-strikes law (New York State 2012; *New York Times* 2012). Many hundreds of laws were enacted that slightly narrowed the scope of severe existing laws, made limited categories of prisoners newly eligible for release, and reduced the frequency of parole and probation revocations (Austin et al. 2013). Drug and other problem-solving courts and prisoner reentry courts proliferated. Various recent initiatives, including drug courts, prisoner reentry programs, and new treatment programs, seek to reduce reoffending. No general theoretical logic is discernible in the crazy quilt of diverging policies; within the theory class, retributivism remains predominant (e.g., von Hirsch and Ashworth 2005; Robinson 2008, 2013). The imprisonment rate continued to increase rapidly for a few years and then slowly until it peaked at 762 per 100,000 in 2007 and fell slightly thereafter (Blumstein and Wallman 2006; Sabol and Couture 2008; Carson and Sabol 2012).

The remainder of this section mostly discusses the second and third periods, summarizing more fully the policies adopted, and what was learned about their effectiveness and effects.

B. The Sentencing Reform Period

By the mid-1970s every major element of indeterminate sentencing was contested and all of its underlying premises were challenged. Indeterminate sentencing was widely thought to be unjust (e.g., von Hirsch 1976) and to be predicated on a capacity to rehabilitate offenders that did not exist (e.g., Martinson 1974). Broad, unregulated discretions were said to permit idiosyncratic, arbitrary, and racist decisions (e.g., American Friends Service Committee 1971; Fogel 1979). Unwarranted sentencing disparities were seen as inherent in the system (Frankel 1973). Procedural informality was seen as fundamentally unfair (Davis 1969).

The solutions seemed obvious: constrain judicial discretion, establish rules for sentencing, abolish or systematize parole release, and allow offenders to file appeals (Morris 1974; Dershowitz 1976). The primary

[5] I know only of Alaska's adoption in 2006—the first in any state since 1996—of a three-strikes law (Chen 2008, table 1).

aims were to make sentencing and parole fairer, more consistent, and more just: reduction in unwarranted sentencing disparities was the mantra. Although law and order had begun to emerge as a partisan political issue, the major goals of the early sentencing reform movement were fairness and consistency. This can be seen in the work of the National Academy of Sciences Panel on Sentencing Research; the primary emphases of its report and the literature reviews it commissioned were on the determinants of sentencing, disparity, and discrimination and the effects on disparities and court operations of recent reform initiatives; effects on crime rates, recidivism, and prevention received little attention (Blumstein et al. 1983, chaps. 1, 4). The focus on procedural fairness and disparities can also be seen in the work of the earliest sentencing commissions. The Minnesota commission deliberated over two guidelines options—the Just Deserts and Modified Just Deserts Models—before selecting the latter. The Oregon guidelines enabling legislation unambiguously indicated that "punishment" was the purpose of sentencing (von Hirsch, Knapp, and Tonry 1987, chap. 4).

In the aftermath of the implosion of indeterminate sentencing and its primarily rehabilitative rationale, sentencing reform initiatives proliferated. The process was primarily technocratic—systematic, evidence-based, and cumulative. The earliest and most incremental initiatives sought to reduce disparities through development and use of parole guidelines and "voluntary" sentencing guidelines. These were followed by statutory determinate sentencing systems and presumptive sentencing guidelines.

1. *Parole Guidelines.* The early pilot projects for development of parole guidelines took place under the aegis of the US Parole Commission.[6] The logic of a team headed by Leslie Wilkinson and Don M. Gottfredson was that, with the use of "salient factors" that predict recidivism, parole release guidelines could be developed that would simultaneously reduce disparities in release dates and tie decisions to predictions of parolees' prospects of living law-abiding lives. They reasoned that a well-run administrative agency could supervise parole ex-

---

[6] Many states today use risk prediction instruments of various sorts in making release decisions. Sometimes they are referred to as "parole guidelines." Unlike the systems developed in the 1970s, however, they are not typically meant to serve as primary means to achieve greater procedural fairness and greater consistency in time served but to classify offenders on the basis of risks of recidivism (Burke and Tonry 2006).

aminers and operate a system of administrative appeals that would allow prisoners to contest their decisions. Evaluation of the pilot project showed that the system worked as intended and, compared with prior practice, produced more consistent decisions. The US Parole Commission formally adopted a guideline system. Parole boards in Minnesota, Oregon, and Washington did likewise. All sought to increase procedural fairness, reduce unwarranted disparities in time served, and make the release system more transparent and predictable (Gottfredson, Wilkins, and Hoffman 1978). A federally funded evaluation concluded that the federal and Minnesota systems operated as intended and improved consistency in release dates and time served; the Oregon and Washington systems were less effective (Arthur D. Little and Goldfarb and Singer 1981; Blumstein et al. 1983).

Parole guidelines have two important potential advantages as a sentencing policy mechanism and one major disadvantage. One advantage is that case-by-case decision making within a well-run administrative agency can be expeditious and economical—faster, less costly, and more easily appealable than are decisions by judges. There is nothing inherently complicated about establishing an effective system of management controls. A second advantage is that, as commonly happened during the indeterminate sentencing era, parole boards can expeditiously address prison overcrowding problems by adjusting release dates (e.g., Messinger et al. 1985). The disadvantage is that parole boards have authority only over offenders sentenced to imprisonment. Parole guidelines can reduce disparities among people sentenced to imprisonment, but not between them and people sentenced to local jails or community punishments.

The logical next step was to create comparable but more comprehensive guidelines for judges. That was attempted in all four of the pioneering jurisdictions. Parole guidelines in each were succeeded by presumptive sentencing guidelines systems. I discuss them below, but in the interest of chronology, I take a detour first to discuss an earlier generation of "voluntary" sentencing guidelines and a separate reform approach generally referred to as "statutory determinate sentencing."

2. *Voluntary Sentencing Guidelines.* The team of researchers who created the federal parole guidelines persuaded judges in Colorado and Vermont to collaborate with them in developing guidelines for sentencing. They hypothesized that judges are less likely than parole examiners to accept guidelines whose existence might give rise to appeals.

As a consequence, the guidelines were to be "voluntary" and thereby to pose no threat to judges' discretionary authority. Moreover, they would be based on research on past sentencing practices in the jurisdiction and would do no more than indicate ranges of sentences that encompassed 80 percent of those previously imposed on people convicted of particular offenses and having similar records of prior convictions. The modest goal was to highlight past outliers and lessen their future frequency. The developers reasoned that judges would want to comply with local sentencing patterns once guidelines made them evident and that over time compliance with the guidelines would become part of the local judicial culture and make outliers less common and sentencing disparities less pronounced (Gottfredson, Wilkins, and Hoffman 1978).

The underlying assumptions proved to be wrong. Judges were not much interested in knowing about past sentencing patterns nor in taking them into account in making their own decisions.[7] An evaluation of the first federally funded pilot projects in Vermont and Colorado concluded that the guidelines had no effect on sentencing disparities or consistency (Rich et al. 1982). One possible reason was that the participating judges felt little sense of local ownership or commitment because the initiative for the guidelines had come from the research team. However, a subsequent evaluation of statewide voluntary guidelines in Florida and Maryland developed at the initiative of the state judiciaries reached the same conclusions (Carrow et al. 1985).

Those evaluations were not finished or published until the 1980s. In the meantime, voluntary guidelines had been established at state or local levels in every state (Blumstein et al. 1983; Tonry 1996, chap. 3). Nearly all of those early voluntary guidelines systems were abandoned or fell into desuetude.

Even so, a number of states established voluntary guidelines systems in the 1980s and 1990s, despite a continuing absence of evidence from credible evaluations or other research showing that they reduce the

---

[7] A parallel initiative in the Canadian provinces of British Columbia, Manitoba, Newfoundland, and Saskatchewan, creating "sentencing information systems" that informed judges of patterns of sentences previously imposed for particular offenses in their courts, was no more successful (Doob and Park 1987; Doob 1989, 1990). It was terminated after several years of pilot projects. The problem was that a key premise— that judges would want to know what sentences other judges had imposed in similar cases—proved to be faulty. In the project's final report, the director, Anthony N. Doob, observed, "Judges do not, as a rule, care to know what sentences other judges are handing down in comparable cases" (1989, p. 6).

extent of unwarranted sentencing disparities. Prison population increases in two especially well-known voluntary guidelines systems, in Delaware and Virginia, have been less than elsewhere, and their proponents claim and believe that they have managed to improve consistency and reduce disparity. If that is true, Gottfredson, Wilkins, and Hoffman (1978) in the long term may have been correct in their hope that compliance with guidelines would eventually become part of the local judicial culture and part of what judges believe is a component of doing their work responsibly.

Voluntary guidelines have attracted renewed interest in recent years because of two US Supreme Court decisions (*U.S. v. Booker*, 543 U.S. 220 [2005], and *Blakely v. Washington*, 542 U.S. 296 [2004]), which created new procedural requirements for presumptive sentencing guidelines systems. Presumptive guidelines, discussed below, have been shown to be capable of reducing disparities and achieving other sought-after goals. Ohio in 2006 nonetheless converted its presumptive guidelines system into a voluntary one.

3. *Statutory Determinate Sentencing.* Some states followed another path, although to a dead end. The most influential reform proposals called for abolition of parole release and creation of enforceable standards to guide judges' decisions in individual cases (e.g., Morris 1974; von Hirsch 1976). Policy makers in some states responded by building standards into their criminal codes. Maine in 1975 went part way, abolishing parole release and thereby becoming the first modern "determinate" sentencing state in the sense that the length of time to be served under a prison sentence could be known, "determined," when it was imposed. Maine, however, did not establish standards for sentencing. California did. It enacted the Uniform Determinate Sentencing Act of 1976, abolishing parole release and specifying normal, aggravated, and mitigated sentences for most offenses in statutes. Other states—including Arizona, Indiana, Illinois, and North Carolina—quickly followed California's lead, though in somewhat different ways. Evaluations concluded, however, that such laws had little if any effect on sentencing disparities.[8] No additional states since the mid-1980s have created statutory determinate sentencing systems.

4. *Presumptive Sentencing Guidelines.* Acting on Judge Marvin

---

[8] The evaluations are discussed in detail and citations to them are provided in Cohen and Tonry (1983) and Tonry (1987).

Frankel's proposal in *Criminal Sentences—Law without Order* (1973), Minnesota in 1978 enacted legislation to create a specialized administrative agency, a "sentencing commission," with authority to promulgate "presumptive" sentencing guidelines. They were to be presumptive in the sense that judges had to provide reasons for imposing sentences that were not encompassed in the guidelines; the adequacy of those reasons could be reviewed by appellate courts. Judge Frankel argued that permanent administrative agencies would be much better situated than legislatures—afflicted by high turnover, short attention spans, and tendencies to react impulsively to short-term emotions and political concerns—to develop rational, evidence-based policies. An independent sentencing commission, he hoped, would be somewhat insulated from political pressures. Because of its permanence, a commission over time would develop specialized expertise and an institutional memory and could revise and amend the guidelines to respond to changing priorities and conditions.[9]

Minnesota's guidelines took effect in 1980. The Minnesota commission made a number of unprecedented decisions. It sought—the first time a jurisdiction did this explicitly—to base its guidelines on an agreed normative framework, which it called "Modified Just Deserts." It developed comprehensive guidelines for all felony offenses, classifying them into groups on the basis of assessments of each offense category's seriousness, and not on the basis of statutory maximum sentences, which were highly inconsistent. It construed ambiguous language in its enabling legislation to require that a "capacity constraint" guide its decisions and accordingly that the projected application of its guidelines not produce a prison population exceeding 95 percent of the rated capacity of Minnesota's existing or planned prisons. This meant that the commission forced itself to make trade-offs. If commissioners wanted to increase sentence lengths for particular offenses, they would have to be reduced for others. In order to monitor compliance with the guidelines, the commission required that judges, or clerks working for them, prepare a report on each sentence imposed; commission chair Douglas Amdahl, later Minnesota Supreme Court Chief Justice, personally telephoned laggards to obtain the reports. This meant that for the first time, a state had comprehensive data on statewide sentencing

---

[9] Frase (2013) provides a comprehensive summary of state presumptive guidelines systems.

patterns. The statute authorized defense and prosecution appeals of sentences; judges who imposed a sentence inconsistent with the guidelines were required to offer "substantial and compelling" reasons for doing so (Knapp 1984; Parent 1988).

The guidelines worked. Judges complied with the guidelines in most cases and gave reasons when they did not. Racial and other unwarranted disparities were reduced. The commission from time to time revised the guidelines to change presumptive sentences for particular offenses and altered sentences for other offenses to comply with the capacity constraint. Minnesota prisons operated within their capacities, during a period when prison populations were rising rapidly in most states and prisons in most states were overcrowded. The prison population increased during the 1980s, but in line with increased capacity resulting from construction of new prisons. The appellate courts created a sentencing appeal jurisprudence (Parent 1988; Reitz 1997; Frase 2005).

Pennsylvania, Oregon, and Washington created similar systems in the 1980s, and Florida, Kansas, North Carolina, and Ohio in the 1990s. Their experiences differed, but Washington (Boerner and Lieb 2001), Oregon (Bogan and Factor 1997), and North Carolina (Wright 2002) had successes comparable to Minnesota's.

Evaluations showed that well-designed and well-implemented presumptive guidelines systems can make sentencing more predictable, reduce racial and other unwarranted disparities, facilitate systems planning, and control correctional spending. "Population constraint" policies in Minnesota, Washington, and North Carolina worked. During the periods when they were in effect, prison systems in all three states operated within capacity and limited prison population growth well below national and regional averages (Tonry 1996).

North Carolina has been the most successful at controlling prison population growth. In 1970, North Carolina had the highest incarceration rate in the country but had fallen to thirty-first by 1999 (Wright 2002). It ranked thirtieth or thirty-first for the following 10 years and was thirty-third in 2011 (Carson and Sabol 2012). From 1994, when the guidelines took effect, through 2011, the North Carolina imprisonment rate was essentially flat, fluctuating between 340 and 370 per 100,000 population and well below the rising national rate.

A handful of studies have concluded that presumptive guidelines, especially with population constraints, help control prison population size (Marvell 1995; Nicholson-Crotty 2004; Stemen, Rengifo, and Wilson 2006). Marvell (1995) examined prison population growth from 1976 to 1993 in nine guidelines states, compared with the national average, and concluded that guidelines based on population constraints produced lower rates of increase. Nicholson-Crotty (2004), using 1975–98 prison data in a 50-state analysis, concluded that guidelines incorporating capacity constraints tend to moderate imprisonment growth and that those not based on constraints exacerbate it. Stemen, Rengifo, and Wilson (2006) analyzed state sentencing patterns in the period 1975–2002 and concluded that states that adopted presumptive guidelines and abolished parole release had lower incarceration rates and lower rates of prison population growth than other states.

Notwithstanding those positive findings, things quickly changed. The successes of presumptive sentencing guidelines proved much less important to policy makers after the early 1990s than in earlier years. Presumptive sentencing guidelines fell from favor. The three most recent presumptive systems, in Kansas, North Carolina, and Ohio, were established in 1993–96. A few voluntary or advisory systems have been developed since then. In Oregon, the committee that drafted and monitored the guidelines was closed down (Bogan and Factor 1997). Sentencing commissions in Florida, Louisiana, Tennessee, and Wisconsin were abolished and Washington's lost its staff and budget in 2011 (Frase 2013). The Pennsylvania Commission on Sentencing survived, but Pennsylvania Supreme Court decisions effectively converted the nominally presumptive guidelines into voluntary ones (Reitz 1997; Kramer and Ulmer 2008).

Policy making ceased to be greatly concerned with evidence, fairness, and consistency. In Minnesota, the legislature in 1989 instructed the commission to give much less weight to its population constraint policy (Frase 2005). In Oregon, a broad-based mandatory minimum sentence law was enacted in 1994 that trumped the guidelines (Merritt, Fain, and Turner 2006). The Washington commission gave up the policy on its own (Boerner and Lieb 2001). The Ohio guidelines were converted from presumptive to voluntary in 2006 (Frase 2013). The North Carolina and Minnesota commissions continue, however, to develop correctional impact projections of proposed new sentencing laws; the projections are commonly believed to have slowed the enactment of laws that would have required additional prison space (Frase 2013).

The presumptive guidelines systems in the 1980s were developed in a period before American crime control policy became highly politicized and when the primary policy goal was to reduce disparities and unfairness. They focused primarily on developing systems for achieving greater fairness and consistency and on the use of population projection methods for financial and facilities planning. Population constraint policies made obvious sense to the early guidelines commissions and to the legislatures that established them. Concern for managing prison population growth and corrections budgets, not reduction of sentencing disparities, was the primary policy goal underlying creation of the North Carolina, Kansas, and Ohio commissions in the 1990s.

The promulgation of federal sentencing guidelines, which took effect in 1987, signaled the beginning of the end of the sentencing reform period that targeted disparities and the beginning of the tough on crime period that sought increased certainty and severity. The Sentencing Reform Act of 1984 created the US Commission on Sentencing and directed it to develop guidelines to reduce disparities, to provide for use of nonincarcerative punishments for most first offenders, and to develop population constraint–based guidelines that would not result in larger numbers of prisoners than federal prisons could accommodate. The commission ignored the directives concerning first offenders and the prison population constraint and instead promulgated "mandatory" guidelines that greatly increased the percentage of offenders receiving prison sentences and greatly increased sentence lengths for many offenses (Tonry 1996, chap. 2; Stith and Cabranes 1998). The federal guidelines were converted from presumptive to voluntary by *U.S. v. Booker* (543 U.S. 220 [2005]), a US Supreme Court decision that declared some of their features unconstitutional.

The sentencing reform period basically ended by the mid-1980s. Nominally, the tough on crime initiatives aimed at crime prevention through deterrence and incapacitation. Partisan political considerations were at least equally important (Windlesham 1998; Gest 2001).

C. Tough on Crime

Between the passage of the federal Sentencing Reform Act of 1984 and the October 1, 1987, implementation of federal sentencing guidelines, the US Congress enacted the Anti–Drug Abuse Act of 1986. It created a new set of mandatory minimum sentences for drug and violent crimes, including the federal 100-to-1 law that mandated sentence lengths for crack offenses that were the same as for powder cocaine offenses involving quantities 100 times larger (e.g., 5 grams of crack compared with 500 grams of powder). Two years later, the Congress enacted a more comprehensive and severe set of mandatory minimums in the Omnibus Anti–Drug Abuse Act of 1988. In 1994, the Congress enacted the Violent Crime Control and Law Enforcement Act of 1994, which promised federal funding for state prison construction to states that enacted "truth-in-sentencing laws" requiring selected prisoners to serve 85 percent of their nominal prison sentences. It also enacted additional mandatory minimum laws, including the federal three-strikes law. The federal laws paralleled, presaged, and encouraged passage of mandatory minimum laws in all 50 states and three-strikes and truth-in-sentencing laws in (slightly different) majorities of the states.

Sentencing policy changes developed during the sentencing reform period primarily sought to make sentencing processes fairer and more transparent and to make sentences more predictable and consistent. In those ways they were centered on the offender and whether he or she was sentenced fairly, justly, and appropriately. Most policy initiatives during the tough on crime period sought to make sentences harsher and more certain and, implicitly or explicitly, to prevent crime through deterrence and incapacitation. The primary focus shifted from fairness to offenders to harshness, crime prevention, and symbolic denunciation of crime and criminals.

The policy initiatives of the tough on crime period undermined pursuit of the aims of the preceding period. Two centuries of experience have shown that mandatory punishments foster circumvention by prosecutors, juries, and judges and thereby produce extreme inconsistencies between cases (Dawson 1969; Hay 1975; Tonry 2009b). They also transfer dispositive discretion about the handling of cases from judges, who are expected to be nonpartisan and dispassionate, to prosecutors, who are comparatively more vulnerable to influence by political considerations and public emotion (Tonry 2012). This transfer did not trouble legislators, David Boerner (1995), a former Seattle (King County) deputy district attorney explained, because they trusted prosecutors to be tough on crime and insist on severe sentences but were much less trustful of judges.

Federal legislation highlights the problems of foreseeable injustice associated with mandatory minimum sentencing laws. The 1984 Sentencing Reform Act contemplated that guidelines aimed at reducing disparities would be developed and implemented. One principal element of guidelines development is to agree on rankings of crimes by seriousness and of punishments by severity so that a rational, proportionate sentencing system can be developed that will punish serious crimes more harshly than less serious ones. The Anti–Drug Abuse Act of 1986, however, mandated minimum sentences for many drug crimes that trumped the guidelines and made the development of a comprehensive set of proportionate sentencing standards impossible (Stith and Cabranes 1998).

In this subsection I discuss sentencing policy initiatives during the tough on crime period. It is difficult to provide a comprehensive summary of the numbers of states that adopted particular kinds of laws. Because state laws vary substantially, the writers of summary reports define initiatives in different ways. For example, a Vera Institute of Justice analysis of the effects of sentencing law changes since 1975 defined as three-strikes laws all described by that term that were enacted in the 1990s but also included states that enacted "habitual offender" laws from the 1920s onward (Stemen, Rengifo, and Wilson 2006). In most states, such laws long ago largely fell into disuse and in any case were usually applied to chronic property offenders, not to the violent and drug offenders targeted by modern three-strikes laws. Likewise, an Urban Institute analysis of the effects of truth-in-sentencing laws cites 42 states with some form of such laws as the evaluators defined them, although many were not characterized that way when enacted, and only 28 (plus the District of Columbia) satisfied criteria for federal prison construction funding (Sabol et al. 2002).

1. *Truth-in-Sentencing Laws.* The term, a 1980s neologism, is a play on words alluding to the development in the 1970s of federal "truth-in-lending" laws that required consumer lenders and merchants to disclose interest rates and other key financing terms in order to eliminate deceptive lending practices. The implication is that there is something untruthful about discretionary parole release. Under the indeterminate sentencing systems that blanketed the United States for more than four decades before 1975, however, there was nothing unwarranted or untruthful about parole release. The system was meant to allow for individualized sentences tailored to the rehabilitative prospects and other circumstances of individual offenders; maximum prison sentences were not meant to indicate how long an individual would remain in prison but to set an absolute final date by which he or she must be released

(e.g., in the American Law Institute's *Model Penal Code* [1962] and the *Model Sentencing Act* [1972] of the Advisory Council of Judges of the National Council on Crime and Delinquency).

Conservative policy advocates in the tough on crime period, however, defined the differences between the sentences judges announced and the times prisoners served as a problem that needed fixing. A Department of Justice report called *The Case for More Incarceration* (1992), promoted by US Attorney General William Barr, for example, argued that "prison works," urged that the number of people in prison be increased, proposed a major national program of prison construction, and called for the abolition of parole release.[10] Barr's proposals were embodied in proposed legislation that became the Violent Crime Control and Law Enforcement Act of 1994, as amended in 1996. The law unambiguously sought to increase the number of people in prison and the times they spent there. To obtain federal funds for prison construction, a state had to demonstrate that it "(A) has increased the percentage of convicted violent offenders sentenced to prison; (B) has increased the average prison time which will be served in prison by convicted violent offenders sentenced to prison; (C) has increased the percentage of sentence which will be served in prison by violent offenders sentenced to prison." To qualify for funding, states were required to demonstrate that violent offenders would be required to serve at least 85 percent of the sentence imposed.

Evaluators at the Urban Institute sought to determine how truth-in-sentencing laws affected sentencing patterns and prison populations. They used Bureau of Justice Statistics prison data for 1991, 1993, and 1996 (1998 for Ohio). They were unable "to draw general conclusions about the effects of truth-in-sentencing on sentencing practices throughout the nation" (Sabol et al. 2002, p. vi). However, they did find that truth-in-sentencing laws had large projected effects in some of the seven states they examined closely. When implemented as part of a comprehensive change to the sentencing system, "truth-in-sentencing laws were associated with large changes in prison populations" (p. vii). Patterns varied in states where truth-in-sentencing was

---

[10] Parole abolition was also a goal of policy advocates in the first sentencing reform phase but for different reasons: because parole release disparities were unfair to prisoners and frustrated goals of consistency and proportionality (Morris 1974; von Hirsch and Hanrahan 1979). Sixteen states abolished parole for those reasons in the 1970s through the 1990s. Barr's reasons were different: he wanted to make sentences harsher and more effective at incapacitating offenders.

TABLE 2

Estimated Percentage of Sentence Served Prior to Enactment of
Truth-in-Sentencing and Expected to Be Served in Future

State	Percentage of Sentence Served by Offenders Released from Prison during 1993	Estimated Percentage for Offenders Entering Prison during 1991	Expected Percentage under Truth-in-Sentencing
Georgia	42	51	100
Washington	76	76	85
Illinois	44	43	85
Ohio	26	83*	97
New Jersey	39	37	85
Pennsylvania	46	108*	100*
Utah	36	32	Indeterminate

SOURCE.—Ditton and Wilson (1999); Sabol et al. (2002, table 3.3).

* Minimum sentences (all others refer to maximum sentences).

not embedded in a comprehensive sentencing system overhaul, but in
one such instance, "the increase in the percentage of sentences required
to be served before release led to larger increases in length of stay and
consequently a larger effect of length of stay on the expected number
of prisoners" (p. vii). Truth-in-sentencing and lengthy mandatory minimum sentence laws have a sleeper effect that has contributed heavily
to increases in prison populations: prisoners subject to them accumu-
late year by year, and many years pass before the first of them are
eligible for release.

Table 2 shows that the percentages of sentences projected to be
served in the seven states under truth-in-sentencing were much higher
than for those released in 1991 and 1993. In most states they at least
doubled. The Urban Institute evaluators observed that the effects of
truth-in-sentencing on prison population were much less than they
would have been had violent crime rates not begun a substantial decline
after 1991. They elaborated: "Were the sentencing practices of 1996
to persist during a time when the number of violent offenses increases,
the impacts on prison populations and corrections management could
be dramatic" (Sabol et al. 2002, p. 31).

The Urban Institute's was the most comprehensive assessment of
the effects of truth-in-sentencing laws. A Vera Institute of Justice study
in a 50-state analysis looked at the effects on prison populations of a
wider range of sentencing policy changes during the period 1975–2002

(Stemen, Rengifo, and Wilson 2006). Truth-in-sentencing laws were included among a larger set of changes that increased time-served requirements for violent crimes; they concluded that "states with separate time served requirements for violent offenders had higher incarceration rates than other states" (p. iii).

The RAND Corporation also carried out a federally funded evaluation of the effects of the federal truth-in-sentencing initiative (Turner et al. 2001). It covered data only through 1997, however. Even so, it concluded, "We do know that nationwide, the imposed maximum sentence length, the average length of prison term, and the percent of term served for violent offenses have increased for TIS states between 1993 and 1997. For non-TIS states, sentence lengths have been dropping, and months served have dropped slightly" (p. 134).

The Urban Institute, Vera, and RAND studies inevitably underestimate the effects of truth-in-sentencing laws on prison population growth because their data cover periods ending, respectively, in 1996 (1998 for Ohio), 2002, and 1997. Because of the sleeper effect mentioned above, the ultimate effects of enactment of truth-in-sentencing legislation are not yet apparent. This is also true of all laws enacted during the tough on crime period that mandated sentences of historically unprecedented lengths. Under California's and other states' three-strikes laws mandating 25-year minimum sentences, mostly enacted in the period 1993–96, not a single prisoner's 25-year term had expired by 2013. Under an 85 percent rule, a prisoner serving a 25-year sentence is not eligible for release before serving at least 21 years and 3 months. Each year's entry cohort so far has been a net addition to the state's prison populations. Only after the passage of several more years will prisoners newly admitted begin to be offset by the release of prisoners admitted two or more decades earlier.

The Urban Institute study defined any state that had eliminated the possibility of parole release for some or all prisoners as a "truth-in-sentencing state." Marvell and Moody (1996) examined prison population effects of parole abolition and, using 1971–93 state prison data, found that only one of 10 abolition states experienced a higher rate of increase than the 50-state average. The lowest rates of growth were in Minnesota and Washington. The states included in that study, however, abolished parole release as part of the sentencing reform period, and none during that period had enacted a modern truth-in-sentencing law with a requirement that at least 85 percent of the sentence be

served. The early parole abolition initiatives aimed at greater transparency and in some cases at reductions in unwarranted sentencing
disparities. Several abolition states had adopted presumptive sentencing
guidelines that incorporated prison capacity constraints in their policy
development processes. Findings that the early abolitions of parole release operated to restrain prison population growth are thus not inconsistent with the Urban Institute, Vera, and RAND findings that
truth-in-sentencing laws operated to increase it. Unlike the truth-in-
sentencing initiatives, the earlier abolitions of parole were not typically
intended to increase durations of prison sentences.

2. *Mandatory Minimum Sentence and Three-Strikes Laws.* Between
1975 and 1996, mandatory minimums were America's most frequently
enacted sentencing law changes. By 1983, 49 of the 50 states had
adopted mandatory sentencing laws for offenses other than murder or
drunk driving (Shane-DuBow, Brown, and Olsen 1985, table 30). By
1994, every state had adopted mandatory penalties; most had several
(Austin et al. 1994). Most mandatory penalties apply to drug offenses,
murder or aggravated rape, felonies involving firearms, or felonies
committed by people who have previous felony convictions. Between
1985 and mid-1991, the US Congress enacted at least 20 new mandatory penalty provisions; by 1991, more than 60 federal statutes subjected more than 100 crimes to mandatory penalties (US Sentencing
Commission 1991, pp. 8–10). More followed.

Three-strikes and mandatory minimum sentence laws are variations
on the same theme: conviction of an offense triggers a statutory mandate that the judge impose a prison sentence of a specified minimum
length. Knowledge about mandatory minimum sentences has changed
remarkably little in the past 30 years. Their ostensible primary rationale is deterrence. Although it would not be unreasonable for someone
new to the subject to assume that the threat of a mandatory prison
sentence deters would-be offenders—after all, nearly everyone is careful to avoid overstaying a parking meter when there is a tow truck or
a traffic officer nearby, and slows down when seeing a police car—the
overwhelming weight of the evidence is that they have few if any deterrent effects. Those surveys that conclude that deterrent effects can
sometimes be demonstrated also note that existing knowledge is too
fragmentary or the estimated effect so small as to have no relevance to
policy making. The evidence is equally overwhelming that practitioners
often evade or circumvent mandatory penalties, that they create stark

disparities between cases in which they are circumvented and cases in which they are not, and that they often result in imposition of sentences in individual cases that everyone directly involved believes are unjust. Here I discuss evidence on implementation of mandatory penalty laws. The evidence concerning their deterrent effects is discussed in Section III.

The evidence concerning case processing comes primarily from six major studies. One is an evaluation of the Rockefeller Drug Laws, which required lengthy mandatory minimum sentences for a wide range of drug offenses (Joint Committee on New York Drug Law Evaluation 1978). One concerns a Michigan law requiring imposition of a 2-year mandatory prison sentence on persons convicted of possession of a gun during commission of a felony (Loftin and McDowall 1981; Loftin, Heumann, and McDowall 1983). Two concern a Massachusetts law requiring a 1-year prison sentence for persons convicted of carrying a firearm unlawfully (Beha 1977; Rossman et al. 1979). One concerns a 1994 Oregon law that established lengthy minimum sentences for 16 offenses (Merritt, Fain, and Turner 2006). The last is an evaluation of the effects of a truth-in-sentencing law in New Jersey (McCoy and McManimon 2004). All six studies found that prosecutors and judges (and sometimes police) in many cases in various ways changed their practices to avoid imposition of the mandatory penalties, that the harsher punishments were imposed in the remaining cases, and that overall there were no effects on conviction rates.

The Massachusetts, Michigan, and New York laws are especially good illustrations of the operation of mandatory sentencing laws. Vigorous and highly publicized efforts were made to make them effective. The New York law attracted massive media attention of which prospective drug dealers could not have been unaware. Amid enormous publicity, the legislature authorized and funded 31 new courts to handle drug cases and expressly forbade some kinds of plea bargaining to assure that the mandatory sentences were imposed. The Massachusetts statute expressly forbade "diversion in the form of continuance without a finding or filing of cases," both devices used in the Boston Municipal Court for disposition of cases other than on their merits.[11] In Michigan, the Wayne County prosecutor established and enforced a ban on

---

[11] Filing is a practice in which cases are left open with no expectation that they will ever be closed; continuance without finding leaves the case open in anticipation of eventual dismissal if the defendant avoids further trouble.

plea bargaining. He also launched a major publicity campaign, promising on billboards and bumper stickers that "One with a Gun Gets You Two."

a. Rockefeller Drug Laws. Practitioners made vigorous efforts to avoid application of the mandatory sentences and often succeeded; the remaining cases were dealt with as the law dictated (Blumstein et al. 1983, pp. 188–89). Drug felony arrests, indictment rates, and conviction rates all declined after the law took effect. For those who were convicted, the likelihood of being imprisoned and the average length of prison term increased. The likelihood that a person arrested for a drug felony was imprisoned was the same after the law took effect— 11 percent—as before (Joint Committee on New York Drug Law Evaluation 1978).

b. Massachusetts's Bartley-Fox Amendment. Massachusetts's Bartley-Fox Amendment required imposition of a 1-year mandatory minimum prison sentence, without suspension, furlough, or parole, for anyone convicted of unlawful carrying of an unlicensed firearm. An offender need not have committed any other crime. Two major evaluations were conducted.

The primary findings: Police altered their behavior, becoming more selective about whom to frisk, decreasing the number of drug offense arrests, and seizing many more weapons without making an arrest. Both charge dismissals and acquittals increased significantly. The percentage of defendants who entirely avoided a conviction rose from 53.5 percent to 80 percent. Of those finally convicted, the probability of receiving an incarcerative sentence increased from 23 percent to 100 percent (Beha 1977; Rossman et al. 1979; Carlson 1982).

c. The Michigan Felony Firearms Statute. This statute created a new offense of possessing a firearm while engaging in a felony and specified a 2-year mandatory prison sentence that could not be suspended or shortened by release on parole and had to be served consecutively to a sentence imposed for the underlying felony. The law took effect on January 1, 1977. The Wayne County prosecutor banned charge bargaining in firearms cases and took measures to enforce the ban.

The findings paralleled those in the earlier studies. There were sizable increases in dismissals. Conviction probabilities declined. The probability of imprisonment did not increase, but lengths of sentences increased for those sent to prison. Overall, the percentage of defendants incarcerated among those potentially covered by the law did not change markedly (Heumann and Loftin 1979; Loftin, Heumann, and McDowall 1983).

Trial rates remained roughly comparable except for the least serious category of offenses, felonious assaults, for which the percentage of cases resolved at trial increased from 16 percent to 41 percent of cases (Heumann and Loftin 1979, table 4). This was attributed to an innovative adaptive response, the "waiver trial." The judge would convict the defendant of a misdemeanor rather than the charged felony (the firearms law applied only to felonies) or, with the prosecutor's acquiescence, acquit the defendant on the firearms charge. Another circumvention technique was to decrease the sentence that otherwise would have been imposed by 2 years and then add the 2 years back in compliance with the firearms law (Heumann and Loftin 1979, pp. 416–24).

d. Oregon's Measure 11.   The measure, adopted by referendum in 1994, required imposition of mandatory minimum prison sentences from 70 to 300 months on anyone convicted of any of 16 designated crimes. The law's coverage was later extended to include five additional crimes.

On the basis of the earlier research findings, RAND Corporation evaluators supposed that judges and lawyers would alter previous ways of doing business, especially in filing charges and negotiating plea bargains, in order to achieve results that seemed to them sensible and just (Merritt, Fain, and Turner 2006). They expected that relatively fewer people than before would be convicted of Measure 11 offenses and more of non–Measure 11 offenses and that those convicted of Measure 11 offenses would receive harsher sentences. The research confirmed the hypotheses and showed that the changed sentencing patterns resulted primarily from changes in charging (fewer Measure 11 crimes, more lesser crimes) and plea bargaining (fewer pleas to initially charged offenses, more to lesser included offenses).

e. New Jersey Truth-in-Sentencing.   McCoy and McManimon (2004) examined sentencing patterns and case processing in New Jersey following enactment of a truth-in-sentencing law requiring people convicted of designated offenses to serve 85 percent of the announced sentence. This was not a mandatory minimum sentence law, but similar hypotheses apply: that charging and bargaining patterns would change to shelter some defendants from the new law and that sentences would be harsher for those not sheltered. Both hypotheses were confirmed.

Truth-in-sentencing and mandatory minimum sentence (including three-strikes) laws contributed substantially to prison population growth. These laws are difficult to reconcile with any mainstream, or even coherent, theory of punishment, as Section II shows. Many require sentences that are highly disproportionate to sentences received by prisoners convicted of other offenses and, as Section III shows, are impossible to justify on the basis of their crime-preventive effects.

II. Normative Analyses

Changing ideas about justice were an important part of the changes associated with the decline in support for indeterminate sentencing in the 1970s and with the initiatives adopted during the sentencing reform period. In legal, philosophical, and policy worlds, utilitarian ideas were predominant in the English-speaking countries from the middle of the nineteenth century through the 1960s. For a time, in the 1970s and early 1980s, it appeared that retributivism might replace the utilitarian framework that long shaped policies and practices and the thinking of philosophers and other theorists. That did not happen.

The major tough on crime initiatives of the 1980s and 1990s neither implicitly nor explicitly take into account the interests of affected offenders. None of them is predicated on the retributive premise that responses to crime—if they are to be just—must take account of concerns about horizontal (treat like cases alike) and vertical (treat different cases differently) equity in the distribution of punishment. Nor do they honor the two utilitarian "parsimony" principles that punishments should not be more painful or intrusive than is necessary to achieve their preventive aims and that punishments are not justifiable if their aims can be achieved as well or better through other nonpunitive means (Frase 2009).[12] Nor do they honor the utilitarian "least restrictive alternative" idea that the draftsmen of the *Model Penal Code* (1962) and the *Model Sentencing Act* (1972) regarded as fundamental.

The harshest contemporary laws prescribe prison sentences measured in decades and lifetimes. Drug laws often mandate sentences for

---

[12] The two utilitarian principles are predicated on the belief that causing suffering, including to offenders in the name of punishment, is an evil to be avoided. The ends-benefits test requires that the pain to victims to be avoided by punishment be greater than the pain the offender would suffer. The alternative means test requires that there be no less costly way to achieve the sought-after goal. No punishment may properly be imposed if some approach other than punishment would do as well. If not, punishment cannot be justified.

minor trafficking offenses far longer than many that are imposed on violent and sexual offenders. Three-strikes laws typically require minimum 25-year sentences for a wide range of violent offenses but also for some property and drug offenses (Zimring, Hawkins, and Kamin 2001). LWOPs are often imposed for offenses other than murder (Ogletree and Austin 2012, chap. 1). None of that can be squared with either the retributive proportionality principle or the utilitarian parsimony principle.

Failure to satisfy requirements of traditional frameworks for thinking about just punishments is not necessarily a fundamental defect if there is some other plausible set of normative justifications. It is conceivable—though unlikely inasmuch as, from Aristotle and Plato on, no one has developed a third framework—that the severe and disproportionate burdens recent laws impose on offenders can be justified in other ways. No one, however, has offered any. Below I discuss what I call "anormative" theories of punishment, but as the term indicates, these are not normative ideas about punishing individual offenders.

People offer political justifications for tough on crime policies, such as that the public wants or is reassured by harsh sentencing laws, is morally affronted by drug use and trafficking, or supports electoral candidates who are tough on crime, and assert that programs should be adopted for those reasons. Some observers assert that criminal justice policies are often adopted as much or more for expressive reasons—to reassure a frightened public, to acknowledge public anger or hatred, to demonstrate that something is being done—as because policy makers believe that they will have any effects on crime (e.g., Garland 2001; Freiberg 2007; Simon 2007). None of these political and policy arguments, however, addresses the question, "How can we justify doing *that* to *this particular* offender?" Both the traditional frameworks viewed that as the critical question.

From early in the nineteenth century until the 1970s, punishment theories, institutions, policies, and practices in the English-speaking countries were based largely on consequentialist ideas. The academic and real worlds lined up nicely. Practitioners and policy makers may not have read Cesare Beccaria ([1764] 2007), Jeremy Bentham ([1830] 2008), or Enrico Ferri (1921) or known who they were, but they were in broad agreement with them that the primary purpose of punishment is to minimize harms associated with crime and state responses to it. Most of the institutions that constitute contemporary criminal justice systems—penitentiaries, training schools, reformatories, juvenile courts, probation, parole—were invented in the nineteenth century and premised on the pursuit of that purpose (Rothman 1971; Allen 1981). So were individualized and indeterminate sentencing systems for dealing with adult offenders and the *parens patrie* rationale that underlies the juvenile court (Platt 1969; Rothman 1971; Mennel 1983).

Near the end of that 150-year period, the *Model Penal Code* (1962) laid out a blueprint for the mother of all consequentialist punishment systems. Offenses were defined broadly and were categorized only into misdemeanors and three levels of felonies. Precise delineation of the seriousness of crimes was considered unimportant and unnecessary. The only important question was whether the defendant was guilty. Once that was determined, the judge was given broad discretion to decide what sentence to impose. Probation was available for any offense, including murder. If the judge believed that the sentences authorized for a crime were too severe, he or she could sentence the offender as if he had been convicted of something less serious. If a prison sentence was ordered, the parole board decided when the prisoner was released. The prison authorities could award and withdraw time off for good behavior. Consistent with the utilitarian principle of parsimony, presumptions were created to ensure that offenders were not punished more severely than was necessary: judges were directed not to send people to prison, and parole boards were directed to release inmates when first they became eligible, unless specified conditions existed to justify some other decision. Allusions to retributive ideas appear only three times, and faintly. Nonincarcerative penalties should not be imposed or inmates released on parole if doing so would "unduly depreciate the seriousness of the offense." One of the overall purposes of the code was to ensure that disproportionately severe punishments were not imposed (Tonry 2004, chap. 7).

In our time, in contrast, retributive ideas about crime and punishment seem an inherent part of thinking by most philosophers and other theorists, even if those ideas have had little recent influence on policy except in the loose, vindictive sense that policy makers have generally preferred harsher punishments to milder ones. Social and experimental psychologists instruct that human beings are hardwired to react punitively to crime (Darley 2010). Evolutionary psychologists explain that natural selection has favored human beings with that hard wiring. Individuals with clear senses of right and wrong and a willingness to act on them, it is said, are better community members, fostering cohesion, increasing the odds of community survival, and perpetuating the gene pool that predisposed people to be retributive (Robinson, Kurzban, and Jones 2007). Some influential philosophers of criminal law argue that those punitive intuitions justify retributive punishment theories (e.g., Moore 1993).

If retributive ideas and instincts are so common, how can it be that they had so little influence before the 1970s? The answer is that most practitioners and academics in the 1950s and 1960s believed that retributivism was atavistic. Conventional wisdom and intuition can be morally, ethically, and empirically wrong, as widely held beliefs about racial inferiority, homosexuality, and gender roles in earlier times demonstrate. That is what our midcentury predecessors believed about retributive instincts. The instinctual response should be resisted (Michael and Adler 1933, pp. 341, 344; Michael and Wechsler 1940, pp. 7, 11).

Sensibilities, however, were changing during the period when the *Model Penal Code* was being developed. Harbingers of discontent with penal consequentialism had already begun to appear (e.g., Lewis [1949] 2011; Allen 1959) and recurred with increasing frequency (e.g., Burgess 1962; Allen 1964; Davis 1969). By the mid-1970s, dissatisfaction was widespread. Policy makers rejected many features of indeterminate sentencing and favored new approaches based on retributive ideas.

Consequentialism lost ground and influence. Retributivism came into vogue. In the 1950s, Norval Morris (1953), John Rawls (1955), and H. L. A. Hart (1959) attempted to reconcile general utilitarian rationales for punishment as an institution with resort to retributive considerations in individual cases. Numerous philosophers offered diverse retributive punishment theories (Morris 1966, 1981; Feinberg 1970; Kleinig 1973; Murphy 1973; Hampton 1984; Duff 1986). Among the lawyers, Norval Morris (1974) elaborated his theory of limiting retributivism, Alan Dershowitz (1976) his of "fair and certain punishment," and Andrew von Hirsch (1976) his of "just deserts." By the early 1980s, it was not unreasonable to believe that a corner had been turned and that policy makers, practitioners, and theorists would long march to the beat of distant retributive drums.

That did not happen, except for a few years. During the sentencing reform period, some legislatures enacted determinate sentencing laws and abolished parole release in order to ensure that offenders served the proportionate sentences they received. Sentencing commissions adopted presumptive sentencing guidelines based on retributive premises.

The retributive moment quickly passed. By the mid-1980s the tough on crime period was under way. Except in lip service, proportionality largely disappeared as a policy goal. Many of the sentencing laws enacted in the United States in the 1980s and 1990s, including mandatory minimum, three-strikes, truth-in-sentencing, and LWOP laws, paid no heed to the idea that punishments should be proportionate to some plausible assessment of the offender's blameworthiness or the gravity of the offense. If principled rationales were implied by developments such as these, the principles were consequentialist: deterrence by means of threats of harsh punishment, incapacitation by means of lengthy sentences, and moral education by means of the messages severe punishments ostensibly convey about right and wrong. There was, however, as I show in Section III, no credible evidence on the basis of which to believe that those policies would be more effective crime preventatives than the less severe policies they supplanted.

New, less overtly punitive initiatives also paid little heed to proportionality or parsimony. Drug courts and other problem-solving courts targeting mentally ill offenders, domestic violence, and gun crimes began in the early 1990s. By 2010 they numbered in the thousands (Mitchell 2011). Drug courts are predicated on the beliefs that drug treatment can work, that drug dependence is causally related to offending, and that coerced treatment backed up by firm judicial monitoring can break drug dependence and thereby reduce offending. Other problem-solving courts are based on parallel logic. The logic calls not for proportionate punishments but for participation in treatment and behavioral controls as long as needed to maximize their effectiveness.

Other proportionality-defying approaches proliferated, including prison reentry programs predicated on risk prediction and rehabilitative programming. Throughout corrections systems, increased investments were made in cognitive skills, drug abuse, sexual offending, and other treatment programs. Throughout the world, including in the United States, thousands of new restorative justice programs were established. All of these initiatives shared the characteristics that their primary aims were forward-looking—reduce reoffending or drug use; solve problems; restore relations among offenders, victims, and communities—and not much concerned to apportion punishment to offense gravity or blameworthiness (Tonry 2011a).

The rationales of drug courts, correctional treatment programs, and restorative justice are not the same, and they are not the same as the rationales for mandatory minimum sentences, three-strikes laws, and LWOPs. What all these programs and policies share, however, is that they do not give much weight to ideas about proportionality and parsimony in deciding what should be done in individual cases. Committing an offense, particularly a serious violent or sexual offense, in effect makes offenders into outlaws whose interests do not matter.

The ideas encompassed in retributivism and consequentialism are ultimately concerned to explain and justify what happens to convicted offenders in terms that relate to them as individual human beings and that acknowledge their interests and moral autonomy. In many countries at diverse times, however, punishment policies have taken little account of offenders' interests. Prominent contemporary examples include the United States during the tough on crime period, England and Wales since the early 1990s, South Africa, the former socialist states of Eastern and Central Europe, and Russia.

What all those countries share is histories characterized by political cultures in which the interests of some people do or did not count. All of these social categories of people are the targets of laws, policies, and patterns of punishment that suggest that they are seen primarily as social threats and not as people whose interests deserve the concern and respect that traditional retributive and consequentialist theories of punishment would give them.

If such views were given a name, they might be called anormative theories. They are influential in many countries in our time, particularly in the United States and parts of Eastern Europe. They were prevalent in South Africa during apartheid and in the Soviet Union and continue to cast long shadows. Whether offenders were considered "Kaffirs," "class enemies," "social parasites," or something similarly opprobrious, their interests need not be considered. Anormative theories were predominant in Western countries before the nineteenth century as is demonstrated by Foucault's (1977) accounts of punishment under the *ancien regime* and historians' accounts of the use of capital punishment in England (e.g., Hay et al. 1975) and imprisonment throughout Europe and Britain in the sixteenth through eighteenth centuries (Whitman 2003).

The two traditional ways of thinking about punishment focus fully or partly on offenders. Retributive theories link notions of blameworthiness, culpability, or wrongfulness to what happens to them. Consequentialist theories, although by definition concerned with effects, impose limits on what may justly be done to offenders: for example, that the harm done to offenders not exceed the harm thereby averted for others (Frase 2009). Anormative ways of thinking about punishment take no or reduced account of considerations relating to just treatment of offenders. That is the only way that extraordinarily disproportionate punishments—life without possibility of parole for 13-year-old robbers or three-strikes sentences of 25 years to life for adult shoplifters, or in England and Wales indeterminate, potentially lifetime imprisonment of "dangerous" offenders—can be understood. Those policies and practices have little or nothing to do with justice toward offenders. They center instead on denunciation of wrongdoing, reassurance of citizens, acknowledgment of popular outrage and insecurity, and demonstration of government resolve. All of these goals, or functions, involve communication about norms related to wrongdoing, but none is principally concerned with offenders and their circumstances or interests.

In the tough on crime period, in contrast to the two preceding periods, it is impossible to link the main components of sentencing policies and practices to normative ideas about just treatment of convicted offenders. Some contemporary laws, such as presumptive guidelines systems, are broadly consistent with retributive ideas. Others, including drug courts, many treatment programs, and restorative justice, are broadly consistent with different kinds of consequentialist ideas. Still others, such as three-strikes laws, many minimum sentence laws, and LWOPs, are inconsistent with any discernible set of ideas about justice. Anormative thinking may accurately describe the thinking underlying many contemporary sentencing laws, but it can hardly be described as a theory of justice.

III. Does Research Matter?

In recent decades social science evidence was conspicuously absent from legislative policy making processes concerning sentencing and punishment. The consequences have contributed substantially to contemporary patterns of imprisonment.

For much of the century before 1975, faith in good will and good effects, not research findings, underlay indeterminate sentencing. If major developments since 1975 had been predicated on widely accepted research findings, things would have evolved very differently or, as has been true of most other developed countries, not have changed much at all. Most laws were enacted not on the basis of research findings, cost-benefit studies, impact projections, or meta-analyses, however, but because policy makers believed them to be intuitively plausible, morally appropriate, or politically expedient.

Research has interacted with policy in several ways. The developments during the sentencing reform period for a time provided a classic example of evidence-based policy making. Pilot studies suggested that federal parole guidelines might work. Federal parole guidelines were developed, implemented, and evaluated. They were successful at reducing disparities and increasing consistency. On the basis of that experience, voluntary sentencing guidelines were developed (Gottfredson, Wilkins, and Hoffman 1978). They proved unsuccessful but were succeeded by presumptive sentencing guidelines, which were a success.

That instance of admirably evidence-based policy making proved short-lived. By the mid-1980s, credible evaluations showed that *voluntary* sentencing guidelines had little effect on sentencing patterns and did not reduce disparities. By contrast, *presumptive* sentencing guidelines developed by a sentencing commission were shown to reduce racial and other unwarranted sentencing disparities, bringing greater consistency to plea bargaining, and enabling states to improve resource planning (e.g., Knapp 1984; Tonry 1996, chap. 2). From an evidence-based policy perspective, the implications were straightforward: parole and presumptive sentencing guidelines work, voluntary guidelines do not. Nonetheless, parole guidelines, despite their successes, withered away, and voluntary sentencing guidelines became the industry standard.

Mandatory minimum sentence and three-strikes laws offer a diametrically opposed example of the limited influence of research findings. Little solid research evidence was ever available to justify their enactment or their survival.

A. Deterrence

Some of the laws enacted during the tough on crime period were ostensibly premised on beliefs or assumptions about the deterrent effects of mandatory and severe punishments. From a crime control perspective, such beliefs and assumptions were largely misguided. There are three main sources of evidence: government reviews for policy making, scholarly surveys, and evaluations of mandatory minimum and three-strikes laws. All point in the same direction.

1. *Government Reviews.* Governments in many countries have asked advisory committees or national commissions to survey knowledge of the deterrent effects of criminal penalties generally. After the most exhaustive examination of the question ever undertaken, the National Academy of Sciences Panel on Research on Deterrent and Incapacitative Effects concluded, "In summary . . . we cannot assert that the evidence warrants an affirmative conclusion regarding deterrence" (Blumstein, Cohen, and Nagin 1978, p. 7). The 2012 National Academy of Sciences Panel on Deterrence and the Death Penalty concluded that there is no credible evidence that the death penalty is a deterrent to homicide (Nagin and Pepper 2012).

Similar bodies in other Western countries have reached similar conclusions. An English Home Office advisory committee on criminal penalties, explaining the rationale for the Criminal Justice Act 1991, expressed deep skepticism: "Deterrence is a principle with much immediate appeal. . . . But much crime is committed on impulse, given the opportunity presented by an open window or unlocked door, and it is committed by offenders who live from moment to moment; their crimes are as impulsive as the rest of their feckless, sad, or pathetic lives. It is unrealistic to construct sentencing arrangements on the assumption that most offenders will weigh up the possibilities in advance and base their conduct on rational calculation" (Home Office 1990, p. 6). The Home Office commissioned a follow-up survey of the literature a decade later. It concluded that "there is as yet no firm evidence regarding the extent to which raising the severity of punishment would enhance deterrence of crime" (von Hirsch et al. 1999, p. 52).

The Canadian Sentencing Commission (1987) expressed a similar view: "Evidence does not support the notion that variations in sanctions (within a range that reasonably could be contemplated) affect the deterrent value of sentences. In other words, deterrence cannot be used with empirical justification, to guide the imposition of sentences" (p. xxvii). The Finnish National Research Institute of Legal Policy, explaining a national policy decision to reduce use of imprisonment substantially, observed, "Can our long prison sentences be defended on the basis of a cost/benefit assessment of their general preventative effect? The answer of the criminological expertise was no" (Törnudd 1993, p. 3).

2. *Scholarly Surveys.* A sizable number of comprehensive reviews of the deterrence literature have been published. The heavy majority reach similar conclusions. In a classic, much-cited survey, Cook (1980) concluded that existing studies showed that "there exist feasible actions on the part of the criminal justice system that may be effective in deterring [certain] crimes, . . . [but the studies] do *not* demonstrate that all types of crimes are potentially deterrable, and certainly they provide little help in predicting the effects of any specific governmental action" (p. 215; emphasis in original).

Updating the work of the 1978 National Academy of Sciences panel, Nagin (1998) observed that he "was convinced that a number of studies have credibly demonstrated marginal deterrent effects" but concluded that it was "difficult to generalize from the findings of a specific study because knowledge about the factors that affect the efficacy of policy is so limited" (p. 4).

Doob and Webster (2003) concluded, "There is no plausible body of evidence that supports policies based on this premise [that increased penalties reduce crime]. On the contrary, standard social scientific norms governing the acceptance of the null hypothesis justify the present (always rebuttable) conclusion that sentence severity does not affect levels of crime" (p. 146).

A meta-analysis by Pratt et al. (2006) produced a main finding on deterrence, one "noted by previous narrative reviews of the deterrence literature," that "the effects of severity estimates and deterrence/sanctions composites, even when statistically significant, are too weak to be of substantive significance (consistently below −.1)" (p. 379).

Nagin and Durlauf (2011) in an influential recent article examined evidence on the deterrent effects of sanctions and the effects on crime of imprisonment and policing. About deterrence, they concluded, "In summary, the literature on whether increases in prison sentence length serve as a deterrent is not large, but several persuasive studies do exist. These studies suggest that increases in the severity of punishment have at best only a modest deterrent effect" (p. 31). They also concluded that the effects of imprisonment on prisoners might on average be criminogenic rather than crime-preventative (e.g., Nagin, Cullen, and Jonson 2009) but that a sizable literature indicates that some police actions have preventive effects (e.g., Evans and Owens 2007). As a result, they proposed that prison use be reduced and saved funds be transferred to more effective police crime-prevention efforts.

3. *Impact Evaluations.* Evaluations have been conducted of the deterrent effects of newly enacted mandatory penalty laws. The evaluators of the Rockefeller Drug Laws in New York, which required lengthy prison sentences for drug crimes, devoted most of their energies to trying to identify effects on drug use or drug-related crime. They found none (Joint Committee on New York Drug Law Evaluation 1978).

A number of studies were made of the crime-preventive effects of a Massachusetts law requiring a 1-year minimum sentence for people convicted of possession of an unregistered firearm. The studies concluded that it had either no deterrent effect on the use of firearms in violent crimes (Beha 1977; Rossman et al. 1979; Carlson 1982) or a small short-term effect that quickly disappeared (Pierce and Bowers 1981).

Studies in other states reached similar results. An evaluation of a mandatory sentencing law for firearms offenses in Detroit concluded, "the mandatory sentencing law did not have a preventive effect on crime" (Loftin, Heumann, and McDowall 1983, pp. 304–5). Assessments of the deterrent effects of mandatory penalty laws in Tampa, Jacksonville, and Miami "concluded that the results did not support a preventive effect model" (Loftin and McDowall 1984, p. 259). The results of evaluations of the effects of mandatory penalty laws in Pittsburgh and Philadelphia "do not strongly challenge the conclusion that the statutes have no preventive effect" (McDowall, Loftin, and Wiersema 1992, p. 352).[13]

Most credible empirical assessments of California's three-strikes law's effects on crime rates and patterns have concluded that none can be shown. In 2005, the Legislative Analyst's Office, after analyzing

---

[13] McDowall, Loftin, and Wiersema (1992), the team of researchers who conducted the Michigan, Florida, and Pennsylvania deterrence analyses mentioned in the text, combined the data from all three states and concluded that mandatory penalties for gun crimes reduced gun homicides but not assaults or robberies involving guns. This is counterintuitive. Homicides by definition are lethal assaults, and the ratios of assaults and robberies that involve guns and result in deaths should be relatively stable, assuming that there have been no substantial changes in the availability or lethality of weapons. If the proportions of assaults and robberies involving guns decline, gun homicides should decline commensurately, and vice versa. If a deterrent effect can be shown for relatively small numbers of homicides, it should be much easier to demonstrate for vastly larger numbers of assaults and robberies. Nagin and Durlauf (2011, p. 28) provide other reasons to be skeptical.

declines in overall and violent crime rates, concluded, "For now, it remains an open question as to how much safer California's citizens are as a result of Three Strikes" (Analyst's Office 2005, p. 33).

There have been more than 20 published assessments of the crime-preventive effects of three-strikes laws, most focusing on California's experience.[14] Only four conclude that three-strikes laws have crime reduction effects (Chen 2000, 2008; Zimring, Hawkins, and Kamin 2001; Shepherd 2002; Helland and Tabarrok 2007). Of these, Zimring, Hawkins, and Kamin found a small effect and only for second-strike offenders; Helland and Tabarrok also found only a small effect and concluded that it fell far short of what would be required to justify the law's effects on prison budgets in cost-benefit terms; Chen's findings were weak and her conclusions were hedged;[15] and Shepherd's findings are not credible.[16] Three studies concluded that enactment of three-strikes laws produced increases in homicide rates (Marvell and Moody 2001; Kovandzic, Sloan, and Vieraitis 2002; Moody, Marvell, and Kaminski 2002). One concluded that they result in increases in killings of police (Moody, Marvell, and Kaminski 2002).

No matter which body of evidence is consulted—the general literature on the deterrent effects of criminal sanctions, research on marginal deterrence effects, or the evaluation literature on mandatory penalties—the conclusion is the same. There is little basis for believing that mandatory penalties or severe penalties have significant marginal deterrent effects.

[14] Most are shown in Tonry (2011b, table 6.3).

[15] "The approach taken in California has not been dramatically more effective at controlling crime than other states' efforts. . . . [California's law] is not considerably more effective at crime reduction than alternative methods that are narrower in scope" (Chen 2008, pp. 362, 365). Doob and Webster (2003) have demonstrated fundamental problems with her analysis.

[16] Shepherd (2002) concluded, "During the first 2 years after the legislation's enactment, approximately eight murders, 3,952 aggravated assaults, 10,672 robberies, and 384,488 burglaries were deterred in California by the two- and three-strikes legislation" (p. 174). The fundamental problem, however, is that Shepherd, like most economists, assumed what other social scientists investigate: that increased penalties reduce crime rates. Shepherd's findings correspond to her findings on the deterrent effects of capital punishment (e.g., Dezhbakhsh, Rubin, and Shepherd 2003). Other economists have demonstrated why those findings are not credible (e.g., Donohue and Wolfers 2005; Donohue 2006). Problems recurringly identified are reliance solely on official data analyzed at county or state levels, lack of awareness of case processing differences at local levels, and poorly specified models. On California's three-strikes law, however, Shepherd is an outlier; most other economists' analyses concur with the no deterrent effect conclusions of noneconomists (Marvell and Moody 2001; Kovandzic, Sloan, and Vieraitis 2002; Moody, Marvell, and Kaminski 2002).

B. Incapacitation

Research on incapacitative effects provides no firmer underpinnings to the proliferation of laws mandating lengthy prison sentences during the tough on crime period. Some of them were ostensibly premised on beliefs or assumptions about incapacitation. From a crime control perspective, however, such beliefs and assumptions were largely misguided. Three major bodies of evidence are particularly relevant: research on replacement effects, criminal careers, and the overbreadth of "selective incapacitation."

1. *Replacement Effects.* For some categories of offenders, an incapacitation strategy necessarily failed because most or all of the individuals sent to prison were rapidly replaced in the criminal networks of which they were a part. Confining those individuals did not diminish future offending. Drug trafficking is the paradigm case. Drug dealing is part of a large complex illegal market with low barriers to entry. The net earnings of street-level dealers are low and the probabilities of eventual arrest and imprisonment are high (Levitt and Venkatesh 2000; Cook et al. 2007). Even so, arrested dealers are quickly replaced by new recruits (Dills, Miron, and Summers 2008; MacCoun and Martin 2009). At the corner of Ninth and Concordia in Milwaukee in the mid-1990s, for example, 94 drug arrests were made within a 3-month period. "These arrests, [the police officer] pointed out, were easy to prosecute and to convict. But . . . the drug market continued to thrive at the intersection" (Smith and Dickey 1999, p. 8).

Disadvantaged young people tend to overestimate the benefits of drug dealing and to underestimate the risks (Reuter, MacCoun, and Murphy 1990; Kleiman 1997). This is compounded by peer influences, social pressures, and deviant role models provided by successful dealers who live conspicuously affluent lives and manage to avoid arrest. This impression can be strong because the likelihood of arrest for any individual sale of crack, cocaine, heroin, or methamphetamine is low even though the likelihood of eventual arrest and imprisonment is very high (Caulkins and MacCoun 2003; Reuter, in this volume). Similar analyses apply to many members of deviant youth groups and gangs: as members and even leaders are arrested and removed from circulation, others step into the newly opened positions. The arrests and imprisonments of street-level dealers and, often, of gang members create illicit "opportunities" for others.

2. *Criminal Careers Research.* Research on "criminal careers" pro-

vides other reasons to be skeptical of using long sentences to incapacitate offenders. Many of those confined would have ceased offending
long before their prison terms expire. Criminal careers were a major
focus of federally funded crime research in the 1980s and the subject
of a National Research Council panel report (Blumstein et al. 1986).
Researchers investigated patterns of onset, continuation, desistance,
specialization, acceleration, and deceleration in criminal careers. One
strand of that literature documented "age-crime curves" (Farrington
1986). Another strand investigated and documented the phenomenon
of "residual career length," the period during which an active offender
will continue to commit offenses (Blumstein, Cohen, and Hsieh 1982).
A third examined the effects of incapacitation strategies (Cohen 1983),
including strategies of "selective incapacitation," which target especially serious offenders (Greenwood and Abrahamse 1982). The findings of none of those literatures justify reliance on incapacitation as a
crime control strategy.

   a. Age-Crime Curves.   The work on age-crime curves shows that
very large percentages of young people commit offenses; rates peak in
the midteenage years for property offenses and the late teenage years
for violent offenses followed by rapid declines (e.g., Farrington 1986;
Sweeten, Piquero, and Steinberg 2013). For most offenders, a process
of natural desistance results in cessation of criminal activities in the
late teens and early 20s. Confining people after they would have desisted from crime is in any case inefficient; it also may be criminogenic
and operate to extend criminal careers of people who would otherwise
have desisted (Nagin, Cullen, and Jonson 2009).

   b. Residual Criminal Career Lengths.   Most active career offenders
desist from crime at relatively early ages—typically in their 30s (Farrington 2003). This means that most—even active—criminal careers
are short. In the federal system and most states, first offenders are
punished less severely—usually much less severely—than repeat offenders. Under three-strikes laws, dangerous offender statutes, and all
sentencing guidelines, criminal history considerations substantially increase sentence lengths, often doubling or tripling sentence lengths for
first offenders (e.g., Reitz 2010; Frase 2013). Under three-strikes and
"career criminal" or "dangerous offender" laws, the multiplier is often
vastly greater. The short "residual career lengths" of most offenders
mean that there is little incapacitative gain to be realized from holding
repeat offenders for increasingly long terms.

c. Selective Incapacitation. Longitudinal research on offending has long shown that relatively few offenders commit a large percentage of offenses (e.g., Wolfgang, Figlio, and Sellin 1972; Farrington 1979). Research in the 1980s based on interviews with prison inmates seemed to show that identifying and confining high-rate offenders would be a viable crime-prevention strategy (Chaiken and Chaiken 1982; Greenwood and Abrahamse 1982). The results, however, did not withstand scrutiny. The early research was retrospective; offenders were asked to detail their past behavior. The overriding difficulty was that it is easy to identify high-rate serious offenders retrospectively but exceedingly difficult to identify them prospectively. When researchers tested prospective application of selective incapacitation by developing instruments for use in predicting high-rate offenders, they discovered that they were unable to identify high-rate offenders with sufficient accuracy for the strategy to be viable (Blumstein et al. 1986). Too many of the people confined on the basis that they were predicted to be active offenders in the future proved to be "false positives," people who would not have committed new serious offenses. The age-crime curve and short residual lengths of criminal careers are principal reasons for the inadequate prediction capacity.

Evidence has not made much difference in recent decades in relation to sentencing laws and policies. Initiatives that largely achieved their goals—notably parole and presumptive sentencing guidelines—have not notably influenced policy making outside the pioneering jurisdictions and within them have suffered abandonment and retrenchment. Sentencing laws and policies putatively aimed at deterrence and incapacitation could not have been justified when they were adopted on the basis of then-available research findings, and their retention cannot be justified now. Whatever it is that has been driving sentencing policy in the United States has been something other than evidence.

IV. What's It All About?

Evidence and mainstream normative ideas about just punishments have been conspicuously absent from policy making about sentencing since the mid-1980s. Something else has been driving policy.

A number of master narratives are available to explain what that might be. One focuses on rises in crime rates, most importantly for homicide, which began in the 1960s and began to fall, after some intermediate fluctuations, only in 1991. Americans became angry and fearful. Policy makers and practitioners responded. The rest, the narratives proponents argue, is obvious. The public was angry and frightened and policy makers responded (Zimring and Hawkins 1999; Ruth and Reitz 2003).

A second master narrative is that it's partly about crime but it's also about the existential agonies of contemporary society. The final third of the twentieth century was a period of instability and rapid social and economic change. Politicians responded opportunistically. On one influential account, crime and criminals were convenient symbols of the forces of instability. American (and English) politicians promoted punitive, expressive legislation in order to acknowledge public anxieties, protect the legitimacy of the state, and promote political self-interest (Garland 2001). In another, politicians manipulated public anxieties in order to gain or preserve power that could be used to pursue other ends (Simon 2007). In yet another, increases in crime and insecurity created an atmosphere of "populist punitivism" (Bottoms 1995) or "penal populism" (Pratt 2007) to which politicians responded. In still another account, public anxieties, exacerbated by global mass media, fostered a climate of risk aversion to which politicians responded, harsh anticrime policies being but one of many responses to heightened perceptions of risk (Douglas 1992).

A third master narrative is that the tough on crime period in the United States and similar developments since the early 1990s in England and Wales and New Zealand are consequences of the growing global influence of neoliberalism and globalization and their political emanations. Declining social welfare expenditure has reduced governmental capacity to shelter citizens from adversity. Increasing emphasis on personal responsibility for economic and social disadvantage, what former British Prime Minister Tony Blair called "responsibilization," has exposed individuals to more extreme disadvantage and heightened willingness to react harshly to criminal and other nonconforming behavior (Cavadino and Dignan 2005; Lacey 2008).

None of the master narratives suffices to explain American developments. All wealthy developed countries except Japan experienced steep rises in crime rates, including homicide rates, from the 1960s to the 1990s, but only a handful adopted harshly punitive criminal justice policies: the United States during the tough on crime period, England and Wales after 1993 (Morgan 2006; Downes and Morgan 2012), and

New Zealand since the late 1990s (Pratt and Clark 2005). Most others, including Germany, Australia, Belgium, Canada, Switzerland, and the Scandinavian countries except Finland, had stable or only slightly rising imprisonment rates during the period of sharply rising crime rates (Lappi-Seppälä 2008).

Countries have different criminal justice policies and practices for reasons of political culture and history, not because of crime levels, crime trends, or larger social and economic forces. Anglo-Saxon countries have higher imprisonment rates than Scandinavian ones. French and Italian governments regularly reduce their prison populations by use of large-scale collective pardons and amnesties (Lévy 2007). The United States responded to the rising crime rates from the 1960s to the 1990s with harsher laws and larger prisons. Most European countries responded to similar crime rises with diversion programs and alternatives to imprisonment (Tonry 2007).

Countries and, within the United States, states have the policies and prison populations they choose to have. Politicians in Finland decided to reduce the Finnish imprisonment rate by two-thirds between 1965 and 1990, a period when overall and violent crime rates tripled. In the face of similar rising crime rates, German politicians chose to hold the imprisonment rate flat, and American politicians allowed American rates to quintuple (Tonry 2001). All American states experienced large crime rate increases in the 1970s and 1980s, but their responses were substantially different. Not surprisingly, politicians in states such as Maine, Vermont, and Minnesota resisted calls for enactment of the harshest laws and politicians in states such as California, Oklahoma, Florida, and Georgia responded with enthusiasm.

The words "politicians chose . . ." are at the beginning, not the end, of the story. The next question is why politicians in one country or state chose one thing and those in another country or state chose another. I have my own explanation for what happened in the United States. It includes the history of American race relations, the continuing influence of Protestant fundamentalism, constitutional arrangements that give short-term emotions and politics greater influence on policy than elsewhere, and what historian Richard Hofstadter (1965) called the "paranoid style" in American politics (Tonry 2009a).

The basic story is simple. Republican presidential candidate Barry Goldwater in 1964, a time when crime rates had been rising for several years, made "crime in the streets" into a partisan political issue. The victories of the civil rights movement increased opportunities for black people but also offered conservative Republicans an opportunity to appeal to white voters in the formerly solidly Democratic South. In *The Emerging Republican Majority* (1969), Goldwater staffer Kevin Phillips proposed that Republicans take advantage of the opportunity. Throughout the United States, they did, using crime, welfare fraud, and affirmative action as facially neutral but racially tinged "wedge issues" to undermine traditional working class and southern white support for Democrats (Edsall and Edsall 1991). All three issues proved potent, but especially crime. Simplistic sound bite proposals, campaign advertisements with images of jailhouse doors slamming shut, and accusations that opponents were "soft on crime" proved potent. Democrats eventually learned that they could seldom win head-to-head electoral contests in which Republicans made crime a major issue, unless they too became "tough on crime." They did, most famously when soon-to-become president Bill Clinton and his Democratic Leadership Council decided never to let the Republicans get to the right of Democrats on crime issues (Windlesham 1998; Gest 2001).

Until the politics of law and order settled into a stalemate, American criminal justice policy making from the mid-1980s through the mid-1990s was a one-way ratchet. Sentencing laws only became harsher and prison populations larger. Once the stalemate was in place, relatively few major new punitive laws were enacted. However, at least when these words were written, the laws enacted during the tough on crime period largely remain in place.

The seemingly odd sentencing policy developments of the 1980s and 1990s in retrospect are intelligible, even if regrettable. The successful policy initiatives of the 1970s and early 1980s—parole and presumptive sentencing guidelines—fell from favor because their accomplishments ceased being strategically important to politicians. Reducing racial and other unwarranted disparities and enhancing consistency and predictability were not major aims of the tough on crime period.

By contrast, however, once crime became a galvanizing issue in partisan politics, it is not surprising that evidence ceased to matter. The main findings of the research on mandatory minimum sentences, deterrence, and incapacitation were known in the mid-1980s before lengthy minimum sentence, three-strikes, LWOP, and truth-in-sentencing laws proliferated. The proponents of those laws aimed to win elections and gain political power; they did not let evidence, or its absence, get in the way.

Making predictions about the future is a highly uncertain business, possibly more so in relation to sentencing policy than to other criminal justice subjects such as policing or juvenile justice. Conceivably, the recent flattening out of the American prison population, many nibbles at the edges of harsh laws, and the emergence of programs aiming at rehabilitation of offenders signal a major change of direction. Or maybe the Great Recession of recent years has created pressures for modest reforms meant to save money that will abate when the good times again roll, and the march toward continued or greater toughness will resume. Or maybe a major shift in sensibilities is under way and American penal attitudes will shift back toward the greater degrees of moderation and optimism that predated the last 30 years' developments.

If a sea change is coming, the steps necessary to move American sentencing policies and patterns back into the mainstream with those of other Western countries are straightforward: repeal all mandatory minimum, three-strikes, and LWOP laws so that judges can decide case by case what justice requires; establish presumptive sentencing guidelines systems to provide standards to guide those decisions, subject to appellate court review; and either reestablish parole release systems for use across the board or establish administrative systems of regular review of the need for continued detention of any prisoner serving a sentence longer than some designated period such as 5 or 7 years. If those things happen, American sentencing policy may in time become both evidence-based and compatible with mainstream notions of justice.

REFERENCES

Advisory Council of Judges. National Council on Crime and Delinquency. 1972. *Model Sentencing Act.* 2nd ed. Hackensack, NJ: National Council on Crime and Delinquency.

Allen, Francis A. 1959. "Legal Values and the Rehabilitative Ideal." *Journal of Criminal Law, Criminology, and Police Science* 50:226–32.

———. 1964. *The Borderland of Criminal Justice: Essays in Law and Criminology.* Chicago: University of Chicago Press.

———. 1981. *The Decline of the Rehabilitative Ideal*. New Haven, CT: Yale University Press.

American Friends Service Committee. 1971. *Struggle for Justice: A Report on Crime and Punishment in America*. New York: Hill & Wang.

American Law Institute. 1962. *Model Penal Code—Proposed Official Draft*. Philadelphia: American Law Institute.

Analyst's Office. California Legislature. 2005. *Three Strikes: The Impact after More than a Decade*. Sacramento: Legislative Analyst's Office.

Anderson, David C. 1995. *Crime and the Politics of Hysteria: How the Willie Horton Story Changed American Justice*. New York: Crown.

Arthur D. Little, Inc., and Goldfarb and Singer, Esqs. 1981. *An Evaluation of Parole Guidelines in Four Jurisdictions*. Washington, DC: National Institute of Corrections.

Austin, Adrienne. 2010. *Criminal Justice Trends—Key Legislative Changes in Sentencing Policy, 2000–2010*. New York: Vera Institute of Justice.

Austin, James, Eric Cadora, Todd R. Clear, Kara Dansky, Judith Greene, Vanita Gupta, Marc Mauer, Nicole Porter, Susan Tucker, and Malcolm C. Young. 2013. *Ending Mass Incarceration: Charting a New Justice Reinvestment*. Washington, DC: Sentencing Project.

Austin, James, Charles Jones, John Kramer, and Phil Renninger. 1994. *National Assessment of Structured Sentencing*. Washington, DC: US Department of Justice, Bureau of Justice Assistance.

Barr, William. 1992. *The Case for More Incarceration*. Washington, DC: US Department of Justice, Office of Policy Development.

Beccaria, Cesare. 2007. *Dei delitti e delle pene* [On crimes and punishments]. Translated by Aaron Thomas and Jeremy Parzen. Toronto: University of Toronto Press. (Originally published 1764.)

Beha, James A., II. 1977. "'And Nobody Can Get You Out': The Impact of a Mandatory Prison Sentence for the Illegal Carrying of a Firearm on the Use of Firearms and on the Administration of Criminal Justice in Boston." Pts. 1 and 2. *Boston University Law Review* 57:96–146, 289–333.

Bentham, Jeremy. 2008. *The Rationale of Punishment*. Amherst, NY: Kessinger. (Originally published 1830.)

Blumstein, Alfred, and Allen J. Beck. 1999. "Population Growth in the U.S. Prisons, 1980–1996." In *Prisons*, edited by Michael Tonry and Joan Petersilia. Vol. 26 of *Crime and Justice: A Review of Research*, edited by Michael Tonry. Chicago: University of Chicago Press.

Blumstein, Alfred, and Jacqueline Cohen. 1973. "A Theory of the Stability of Punishment." *Journal of Criminal Law and Criminology* 64(2):198–206.

Blumstein, Alfred, Jacqueline Cohen, and P. Hsieh. 1982. *The Duration of Adult Criminal Careers*. Final report submitted to the National Institute of Justice, US Department of Justice. Pittsburgh: Heinz School of Urban and Public Affairs, Carnegie-Mellon University.

Blumstein, Alfred, Jacqueline Cohen, Susan E. Martin, and Michael Tonry, eds. 1983. *Research on Sentencing: The Search for Reform*. Vol. 1. Washington, DC: National Academy Press.

Blumstein, Alfred, Jacqueline Cohen, and Daniel Nagin, eds. 1978. *Deterrence and Incapacitation: Estimating the Effects of Criminal Sanctions on Crime Rates.* Washington, DC: National Academy of Sciences.

Blumstein, Alfred, Jacqueline Cohen, Jeffrey A. Roth, and Christy A. Visher, eds. 1986. *Criminal Careers and "Career Criminals."* Washington, DC: National Academies Press.

Blumstein, Alfred, and Joel Wallman. 2006. "The Crime Drop and Beyond." *Annual Review of Laws and Social Sciences* 2:125–46.

Boerner, David. 1995. "Sentencing Guidelines and Prosecutorial Discretion." *Judicature* 78:196–200.

Boerner, David, and Roxanne Lieb. 2001. "Sentencing Reform in the Other Washington." In *Crime and Justice: A Review of Research*, vol. 28, edited by Michael Tonry. Chicago: University of Chicago Press.

Bogan, Kathleen, and David Factor. 1997. "Oregon Guidelines, 1989–1994." In *Sentencing Reform in Overcrowded Times*, edited by Michael Tonry and Kathleen Hatlestad. New York: Oxford University Press.

Bottoms, Anthony E. 1995. "The Philosophy and Politics of Punishment and Sentencing." In *The Politics of Sentencing Reform*, edited by Chris Clarkson and Rod Morgan. Oxford: Oxford University Press.

Burgess, Anthony. 1962. *A Clockwork Orange.* London: Heinemann.

Burke, Peggy, and Michael Tonry. 2006. *Successful Transitions and Reentry for Safer Communities: A Call to Action for Parole.* Silver Spring, MD: Center for Effective Public Policy.

Canadian Sentencing Commission. 1987. *Sentencing Reform: A Canadian Approach.* Ottowa: Canadian Government Publishing Centre.

Carlson, Kenneth. 1982. *Mandatory Sentencing: The Experience of Two States.* National Institute of Justice, U.S. Department of Justice. Washington, DC: US Government Printing Office.

Carrow, Deborah M., Judith Feins, Beverly N. W. Lee, and Lois Olinger. 1985. *Guidelines without Force: An Evaluation of the Multi-Jurisdictional Sentencing Guidelines Field Test.* Report to the National Institute of Justice. Cambridge, MA: Abt Associates.

Carson, Ann E., and William J. Sabol. 2012. *Prisoners in 2011.* Washington, DC: US Department of Justice, Bureau of Justice Statistics.

Caulkins, Jonathan P., and Robert MacCoun. 2003. "Limited Rationality and the Limits of Supply Reduction." *Journal of Drug Issues* 33(2):433–64.

Cavadino, Michael, and James Dignan. 2005. *Penal Systems: A Comparative Approach.* London: Sage.

Chaiken, Jan M., and Marcia Chaiken. 1982. *Varieties of Criminal Behavior.* Santa Monica, CA: RAND Corporation.

Chen, Elsa Y. 2000. "'Three Strikes and You're Out' and 'Truth in Sentencing': Lessons in Policy Implementation and Impacts." PhD dissertation, University of California, Los Angeles, Department of Political Science.

———. 2008. "Impacts of 'Three Strikes and You're Out' on Crime Trends in California and throughout the United States." *Journal of Contemporary Criminal Justice* 24:345–70.

Cohen, Jacqueline. 1983. "Incapacitation as a Strategy for Crime Control: Possibilities and Pitfalls." In *Crime and Justice: An Annual Review of Research*, vol. 5, edited by Michael Tonry and Norval Morris. Chicago: University of Chicago Press.

Cohen, Jacqueline, and Michael Tonry. 1983. "Sentencing Reforms and Their Impacts." In *Research on Sentencing: The Search for Reform*, vol. 2, edited by Alfred Blumstein, Jacqueline Cohen, Susan E. Martin, and Michael Tonry. Washington, DC: National Academy Press.

Cook, Philip J. 1980. "Research in Criminal Deterrence: Laying the Groundwork for the Second Decade." In *Crime and Justice: An Annual Review of Research*, vol. 2, edited by Norval Morris and Michael Tonry. Chicago: University of Chicago Press.

Cook, Philip J., Jens Ludwig, Sudhir Alladi Venkatesh, and Anthony A. Braga. 2007. "Underground Drug Markets." *Economic Journal* 117(November):F1–F29.

Darley, John M. 2010. "Citizens' Assignments of Punishments for Moral Transgressions: A Case Study in the Psychology of Punishment." *Ohio State Journal of Criminal Law* 8:101–17.

Davis, Kenneth Culp. 1969. *Discretionary Justice: A Preliminary Inquiry*. Baton Rouge: Louisiana State University Press.

Dawson, Robert O. 1969. *Sentencing*. Boston: Little, Brown.

Dershowitz, Alan. 1976. *Fair and Certain Punishment*. New York: Twentieth Century Fund.

Dezhbakhsh, Hashem, Paul H. Rubin, and Joanna M. Shepherd. 2003. "Does Capital Punishment Have a Deterrent Effect? New Evidence from Postmoratorium Panel Data." *American Law and Economics Review* 5:344–76.

Dills, Angela K., Jeffrey A. Miron, and Garrett Summers. 2008. "What Do Economists Know about Crime?" NBER Working Paper no. 13759. Cambridge, MA: National Bureau of Economic Research.

Ditton, Paula M., and Doris James Wilson. 1999. *Truth in Sentencing in State Prisons*. Washington, DC: US Department of Justice, Bureau of Justice Statistics.

Donohue, John J. 2006. "The Death Penalty: No Evidence for Deterrence." *Economists' Voice* (April):1–6.

Donohue, John J., and Justin Wolfers. 2005. "Uses and Abuses of Empirical Evidence in the Death Penalty Debate." *Stanford Law Review* 58:791–846.

Doob, Anthony N. 1989. "Sentencing Aids Final Report." Unpublished manuscript. Toronto: University of Toronto, Institute of Criminology.

———. 1990. "Computerized Sentencing Information for Judges: An Overview of Progress Reports on the Sentencing Aids Project." Unpublished report. Toronto: University of Toronto, Institute of Criminology.

Doob, Anthony N., and Norman W. Park. 1987. "Computerized Sentencing Information for Judges: An Aid to the Sentencing Process." *Criminal Law Quarterly* 30(1):54–72.

Doob, Anthony N., and Cheryl Marie Webster. 2003. "Sentence Severity and Crime: Accepting the Null Hypothesis." In *Crime and Justice: A Review of*

Research, vol. 30, edited by Michael Tonry. Chicago: University of Chicago Press.

Douglas, Mary. 1992. *Risk and Blame: Essays in Cultural Theory*. London: Routledge.

Downes, David, and Rod Morgan. 2012. "Overtaking on the Left: The Politics of Law and Order in the 'Big Society.'" In *The Oxford Handbook of Criminology*, 4th ed., edited by Mike Maguire, Rod Morgan, and David Downes. Oxford: Oxford University Press.

Duff, R. Antony. 1986. *Trials and Punishments*. Cambridge: Cambridge University Press.

Edsall, Thomas, and Mary Edsall. 1991. *Chain Reaction: The Impact of Race, Rights, and Taxes on American Politics*. New York: Norton.

Evans, William N., and Emily G. Owens. 2007. "COPS and Crime." *Journal of Public Economics* 91:181–201.

Farrington, David P. 1979. "Longitudinal Research on Crime and Delinquency." In *Crime and Justice: An Annual Review of Research*, vol. 1, edited by Norval Morris and Michael Tonry. Chicago: University of Chicago Press.

———. 1986. "Age and Crime." In *Crime and Justice: An Annual Review of Research*, vol. 7, edited by Michael Tonry and Norval Morris. Chicago: University of Chicago Press.

———. 2003. "Developmental and Life-Course Criminology: Key Theoretical and Empirical Issues." *Criminology* 41:221–55.

Feinberg, Joel. 1970. "The Expressive Function of Punishment." In *Doing and Deserving: Essays in the Theory of Responsibility*. Princeton, NJ: Princeton University Press.

Ferri, Enrico. 1921. *Relazione sul progetto preliminare di Codice Penale Italiano*. Rome: L'Universelle.

Fogel, David. 1979. *We Are the Living Proof: The Justice Model for Corrections*. Cincinnati: Anderson.

Foucault, Michel. 1977. *Discipline and Punish: The Birth of the Prison*. Harmondsworth, UK: Penguin.

Frankel, Marvin. 1973. *Criminal Sentences—Law without Order*. New York: Hill & Wang.

Frase, Richard S. 2005. "Sentencing Guidelines in Minnesota, 1978–2003." In *Crime and Justice: A Review of Research*, vol. 32, edited by Michael Tonry. Chicago: University of Chicago Press.

———. 2009. "Limiting Excessive Prison Sentencing." *University of Pennsylvania Journal of Constitutional Law* 11(1):43–46.

———. 2013. *Just Sentencing: Principles and Procedures for a Workable System*. New York: Oxford University Press.

Freiberg, Arie. 2007. "Jurisprudential Miscegenation: Strict Liability and the Ambiguity of Crime." In *Governance and Regulation in Social Life: Essays in Honour of WG Carson*, edited by A. Brannigan and G. Pavlich. Oxford: Routledge-Cavendish.

Garland, David. 2001. *The Culture of Control*. Chicago: University of Chicago Press.

Gest, Ted. 2001. *Crime and Politics: Big Government's Erratic Campaign for Law and Order*. New York: Oxford University Press.

Gilliard, Darrell K., and Allen J. Beck. 1997. *Prison and Jail Inmates at Midyear 1996*. Washington, DC: Bureau of Justice Statistics, US Department of Justice.

Gottfredson, Don M., Leslie T. Wilkins, and Peter B. Hoffman 1978. *Guidelines for Parole and Sentencing*. Lanham, MD: Lexington.

Greenwood, Peter W., and Allan Abrahamse. 1982. *Selective Incapacitation*. Santa Monica, CA: RAND Corporation.

Hampton, Jean. 1984. "The Moral Education Theory of Punishment." *Philosophy and Public Affairs* 13(3):208–38.

Hart, H. L. A. 1959. "Prolegomenon to the Principles of Punishment." *Proceedings of the Aristotelian Society*, n.s., 60:1–26.

Hay, Douglas. 1975. "Property, Authority, and the Criminal Law." In *Albion's Fatal Tree: Crime and Society in Eighteenth Century England*, edited by Douglas Hay, Peter Linebaugh, John G. Rule, E. P. Thompson, and Cal Winslow. New York: Pantheon.

Hay, Douglas, Peter Linebaugh, John G. Rule, E. P. Thompson, and Cal Winslow, eds. 1975. *Albion's Fatal Tree: Crime and Society in Eighteenth-Century England*. New York: Pantheon.

Helland, Eric, and Alexander Tabarrok. 2007. "Does Three Strikes Deter? A Nonparametric Estimation." *Journal of Human Resources* 42:309–30.

Heumann, Milton, and Colin Loftin. 1979. "Mandatory Sentencing and the Abolition of Plea Bargaining: The Michigan Felony Firearms Statute." *Law and Society Review* 13:393–430.

Hofstadter, Richard. 1965. *The Paranoid Style in American Politics and Other Essays*. Chicago: University of Chicago Press.

Home Office. 1990. *Crime, Justice, and Protecting the Public*. London: Home Office.

Joint Committee on New York Drug Law Evaluation. 1978. *The Nation's Toughest Drug Law: Evaluating the New York Experience*. Project of the Association of the Bar of the City of New York and the Drug Abuse Council. Washington, DC: US Government Printing Office.

Kassebaum, Gene, David Ward, and Daniel Wilner. 1971. *Prison Treatment and Parole Survival: An Empirical Assessment*. New York: Wiley.

Kleiman, Mark A. R. 1997. "The Problem of Replacement and the Logic of Drug Law Enforcement." *Drug Policy Analysis Bulletin* 3:8–10.

Kleinig, John. 1973. *Punishment and Desert*. New York: Springer.

Knapp, Kay A. 1984. *The Impact of the Minnesota Sentencing Guidelines: Three-Year Evaluation*. St. Paul: Minnesota Sentencing Guidelines Commission.

Kovandzic, Tomislav, John Sloan, and Lynne Vieraitis. 2002. "Unintended Consequences of Politically Popular Sentencing Policy: The Homicide Promoting Effects of 'Three Strikes' in US Cities (1980–1999)." *Criminology and Public Policy* 1(3):399–424.

Kramer, John H., and Jeffrey T. Ulmer. 2008. *Sentencing Guidelines: Lessons from Pennsylvania*. Boulder, CO: Lynne Rienner.

Lacey, Nicola. 2008. *The Prisoner's Dilemma—Political Economy and Punishment in Contemporary Democracies.* Cambridge: Cambridge University Press.

Lappi-Seppälä, Tapio. 2008. "Trust, Welfare, and Political Culture: Explaining Differences in National Penal Policies." In *Crime and Justice: A Review of Research*, vol. 37, edited by Michael Tonry. Chicago: University of Chicago Press.

Levitt, Steven D., and Sudhir Alladi Venkatesh. 2000. "An Economic Analysis of a Drug Selling Gang's Finances." *Quarterly Journal of Economics* 115(3): 755–89.

Lévy, René. 2007. "Pardons and Amnesties as Policy Instruments in Contemporary France." In *Crime, Punishment, and Politics in Comparative Perspective*, edited by Michael Tonry. Vol. 36 of *Crime and Justice: A Review of Research*, edited by Michael Tonry. Chicago: University of Chicago Press.

Lewis, C. S. 2011. "The Humanitarian Theory of Punishment." In *Why Punish? How Much?*, edited by Michael Tonry. New York: Oxford University Press. (Originally published in *20th Century: An Australian Quarterly Review* 3, no. 3[1949]:5–12.)

Loftin, Colin, Milton Heumann, and David McDowall. 1983. "Mandatory Sentencing and Firearms Violence: Evaluating an Alternative to Gun Control." *Law and Society Review* 17:287–318.

Loftin, Colin, and David McDowall. 1981. "'One with a Gun Gets You Two': Mandatory Sentencing and Firearms Violence in Detroit." *Annals of the American Academy of Political and Social Science* 455:150–67.

———. 1984. "The Deterrent Effects of the Florida Felony Firearm Law." *Journal of Criminal Law and Criminology* 75:250–59.

MacCoun, Robert, and Karin D. Martin. 2009. "Drugs." In *Handbook on Crime and Public Policy*, edited by Michael Tonry. New York: Oxford University Press.

Martinson, Robert. 1974. "What Works?—Questions and Answers about Prison Reform." *Public Interest* 35(2):22–54.

Marvell, Thomas B. 1995. "Sentencing Guidelines and Prison Population Growth." *Journal of Criminal Law and Criminology* 85:696–706.

Marvell, Thomas B., and Carlisle E. Moody. 1996. "Determinate Sentencing and Abolishing Parole: The Long-Term Impacts on Prisons and Crime." *Criminology* 34:107–38.

———. 2001. "The Lethal Effects of Three Strikes Laws." *Journal of Legal Studies* 30:89–106.

McCoy, Candace, and Patrick McManimon. 2004. "New Jersey's 'No Early Release Act': Its Impact on Prosecution, Sentencing, Corrections, and Victim Satisfaction." Final Report to the National Institute of Justice, US Department of Justice. Rutgers University, School of Criminal Justice.

McDowall, David, Colin Loftin, and Brian Wiersema. 1992. "A Comparative Study of the Preventative Effects of Mandatory Sentencing Laws for Gun Crimes." *Journal of Criminal Law and Criminology* 83:378–94.

Mennel, Robert M. 1983. *Thorns and Thistles: Juvenile Delinquents in the United States, 1825–1940.* Hanover: University of New Hampshire Press.

Merritt, Nancy, Terry Fain, and Susan Turner. 2006. "Oregon's Get Tough Sentencing Reform: A Lesson in Justice System Adaptation." *Criminology and Public Policy* 5(1):5–36.

Messinger, Sheldon L., John E. Berecochea, David Rauma, and Richard A. Berk. 1985. "Foundations of Parole in California." *Law and Society Review* 19:69–106.

Michael, Jerome, and Mortimer Adler. 1933. *Crime, Law, and Social Science.* New York: Harcourt Brace.

Michael, Jerome, and Herbert Wechsler. 1940. *Criminal Law and Its Administration.* Chicago: Foundation Press.

Minton, Todd D. 2012. *Jail Inmates at Mid-year 2011.* Washington, DC: US Department of Justice, Bureau of Justice Statistics.

Mitchell, Ojmarrh. 2011. "Drug and Other Problem-Solving Courts." In *The Oxford Handbook of Crime and Criminal Justice*, edited by Michael Tonry. New York: Oxford University Press.

Moody, Carlisle E., Thomas B. Marvell, and Robert J. Kaminski. 2002. "Unintended Consequences: Three-Strikes Laws and the Murders of Police Officers." http://www.ncjrs.gov/App/Publications/abstract.aspx?ID=203649.

Moore, Michael S. 1993. "Justifying Retributivism." *Israeli Law Review* 27:15–36.

Morgan, Rod. 2006. "With Respect to Order, the Rules of the Game Have Changed: New Labour's Dominance of the 'Law and Order' Agenda." In *The Politics of Crime Control: Essays in Honour of David Downes*, edited by Tim Newburn and Paul Rock. Oxford: Oxford University Press.

Morris, Herbert. 1966. "Persons and Punishment." *Monist* 52:475–501.

———. 1981. "A Paternalist Theory of Punishment." *American Philosophical Quarterly* 18:263–71.

Morris, Norval. 1953. "Sentencing Convicted Criminals." *Australian Law Review* 27:186–208.

———. 1974. *The Future of Imprisonment.* Chicago: University of Chicago Press.

Murphy, Jeffrey. 1973. "Marxism and Retribution." *Philosophy and Public Affairs* 2:217–43.

Musto, David. 1999. *The American Disease: The Origins of Narcotic Control.* 3rd ed. New York: Oxford University Press.

Nagin, Daniel S. 1998. "Criminal Deterrence Research at the Outset of the Twenty-First Century." In *Crime and Justice: A Review of Research*, vol. 23, edited by Michael Tonry. Chicago: University of Chicago Press.

Nagin, Daniel S., Francis Cullen, and Cheryl Lero Jonson. 2009. "Imprisonment and Reoffending." In *Crime and Justice: A Review of Research*, vol. 38, edited by Michael Tonry. Chicago: University of Chicago Press.

Nagin, Daniel S., and Steven N. Durlauf. 2011. "Imprisonment and Crime Can Both Be Reduced?" *Criminology and Public Policy* 10(1):13–54.

Nagin, Daniel S., and John V. Pepper, eds. 2012. *Deterrence and the Death Penalty.* Washington, DC: National Academies Press.

National Commission on Reform of Federal Criminal Law. 1971. *Report.* Washington, DC: US Government Printing Office.

New York State. Division of Criminal Justice Services. 2012. *2009 Drug Law Changes—June 2012 Update.* Albany, NY: Division of Criminal Justice Services.

New York Times. 2012. "Three Strikes Made Fairer." November 9.

Nicholson-Crotty, Sean. 2004. "The Impact of Sentencing Guidelines on State-Level Sanctions: An Analysis over Time." *Crime and Delinquency* 50(3): 395–411.

Ogletree, Charles J., Jr., and Sara Austin, eds. 2012. *Life without Parole: America's New Death Penalty?* New York: NYU Press.

Parent, Dale G. 1988. *Structuring Criminal Sentences: The Evolution of Minnesota's Sentencing Guidelines.* New York: LEXIS Law Publications.

Phillips, Kevin P. 1969. *The Emerging Republican Majority.* New Rochelle, NY: Arlington.

Pierce, Glenn L., and William J. Bowers. 1981. "The Bartley-Fox Gun Law's Short-Term Impact on Crime in Boston." *Annals of the American Academy of Political and Social Science* 455:120–37.

Platt, Anthony M. 1969. *The Child Savers: The Invention of Delinquency.* Chicago: University of Chicago Press.

Porter Nicole D. 2013. *The State of Sentencing 2012—Developments in Policy and Practice.* Washington, DC: Sentencing Project.

Pratt, John. 2007. *Penal Populism.* London: Routledge.

Pratt, John, and M. Clark. 2005. "Penal Populism in New Zealand." *Punishment and Society* 7(30):303–22.

Pratt, Travis C., Francis T. Cullen, Kristie R. Blevins, Leah H. Daigle, and Tamara D. Madensen. 2006. "The Empirical Status of Deterrence Theory: A Meta-Analysis." In *Taking Stock: The Status of Criminological Theory*, edited by Francis T. Cullen, John Paul Wright, and Kristie R. Blevins. New Brunswick, NJ: Transaction.

Rawls, John. 1955. "Two Concepts of Rules." *Philosophical Review* 44:3–13.

Reitz, Kevin. 1997. "Sentencing Guideline Systems and Sentence Appeals: A Comparison of Federal and State Experiences." *Northwestern University Law Review* 91:1441–1506.

———. 2010. "The Illusion of Proportionality: Desert and Repeat Offenders." In *Previous Convictions at Sentencing: Theoretical and Applied Perspectives*, edited by Julian V. Roberts and Andrew von Hirsch. Oxford: Hart.

Reuter, Peter. In this volume. "Why Has US Drug Policy Changed So Little over 30 Years?"

Reuter, Peter, Robert J. MacCoun, and Patrick Murphy. 1990. *Money from Crime: The Economics of Drug Dealing in Washington, DC.* Santa Monica, CA: RAND Corporation, Drug Policy Research Center.

Rich, William D., L. Paul Sutton, Todd D. Clear, and Michael J. Saks. 1982. *Sentencing by Mathematics: An Evaluation of the Early Attempts to Develop Sentencing Guidelines.* Williamburg, VA: National Center for State Courts.

Robinson, Paul H. 1987. "Hybrid Principles for the Distribution of Criminal Sanctions." *Northwestern Law Review* 82:19–42.

———. 2008. *Distributive Principles of Criminal Law: Who Should Be Punished How Much?* New York: Oxford University Press.

———. 2013. *Intuitions of Justice and the Utility of Desert*. New York: Oxford University Press.

Robinson, Paul H., Robert Kurzban, and Owen D. Jones. 2007. "The Origins of Shared Intuitions of Justice." *Vanderbilt Law Review* 60:1633–88.

Rossman, David, Paul Froyd, Glenn Pierce, John McDevitt, and William Bowers. 1979. *The Impact of the Mandatory Gun Law in Massachusetts*. Report to the National Institute of Law Enforcement and Criminal Justice. Washington, DC: US Government Printing Office.

Rothman, David. 1971. *The Discovery of Asylum: Social Order and Disorder in the New Republic*. Boston: Little, Brown.

Ruth, Henry S., and Kevin R. Reitz. 2003. *The Challenge of Crime: Rethinking Our Response*. Boston: Harvard University Press.

Sabol, William J., and Heather Couture. 2008. *Prison Inmates at Midyear 2007*. Washington, DC: Bureau of Justice Statistics, US Department of Justice.

Sabol, William J., Katherine Rosich, Kamala Mallik Kane, David Kirk, and Glenn Dubin. 2002. *Influences of Truth-in-Sentencing Reforms on Changes in States' Sentencing Practices and Prison Populations*. Washington, DC: Urban Institute.

Shane-DuBow, Sandra, Alice P. Brown, and Erik Olsen. 1985. *Sentencing Reform in the United States: History, Content, and Effect*. Washington, DC: US Government Printing Office.

Shepherd, Joanna M. 2002. "Fear of the First Strike: The Full Deterrent Effect of California's Two- and Three-Strike Legislation." *Journal of Legal Studies* 31:159–201.

Simon, Jonathan. 2007. *Governing through Crime: How the War on Crime Transformed American Democracy and Created a Culture of Fear*. New York: Oxford University Press.

Smith, Michael E., and Walter J. Dickey. 1999. *Reforming Sentencing and Corrections for Just Punishment and Public Safety*. Washington, DC: US Department of Justice, National Institute of Justice.

Spelman, William. 2009. "Crime, Cash, and Limited Options: Explaining the Prison Boom." *Criminology and Public Policy* 8(1):29–77.

Stemen, Don, Andres Rengifo, and James Wilson. 2006. *Of Fragmentation and Ferment: The Impact of State Sentencing Policies on Incarceration Rates, 1975–2002*. Final Report to the National Institute of Justice. Washington, DC: National Institute of Justice.

Stith, Kate, and José Cabranes. 1998. *Fear of Judging: Sentencing Guidelines in the Federal Courts*. Chicago: University of Chicago Press.

Sweeten, Gary, Alex R. Piquero, and Laurence Steinberg. 2013. "Age and the Explanation of Crime, Revisited." *Journal of Youth and Adolescence*. DOI: 10.1007/s10964-013-9926-4.

Tonry, Michael. 1987. *Sentencing Reform Impacts*. Washington, D.C.: US Government Printing Office.

———. 1996. *Sentencing Matters*. New York: Oxford University Press.

———. 2001. "Punishment Policies and Patterns in Western Countries." In *Sentencing and Sanctions in Western Countries*, edited by Michael Tonry and Richard S. Frase. New York: Oxford University Press.

———. 2004. *Thinking about Crime: Sense and Sensibility in American Penal Culture*. New York: Oxford University Press.

———. 2007. "Determinants of Penal Policies." In *Crime, Punishment, and Politics in Comparative Perspective*, edited by Michael Tonry. Vol. 36 of *Crime and Justice: A Review of Research*, edited by Michael Tonry. Chicago: University of Chicago Press.

———. 2009a. "Emerging Explanations of American Punishment Policies—a Natural History." *Punishment and Society* 11:377–94.

———. 2009b. "The Mostly Unintended Effects of Mandatory Penalties: Two Centuries of Consistent Findings." In *Crime and Justice: A Review of Research*, vol. 38, edited by Michael Tonry. Chicago: University of Chicago Press.

———. 2011a. "Can Twenty-First Century Punishment Policies Be Justified in Principle?" In *Retributivism Has a Past: Has It a Future?*, edited by Michael Tonry. New York: Oxford University Press.

———. 2011b. *Punishing Race: An American Dilemma Continues*. New York: Oxford University Press.

———. 2012. "Prosecutors and Politics in Comparative Perspective." In *Prosecutors and Politics: A Comparative Perspective*, edited by Michael Tonry. Vol. 41 of *Crime and Justice: A Review of Research*, edited by Michael Tonry. Chicago: University of Chicago Press.

Törnudd, Patrik. 1993. *Fifteen Years of Declining Prisoner Rates*. Research Communication no. 8. Helsinki: National Research Institute of Legal Policy.

Turner, Susan, Terry Fain, Peter W. Greenwood, Elsa Y. Chen, and James R. Chiesa. 2001. *National Evaluation of the Violent Offender Incarceration/Truth-in-Sentencing Incentive Grant Program*. Final Report to the U.S. National Institute of Justice. Santa Monica, CA: RAND Corporation.

US Sentencing Commission. 1991. *Special Report to the Congress: Mandatory Minimum Penalties in the Federal Criminal Justice System*. Washington, DC: US Sentencing Commission.

von Hirsch, Andrew. 1976. *Doing Justice*. New York: Hill & Wang.

———. 1985. *Past and Future Crimes: Deservedness and Dangerousness in Sentencing Criminals*. New Brunswick, NJ: Rutgers University Press

von Hirsch, Andrew, and Andrew Ashworth. 2005. *Proportionate Sentencing: Exploring the Principles*. Oxford: Oxford University Press.

von Hirsch, Andrew, Anthony E. Bottoms, Elizabeth Burney, and P.-O. Wikström. 1999. *Criminal Deterrence and Sentence Severity: An Analysis of Recent Research*. Oxford: Hart.

von Hirsch, Andrew, and Kathleen J. Hanrahan. 1979. *The Question of Parole: Retention, Reform, or Abolition?* Cambridge, MA: Ballinger.

von Hirsch, Andrew, Kay A. Knapp, and Michael Tonry. 1987. *The Sentencing Commission and Its Guidelines*. Boston: Northeastern University Press.

Whitman, James. 2003. *Harsh Justice*. New York: Oxford University Press.

Windlesham, Lord David. 1998. *Politics, Punishment, and Populism*. New York: Oxford University Press.

Wolfgang, Marvin E., Robert M. Figlio, and Thorsten Sellin. 1972. *Delinquency in a Birth Cohort*. Chicago: University of Chicago Press.

Wright, Ronald F. 2002. "Counting the Cost of Sentencing in North Carolina, 1980–2000." In *Crime and Justice: A Review of Research*, vol. 29, edited by Michael Tonry. Chicago: University of Chicago Press.

Zimring, Franklin E., and Gordon Hawkins. 1999. *Crime Is Not the Problem: Lethal Violence in America*. New York: Oxford University Press.

Zimring, Franklin E., Gordon Hawkins, and Sam Kamin. 2001. *Punishment and Democracy: Three Strikes and You're Out in California*. New York: Oxford University Press.

Daniel S. Nagin

Deterrence in the Twenty-First Century

ABSTRACT

The evidence in support of the deterrent effect of the certainty of punishment is far more consistent than that for the severity of punishment. However, the evidence in support of certainty's effect pertains almost exclusively to apprehension probability. Consequently, the more precise statement is that certainty of apprehension, not the severity of the ensuing legal consequence, is the more effective deterrent. This conclusion has important policy implications among which are that lengthy prison sentences and mandatory minimum sentencing cannot be justified on deterrence. There are four major research gaps. The first concerns the mechanism by which police affect perceptions of the probability of apprehension. The second concerns the inextricable link between the deterrent effect of the threat of punishment and the potentially criminogenic effect of the experience of punishment. The third concerns the concept of a sanction regime defined by the sanctions legally available and how that legal authority is administered. Theories of deterrence conceive of sanctions in the singular, not the plural, and do not provide a conceptual basis for considering the differential deterrent effects of different components of the sanction regime. The fourth involves sanction risk perceptions. Establishing the link between risk perceptions and sanction regimes is imperative; unless perceptions adjust, however crudely, to changes in the sanction regime, desired deterrent effects will not be achieved.

Three enduring questions have occupied centuries of scholarship on crime and punishment. Does punishment prevent crime? How does punishment prevent crime? And should punishment be used to prevent crime? This essay is concerned with the first two of these questions.

Daniel S. Nagin is the Teresa and H. John Heinz III University Professor of Public Policy and Statistics at Carnegie Mellon University.

The criminal justice system dispenses justice by apprehending, prosecuting, and punishing individuals who break the law. These activities may prevent crime by three distinct mechanisms: incapacitation, specific deterrence, and general deterrence. Convicted offenders are sometimes punished with imprisonment. Incapacitation concerns crimes averted by their physical isolation during the period of their incarceration. Specific and general deterrence involve possible behavioral responses. General deterrence refers to the crime prevention effects of the threat of punishment. Specific deterrence concerns the aftermath of the failure of general deterrence—the effect on reoffending, if any, that results from the experience of actually being punished.

In this essay, I consider the theoretical and evidentiary basis for general deterrence. In another recent *Crime and Justice* essay (Nagin, Cullen, and Jonson 2009), I surveyed the evidence on the specific deterrence effects of imprisonment. Here, I draw heavily from recent and prior deterrence reviews by me and others.

My aim is to provide a succinct summary of the current state of theoretical and empirical knowledge about deterrence in support of several interrelated objectives. The first is to provide a selective intellectual history of deterrence research that identifies important recurring themes. I highlight both what has been learned and persistent flaws that should be addressed in future research.

The second objective concerns the framing of discourse on deterrence, which often takes the same pattern, particularly in policy discussions: one group arguing that sanction threats always deter and another group arguing that sanction threats never deter. When deterrence effects are unpacked, it is clear that sanction threats are not universally efficacious: magnitudes of deterrent effects range from none to seemingly very large. Thus, another primary objective is to move discourse about deterrence away from the equally indefensible positions that deterrence effects are always or never present to a more nuanced and useful inquiry into the basis for variation in the existence and size of deterrent effects.

The third objective is policy related. Prison populations have been rising in the United States for four decades. Only recently have there been signs that the increase is abating. In 2009 and 2010, state-level prison population declined but federal-level population continued to increase (Bureau of Justice Statistice 2012). Less well recognized is that prison populations have risen elsewhere in the world, for example, in the Netherlands since 1975 and more recently in England and Wales, Portugal, Spain, and New Zealand. An incarceration-based sanction policy that reduces crime solely by incapacitation will necessarily increase the rate of imprisonment. In contrast, if the crime control policy also prevents crime by deterrence, it may be possible to reduce both imprisonment and crime; successful prevention by any mechanism, whether by deterrence or otherwise, has the virtue of averting not only crime but also the punishment of perpetrators. Hence, it is important to identify policies that increase imprisonment but have only negligible effects on crime rates.

My main conclusions are as follows: First, there is little evidence that increases in the length of already long prison sentences yield general deterrent effects that are sufficiently large to justify their social and economic costs. Such severity-based deterrence measures include "three strikes, you're out," life without the possibility of parole, and other laws that mandate lengthy prison sentences.

Second, on the basis of the earlier noted *Crime and Justice* review (Nagin, Cullen, and Jonson 2009), I have concluded that there is little evidence of a specific deterrent effect arising from the experience of imprisonment compared with the experience of noncustodial sanctions such as probation. Instead, the evidence suggests that that reoffending is either unaffected or increased.

Third, there is substantial evidence that increasing the visibility of the police by hiring more officers and allocating existing officers in ways that materially heighten the perceived risk of apprehension can deter crimes. This evidence is consistent with the perceptual deterrence literature that surveys individuals on sanction risk perceptions and relates these perceptions to their actual or intended offending behavior. This literature finds that perceived certainty of punishment is associated with reduced self-reported or intended offending.

Thus, I conclude, as have many prior reviews of deterrence research, that evidence in support of the deterrent effect of various measures of the certainty of punishment is far more convincing and consistent than for the severity of punishment. However, the certainty of punishment is conceptually and mathematically the product of a series of conditional probabilities: the probability of apprehension given commission of a crime, the probability of prosecution given apprehension, the probability of conviction given prosecution, and the probability of sanction given conviction. The evidence in support of certainty's deterrent effect pertains almost exclusively to apprehension probability. Consequently, the conclusion that certainty, not severity, is the more effective deterrent is more precisely stated as *certainty of apprehension* and not the severity of the legal consequence ensuing from apprehension is the more effective deterrent. This more precise statement has important policy implications; the empirical evidence from the policing and perceptual deterrence literature is silent on the deterrent effectiveness of policies that mandate incarceration after apprehension. These include policies such as mandatory minimum sentencing laws or sentencing guidelines that mandate incarceration. Thus, this revised conclusion about the deterrent effect of punishment certainty should not be construed as implying that policies mandating severe legal consequences have been demonstrated to achieve deterrent effects.

Together these conclusions have a range of policy implications, particularly as they relate to the United States (Durlauf and Nagin 2011*b*). First, it is clear that lengthy prison sentences cannot be justified on a deterrence-based, crime prevention basis. Thus, the case for crime prevention benefits of measures requiring lengthy prison sentences such as California's three-strikes law must rest on incapacitation. Another implication is that crime prevention would be enhanced by shifting resources from imprisonment to policing or, in periods of declining criminal justice system budgets, that policing should get a larger share of a smaller overall budget.

While accumulation of knowledge about deterrence in the past four decades has been impressive, much remains to be learned. There are four major theoretical and related empirical gaps. The first concerns the deterrent effect of the certainty of apprehension. There are two distinct mechanisms by which the police may deter crime. One stems from their effectiveness in apprehending perpetrators of crimes; by definition this activity involves occurrences in which deterrence has failed. Thus, police effectiveness in successfully apprehending criminal perpetrators can have a deterrent effect only on others or on the perpetrator's future behavior. The second mechanism involves the effect of the intensity of police presence in creating a perception that apprehension risk is sufficiently high that no crime is committed in the first place. I speculate that this second mechanism is the primary source of police effectiveness in deterring crime whereas the first role primarily prevents crime by capturing and incapacitating crime-prone individuals. The research gap involves developing rigorous empirical tests of this contention and developing improved theoretical models of how police presence and tactics can reduce the attractiveness of criminal opportunities by increasing the perceived risk of apprehension.

The second gap concerns the distinction between specific and general deterrence. The two are inextricably linked because the experience of punishment is a consequence of the failure of the threat of punishment to deter crime, yet no theory of deterrence explicitly addresses how the experience of punishment influences the deterrent effect of the threat of punishment. Relevant issues include how the experience of punishment affects the proclivity to commit crime due to potential stigma effects, sustained contacts with criminals in a prison setting, or participation in rehabilitative programs as well as the effect of the experience of punishment on perceptions of the certainty and severity of sanctions. Analysis of these and other related issues will require longitudinal data on individuals who do and do not have the experience of punishment.

The third theoretical gap concerns the concept of a sanction regime. A sanction regime defines the sanctions that are legally available for the punishment of various types of crime and how that legal authority is administered. Depending on the crime and characteristics of the offenders, such as age or prior record, available sanctions range in severity from verbal reprimands to fines and different forms of community service to lengthy terms of imprisonment and execution. How the legal authority is administered determines the relative frequency with which the available sanction options are used and also the swiftness of their application. Thus, both dimensions of the sanction regime—the legal authority for different types of sanctions and how that authority is administered—combine to determine the certainty, severity, and celerity of sanctioning options available for punishment of a specific type of crime.

Theories of deterrence, however, specify sanction threats in the singular, not the plural. For example, a sizable number of studies examine the question whether capital punishment deters murder. Yet properly understood, the relevant question is the differential or marginal deterrent effect of execution over the deterrent effect of other available or commonly used penalties. In this case the alternative penalty would be a lengthy prison sentence—sometimes life without the possibility of parole. Yet none of the capital punishment studies take account of differences across states and over time in the severity of noncapital punishments for murder (Nagin and Pepper 2012). Theories of deterrence that conceive of sanctions in the singular do not provide a conceptual basis for considering the differential deterrent effect of different types of sanction options. The empirical companion to this theoretical expansion involves assembling the data required to measure sanction regimes. At least in the United States, such data are largely unavailable.

The fourth theoretical and empirical gap involves sanction risk perceptions, an issue that I emphasized in an earlier review of the deterrence literature (Nagin 1998). Deterrence is the behavioral response to the perception of sanction threats. Establishing the link between risk perceptions and sanction regimes is imperative; the conclusion that crime decisions are affected by sanction risk perceptions is not sufficient to conclude that policy can deter crime. Policy cannot directly manipulate perceptions. It can affect only the variety and severity of sanctions legally available in the sanction regime and the manner of their administration. Unless perceptions adjust, however crudely, to changes in the sanction regime, the desired deterrent effect will not be achieved.

Since the publication of Nagin (1998), valuable headway has been made in how the experience of apprehension or not following commission of a crime affects sanction risk perceptions. This research is valuable for specification of a theory that combines the concepts of general and specific deterrence. However, it does not address how perceptions are formed about the two key dimensions of a sanction regime: the legal authority for different types of sanctions and how that authority is administered. Numerous surveys have been conducted of the general public's knowledge of sanction regimes, especially concerning the legal authority for different types of sanctions (Apel 2013). Not surprisingly, the surveys find that knowledge of sanction regimes is poor. However, the fundamental flaw with these surveys is that knowledge of the potential legal consequences of lawbreaking is unnecessary for most people; their decisions to refrain from crime are based on the mere knowledge that the behavior is legally prohibited or for other nonlegal considerations such as morality or fear of social censure (Packer 1968; Zimring and Hawkins 1973; Andenaes 1974; Wikström et al. 2012). That said, for individuals for whom sanction threats might affect their behavior, it is preposterous to assume that their perceptions conform to the realities of the legally available sanction options and their administration. More than a decade after my earlier review, it remains the case that little is known about how individuals form perceptions of the sanction regimes they confront.

This essay is organized in the following sections. Key concepts of deterrence are discussed in Section I, where I also set out a simplified model of deterrence that is referred to throughout the essay. Section II provides a brief summary of the themes, conclusions, and flaws of research on the deterrent effects of prison and the police up to about 1990. In Section III, I summarize the evidence on the deterrent effects of capital punishment. I discuss the capital punishment literature separately because of its distinctive features and salience. I then examine in Section IV post-1990 studies of the crime prevention effects of imprisonment and in Section V post-1990s studies of the police effects on crime. Section VI discusses the survey-based literature on the accuracy of sanction risk perceptions, their formation, and their relationship to self-reported criminality. Section VII offers conclusions.

I. Key Concepts

Deterrence is a theory of choice in which would-be offenders balance the benefits and costs of crime. Benefits may be pecuniary, as in the case of property crime, but may also involve intangible benefits such as defending one's honor, expressing outrage, demonstrating dominance, cementing a reputation, or seeking a thrill. The potential costs of crime are comparably varied. Crime can entail personal risk if the victim resists. It may also invoke pangs of conscience or shame (Braithwaite 1989). I am mainly concerned with offender responses to the costs that attend the imposition of official sanctions such as arrest, imprisonment, execution, fines, and other restrictions on freedom and liberty such as mandated drug testing or electronic monitoring.

The origins of most modern theories of deterrence can be traced to the work of the Enlightenment-era legal philosophers (Beccaria 1764; Bentham 1789). The motivation for their work was their mutual abhorrence of the administration of punishment without constructive purpose. For them the constructive purpose was preventing crime. As Beccaria observed, "it is better to prevent crimes than punish them" ([1764] 1986, p. 93). Beccaria and Bentham argued that there are three key ingredients to the deterrence process: the severity, certainty, and celerity of punishment. These concepts, particularly the certainty and severity of punishment, form the foundation of nearly all contemporary theories of deterrence. The enduring impact of their thinking is remarkable testimony to their innovation.

The theory of deterrence is predicated on the idea that if state-imposed sanction costs are sufficiently severe, criminal activity will be discouraged, at least for some. Thus, one of the key concepts of deterrence is the severity of punishment. Severity alone, however, cannot deter. There must also be some possibility that the sanction will be incurred if the crime is committed. Indeed the argument that the probability of punishment, not severity, is the more potent component of the deterrence process goes back to Beccaria, who observed that "one of the greatest curbs on crime is not the cruelty of punishments, but their infallibility. . . . The certainty of punishment even if moderate will always make a stronger impression" ([1764] 1986, p. 58).

In the lifetimes of Beccaria and Bentham there was no criminal justice system as we know it. Punishment for lawbreaking was almost certainly less regular and more haphazard than it is today. Punishment in contemporary society, however, also still remains far from guaranteed. In order for a formal sanction—whether moderate or severe—to be imposed, the offender must first be apprehended, usually by the police.[1] He must next be charged and successfully prosecuted and, finally, sentenced by the judge. Successful passage through all of these stages is far from certain. The most important set of actors affecting certainty is the police: without detection and apprehension, there is no possibility of conviction or punishment. For this reason special attention is given to discussing what is known about the deterrent effect of police activities and presence.

The third conceptual component of the theory of deterrence advanced by Bentham and Beccaria is the swiftness of punishment, which Bentham referred to as celerity. Celerity is the least studied of the conceptual troika underlying deterrence theory. The theoretical basis for its effect on deterrence is ambiguous, as is the empirical evidence on its effectiveness. Even Beccaria seemed to base his case for celerity more on normative considerations of just punishment than on deterrence effectiveness. He observed that "the more promptly and the more closely punishment follows upon the commission of a crime, the more just and useful will it be. I say more just, because the criminal is

---

[1] Crime may also be sanctioned entirely outside of the criminal justice system through retaliation by the victim or by others on his or her behalf (Jacobs and Wright 2006).

thereby spared the useless and cruel torments of uncertainty, which increase with the vigor of imagination and with the sense of personal weakness" (Beccaria [1764] 1986, p. 36).

In 1968 economist Gary Becker published the first modern formalization of the Beccaria-Bentham conception of the deterrence process (Becker 1968). Since then, other formalizations have appeared in economics, criminology, law, and sociology—some in the form of mathematical models and others in the form of nonmathematical conceptual theories (Cornish and Clarke 1986).

For the purposes of this essay still another formalization is provided. I have two purposes. One is to provide a conceptual structure for framing results that are well established in the literature. The second is more ambitious. I earlier indicated that the seemingly greater deterrent effect of certainty rather than severity of punishment reflected a response to the certainty of apprehension. In this regard, I distinguished two distinct functions of the police: apprehending the perpetrators of crime and serving in a sentinel function that deters crime from happening in the first place. The second purpose is to formalize this distinction. In so doing I link situational crime prevention theory with deterrence theory.

Bentham's conception of criminal choice involved the would-be offender balancing the potential pains of punishment against the pleasures of the offense. In this spirit the model formalizes the decision of a would-be offender to victimize a potential criminal opportunity, whether that opportunity is a person in the form of a potential robbery victim or property that might be stolen or vandalized.

The choice model is depicted in figure 1. It distinguishes four possible outcomes if the target is victimized: the criminal act is successfully completed, the act is not successfully completed and the perpetrator is not apprehended, the act is not successfully completed and the perpetrator is apprehended but not convicted, and the act is not successfully completed and the perpetrator is both apprehended and convicted. The probability of each of these outcomes is determined by the following probabilities.

Perceived Probability of Successful Completion of the Act. This probability, which is denoted by P_s, measures the would-be offender's perception of the chances the target can be successfully victimized. This perception will be affected by how effectively the opportunity is protected. For property targets, the level of protection is determined by

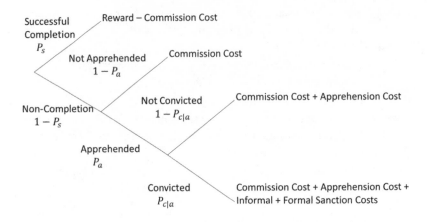

Fig. 1.—The decision to victimize a target

technological safeguards such as alarm and surveillance systems and use of physical protection such as locked showcases. For human targets, the protection level is affected by the care with which valuable property is secured, for example, by keeping it out of sight. Protection may also be provided by what Cohen and Felson (1979) call capable guardians such as security guards, vigilant employees, or onlookers who are willing to intervene. Importantly, the police may also serve as a guardian. I refer to police as acting as sentinels when acting in this role. An idling police car outside a liquor store greatly reduces the chance, probably to zero, that the store can be successfully robbed. This brings me to the risk of apprehension.

Perceived Probability of Apprehension Given Noncompletion.   Police perform another crime control function that is distinct from their role as official guardians. They apprehend those offenders who chose to act on a criminal opportunity. When acting in this role, police are described as "apprehension agents." The sentinel and apprehension roles of the police are conceptually linked but distinct. They are conceptually linked because both roles are based on the legal authority of the police to arrest persons suspected of committing a crime. Because a contributing factor to P_s is the risk of apprehension, arrest authority is one source of police influence on P_s in their sentinel role. However, the sentinel role of police is distinct from their apprehension role because the latter comes into play only when deterrence has failed and a would-be offender becomes an actual offender. Thus, at one moment police can be functioning as a sentinel and in the next moment they can be acting as an apprehension agent. The would-be offender's perception of the probability of apprehension given commission of the crime is denoted by P_a.

In this model I assume that the risk of apprehension is limited to acts that are not successfully completed. I make this assumption for several reasons. First, it is useful for clarifying the distinction between police acting as sentinels and police acting as apprehension agents. Second, it conforms to the seeming reality that most offenders are apprehended at the scene of the crime or soon thereafter. I say seeming because I have been able to identify only two studies (Greenwood, Chaiken, and Petersilia 1977; Blake and Coupe 2001) that report relevant data. Data reported in both support this assumption.

Perceived Probability of Conviction Given Apprehension. The offender's perception of the probability that apprehension will actually result in conviction is denoted by $P_{c|a}$.

Under this setup, the probability of successful completion is P_s, the probability of nonsuccessful completion but with apprehension avoidance is $(1 - P_s)(1 - P_a)$, the probability of nonsuccessful completion followed by apprehension but not conviction is $(1 - P_s)(P_a)(1 - P_{c|a})$, and the probability of nonsuccessful completion followed by apprehension and conviction is $(1 - P_s)(P_a)(P_{c|a})$.

The benefits and costs of each of these outcomes are assumed to be determined by the following factors:

- *Rewards.* Rewards measures the total benefits of victimizing a target. For a crime with a property motive, the value of the property to the perpetrator likely accounts for all or a major share of the total reward. However, the thrill of offending or—in the case of violent crimes without a property motive—the satisfaction of humiliating, physically hurting, or killing the victim may also be relevant to the reward value of a target.
- *Crime commission cost.* Crime commission cost measures the total cost of committing the crime separate from the sanction cost defined below. Commission cost includes time searching for the opportunity, planning time, if any, and the effort required to commit the crime itself. Importantly, it also includes the potential costs to the perpetrator of victim retaliation or resistance. Finally, commission cost includes Raskolnikov-like feelings of guilt or shame that

may affect the perpetrator, whether or not he is apprehended and sanctioned.

- *Perceived formal sanction cost.* Perceived sanction cost measures the would-be perpetrator's assessment of the formal sanction cost that might be imposed if convicted. These costs include the loss of freedom if imprisoned and the unpleasantness of other restrictions on freedom due to conditions of parole or probations and fines.
- *Perceived informal sanction cost.* The imposition of formal sanctions may also trigger informal sanctions by family, friends, and the community at large, which for some offenders may be even more costly than the formal sanctions. Informal sanction cost may also involve large economic costs due to job loss.
- *Perceived cost of apprehension.* Apprehension imposes costs that are distinct from formal and informal sanction costs. These include the unpleasantness of the apprehension itself, possible loss of liberty due to pretrial detention, and legal fees. Perceived cost of apprehension also includes the social and economic costs triggered by arrest, even without conviction, such as disapproval of family, friends, and the community at large, as well as job loss.

At the end of each branch, figure 1 shows the costs that attend the various forms of an unsuccessful attempt or the benefit of a successful attempt. If the individual chooses to act on a criminal opportunity, the benefits and costs of the four possible outcomes and their attendant probabilities are as follows:

1. The offender successfully completes the criminal act. This occurs with probability P_s, and the net benefit to the offender is reward less commission cost. Thus, the expected benefit of victimization is P_s(Reward − Commission Cost), which is denoted as $P_s(R - CC)$.

2. The offender is not successful and is not apprehended. This occurs with probability $(1 - P_s)(1 - P_a)$. The cost to the offender is that much, or all, of the commission cost is incurred but with no reward. For simplicity it is assumed that all of the commission cost is incurred. Thus, the contribution of this outcome to expected cost is $(1 - P_s)(1 - P_a)$(Commission Cost), which is denoted as $(1 - P_s)(1 - P_a)CC$.

3. The offender is not successful and is apprehended but is not convicted and formally sanctioned. This occurs with probability

$(1 - P_s)(P_a)(1 - P_{a|c})$. In this case the cost to the offender is commission cost plus apprehension cost. Thus the contribution of this outcome to expected cost is $(1 - P_s)(P_a)(1 - P_{c|a})$(Commission Cost + Apprehension Cost), which is denoted as $(1 - P_s)(P_a)(1 - P_{c|a})(CC + AC)$. Because, as already noted, most apprehensions occur at the scene of the crime or shortly thereafter, it is assumed that the perpetrator does not have the opportunity to enjoy the rewards provided by the act.

4. The offender is not successful but is apprehended, convicted, and formally sanctioned. This occurs with probability $(1 - P_s)(P_a)(P_{c|a})$. In this case the cost to the offender is commission cost plus apprehension cost plus formal and informal sanction cost. Thus, the contribution of this outcome to expected cost, again assuming that the rewards are not enjoyed, is $(1 - P_s)(P_a)[P_{c|a}$(Commission Cost + Apprehension Cost + Formal Sanction + Informal Sanction Cost)], which is denoted as $(1 - P_s)(P_a)(P_{c|a})(CC + AC + FS + ISC)$.[2]

An arrow at the top of figure 1 highlights that the possible events depicted occur over time. Success or failure at completion is typically immediate, whereas the down tree events occur later, often months after the criminal event in the case of conviction and sentencing. I return to this observation in the discussion of the celerity of punishment.

It is assumed that the crime will be committed if the expected benefits from a successful completion exceed the expected cost of an unsuccessful attempt, namely, if

$$P_s(R - CC) > (1 - P_s)(1 - P_a)CC + (1 - P_s)(P_a)(1 - P_{c|a})(CC + AC) \quad (1)$$

$$+ (1 - P_s)(P_a)(P_{c|a})(CC + AC + FS + ISC).$$

An equivalent form of this relationship moves P_s on the left-hand side to the right-hand side, in which case the crime will be committed if

$$(R - CC) > \left(\frac{1 - P_s}{P_s}\right)[(1 - P_a)CC + (P_a)(1 - P_{c|a})(CC + AC) \quad (2)$$

$$+ (P_a)(P_{c|a})(CC + AC + FS + ISC)].$$

The left-hand side of equation (2) measures the net benefits of com-

[2] This model assumes that success precludes the possibility of subsequent apprehension and the attendant risk of formal sanction.

mitting the crime and the right-hand side measures the costs. Several observations about this relationship are relevant to the remainder of the discussion.

First, unless the net benefit of crime commission is positive (i.e., $R - C > 0$),[3] the offense will not be committed regardless of the formal and informal sanction costs specified on the right-hand side of equation (2). Particularly if commission cost is understood to include the shame of committing an act that involves taking another person's property or doing violence to that person, for most people sanction costs are irrelevant to the decision to refrain from crime. For example, Bachman, Paternoster, and Ward (1992) found in a study of sexual assault that sanction risk perceptions were relevant to self-reported intentions to offend only for the least morally committed. The absence of an effect for those with higher levels of moral commitment, however, should not be construed as their being impervious to incentives but to their moral commitment being a sufficient basis for refraining from sexual assault.[4] This elementary but fundamental point has been made repeatedly in the discussion about to the degree to which sanction threats affect behavior among different individuals. See, for example, Zimring and Hawkins (1973) and more recently Piquero et al. (2011) and Wikström et al. (2012). I return to this point in the discussion of sanction risk perceptions and their influence on behavior in Section VI.

Second, the bottom three branches of the tree pertain to the consequences of failure to complete the crime. Commission cost contributes to the total cost of all three of these branches, apprehension cost contributes to two of the three branches—apprehension with and without conviction—and informal and formal sanction costs contribute only to the final branch, apprehension with conviction. This implies that increases in perceived commission cost will have a greater deterrent effect than equal increases in either perceived apprehension cost or perceived formal and informal sanction costs. In turn the structure of the tree implies that increases in apprehension cost will have a greater deterrent effect than equal increases in either formal or informal sanction cost. This observation helps to explain the longstanding conclusion from the perceptual deterrence literature that shame, a key component of commission cost and apprehension cost, plays a more

---

[3] Rewards and commission cost may also be affected by risk preferences.

[4] Knowledge of potential punishment may also reinforce a normative sense of wrongfulness.

decisive role in the deterrence process than sanction cost. This issue is discussed further in Section III. It also explains the seeming effectiveness of situational crime prevention tactics, a topic I allude to in Section V.

Third, the structure of the tree also implies that decreases in P_s will have larger deterrent effects than equal-sized increases in either P_a or $P_{s|a}$ and that increases in P_a will have a bigger deterrent impact than an equal increase in $P_{s|a}$. This observation is consistent with the longstanding belief dating back to Beccaria that the certainty of punishment is a more effective deterrent than the severity of punishment. However, I earlier noted that the evidence suggests that a more precise statement of the certainty conclusion pertains to the certainty of apprehension. The decision model laid out here provides a still more precise statement of that conclusion. Decreases in P_s provide more effective deterrence than equal increases in P_a. Concerning the distinction between police serving as sentinels or as apprehension agents, when serving in their role as sentinels, they affect P_s, whereas when serving as apprehension agents, they affect P_a. This implies that the sentinel role of policing is more effective in deterring crime than their apprehension agent role. This observation is relevant to the discussion in Section V of the varying findings on police effectiveness in preventing crime.

II. Deterrence Research to the 1990s

Empirically based deterrence research began in earnest in the late 1960s. There were three major instigators. One was technological: the growing availability of computers and statistical software for analyzing crime data, which were also growing in availability. The second was social: the steady growth of crime rates during the 1960s. The third was intellectual, especially within economics, with the publication in 1968 of Becker's seminal article "Crime and Punishment: An Economic Approach."

Deterrence studies up to the 1990s are usefully grouped into three categories: experimental and quasi-experimental studies, aggregate studies, and perceptual deterrence studies. My 1998 *Crime and Justice* review provided an extended discussion of the three types of studies (Nagin 1998). This section summarizes conclusions of the experimental and quasi-experimental studies and aggregate studies of this research era that are most relevant to this review. Because of the persistence of themes in the pre- and post-1990s perceptual deterrence research and the continuity of the research methods used, I discuss this body of research without reference to era in Section VI.

A. Experimental and Quasi-Experimental Studies

This category of studies examines the effect of targeted policy interventions such as police crackdowns or implementation of statutes changing penalties. In the experimental studies the intervention and control treatments are randomly assigned. A classic example is the Minneapolis Domestic Violence Experiment (Sherman and Berk 1984) in which police responded to misdemeanor incidents of domestic violence with one of three randomly chosen responses. The arrest response was found to be most effective in preventing recidivism, but as discussed in Section V, this finding was not consistent across replications of the experiment in other localities.

True experiments, however, compose only a small fraction of the studies in this category. Most are quasi experiments. The best-designed quasi-experimental studies attempt to incorporate important features of a true experiment: a well-defined treatment regime, measurement of response before and after treatment, and a control group. Two classic studies of this genre are Ross's studies of the effects on drunk driving of the British Road Safety Act (Ross 1973) and of Scandinavian-style drunk driving laws. Most studies in this group examine the effects of police crackdowns on drug markets, disorderly behavior, and drunk driving. Excellent reviews of these studies are available in Sherman (1990) and Ross (1982). Both Sherman and Ross conclude that the interventions were generally successful in generating an initial deterrent effect. For instance, in drunk-driving interventions, this was evidenced by a reduction in fatalities in which the driver was intoxicated or in drug market crackdowns by reduced dealing. However, they also concluded that the effect was generally only transitory: the initial deterrent effect typically began decaying even while the intervention was in effect. One exception to this finding of at least initial deterrent effectiveness concerned studies of increases in sentence severity. Ross (1982) discusses the ineffectiveness of severity enhancements in three very different places: Finland, Chicago, and New South Wales, Australia. Evidence even of an initial effect is less consistent than in studies of interventions that increased the certainty of apprehension.

I take away three important lessons from this literature. First, the generally more consistent findings of initial effectiveness in the apprehension-based interventions, compared to the severity-based interventions, provide more evidence in support for my modified version of the certainty effect, namely, that certainty of apprehension is a more effective deterrent than the severity of the ensuing legal consequences, but with an important proviso. Ross (1982) attributed the ineffectiveness of severity-enhancing policies to the fact that they trigger a system response that reduced certainty of punishment. He pointed out that if judges or juries believed the penalties too harsh, they may have responded by refusing to convict guilty defendants. Police and prosecutors may respond similarly. Thus, any potential deterrent effect of the severity enhancement may be canceled by the reduction in certainty. This result is a reminder not only of the difficulty of enforcing penalties that are deemed unjust but also that certainty and severity do not operate independently—they interact. Tonry (2009) forcefully elaborates on many of these points.

Second, Sherman (1990) offers useful nomenclature for describing the finding of only transitory effects. He uses the term "initial deterrence decay" to describe the decline in the deterrent response as "potential offenders learn through trial and error that they had overestimated the certainty of getting caught at the beginning of the crackdown" and "residual deterrence," which is a crime suppression effect that extends beyond the intervention until offenders learn by experience or word of mouth that "it is once again 'safe' to offend" (p. 10). Sherman's observations are a reminder that deterrence is a perceptual phenomenon. In Sherman (1990) and Nagin (1998), we both discuss the decay of initial deterrence as a possible response to what behavioral economists call ambiguity aversion. People consistently prefer gambles in which the risks are clearly comprehensible compared to equivalent gambles in which the risks are less transparent. Initial deterrence may be a response to perceptions of uncertainty about true risk rather than to any change in the true risk of apprehension. Thus, unless policy can affect perceptions, there will be no behavioral response. It is also a reminder that perceptions may be updated in response to cues from the environment and therefore will not necessarily be stable. I return to this important issue in the discussion of the perceptions studies in Section VI.

Third, the findings from these studies have stood the test of time. In my judgment, well-conducted experimental and quasi-experimental studies of deterrence provide the most convincing evidence of the circumstances under which deterrence is and is not effective. This holds for both the post-1990s and the pre-1990s literatures.

B. Aggregate Studies

The pre-1990s aggregate studies generally analyzed the association of crime rates across geographic units, usually states, with measures of the certainty and severity of punishment. The most basic form of these analyses involved bivariate correlations across states of crimes rates for the crime categories composing the FBI part I crime index (e.g., murder and nonnegligent homicide, robbery, burglary) with certainty of punishment, measured by prison admissions per reported crime, and severity of punishment, measured by median time served. More elaborate analyses were conducted in a regression format. These analyses added various state characteristics known to be correlated with crime (e.g., age and racial composition, urbanization) to the base regression model relating crime rate to the certainty and severity measures. Negative and significant associations were generally found between the crime rate and the certainty of imprisonment ratio. The association of time served with the crime rate was generally insignificant.

Reviews of these studies, including a high-visibility National Research Council (NRC) report (Blumstein, Cohen, and Nagin 1978), concluded that the aggregate studies suffered from such grave flaws that they did not provide a basis for valid inference about deterrent effects. Two flaws are particularly noteworthy because they remain relevant to the interpretation of a successor strand of post-1990 aggregate studies discussed in Section IV. The first is that the associations do not distinguish the behavioral response to sanction threats, deterrence, from incapacitation. The second is more fundamental—distinguishing cause from effect. All forms of nonexperimental data are vulnerable to the criticism that the outcome of interest, in this case the crime rate, is the cause of the predictor of interest, in this case sanctions, and not vice versa. High crime rates, for example, might prompt a police crackdown followed by crime rates declining for other reasons. Cross-polity studies of natural variations in crime rates and sanction levels are particularly vulnerable to this concern because there is generally no basis for assessing whether the variations in sanction levels are the result of factors independent of the crime rate. By contrast, for quasi-experimental studies, institutional research can reveal whether the intervention was prompted by rising crime rates.

III. Capital Punishment

Studies of the deterrent effect of capital punishment have been and continue to be the source of bitter contention. Isaac Ehrlich's 1975 study, in which he concluded that each execution averted seven to eight homicides, is undoubtedly the most-cited study of this kind. The 1978 NRC report (Blumstein, Cohen, and Nagin 1978) and an accompanying commissioned paper (Klein, Forst, and Filatov 1978) laid out a lengthy list of criticisms of the Ehrlich analysis. The NRC report concluded that "available studies [including Ehrlich's] provide no useful evidence on the deterrent effect of capital punishment" (p. 9).

Coincidentally, that report was issued shortly after the 1976 Supreme Court decision *Gregg v. Georgia* ended the moratorium on execution in the United States. In the 35 years since publication of the 1978 report, and more especially in recent years, a considerable number of post-*Gregg* studies have attempted to estimate the effect of the legal status or the actual implementation of the death penalty on homicide rates. These studies have reached widely varying conclusions and have resulted in often bitter disagreement about their interpretation.

This more recent literature has been the subject of still another NRC report titled *Deterrence and the Death Penalty*, which I coedited (Nagin and Pepper 2012), as well as two reviews of the literature commissioned by the NRC committee (Chalfin, Haviland, and Raphael 2013; Charles and Durlauf 2013) and two valuable reviews by Donohue and Wolfers (2005, 2009). The NRC report and all of the reviews are highly critical of the post-*Gregg* research. The report concluded, "Research to date on the effect of capital punishment on homicide is not informative about whether capital punishment decreases, increases, or has no effect on homicide rates. Therefore, the Committee recommends that these studies not be used to inform deliberations requiring judgments about the effect of the death penalty on homicide. Consequently, claims that research demonstrates that capital punishment decreases or increases the homicide rate by a specified amount or has no effect on the homicide rate should not influence policy judgments about capital punishment" (Nagin and Pepper 2012, p. 3).

The NRC report leveled two key criticisms of the post-*Gregg* capital punishment deterrence research that transcend the high-profile but still narrow issue of the deterrent effect of capital punishment. They also apply to studies of the deterrent effect of other forms of sanction—prison, fines, and community control—that form the backbone of contemporary sanction policy in the United States and most other countries.

One criticism concerned the incomplete specification of the sanction regime for homicide. Even for capital-eligible convictions for homicide, only a minority of cases result in a sentence of death, let alone an execution (Nagin and Pepper 2012). This is true even for states such as Texas and Virginia that make the most intense use of capital punishment. Instead, most homicides result in a lengthy prison sentence, sometimes life without parole. A study by Cook (2009) illustrates this point. Of 274 cases prosecuted as capital cases, only 11 resulted in a death sentence. Another 42 resulted in dismissal or a verdict of not guilty, which left 221 cases resulting in conviction and sentences to a noncapital sanction.

None of the post-*Gregg* studies take into account the noncapital component of the sanction regime. As discussed in Nagin and Pepper (2012) and Chalfin, Haviland, and Raphael (2013), there are sound reasons for expecting that the severity of the noncapital sanctions for homicide varies systematically with the availability and the intensity of use of capital punishment. For example, the political culture of a state may affect the frequency of use of capital punishment and also the severity of noncapital sanctions for homicide. Thus, any effect that these noncapital sanctions have on homicide may contaminate the estimated effect of capital punishment on homicide. In capital punishment studies the potential for such bias is particularly strong because, as noted, noncapital sanctions remain the dominant sanction response to capital-eligible murders, even in states that make the most intense use of capital punishment.

Homicide is not the only criminal offense punishable by a range of qualitatively different sanction alternatives. Indeed the sanction regimes for most other criminal offenses, even felonies, include more than one sanction option for their punishment. This point is returned to in Section IV.

A second key criticism elaborated in the NRC report concerned the specification of perceptions of the capital punishment component of the sanction regime. Studies typically suppose that people who are contemplating murder perceive sanction risks as subjective probabilities of arrest, conviction, and execution. Lacking data on these subjective probabilities, researchers presume that they are somehow based on the observable frequencies of arrest, conviction, and execution.

The report concluded that several factors made the attempts by the panel studies to specify the capital component of state sanction regimes uninterpretable. First, the findings are very sensitive to the way in which the risk of execution is specified. For example, because of delays between the imposition of a death sentence and its being carried out, if ever, researchers routinely computed ratios in which the numerator was the number of executions in a given state and year divided by the number of death sentences imposed in that state in some prior year. Results are very sensitive to how that ratio is computed (Chalfin, Haviland, and Raphael 2013), and there is no logical basis for resolving disagreements about how the true risk of execution should be measured. Among the difficulties is that only 15 percent of those sentenced to death in the United States since 1977 have been executed, with close to 40 percent leaving death row for other reasons (vacated sentences or convictions, commutations, a successful appeal, or death by other causes) and 45 percent still awaiting execution (Snell 2010). Available information for calculating the risk depends on the size of the state: for large states such as Texas and California, there are far more data for calibrating risk than for small states such as Delaware and Montana. Further complicating matters, policies can change as a result of court decisions and administrative decrees of elected officials. This unpredictability calls into question the usefulness of prior data on the death penalty when calculating present and future risk. Because none of the measures used has any clear relationship with the correct measure, there is no reasoned basis for arbitrating competing claims about which study provides the better estimate of the deterrent effect of the death penalty.

Even if it were possible to judge which measure more closely corresponds to true risk, there is no evidence that the perceptions of potential murderers correspond to this risk. The above discussion concerns only one aspect of sanction regime, the risk of execution given conviction. Other relevant dimensions of the sanction regime are the risk of conviction given commission of a murder and the certainty and severity of the noncapital component alternatives to the death penalty. The assumption that potential murderers have accurate perceptions of these risks and consequences is not credible: indeed it is preposterous. I return to the issue of sanction risk perceptions in Section VI.

IV. Imprisonment and Crime

There have been two distinct waves of aggregate studies of the relationship between imprisonment and crime. Studies in the 1960s and 1970s described in Section II examined associations of state-level crime rates to state-level certainty of punishment, measured by the ratio of prison admissions to reported crimes, and to state-level severity of punishment as measured by median time served. These studies suffered from fundamental deficiencies laid out in the 1978 NRC report (Blumstein, Cohen, and Nagin 1978) and elsewhere. As a consequence, aggregate-level deterrence research went largely "silent" for more than a decade.

A. Post-1990s Aggregate Studies

By the mid-1990s, a second generation of studies emerged. Unlike the first-generation studies, which primarily involved cross-sectional analyses of states, second-generation studies had a longitudinal component in which data were analyzed across states and over time. Another important difference in the second-generation studies is that they did not attempt to estimate certainty and severity effects separately. Instead they examined the relationship between the crime rate and the rate of imprisonment as measured by prisoners per capita.

A review by Donohue (2009) identifies six studies of the relationship of crime rates to imprisonment rates. All find statistically significant negative associations between imprisonment rates and crime rates, implying a crime prevention effect for imprisonment. However, the magnitude of the estimate varied widely: from nil for a study that allowed for the possibility that prevention effects decline as the scale of imprisonment increases (Liedka, Piehl, and Useem 2006) to −0.4 percent for each 1 percent increase in the imprisonment rate (Spelman 2000).

Apel and Nagin (2009), Donohue (2009), and Durlauf and Nagin (2011a, 2011b) discuss important flaws in these studies. One is that they are necessarily measuring the combined effect of deterrence and incapacitation on crime rates and thus cannot be interpreted as measuring the deterrent effect of imprisonment. At best they can be said to estimate the upper bound of that effect.

Other shortcomings are even more fundamental. One concerns the same fundamental flaw of the first-generation studies—distinguishing cause from effect. While imprisonment prevents crime through a combination of deterrence and incapacitation, crime also generates the prison population. The object of interest is the effect of the imprisonment rate on the crime rate, but data available for estimation of that effect also reflect the effect of the crime rate on the imprisonment rate. Thus, statistical isolation of the crime prevention effect requires properly accounting for the effect of crime on imprisonment.

The shortcomings in the statistical strategies used in these studies to identify the crime prevention effect of imprisonment are discussed at length in Durlauf and Nagin (2011*a*, 2011*b*). To summarize, with the exception of Levitt (1996) and Johnson and Raphael (2012), the conclusions of the studies rest on a form of statistical analysis pioneered by the Nobel laureate Clive Granger (1969). Granger's method is often mistakenly interpreted as providing estimates with a causal interpretation, which in the context of the aggregate imprisonment studies would be the expected change in the crime rate resulting from a policy that changes the imprisonment rate by a specified amount. In fact, the results are not in general amenable to this interpretation. Instead, application of Granger's method provides only a basis for forecasting future changes in the crime rate as a function of prior changes in the imprisonment rate and the crime rate. While valid forecasts can be based on correlations alone, valid causal interpretation requires more than establishing correlation.

Figure 2 illustrates the problem. Panel *A* depicts hypothetical crime and imprisonment functions. The crime function $C(I)$ describes the crime rate as a function of the imprisonment rate, I, and the imprisonment function $I(C)$ measures the imprisonment rate as a function of the crime rate, C. The function $C(I)$ is shown to be downward sloping in I to reflect the crime reduction effects of imprisonment via some combination of deterrence and incapacitation. Studies of the relationship of the crime rate to the imprisonment rate aim to measure whether this line is in fact downward sloping and, if so, by how much. The function $I(C)$ is depicted as upward sloping because for any fixed set of policies determining the certainty and severity of punishment, imprisonment rates will be a rising function of the crime

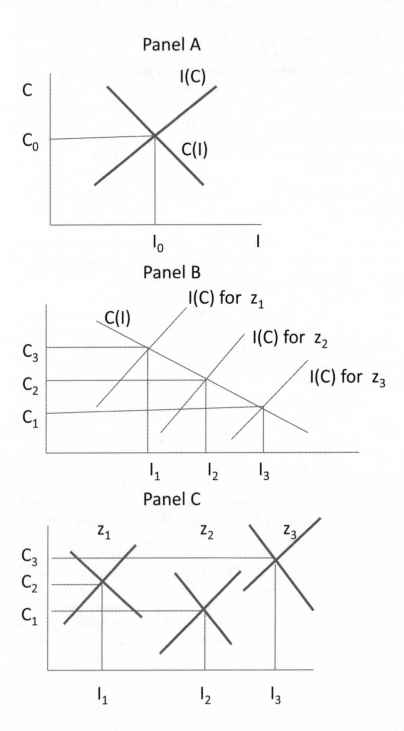

FIG. 2.—The challenge of identifying the effect of the imprisonment rate on the crime rate

rate.[5] The intersection of the $C(I)$ and $I(C)$ functions at I_0 and C_0 measures the observed level of crime and imprisonment.

Crime rates and imprisonment rates are, of course, affected by a multitude of other factors beyond their mutual interaction as depicted in panel A. The key to estimating $C(I)$ is identifying some factor, called an instrumental variable (IV), that is thought to affect the imprisonment rate but that affects the crime rate only via its effect on shifting the location of imprisonment rate function. Suppose that such an IV were identified and denoted by z. Panel B demonstrates how changing values of z from z_1 to z_2 to z_3 shifts the $I(C)$ function and, in so doing, traces out the $C(I)$ function. Connecting the points (I_1, C_1), (I_2, C_2), and (I_3, C_3) estimates $C(I)$. In this fashion, IV regression models can be said to identify $C(I)$ and thereby the crime reduction effect of the imprisonment rate on the crime rate. However, the key to IV regression successfully isolating this effect is that $C(I)$ is not directly affected by z. Panel C illustrates the failure of this assumption. If z also shifts $C(I)$, the changing equilibrium values of the imprisonment rate and crime rate no longer trace out the $C(I)$ function.

Only Levitt (1996) and Johnson and Raphael (2012) use an IV regression approach to identify the causal effect of imprisonment on crime. Levitt uses court-ordered prison releases to form a set of IVs. He argues that such court orders meet the test for providing a valid estimate of the effect of the imprisonment rate on the crime rate: the orders have no direct effect on the crime rate and affect it only insofar as the court orders affect the imprisonment rate, which in turn affects the crime rate.

Even if one accepts this argument, the estimated effect has only limited policy value. By its construction, it is likely measuring the effect on crime of the early release of selected prisoners, probably those nearing the end of their sentenced terms. It may also be reflecting the effect of diversion of individuals convicted of less serious crimes either to local jails or to community supervision. In either case, the estimates are not informative about the crime prevention effects, whether by deterrence or incapacitation, of sentence enhancements related to the manner in which a crime is committed (e.g., weapon use), the characteristics of the perpetrator (e.g., prior record), or policies affecting the likelihood of incarceration. More generally, the uncertainty about what is actually being measured inherently limits the value of the estimated effects for both policy and social science.

A more recent study by Johnson and Raphael (2012) is based on a technically complex IV regression model. Identification is based on the assumption that prison populations do not change instantaneously in response to changes in the size of the criminal population. Similarly to the non-IV-based analysis of Liedka, Piehl, and Useem (2006), Johnson and Raphael conclude that the crime prevention effect of imprisonment has diminished with the scale of imprisonment, which was rising steadily over the period of their analysis, 1978–2004.

One explanation for the Johnson and Raphael finding is that the states and the federal government over this period collectively implemented policies with steadily declining average deterrent effectiveness. Given that knowledge of the deterrent effectiveness of alternative sanction policies is so limited, this explanation is not credible. An alternative explanation involving incapacitation is more credible. If the crime reduction effect of incarceration primarily stems from incapacitation, the Johnson and Raphael finding is consistent with the concept of "stochastic selectivity" (Canela-Cacho, Blumstein, and Cohen 1997), whereby high-rate offenders are more likely to be apprehended and incarcerated than low-rate offenders. Thus, as the scale of imprisonment increases, higher-rate offenders will be less likely to be at large committing crimes. Johnson and Raphael's finding is replicated by Vollaard (2013) in an analysis of the Netherlands' Habitual Offender Law. Vollaard attributes the entirety of the crime prevention effect that he estimates to incapacitation. Also of note, Owens (2009) in her analysis of 2003 data from Maryland finds modest incapacitation effects.

The incapacitation interpretation of the Johnson and Raphael finding of decreasing crime prevention returns with the scale of imprisonment is more credible than the deterrence interpretation. This interpretation also implies that the study is not useful for learning about deterrence. However, even the incapacitation interpretation is cast in doubt by the aging of the US prison population. Between 1991 and 2010, the percentage of prisoners in state and federal prisons over 45 years old has nearly tripled from 10.6 percent to 27.4 percent (Bureau of Justice Statistics 1999, 2011). Thus, the seeming decline in the incapacitative effectiveness of prison with scale may be reflecting only the aging of the prison population, which coincides with rising imprisonment rates. Further complicating the decreasing returns interpretation is the changing composition of the prison population in terms of the composition of prisoner conviction offense. Over the past four decades, the percentage of prisoners incarcerated for non–part I FBI index crimes has increased substantially (Blumstein and Beck 1999, 2005). Thus, the reduction in crime prevention effectiveness may be due to the types of prisoners incarcerated, not to scale effects.

All of these studies, whether IV based or not, also suffer from an important conceptual flaw that limits their usefulness in understanding deterrence and devising crime control policy. Prison population is not a policy variable per se; rather, it is an outcome of sanction policies dictating who goes to prison and for how long, namely, the certainty and severity of punishment. In all incentive-based theories of criminal behavior, in the tradition of Bentham and Beccaria, the deterrence response to sanction threats is posed in terms of the certainty and severity of punishment, not in terms of the imprisonment rate. Therefore, to predict how changes in certainty and severity might affect the crime rate requires knowledge of the relationship of the crime rate to certainty and severity as separate entities, which is not provided by the literature that analyzes the relationship of the crime rate to the imprisonment rate.

The studies are also conducted at a too-global level. In Nagin (1998), I describe the two-dimensional taxonomy of sanction policies affecting the scale of imprisonment. One dimension labeled "type" distinguishes three broad categories: policies regulating certainty of punishment such as laws requiring mandatory imprisonment, policies influencing sentence length such as determinate sentencing laws, and policies regulating parole powers. The second dimension of the taxonomy, "scope," distinguishes policies that cast a wide net, such as a general escalation of penalties for broad categories of crime, compared to policies that focus on targeted offenses (e.g., drug dealing) or offenders (e.g., three-strikes laws).

The nearly 500 percent growth in prison population over the last two decades is attributable to a combination of policies belonging to all cells of this matrix. Parole powers have been greatly curtailed; sentence lengths increased, both in general and for particular crimes (e.g., drug dealing); and judicial discretion to impose nonincarcerative sanctions has been reduced (Tonry 1996; Blumstein and Beck 1999, 2005; Raphael and Stoll 2009). Consequently, any effect on the crime rate of the increase in prison population reflects the effects of an amalgam of potentially interacting treatments.

There are good reasons for predicting differences in the crime reduction effects of different types of sanctions (e.g., mandatory minimums for repeat offenders vs. prison diversion programs for first-time offenders). Obvious sources of heterogeneity in offender response include factors such as prior contact with the criminal justice system, demographic characteristics, and the mechanism by which sanction threats are communicated to their intended audience. Indeed, available evidence on the deterrent effect of sentence enhancements, the next topic of discussion, demonstrates such heterogeneity.

B. Policy Evaluation Studies of Sentence Enhancements

There have been comparatively few studies of the deterrent effects of sentence enhancements, judged relative to their importance in contemporary crime control policy. The earliest post-1970s attempts to measure severity effects analyzed the deterrent impact of sentence enhancements for gun crimes. In a series of studies, Loftin, McDowell, and colleagues (Loftin and McDowall 1981, 1984; Loftin, Heumann, and McDowall 1983) examined whether sentence enhancements for gun use in committing another type of crime such as robbery deter gun use in the commission of crime. While the findings are mixed, this body of research has generally failed to uncover evidence of a deterrent effect (but see McDowall, Loftin, and Wiersema 1992).

However, one important caveat remains with respect to extrapolating these studies to understanding the link between deterrence and severity. The same literature that found that gun penalty enhancements were ineffective also found that these laws generally failed to increase the sentences actually received in gun-related crime prosecutions. Thus, gun-using criminals may not have responded because the real incentives were not changed. This again is a reminder of Tonry's (2009) commentary on the highly inconsistent administration of mandatory minimum sentencing.

Kessler and Levitt (1999) examine the deterrent impact of another California sentence enhancement law, Proposition 8, passed in 1982. Proposition 8 anticipated the three-strikes laws passed by many states in the 1990s. They estimate a 4 percent decline in crime attributable to deterrence in the first year after enactment. Within 5–7 years, the effect grows to a 20 percent reduction. As acknowledged by Kessler and Levitt, the longer term estimate includes incapacitation effects.

Webster, Doob, and Zimring (2006) challenged the basic finding of any preventive effects. Kessler and Levitt examine data from every other year. When all annual data are used, Webster, Doob, and Zimring find that the decline in crime rates in the affected categories begins before Proposition 8's enactment, and the slope of this trend remains constant through implementation. But see Levitt (2006) for a response and commentary supporting Webster et al. by Raphael (2006).

One exception to the scarcity of studies on the crime prevention effects of sentence enhancements concerns analyses of the deterrent effect of California's "three strikes, you're out" law, which mandated a minimum sentence of 25 years upon conviction for a third-strike offense. Zimring, Hawkins, and Kamin (2001) concluded that the law reduced the felony crime rate by at most 2 percent. They also conclude that only those individuals with two convictions for two offenses qualifying as "strikes" showed any indication of reduced offending. Other studies by Stolzenberg and D'Alessio (1997) and Greenwood and Hawken (2002), who like Zimring, Hawkins, and Kamin (2001) examine before and after trends, conclude that the crime prevention effects were negligible.

I turn now to six studies that in my judgment report particularly convincing evidence on the deterrent effect of incarceration. They also nicely illustrate heterogeneity in the deterrence response to the threat of imprisonment.[6] Weisburd, Einat, and Kowalski (2008) and Hawken and Kleiman (2009) study the use of imprisonment to enforce fine payment and conditions of probation, respectively, and find substantial deterrent effects; Helland and Tabarrok (2007) analyze the deterrent effect of California's third-strike provision and find a modest deterrent effect; Raphael and Ludwig (2003) examine the deterrent effect of prison sentence enhancements for gun crimes and find no effect; and Hjalmarsson (2009) and Lee and McCrary (2009) examine the heightened threat of imprisonment that attends coming under the jurisdiction of the adult courts at the age of majority and find no deterrent effect.

Weisburd, Einat, and Kowalski (2008) report on a randomized field

---

[6] For further discussion of heterogeneity in deterrence response, see Paternoster (2010) and Piquero et al. (2011).

trial of alternative strategies for incentivizing the payment of court-ordered fines. The most salient finding involves the "miracle of the cells," namely, that the imminent threat of incarceration provides a powerful incentive to pay delinquent fines, even when the incarceration is for only a short period. The miracle of the cells provides a valuable perspective on the conclusion that the certainty, rather than the severity, of punishment is the more powerful deterrent. Consistent with the "certainty principle," the common feature of treatment conditions involving incarceration is a high certainty of imprisonment for failure to pay the fine. However, that Weisburd et al. label the response the "miracle of the cells" and not the "miracle of certainty" is telling. Their choice of label is a reminder that certainty must result in a distasteful consequence in order for it to be a deterrent. The consequences need not be draconian, just sufficiently costly, to deter the proscribed behavior.

The deterrence strategy of certain but nondraconian sanctions has been applied with apparently great success in Project HOPE, an intervention heralded in Hawken and Kleiman (2009), Kleiman (2009), and Hawken (2010). Project HOPE is a Hawaii-based probation enforcement program. In a randomized experiment, probationers assigned to Project HOPE had much lower rates of positive drug tests and missed appointments and—most importantly—were significantly less likely to be arrested and imprisoned. The cornerstone of the HOPE intervention was regular drug testing, including random tests, and certain but short punishment periods of confinement (e.g., 1–2 days) for positive drug tests or other violation of conditions of probation. Thus, both the Weisburd, Einat, and Kowalski (2008) fine experiment and Project HOPE show that highly certain punishment can be an effective deterrent in cases in which deterrence has previously been ineffective in averting crime.

Helland and Tabarrok (2007) examine whether California's "three strikes, you're out" law deters offending among individuals previously convicted of strike-eligible offenses. The future offending of individuals convicted of two previous eligible offenses was compared with that of individuals who had been convicted of only one eligible offense but who, in addition, had been tried for a second eligible offense but were ultimately convicted of a noneligible offense. The two groups of individuals were comparable on many characteristics such as age, race, and time in prison. Even so, Helland and Tabarrok find that arrest rates were about 20 percent lower for the group with convictions for two eligible offenses. The authors attribute this to the greatly enhanced sentence that would have accompanied conviction for a third eligible offense.

Raphael and Ludwig (2003) examine the deterrent effect of sentence enhancements for gun crimes that formed the basis for a much publicized Richmond, Virginia, federal program called Project Exile. Perpetrators of gun crimes, with a particular emphasis on those with a felony record, were the targets of federal prosecution that provided for far more severe sanctions for weapon use than were provided by Virginia state law. In a careful and thorough analysis involving comparisons of adult homicide arrest rates with juvenile homicide arrest rates within Richmond and comparisons of gun homicide rates between Richmond and other cities with comparable pre-intervention homicide rates, Raphael and Ludwig conclude that the threat of an enhanced sentence had no apparent deterrent effect.

For most crimes, the certainty and severity of punishment increase discontinuously upon reaching the age of majority, when jurisdiction for criminal wrongdoing shifts from the juvenile to the adult court. In an extraordinarily careful analysis of individual-level crime histories from Florida, Lee and McCrary (2009) attempt to identify a discontinuous decline in offending at age 18, the age of majority in Florida. Their point estimate of the discontinuous change is negative as predicted but is minute in magnitude and not even remotely close to achieving statistical significance.[7]

Another analysis of the effect, if any, of moving from the jurisdiction of the juvenile to adult courts by Hjalmarsson (2009) uses the 1997

---

[7] The finding that the young fail to respond to changes in penalties associated with the age of majority is not uniform across studies. An earlier analysis by Levitt (1998) finds a large drop in the offending of young adults when they reach the age of jurisdiction for adult courts. For several reasons, Durlauf and Nagin (2011a, 2011b) judge the null effect finding of Lee and McCrary (2009) more persuasive in terms of understanding deterrence. First, Levitt focuses on differences in age measured at annual frequencies, whereas Lee and McCrary measure age in days or weeks. At annual frequencies, the estimated effect is more likely to reflect both deterrence and incapacitation; hence Levitt's results may be driven by incapacitation effects rather than by deterrence per se. Second, the Lee and McCrary analysis is based on individual-level data and so avoids problems that can arise because of aggregation (Durlauf, Navarro, and Rivers 2008; Durlauf and Nagin 2011a). On their own terms, the individual-level data studied by Lee and McCrary are unusually informative since they also contain information on the exact age of arrestees, which allows for the calculation of very short-run effects of the discontinuity in sentence severity, e.g., effects within 30 days of turning 18.

National Longitudinal Survey of Youth to examine whether young males' perception of incarceration risk changed at the age of criminal majority. Youths were asked, "Suppose you were arrested for stealing a car; what is the percent chance that you would serve time in jail?" She found that subjective probabilities of being sent to jail increased discontinuously on average by 5.2 percentage points when youths reached the age of majority in their state of residence. While youths perceived an increase in incarceration risk, she found no convincing evidence of an effect on their self-reported criminal behavior.

C. Summary

In combination, these six studies demonstrate that debates on the effectiveness of deterrence are poorly conceived. Instead, the discussion should be framed in terms argued by Beccaria and Bentham more than two centuries ago: Does the specific sanction deter or not, and if it does, are the crime reduction benefits sufficient to justify the costs of imposing the sanction? Helland and Tabarrok's (2007) study is an exemplar of this type of analysis. They conclude that California's third-strike provision does indeed have a deterrent effect, a point even conceded by Zimring, Hawkins, and Kamin (2001). However, Helland and Tabarrok also conclude, on the basis of a cost-benefit analysis, that the crime-saving benefits are so much smaller than the increased costs of incarceration that the lengthy prison sentences mandated by the third-strike provision cannot be justified by means of a cost-benefit criterion.

The six exemplar studies suggest several important sources of the heterogeneity of the deterrent effect of imprisonment. One concerns the length of the sentence itself. Figure 3 depicts two alternative forms of the response function relating crime rate to sentence length. Both are downward sloping, which captures the idea that increases in severity deter crime. At the status quo sentence length, S_1, the crime rate, C_1, is the same for both curves. The curves are drawn so that they predict the same crime rate for a zero sanction level. Thus, the absolute deterrent effect of the status quo sanction level is the same for both curves. But because the two curves have different shapes, they also imply different responses to an incremental increase in sentence level to S_2. The linear curve (A) is meant to depict a response function in which there is a material deterrent effect accompanying the increase to S_2, whereas the nonlinear curve (B) is meant to depict a small crime

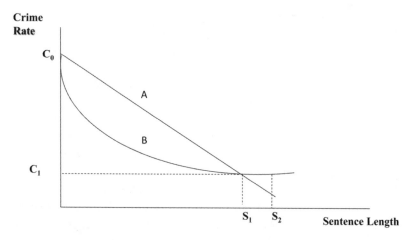

FIG. 3.—Marginal versus absolute deterrent effects

reduction response due to diminishing deterrent returns to increasing sentence length.

My reading of the evidence on the deterrent effect of sentence length is that it implies that the relationship between crime rate and sentence length more closely conforms to curve *B* than to curve *A*. Raphael and Ludwig (2003) find no evidence that gun crime enhancement deters, Hjalmarsson (2009) and Lee and McCrary (2009) find no evidence that the greater penalties that attend moving from the juvenile to the adult justice systems deter, and Helland and Tabarrok (2007) find only a small deterrent effect from California's third strike. As a consequence, the deterrent return to increasing an already long sentence is small, possibly zero. This interpretation forms the basis for my conclusion that mandatory minimum sentencing is unlikely to have a material deterrent effect.

The fine payment and Project HOPE experiments also suggest that curve *B*, not curve *A*, more closely resembles what in medical jargon would be described as the dose-response relationship between crime and sentence length. While neither of these studies is directed at the deterrence of criminal behavior, both suggest that, unlike increments in long sentences, increments in short sentences do have a material deterrent effect on a crime-prone population.

Notwithstanding their strengths, these six exemplar studies do not address several important aspects of the offender response, if any, to the sanction regime. Except for the most trivial offenses, the question at hand is not the deterrent effect of some particular sanction compared to no sanction whatsoever. Instead, it is the deterrent effectiveness of a specified sanction relative to alternative sanction options. In the case of the death penalty, the alternative is a very lengthy prison sentence. For less serious crimes, sanction options to incarceration include fines and various forms of community supervision, or some combination that may also include a period of incarceration. In 2006, for example, 10 percent of felony defendants were diverted to programs such as mandatory drug treatment prior to adjudication. Of those convicted, 29 percent did not receive a jail or prison sentence (Bureau of Justice Statistics 2010) but instead were sentenced to some form of community control, paid a fine, or both.

Theories of deterrence need to be generalized to specify how offenders perceive and respond to the multiplicity of sanction options available for the punishment of most crimes. The theories also need to account for the possibility that offender perceptions of the severity of sanction options may differ. For example, some may view the possibility of life without parole as worse than execution, and still others may view strict community supervision as more onerous than a short period of incarceration (Wood and May 2003). The multiplicity of sanction options and heterogeneity in the response to these options greatly complicate the specification of a deterrence model, but both features are essential to the deterrence phenomenon.

I also note that testing such generalized models of deterrence will require a major expansion of the criminal justice data collection infrastructure at least in the United States. It is currently not possible to measure the availability and frequency of use of sanction alternatives at the state level because the required data are not available. Available data include those from the Bureau of Justice Statistics, which publishes nationwide statistics on sentences for prison admissions and time served for prison releases, based on data collected as part of the National Corrections Reporting Program initiated in the early 1980s. More than 40 states now report annual data on sentences for admissions and time served for releases. Individual-level demographic characteristics are also reported. In principle, these data could be used to measure the administration of the legally authorized dimensions of most state sanction regimes by type of crime. The difficulty is that the data are often extremely incomplete. In some years, some states fail to report any data, and the data that are sent to the bureau are often so incomplete that it is impossible to construct valid state-level measures of the administration of the sanction regime.

V. Police and Crime

The police may prevent crime through many possible mechanisms. Apprehension of active offenders is a necessary first step for their conviction and punishment. If the sanction involves imprisonment, crime may be prevented by the incapacitation of the apprehended offender. The apprehension of active offenders may also deter would-be criminals by increasing their perception of the risk of apprehension. Many police tactics, such as rapid response to calls for service at crime scenes or postcrime investigation, are intended not only to capture the offender but to deter others by projecting a tangible threat of apprehension. Police may, however, deter without actually apprehending criminals: their very presence may deter a motivated offender from carrying out a contemplated criminal act.

Research on the deterrent effect of police has evolved in two distinct literatures. One has focused on the deterrent effect of the level of police numbers or resources, for example, by examining the relationship between police per capita and crime rates. The other has focused on the crime prevention effectiveness of different strategies for deploying police.

A. Studies of Levels of Police Numbers and Resources

Studies of the effect of police numbers and resources come in two forms. One is an analogue of the imprisonment rate and crime rate studies described in the preceding section. These studies are based on panel data sets, usually of US cities over the period circa 1970–2000. They relate crime rates to the resources committed to policing as measured by police per capita or police expenditures per capita. The second form of study is more targeted. These studies analyze the effect on crime from abrupt changes in the level of policing due, for example, to terror alerts.

1. *Panel Studies.* Panel studies include Marvell and Moody (1994), Levitt (1997, 2002), McCrary (2002), and Evans and Owens (2007). With the exception of McCrary's study, these studies consistently find

evidence that larger resource commitments to policing are associated with lower crime rates.[8]

The studies use different statistical strategies for estimating the effect of police resource levels on crime. For example, Marvell and Moody (1996) analyze two panel data sets and apply Granger-causality type statistical models to these data. Levitt (1997, 2002) uses IV-type regression models. In Levitt (1997), election cycles are used as an IV to untangle the cause-effect relationship between crime rates and police manpower. Levitt (2002) uses the number of firefighters and civil service workers as IVs for the same purpose.

The panel studies consistently find evidence that higher levels of police resources are associated with lower crime rates. Durlauf and Nagin (2011a, 2011b) discuss important qualifications to the interpretation and validity of this form of analysis. One is that the police panel studies, like the studies of imprisonment and crime, do not distinguish between incapacitation and deterrent effects. The negative associations between police numbers and crime rates identified in these studies may reflect increased effectiveness in apprehending and incarcerating active offenders rather than in deterring crime. More importantly, an underappreciated limitation of these analyses is the assumption that the effect of police levels on crime rates is the same across place and time. As the discussion of studies of the effects of police deployment strategies on crime makes clear, this assumption is not tenable. Nevertheless, the findings of these studies are consistent with those of studies of abrupt changes in police presence that police numbers do matter.

2. *Abrupt Change Studies.*   Studies of this type, which are sometimes called "interrupted time series" or "regression discontinuity" studies, examine the effects of abrupt changes in police presence. If the change in police presence is attributable to an event unrelated to the crime rate, studies of this type can provide particularly convincing evidence of deterrence. For example, in September 1944, German soldiers occupying Denmark arrested the entire Danish police force. According to an account by Andenaes (1974), crime rates rose immediately but not uniformly. The frequency of street crimes such as robbery, whose

[8] McCrary identified an error in the computation of standard errors in Levitt (1997) that when corrected nullified the finding of a crime prevention effect of police numbers. Levitt (2002) argues that McCrary's findings do not overturn his general claim that increased numbers of police reduce crime rates and presents new evidence to that effect.

control depends heavily on visible police presence, rose sharply. By contrast, crimes such as fraud were less affected. See Sherman and Eck (2002) and Sherman (in this volume) for other examples of crime increases following a collapse of police presence.

The Andenaes anecdote illustrates several important points. It provides a useful reminder of the difference between absolute and marginal deterrence. As shown in figure 3, absolute deterrence refers to the difference in the crime rate between the status quo level of sanction threat, S_1, and a complete (or near) absence of sanction threat, S_0. The Andenaes anecdote is a compelling demonstration that the absolute deterrent effect is large. However, from a policy perspective, the issue is not the absolute deterrent effect posed by police presence. The question is whether, on the margin, crime can be prevented by incremental increases in police numbers or by changes in the way police are deployed. Also, the anecdote is another useful reminder that deterrent effects are heterogeneous: sanction threats (or the absence thereof) do not uniformly affect all types of crime or, more generally, all types of people.

Contemporary tests of the police-crime relationship based on abrupt decreases in police presence investigate the effect on the crime rate of reductions in police presence and productivity as a result of large budget cuts or lawsuits following racial profiling scandals. Such studies have examined the Cincinnati Police Department (Shi 2009), the New Jersey State Police (Heaton 2010), and the Oregon State Police (DeAngelo and Hansen 2008). Each concludes that decreases in police presence and activity substantially increase crime. Shi (2009) studies the fallout from an incident in Cincinnati in which a white police officer shot and killed an unarmed African American suspect. The incident was followed by 3 days of rioting, heavy media attention, the filing of a class action lawsuit, a federal civil rights investigation, and the indictment of the officer in question. These events created an unofficial incentive for officers from the Cincinnati Police Department to curtail their use of arrest for misdemeanor crimes, especially in communities with higher proportional representation of African Americans, out of concern for allegations of racial profiling. Shi finds measurable declines in police productivity in the aftermath of the riot and also documents a substantial increase in criminal activity. The estimated elasticities of crime to policing based on her approach were -0.5 for violent crime and -0.3 for property crime.

The ongoing threat of terrorism has also provided a number of unique opportunities to study the effect of police resource allocation in cities around the world, including the District of Columbia (Klick and Tabarrok 2005), Buenos Aires (Di Tella and Schargrodsky 2004), Stockholm (Poutvaara and Priks 2006), and London (Draca, Machin, and Witt 2008). The Klick and Tabarrok (2005) study examines the effect on crime of the color-coded alert system devised by the US Department of Homeland Security in the aftermath of the September 11, 2001, terrorist attack. Its purpose was to signal federal, state, and local law enforcement agencies to occasions when it might be prudent to divert resources to sensitive locations. Klick and Tabarrok use daily police reports of crime collected by the district's Metropolitan Police Department for the period March 2002 to July 2003, when the terrorism alert level rose from "elevated" (yellow) to "high" (orange) and back down to "elevated" on four occasions. During high alerts, anecdotal evidence suggested that police presence increased by 50 percent. The authors estimate that each 1 percent increase in number of police during the terror alert reduced total crime by 0.3 percent.

To summarize, studies of police presence conducted since the mid-1990s consistently find that putting more police officers on the street—either by hiring new officers or by reallocating existing officers to put them on the street in larger numbers or for longer periods of time—has a substantial deterrent effect on serious crime. There is also consistency with respect to the size of the effect. Most estimates reveal that a 10 percent increase in police presence yields a reduction in total crime of about 3 percent. Yet these police manpower studies speak only to the number and allocation of police officers and not to what police officers actually do on the street beyond making arrests.

B. Police Deployment and Crime

Much research has examined the crime prevention effectiveness of alternative strategies for deploying police resources. This research has mostly been conducted by criminologists and sociologists. Among this group of researchers, the preferred research designs are quasi experiments involving before-and-after studies of the effect of targeted interventions as well as true randomized experiments. The discussion that follows draws heavily on two excellent reviews of this research by Weisburd and Eck (2004) and Braga (2008).

For the most part, deployment strategies affect the certainty of punishment through their effect on the probability of apprehension. One way to increase apprehension risk is to mobilize police in a fashion that increases the probability that an offender is arrested after committing a crime. Strong evidence of a deterrent as opposed to an incapacitation effect resulting from the apprehension of criminals is limited. Studies of the effect of rapid response to calls for service (Kansas City Police Department 1977; Spelman and Brown 1981) do not directly test for deterrence but found no evidence of improved apprehension effectiveness. The reason may be that most calls for service occur well after the crime event, with the result that the perpetrator has fled the scene. Thus, it is doubtful that rapid response materially affects crime. Similarly, apprehension risk is probably not materially affected by improved investigations. Eck concluded that "it is unlikely that improvements in the way investigations are conducted or managed have a dramatic effect on crime or criminal justice" (1992, p. 33). The reason is that most crimes are solved either by the offender being apprehended at the scene or by eyewitness identification of the perpetrator (Greenwood, Chaiken, and Petersilia 1977). Modern forensic methods may ultimately improve the effectiveness of postcrime investigations, but as Braga et al. (2011) note, clearance rates have remained stubbornly stable over the period 1970–2007.

The second source of deterrence from police activities involves averting crime in the first place. In this circumstance, there is no apprehension because there was no offense. In my view, this is the primary source of deterrence from the presence of police. Thus, measures of apprehension risk based only on enforcement actions and crimes that actually occur, such as arrests per reported crime, are not valid measures of the apprehension risk represented by criminal opportunities not acted on because the risk was deemed too high (Cook 1979).

One example of a police deployment strategy for which there is good evidence of effectiveness is "hot spots" policing. The idea of hot spots policing stems from a striking empirical regularity uncovered by Sherman and colleagues. Sherman, Gartin, and Buerger (1989) found that only 3 percent of addresses and intersections ("places," as they were called) in Minneapolis produced 50 percent of all calls to the police. Weisburd and Green (1995) found that 20 percent of all disorder crime and 14 percent of crimes against persons in Jersey City, New Jersey, arose from 56 drug-related crime hot spots. Twenty-five years later in a study of Seattle, Weisburd et al. (2004) reported that between 4 and

5 percent of street segments in the city accounted for 50 percent of crime incidents for each year over a 14-year period. Other, more recent studies finding comparable crime concentrations include Brantingham and Brantingham (1999), Eck, Gersh, and Taylor (2000), and Roncek (2000).

The rationale for concentrating police in crime hot spots is to create a prohibitively high risk of apprehension. The first test of the efficacy of concentrating police resources on crime hot spots was conducted by Sherman and Weisburd (1995). In this randomized experiment, hot spots in the experimental group were subjected to, on average, a doubling of police patrol intensity compared with hot spots in the control group. Declines in total crime calls ranged from 6 to 13 percent. In another randomized experiment, Weisburd and Green (1995) found that hot spots policing was similarly effective in suppressing drug markets.

Braga's (2008) informative review of hot spots policing summarizes the findings from nine experimental or quasi-experimental evaluations. The studies were conducted in five large US cities and one suburb of Australia. All but two found evidence of significant reductions in crime. Further, no evidence was found of material crime displacement to immediately surrounding locations. On the contrary, some studies found evidence of crime reductions, not increases, in the surrounding locations but a "diffusion of crime-control benefits" to nontargeted locales. Note also that the findings from the previously described econometric studies of focused police actions—for example, in response to terror alert level—buttress the conclusion that the strategic targeting of police resources can be very effective in reducing crime.

Another example of a police deployment strategy for which there is credible evidence of effectiveness, albeit less consistent than for hot spots policing, is problem-oriented policing. One of the most visible instances of problem-oriented policing is Boston's Operation Ceasefire (Kennedy et al. 2001). The objective of the collaborative operation was to prevent intergang gun violence using two deterrence-based strategies. The first strategy was to target enforcement against weapons traffickers who were supplying weapons to Boston's violent youth gangs. The second involved a more novel approach. The youth gangs themselves were assembled by the police on multiple occasions in order to send the message that the law enforcement response to any instance of serious violence would be "pulling every lever" legally available to punish gang members collectively. This included a salient severity-related dimension: vigorous prosecution for unrelated, nonviolent crimes such as drug dealing. Thus, the aim of Operation Ceasefire was to deter violent crime by increasing the certainty and severity of punishment, but only in targeted circumstances—specifically, if the gang members committed a violent crime.

Since Operation Ceasefire, the strategy of "pulling every lever" has been the centerpiece of field interventions in many large and small US cities including Richmond, Virginia; Chicago; Stockton, California; High Point, North Carolina; and Pittsburgh. See Kennedy (2009), one of the architects of the pulling every lever strategy, for an extended description of these interventions and the philosophy behind them. Independent evaluations have also been conducted of many of these interventions.[9] As part of the Campbell Collaboration review process, Braga and Weisburd (2012) identified 10 studies of pulling levers focused policing strategies that met their criteria of rigor and relevance to be included in the review. Nine of these studies reported statistically significant reductions in crime. They concluded that "pulling levers focused deterrence strategies are associated with an overall statistically-significant, medium-sized crime reduction effect" (p. 7). However, they caution that focused deterrence has yet to be tested with a randomized control trial. Their caution is also shared by others. In Cook's (2012) commentary on the High Point focused deterrence intervention, he observes that initial conclusions of eye-catchingly large effects have been replaced with far more modest assessments of effect sizes and cautions about the generalizability of the results. Reuter and Pollack (2012) wonder whether a successful intervention in a small urban area such as High Point can be replicated in a large city such as Chicago. Ferrier and Ludwig (2011) point out the difficulty in understanding the mechanism that underlies a seemingly successful intervention that pulls many levers. Despite concerns, these interventions illustrate the potential for combining elements of both certainty and severity enhancements to generate a targeted deterrent effect. Additional evaluations of the efficacy of these multipronged strategies should be a high priority, with the proviso that any designs implemented be amenable to rigorous evaluation as emphasized by commentators. For a useful

---

[9] For Boston, see Cook and Ludwig (2006); for Richmond, see Raphael and Ludwig (2003); for Chicago, see Papachristos, Meares, and Fagan (2007); for Pittsburgh, see Wilson and Chermak (2011); and for High Point, see Corsaro et al. (2012).

discussion of the importance of understanding mechanisms, see Ludwig, Kling, and Mullainathan (2011). The theory behind focused deterrence interventions includes attention to, among other things, deterrence, police legitimacy, informal social control, police/community relations, the provision of social services, and addressing situational factors. Existing evaluations do not address either the contribution (if any) of individual elements or their likely interplay.

C. Summary

The evidence is clear that large changes in police presence do affect crime rates. The change in presence may be the result of an unplanned event, such as a terror alert that triggers a large increase in police officers in public spaces, or it may be a strategic response to a known crime problem, such as in hot spots policing deployments. In either case, crime rates are reduced in places where police presence has been materially increased. While far from definitive, there is no evidence of displacement of crime to places contiguous to the heightened police presence, at least in the short run. Indeed, there is some evidence of crime reductions in the areas immediately surrounding the heightened presence. By contrast, there is no evidence that the rapidity of the response to crime or the thoroughness of the postcrime investigation has a material influence on crime rates. Combined, these two sets of findings suggest that how police are deployed is as important as the number of police deployed in their influence on crime rates.

Notwithstanding these important findings, some additional issues about police presence remain unresolved. The finding from the hot spots policing evaluations that crime is not displaced to adjacent places may not hold up in the long run. The seeming diffusion of crime control benefits may evaporate as offenders become aware that the heightened patrol activity is not present in adjacent places. More fundamentally, the hot spot itself may be displaced to some new location, for example, to a bar that had not previously been a crime hot spot. A longer-term perspective on the effectiveness of hot spots policing is required.

While the evaluations of hot spots policing provide important evidence that police presence can be a deterrent, overall crime control policy cannot be built around such a narrowly formulated tactic. Evaluations of problem-oriented policing suggest police effectiveness in a wider set of circumstances than intensive patrol of high crime micro-places. However, these evaluations do not reveal the mechanism by which prevention is achieved.

The introduction distinguished two distinct crime prevention functions of the police: their role as apprehension agents following the commission of a crime and their role as sentinels. In their sentinel role the police are acting, in the parlance of Cohen and Felson (1979), as "capable guardians." Capable guardians are persons whose presence discourages a motivated offender from victimizing a criminal opportunity. Capable guardians include persons with no official crime control authority who nonetheless are personally willing to intervene or to summon those with the authority to intervene. The police themselves also serve as capable guardians in their conventional patrol and monitoring functions.

For many reasons the apprehension agent role is the most scrutinized and recognized crime control function of the police. The apprehension agent function has been and continues to be glamorized by television in long-running programs such as *Dragnet* in the 1950s and 1960s, *Hawaii Five-0* in the 1970s, *Hill Street Blues* in the 1980s, *Homicide Life on the Streets* in the 1990s, and *CSI* and *Law and Order* in the present. The apprehension role is also salient because it involves the police response to real victims of sometimes horrendous crimes and the ensuing efforts to bring the perpetrators to justice. From a technocratic perspective, police effectiveness in this role can be measured with statistics like the clearance rate. From a crime control perspective, the apprehension agent function protects public safety by capturing and incapacitating sometimes dangerous and repetitive offenders. However, as yet there is no evidence that the apprehension agent role results in a material deterrent effect. By contrast, the evidence on police presence suggests that in their sentinel role police can have a very large deterrent effect. While the differential deterrent effect of the police in their apprehension and sentinel roles has not been demonstrated, there is sufficient evidence to characterize it as a hypothesis with sufficient empirical support to make it credible.

What then is the explanation for the differential deterrent effectiveness of the sentinel/guardian and apprehension roles of the police? The model of the decision to victimize a criminal opportunity laid out in the introduction, I believe, provides useful perspective on the answer. The model distinguishes two key probabilities: the probability that the opportunity can be successfully completed, P_s, and the probability of apprehension conditional on the victimization of the target, P_a. In this model, activities that enhance police visibility, such as concentration of police at crime hot spots, affect P_s, whereas actions such as rapid response to calls for service or improved investigation methods affect P_a. The sentinel role of police is distinct from the apprehension role because the latter comes into play only when deterrence has failed and a would-be offender becomes an actual offender. Thus, at one moment police can function as sentinels and in the next as apprehension agents.

The depiction of the decision to victimize a criminal opportunity in figure 1 provides an explanation for the greater deterrent effectiveness of the police in their sentinel role than in their apprehension role. The police in their sentinel role influence P_s and thereby the probability of all four outcome branches. In particular, improved guardianship reduces the probability that the target can be successfully victimized and increases the probability of the three outcomes that represent failure from the offender's perspective. In contrast, improved effectiveness in the apprehension agent role comes into play only after a crime is committed and can affect only the three branches of the tree related to failure. Thus, innovations that make police more effective sentinels will tend to be more influential in the decision process characterized by this model than innovations in apprehension effectiveness.

The model is also useful in clarifying the basis for the effectiveness of situational crime prevention (Clarke 1995), many forms of which can be construed as reducing P_s. Just as police in their sentinel role reduce the attractiveness of a criminal opportunity, situational crime prevention works by affecting all four branches of the tree.

VI. Perceptual Deterrence and Sanction Risk Perceptions Studies

Analyses of perceptual deterrence examine the association between perceptions of sanction risk, whatever their source, and self-reported illegal behavior or intent to engage in illegal behavior. Analyses of sanction risk perceptions examine the relationship of an individual's perceptions with experience (e.g., being arrested as well as factors external to the individual such as statutorily defined penalties). Some studies address both topics, but most emphasize one or the other.

A. Perceptual Deterrence

The perceptual deterrence literature was spawned by a cadre of researchers (Meier and Johnson 1977; Minor 1977; Tittle 1977, 1980; Grasmick and Bryjak 1980) interested in probing the perceptual underpinnings of the deterrence process.

Perceptual deterrence studies have been based on three types of data: cross-sectional survey studies, panel survey studies, and scenario-based studies. In cross-sectional survey studies, individuals are questioned about their perceptions of the certainty and severity of sanctions and about either their prior offending behavior or their future intentions to offend. For example, Grasmick and Bryjak (1980) queried a sample of city residents about their perceptions of the risk of arrest for offenses such as a petty theft, drunk driving, and tax cheating. They also asked respondents whether they thought they would commit any of these acts in the future. In panel survey studies the sample is repeatedly surveyed on risk perceptions and criminal behavior. For example, Paternoster et al. (1982) followed a sample of students through their 3 years in high school and surveyed them on the frequency with which they engaged in various delinquent acts and their perceptions of the risks and consequences of being caught. In scenario-based studies, individuals are questioned about their perception of the risks of committing a crime that is described to them in detail. They are also asked about their own behavior should they find themselves in that situation. Bachman, Paternoster, and Ward (1992), for instance, constructed a scenario describing the circumstances of a date rape. They then surveyed a sample of college males about their perceptions of the risk of the scenario male being arrested for sexual assault and what they themselves would do in the same circumstance.

Perceptional deterrence research has been faulted with some justification on a number of grounds. One is that the sampled populations are typically high school or college students who do not, by and large, engage in serious crime and delinquency. Other concerns are related to the veracity of the data collected. How well can respondents actually calibrate sanction risks? Do the ways in which questions about perceptions of morality and sanction cost are structured prime responses about actual or projected offending? Despite these questions, in my judgment this class of studies has provided enduring contributions to our understanding of deterrence processes.

One contribution is that, with the exception of the early panel studies, perception studies consistently find that actual or projected offending is negatively related to perceptions of sanction certainty. Findings of a deterrence-like relationship of self-reported offending with perceptions of sanction severity are less consistent. When combined, these two findings provide still further support for the "certainty" principal, but with a proviso that certainty results in a negative but not necessarily draconian consequence. Grasmick and Bryjak (1980) show that when respondents' assessments of the personal costs of the sanction are incorporated into the analysis, perceptions of severity are negatively associated with self-reported behavior.

A second contribution of the perceptual deterrence literature, which may also be its most important, does not involve the evidence it has amassed on deterrence effects per se. Rather it has focused its attention on the links between formal and informal sources of social control. Recognition of this connection predates the perceptual deterrence literature. Zimring and Hawkins (1973) observe that "official *actions* can set off societal *reactions* that may provide potential offenders with more reason to avoid conviction than the officially imposed unpleasantness of punishment" (p. 174; emphasis in original). See also Andenaes (1974), Gibbs (1975), Blumstein and Nagin (1976), and Williams and Hawkins (1986) for this same argument. Perceptual deterrence research has consistently found that individuals who report higher stakes in conventionality are more deterred by perceived risk of public exposure for lawbreaking.

A salient finding in this regard concerns my own research on tax evasion. Enforcement actions by tax authorities are private matters. Criminal prosecutions, however, are the exception to this rule. They necessarily involve public exposure. Thus, from the taxpayer's perspective, civil enforcement actions jeopardize money but not reputation whereas criminal prosecution jeopardizes both. In Klepper and Nagin (1989a, 1989b), we found that if respondents perceived no risk of criminal prosecution, a majority of respondents reported a material probability of taking advantage of noncompliance opportunities. However, the perception of a nonzero risk of criminal prosecution was sufficient to deter most of the middle-class respondents to the survey. Stated differently, if the tax evasion gamble also involved putting reputation and community standing at risk, the middle-class respondents to the survey were less likely to consider taking the gamble.

While my tax evasion research does not pin down the specific sources of these costs, other research on the effects of a criminal record on access to legal labor markets suggests a real basis for the fear of stigmatization (Freeman 1991; Bushway 1996). Freeman estimates that a record of incarceration depresses probability of work by 15–30 percent, Waldfogel (1994) estimates that conviction for fraud reduces income by as much as 40 percent, and Bushway (1996) concludes that even an arrest for a minor offense impairs access to legal labor markets, at least in the short run.

The findings from the perceptual deterrence studies directly relate to two of the main themes of this essay. The first concerns the source of the "certainty" effect. In laying out the implications of the model of the decision to victimize a target, it was pointed out that the cost of apprehension appeared in two of the terms on the right-hand side of equation (2). This side of the equation measures the potential cost of offending: the term measuring the cost of apprehension without conviction and the term measuring the cost of apprehension with conviction. Formal and informal sanction costs appeared only in the second of these terms. Stated differently, apprehension cost is incurred regardless of whether a conviction ensues, whereas sanction costs can be incurred only if apprehension is followed by conviction. This structure formalizes the argument of Williams and Hawkins (1986) that what they call "fear of arrest" serves as a greater deterrent than formal sanction cost. It is also consistent with the conclusion of my own research with coauthors Paternoster (Nagin and Paternoster 1993, 1994) and Pogarsky (Nagin and Pogarsky 2001, 2003) that individuals with the greatest stakes in conformity were the most deterred by informal sanction costs.

The fourth branch of figure 3 is the total cost of formal and informal sanctions. The perceptions research combined with the criminal record research suggests that, for people without a criminal record, informal sanction cost makes a large contribution to this total. That contribution may be substantially reduced once an individual has had contact with the criminal justice system and obtains a criminal record. This observation relates back to a point I emphasized in Nagin (1998). If fear of stigma is a key component of the deterrence mechanism, punishment must be a relatively rare event. Just as the stigma of Hester Prynne's scarlet "A" depended on adultery being uncommon in Puritan America, a criminal record cannot be socially and economically isolating if it is commonplace. For that reason, policies that work well in the short term may erode their effectiveness over the long run if they increase the proportion of the population who are stigmatized.

This observation is also germane to the recommendation that future empirical research and theorizing should take account of whether and how the experience of punishment (which in my view is inappropriately referred to as specific deterrence) affects the response to the threat of punishment, or general deterrence. The experience of punishment may affect general deterrence in two distinct ways. First, it may affect perceptions of sanction risks. Second, it may affect the basic proclivity for offending. Proclivity could be reduced by effective rehabilitation programs or an individual's conclusion that prison is not an experience to be repeated. However, proclivity could also be increased by stigmatization, erosion of human capital during a spell of incarceration, or the social influence of close contact with a mostly crime-prone population. Nagin, Cullen, and Jonson (2009) provide a detailed discussion of this issue.

B. Sanction Risk Perceptions Studies

Studies of sanction risk perception come in three primary forms: surveys of the general public's knowledge of the sanction regime, studies of the effect of apprehension (or nonapprehension) on risk perceptions and subsequent behavior, and scenario-based studies in which respondents are questioned about their perceptions of the risk of apprehension and punishment in specific circumstances.[10]

1. *General Population Surveys.* Apel (2013) identifies only two surveys of the general public's knowledge of the statutory penalties for the types of crime that compose the FBI's crime index (e.g., murder, robbery). Both are dated. A survey of Tucson, Arizona, residents conducted in the 1970s suggests generally good knowledge of the types of sanctions (e.g., fine, prison) available for the punishment of the 14 types of crime surveyed (Williams, Gibbs, and Erickson 1980). Erickson and Gibbs (1979) also find that respondents were reasonably well calibrated on the relative severity of punishments across types of crime (e.g., punishment for robbery is generally more severe than for larceny). However, a 1960s study commissioned by the California Assembly Committee on Criminal Procedure (1968) found that the general

[10] For an exhaustive and thoughtful review, on which this discussion draws heavily, see Apel (2013).

public's knowledge of the statutorily prescribed level of punishment was poor. Only about a quarter of the sample correctly identified the maximum prison sentence available for the punishment of the various crimes included in the survey. However, 62 percent of incarcerated adults correctly identified the maximum. I return to the large difference in knowledge between the incarcerated and not-incarcerated samples below.

There have also been general population surveys of sanction perceptions for two types of crimes—marijuana use and drunk driving—that are far more prevalent in the general population than crimes such as robbery or burglary. The surveys suggest far better, although hardly perfect, knowledge of the legally available sanctions for these two offenses. MacCoun et al. (2009) describe a study by Johnston Lloyd, O'Malley, and Bachman (1981) of student knowledge of punishment for marijuana possession. In states that decriminalized possession between 1976 and 1980, the percentage reporting a possible jail sentence declined from 58 percent to 18 percent. Corresponding changes for students living in states that did not decriminalize were not as large. This finding suggests that for populations in which there is greater need-to-know of sanction risks, knowledge of the risks is better but still crude. For example, MacCoun et al. (2009) also report that knowledge of the maximum penalties for marijuana use was not good. Surveys of knowledge among adults of drunk-driving penalties by Ross (1973) and Grube and Kearney (1983) also suggest greater awareness of the drunk-driving sanctions and available enforcement tools (e.g., Breathalyzers) than corresponding knowledge for street-type crimes.

The Tucson-based survey and more recent surveys by Kleck and colleagues (Kleck et al. 2005; Kleck and Barnes, forthcoming) attempt to assess the accuracy of sanction risk perceptions. Kleck et al. (2005), for example, survey adults residing in 54 large urban counties. For crimes such as homicide and robbery, they correlate respondent estimates of quantities such as arrests per crime and convictions per crime with ratios based on the actual data. They find that the correlation is close to zero.

The results of the surveys by Kleck and colleagues are not surprising on several counts. First, for the reasons elaborated long ago by Beccaria and Bentham and most recently by Wikström et al. (2012) and Apel (2013), most of the general public has no intention of committing the types of crime surveyed in these studies.[11] Thus, there is no reason for them to be aware of the sanction regime for these types of crime. Consequently, their ignorance of the sanction regime is not informative about whether people who have a potential need-to-know of the sanction regime obtain that knowledge, however crudely, and take it into account in the decision whether or not to offend. Second, the ratios calculated by Kleck and colleagues pertain only to criminal opportunities that have actually been acted on. As first pointed out by Cook (1979), the ratio of arrest per crime is not a valid measure of the risk of apprehension for criminal opportunities that are not acted on. Third, statistics such as arrests per crime are calculated at the county or city level and may be very poor indicators of risk at the specific locations where would-be offenders are plying their trade (Apel 2013).

2. *Studies of the Effect of Experience on Perceptions.* Salient findings of the early panel perceptual deterrence studies include considerable instability in sanction risk perceptions and that nonoffenders and novice offenders have higher sanction risk perceptions than experienced offenders. Paternoster and colleagues (Paternoster et al. 1982; Paternoster 1983) called this an experiential effect whereby delinquent youths learned that sanction risks were lower than initially anticipated.

An important study by Horney and Marshall (1992) of serious offenders finds that subjects who had higher arrest ratios, that is, self-reported arrests to self-reported crime, reported higher risk perception. Since that time a large number of studies have used longitudinal data to analyze whether the effect of success or failure in avoiding apprehension influences sanction risk perceptions. The analytical strategy involves relating experience with success or failure in prior survey waves with perceptions of apprehension risk in later survey waves. Studies of this type by criminologists were prompted by an influential article by Stafford and Warr (1993), who distinguished between two sources of information on sanction risk: one's own experience and the experience of peers. A parallel literature has also appeared in economics based on the concept of "Bayesian updating."

The Bayesian updating model and the arguments of Stafford and Warr are complementary. Bayesian updating formalizes their arguments. The Bayesian updating model is designed to describe the pro-

---

[11] In the context of the decision model laid out in Sec. I, these are individuals for whom the net reward of committing a crime is negative even without consideration of sanction costs.

cess by which people update their perceptions of a phenomenon of interest on the basis of new information about that phenomenon. In this case, individuals would update their perceptions of sanction risk with new information regarding success or failure of themselves or their peers in avoiding apprehension. The predictions of the model depend on the specifics of its mathematical specification, but models of this type make predictions about the updating process that are intuitively sensible. The models predict that people generally do not entirely abandon prior beliefs as a result of new information. Most commonly, they only incrementally adjust them.[12]

In the case of perception of apprehension risk, this implies that the experience of apprehension will result in an incremental upward shift in risk perception, and experience of what Stafford and Warr (1993) call "apprehension avoidance" will result in an incremental reduction in risk. A second prediction of the Bayesian updating model is that the magnitude of the change will depend on the depth of prior knowledge. Individuals with more prior knowledge will tend to adjust less to new information than individuals with less prior knowledge. In the context of sanction risk perceptions, this implies that individuals with more experience with offending will make smaller adjustments in their risk perceptions based on current experience with apprehension than will individuals with less experience. Both of these predictions are supported by studies of risk perception updating.

Concerning the first prediction, numerous studies find that increases (or decreases) in perceived apprehension risk are associated with failure (success) in avoiding apprehension (Bridges and Stone 1986; Piliavin et al. 1986; Paternoster and Piquero 1995; Pogarsky, Piquero, and Paternoster 2004; Pogarsky, Kim, and Paternoster 2005; Matsueda, Kreager, and Huizinga 2006; Lochner 2007; Hjalmarsson 2008). There are, however, exceptions to this finding. Apospori and Alpert (1993) and Pogarsky and Piquero (2003) report evidence that is the reverse of this prediction. Pogarsky and Piquero attribute this to a variant of what is called the "gambler's fallacy" whereby offenders believe that bad luck is not followed by bad luck. This is an interesting possibility, but the evidence is overwhelmingly consistent with the Bayesian updating model.

---

[12] Prior history may be ignored if a regime change (e.g., the occupying German army arresting the Danish police force) makes it irrelevant.

Evidence consistent with the second prediction is reported in Pogarsky, Piquero, and Paternoster (2004), Matsueda, Kreager, and Huizinga (2006), and Anwar and Loughran (2011). Anwar and Loughran conducted a particularly thorough test of this prediction. They analyzed a sample composed of about 1,300 adjudicated/convicted youths from Arizona and Pennsylvania enrolled in the Pathways to Desistance study who were interviewed eight times in 5 years (Mulvey 2011). Being arrested significantly increased subjective probabilities (prediction 1), but the magnitude of the change was less for more experienced offenders (prediction 2). Specifically, they showed that experienced offenders placed relatively more weight on their prior subjective probabilities and therefore updated less in response to new arrests. Inexperienced offenders, by contrast, updated more by placing more weight on their current arrest ratios and less weight on their prior subjective probabilities. It is also noteworthy that they concluded that the effect of arrest on subjective probabilities was specific within classes of criminal behaviors: youths arrested for aggressive crimes did not update their subjective probabilities concerning income-generating crimes. This finding implies that there are not spillover effects across classes of crime.

3. *Studies of Situational Effects on Risk Perceptions.* This grouping of studies examines the effect of situational factors on risk perceptions. Particularly important in this regard are situational factors that can be manipulated by policy, such as official sanctions and police presence.

As already noted, knowledge of official sanctions seems to be strongly affected by the need-to-know principle. Knowledge is better, but hardly perfect, among populations with the greatest involvement in the illegal activity. On the basis of the California assembly study, for example, knowledge of maximum penalties for various FBI index-type crimes was far better for incarcerated sample members than for not-incarcerated sample members.

Other interesting evidence of awareness of official sanctions is the previously discussed study by Hjalmarsson (2009) of the effect of reaching the age of majority on perceptions of the risk of incarceration for auto theft. She found that male respondents in the 1997 National Longitudinal Survey of Youth increased that risk by 5.2 percentage points upon reaching their age of majority. The increase, however, had no statistically significant effect on behavior.

Evidence on how police presence affects perceptions of apprehension risk is scant. In my own work with Paternoster, we constructed scenarios and examined how respondent perceptions of sanction risks were affected by scenario conditions (Nagin and Paternoster 1993). We found that respondent perceptions of sanction cost in a drunk-driving scenario were higher in the scenario condition involving a police crackdown on drunk driving versus a scenario condition described as involving state police cutbacks. In addition, perceptions of sanction cost were lower if surveillance could be avoided by driving on back roads. In scenarios concerning peer provocation, Wikström et al. (2012) found that adolescents reported a lower likelihood of violent response in scenario conditions in which adult monitors were present. Evidence from ethnographic studies suggests that offenders are very conscious of police presence when selecting targets. Wright and Decker (1994) report that burglars avoid neighborhoods with a heavy police presence and that robbers prefer to target individuals unlikely to report the crime to the police, such as drug dealers.

C. Summary

Perceptual deterrence research has established that self-reported offending or intention to do so is linked to sanction risk perceptions. The outstanding question is whether those perceptions are grounded in reality. If they are not, behavior is beyond the reach of public policy. The evidence on the sources of sanction risk perceptions suggests that risk perceptions are affected by an individual's own experience with success or failure at averting apprehension. The link between perception and the legally authorized sanctions is less compelling but does indicate that there is at least a rough awareness among individuals in a need-to-know scenario. The other key component of the sanction regime is the intensity of application of the legally authorized sanctions. Research on this topic is based on general population studies of the correlations of perceptions of quantities of the ratio of arrest to crimes with estimates of these ratios calculated from official statistics. For reasons discussed above, in my judgment these studies are not informative about whether perceptions of intensity among the population with need-to-know sanction risks are affected by the actual intensity of application of legally authorized sanctions.

Pogarsky (2007) offers a useful taxonomy of responsiveness to legal threats for considering the implications of these summary observations. The taxonomy distinguishes three groups: acute conformists, deterrables, and incorrigibles. In the context of the decision model laid out in Section I, conformists are individuals for whom reward minus commission cost is negative. For reasons I have already discussed, they have no need to gain knowledge of sanction risks because there is no profit in crime even without potential sanction costs. Deterrables are individuals for whom reward minus commission cost is positive and who are attentive to sanction threats. For such individuals the issue is whether the net benefit of successful commission exceeds the potential costs attending failure. The incorrigible group is also composed of individuals for whom crime is profitable but who for whatever reason are not attentive to sanction threats. The relative sizes of the incorrigible and deterrable groups and the specific form of the sanction regime will determine the effectiveness of criminal justice public policy in preventing crime via deterrence and thereby avoiding the sanction costs of incapacitation.

Future research on sanction risk perceptions needs to target Pogarsky's deterrables and incorrigibles to gain better knowledge of their awareness of the two key elements of the sanction regime: the legally authorized sanctions and the intensity of their application. For the types of crime in the FBI index this will require abandoning surveys of the general population and instead sampling populations with a large representation of deterrables and incorrigibles. An example of such a survey is the Pathways to Desistance project used in the Anwar and Loughran (2011) analysis, which sampled juveniles adjudicated for felony offenses in Philadelphia and Phoenix.

Surveys targeting deterrables and incorrigibles should also include batteries of questions designed to learn how the actions of the police and other guardians affect perceptions of the probability of success, which, for the reasons described in Section V, is likely to be particularly decisive in the deterrence process.

VII. Conclusions

Over the past four decades, much has been learned about the foundations of deterrence that were laid out more than two centuries ago by Cesare Beccaria and Jeremy Bentham. We now know that deterrence is ubiquitous but that the effects are heterogeneous, ranging in size from seemingly null to very large. There is little evidence that increasing already long prison sentences has a material deterrence effect. Evidence on the deterrent effect of the certainty of punishment is more consistent, but the source of the effect is less clear. In this essay I have argued that the certainty effect stems primarily from police functioning in their official guardian role rather than in their apprehension agent role.

These conclusions have important policy implications that are developed in detail in Durlauf and Nagin (2011*b*). They suggest that lengthy prison sentences cannot be justified on deterrent grounds, but rather must be justified either on crime prevention through incapacitation or on retributive grounds. The crime prevention efficiency of incapacitating aged criminals is dubious, and thus the case for lengthy prison sentences must rest on retributive considerations. The conclusions also suggest that crime control effectiveness would be improved by shifting resources from corrections to policing methods that enhance the effectiveness of police in their official guardian role.

While much progress has been made in understanding sources of deterrence and the circumstances in which deterrence is and is not effective, much remains to be learned. Theory needs to be generalized to combine the response to the threat of punishments, known as general deterrence in criminology, and the response to the experience of punishment, which I have argued is inappropriately labeled specific deterrence. A second theoretical and empirical gap concerns the concept of a sanction regime and its two dimensions: the legal authority for different types of sanctions and the way in which authority is administered. These two dimensions combine to determine the certainty, severity, and celerity of sanction options available for punishment of a specific type of crime. Theories of deterrence, however, specify sanction threats in the singular, not in the plural. Theories of deterrence that conceive of sanctions in the singular do not provide the conceptual basis for considering the differential deterrent effect of different types of sanction options. The empirical companion to this theoretical expansion involves assembling the data required to measure sanction regimes.

A third theoretical and empirical gap involves sanction risk perceptions. Deterrence is the behavioral response to the perception of sanction threats. Establishing the link between risk perceptions and actual sanction regimes is imperative because policy cannot directly manipulate perceptions. Unless perceptions adjust, however crudely, to changes in the sanction regime, the desired deterrent effect will not be achieved. More research on the sources of sanction risk perceptions in crime-prone populations is likely to pay large dividends for theory and policy.

The fourth major gap in theory and empirical knowledge involves a thorough testing of my contention that the guardian role, not the apprehension role, of the police is the most important source of their effectiveness in crime prevention. This theory also needs to be expanded to account for how the police and other guardians affect the distribution of criminal opportunities.

REFERENCES

Andenaes, Johannes. 1974. *Punishment and Deterrence*. Ann Arbor: University of Michigan Press.
Anwar, Shamena, and Thomas A. Loughran. 2011. "Testing a Bayesian Learning Theory of Deterrence among Serious Juvenile Offenders." *Criminology* 49:667–98.
Apel, Robert. 2013. "Sanctions, Perceptions, and Crime: Implications for Criminal Deterrence." *Journal of Quantitative Criminology* 29(1):87–101.
Apel, Robert, and Daniel S. Nagin. 2009. "Deterrence." In *Crime*, edited by James Q. Wilson and Joan Petersilia. Oxford: Oxford University Press.
Apospori, Eleni, and Geoffrey Alpert. 1993. "Research Note: The Role of Differential Experience with the Criminal Justice System in Changes in Perceptions of Severity of Legal Sanctions over Time." *Journal of Research in Crime and Delinquency* 39:184–94.
Assembly Committee on Criminal Procedure. 1968. *Deterrent Effects of Criminal Sanctions*. Sacramento: Assembly of the State of California.
Bachman, Ronet, Raymond Paternoster, and Sally Ward. 1992. "The Rationality of Sexual Offending: Testing a Deterrence/Rational Choice Conception of Sexual Assault." *Law and Society Review* 26(2):343–72.
Beccaria, Cesare. 1986. *On Crimes and Punishments*. Translated by Henry Paolucci. New York: Macmillan. (Originally published 1764.)
Becker, Gary S. 1968. "Crime and Punishment: An Economic Approach." *Journal of Political Economy* 76(2):169–217.
Bentham, Jeremy. 1988. *An Introduction to the Principles of Morals and Legislation*. Amherst, NY: Prometheus Books. (Originally published 1789.)
Blake, L., and R. T. Coupe. 2001. "The Impact of Single and Two-Officer Patrols on Catching Burglars in the Act." *British Journal of Criminology* 41:381–96.
Blumstein, Alfred, and Allen J. Beck. 1999. "Population Growth in the U.S. Prisons, 1980–1996." In *Prisons*, edited by Michael Tonry and Joan Petersilia. Vol. 26 of *Crime and Justice: A Review of Research*, edited by Michael Tonry. Chicago: University of Chicago Press.

———. 2005. "Reentry as a Transient State between Liberty and Recommitment." In *Prisoner Reentry and Crime in America*, edited by Jeremy Travis and Christy Visher. Cambridge: Cambridge University Press.

Blumstein, Alfred, Jacqueline Cohen, and Daniel Nagin, eds. 1978. *Deterrence and Incapacitation: Estimating the Effects of Criminal Sanctions on Crime Rates.* Washington, DC: National Academies Press.

Blumstein, Alfred, and Daniel Nagin. 1976. "The Deterrent Effect of Legal Sanctions on Draft Evasion." *Stanford Law Review* 29(2):241–75.

Braga, Anthony A. 2008. *Police Enforcement Strategies to Prevent Crime in Hot Spot Areas.* Edited by Office of Community Oriented Policing. Washington, DC: US Department of Justice.

Braga, Anthony A., Edward A. Flynn, George L. Kelling, and Christine M. Cole. 2011. "Moving the Work of Criminal Investigators towards Crime Control." *New Perspectives in Policing.* Washington, DC: US Department of Justice, National Institute of Justice.

Braga, Anthonly A., and David L. Weisburd. 2012. "The Effects of 'Pulling Levers' Focussed Deterrence Strategies on Crime." Campbell Systematic Reviews. http://campbellcollaboration.org/lib/project/96/.

Braithwaite, John. 1989. *Crime, Shame, and Reintegration.* Cambridge: Cambridge University Press.

Brantingham, Patricia L., and Paul J. Brantingham. 1999. "Theoretical Model of Crime Hot Spot Generation." *Studies on Crime and Crime Prevention* 8:7–26.

Bridges, George S., and James A. Stone. 1986. "Effects of Criminal Punishment on Perceived Threat of Punishment: Toward an Understanding of Specific Deterrence." *Journal of Research in Crime and Delinquency* 23:207–39.

Bureau of Justice Statistics. 1999. *Prisoners in 1998.* Edited by Allen J. Beck and Christopher J. Mumola. Washington, DC: Bureau of Justice Statistics.

———. 2010. *Felony Defendants in Large Urban Counties, 2006.* Edited by Thomas H. Cohen and Tracey Kyckelhahn. Washington, DC: Bureau of Justice Statistics.

———. 2011. *Prisoners in 2010 (Revised).* Edited by Paul Guerino, Paige M. Harrison, and William J. Sabol. Washington, DC: Bureau of Justice Statistics.

———. 2012. *Correctional Populations in the United States, 2011.* Edited by Lauren E. Glaze and Erika Parks. Washington, DC: Bureau of Justice Statistics.

Bushway, Shawn. 1996. "The Impact of a Criminal History Record on Access to Legitimate Employment." PhD dissertation, Carnegie Mellon University.

Canela-Cacho, Jose A., Alfred Blumstein, and Jacqueline Cohen. 1997. "Relationship between the Offending Frequency of Imprisoned and Free Offenders." *Criminology* 35(1):133–76.

Chalfin, Aaron, Amelia M. Haviland, and Steven Raphael. 2013. "What Do Panel Studies Tell Us about a Deterrent Effect of Capital Punishment? A Critique of the Literature." *Journal of Quantitative Criminology* 29(1):5–43.

Charles, Kerwin K., and Steven N. Durlauf. 2013. "Pitfalls in the Use of Time

Series Methods to Study Deterrence and Capital Punishment." *Journal of Quantitative Criminology* 29(1):45–66.

Clarke, Ronald V. 1995. "Situational Crime Prevention." In *Building a Safer Society: Strategic Approaches to Crime Prevention*, edited by Michael Tonry and David P. Farrington. Vol. 19 of *Crime and Justice: A Review of Research*, edited by Michael Tonry. Chicago: University of Chicago Press.

Cohen, Lawrence E., and Marcus Felson. 1979. "Social Change and Crime Rate Trends: A Routine Activity Approach." *American Sociological Review* 44(4):588–608.

Cook, Philip J. 1979. "The Clearance Rate as a Measure of Criminal Justice System Effectiveness." *Journal of Public Economics* 11:135–42.

———. 2009. "Potential Savings from Abolition of the Death Penalty in North Carolina." *American Law and Economics Review* 11(2):498–529.

———. 2012. "The Impact of Drug Market Pulling Levers Policing on Neighborhood Violence: An Evaluation of the High Point Drug Market Intervention." *Criminology and Public Policy* 11(2):161–64.

Cook, Philip J., and Jens Ludwig. 2006. "Aiming for Evidence-Based Gun Policy." *Journal of Policy Analysis and Management* 48:691–735.

Cornish, Derek B., and Ronald V. Clarke. 1986. *The Reasoning Criminal: Rational Choice Perspectives on Offending*. Secausus, NJ: Springer-Verlag.

Corsaro, N., E. D. Hunt, N. K. Hipple, and E. F. McGarrell. 2012. "The Impact of Drug Market Pulling Levers Policing on Neighborhood Violence." *Criminology and Public Policy* 11:167–99.

DeAngelo, Greg, and Benjamin Hansen. 2008. "Life and Death in the Fast Lane: Police Enforcement and Roadway Safety." Unpublished manuscript. University of California, Santa Barbara, Department of Economics.

Di Tella, Rafael, and Ernesto Schargrodsky. 2004. "Do Police Reduce Crime? Estimates Using the Allocation of Police Forces after a Terrorist Attack." *American Economic Review* 94:115–33.

Donohue, John J. 2009. "Assessing the Relative Benefits of Incarceration: The Overall Change over the Previous Decades and the Benefits on the Margin." In *Do Prisons Make Us Safer? The Benefits and Costs of the Prison Boom*, edited by Steven Raphael and Michael A. Stoll. New York: Sage.

Donohue, John J., and Justin Wolfers. 2005. "Uses and Abuses of Empirical Evidence in the Death Penalty Debate." *Stanford Law Review* 58:791–846.

———. 2009. "Estimating the Impact of the Death Penalty on Murder." *American Law and Economic Review* 11(2):249–309.

Draca, Mirko, Stephen Machin, and Robert Witt. 2008. *Panic on the Streets of London: Police, Crime, and the July 2005 Terror Attacks*. Bonn: Institute for the Study of Labor.

Durlauf, Steven N., and Daniel S. Nagin. 2011*a*. "The Deterrent Effect of Imprisonment." In *Controlling Crime: Strategies and Tradeoffs*, edited by Philip J. Cook, Jens Ludwig, and Justin McCrary. Chicago: University of Chicago Press.

———. 2011*b*. "Imprisonment and Crime: Can Both Be Reduced?" *Criminology and Public Policy* 10:9–54.

Durlauf, Steven, S. Navarro, and D. Rivers. 2008. "On the Interpretation of Aggregate Crime Regressions." In *Crime Trends*, edited by A. Goldberger and R. Rosenfeld. Washington DC: National Academy of Sciences Press.

Eck, John E. 1992. "Criminal Investigation." In *What Works in Policing? Operations and Administrations Examined*, edited by Gary W. Cordner and Donna C. Hale. Cincinnati: Anderson.

Eck, John E., Jeffrey S. Gersh, and Charlene Taylor. 2000. "Finding Crime Hot Spots through Repeat Address Mapping." In *Analyzing Crime Patterns: Frontiers of Practice*, edited by Victor Goldsmith, Philip G. McGuire, John H. Mollenkopf, and Timothy A. Ross. Thousand Oaks, CA: Sage.

Ehrlich, Isaac. 1975. "The Deterrent Effect of Capital Punishment: A Question of Life and Death." *American Economic Review* 65(3):397–417.

Erickson, Maynard L., and Jack P. Gibbs. 1979. "On the Perceived Severity of Legal Penalties." *Journal of Criminal Law, Criminology, and Police Science* 70: 102–16.

Evans, William N., and Emily G. Owens. 2007. "COPS and Crime." *Journal of Public Economics* 91:181–201.

Ferrier, M., and Jens Ludwig. 2011. "Crime Policy and Informal Social Control." *Criminology and Public Policy* 10:1029–36.

Freeman, Richard B. 1991. *Crime and the Employment of Disadvantaged Youths.* Cambridge, MA: National Bureau of Economic Research.

Gibbs, Jack P. 1975. *Crime, Punishment, and Deterrence.* New York: Elsevier.

Granger, C. W. J. 1969. "Investigating Causal Relations by Econometric Models and Cross-Spectral Methods." *Econometrica* 37:424–38.

Grasmick, Harold, and George Bryjak. 1980. "The Deterrent Effect of Perceived Severity of Punishment." *Social Forces* 59(2):471–91.

Greenwood, Peter, Jan Chaiken, and Joan Petersilia. 1977. *The Investigation Process.* Lexington, MA: Lexington.

Greenwood, Peter, and Angela Hawken. 2002. *An Assessment of the Effect of California's Three-Strikes Law.* Toronto: Greenwood Associates.

Grube, Joel W., and Kathleen A. Kearney. 1983. "A 'Mandatory' Jail Sentence for Drinking and Driving." *Evaluation Review* 7:235–46.

Hawken, Angela. 2010. "Behavioral Triage: A New Model for Identifying and Treating Substance-Abusing Offenders." *Journal of Drug Policy Analysis* 3: 1–5.

Hawken, Angela, and Mark Kleiman. 2009. *Managing Drug-Involved Probationers with Swift and Certain Sanctions: Evaluating Hawaii's HOPE.* Washington, DC: National Institute of Justice.

Heaton, Paul. 2010. "Understanding the Effects of Antiprofiling Policies." *Journal of Law and Economics* 53(1):29–64.

Helland, E., and A. Tabarrok. 2007. "Does Three Strikes Deter? A Nonparametric Estimation." *Journal of Human Resources* 42(2):309–30.

Hjalmarsson, Randi. 2008. "Criminal Justice Involvement and High School Completion." *Journal of Urban Economics* 63:613–30.

———. 2009. "Crime and Expected Punishment: Changes in Perceptions at the Age of Criminal Majority." *American Law and Economics Review* 7:209–48.

Horney, Julie, and Ineke Haen Marshall. 1992. "Risk Perceptions among Serious Offenders: The Role of Crime and Punishment." *Criminology* 30:575–93.

Jacobs, Bruce A., and Richard Wright. 2006. *Street Justice: Retaliation in the Criminal Underworld*. New York: Cambridge University Press.

Johnson, Rucker, and Steven Raphael. 2012. "How Much Crime Reduction Does the Marginal Prisoner Buy?" *Journal of Law and Economics* 55(2):275–310.

Johnston Lloyd, D., Patrick M. O'Malley, and Jerald G. Bachman. 1981. "Cannabis Decriminalization: The Impact on Youth 1975–1980." In *Monitoring the Future: Occasional Paper*. Ann Arbor, MI: Institute for Social Research.

Kansas City Police Department, eds. 1977. *Response Time Analysis*. Kansas City: Kansas City Police Department.

Kennedy, David M. 2009. *Deterrence and Crime Prevention: Reconsidering the Prospect of Sanction*. New York: Routledge.

Kennedy, David M., Anthony A. Braga, Anne Morrison Piehl, and Elin J. Waring. 2001. *Reducing Gun Violence: The Boston Gun Project's Operation Ceasefire*. Washington, DC: US National Institute of Justice.

Kessler, Daniel, and Steven Levitt. 1999. "Using Sentence Enhancements to Distinguish between Deterrence and Incapacitation." *Journal of Law and Economics* 42:348–63.

Kleck, Gary, and J. C. Barnes. Forthcoming. "Do More Police Lead to More Crime Deterrence?" *Crime and Delinquency*. doi: 10.1177/0011128710382263.

Kleck, Gary, Brion Sever, Spencer Li, and Marc Gertz. 2005. "The Missing Link in General Deterrence Research." *Criminology* 46:623–59.

Kleiman, Mark. 2009. *When Brute Force Fails, How to Have Less Crime and Less Punishment*. Princton, NJ: Princeton University Press.

Klein, Lawrence R., Brian Forst, and Victor Filatov. 1978. "The Deterrent Effect of Capital Punishment: An Assessment of the Estimates." In *Deterrence and Incapacitation: Estimating the Effects of Criminal Sanctions on Crime Rates*, edited by Alfred Blumstein, Jacqueline Cohen, and Daniel S. Nagin. Washington, DC: National Academy of Sciences.

Klepper, Steven, and Daniel Nagin. 1989a. "The Deterrent Effect of Perceived Certainty and Severity of Punishment Revisited." *Criminology* 27(4):721-46.

———. 1989b. "Tax Compliance and Perceptions of the Risks of Detection and Criminal Prosecution." *Law and Society Review* 23:209–40.

Klick, Jonathan, and Alexander Tabarrok. 2005. "Using Terror Alert Levels to Estimate the Effect of Police on Crime." *Journal of Law and Economics* 46:267–79.

Lee, David S., and Justin McCrary. 2009. *The Deterrent Effect of Prison: Dynamic Theory and Evidence*. Princeton, NJ: University of Princeton, Industrial Relations Section.

Levitt, Steven D. 1996. "The Effect of Prison Population Size on Crime Rates:

Evidence from Prison Overcrowding Legislation." *Quarterly Journal of Economics* 111:319–52.

———. 1997. "Using Electoral Cycles in Police Hiring to Estimate the Effect of Police on Crime." *American Economic Review* 87:270–90.

———. 1998. "Juvenile Crime and Punishment." *Journal of Political Economy* 106:1156–85.

———. 2002. "Using Electoral Cycles in Police Hiring to Estimate the Effect of Police on Crime: Reply." *American Economic Review* 92:1244–50.

———. 2006. "The Case of the Critics Who Missed the Point: A Reply to Webster et al." *Criminology and Public Policy* 5:449–60.

Liedka, Raymond V., Anne Morrison Piehl, and Bert Useem. 2006. "The Crime-Control Effect of Incarceration: Does Scale Matter?" *Criminology and Public Policy* 5:245–76.

Lochner, Lance. 2007. "Individual Perceptions of the Criminal Justice System." *American Economic Review* 97:444–60.

Loftin, Colin, Milton Heumann, and David McDowall. 1983. "Mandatory Sentencing and Firearms Violence: Evaluating an Alternative to Gun Control." *Law and Society Review* 17:287–318.

Loftin, Colin, and David McDowall. 1981. "'One with a Gun Gets You Two': Mandatory Sentencing and Firearms Violence in Detroit." *Annals of the American Academy of Political and Social Science* 455(1):150–67.

———. 1984. "The Deterrent Effects of the Florida Felony Firearm Law." *Journal of Criminal Law and Criminology* 75:250–59.

Ludwig, Jens, Jeffrey R. Kling, and Sendhil Mullainathan. 2011. "Mechanism Experiments and Policy Evaluations." *Journal of Economic Perspectives* 25(3): 17–38.

MacCoun, Robert, Rosalie Liccardo Pacula, Jamie Chriqui, Katherine Harris, and Peter Reuter. 2009. "Do Citizens Know Whether Their State Has Decriminalized Marijuana? Assessing the Perceptual Component of Deterrence Theory." *Review of Law and Economics* 5:347–71.

Marvell, Thomas B., and C. Moody Jr. 1994. "Prison Population Growth and Crime Reduction." *Journal of Quantitative Criminology* 10:109–40.

———. 1996. "Specification Problems, Police Levels, and Crime Rates." *Criminology* 34:609–46.

Matsueda, Ross L., D. A. Kreager, and D. Huizinga. 2006. "Deterring Delinquents: A Rational Choice Model of Theft and Violence." *American Sociological Review* 71:95–122.

McCrary, Justin. 2002. "Using Electoral Cycles in Police Hiring to Estimate the Effect of Police on Crime: Comment." *American Economic Review* 92: 1236–43.

McDowall, D., C. Loftin, and B. Wiersema. 1992. "A Comparative Study of the Preventive Effects of Mandatory Sentencing Laws for Gun Crimes." *Journal of Criminal Law and Criminology* 83:378–94.

Meier, R. F., and W. T. Johnson. 1977. "Deterrence as Social Control: The Legal and Extralegal Production of Conformity." *American Sociological Review* 42:292–304.

Minor, W. W. 1977. "A Deterrence-Control Theory of Crime." In *Theory of Criminology*, edited by R. F. Meier. Beverly Hills, CA: Sage.

Mulvey, E. P. 2011. *Highlights from Pathways to Desistance: A Longitudinal Study of Serious Adolescent Offenders*. Juvenile Justice Fact Sheet. Washington, DC: Department of Justice.

Nagin, Daniel S. 1998. "Criminal Deterrence Research at the Outset of the Twenty-First Century." In *Crime and Justice: A Review of Research*, vol. 23, edited by Michael Tonry. Chicago: University of Chicago Press.

Nagin, Daniel S., Francis T. Cullen, and Cheryl Lero Jonson. 2009. "Imprisonment and Reoffending." In *Crime and Justice: A Review of Research*, vol. 38, edited by Michael Tonry. Chicago: University of Chicago Press.

Nagin, Daniel S., and Raymond Paternoster. 1993. "Enduring Individual Differences and Rational Choice Theories of Crime." *Law and Society Review* 27:467–99.

———. 1994. "Personal Capital and Social Control: The Deterrence Implications of Individual Differences in Criminal Offending." *Criminology* 32: 581–606.

Nagin, Daniel S., and John V. Pepper, eds. 2012. *Deterrence and the Death Penalty*. Washington, DC: National Academies Press.

Nagin, Daniel S., and Greg Pogarsky. 2001. "Integrating Celerity, Impulsivity, and Extralegal Sanction Threats into a Model of General Deterrence: Theory and Evidence." *Criminology* 39:865–92.

———. 2003. "An Experimental Investigation of Deterrence: Cheating, Self-Serving Bias, and Impulsivity." *Criminology* 41:167–93.

Owens, Emily G. 2009. "More Time, Less Crime? Estimating the Incapacitative Effects of Sentence Enhancements." *Journal of Labor Economics* 53(3): 551–79.

Packer, H. L. 1968. *The Limits of the Criminal Sanction*. Stanford, CA: Stanford University Press.

Papachristos, Andrew V., Tracey L. Meares, and Jeffrey Fagan. 2007. "Attention Felons: Evaluating Project Safe Neighborhoods in Chicago." *Journal of Empirical Legal Studies* 4:223–72.

Paternoster, Raymond. 1983. "Estimating Perceptual Stability and Deterrent Effects: The Role of Perceived Legal Punishment in the Inhibition of Criminal Involvement." *Journal of Criminal Law and Criminology* 74:210–97.

———. 2010. "How Much Do We Really Know about Criminal Deterrence?" *Journal of Criminal Law and Criminology* 10(3):765–823.

Paternoster, Raymond, and Alex Piquero. 1995. "Reconceptualizing Deterrence: An Empirical Test of Personal and Vicarious Experiences." *Journal of Research in Crime and Delinquency* 32:251–86.

Paternoster, Raymond, Linda E. Saltzman, Theodore G. Chiricos, and Gordon P. Waldo. 1982. "Perceived Risk and Deterrence: Methodological Artifacts in Perceptual Deterrence Research." *Journal of Criminal Law and Criminology* 73:1238–58.

Piliavin, Irving, Craig Thornton, Rosemary Gartner, and Ross L. Matsueda.

1986. "Crime, Deterrence, and Rational Choice." *American Sociological Review* 51:101–19.

Piquero, Alex, Raymond Paternoster, Greg Pogarsky, and Thomas A. Loughran. 2011. "Elaborating the Individual Difference Component in Deterrence Theory." *Annual Review of Law and Social Science* 7:355–60.

Pogarsky, Greg. 2007. "Deterrence and Individual Differences among Convicted Offenders." *Quantitative Criminology* 23(1):59–74.

Pogarsky, Greg, KiDuek Kim, and Raymond Paternoster. 2005. "Perceptual Change in the National Youth Survey: Lessons for Deterrence Theory and Offender Decision-Making." *Justice Quarterly* 22:1–29.

Pogarsky, Greg, and Alex R. Piquero. 2003. "Can Punishment Encourage Offending? Investigating the 'Resetting' Effect." *Journal of Research in Crime and Delinquency* 40:95–120.

Pogarsky, Greg, Alex R. Piquero, and Raymond Paternoster. 2004. "Modeling Change in Perceptions about Sanction Threats: The Neglected Link in Deterrence Theory." *Journal of Quantitative Criminology* 20:343–69.

Poutvaara, Panu, and Mikael Priks. 2006. "Hooliganism in the Shadow of a Terrorist Attack and the Tsunami: Do Police Reduce Group Violence?" Working Paper no. 1882. Munich: Center for Economic Studies and Ifo Institute for Economic Research.

Raphael, Steven. 2006. "The Deterrent Effects of California's Proposition 8: Weighing the Evidence." *Criminology and Public Policy* 5:471–78.

Raphael, Steven, and Jens Ludwig. 2003. "Prison Sentence Enhancements: The Case of Project Exile." In *Evaluating Gun Policy: Effects on Crime and Violence*, edited by Jens Ludwig and Philip J. Cook. Washington, DC: Brookings Institution Press.

Raphael, Steven, and Michael A. Stoll. 2009. "Why Are So Many Americans in Prison?" In *Do Prisons Make Us Safer? The Benefits and Costs of the Prison Boom*, edited by Steven Raphael and Michael A. Stoll. New York: Sage.

Reuter, Peter, and Howard Pollack. 2012. "Good Markets Make Bad Neighbors: Regulating Open-Air Drug Markets." *Criminology and Public Policy* 11(2):211–20.

Roncek, Dennis W. 2000. "Schools and Crime." In *Analyzing Crime Patterns: Frontiers of Practice*, edited by Victor Goldsmith, Philip G. McGuire, John H. Mollenkopf, and Timothy A. Ross. Thousand Oaks, CA: Sage.

Ross, H. Laurence. 1973. "Law, Science, and Accidents: The British Road Safety Act of 1967." *Journal of Legal Studies* 2:1–78.

———. 1982. *Deterring the Drinking Driver: Legal Policy and Social Control.* Lexington, MA: Lexington.

Sherman, Lawrence W. 1990. "Police Crackdowns: Initial and Residual Deterrence." In *Crime and Justice: A Review of Research*, vol. 12, edited by Michael Tonry and Norval Morris. Chicago: University of Chicago Press.

———. In this volume. "The Rise of Evidence-Based Policing: Targeting, Testing, and Tracking."

Sherman, Lawrence W., and Richard A. Berk. 1984. "The Specific Deterrent

Effects of Arrest for Domestic Assault." *American Sociological Review* 49:261–72.

Sherman, Lawrence W., and John E. Eck. 2002. "Policing for Prevention." In *Evidence Based Crime Prevention*, edited by Lawrence W. Sherman, David Farrington, and Brandon Welsh. New York: Routledge.

Sherman, Lawrence W., Patrick Gartin, and Michael Buerger. 1989. "Hot Spots of Predatory Crime: Routine Activities and the Criminology of Place." *Criminology* 27:27–55.

Sherman, Lawrence, and David Weisburd. 1995. "General Deterrent Effects of Police Patrol in Crime 'Hot Spots': A Randomized Study." *Justice Quarterly* 12:625–48.

Shi, Lan. 2009. "The Limits of Oversight in Policing: Evidence from the 2001 Cincinnati Riot." *Journal of Public Economics* 93:99–113.

Snell, T. L. 2010. *Capital Punishment 2009—Statistical Tables*. Washington, DC: US Department of Justice.

Spelman, William. 2000. "What Recent Studies Do (and Don't) Tell Us about Imprisonment and Crime." In *Crime and Justice: A Review of Research*, vol. 27, edited by Michael Tonry. Chicago: University of Chicago Press.

Spelman, William, and Dale K. Brown. 1981. *Calling the Police: A Replication of the Citizen Reporting Component of the Kansas City Response Time Analysis*. Washington, DC: Police Executive Research Forum.

Stafford, Mark C., and Mark Warr. 1993. "A Reconceptualization of General and Specific Deterrence." *Journal of Research in Crime and Delinquency* 30:123–35.

Stolzenberg, Lisa, and Stewart J. D'Alessio. 1997. "'Three Strikes and You're Out': The Impact of California's New Mandatory Sentencing Law on Serious Crime Rates." *Crime and Delinquency* 43(4):457–69.

Tittle, Charles. 1977. "Sanction Fear and the Maintenance of Social Order." *Social Forces* 55:579–96.

———. 1980. *Sanctions and Social Deviance: The Question of Deterrence*. New York: Praeger.

Tonry, Michael. 1996. *Sentencing Matters*. Oxford: Oxford University Press.

———. 2009. "The Mostly Unintended Effects of Mandatory Penalties: Two Centuries of Consistent Findings." In *Crime and Justice: A Review of Research*, vol. 38, edited by Michael Tonry. Chicago: University of Chicago Press.

Vollaard, Ben. 2013. "Preventing Crime through Selective Incapacitation." *Economic Journal* 123(567):262–84.

Waldfogel, Joel. 1994. "The Effect of Criminal Conviction on Income and the Trust 'Reposed in the Workmen.'" *Journal of Human Resources* 29:62–81.

Webster, Cheryl Marie, Anthony Doob, and Franklin Zimring. 2006. "Proposition 8 and Crime Rates in California: The Case of the Disappearing Deterrent." *Criminology and Public Policy* 5:417–48.

Weisburd, David, Shawn Bushway, Cynthia Lum, and Su-Ming Yang. 2004. "Trajectories of Crime at Places: A Longitudinal Study of Street Segments in the City of Seattle." *Criminology* 42:238–320.

Weisburd, David, and John Eck. 2004. "What Can Police Do to Reduce

Crime, Disorder, and Fear?" *Annals of the American Academy of Political and Social Science* 593:42–65.

Weisburd, David, Tomar Einat, and Matt Kowalski. 2008. "The Miracle of the Cells: An Experimental Study of Interventions to Increase Payment of Court-Ordered Financial Obligations." *Criminology and Public Policy* 7:9–36.

Weisburd, David, and Lorraine Green. 1995. "Policing Drug Hot Spots: The Jersey City Drug Market Analysis Experiment." *Justice Quarterly* 12:711–35.

Wikström, Per-Olof H., D. Oberwittler, K. Treiber, and B. Hardie. 2012. *Breaking Rules: The Social and Situational Dynamics of Young People's Urban Crime*. Oxford: Oxford University Press.

Williams, Kirk R., Jack P. Gibbs, and Maynard L. Erickson. 1980. "Public Knowledge of Statutory Penalties: The Extent and Basis of Accurate Perception." *Sociological Review* 23:105–28.

Williams, Kirk R., and Richard Hawkins. 1986. "Perceptual Research on General Deterrence: A Critical Overview." *Law and Society Review* 20:545–72.

Wilson, J. M., and S. Chermak. 2011. "Community-Driven Violence Reduction Programs." *Criminology and Public Policy* 10:993–1027.

Wood, Peter B., and David C. May. 2003. "Racial Differences in Perceptions of Severity of Sanctions: A Comparison of Prison with Alternatives." *Justice Quarterly* 20(3):605–31.

Wright, Richard T., and Scott H. Decker. 1994. *Burglars on the Job: Streetlife and Residential Break-ins*. Boston: Northeastern University Press.

Zimring, Franklin, and Gordon Hawkins. 1973. *Deterrence: The Legal Threat in Crime Control*. Chicago: University of Chicago Press.

Zimring, Franklin E., Gordon Hawkins, and Sam Kamin. 2001. *Punishment and Democracy: Three Strikes and You're Out in California*. New York: Oxford University Press.

Franklin E. Zimring

American Youth Violence: A Cautionary Tale

ABSTRACT

Violence by young offenders has long been a concern of students of juvenile delinquency. Until the 1980s, juveniles had high rates of committing less serious assaults but accounted for less than 10 percent of homicides, a proportion to which they have since returned. But the late 1980s produced an epidemic of gun homicides by juveniles and young adults, which led in the mid-1990s to warnings about an emerging group of "superpredators" and to fabulously inaccurate predictions of "a coming storm of juvenile violence." Just as the rhetoric was reaching its crescendo, youth homicide rates began their largest drop in modern history. Several problematic assumptions underlay the faulty predictions and offer lessons about how to avoid catastrophic errors in the prediction of crime rates. Some of the same problems reappear in more recent scholarly analyses.

Acts of life-threatening violence by young persons are important and troublesome events in developed nations for a variety of reasons: they are the most serious crimes young persons commit and thus test the degree to which legal principles can mitigate penal responses; they happen at the beginning of social and criminal careers and thus may be signals of protracted dangerousness; and they follow closely on periods of child development and dependence so that the crimes of the young also clearly implicate failures of family, government, and society. It is therefore no surprise that youth violence has been the focus of

Franklin E. Zimring is the William G. Simon Professor of Law and Wolfen Distinguished Scholar at the University of California, Berkeley, Law School. Stephen Rushin provided research help on this venture, and Barry Feld was the godfather of fig. 12.

scholarly concern in the pages of *Crime and Justice* on a consistent basis throughout 35 years of publication (see the list of articles in App. A).

But there were three special developments in the United States over the period since 1975 that compelled special scholarly concern with youth violence. The first special feature of the late twentieth century was a baby boom that propelled an expansion of children and adolescents all through the 1960s and early 1970s just as crime rates in urban America were also expanding. Youth violence had become a much more important concern simply because there were so many more young people in the American mix.

The second special element of the period was an explosion of rates of youth homicide in urban areas during the 8 years after 1984. The escalating rates of youth homicide started after the youth population peak (in 1975) during a period when the population of older juveniles was declining.

This explosive increase in youth homicide touched off the third element of the story, predictions of continuing growth in American violence on the horizon, a moral panic in the media and government inspired by PhDs warning that "a bloodbath" was on the horizon that would be the result of an emerging generation of "juvenile superpredators." While the ink was still wet on these dire predictions, rates of youth homicide were already dropping—the beginning of an era of declining rates of lethal violence by youth unprecedented in magnitude in the modern era. The contrast between predicted and actual rates of homicide arrests for the middle term was five to one. James Alan Fox had projected a volume of juvenile homicide arrests of "almost 5,000 per year by 2005, as a result of demographic growth alone" but then concluded that "we will likely have many more than 5,000 teen killers" (1996, p. 3). Yet the actual number of arrests in that age group in 2005 was 1,073.

This essay focuses on trends over time in serious youth violence since 1975 and on what the catastrophic errors of the 1990s teach us about youth violence and the limits of criminological projection. The first section provides a profile of statistical sources on youth violence with emphasis on the distinctive features of violent crime during adolescence. The second then profiles the age-specific trends in homicide after 1980 that provoked the moral panic in the 1990s and provides details on the assumptions used to project future problems. A third section details the trends of homicide after 1994 for different age groups and suggests substantive reasons why the direction and magnitude of juvenile homicide were the reverse of what was predicted. A brief concluding section applies the lessons learned since 1995 to a risk-averse discussion of future trends in youth homicide.

The jump in youth homicide in the mid-1980s was tied to a sharp increase in gun use by younger offenders. What happened after 1995 was a classic regression toward prior proportions of youths to total homicide that interacted with general declines to produce huge drops in youth violence. The regression scenario was not considered by the superpredator predictors of the mid-1990s. That error should not be repeated. The prospects for future trends in youth violence are most likely to be in the same direction and have the same magnitude as the rates for offenders over 20.

I. Youth Violence: A Profile

Two sources of information are available about the incidence and character of youth violence in the United States: official statistics from police and health departments and survey research estimates that come from interviews with samples of the population about whether and in what respects they have been crime victims in the recent past.

Because the victims of an offense will frequently not know much about the offender, there are important limits to using such surveys to determine offender characteristics, even in violent episodes in which the victim comes in contact with the offender. So most of the information available about the incidence and character of youth violence in the United States comes from police statistics.

But police statistics on the age of criminal offenders will not be available for the majority of all the offenses known to the police because an offender has not been identified. Detailed and accurate information on the age of criminal offenders can be taken only from cases in which a particular suspect has been arrested or otherwise identified, and, as I show later in this section, estimating the true prevalence of criminal offense responsibility from arrest or suspect counts is often problematic.

A. Official Statistics

There are five crime categories used in uniform crime reporting statistics that involve the immediate threat or imposition of personal

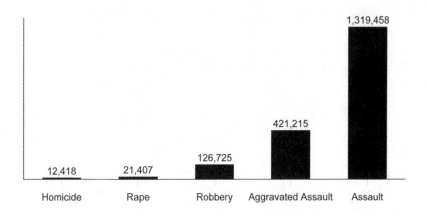

FIG. 1.—Police-defined crimes of violence in the United States, 2009. Source: FBI Uniform Crime Reports, 2009.

injury: homicide, rape, robbery, aggravated assault, and assault. Homicide and rape are the most serious of the police-classified offenses and also the lowest-incidence crimes. The total number of intentional killings estimated by police statistics is around 13,000 per year, and health department death statistics stay quite close to this level. The number of rapes reported in the United States by the FBI's Uniform Crime Reports is also small at just over 20,000, though this is regarded as a very substantial undercount. The two more frequent "index" crimes of violence, robbery and aggravated assault are heterogeneous in severity. Robberies vary from unarmed extortions to dangerous encounters with loaded guns. While assaults must be "aggravated" by either an intent to injure or the threat to use a deadly weapon to be upgraded to the index categories, they vary in severity. Figure 1 shows the varying scale for police-defined crimes of violence in the United States in reports for 2009.

With arrests used as one measure of crime (because age-specific detail can be added to it), homicides produced 2 percent of all index violent crime arrests in 2009. When arrests for the less serious assault category are added into the mix, homicide arrests are just over 0.6 percent of violence arrests.

Figure 2 provides some measure of the concentration of various violent crimes among younger adolescents by showing the percentage of all arrests for the eight index crimes and for nonindex assault in 2009.

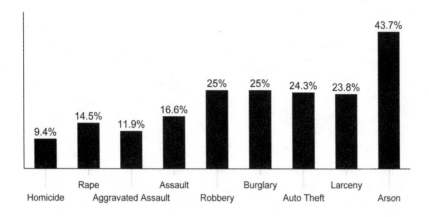

FIG. 2.—Under-18 share of arrests, nine offenses, United States, 2009. Source: FBI Uniform Crime Reports, 2009.

The youth share of violent crimes is at the low end of index offenses for four of the five violent crimes. The fifth, robbery, at 25 percent, clusters with burglary and the other property crimes at almost twice the concentration of murder, aggravated assault, and rape.

But these police-based statistics both underestimate the amount and the concentration of violence among the young and overstate the youth share of violence. The first reason the "under-18" share of arrests understates the relationship between youth and violence is that it cuts off the youth category pretty early in the developmental process. Adding in violent crimes up to age 21 or 23 would more than double the youth segment. The second reason that the under-18 share of arrests is an undercount is that official statistics do not fully reflect the assaults and fights among teens that are frequent during middle and late adolescence. Victim surveys identify the ages 15–19 as the highest-assault age group, and 12–15 ties with young adulthood for second place (Zimring 1998, chap. 2). Teen males often do not report such conflict to the police, and police will often take such events lightly if injuries are not severe. In one sense, however, arrest statistics exaggerate the amount of youth violence because younger offenders get arrested in groups, an issue I return to later in this section (see fig. 4).

B. Is Youth Violence Different?

For the most part, patterns of youth violence resemble patterns of violence by older persons: concentrated in the same genders (males), the same kinds of conflicts, and the same disadvantaged minority segments of the community (Zimring 1998, pp. 20–30). There are three important respects in which youth violence, particularly under age 18, differs from the behaviors found among older populations: high volume, low seriousness, and group involvement.

The high volume of violence during adolescence is not in serious dispute in the United States, but the extent to which it crosses gender and class boundaries and the degree to which very serious violence is broadly distributed among boys is not clear. The prevalence of assault among boys is substantial, but how serious are most of these male peer assaults? And while fighting is a relatively common rite of passage among boys in the teen years, we are less confident about the extent and severity of assaults initiated by adolescent girls. If arrest statistics are an accurate measure, assaultive behavior is even more concentrated in males during teen years than after (see Zimring 1998, chap. 3). But is the arrest rubric itself a product of police discounting of girl violence?

The high rates of youth assaults that are common are usually counterbalanced by the relatively low severity of most youth assaults. Figure 3 contrasts homicide and self-reported assault victimization rates for three age groups. I use data for 1991, a year that was close to the high point for youth homicide discussed in the next section. The best evidence that youth assaults are less serious is that the youngest group in the figure has the same reported incidence of self-reported assault victimization (7.5 per 1,000) as 20–24-year-olds but a much lower homicide victimization rate (6.8 vs. 41 per 100,000).

The third specific marker of youth violence is the very high prevalence of group involvement. The official statistics on almost all forms of adolescent criminality show high levels of group involvement. Figure 4 demonstrates this pattern for homicide by showing the ratio of homicide arrests to victims associated with the arrests for three different age groups in the United States in 2008–9.

The group involvement and multiple arrests of juvenile offenders produce two arrests for every victim of this age group, while the oldest age group produces what is essentially a one-to-one ratio. The young adult rate is 1.44, between the juvenile and older-adult ratios.

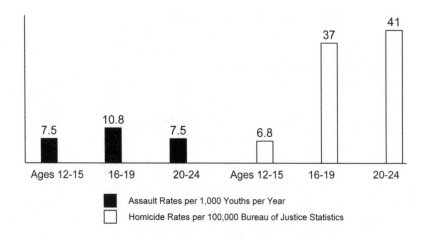

FIG. 3.—Male homicide and assault victimization rates by age, 1991. Source: National Center for Health Statistics (1991, p. 36); US Department of Justice, Bureau of Justice Statistics (1991, p. 24, table 5).

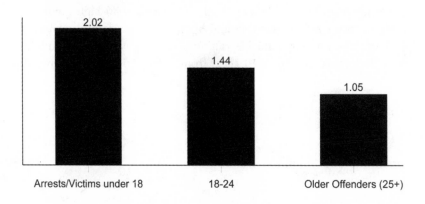

FIG. 4.—Ratio of arrests for homicide to homicide victims, United States, 2008–9. Source: FBI Uniform Crime Reports, Supplementary Homicide Reports.

For most nonserious assaults, the net effect of undercounting offenses and multiple arrests is almost certainly to undercount total juvenile assaults and to underestimate the proportionate share of assaults committed by youths. For homicides, however, there is no undercount, and the much larger role of multiple arrests in the 1990s produces a significant overestimate of the proportionate share of homicides.

For homicides a comparison of homicide arrest rates for juveniles with homicide arrest rates for persons over 25 is a very misleading indication of the risk to victims posed by the two age groups because the number of victims generated by each 100 homicide arrests of juveniles is half that of the over-25 offender set. The impact of multiple arrests and the clearest way to correct the distortions produced by arrest patterns are discussed later in this analysis.

II. The Late 1980s Homicide Epidemic and the
Projections It Produced

The pattern of violent crime in the last four decades of the twentieth century breaks into three distinct suberas, as shown in figure 5. The first era of homicide experience was during the decade after 1964, when homicide rates doubled in the United States. The second era of fluctuation without clear trend lasted from the mid-1970s to the early 1990s, when rates first dropped in the mid-1970s, then climbed back to the 1974 high in 1980, and then dropped in the early 1980s, only to go up again after 1985 to near the 1974 and 1980 high points in 1991. This second era was followed by nearly a decade of decline.

The trend line for homicide victimization between ages 15 and 19 provides reports for every 10 years from 1950 until 1980 and annual

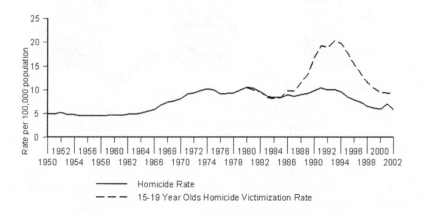

FIG. 5.—Homicide rates by year and 15–19-year-olds' homicide victimization rate in the United States, 1960–2002. Source: National Center for Health Statistics (2005); Centers for Disease Control and Prevention (2004, table 45).

reports thereafter. The early 1980s level is approximately twice the 1950 rate but then spikes sharply after 1985 to peak at 20 per 100,000.

The last half of the 1980s was a particularly sharp disappointment in the United States when homicide rates increased. Rates of imprisonment had expanded as never before and were expected to reduce crime through substantial incapacitation (Zimring and Hawkins 1995), and the aging of baby boomers also had reduced the proportion of the population in high-risk youth ages. Yet homicide and life-threatening violence increased almost as much as during the late 1970s, and the rebound of the late 1980s was concentrated among younger offenders. Some of the most dramatic contrasts over time were based on the increases in cases in which municipal police identified the suspect as under 18 when the crime was committed. The sharpest increases were noted in the monthly supplemental homicide reports that were the basis for Fox's (1996) analysis:

> Since 1985, the rate of homicide committed by adults, ages 25 and older, has declined 25 percent, from 6.3 to 4.7 per 100,000 as the baby boomers matured into their middle-age years. At the same time, however, the homicide rate among 18 to 24-year-olds has increased 61 percent from 15.7 to 25.3 per 100,000. Even more alarming and tragic, homicide is now reaching down to a much younger age group—children as young as 14–17. Over the past decade, the rate of homicide committed by teenagers ages 14–17 has more than doubled, increasing 172 percent, from 7.0 per 100,000 in 1985 to 19.1 in 1994. (Fox 1996, p. 2)

Fox's 1996 report created a figure from Supplementary Homicide Report (SHR) data adjusted to cover missing reporting sites, reproduced here as figure 6. The data in Fox's table present an estimated rate of offending and show a clear contrast after 1985 between sharp upward trends for juveniles and young adults and low rates for older groups with some downward draft. In this analysis, the rates of homicide offending were the highest for the young adult group, but the sharpest increase after 1985 occurred for the 14–17-year-old group, with a peak rate 172 percent higher. Fox then constructed two projections, a "high" and a "low" projection for 2010, using the pre-1995 trends in his table. The low projection assumed that rates per 100,000 youths would stay at their peak 1994 rates for the next 15 years and then adjusted the volume for each protected year by that year's pop-

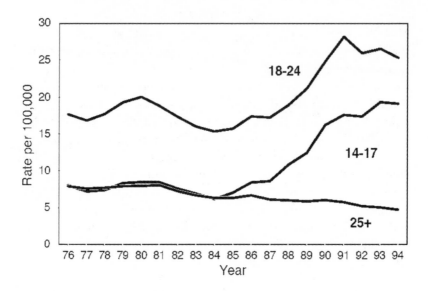

FIG. 6.—Homicide offending rate by age. Source: Fox 1996 (based on FBI Supplementary Homicide Reports and Current Population Survey).

ulation 14–17. Because the population in the age group expands, this method produces Fox's "almost 5,000 per year as a result of demographic growth alone" (Fox 1996, p. 3). The second projection (Fox labels this one "high") assumes that the offending rate will continue to expand as it had in recent years. This method produces a projected 8,000 "juvenile killers" by 2005. There is no express rationale for assuming the continued expansion of this peak rate for another decade. Perhaps Fox was trying to imagine the worst outcome of any likelihood. There are a variety of indications that he was presenting these two versions of the future as exhausting the likely or possible trends. He labels one "low" even though it produces the highest volume of juvenile homicide offending ever by 2005 and calls the other (and even higher) projection "high," suggesting that he is exhausting the field of choice. But he never says why his low total assumes no decline from the peak rate in his historical series.

While Fox spent most of his mid-1990s analysis on the arrest and suspect statistics of the prior decade, John DiIulio of Princeton emphasized the interaction of high mid-1990s crime rates with changes that were taking place in the age structure of the US population. Reviewing the SHR numbers in the Fox analysis, DiIulio concluded that "the youth crime wave has reached horrific proportions" but added, "what is really frightening everyone from D.A.s to demographers . . . is not what's happening now but what's just around the corner— namely a sharp increase in the number of super crime-prone males. . . . By 2005, the number of males in this age group [14–17] will have risen about 25 percent overall and 50 percent for blacks. . . . Americans are sitting atop a demographic time bomb" (DiIulio 1995, pp. 23–24).

DiIulio's demographic time bomb was based on two substantially inconsistent projection techniques. The first method was based on an assumption that fixed proportions of a youth population become serious offenders. The origination of this formula was DiIulio's teacher at Harvard, James Q. Wilson, who assumed that the 6 percent of Philadelphia boys born in 1945 who had five or more police contacts prior to age 18 were a fixed proportion of serious offenders (Wolfgang, Figlio, and Sellin 1972). Wilson then argued that an expansion in the youth population of 1 million produces 500,000 extra adolescent males. Extrapolating from the 6 percent chronic finding, Wilson tells us to expect "30,000 more muggers, killers, and thieves than we have now" (1995, p. 507).

DiIulio used this logic but with different time horizons and adjectives. He notes that the total population of boys under 18 is expected to grow from 32 million to 36.5 million, a total of 4.5 million prior to 2010. Using the Philadelphia cohort 6 percent finding, he multiplies the 4.5 million additional male children under 18 in the United States by 2010 to project "approximately 270,000 more super-predators" (DiIulio 1995). The ninefold increase between the Wilson and DiIulio totals happens because the time period and number of extra youths are expanded but also, and more importantly, because Wilson confines his analysis to adolescents while DiIulio assumes that 6 percent of all children alive in 2010 will be superpredators. The logic is still a fixed proportion of a variable population. That slightly more of these superpredators would be under age 4 in 2010 than over age 14 I had reason to point out (Zimring 1996).

But DiIulio is not content to assume only a fixed proportion of criminal threats, noting that the offense severity profile increased between the two Philadelphia birth cohort juvenile eras: "Each generation of crime-prone boys has been about three times as dangerous as the one before it. For example, the crime-prone boys born in Philadelphia in

1958 went on to commit about three times as much serious crime per capita as their older cousins in the [first Philadelphia birth cohort]" (1995, p. 24). So DiIulio is ready to argue that the rate of serious youth crime is dynamic rather than constant and things have been getting worse. But if the rate and seriousness of youth crime vary over time, why should we assume that the 6 percent estimate of serious offenders is constant or for that matter that the size of the youth population is a major variable in predicting the criminological future?

By the middle of 1996, complaints based on what Philip Cook and John Laub call cohort effects were taking center stage—allegations that the current youth generation were a breed apart (Cook and Laub 1998). In the coauthored volume *Body Count*, published in 1996, Bennett, DiIulio, and Walters argue that the concentrated social disadvantages of fatherless families had created a high incidence of what they call "moral poverty," which all but guarantees violent criminal careers. "Four of 10 children go to sleep without fathers who live in their homes. . . . We have come to the point in America where we are asking prisons to do what fathers used to do" (1996, p. 196).

The impact of predictions based on projections of increasing youth violence on the political process was not small. In 1996, Representative Bob McCollum of Florida, the chairman of the House Subcommittee on Crime, testified at a Senate hearing: "Today's enormous cohort of 5-year-olds will be tomorrow's teenagers. This is ominous news given that most violent crime is committed by older juveniles. . . . Put these demographic facts together and brace yourself for the coming generation of 'super-predators'" (McCollum 1996, p. 2).

I do not mean to suggest that projections of increasing juvenile homicides let alone nightmare predictions of coming generations of juvenile superpredators met with universal academic acceptance. The Cook and Laub analysis in these pages separated fact from science fiction with clarity and vigor (Cook and Laub 1998, 2002; Zimring 1998). For the most part, however, the academic reaction to the demographic time bomb rhetoric was silence, whether respectful or not. The empirical criminologists whose cohort findings provided a framework for the Wilson and DiIulio predictions apparently did not participate in the public discourse about juvenile crime futures. And the prospect of impending juvenile risk seemed to offer rhetorical opportunities for the left (Fox complaining about inadequate support for youth services) as well as Bennett and DiIulio's right-wing diagnosis of moral poverty and prescription of prison expansion. The "demographic time bomb" looked to be the next big thing in a period that had already endured the War on Drugs and three-strikes-and-you're-out phenomena.

What Happened Next?   But what happened next was the most sustained and substantial decline in youth homicide in modern US history. Youth homicide arrests had actually begun to drop in 1994 so that the "low" estimate in Fox's figure 6 projection for 1996—the year his analysis was published—was already 33 percent higher than the actual FBI numbers. By 2005 the total volume of SHR homicide arrests and suspects under 18 had dropped by two-thirds instead of increasing by almost 40 percent, and this very large decline in homicide volume took place even as the youth population had expanded and the proportion of the youth population from traditional high-rate minority groups had also expanded. Every demographic determinant in the predictions made by Fox, Wilson, and DiIulio had come to pass, but the violent crime outcomes had been turned upside down. What turned Fox's 40 percent increase into a 67 percent decrease was only one variable: the rate of juvenile homicide involvement. Figure 7 tells the tale by tracing the rate per 100,000 for ages 13–17 through more than a quarter century.

After rising in the late 1970s, the youth homicide rate turns down sharply through the early 1980s before beginning the ascent that was the centerpiece of the Fox and DiIulio concerns. Even as the alarms of the mid-1990s were being sounded, the rate of homicide attributable to juveniles began its steep and sustained drop.

In both the increase after the mid-1980s and its decline after 1993, the homicide patterns of ages 18–24 paralleled the roller-coaster ride of age-specific homicide rates as shown in figure 8. The timing of the ups and downs for the two groups is very close, with a correlation over time of .95 (Zimring and Rushin 2013, p. 13).

In retrospect, the predictions of a coming storm of juvenile violence were classic false predictions on a par with pushing Internet stocks in 2000 or recommending Greek government bonds in 2007. But was this simply bad timing or was it also problematic criminology? The question is an important one because discovering mistakes that should have been foreseen in 1995 can reduce the margin of error as we think about what should determine the character and rate of youth violence in the

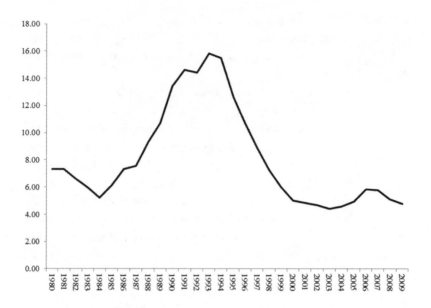

FIG. 7.—Rate of juvenile homicide arrest rates. Source: FBI Uniform Crime Reports, Supplementary Homicide Reports.

coming decades. Are there lessons to be learned, or is the recent history of forecasting on this topic an uncorrectable blind gamble?

III. An Anatomy of Catastrophic Error

The previous section of this essay mentioned a few ways in which the methods and assumptions in Fox's projections differed from those by Wilson and DiIulio. There were, however, four problems manifest in all of the "coming storm" predictions that were errors in judgment even from the perspective of 1996: failing to recognize the plenary power of rate fluctuations in determining homicide trends, failing to account for regression to historically typical levels as a probable future outcome, assuming that fluctuations in the number and demographic character of future population were a major influence on crime volume, and mistaking simultaneous movements in youth and young adult violence for juvenile-only cohort effects that signal long-term changes in rates of crime and violence as a group ages through the life cycle.

FIG. 8.—Young adult homicide arrest rates. Source: FBI Uniform Crime Reports, Supplementary Homicide Reports.

A. The Plenary Power of Rate Variations in Juvenile Homicide

What I am calling the plenary power of rates on the volume of juvenile violence was a central fact in the epidemic that led to "coming storm" predictions. The youth population actually decreased in the 7 years after 1984, when killings committed by juveniles increased. All the extra killings come from higher rates of killings attributed to juveniles. As a matter of strict arithmetic, more than 100 percent of the increase in youth homicide after 1984 came from rates going up because the higher rates had to compensate for fewer kids. Since the period just prior to the mid-1990s had been dominated by variability in rates, the people making future projections should have been on notice that the dominant factor in future homicide rates would not be the number of juveniles at risk but rather the trends in homicide rates per 100,000.

Sure enough, more than 100 percent of the decline in juvenile homicide that followed the dire predictions of the mid-1990s was also the result of rate changes because the youth population had expanded modestly. The extreme variability of homicide rates—almost tripling

then declining by two-thirds in just over 20 years—means that 15 percent or 20 percent variations in total population will probably play a
minor part in the total volume of serious youth violence. So what can
be precisely estimated 10 and 15 years in the future—the population
of youths and young adults—will not make much difference, and what
will be the largest determinant of youth homicide—trends in rates—
cannot be predicted with any confidence.

The extreme variability in homicide rates that produced the Fox and
DiIulio projections also should have worried Wilson and DiIulio away
from expecting a fixed 6 percent of the youth population as violent.
The variability of homicide rates from 1980 to 1994 undercut Fox's
assumptions in a slightly different way. At no point in his analysis of
the growth of youth homicide from 1984 onward does Fox suggest
either an explanation for the upward slope or a behavioral model of
what determines rate fluctuations. So he cannot explain the extreme
fluctuations that he documents. But how can he predict future variations if he cannot explain past variations? He never discloses this. Instead, he produces two straight-line models, each of which is based on
a single assumption never justified. The "low" future merely assumes
that the rate per 100,000 of juvenile homicides will stay at its 1994
level (an all-time high) for the foreseeable future. The high-projection
model assumes that the upward growth in homicide rates will continue
without interruption for the projectable future. A look back at figure
7 will demonstrate that the actual variations in rates since 1980 conform to neither of these assumptions, with some downward variation
after 1980 before an upward shift. So Fox had no behavioral or historical model to project future rates, despite the fact that rate fluctuations are the dominant feature in the magnitude of youth violence.

Both Fox and DiIulio believed that rates of youth violence would go
up from 1994 levels. DiIulio mentions that the incidence of serious
crime went up between the juvenile years of the 1945 Philadelphia
birth cohort (1957–63) and the juvenile years of the 1958 Philadelphia
cohort (1970–76) and suggests that this is likely to continue.

The behavioral emptiness of the Fox projections published in 1995
can best be illustrated by a parallel exercise of projecting juvenile homicide rates using 2005 as the base year. The high estimate, shown in
figure 9, parallel to that of Fox in 1996, would take the 2006 rate of
SHR juvenile homicides and assume that it will continue with adjust-

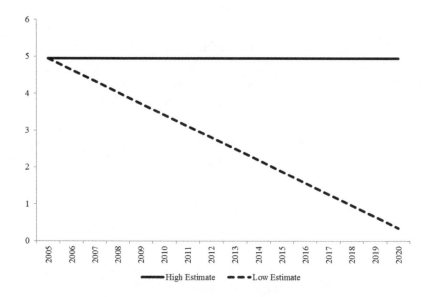

FIG. 9.—High and low volumes of juvenile homicide offending, 2005–20. Source: Author's projections.

ments only for anticipated changes in the population aged 13–17. The low estimate would project continued downward rate levels.

Each of these projections assumes that juvenile homicide rate trends will do something they have never done before: either continue without significant change for 12 years or follow an uninterrupted downward trend for more than 20 years. Neither projection allows for an increase in juvenile homicide offending. Why? Have social or economic trends improved? No. But the crime trends preceding year 1 have changed.

For DiIulio, the 1995 assumption that crime trends would continue to get worse has been falsified. Will he still believe that a fixed percentage of the youth population will be "juvenile superpredators"? So one important vice of all the 1995 and 1996 predictions was that they did not allow for the known variability of crime rates despite the fact that rate changes had been the only significant moving part in the decade that produced their alarm.

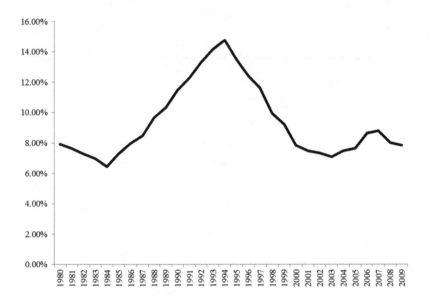

FIG. 10.—Juveniles as a percentage of total homicide arrests. Source: FBI Uniform Crime Reports, Supplementary Homicide Reports.

B. Regression and the Lessons of History

When historical patterns have been cyclical, any "straight-line" projections that either forbid variation (the Fox low projection in fig. 6) or push it all in one direction (Fox's high projection) must assume that long-term historical trends have changed. And this ignores a common pattern of statistical accounts of crime over time: regression toward long-term mean patterns. With respect to youth homicide, a good illustration is a charting of the share of all homicide arrests attributable to persons under 18 in the United States. Figure 10 tells this story for the period 1980–2009.

What figure 10 shows is that the percentage of total homicide arrests or attributions in the SHR increased over the period after 1984 to a rate double the level in the early years of the series and then returned to near the beginning proportion. The steep increase in the share of all arrests attributed to juveniles in the years after 1984 does not translate into any direct information on the future rate of juvenile offending, of course, because we would have to know future homicide offense rates for older offenders to translate any guesses we might have about the juvenile share of homicide arrests into estimates of juvenile rates. But the clear departure from historic patterns in 1984 onward puts forecasters on notice of important implications in assumptions they make about future trends. Take Fox's high projection for 2005 from the perspective of 1994. To maintain straight-line continuity from 1994, the historical pattern tells us that the proportion of total arrests attributable to juveniles would have to keep diverging from its historical levels. But we are also on notice that what had already diverged from a historic mean might also return to it. The perspective of a longer-term history should thus provide a caution against future assumptions radically different from historic relationships.

Paying close attention to historic relationships can also provide important information about the substantive implications of later changes. The pattern revealed in figure 10 speaks directly to the substantive argument made by Donohue and Levitt in their now-famous conclusion that about one-half the 1990s crime decline in the United States should be attributable to the changes in the quality of those born generated by the US Supreme Court abortion *Roe v. Wade* (410 U.S. 113 [1973]) decision (Donohue and Levitt 2001). I have extensively analyzed this study elsewhere (Zimring 2006, pp. 88–103) and do not here revisit most of the wide range of issues that analysis covered. But one argument made by Donohue and Levitt seems to me a textbook case in the substantive implications of regression. The clinching argument for these authors that crime declines in the 1990s were the result of 1973 changes in abortion rules was that arrest data showing crime declines in the 1990s were concentrated in younger age groups: "virtually all of the abortion-related crime decrease can be attributed to reductions in crime among the cohorts born after the abortion legalization. There is little change among older cohorts" (Donohue and Levitt 2001, p. 382).

But recall that Donohue and Levitt are examining the period after the early 1990s in figure 10, when the proportion of arrests for homicide attributable to youths is dropping, and they are noticing the same pattern for young adults. What they argue is that this "youth-only" pattern of decline shows that the lower rate of unwanted births produced a lower rate of crime and violence among teens and young adults in the 1990s.

But figure 10's data provide a new perspective for evaluating this claim: lower than what? If the arrest share of youths had declined to levels in the late 1990s that were much lower than in earlier eras, that would be evidence that crime tendencies of the young had shifted from normal expectations. But what figure 10 actually shows for juveniles is a return to normal patterns of juvenile homicide market share—7.3 percent in 1983 versus 9.7 percent in 2009—after peaking in the intervening years. The problem is that there was no *Roe v. Wade* to hold the 1983 levels down, so why should we conclude that it was a *Roe v. Wade* effect that pushed the youth share back to near its 1983 level in the late 1990s?

Figure 11 shows trends over time in the percentage of total arrests attributable to suspects under 18 for violent index offenses. The first lesson from figure 11 is that homicide and robbery have much larger increases and subsequent drops. The second pattern is that any increase in the juvenile share for violent crimes, much more modest than homicides, also falls back in the late 1990s, but the level of violence arrests for juveniles does not return to its 1983 level for violence—not good news for the Donohue and Levitt expectation of a uniquely large drop for the young. For property crime, by contrast, the concentration of arrests under age 18 declines in the 1990s to levels below the 1983 starting rates—better news for an argument that expects lower-than-historical concentrations for the post-*Roe* cohorts.

C. Gun and Nongun Juvenile Trends

One important disaggregation of trends in youth homicide provides important information on the source of the sharp increase in total youth homicide. Figure 12 separately shows trends over time in firearm and nonfirearm killings involving at least one offender under age 18.

All of the growth of homicide cases involving youths after 1980 was for firearm homicide. The three decades of nongun killings show no pronounced increases ever and a downward tendency throughout. Gun homicides first drop in the early 1980s and then triple during the decade after 1984, before dropping below the 1990 rate for every year after 1998. That the entirety of the increase occurs in gun cases suggests that the increase after 1984 is not due to a change in the character of the youth population but rather to the interaction of kids and guns. And the sharp and restricted nature of this increase is also a further suggestion that a regression, in this case a gun-specific regression, might be on the horizon. Figure 12 is pretty convincing evidence that

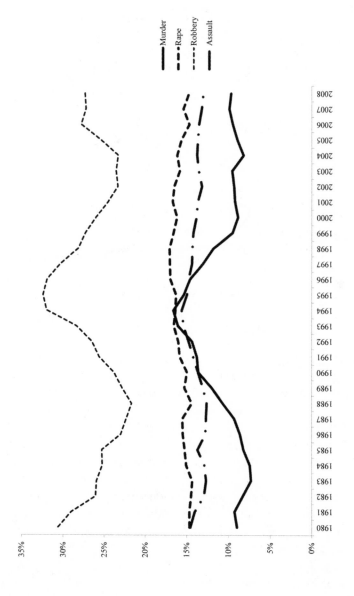

FIG. 11.—Juveniles as a percentage of total arrests for violent crimes. Source: FBI Uniform Crime Reports, Supplementary Homicide Reports.

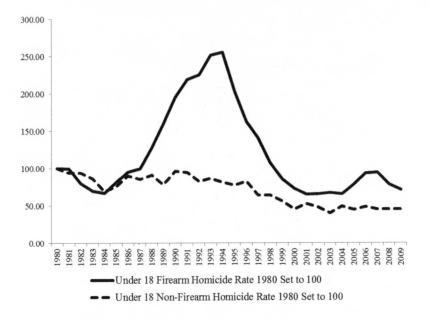

FIG. 12.—Trends in juvenile firearm and nonfirearm homicide rates, 1980 set to 100. Source: FBI Uniform Crime Reports, Supplementary Homicide Reports.

the character of the juvenile population did not change in the 1990s, only the character of instruments used in many violent assaults.

As a precautionary principle, for any projections based on historically atypical periods, regression toward more normal statistical values must be regarded as a plausible rival hypothesis to consider. The possibility of a return to historically normal patterns is so obvious that any set of projections that do not provide this alternative is presumptively deficient. Only convincing evidence of irreversible structural change should rebut the presumption that regression cannot be ignored. There were no such indications in the 1990s, only anecdotes and adjectives to the effect that this generation was very dangerous and the next one would be even worse.

D. The Folly of Demographic Determinism

This is not an appropriate venue for a comprehensive discussion of the relationship between population fluctuations and rates of youth crime in the United States. But one aspect of the moral panic of the

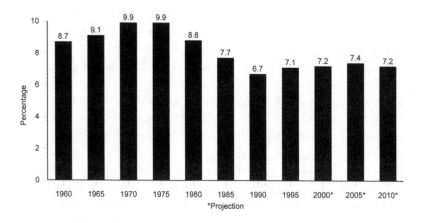

F<small>IG</small>. 13.—Proportion of US population, aged 13–17, 1960–2010. Source: Zimring (2005, fig. 8.2), based on 1960–95 census data.

1990s makes a brief excursion into demography necessary. The academic and political vendors of "the coming storm of juvenile violence" all argued that a major expansion of adolescents was on the American horizon. Wilson opened the bidding with a million more teenagers in the short term; DiIulio upped the ante to 4.5 million extra young people to derive his 270,000 juvenile superpredators and characterized the population developments on top as "a demographic time bomb." McCollum prophesied that "today's enormous cohort of 5-year-olds will be tomorrow's teenagers" (1996, p. 2) and places the major emphasis for his "coming storm" prediction on the expansion of the youth population.

There are two empirical puzzles that stand out when looking back at this particular American moral panic. The first puzzle is that the population trends that were on the horizon for the 20 years after 1990 were really quite modest. Figure 13 reproduces a figure from an earlier analysis of the 1990s panic, based on 1960–95 census data, that shows the share of total population aged 13–17 at 5-year intervals.

The proportion of the US population aged 13–17 varies over the 50 years after 1960 from a low of 6.7 percent of the population to a high of 9.9 percent. The demographic projections viewed with alarm in the 1990s were a very modest increase in the youth share: from the 6.7 percent low point in 1990 to 7.2 percent in 2010. The post–"demographic time bomb" youth cohort would be a much smaller share of the total population than 13–17-year-olds had been in the low-crime era of 1960 (7.2 percent vs. 8.7 percent). There were only two reasons why the numerical count of teens would go up at all by 2010: that total population was expanding and the significant fact that 1990 was the very lowest youth share of the time series. The 7.2 percent concentration projected for 2010 would be the third-lowest in the half century after 1960. By post–World War II American standards, the concentration of youths expected for 2010 was below average. And that should have been easy to determine in 1995.

The second reason that worry about the size of the youth population was an odd concern for 1995 was the lack of any indication in the years after 1975 that the size of the youth cohort was a major determinant of the youth violence problem. Recall that 1990 was the post-1960 low point in the youth share of total population. It was also the middle of the youth violence epidemic that launched the moral panic. A corollary to the fact discussed earlier that more than 100 percent of the rise in youth homicide was caused by changes in rates per 100,000 kids is that the size of the youth population played no role in the process. It turns out that the post-1990 modest expansion that McCollum worried about also played no role in the decline of youth violence, but the worry merchants of 1996 had no reason to know this. They did know, how-ever, that crime rates had been the only problematic moving part in producing the epidemic of the late 1980s. Why didn't the lack of any demographic impact on the crime upswing deter them from assuming the negative impact of any future population growth? Some speculation is required to answer this question, and that brings me to the final element of this methodological autopsy.

E. The Case of the Counterfeit Crime Cohort

The American birth cohort that was the subject of the projections by Fox, Wilson, DiIulio, and McCollum was too young to have any track record of criminal behavior in 1996. McCollum was predicting violence for 5-year-olds. Fox was projecting the number of appre-hended killers in a group of children between 3 and 7 years old for the period a decade in the future, and he asserted that the lowest vol-ume this new group would generate would be at the highest rate that age group had experienced in the 15 years in his chart. Why? He was projecting this 1994 rate (at minimum) on a 2005 set of 13–17-year-olds because he must have been assuming that the forces that pushed up the rates of adolescents in the 1980s and 1990s were structural shifts in urban settings or populations that would not be reversed in the proximate future. But what were those changes? The report complains about the lack of public support for child development in general terms but presents no model. The only data to inform the future in Fox's calculations were previous years' rates. Why shouldn't the average rate from 1980 to 1994 be his middle-range forward estimate? Because Fox assumed that things had been changing, but the evidence for this is missing from the analysis and it was literally off his chart.

DiIulio and associates had a verbal description for what they thought had driven up the homicide rate—"moral poverty"—and they argued that these social and demographic features are the cause of the sharp increases in the rate. But this is an assumption made by DiIulio, and there is no discussion of one-off environmental and situation features of the 1980s that might not have a similar impact in future years. Two examples of potentially nonpermanent impacts of the era mentioned by others were crack cocaine (Blumstein 2000) and sharp fluctuation in gun use (Cook and Laub 1998). For the cohort of kids born after 1985, the assumption in the "coming storm" warnings was that permanent social or demographic changes made a peak rate in an older generation the minimum legacy for the new generation.

Because the evidence for the permanent impact of the 1980s and 1990s changes was so weak, the out-of-hand rejection of regression or return to normal ratios is unjustified. But this must have been why intelligent people made simple mistakes.

The supreme irony is that this same generation of kids, "the enormous cohort of 5-year-olds" that scared McCollum and presidential nominee Robert Dole, became a blessed low-crime population group of wanted children 5 years later when economists Donohue and Levitt published their statistical argument that legal changes creating abortion on demand for pregnant women had reduced the probable crime rates of the post–*Roe v. Wade* birth cohorts by reducing the number and proportion of unwanted births. What had changed between 1995 and 2001 was first that a national crime drop of approximately 40 percent that started in the early 1990s generated attention by the late 1990s, so that many of the same social scientists who had been trying to explain unexpected bad news in the early 1990s were now trying to explain unexpected good crime news in 2001. As I showed earlier, Donohue and Levitt noticed that the arrest rates of younger segments of the population had dropped more than among older age groups. And this was taken as the distinctive fingerprint of the *Roe v. Wade* effect.

In less than a decade, future superpredators had become pioneer leaders in the great American crime decline. All during this transition the kids born around 1985 were too young to have been a major feature in the crime rates projected for their futures during either the *Roe v. Wade* or superpredator fads. To be fair, Donohue and Levitt did have older cohorts of post-*Roe* kids to assess effects on arrest rates. But assuming these 1990s arrest rate declines were *Roe* effects and therefore were also the legacy for the children born in 1990 was then and still is open to serious question.

But historians of science should take note of this episode. The criminological career of this cohort of US kids born in 1990 seems worthy of the *Guinness Book of World Records*. Before these kids turned 7, they were blamed for being a "demographic time bomb" certain to trouble our cities and fill our prisons. Yet before they turned 12, they were credited with leading a substantial reduction in American crime. The path from fatherless moral poverty to mother-loved wanted children was paved with crime statistics involving other age groups manipulated by creative theorists. Has there ever been a reversal of criminological fortune of this extremity?

IV. Youth Violence in 2025

To have read this far is to know that projecting rates and trends in life-threatening youth violence has been a hazardous occupation for more than a quarter century. As I write in 2012, is there any more concrete wisdom available about what will happen in the next 13 years than Norval Morris's refrain from the mid-1990s, "I don't know and you don't know and neither does DiIulio"? Nothing is certain, but I argue here that three elements of the American near future will produce much less variation in rates of youth homicide and life-threatening assaults than occurred in the roller-coaster years after 1985. This is good news for analysts—because less variation reduces the margin of error—and very good news for the citizenry because the 2011 base rate from which I predict only modest variability is as low as youth homicide has been in a generation.

The three features I expect to observe over the period 2012–25 are as follows:

1. diminished volatility in the proportion of total homicide attrib-
    utable to juvenile offenders;
2. minimal impact of demographic changes on youth homicide vol-
    ume from either the number of youths or the population com-
    position by race and ethnicity;
3. a pronounced tendency for the modest changes to come in ju-
    venile homicide to show the same direction and approximate
    magnitude as the trends for homicide by offenders in their 20s
    and 30s.

Two of the three features for the near future (numbers 1 and 3) were
not in evidence during the period from 1985 to 1994. Why, then, do
I now suspect that the wild swings of the 1980s and 1990s are over?

My first prediction is that the wide variations observed in the proportion of all homicides that were committed by juveniles are not likely
to happen again soon. The pattern shown in figure 10 of juvenile homicide arrests accounting for less than 8 percent of total homicides in
1983, more than 20 percent in 1994, and then less than 10 percent in
2008 and 2009 is a major reason why juvenile killings rose so swiftly
and then dropped so substantially. But the shape of figure 10 is also
why I expect much less volatility from now on. The story that figure
10 tells us is of a one-of-a-kind expansion of juvenile homicide involvement in the late 1980s and early 1990s that was followed by a major
drop back into the more normal level of close to 10 percent. Having
quickly returned to near-normal levels, it will take another Black Swan
dislocation to launch more volatile swings of the type we experienced
in the twentieth century's last 15 years. Without that sort of dislocation, we can expect the juvenile share of total homicide to stay close
to its current levels.

And the impact of population trends on youth violence rates will be
modest for two reasons. First, the projected shifts in the age structure
of the population will be rather modest in the period 2012–15. Youths
aged 13–17 will expand 6.6 percent from 2010 to 2025, but that is
about half the rate of total population expansion (13 percent), so the
share of the population in the age bracket will drop slightly. (Detailed
youth population estimates are presented in App. fig. B1.) This is
hardly "a demographic time bomb" (but then neither was the 16 percent expansion between 1995 and 2010 that provoked the figure of
speech). Second, changes in youth population levels have not played a
significant role in crime trends since 1975. Why should the ripples

projected for youth population in the near future break the pattern of lack of influence over the last generation?

So what might change levels of youth violence and in what direction? The most likely influence on future trends in youth violence is whether and to what extent there are changes in the homicide rates of persons over 18 in the coming years. When examining the proportion of total homicide arrests attributable to offenders under 18, Jeff Fagan and I found relatively similar percentages of total homicide rates for juveniles in the United States, Canada, New South Wales, Australia, and the United Kingdom. This did not mean that youth homicide rates were the same across these nations; they varied widely, but the variance in youth homicide was well predicted by the general homicide rate in each country (Zimring and Fagan 2005). We call this phenomenon "general rate dependence" and do not believe that it means that adult violence directly conditions the rate of youth violence. Instead, it seems likely that the same environmental factors that influence general homicide rates—culture, handgun availability, access to emergency medicine, law enforcement—influence juvenile rates as well. It seems likely that fluctuations in environmental conditions over time should have simultaneous and similar impacts on juvenile and older age group violence over time. This did not happen for population groups 25 and older in the decade after 1984, but that may have been the exception that proves the rule; witness the restoration of the previous pattern by 2000.

So I expect that juvenile homicide rates will move in the same direction as adult homicide rates. Both juvenile and adult rates were close to 45-year low points in 2011, but the widespread emulation of drops of the magnitude experienced by New York and more recently Los Angeles could produce even lower general (and juvenile) levels. There is no iron law that juvenile rates must conform to general patterns, but that is the most plausible default expectation for the near future. Perhaps American youth violence has arrived at a "new normal" after an exciting and peculiar 25-year interlude.

APPENDIX A

Articles Concerning Juvenile Crime and Justice in *Crime and Justice* by Year

Zimring, Franklin E. 1979. "American Youth Violence: Issues and Trends." In *Crime and Justice: An Annual Review of Research*, vol. 1, edited by Norval Morris and Michael Tonry. Chicago: University of Chicago Press.

Klein, Malcolm W. 1979. "Deinstitutionalization and Diversion of Juvenile Offenders: A Litany of Impediments." In *Crime and Justice: An Annual Review of Research*, vol. 1, edited by Norval Morris and Michael Tonry. Chicago: University of Chicago Press.

Mennel, Robert M. 1983. "Attitudes and Policies toward Juvenile Delinquency in the United States: A Historiographical Review." In *Crime and Justice: An Annual Review of Research*, vol. 4, edited by Michael Tonry and Norval Morris. Chicago: University of Chicago Press.

Loeber, Rolf, and Magda Stouthamer-Loeber. 1986. "Family Factors as Correlates and Predictors of Juvenile Conduct Problems and Delinquency." In *Crime and Justice: An Annual Review of Research*, vol. 7, edited by Michael Tonry and Norval Morris. Chicago: University of Chicago Press.

Greenwood, Peter W. 1986. "Differences in Criminal Behavior and Court Responses among Juveniles and Young Adult Defendants." In *Crime and Justice: An Annual Review of Research*, vol. 7, edited by Michael Tonry and Norval Morris. Chicago: University of Chicago Press.

Moffitt, Terrie E. 1990. "The Neuropsychology of Juvenile Delinquency: A Critical Review." In *Crime and Justice: A Review of Research*, vol. 12, edited by Michael Tonry and Norval Morris. Chicago: University of Chicago Press.

Spergel, Irving A. 1990. "Youth Gangs: Continuity and Change." In *Crime and Justice: A Review of Research*, vol. 12, edited by Michael Tonry and Norval Morris. Chicago: University of Chicago Press.

Feld, Barry C. 1993. "Criminalizing the American Juvenile Court." In *Crime and Justice: A Review of Research*, vol. 17, edited by Michael Tonry. Chicago: University of Chicago Press.

Moore, Mark H., and Stewart Wakeling. 1997. "Juvenile Justice: Shoring Up the Foundations." In *Crime and Justice: A Review of Research*, vol. 22, edited by Michael Tonry. Chicago: University of Chicago Press.

Pfeiffer, Christian. 1998. "Juvenile Crime and Violence in Europe." In *Crime and Justice: A Review of Research*, vol. 23, edited by Michael Tonry. Chicago: University of Chicago Press.

Moore, Mark H., and Michael Tonry. 1998. "Youth Violence in America." In *Youth Violence*, edited by Michael Tonry and Mark H. Moore. Vol. 24 of *Crime and Justice: A Review of Research*, edited by Michael Tonry. Chicago: University of Chicago Press.

Cook, Philip J., and John H. Laub. 1998. "The Unprecedented Epidemic in Youth Violence." In *Youth Violence*, edited by Michael Tonry and Mark H. Moore. Vol. 24 of *Crime and Justice: A Review of Research*, edited by Michael Tonry. Chicago: University of Chicago Press.

Anderson, Elijah. 1998. "The Social Ecology of Youth Violence." In *Youth Violence*, edited by Michael Tonry and Mark H. Moore. Vol. 24 of *Crime and Justice: A Review of Research*, edited by Michael Tonry. Chicago: University of Chicago Press.

Fagan, Jeffrey, and Deanna L. Wilkerson. 1998. "Guns, Youth Violence, and Social Identity in Inner Cities." In *Youth Violence*, edited by Michael Tonry and Mark H. Moore. Vol. 24 of *Crime and Justice: A Review of Research*, edited by Michael Tonry. Chicago: University of Chicago Press.

Feld, Barry C. 1998. "Juvenile and Criminal Justice Systems' Responses to Youth Violence." In *Youth Violence*, edited by Michael Tonry and Mark H. Moore. Vol. 24 of *Crime and Justice: A Review of Research*, edited by Michael Tonry. Chicago: University of Chicago Press.

Farrington, David P. 1998. "Predictors, Causes, and Correlates of Male Youth Violence." In *Youth Violence*, edited by Michael Tonry and Mark H. Moore. Vol. 24 of *Crime and Justice: A Review of Research*, edited by Michael Tonry. Chicago: University of Chicago Press.

Zimring, Franklin E. 1998. "Toward a Jurisprudence of Youth Violence." In *Youth Violence*, edited by Michael Tonry and Mark H. Moore. Vol. 24 of *Crime and Justice: A Review of Research*, edited by Michael Tonry. Chicago: University of Chicago Press.

Howell, James C., and J. David Hawkins. 1998. "Prevention of Youth Violence." In *Youth Violence*, edited by Michael Tonry and Mark H. Moore. Vol. 24 of *Crime and Justice: A Review of Research*, edited by Michael Tonry. Chicago: University of Chicago Press.

Bishop, Donna M. 2000. "Juvenile Offenders in the Adult Criminal System." In *Crime and Justice: A Review of Research*, vol. 27, edited by Michael Tonry. Chicago: University of Chicago Press.

Cook, Philip J., and John H. Laub. 2002. "After the Epidemic: Recent Trends in Youth Violence in the United States." In *Crime and Justice: A Review of Research*, vol. 29, edited by Michael Tonry. Chicago: University of Chicago Press.

Bottoms, Anthony, and James Dignan. 2004. "Youth Justice in Great Britain." In *Youth Crime and Youth Justice: Comparative and Cross-National Perspectives*, edited by Michael Tonry and Anthony N. Doob. Vol. 31 of *Crime and Justice: A Review of Research*, edited by Michael Tonry. Chicago: University of Chicago Press.

Doob, Anthony N., and Jane B. Sprott. 2004. "Youth Justice in Canada." In *Youth Crime and Youth Justice: Comparative and Cross-National Perspectives*, edited by Michael Tonry and Anthony N. Doob. Vol. 31 of *Crime and Justice: A Review of Research*, edited by Michael Tonry. Chicago: University of Chicago Press.

Morris, Allison. 2004. "Youth Justice in New Zealand." In *Youth Crime and Youth Justice: Comparative and Cross-National Perspectives*, edited by Michael Tonry and Anthony N. Doob. Vol. 31 of *Crime and Justice: A Review of Research*, edited by Michael Tonry. Chicago: University of Chicago Press.

Junger-Tas, Josine. 2004. "Youth Justice in the Netherlands." In *Youth Crime and Youth Justice: Comparative and Cross-National Perspectives*, edited by Michael Tonry and Anthony N. Doob. Vol. 31 of *Crime and Justice: A Review of Research*, edited by Michael Tonry. Chicago: University of Chicago Press.

Kyvsgaard, Britta. 2004. "Youth Justice in Denmark." In *Youth Crime and Youth Justice: Comparative and Cross-National Perspectives*, edited by Michael Tonry and Anthony N. Doob. Vol. 31 of *Crime and Justice: A Review of Research*, edited by Michael Tonry. Chicago: University of Chicago Press.

Janson, Carl-Gunnar. 2004. "Youth Justice in Sweden." In *Youth Crime and Youth Justice: Comparative and Cross-National Perspectives*, edited by Michael Tonry and Anthony N. Doob. Vol. 31 of *Crime and Justice: A Review of Research*, edited by Michael Tonry. Chicago: University of Chicago Press.

Albrecht, Hans-Jörg. 2004. "Youth Justice in Germany." In *Youth Crime and Youth Justice: Comparative and Cross-National Perspectives*, edited by Michael Tonry and Anthony N. Doob. Vol. 31 of *Crime and Justice: A Review of Research*, edited by Michael Tonry. Chicago: University of Chicago Press.

Roberts, Julian V. 2004. "Public Opinion and Youth Justice." In *Youth Crime and Youth Justice: Comparative and Cross-National Perspectives*, edited by Michael Tonry and Anthony N. Doob. Vol. 31 of *Crime and Justice: A Review of Research*, edited by Michael Tonry. Chicago: University of Chicago Press.

Walgrave, Lode. 2004. "Restoration in Youth Justice." In *Youth Crime and Youth Justice: Comparative and Cross-National Perspectives*, edited by Michael Tonry and Anthony N. Doob. Vol. 31 of *Crime and Justice: A Review of Research*, edited by Michael Tonry. Chicago: University of Chicago Press.

Weerman, Frank M. 2006. "Juvenile Offending." In *Crime and Justice in the Netherlands*, edited by Michael Tonry and Catrien Bijleveld. Vol. 35 of *Crime and Justice: A Review of Research*, edited by Michael Tonry. Chicago: University of Chicago Press.

Loeber, Rolf, and Wim Slot. 2006. "Serious and Violent Juvenile Delinquency: An Update." In *Crime and Justice in the Netherlands*, edited by Michael Tonry and Catrien Bijleveld. Vol. 35 of *Crime and Justice: A Review of Research*, edited by Michael Tonry. Chicago: University of Chicago Press.

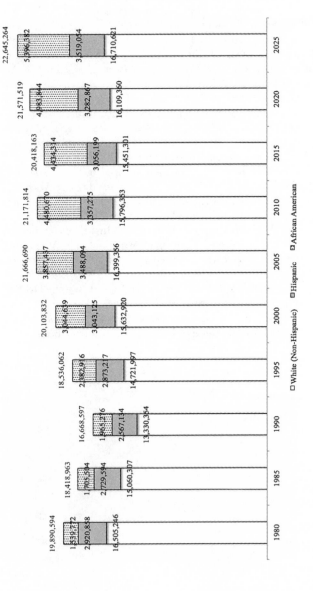

FIG. B1.—Youths aged 13–17: populations and projections, 1980–2025. Source: US Census (various years) and projections.

REFERENCES

Bennett, William J., John J. DiIulio, and John P. Walters. 1996. *Body Count: Moral Poverty . . . and How to Win America's War against Crime and Drugs.* New York: Simon & Schuster.

Blumstein, Alfred. 2000. "Disaggregating the Violence Trends." In *The Crime Drop in America*, edited by Alfred Blumstein and Joel Wallman. Cambridge: Cambridge University Press.

Centers for Disease Control and Prevention. 2004. *Health, United States 2004, with Chartbook on Trends in the Health of Americans.* http://www.cdc.gov/nchs/data/hus/hus04trend.pdf.

Cook, Philip J., and John H. Laub. 1998. "The Unprecedented Epidemic in Youth Violence." In *Youth Violence*, edited by Michael Tonry and Mark H. Moore. Vol. 24 of *Crime and Justice: A Review of Research*, edited by Michael Tonry. Chicago: University of Chicago Press.

———. 2002. "After the Epidemic: Recent Trends in Youth Violence in the United States." In *Crime and Justice: A Review of Research*, vol. 29, edited by Michael Tonry. Chicago: University of Chicago Press.

DiIulio, John. 1995. "The Coming of the Super-Predators." *Weekly Standard*, November 27.

Donohue, John, and Steven Levitt. 2001. "The Impact of Legalized Abortion on Crime." *Quarterly Journal of Economics* 116(2):379–420.

Fox, James Alan. 1996. *Trends in Juvenile Violence: A Report to the United States Attorney General on Current and Future Rates of Juvenile Offending.* Washington, DC: US Bureau of Justice Statistics.

McCollum, Bill. 1996. *Testimony before the House Subcommittee on Crime.* 104th Cong., 2nd sess., June 27.

National Center for Health Statistics. 1991. *Vital Statistics of the United States.* Washington, DC: US Government Printing Office.

US Department of Justice. Bureau of Justice Statistics. 1991. *Criminal Victimization in the United States.* Washington, DC: US Government Printing Office.

US National Center for Health Statistics. 2005. *Health, United States, 2005.* Hyattsville, MD: US National Center for Health Statistics.

Wilson, James Q. 1995. "Crime and Public Policy." In *Crime: Public Policies for Crime Control*, edited by James Q. Wilson and Joan Petersilia. San Francisco: Institute for Contemporary Studies.

Wolfgang, Marvin E., Robert M. Figlio, and Thorsten Sellin. 1972. *Delinquency in a Birth Cohort.* Chicago: University of Chicago Press.

Zimring, Franklin E. 1996. "Crying Wolf over Teen Demons." *Los Angeles Times*, August 19.

———. 1998. *American Youth Violence.* New York: Oxford University Press.

———. 2005. *American Juvenile Justice.* New York: Oxford University Press.

———. 2006. *The Great American Crime Decline.* Oxford: Oxford University Press.

Zimring, Franklin E., and Jeffrey Fagan. 2005. "Two Patterns of Age Progression in Adolescent Crime." In *American Juvenile Justice*, edited by Franklin E. Zimring. New York: Oxford University Press.

Zimring, Franklin E., and Gordon Hawkins. 1995. *Incapacitation: Penal Confinement and the Restraint of Crime*. New York: Oxford University Press.

Zimring, Franklin E., and Stephen Rushin. 2013. "Did Changes in Juvenile Sanctions Reduce Juvenile Crime Rates? A Natural Experiment." *Ohio State Journal of Criminal Law*, forthcoming.

Francis T. Cullen

Rehabilitation: Beyond Nothing Works

ABSTRACT

By 1975, the long-standing rehabilitative ideal had collapsed, a demise that was sudden and advocated by conservatives and liberals alike. Through the prism of the author's personal involvement in the issue of correctional rehabilitation, what occurred from this time to the present is recounted. This story includes identifying a period of pessimism in which a "nothing works" doctrine was widely embraced and a period of optimism in which knowledge has grown about the effectiveness of offender treatment. Given the current context, eight developments are likely to unfold in coming years: the continued policy appeal of rehabilitation, widening influence of the risk-need-responsivity paradigm, popularity of desistance-based treatment models, use of reentry programs as a conduit for rehabilitation, integration of early intervention with correctional intervention, use of financial incentives to fund effective programs, spread of rehabilitation ceremonies, and growth of specialty courts that target treatment to specific categories of offenders. For the rehabilitative ideal to retain legitimacy, however, two major challenges will need to be addressed. First, with support from policy makers, practitioners must embrace evidence-based corrections and professionalism. And second, criminologists must take seriously their obligation to develop a correctional science that can invent treatment interventions capable of reducing offender recidivism.

If my memory serves me correctly—and who can be sure after nearly 40 years?—I first met Robert Martinson on a chilly but sunny Saturday

Francis T. Cullen is Distinguished Research Professor of Criminal Justice at the University of Cincinnati. He is grateful to Cheryl Lero Jonson, Jennifer L. Lux, Hyung Jin Lim, Ted Palmer, Michael Tonry, and an anonymous reviewer for their assistance. Valuable comments were also provided by Anthony Doob, Barry Feld, Richard Frase, Joshua Page, Alex Piquero, Lawrence Sherman, and other participants in the April 27–28, 2012, Robina Institute Conference at the University of Minnesota Law School.

morning in the fall of 1975. I was a doctoral student in sociology and education at Columbia University. I had found my way into criminology, however, after taking a course with Richard Cloward at the School of Social Work and, subsequently, being invited to pursue my dissertation under his direction. As I traveled to see Professor Martinson, I was aware that he had driven the final nail into rehabilitation's coffin through his 1974*b* essay, published in *The Public Interest*, that was widely understood to show that "nothing works" in correctional programming to reform offenders. Now he was embarking on a follow-up evaluation study in which he would revisit the issue of treatment effectiveness (Martinson 1979). I had seen an advertisement for a research assistant's position and, after applying, was asked to come and talk with him.

How excited I was as I knocked on the door of a brownstone in Manhattan. I was met, I believe, by Judith Wilks—a coauthor on Martinson's previous project (Lipton, Martinson, and Wilks 1975)—and ushered into a living room. Soon thereafter, Martinson appeared, wearing a white T-shirt and seeming as though he had just awakened for our 10:00 appointment. I was given a reprint of the article in *The Public Interest* and two other writings—all of which I retain in my "Martinson file" today. The meeting was cordial, and then I was asked whether I had computer skills. My dissertation with Cloward, however, was theoretical and, while it subsequently resulted in a published book (Cullen 1984), its content showed my lack of interest in honing my quantitative skills (I have never had SPSS on my computer). It was clear that my answer of, "No, but I can learn them," was not going to earn me the research position. Despite Martinson's faint promise that I would soon hear from him, I never did.

I was not terribly disappointed. Mostly, I was pleased to have met Professor Martinson, for by that time I had become an ardent opponent of rehabilitation, whether it was with the mentally ill or with criminals. I had read virtually everything written on labeling theory (for one fruit of these labors, see Cullen and Cullen [1978]), and thus was well acquainted with the unanticipated consequences of efforts to save the wayward. Furthermore, Cloward's course, "Deviance and the Social Structure," was not, as I had anticipated, a discussion of *Delinquency and Opportunity* (Cloward and Ohlin 1960) and theoretical criminology. Rather, it was a fascinating account of how social welfare ideology was used to control poor and deviant populations; we read titles such as *The Right to Be Different* (Kittrie 1971), *The Manufacture of Madness* (Szasz 1970), and *The Discovery of the Asylum* (Rothman 1971; see also Piven and Cloward 1977). Disappointed at not getting hired by Martinson? No. Just to meet the scholar who proved that rehabilitation was quackery was a privilege.

A little over 3 years earlier, however, I was a psychology major at Bridgewater State College, not far from my boyhood home in Boston. I entered college in 1968 as a history major, intending to become a high school teacher and coach. My exposure to psychology (as well as to sociology), which was not taught in high school, unlocked my imagination and enthusiasm. Whereas history was largely the study of dead people, it seemed so much more fun to investigate the behavior of living people, whom one could talk to—and even help. Majoring in psychology had another benefit. To avoid doing some onerous assignment, psychology classes offered students the option to participate in experiments (I was a confederate in a replication of a classic Solomon Asch conformity study) and, due to the college's proximity to the institution, the option to travel to the local mental hospital for the criminally insane each week to talk with an offender. I took advantage of this latter opportunity during, I believe, the 1970–71 academic year. One semester, I was assigned a "defective delinquent," a mentally challenged offender for whom I felt quite sorry. Another semester, I was assigned a sex offender who, when he talked about women, stuttered and referred to them as squaws. Given my youth and the less politically correct environment of the time, this struck me as a touch amusing.

Again, my motivation for traveling to the local "hospital" was mostly to avoid assignments. Still, I had another incentive: voyeurism—a chance to peek into the hidden world where unfortunate people were detained. I was not so naive as to believe that my weekly hourly visit would have a transformative effect on my "clients." But I did think that such contacts could be part of a larger effort to humanize these offenders' institutional lives and eventually return them to society less troubled. They should be rehabilitated, and we should do all in our power to save them. My faith in treatment was so unblinking that I fully intended to become a counseling or clinical psychologist and, had not modest GRE scores prompted nearly all the graduate programs to which I applied to decline my admission, I would have. At that point, sociology—which welcomed my talents—seemed a better option, and it was off to graduate school for a year at the University of Rhode Island and then to Columbia.

As it turned out, the site of my visitation—Bridgewater State Hospital for the Criminally Insane—was a notoriously awful institution. The facility's failings were captured in Frederick Wiseman's classic exposé, *Titicut Follies*, first shown at the 1967 New York Film Festival at Lincoln Center. The documentary took its title from the name of the patients' annual talent contest, with the label of "Titicut" itself a Native American designation for the local area. In his *New York Times* review, Vincent Canby (1967) described the film as providing "a calm, cool and ultimately horrifying look at conditions in the state prison" and "an extraordinarily candid picture of a modern Bedlam, where the horrors are composed of indifference and patronizing concern."

My trips to the hospital were circumscribed—taking approved routes through the institution to a small private room where my visits with offenders were held—but I was vaguely aware how difficult life was in aged buildings whose every inch seemed painted in gray. I also heard rumors that the patients saw psychiatrists only briefly and perfunctorily, and that if a paroled hospital inmate offended, nobody's release would be approved for six months. I had no idea if any of this was true. But the strange thing was that none of these experiences in 1971 caused me to doubt the legitimacy of treatment. The challenge was to do it better—whether that was to design a more colorful and therapeutic facility or, in my case, to become a counseling psychologist who cared enough to save the wayward. Within 2 years, however, I had undergone a fundamental cognitive transformation. I now understood the true message of *Titicut Follies*: Rehabilitation could never work.

My biography is of little substantive importance in and of itself but, writ large, it reflects a common and profound change that occurred in the 1970s: Not only Frank Cullen, but virtually everyone came to forsake the rehabilitative ideal. Through an intersection of cataclysmic social events and strong intellectual currents, a social movement of sorts had risen up to purge systems of control of the insidious social welfare ideology that used the rhetoric of benevolence to mask the abuse of power. Martinson's (1974*b*) study did not spark such thinking; its publication served only to confirm what we already knew.

Looking back, what is perhaps more remarkable is that I ever escaped the clutches of this new way of thinking about rehabilitation. A Kuhnian scientific and policy revolution had taken place. Those who persisted in embracing offender treatment were excommunicated from the criminological faith—a shunning that involved being either ignored or vigorously attacked (Gottfredson 1979). It is perhaps tempting to accuse me of hyperbole; but I am not guilty of this charge. In the early days of my academic career, I was one of those who mocked anyone stupid enough to retain any belief in the capacity of the state to improve anyone's life—let alone those sitting in dreary cages behind thick, impenetrable walls.

In 1979, however, I changed my mind. It was one of those St. Paul moments. I was converted from persecutor to apostle. No, I was not riding a horse and the God of Truth did not speak unto me. But there was a flash of light—or a flash of something—that enveloped my consciousness and revealed a new reality. In a moment, my understanding of the correctional world was reversed in a fresh and uplifting way. I was attending a National Endowment for the Humanities seminar at the University of Virginia conducted by Gresham Sykes. I thought that I would simply hang out with a famous scholar and play tennis in my free time—expectations that came to fruition. But Grex, as he was known, also wished us to do some work and surprisingly assigned a 10-page paper. I was confronted with the anxiety that my students must feel when they have no idea what topic to choose. Relief came shortly, however, when it dawned on me that I could write about rehabilitation.

For some unknown reason, a thought I had never had before came to mind. When rehabilitation is eliminated as the guiding correctional theory, will the alternative paradigm and its accompanying policies be better? Until this point, I had lacked the reflexivity to question the received wisdom about rehabilitation. But once the question was posed, the answer seemed stunningly obvious—No. Why would a system that overtly intends to inflict pain on offenders be preferable to one that at least pretends to try to improve their lives? I strained to find any reason to believe that the explicit embrace of punishment would yield a more humane and effective system than the embrace of rehabilitation. Shortly thereafter, Grex had his 10-page paper outlining the unanticipated consequences of forfeiting the rehabilitative ideal. Three years later, with Karen Gilbert as a collaborator, I wrote *Reaffirming Rehabilitation* (1982).

By coincidence, *Reaffirming Rehabilitation* was published by Anderson, then based in Cincinnati, on the very day that I interviewed for my current position at the University of Cincinnati. My great fear was

that the plane would crash on the way to the interview, and I would never see my first book! Because two other applicants had turned down the job offer and it was late in the academic year—May of 1982—I was offered the position before leaving campus (my first offer after, by a conservative estimate, having applications rejected 150 times over the previous 6 years). I returned to Western Illinois University with book and job in hand.

Moving to Cincinnati was important because it placed me in what Merton (1995, p. 5) terms a "cognitive micro-environment"—a location where "direct interaction among teachers, students, and colleagues" allows fresh ideas to "emerge and develop." Of the six faculty in my new academic home (we now have over 20), three were avowed advocates of offender treatment—me, of course; Edward Latessa, who joined the department just before me; and Patricia Van Voorhis, who joined just after me. With some amusement—but also with more than a kernel of truth—it was often said that the only three people who still believed in rehabilitation were the Cincinnati trinity of Ed, Pat, and Frank. Eventually, we helped build a major center and training ground for correctional research and practice (Ed and Pat would win the ASC Vollmer Award for their efforts to develop and disseminate evidence-based practices). Personally, my association with my colleagues nourished my commitment to rehabilitation and expanded my insights into the fate of offender rehabilitation in the past quarter century.

Reaffirming Rehabilitation had one other significant by-product. Upon reading this volume, Paul Gendreau—now an internationally respected rehabilitation scholar—sent a letter of praise to my publisher, who passed it on to me. I answer my mail and so does Paul, and thus we were soon corresponding, which resulted in mutual lecture invitations and scholarly collaboration. Paul's friendship proved important because it was how I became acquainted with a network of Canadian psychologists who developed the field's most vital treatment paradigm (see Andrews and Bonta 2010; Cullen 2012). My associations with this scholarly crew challenged my sociological biases and allowed me to interpret their contributions in ways that were not common among criminologists.

The point of my story is that by choice and by serendipity, I have found myself at the intersection of key rehabilitation ideas, figures, and networks that have shaped the development of correctional treatment policy and practice since 1975. My belief is that despite its idiosyncratic elements, my autobiography has afforded me close insights into core developments in this area. Although not always explicitly revealed, I draw on these experiences in this essay to recount the story of rehabilitation—how, in a sense, we have arrived at the current state of affairs in corrections. These understandings also inform my predictions of the major developments that will direct offender treatment as the United States moves toward 2025.

Section I briefly discusses the rise and power of the rehabilitative ideal, which has implications even today for offender treatment's remarkable tenacity. The concept embodies core reasons for its appeal—its embrace of a noble ideal and its pragmatic understanding that offender deficits must be addressed to avoid recidivism. Section II considers why rehabilitation by 1975 had experienced a sudden reversal of fortune, moving from decades-long ideological hegemony to complete disrepute. Although treatment's failures were real, its rejection was inspired mainly by a broader loss of confidence in the social welfare state to live up to its promises to do good. The special effects of Robert Martinson's "nothing works" essay are discussed, especially how he reframed the focus of the treatment debate from the failure of the corrections system to the ineffectiveness of rehabilitation interventions.

Section III proposes that a more optimistic "what works" movement arose in the late 1970s and early 1980s that, in the shadows of "nothing works" dominance, grew incrementally until the past decade when it emerged to shape correctional policy and practice. Its legitimacy came from its capacity to demonstrate empirically, especially through meta-analyses, that offender treatment reduces recidivism—and does so far more than do punitively based interventions. This approach was advanced further by the risk-need-responsivity (RNR) model developed by Andrews, Bonta, Gendreau, and other Canadian psychologists (e.g., Gendreau 1996; Andrews and Bonta 2010). The RNR paradigm offered core principles of effective intervention and the technology to implement them; it also produced positive treatment outcomes (Andrews and Bonta 2010). The emergence and growth of the evidence-based corrections movement proved important as well, focusing attention on the need to implement programs that worked. As the evidence showed, these were interventions with a rehabilitative component.

Section IV uses current developments to predict the likely arc of rehabilitation policy until 2025. Thus, in the immediate future—but likely for the foreseeable future—the rehabilitative ideal will remain popular with the public and will shape correctional policy and practice. In terms of treatment paradigms, the Canadians' RNR model is likely to dominate the field, although its supremacy will be challenged by perspectives derived for desistance research (such as the Good Lives Model; see Ward and Maruna 2007). Reentry programs are likely to continue to spread and, although used for many purposes, could be a conduit for the delivery of evidence-based treatment. As biosocial and life-course criminology continue to unravel trajectories into persistent offending, the line between antisocial and criminal behavior will become less distinct. Calls to integrate early intervention and correctional treatment will expand. Some of these programs will be funded with innovative strategies, such as social impact bonds, that will reward vendors of effective initiatives with profits to be shared with investors. It also is possible that more attention will be paid to "deserving" offenders. If so, there should be a growth of rehabilitation ceremonies that certify that offenders are reformed and a growth of specialty courts (e.g., drug, mental health, veterans) that seek to keep troubled offenders away from the traditional justice system.

Section V concludes by identifying two challenges. The first challenge is to policy makers and practitioners: They must embrace evidence-based corrections. Promising programs exist, but only sustained research to identify what works and how to make interventions work will produce meaningful reductions in recidivism. Rehabilitation is an evolving science. Respect for expertise also is a prelude to the requirement that correctional practice, much like medicine, become, and come to be seen as, a profession. We need a "Correctional Hippocratic Oath" that embraces science and an ethic of care that promises to do no needless harm to offenders or the public. The second challenge is to academic criminologists. As is happening in the emerging field of "crime science" (Clarke 2010), scholars should envision themselves as capable of constructing knowledge that has the practical utility of inventing programs that take rehabilitation seriously (Cullen 2012).

Before embarking on this excursion into the past and then on to the future of correctional policy, some conceptual housekeeping is in order. The concept of rehabilitation is typically used in three logically related ways. First, rehabilitation refers to the goal or purpose of corrections, typically juxtaposed to other "philosophies of punishment," such as retribution/just deserts, deterrence, and incapacitation. In Allen's (1981, p. 2) words, rehabilitation "is the notion that the purpose of penal treatment is to effect changes in the characters, attitudes, and behaviors of convicted offenders, so as to strengthen the social defense against unwanted behavior, but also to contribute to the welfare and satisfaction of others." Second, rehabilitation refers to a correctional theory that articulates an overarching blueprint for the correctional system. Thus, the concept would specify the practices that should be used to change offenders and the organizational forms and policies for achieving the goal of offender reform (e.g., indeterminate sentencing, probation, parole release based on treatment progress). Third, rehabilitation refers to a particular kind of intervention—one defined as a "planned correctional intervention that targets for change internal and/ or social criminogenic factors with the goal of reducing recidivism and, where possible, of improving other aspects of an offender's life" (Cullen and Jonson 2012, p. 149; see also Cullen and Jonson 2011). This definition includes under its conceptual umbrella interventions that are undertaken within the correctional system, that are designed to be responsive to certain treatment targets, and that seek to produce definable outcomes. It excludes general aspects of the correctional system (e.g., exercise in prison, being on probation) that might have behavioral effects. It also excludes influences and behavioral changes that might be due to fortuitous life events (e.g., marriage).

The three definitions—correctional goal, theoretical blueprint, treatment intervention—are typically interrelated, which is perhaps why they are rarely differentiated in scholarly writings. Thus, the goal of rehabilitation leads to a specific blueprint for how to achieve the goal, and this blueprint in turn includes interventions or programs that seek to effect planned correctional change through treatment strategies. In the pages to follow, the specific usage of "rehabilitation" will be transparent from the context of the text. Still, should a distinction in usage be relevant to a substantive point, I try to make this clear.

I. The Rehabilitative Ideal

It is a remarkable fact that, despite a four-decade mean season in corrections and widespread endorsement of the idea that nothing works, rehabilitation remains integral to contemporary policy discussions (Cullen 2006). As a prelude to understanding the present, it may be helpful to discuss why the rehabilitative ideal is powerful and how it became ingrained in correctional policy and practice.

A. Power of Rehabilitation

Offender treatment is not merely called "offender treatment"—or something similar. Rather, it is subsumed under the classic phrase of "the rehabilitative ideal" (Allen 1964, 1981). Until very recently, I did not give this construct a second thought, but I should have. For its two words—"ideal" and "rehabilitation"—reveal why treatment remains a vital part of public policy preferences. As I discuss in Section V, Americans' support for reforming the criminally wayward is longstanding and stable—a fundamental component of the national culture (Cullen, Fisher, and Applegate 2000; Cullen et al. 2007). Each word has special meaning. When combined, they constitute a way of thinking—a "sensibility" (Tonry 2004)—that is powerful and has the capacity to remain persuasive across diverse historical eras.

The word "ideal" suggests that treatment is intended to be an enlightened enterprise—a noble attempt to surmount our baser desires to inflict pain on those who have inflicted pain on others. Rehabilitation is meant to serve a broad social purpose, which includes reforming the wayward and, symbolically, announcing what kind of people we are. Here, the secular and the sacred intersect (Allen 1981). The secular message is that we are a civilized nation that has relinquished the brutal and the barbaric—the whip and the gallows. The sacred message is that we are capable of turning our collective cheek in hopes of effecting redemption.

Belief in this idea is not all-enveloping. It can ring hollow in the face of a heinous crime or when victims are trumpeted as the more deserving object of our sympathies. Still, the notion that corrections should do more than punish and warehouse—that it should serve a nobler purpose—is difficult to relinquish. The call to be a better people tugs at our hearts and minds. This ideal is a fundamental part of rehabilitation's continued appeal.

The word "rehabilitation" is pregnant with the understanding that offenders are not like us—normal people who do not break the law. There is something wrong with them that needs to be fixed. If not, then these crime-producing deficits will continue to exist and to produce what they have in the past—criminal involvement. These individuals would be consigned to a life in crime and public safety would be jeopardized. Not to "rehabilitate" offenders thus is irrational.

Of course, this is the logic that inheres in the so-called medical model. Unless sick people are treated, they will not be cured. This idea leads to three interrelated components of how rehabilitation must be accomplished. First, similar to medicine, we cannot fix offenders if we do not know what is wrong with them. To diagnose accurately, we must have the scientific expertise to know what causes crime and then how to treat offenders effectively. Second, just as people may become ill for different reasons, they commit crimes for different reasons. One person may rob due to economic need, another due to peer pressure. This means that diagnosis and treatment must be based on the criminal and not the crime. Third and closely related, a focus on the offender means that, as in medicine, the treatment must be individualized. We see a physician to be examined as an individual. Some medications might be effective for many people who share our specific malady, but this is not always true. We may have more than one thing wrong with us, we may be allergic to some medications, our problems may be genetic or due to poor lifestyle choices, and so on. We need to be treated as the unique individuals we are. To cure criminals, the same process is needed (Rothman 1980).

Rehabilitation's contentions resonate because they are based on a criminological reality that also is reflected in public opinion. Criminology as a discipline is devoted to discovering the conditions that separate lawbreakers from law-abiders. Theories are competing wagers as to which criminogenic conditions matter most and how they might be sequenced over time. Empirical studies, some guided by theory and some not, have produced a vast amount of evidence on the risk factors that heighten criminal participation (see, e.g., Gendreau, Little, and Goggin 1996; Farrington, Loeber, and Ttofi 2012; Tanner-Smith, Wilson, and Lipsey 2013). Successful treatment programs take note of these risk factors and target them for change (Andrews and Bonta 2010). The connection between cause and treatment is fundamental. It is a reality that citizens appear to understand.

In a corresponding way, public opinion research shows that attributions of crime causation affect policy preferences. Dispositional attributions, which see crime as due to choice or traits, justify punitive policies aimed at making bad choices less profitable or at keeping those with bad seeds incapacitated. These attributions are expressed by survey respondents, but so are situational attributions—and often more strongly and typically by the same individuals (Unnever et al. 2010). This situational worldview links crime to more malleable social factors, such as ineffective parenting, family breakdown, exposure to delinquent peers, neighborhood disorganization, poverty, and unemployment. In turn, these explanations provide the public with the logic for endorsing—which they do in large percentages—correctional rehabilitation and human-services prevention programs (e.g., early intervention): Unless the risk factors that create deficits in offenders are addressed and their effects reversed, recidivism will ensue (Peter D. Hart Research Associates 2002; Princeton Survey Research Associates International 2006; Unnever et al. 2010).

Thus, the rehabilitative ideal draws its power from its nobility and its rationality—from the promise that compassionate science, rather than vengeful punishment, is the road to reducing crime. Rehabilitation allows us to be a better and safer people—a bargain that an aspirational and utilitarian nation finds hard to turn down. Still, two potential weaknesses lie within the rehabilitative ideal—shortcomings I discuss in Section II. One is that the ideal is a lie; we promise to save offenders but in reality intend often only to control and coerce them. The second is quackery; we claim to have the expertise to cure offenders but often do not.

B. Rise of Rehabilitation

Although the task at hand is more to explore the recent than the distant past of rehabilitation, four points need to be made. First, Americans' public embrace of rehabilitation extends back more than 200 years. It was perhaps first evident prominently in the 1820s, when reformers in New York and Pennsylvania invented the "penitentiary" (Rothman 1971). The name penitentiary is instructive because it expresses the aim to create an institution that would be an instrument of reformation, not punishment. The critical debate in the two states was over not goals but methods—especially how to prevent inmates from corrupting one another when confined together behind thick and insurmountable walls. Pennsylvania placed its inmates in solitary confinement. New York allowed inmates to congregate but enforced a strict code of silence. In both cases, reformers claimed that the internal regimen of their institutions—an orderly community based on religion, hard work, freedom from criminal influence, and discipline—would reverse the criminogenic effects of life in the disorderly environments from which offenders were drawn.

Second, the outlines of the modern rehabilitative ideal, called the "new penology," were articulated in the "Declaration of Principles" promulgated at the inaugural meeting, held in 1870 in Cincinnati, of the National Congress on Penitentiary and Reformatory Discipline (later called the American Correctional Association). By this time, the penitentiary model had fallen into disrepute. Crowding made solitary confinement and enforced silence impractical. Institutions were increasingly populated by members of the so-called dangerous class—poor, urban, immigrants—whose behavior might be explained in terms of social Darwinism (Werth 2009). But the Congress's 130 or so participants—arriving from 24 states and other nations—greeted such challenges not with despair but by reaffirming the ideal. They were, as described by McKelvey (1977, p. 89), a group of "wardens, chaplains, judges, governors, and humanitarians," and they proclaimed that "the supreme aim of prison discipline is the reformation of criminals, not the infliction of vindictive suffering" (Wines 1910, p. 39). "Criminals on conviction" should not be "cast off" but "made the objects of a generous parental care"; they should be "trained to virtue and not merely sentenced to suffering" (p. 40).

The accompanying question was how to rehabilitate more effectively. They started by advocating for, in essence, treatment programs. Religion was still defined as "first in importance" because it is "most potent in its action upon the human heart and life" (Wines 1910, p. 40). But they then called for education and industrial training, and, "to save discharged prisoners," they advocated both "providing them with work and encouraging them to redeem their character and regain their lost position in society" (p. 42). They argued further that corrections must become more professional. Inmates should be classified and managed more with rewards than with punishments. The "prison officer" should receive "special training" and have "high qualities of head and heart," for only when their position "is raised to a dignity of a profession" will "the administration of public punishment become scientific, uniform and successful" (pp. 39–40). Perhaps most critical, sentences should be made indeterminate, with release contingent upon reformation. Only in this way, they asserted, would an offender have the motivation to change. A key obligation was to create circumstances where this was possible. Thus, the "prisoner's destiny should be placed, measurably, in his own hands; he must be put into circumstances where he will be able, through his own exertion, to continuously better his own condition" (p. 39).

Third, the new penology proved to be the foundational blueprint for modern corrections. It was fleshed out further during the Progressive Era when the emerging social sciences provided a means for identifying the social and psychological sources of offending. Such causal insights were to be found in a series of influential books, such as Sophonisba Breckinridge and Edith Abbott's (1912) *The Delinquent Child and the Home* and William Healy's (1915) *The Individual Delinquent*. It was now possible to know what to treat—whether the harsh circumstances of inner-city lives, disrupted families, bad companions, or mental abnormality (Rothman 1980).

More salient, the Progressive Era—roughly the first quarter of the 1900s—was the "age of reform" in which calls for progress were not only made but answered (Hofstadter 1955). During this period, probation, parole, indeterminate sentencing, and the juvenile court went from the exception to close to the rule (Rothman 1980; Cullen and Gilbert 1982). These reforms constituted a coherent effort to implement the rehabilitative ideal. Thus, individual offenders would be assessed case by case; those judged less risky in a presentence report would be placed on probation where they would be supervised and counseled by a probation officer. If sent to prison, offenders would serve an indeterminate length until a parole board judged them cured, at which time they would come under the watchful and helpful eye of a parole officer. The uniqueness and malleability of youngsters justified a separate juvenile court devoted to saving delinquent youths and those at risk of such misconduct (i.e., status offenders and abused and neglected youths). These justice system components remain with us nearly a century later and are invariably involved in discussion of policy and practice reforms.

Fourth, the next 50-year period—following 1920 or so—might be called the era of "corrections." Rehabilitation consolidated its hold. Over time, more sophisticated offender classification systems were introduced, and an array of programs appeared—individual and group counseling, therapeutic communities, token economies, behavioral modification, vocational training, work release and furloughs, college education, halfway houses, and so on. The very use of the term "corrections"—whether in reference to correctional institutions or to community corrections—signaled the ideological dominance of the rehabilitative ideal. Favoring the treatment of offenders became a sign not only of a kind heart but also of a civilized mind.

As Allen (1981, p. 6) notes, "it is remarkable how widely the rehabilitative ideal was accepted in this century as a statement of aspirations for the penal system, a statement largely endorsed by the media, politicians, and ordinary citizens." Take, for example, Lou Gehrig. Following his retirement from the Yankees due to a disease later named after him, Gehrig willingly served on the New York City Parole Commission in 1940–41. He voiced the view that "only a small percentage of men have to go back to prison. I think that many convicted fellows deserve another chance" (quoted in Robinson 2001, p. 32). There is broader confirming evidence: In a 1968 national poll, 73 percent of Americans stated that the main emphasis of prisons should be rehabilitation. Protecting society and punishment were selected by only 12 percent and 7 percent, respectively; "don't know" was 9 percent (Cullen, Fisher, and Applegate 2000).

Moreover, support for rehabilitation among criminologists was nearly universal—so much so that offender treatment was a core part of the discipline's professional ideology or orthodoxy (Allen 1981; Cullen and Gendreau 2001). The view that corrections should be about using the scientific study of crime to save the wayward was unquestioned, as was the view that punishment was ineffective and unjustified. Characterizing textbooks in the early 1960s, Toby (1964, p. 332) concluded that students reading these volumes "might infer that punishment is a vestigial carryover of a barbaric past and will disappear as humanitarianism and rationality spreads." Echoing these views, Gibbons (1999, p. 272) observed that "it seemed to many criminologists that they were about to become 'scholar-princes' who would lead a social movement away from punitive responses to criminals and delinquents and toward a society in which treatment, rehabilitation, and reintegration of deviants and lawbreakers would be the dominant cultural motifs."

Faith in rehabilitation, however, did not mean that scholars were naive to its failings (see, e.g., Menninger 1968). Cressey (1958, p. 371) noted that "most of the 'techniques' used in 'correcting' criminals have not been shown to be effective or ineffective and are only vaguely related to any reputable theory of behavior or criminality." But unmasking the limits of treatment was seen not as falsifying the entire enterprise but as a prelude to identifying how rehabilitation might be improved. Cressey's prescription was to develop a theory-based correctional technique "which can be routinely administered by a rather unskilled worker in the framework of an eight-hour shift" (p. 372).

Sykes (1958) shared this professional ideology. In his classic *The Society of Captives*, he detailed how the "pains of imprisonment" foster an oppositional inmate subculture. This reality argues against hubris, for it is "excessively optimistic to expect the prison to rehabilitate 100 percent of its inmates" (p. 133). Still, cautioned Sykes, the "greatest naiveté, perhaps, lies in those who believe that because progress in methods for reforming the criminal has been so painfully slow and uncertain in the past, little or no progress can be expected in the future" (pp. 133–34).

Again, this was the worldview that I held when I graduated from Bridgewater State College in the spring of 1972. The reality of rehabilitation might not be perfect—or even defensible—but the ideal would energize us to discover the elixir for curing offenders. One year later I did not believe in rehabilitation—an ideological transformation that everyone else seemed to share.

II. Sudden Decline

The decline of support for the rehabilitative ideal was sudden and qualitative (for reviews of this period, see Palmer [1978]; Cullen and Gilbert [1982]; Rotman [1990]). By the mid–1970s, it had become common to ask, "Is rehabilitation dead?" (see, e.g., Serrill 1975; Halleck and Witte 1977). Allen (1981) describes this change in paradigmatic language in which an ideological revolution had quickly transpired (see Kuhn 1970). "In a remarkably short time," he notes, "a new orthodoxy has been established asserting that rehabilitative objectives are largely unattainable" (p. 57). Although taking the opposite position, these "new attitudes resemble in their dominance and pervasiveness those of the old orthodoxy, prevailing only a few years ago, that mandated rehabilitative efforts and exuded optimism about rehabilitative capabilities" (p. 58). How could this occur? Why did people like me change our minds?

A. A Noble Lie

Belief in treatment hinges on the assumption that state officials are able to rehabilitate offenders. The most obvious issue is whether they have the scientific expertise to diagnose and then cure criminogenic propensities. This technical issue is not necessarily a deal breaker. If crime is like cancer, it might simply take a long time to develop effective medicines, and we might have to be satisfied with incremental treatment gains. What matters more, however, is whether those claiming to save the wayward are, in fact, acting in bad faith. If that is true, officials are purporting to live by an ideal but in fact are using claims of benevolence as a mask for more sinister ends. If so, then the rehabilitative ideal is transformed from a humane ideal into what was called a "noble lie" (Morris 1974, p. 20).

Similar to many of my generation, I felt that I had indeed been told a noble lie—that I had been duped by those running the correctional system. Since the mid- to late 1960s, a mounting literature had appeared that detailed the disquieting gap between the ideal and the real in offender treatment—or between what Rothman (1980) termed "conscience and convenience." Rothman poignantly captured the issue at hand. "In the end," he observed, "when conscience and convenience met, convenience won. When treatment and coercion met, coercion won" (1980, p. 10).

These words by Rothman appeared slightly after my 1979 epiphany and reconversion to rehabilitation. But they reflected a theme that, during the 1970s, became increasingly ubiquitous in the correctional literature. For example, a 1978 book coedited by Rothman carried the title, *Doing Good: The Limits of Benevolence* (Gaylin et al. 1978). In any event, as I read commentaries of this sort, I wondered how I could have been blind to the reality that kindhearted therapeutic ideology was masking a host of bad acts. How could I have been so stupid? How could I have traveled to Bridgewater State Hospital for a year—the institution of *Titicut Follies* fame—and been okay with it?

Still, I must layer in one point here: It never dawned on me that Rothman and others could be wrong (see also Rothman 2002). Today, I wonder the opposite: How could I have been so stupid to accept what they had to say so uncritically? How could I replace one orthodoxy with another, with not a hint of reflexivity? Again, I take solace that I was not alone.

Part of the reason for my, and others', cognitive shift is that the criticisms of rehabilitation were powerful, illuminating problems that were real. The cautionary literature was diverse in origin and persuasive in content. Within criminology, labeling theory had become the dominant perspective (Cole 1975; Cullen and Cullen 1978). The theory emphasized the ironic and unanticipated and thus was, as Hagan (1973) called it, the "sociology of the interesting." We learned that the very efforts to sanction offenders legally—whether that involved punishment or treatment—resulted in a self-fulfilling prophecy. Offenders became not what we hoped, nonoffenders, but what we did not expect, "secondary deviants"—as they centered their lives around their stigmatized criminal identities and became entrapped in a stable criminal role. Commentators thus called not for rehabilitation but for "radical non-intervention"—to "leave kids alone whenever possible" (Schur 1973, p. 155).

Legal scholars weighed in by criticizing rehabilitative programs for ignoring the due process rights of offenders. They warned that criminal justice was not therapeutic but in a state of "law without order" (Frankel 1972). The call to "do good" was replaced by the call to "do justice" (see, e.g., von Hirsch 1976; Gaylin et al. 1978; Singer 1979). Historians questioned the march-of-civilization view in which rehabilitation reflected a history of good intentions in which progress was incremental but steady (Ignatieff 1978, 1981; cf. Eriksson 1976; McKelvey 1977). When read together, Rothman's (1971, 1980) two social histories, spanning the 1820s to the 1920s, told a sobering tale of the harms the rehabilitative ideal had justified—and then made possible. Similar lessons were conveyed in Platt's (1969) account of the invention of the juvenile court in which well-meaning Chicago reformers created a system that would eventually descend into state-sponsored child abuse (see also Feld 1999). And Foucault's (1977) *Discipline and Punish* was widely hailed for showing how the therapeutic was more insidious than the physical because it controlled the mind, not the body. I must confess that in reading this dense volume, I had no idea what Foucault was saying most of the time; I also could not understand how rehabilitation could be an instrument of mind control when it supposedly did not work! Still, Foucault's point was widely endorsed, and it added to rehabilitation's demise.

Again, the critique offered by these diverse writings was radical, not reformist. The rehabilitative ideal was not flawed and fixable but rotten to the core. Gaylin (1974, p. 26) expressed this prevailing sentiment: "On the other hand, the rehabilitation mode, with its emphasis on understanding and concern, has dominated our modus operandi so far; under it we have abused our charges, the prisoners, without disabusing our conscience. It is beneath this cloak of benevolence that hypocrisy has flourished, where such new exploitation inevitably has been introduced as an act of grace."

B. *Three Criticisms*

Critics articulated a number of reservations about the rehabilitative ideal, but three were so fundamental as to render the treatment enterprise fully illegitimate. First, prisons—and other "total institutions" such as mental hospitals (Goffman 1961)—were not places in which reform either would be given priority or could be accomplished. Custodial goals—the need to maintain order and to prevent escapes— would always trump the therapeutic. Those in charge might give lip service to rehabilitation, but their jobs hinged on keeping prisons quiet, not curing offenders. They would use whatever methods it took to maintain control. The bloody riot at Attica in September 1971, with over 40 lives lost, made this point clear (Wicker 1975). The state troopers, sheriff's deputies, and guards retaking the prison were so indiscriminate in their use of lethal violence that they shot not only inmates but also 10 correctional officers who had been taken hostage. Is this what American "corrections" had come to? As Sykes (1978, p. 476) noted, this tragedy served as "a symbol for the end of an era in correctional philosophy."

The classic 1971 Stanford Prison Experiment, administered by Zimbardo and his colleagues (1973), cemented the view that prisons were inherently inhumane and thus could not function as therapeutic milieus (see also Zimbardo 2007). A mock prison was constructed in the bottom floor of a Stanford University building, and psychologically healthy subjects were randomly assigned to be inmates or guards. Within a short time, the guards moved to assert their control. They regularly "insulted the prisoners, threatened them, were physically aggressive, used instruments (night sticks, fire extinguishers, etc.) to keep the prisoners in line and referred to them in impersonal, anonymous, deprecating ways" (Zimbardo et al. 1973, pp. 48–49). To avoid serious harm, the experiment had to be halted prematurely. Upon reflection, it sent a chilling message about the absurdity of seeing prisons as settings for inmate improvement:

> The potential social value of this study derives precisely from the fact that normal, healthy, educated young men could be so radically transformed under the institutional pressures of a "prison environment." If this could happen in so short a time, without the excesses that are possible in real prisons, and if it could happen to the "cream-of-the-crop of American youth," then one can only shudder to imagine what society is doing both to the actual guards

and prisoners who are at this very moment participating in this unnatural "social experiment." (Zimbardo et al. 1973, p. 56)

The second criticism focused on abuse of discretion. Under the rehabilitative ideal, correctional officials were given virtually unfettered discretion to diagnose and treat offenders. With the assistance of presentence reports prepared by probation officers, judges would decide whether offenders would be treated in the community or in prison. With the assistance of wardens and counselors, parole boards would decide when a cured offender could be released. Probation and parole officers would decide how to assist their charges in the community or, if an offender proved recalcitrant, when a return to custody was merited.

But this rosy picture proved a mirage. In reality, the decision to send an offender to prison or release one from prison was not based on careful assessment and scientific expertise but on a hunch as to who might, or might not, be dangerous. Worse still, officials were suspected not simply of ignorance but of malice—of engaging in unjust decisions. Research on so-called extralegal factors suggested that racial stereotypes shaped sentencing and subsequent decisions. African Americans were seen as objects for special repression during incarceration, especially if they voiced politically radical ideas. The controversial shooting of "Soledad brother" George Jackson (1970) in an escape attempt inside San Quentin Prison, just days before he was to go on trial for allegedly murdering a correctional officer, was widely seen as a trumped-up execution (for a balanced account of this incident, see Page [2011]).

Special concern was reserved for "bad kids" under the control of the juvenile court (Murphy 1974; Wooden 1976; Ryerson 1978; Feld 1999). Because this system was created to serve as a kindly parent to act in the best interest of the child, wayward youths were accorded few legal rights and could be detained for being in need of supervision—for being a neglected child or being a status offender. A series of exposés showed that juvenile facilities were not cheerful reformatories but dreary and dangerous places in which the incarcerated were "weeping in the playtime of others" (Wooden 1976). They were not instruments of child-saving treatment but of "institutionalized punishment" and "legalized child abuse" (p. 106).

The third criticism was that the treatment was "enforced" (Kittrie 1971). Many suspected that offenders could not be helped against their will and thus that a system of coerced cure was a futile enterprise. But the more significant concern was that in the name of rehabilitation, those state officials claiming to help offenders—or the mentally ill and mentally retarded—could do almost anything they wanted to their charges. Unlike medical treatment, correctional treatment was not a choice. For those incarcerated, the price of refusing rehabilitation was a denial of freedom. But more than this was feared. This was the era of Stanley Kubrick's 1971 film *A Clockwork Orange* and Ken Kesey's (1962) *One Flew over the Cuckoo's Nest*. Commentators worried that new behavior and drug technologies would provide insidious means for dehumanizing mind control. David Fogel (1979, p. 180), a former corrections commissioner in Minnesota, cautioned us to beware of the "behavior modifiers," who were emerging from "animal laboratories and the back wards of hospitals in search of defectives." Their "therapeutic arsenal" included "positive and negative reinforcements, pills, chemicals, electrodes, and neurosurgical instruments" (see also Mitford 1973).

Taken together, these three criticisms comprised a toxic brew. Imagine giving state officials—whether judges or correctional officials—the unfettered discretion to place offenders, including defenseless youngsters, in inherently inhumane, coercive institutions where they received either no or harmful treatment. And to do this in the name of benevolence was particularly galling, if not dangerous. To stop such bad treatment effects, reformers thus felt compelled to relinquish the rehabilitative ideal—an ideological and policy paradigm many had embraced for years. Instead, they called for a "justice model" of corrections (see, e.g., American Friends Service Committee Working Party 1971; Conrad 1973; Morris 1974; von Hirsch 1976; Fogel 1979). The goal was no longer to do good but to do less harm (Gaylin et al. 1978).

Various policy schemes were proposed, but they shared the view that steps must be taken to purge the justice system of the indeterminate sentence. Discretion would be curtailed by penalizing the crime, not the criminal. This was to be accomplished either through determinate sentencing or through sentencing guidelines. Judges would sentence all offenders who committed the same crime to the same sentence—regardless of race, class, or gender. Further, a key principle was that those sent to prison would know the exact length of their term at the time of sentencing. Release would thus be based on paying one's just deserts and not on proving one's cure. Parole would be abolished. To the extent that they existed, rehabilitation programs would be voluntary. Prison communities would instead become just communities, with an emphasis on inmates' rights and self-governance. Finally, because life in the society of captives was painful, reducing harm also meant reducing the use and length of terms behind bars. Custody should only be used as a sanction of last resort. This proposal proved to be wishful thinking.

C. Mistrusting the Welfare State

Although rehabilitation's problems were serious, the question remains why people in the 1970s responded as they did—myself included. Just a few years before, such correctional problems would have been lamented, but the call would have been to reaffirm rehabilitation—to expand services and to make institutions truly therapeutic. This kind of response can be seen in psychiatrist Karl Menninger's widely acclaimed indictment of the legal apparatus, *The Crime of Punishment* (1968).

According to Menninger, although corrections originally embodied reformist ideals, the system had declined to the point where "city jails and inhuman reformatories and wretched prisons are jammed. They are known to be unhealthy, filthy, dangerous, immoral, indecent, crime-breeding dens of iniquity" (1968, p. 143). Menninger suspected that "*all the crimes committed by all the jailed criminals do not equal in total social damage that of the crimes committed against them*" (p. 28; emphasis in the original). Much of the problem stemmed from a ready reliance on common sense: "Catch criminals and lock them up; if they hit you, hit them back. This is common sense, but it does not work" (p. 5). Instead, in an early call for evidence-based corrections, he trumpeted the use of science—what he termed "uncommon sense"—to inform practice (p. 5). The most essential ingredient to renovating the "crime of punishment" is the firm embrace of a "therapeutic attitude" (p. 262). The successes reaped in the medical arena, especially in treating mental illness (his field of expertise), should be reason for optimism. Thus, "change is what medical science always aims for. The prisoner, like the doctor's other patients, should emerge from his treatment experience a different person, differently equipped, differently functioning, and headed in a different direction from when he began the treatment" (p. 258).

By the early to mid-1970s, however, we were all prepared to throw the baby out with the bathwater. Written at that time, my marginal notes on page 111 of *The Crime of Punishment* read, "Ignores the evils done in the name of rehabilitation." This comment stemmed from my readings of labeling theory and the many recently published works critical of the treatment enterprise. But this explanation begs the larger point of why my interpretation of rehabilitation-as-evil was part of criminological orthodoxy at that particular historical juncture. What occurred to produce a collective shift in our thinking? Why reject the rehabilitative ideal?

Our willingness to do so is best explained by understanding the changing social context. By this time, numerous events had transpired to show that the *state could no longer be trusted*. This era has been richly chronicled, and thus the story can be repeated in the barest of details here (see, e.g., Gitlin 1987; Patterson 1996; Brokaw 2007; Collins 2009). It was a period when, in Collins's (2009) words, "everything changed." A cultural revolution swept across the country as music, dress, sexual norms, and gender roles were transformed. Movements of all sorts arose—Civil Rights, consumer, environmental, women's. The nation was rocked by the assassinations in 1963 of John Kennedy and then, just two months apart in 1968, of Robert Kennedy and of Martin Luther King Jr. Riots broke out in major cities that left neighborhoods afire, and insurgency enveloped college campuses. In May 1970, it is estimated that a million students (including me) demonstrated against the Vietnam War following the gunshot killings of four antiwar student protesters by National Guard troops at Kent State University. That year, there were over 9,400 protest incidents across the nation (Gitlin 1987). The era ended with revelations of political corruption. In October 1973, Vice President Spiro Agnew was forced to resign for accepting kickbacks from contractors, which started when he was Maryland's governor. And in August 1974, Richard Nixon resigned from the presidency, a victim of the Watergate scandal (Patterson 1996). I was standing at the library counter at Columbia University when I heard this stunning news.

Transformative shifts in public opinion are often produced when an era is marked by a continuing sequence of adverse events—as happened during this period (Lipset and Schneider 1983). The nature of the changes is captured in the title of Todd Gitlin's book, *The Sixties: Years of Hope, Days of Rage* (1987). Following the post–World War II economic boom, the 1960s began with "great expectations," including the Kennedy administration's embarking on a New Frontier and the Johnson administration's promise to complete the task of building a Great Society (Patterson 1996). By the end of the decade, such rhetoric seemed like grand noble lies. Those in power were commonly depicted as duplicitous or as outright prevaricators. Commentators began to talk about a "legitimacy crisis" or a "confidence gap." As Lipset and Schneider (1983, p. 16) concluded from their analysis of polling data, "from 1964 to 1970, there was a virtual explosion in anti-government feeling." Public confidence in government officials "to do what is right just about always or most of the time" was 73 percent in 1958. By the mid-1970s, it had plummeted to under 40 percent (Pew Research Center for the People and the Press 2010). The state was no longer trusted.

This change in the public mind pertains directly to rehabilitation. Rothman (1978) perceptively analyzed this paradigmatic shift. In brief, the Progressives' model of the rehabilitative ideal was paternalistic, counting on state officials, including those in the legal system, to use their discretion to address troubled people's needs and to sponsor their social mobility. But how could these officials be granted the discretionary power to do good in a context in which there was "a pervasive distrust of all constituted authorities" (Rothman 1978, p. 84)? Reluctantly for Rothman, it was necessary to abandon an "equality model" in favor of a "liberty model" that would limit state power. "The formula is clear," said Rothman; "better that a few should suffer from the inflexibility of a code than that the many should suffer through the discretion of an administrator" (p. 84).

The final piece to this story is to understand which state was being rejected. The only state available to be mistrusted at this time was the "welfare state." The particular concern was that under the cloak of a benevolent human services ideology, state officials were compromising the liberty not only of offenders but also of the poor and other vulnerable populations including the mentally ill, the mentally retarded, students, and welfare recipients. Their so-called betterment was being forced upon them, often in harsh and ineffective ways. It was as though there was a liberal Tea Party at work, with calls to protect liberty and move government out of people's lives. As Glasser worried, the discretionary powers exercised by human service providers traditionally had not been questioned because they were presumed to be acting in their clients' best interests; "they were not cops" (1978, p. 112). Accordingly, few efforts were made to limit the "powers of high school principals, social workers, housing officials, or mental health professionals" (p. 113). In Gaylin's perspective,

These citizens who lived under the jurisdiction of the service professionals were consequently without rights. Students in school,
the poor in public housing, the sick in mental hospitals, the aged
in nursing homes, and the young in foster care institutions all
came to resemble each other in a strange and critical way. All were
enmeshed against their wills in institutions ostensibly designed to
benefit them. (1978, p. 113)

The criticism of correctional rehabilitation was part of this larger critique of the welfare state.

Such views look quaint today even if they retain an important kernel
of truth. The welfare state soon was replaced by the punitive state in
which politicians sought to govern through crime (Simon 2007; see
also Garland 2001). The problem is no longer social welfare's legitimacy but its illegitimacy—its portrayal as giving handouts to the un-
deserving and as a prime target for budget cutting. Notably, part of
rehabilitation's value is that it combats such thinking by providing a
rationale for addressing offenders' needs through human services.
Rothman presciently cautioned that a focus on rights could lead to
neglect. In a comment he attributed to Willard Gaylin, he humorously
observed that the rights movement promised to "substitute for the
hard-nosed, belligerent, and tough-minded psychiatrist the attention
of the gentle, understanding, empathetic lawyer!" (1978, p. 94).

D. The Conservative Critique

In 1972, my father told me that he had voted for Richard Nixon,
the first and only Republican candidate who had earned his support.
(I wonder, as a Boston Irish Catholic, if he could really have checked
Nixon's box on the ballot!) In retrospect—having become a father myself—I am not sure I blame him. I was a good son in that in college I
played sports (hockey and tennis) and earned "A"s. Still, I left the nest
after high school with short hair and geeky black glasses. By the time
I graduated from college, I had longish hair, a beard, and horn-rimmed
glasses; I wore bell-bottom pants, listened to Phil Ochs and the Rolling
Stones, and was angry at the Catholic Church for maximizing my capacity to feel guilt; and, as class president, I helped to shut down my
college with a student strike. My dad was a classic Kennedy liberal, but
he sensed that something was wrong in society and that, in his words,
his son had become a "damn fool." Hard as it was for him to stomach,
Richard Nixon's views resonated far more with him than George Mc-

Govern's. Someone needed to be an adult and put the society back in order.

My father and I both mistrusted the state but for different reasons—and with hopes for different futures. Whereas I saw those in power as corrupt, he saw the government as losing the capacity to maintain order. He was not strongly in favor of the Vietnam War, but he did sense that the ties holding the social order together were fraying and had to be strengthened. Nixon's appeal was not simply that he promised to clamp down on crime but also that he would establish "law and order." The point is that many in my father's generation, especially in more conservative locales than Massachusetts, experienced and interpreted the events of the 1960s differently than my generation did: They felt that things had gotten out of hand. They constituted the so-called silent majority—those who were not protesting in the streets but silently sitting at home and getting angry about what was happening to their great nation. As Beckett (1997, p. 38) notes, "by 1969, 81 percent of those polled believed that law and order had broken down."

In this context, the conservative critique of the welfare state was not that it was overly coercive but that it was overly permissive. Through its policies, the state was rewarding wayward behavior. Single mothers receiving benefits—the "welfare queens"—were a favorite target, because they were portrayed as being paid to have babies so as to avoid going to work. The solution was to build self-reliance by throwing them cold turkey off the dole (see, e.g., Murray 1984). Education was similarly in decline because teachers were not focusing on the so-called basics (the "three Rs"), and principals were sparing the rod and spoiling the child; discipline was needed. And youngsters were entering crime because it paid; they could literally "get away with murder," suffering few consequences for bad acts.

Rehabilitation was the chief culprit for two reasons. First, by focusing on the causes of behavior, such as poverty or family conflict, it provided excuses—readily available techniques of neutralization—for irresponsible choices. Second, and more important, state officials used their discretion to create a revolving door of justice. Judges were placing dangerous predators not in prison but back on the streets, and kindhearted or duped parole boards were being conned into releasing career criminals prematurely.

Among conservatives, promises to institute law and order, which had begun in Barry Goldwater's 1964 presidential campaign, were becoming ever more frequent. A cacophony of voices was now heard calling for the criminal justice system to "get tough on crime." We might even require a "war on crime." The rhetorical thrust was that just as we needed to bring discipline back into the welfare system and the schools—if not even our own homes—we needed to bring discipline back into the correctional process. If judges and parole boards would not protect society by making crime a costly choice and by caging the dangerous, then they should have their discretionary powers taken away.

Perceptive readers will recognize that liberals and conservatives in the 1970s were calling for similar policies—purging state officials' discretion justified by rehabilitation through determinate sentencing—but for different reasons. Liberals believed that rehabilitation allowed for coercive practices that *victimized offenders*; conservatives believed that rehabilitation allowed for permissive practices that *victimized innocent citizens* (Cullen and Gilbert 1982). Liberals were interested in doing justice; conservatives were interested in controlling crime. The key difference was that liberals thought that prison was a severe punishment that should be used sparingly and in small doses; conservatives thought that prisons were a much-needed mechanism—a disincentive for the deterrable and a cage for the wicked—that should be used extensively and in large doses. The conservative vision in due course prevailed. But for that moment, liberals and conservatives joined forces to accomplish what they agreed on: to constrain discretion and to move toward determinacy in sentencing. Meanwhile, nobody was left to defend the rehabilitative ideal.

The conservatives' rejection of rehabilitation was long-standing, not new—though, smelling blood, it was more vehement and tied to a harsh policy agenda. More consequential, however, was the liberals' abandonment of offender treatment. They had been the crucial interest group, including as members of the cultural elite, who had linked support for rehabilitation to modern society's inexorable climb toward greater civility and humanity. Now, they depicted rehabilitation not as the friend but as the enemy of progress—a weapon wielded by the state to protect its narrow interests. Rehabilitation became a political orphan—defenseless against the attacks it was receiving. Its decline was assured.

E. Martinson: Reframing the Debate

Martinson's (1974*b*) "nothing works" essay had an exhilarating effect in policy and academic circles. The case against rehabilitation was complete; science confirmed that offender treatment did not work. He used technical language, but the message was clear—rehabilitation was a failed enterprise: "With these caveats," asserted Martinson, "it is possible to give a rather bald summary of our findings: *With few and isolated exceptions, the rehabilitative efforts that have reported so far have had no appreciable effect on recidivism*" (1974*b*, p. 25; emphasis in the original).

Martinson's critique was powerful in part because of its methodological quality. Along with his collaborators Douglas Lipton and Judith Wilks, Martinson had used rigorous standards to select and analyze 231 evaluation studies (see Lipton, Martinson, and Wilks 1975). The dismal results could not be attributed to shoddy scholarship; later analysts, such as a panel of the National Research Council, would corroborate that Martinson's project "was reasonably accurate and fair in its appraisal of the rehabilitation literature" (Martin, Sechrest, and Redner 1981, p. 9). But the article also drew its appeal from how Martinson constructed its central message.

Thus, the essay's title clearly captured the issue at hand: "What Works?" Some commentators suggest that Martinson never explicitly said that "nothing works," but this claim is disingenuous and gives him an "out" that he would not have taken at the time. His statement that programs "had no appreciable effect" was hardly a ringing endorsement for correctional treatment. The heading of the article's concluding section provocatively asked, "Does Nothing Work?" The first sentence of text followed this question with another: "*Do all of these studies lead us irrevocably to the conclusion that nothing works, that we haven't the faintest clue about how to rehabilitate offenders and reduce recidivism?*" (1974*b*, p. 48; emphasis in the original). Martinson felt compelled to add the caveat that a treatment effect might possibly exist, but that the research was too flawed to detect it or the programs being delivered lacked enough therapeutic integrity to achieve it. But he then proceeded to give the punch line that he clearly favored. "It may be, on the other hand, that there is a more radical flaw in our present strategies—that education at its best, or that psychotherapy at its best, cannot overcome, or even appreciably reduce, the powerful tendency for offenders to continue in criminal behavior" (p. 49).

If there were any doubt about Martinson's views, they vanished in a 1975 interview by Mike Wallace on *60 Minutes* (CBS Television Network 1975, p. 3). The segment was titled, "It Doesn't Work." Here is but one exchange in which Martinson confirmed that nothing works:

Martinson: I looked at all the methods that we could find—vocational, educational—and a variety of other methods. These methods simply have no fundamental effect on the recidivism rate of people who go through . . . the system.

Wallace: No effect at all?

Martinson: No effect, no basic effect.

Notably, Martinson echoed these views elsewhere, saying that, based on "the evidence made available" by his study, he considered rehabilitation a "myth" (Martinson 1974*a*, p. 4) and that the "treatment of offenders is largely impotent in reducing the crime rate" (Wilks and Martinson 1976, p. 5).

In the *60 Minutes* segment, Mike Wallace noted that it "is no understatement to say his [Martinson's] findings are sending shock waves through the correctional establishment" (CBS Television Network 1975, p. 3). And so they did. But it is crucial to remember that for most people—including me—this was not a rational process in which exposure to scientific evidence changed minds. Rather, our "sensibility" had already changed, which led us to forfeit our support for rehabilitation. Tonry notes that "Sensibilities are time- and place-bound ways of thinking that include ideas and express values that are widely shared and little questioned. Sometimes sensibilities change slowly and sometimes they change rapidly, but when a particular sensibility is widespread it influences what people think, say, and believe" (2004, p. 70). As discussed, the prevailing sensibility had changed from a social welfare orthodoxy to a mistrust-the-state orthodoxy. It was thus appealing to latch onto and trumpet Martinson's work because it reinforced "what we already knew"—that therapy enforced by the state was a noble lie.

Psychologists use the term "confirmation bias" to refer to the process of deliberately searching for "confirming evidence . . . people (and scientists quite often) seek data that are likely to be compatible with the beliefs they currently hold" (Kahneman 2011, p. 81). At that time, the confirmation bias was writ so large that any evidence of program success was attacked through an array of selectively applied methodological and ex post facto criticisms that Gottfredson (1979) called "treatment destruction techniques." Despite being on shaky empirical grounds, said Gottfredson, the "conventional wisdom" about rehabilitation's ineffectiveness had become so widespread that it was "agreed upon by criminologists of nearly every persuasion and theoretical orientation" (p. 39).

Three additional considerations show that Martinson's "nothing works" message was so popular in large part because it resonated with the new sensibility. First, numerous scholars previously had reviewed the empirical literature and questioned the effectiveness of rehabilitation, starting in the 1950s and continuing into the early 1970s (for a summary, see Cullen and Gendreau [2000, p. 121]). These works received little attention and evoked few recommendations for undertaking offender treatment with more integrity. They did not lead to calls to rid corrections of the "noble lie" of rehabilitation.

Second, in 1979, Martinson recanted his "nothing works" claim. His follow-up study—the one I had interviewed for unsuccessfully—had come to fruition. Based on an analysis of 555 studies, Martinson now proposed that, "contrary to my previous position, some treatment programs *do* have an appreciable effect on recidivism" (1979, p. 244; emphasis in the original). He went on, "I have often said that treatment added to the networks of criminal justice is 'impotent,' and I withdraw that characterization as well" (p. 254). But the new evidence did not cause others to follow Martinson in reconsidering their rejection of rehabilitation. Indeed, this second essay was largely ignored and changed few, if any, minds. Of course, due to the change in my own confirmation bias in 1979, I uncovered this essay (despite its placement in the *Hofstra Law Review*) and cited it in my work (Cullen and Gilbert 1982).

Third, academic criminologists accepted Martinson's (1974*b*) "nothing works" conclusion uncritically, abandoning the core norm of science that scholars subject empirical claims to organized skepticism (Merton 1973). No study should be assumed to provide the final word. In this case, Martinson's project had limitations. For example, it did not restrict the dependent variable to recidivism but included outcomes such as institutional adjustment and educational achievement. Thus, although Martinson reviewed 231 studies (which reported data on 286 outcomes), the results were based on only 138 measures of recidivism. If interventions without a clear treatment focus are excluded (e.g., imprisonment, probation, leisure-time activities), the critical outcomes plummet to the modest number of 73—less than one-third of the routinely cited and more impressive figure of 231 (Cullen and Gendreau 2000). Further, as Palmer (1975) documented, about half the studies actually showed positive treatment effects. And because there were no evaluations at that time, the project did not have a category for cognitive-behavioral programs, which later research has revealed to be the most effective treatment modality (Andrews and Bonta 2010). But this kind of scrutiny either did not occur or fell on deaf ears. The "nothing works" doctrine, cloaked in the veneer of science, became a matter of almost religious faith. Martinson provided the received wisdom, and only correctional heretics dared question it.

All this is not to suggest that Martinson's work was merely epiphenomenal. It may not have inspired rehabilitation's decline, but it did help to finish it off. Its publication nailed the door shut on rehabilitation's coffin. Critics could hold up Martinson's article aloft—as I did in my classes—and say, "See, nothing works. Rehabilitation is a failure." Those clinging to the rehabilitative ideal were placed at an enormous disadvantage, having no apparent evidence on their side. How could they cling to a falsified ideal? In the face of seemingly indisputable negative empirical evidence, what rejoinder could be made?

In retrospect, I believe that Martinson's work had an even more enduring effect: It transformed the debate on rehabilitation from a broad and complex critique of the welfare state into the narrower and simpler issue of effectiveness. If nothing works, then the rehabilitation debate was decisively settled. My sense is that for critics, citing Martinson—using the "nothing works" slogan—was easier than articulating why discretionary decision making was problematic. They no longer had to show the flaws of rehabilitation as a correctional theory but simply that it failed to deliver as an intervention. By the early 1980s, the publication of major works criticizing state-enforced therapy had slowed to a trickle. In contrast, Martinson's essay continues to be widely cited; as of 2013, its Google Scholar citation count had grown to more than 2,260.

In the short term, the advantage clearly went to the opponents of rehabilitation; they had the data on their side. However, by *reframing the debate* into one over effectiveness, Martinson unwittingly gave advocates of rehabilitation a strategy for turning a losing battle into a winning war. If they could marshal evaluation studies showing that offender treatment *did* reduce recidivism, then the legitimacy of the rehabilitative ideal might be restored (Cullen and Smith 2011).

In Section III, I return to this issue. Although it took many years, a small group of researchers worked to change the conventional wisdom and show that treatment was effective (Cullen 2005). They also developed a coherent paradigm that could provide practical advice on what to do to rehabilitate offenders. Ironically, Martinson sowed the seeds of the "nothing works" doctrine's own destruction. He transformed rehabilitation into an evidence-based contest. In the end, the evidence has piled up in favor of treatment—and not, I might add, in favor of punitive correctional programming (Cullen, Pratt, et al. 2002).

E. Policy Problems

It is difficult to itemize what developments can be tied directly to the decline of the rehabilitative ideal and the advocacy of the justice model. Many bad things emerged in the subsequent decades, but perhaps they would have happened anyway. Indeed, a sizable literature seeks to explain precisely why the United States became a punitive state with mass incarceration as the linchpin of its crime-control policy (for reviews, see Tonry [2004, 2007]). Still, amid all else, the discarding of rehabilitation almost certainly encouraged three unanticipated consequences.

First, sentencing reform opened a Pandora's box that liberals could not close. It is unclear whether desert-based determinate sentencing was an improvement over indeterminate sentencing (Johnson 2011). Sentencing reform in some states, especially when it took the form of presumptive sentencing or sentencing guidelines, may have enhanced the quality of justice, but in others this did not happen (see, e.g., Griset 1991; Frase 2005). But in a broader sense, the move away from indeterminacy backfired, mainly because it politicized sentencing by inviting legislators into the process and encouraging them to fit the punishment to the crime. As Tonry documented, "every state since 1980 has enacted laws mandating minimum prison sentences based on the premises that harsher penalties will reduce crime rates and that judges cannot otherwise be trusted to impose them" (1996, p. 3; see also Tonry 2009). Garland has echoed this point, noting that concerns about fairness and reducing prisons sentences "gave way to more hard-line policies of deterrence, predictive restraint, and imprisonment" (2001, p. 61).

Second, rehabilitation did not vanish from the nation's prisons; most institutions continued to offer some combination of substance abuse treatment, educational programs, and vocational training (Cullen and Jonson 2011). In part, treatment survived because of the correctional staff's continued support of offender treatment (Cullen et al. 1989, 1993) and in part because prison programming kept offenders busy. But even if the status quo tended to persist, the commitment to building therapeutic communities virtually evaporated. Punitive goals ascended in importance and created a context that was unsupportive, if not hostile, to treatment advocates.

Thus, commenting on the effects of the "nothing works" doctrine shortly after its pronouncement, Adams (1976, p. 76) observed that "widely assorted members of the criminal justice field are briskly urging that punishment and incapacitation should be given much higher priority among criminal justice goals" (see also Wilson 1975). Integral to the rehabilitative ideal had been the understanding that offenders have potential value and that their improvement requires a humane environment. Now, however, inmates increasingly were portrayed as prime candidates for lengthy, if not permanent, stays behind bars—labeled as "career criminals" and, still worse, as "super-predators" beyond redemption (Bennett, DiIulio, and Walters 1996). This image of the criminal as "the other" was perhaps more easily accepted because inmates were increasingly African American—for "confidence in rehabilitative effort dwindles when a sense of difference and social distance separates the promoters from the subjects of reform" (Allen 1981, p. 21; see also Wacquant 2001). Meanwhile, policy makers not only increased sentence lengths but also, in hopes of achieving added deterrence, moved to create painful "no-frills" prisons by stripping inmates of amenities such as televisions, exercise equipment, high-quality meals, and access to a college education (Finn 1996; Listwan et al. 2013). In a retrospective assessment of what he had helped bring about, Rothman lamented that "the reformers proved wrong on all counts" (2002, p. 429). In the end, the "distaste for rehabilitation" has "contributed to making prisons into human warehouses" (pp. 429–30).

California's correctional experience illustrates these developments. From the 1940s to the 1960s, the state was at the forefront in advancing the cause of offender rehabilitation (McKelvey 1977; Petersilia 2008; Page 2011). As Petersilia notes, the "department at one time had 80 researchers on staff and developed the nation's first inmate classification system, the first recidivism prediction score system, and an array of model prison and parole programs, including today's well-regarded therapeutic communities for treating drug abusers" (2008, p. 209). Many of the nation's top professionals migrated to California to participate in this grand treatment experiment (McKelvey 1977). There they found wardens who wrote books and held degrees in social work (Petersilia 2008).

As optimism turned to despair, California in 1976 adopted determinate sentencing, abolished parole, and "declared that the goal of imprisonment was punishment and not rehabilitation" (Petersilia 2008, p. 230). Promising to get tough, elected officials enacted a host of mandatory minimum sentence laws and successfully encouraged the public to support the passage of the nation's harshest three-strikes-and-you're-out law. As a result, observes Petersilia, "California legislators and voters have radically transformed the penal system by enacting hundreds of new sentencing laws, building 22 new prisons, and dismantling most rehabilitation programs" (2008, p 211; see also Zimring, Hawkins, and Kamin 2001). To make matters worse, a powerful correctional officers' union, some 30,000 strong, arose and campaigned successfully for "tough penal policies" and institutional expansion (Page 2011, p. 7). Prison populations eventually exceeded 170,000— with conditions so deleterious to inmate mental and physical health that in 2011, the US Supreme Court ordered the number of inmates cut by 46,000 (33,000 by the time the decision was actually issued; *Brown v. Plata*, 131 S.Ct. 1910 [2011]). Life inside prisons became, in Page's words, "increasingly stark, depressing, and punitive," with offenders having "few genuine opportunities to change their lives" (2011, p. 4). Indeed, as of 2006, half of the inmates received no work or treatment program assignment while incarcerated; two-thirds returned to prison (Petersilia 2008). In 2004, then-governor Arnold Schwarzenegger called for a new correctional era based on evidence-based treatment, adding the name "and Rehabilitation" to the former title of "Department of Corrections." But the damage had been substantial and achieving meaningful reform has proven a daunting challenge (Page 2011). According to Petersilia, "California's prison system is in crisis. It has deteriorated from being one of the best systems in the country to being dysfunctional" (2008, p. 231).

Kruttschnitt and Gartner (2005) chronicled the effects of California's correctional developments on female offenders. Their research reveals that although incarceration produces some similar adaptations regardless of historical era, the quality of institutional life is markedly affected by a period's prevailing correctional theory. The California Institution for Women, for example, opened in the 1950s, housed women in cottages and was landscaped to look much like a high school campus. With staff infused with a spirit of optimism and a belief in the rehabilitative ideal, inmates—who were called "residents"—were seen as malleable, were exposed to a therapeutic community, and were given some freedom of movement and clothing style. In sharp contrast, Valley State Prison for Women, a product of the "get tough" era (opened in 1995), had architecture typical of a men's prison, with cell blocks and a perimeter defended by multiple fences, razor wire, armed vehicle patrols, and guard towers. From their study conducted in the 1990s, Kruttschnitt and Gartner (2005, p. 97) observed that a priority was placed on custody, with correctional officers carrying "batons along with pepper spray and handcuffs." Offenders wore uniforms and en-joyed little freedom of movement. Life was strict and bleak, in line with the "pessimistic and austere approach to imprisonment" that was consistent with the "official discourse about the prison's purpose" (p. 100). Most striking was the "relative silence about rehabilitation" on the part of the female inmates, which suggested "that they, like the prison administration, had lowered their expectations for what could be gained from their time in prison" (p. 105). Ideas, in short, do have consequences.

Third, the abandonment of rehabilitation created space for the spread of new forms of correctional quackery—punitive interventions that, if anything, increased recidivism (Latessa, Cullen, and Gendreau 2002). In the 1980s and beyond, boot camps and control-oriented in-tensive supervision probation and parole proved especially popular, promising to discipline and deter offenders into conformity inexpen-sively. Their utter ineffectiveness not only wasted untold millions of dollars but also needlessly endangered public safety (Cullen, Wright, and Applegate 1996; Cullen, Pratt, et al. 2002; Cullen et al. 2005; MacKenzie 2006). There was an enormous opportunity cost. Following Martinson, criminologists and policy makers invested almost no time or expertise in developing effective treatment programs, even as the reach of the American correctional system grew to include—on any given day—one in every 31 adults (Pew Center on the States 2009).

In this latter regard, the "nothing works" doctrine was an important component in the development of a broader view among criminologists that Matthews (2009, p. 357) calls "impossibilism"—the belief that no crime control effort enacted by the state can be effective (see also Cullen 2011a). Rooted in liberal pessimism, the claim was—and, in many quarters, still is—that social control does not simply have no effects "but also that intervention often makes things worse" (p. 357). Concepts such as net widening and displacement were commonly used to show that state intervention had untoward unanticipated consequences (Binder and Geis 1984). Impossibilism became so ingrained in the field's professional ideology that scholars seeking practical ways to reduce crime and victimization were labeled as "tools of the state" or as "administrative criminologists" (Cullen and Gendreau 2001; Clarke and Felson 2011). Commenting on police scholarship, Sherman (1993) was moved to author an essay entitled, "Why Crime Control Is Not Reactionary." Writing almost two decades after the publication of Martinson's "nothing works" article, he noted that "there is still a strong academic bias . . . against police even *trying* to control crime . . . the central thrust of police scholarship for almost two decades was anti-crime control" (p. 174; emphasis in the original).

The effect of this ideology was that, with regard to crime control, many criminologists became far more committed to knowledge destruction (showing what does not work) than to knowledge construction (showing what does). As time progressed, critics no longer worried about rehabilitation; attacks on rehabilitation were beside the point. It became apparent that the problem was not the welfare state but the growing punitive state and its embrace of mass imprisonment. A mean season in criminal justice, including corrections, had arrived.

It must be admitted that scholars did much sound research in showing the flaws of a series of harsh policies and practices (see, e.g., Currie 1985; Clear 1994). Still, apart from work in crime science (Clarke 2010)—especially the areas of problem-oriented policing and situational crime prevention—criminology as a discipline did little to develop effective intervention strategies. Indeed, with regard to offender treatment, efforts to construct knowledge about what works was largely produced by psychologists, especially those residing in Canada, a story to which I now turn.

III. Optimism: What Works

I was part of a small group of scholars who participated in a "cognitive macro-environment" (Merton 1995, p. 5) for the study and advocacy of rehabilitation—a set of loosely coupled academics and corrections researchers who learned about their common support for offender treatment by reading published works, participating together on convention panels, and forming friendship networks (Cullen 2005). In the aftermath of Martinson's article, this group started to challenge the conclusion that nothing works. My own work with Karen Gilbert, *Reaffirming Rehabilitation* (1982), cautioned that the correctional system would be worse off if the treatment ideology was relinquished in favor of punitive policies and if organizations were purged of a commitment to human services. This prediction proved correct (Rothman 2002; see also Cullen and Gilbert 2013).

Unlike me, however, most other group members did not concentrate on this broader system argument but took up the more specific issue of program effectiveness. Their contributions were integral to restoring the legitimacy of rehabilitation as a goal of and practice within corrections. As discussed in this section, two lines of inquiry coalesced to show treatment efficacy: the findings from meta-analyses and the development of principles of effective correctional intervention (for additional details on the "re-emergence of correctional intervention," see Palmer [1992]). In essence, the meta-analyses furnished a persuasive empirical refutation of the "nothing works" doctrine, and the principles paradigm provided a clear blueprint for how efficacious treatment could be accomplished. Further, the development of evidence-based ideology across many fields, including corrections, supplied a context conducive to embracing these messages.

A. Meta-Analysis

When Paul Gendreau, at the time a regional psychologist at Rideau Corrections Centre in Ontario, heard the claims that nothing works, he was appalled. He knew that many interventions could change behavior. Cynics needed an education—they needed "bibliotherapy" (Gendreau and Ross 1979). In two essays, Gendreau and coauthor Robert Ross (1979, 1987) set out to provide that bibliotherapy by reviewing numerous evaluation studies, showing that treatment reduced recidivism. Their 1979 study covered works published after 1973; their 1987 study covered works published after 1981. Gendreau and Ross offered this unambiguous conclusion: "In summary, it is downright ridiculous to say 'Nothing works.' This review attests that much is going on to indicate that offender rehabilitation has been, can be, and will be achieved" (1987, p. 395).

Gendreau and Ross's studies were read and undoubtedly had some effect. But a narrative review of the literature is qualitative in nature because studies are selected, described, and then used to derive some overall conclusion. Any interpretation is open to the criticism of being biased. Scholars can be charged with cherry picking or giving more weight to studies reporting successful programs while ignoring or deemphasizing studies reporting unsuccessful ones. If Gendreau and Ross saw rehabilitation's glass as half full, others saw it as half empty.

One way around this charge is to undertake a meta-analysis, which is a quantitative synthesis of studies. This is similar to a batting average, computing the average effect of treatment on recidivism (the "mean effect size") across all studies. If nothing works, as Martinson contended, then the effect size should be zero or negative; if it is positive, then this means that the treatment modality decreased reoffending (although some authors use positive and negative in the opposite way, defining a negative sign to indicate that the treatment reduces criminal involvement). A meta-analysis is commonly seen as more objective than a narrative review not only because it produces a number—the mean effect size—but also because the coding can be replicated.

In 1990, Gendreau and his colleagues conducted a meta-analysis (Andrews et al. 1990). I was a coauthor of this article, mainly because I had alerted Paul to a published review claiming that treatment did not work with juveniles. I knew this article would make him apoplectic (it did), but I did not know it would motivate him and his Canadian friends to try to rebut these claims by conducting a quantitative synthesis of the literature. The resulting manuscript, which I helped package for a criminological audience, eventually became a correctional research classic, earning more than 1,780 cites on Google Scholar.

In this work, they first set forth three principles of effective intervention—risk, need, and responsivity—which I return to below. Programs that satisfied these principles were coded as "appropriate." The punch line was that the mean effect size (phi coefficient) for appropriate programs was a substantial .30. Inappropriate interventions (−.06) and criminal sanctions without treatment (−.07) slightly increased reoffending. Further, the effects of appropriate treatments were stronger when delivered in community settings (.35) than in institutional or residential settings (.20).

These findings have largely been replicated in other meta-analyses (Andrews and Bonta 2006, 2010; Smith, Gendreau, and Swartz 2009). But soon after its publication, critics warned that meta-analysis could be "misused, like some kind of alchemy, in an attempt to turn the lead of inadequate experiments into the gold of established knowledge" (Logan and Gaes 1993, p. 247). Logan and Gaes (1993) were especially critical of Andrews et al.'s claim of what counted as an "appropriate" program. Raising the possibility of tautology, they asked: "Is treatment effective *because* it is appropriate, or is it *called* 'appropriate' when it is seen to be effective?" (p. 248; emphasis in the original). They suspected the latter—and presented plausible reasons for reaching this conclusion.

Although I have published fairly influential meta-analyses, I must confess that I have no clue of how to do one (I mainly think up the ideas and entice others to compute effect sizes). So, although a collaborator, I was not privy to the coding of evaluations in the Andrews et al. project. Still, my understanding was that they had developed the risk-need-responsivity principles prior to the meta-analysis (Andrews, Bonta, and Hoge 1990) and then used them to code the studies accordingly—a point that Andrews and Bonta (2010, p. 365) have made in print. Even if they had not done so, this would not be a problem so long as the same principles that defined appropriate and inappropriate treatment were used in subsequent analyses, thus providing an independent confirmation of the initial findings. I have always felt that if critics did not trust the findings, they should have reanalyzed the sample of studies and published contrary results in a peer-reviewed journal (to my knowledge, none did).

Regardless, to rehabilitation's opponents, the research conducted by offender-treatment advocates, such as that by Andrews et al., would always warrant special scrutiny and be potentially suspect. Thus, might Andrews and his colleagues be dredging the data to find any positive treatment results they could? Or might they unwittingly shift criteria when coding a study whose effects were disconcertingly inconsistent with hoped-for results? Such things have occurred in science (see Gould 1981; cf. Lewis et al. 2011). As Logan and his colleagues asserted, firm conclusions about treatment effectiveness were not possible until advocates' meta-analyses "have been subjected to critical and painstakingly thorough evaluation by independent experts who do not share the missionary zeal of 'believers' in rehabilitation" (quoted in Lösel 1995, p. 80).

This context of suspicion made the meta-analyses of Mark Lipsey, first published in the 1990s, especially important (see Lipsey 1992, 1995, 1999, 2009; Lipsey and Wilson 1993, 1998; Lipsey, Chapman, and Landenberger 2001; Lipsey and Cullen 2007). Lipsey had two important qualifications for arbitrating rehabilitation's empirical status. First, he was not a participant in the treatment war; and, second, as an expert in meta-analysis, his studies were methodologically beyond reproach. His findings could not easily be attacked as biased or as an artifact of shoddy methods.

Lipsey's meta-analyses, conducted on interventions with juveniles, yielded three findings. First and most important, the view that nothing works in treatment is wrong. Thus, in a study coauthored with David Wilson, he computed the overall effect size to be .12 (Lipsey and Wilson 1998), a finding similar to that reported elsewhere (Lösel 1995). To convey the practical effect of interventions, scholars typically assume a 50 percent recidivism rate for the control group and then report how much programs reduce recidivism from that figure. Most often, the effect size statistic can be interpreted as the direct reduction in recidivism (e.g., .12 would mean a reduction of 12 percentage points from 50 percent to 38 percent). However, Lipsey and Wilson's figures were based on the percentage reduction in recidivism from 50 percent. Thus, a .12 effect size equaled 12 percent of 50 percent, which is 6 percent. This meant that the treatment group's overall recidivism rate would be 44 percent (Lipsey and Wilson 1998; see also Andrews and Bonta 2006, p. 325). This reduction is modest but not inconsequential, especially when dealing with high-risk offenders. More importantly, this overall effect size covered a grab bag of programs, including some with a primarily punitive orientation. But what if different types of interventions had different effects? Might not some programs work better than others?

This question leads to the second conclusion that can be drawn from Lipsey's work: The effects of interventions are heterogeneous, not homogenous (see also Lösel 1995). Lipsey found that the most effective interventions used modalities that were clearly rehabilitation-oriented, including counseling, interpersonal skills, cognitive-behavioral, and multi-model (Lipsey and Wilson 1998; Lipsey, Wilson, and Cothern 2000; see also Lipsey, Chapman, and Landenberger 2001). Lipsey and

Wilson noted that the overall 12 percent figure was "not representative of the impact achieved by the best programs." Indeed, the most effective interventions "were capable of reducing recidivism rates by as much as 40 percent, an accomplishment of considerable practical value in terms of expense and social damage associated with the delinquent behavior of these juveniles" (1998, p. 338).

The third finding involves the other end of the effectiveness continuum: What does not work? A key finding of Lipsey and Wilson is that "deterrence programs," such as shock incarceration, are ineffective. There is now substantial evidence that interventions with a punitive focus (e.g., scared straight programs, control-oriented intensive supervision programs) are ineffective (Cullen, Wright, and Applegate 1996; Cullen, Pratt, et al. 2002; MacKenzie 2006; Andrews and Bonta 2010). Recent evidence also suggests that giving offenders a sentence of imprisonment compared with a noncustodial sanction has either a null or slightly criminogenic effect (Nagin, Cullen, and Jonson 2009; Jonson 2010; Cullen, Jonson, and Nagin 2011). Similar results are found when inmates experience more, rather than less, painful conditions while incarcerated (Listwan et al. 2013). In short, placing offenders in prison, especially harsh ones, or in punitively oriented correctional programs, has no specific deterrent effects.

This last finding is important. We can now revise Martinson's famous "nothing works" conclusion to read as follows: With few and isolated exceptions, the *punitive* efforts that have been reported so far have had no appreciable effect on recidivism. In an evidence-based contest, there are winners and losers—and, in this case, the losers are interventions that are punitive in theory and practice. Critics of rehabilitation are thus bereft of any alternative intervention agenda, short of incapacitation. It is now clear that interventions must include a human services component if offender recidivism is to be reduced.

B. The Canadians' RNR Paradigm

The cumulative impact of treatment program meta-analyses, most notably those by Lipsey and his colleagues, cannot be overstated. Having touted the "nothing works" slogan for years, rehabilitation's critics were rendered speechless in the face of mounting empirical evidence of treatment effectiveness. The crowd in favor of punitive policies faced a particularly daunting reality: The research demonstrated not only positive treatment effects but also tiny, null, or criminogenic effects for punishment. Still, challenges remained.

Meta-analyses might provide good news, but they do not instruct practitioners on precisely how to rehabilitate offenders. It is just this issue—how to do rehabilitation—that a group of Canadian psychologists addressed, most notably, the late Donald Andrews, James Bonta, and Paul Gendreau. Their perspective became known as the "RNR model," named after the approach's three core principles of risk (R), need (N), and responsivity (R). It has since developed into the dominant treatment paradigm (Cullen and Jonson 2011; Cullen and Smith 2011).

Andrews, Bonta, and Gendreau devised the RNR model largely because they started their careers working in correctional agencies and were charged with implementing or evaluating treatment programs. They approached their task as talented PhD-trained psychologists and with an ethic of care toward offenders. As Canadians and as psychologists, they were largely immune to the "nothing works" ideology that permeated American corrections. They believed that intervention could effect behavior change—a core norm of psychology that laboratory experiments demonstrated daily—and that rehabilitation would improve offenders' lives. Most importantly, they were prepared to root their correctional practice in science. Eventually, Andrews and Bonta (2010) published five editions of *The Psychology of Criminal Conduct*. This volume is the RNR bible—a 672-page book that presents the scientific basis for their treatment paradigm (see also Cullen 2005). Scholars should study this book before casually dismissing or leveling charges against the Canadians' paradigm.

Most discussions of rehabilitation focus on treatment modalities, such as individual or group counseling, vocational education or training, skill development, or cognitive-behavioral programs (MacKenzie 2006). These are the kinds of categories used to code program types in meta-analyses (see Lipsey and Wilson 1998). There is nothing inherently wrong with this approach, especially if it is used to guide the selection of effective interventions. Still, this listing tends to portray the rehabilitation enterprise much like entering a cafeteria line, where I might select one program and you another. The guidance is thus general and not specific.

The Canadians, however, reject this strategy. They favor more directive advice—delineating which treatment is "appropriate" and which is "inappropriate." They also favor an approach that situates preferred treatment modalities within broader frameworks. Their approach goes, as my mother used to say, "from soup to nuts." It is in this sense that they have developed a "paradigm," a model that has three core components: criminological, correctional, and technological (Cullen 2011*b*; Cullen and Smith 2011; Smith 2013). As will be explained, it is the integration of these components that produces the possibility for effective practice with offenders.

The RNR model is not the only intervention paradigm. For example, in the field of early intervention—which extends from the prenatal period into the adolescent years—several prominent programs now exist that take a paradigmatic approach to treatment—such as Olds's (2007) nurse-family partnership program, Alexander's functional family therapy (Alexander, Pugh, and Parsons 1998), and Henggeler's (1999) multisystemic therapy. In each case, the intervention focuses on risk, need, and responsivity. Each is based on an explicit causal theory of antisocial conduct, empirically identifies and carefully targets risk factors, and provides a clear protocol on how to deliver evidence-based treatment. It is instructive that by following this coherent approach, these interventions have been shown to be successful (Greenwood 2006; Farrington and Welsh 2007; Cullen and Jonson 2012; Welsh and Farrington 2012).

Andrews, Bonta, and Gendreau started their paradigm with a research-based theory of human behavior. Rejecting Freudian and other psychodynamic theories, they embraced an integrated behavioral (operant conditioning), social learning, cognitive approach. In turn, similar to Sutherland's differential association theory, their "psychology of criminal conduct" emphasizes how illegal behavior is learned much as any behavior is learned (Andrews 1980). Treatment thus largely involves interventions that create learning experiences for offenders in which antisocial cognitions and behaviors are replaced with prosocial cognitions and behaviors (Cullen and Smith 2011). This is the *criminological component* of their paradigm in that it articulates a theory that explains why people offend, which then leads logically to how best to change the conduct.

Second, the *correctional component* presents a blueprint for intervening with offenders. This blueprint is conveyed through the principles of effective correctional treatment (Andrews, Bonta, and Hoge 1990; Andrews 1995; Gendreau 1996; Andrews and Bonta 2010). The RNR principles form the core of the correctional component. First, the *risk principle* advises that services should be provided to high-risk offenders. Interventions with low-risk offenders are either unnecessary (they will seldom reoffend) or can have iatrogenic effects (they will be criminogenic).

The *need principle* is more complicated. The concept of "needs" implies that offenders have "problematic circumstances" or deficits that should be addressed (Andrews and Bonta 2010, p. 49). "Criminogenic needs" are problems or deficits that lead to recidivism. Such deficits are typically referred to as "risk factors." However, Andrews and his colleagues differentiate between two kinds of risk factors. The first are "static" risk factors—characteristics associated with crime that cannot be changed (e.g., age, gender). The second are "dynamic" risk factors. These are aspects of a person that are malleable—that can be changed. If there were no dynamic risk factors—sometimes also called criminogenic needs—there could be no treatment; there would be nothing to change. Fortunately, there are a number of dynamic risk factors that can be targeted for change. Actually, they must be targeted and treated for recidivism to be reduced. If programs focus on noncriminogenic needs (e.g., poor self-esteem)—that is, risk factors not associated with reoffending—they will not work.

The Canadians identified the strongest dynamic risk factors/criminogenic needs through meta-analysis (Gendreau, Little, and Goggin 1996; Andrews and Bonta 2010). Most important are what they term "the Big Four," which include antisocial cognitions or attitudes, antisocial associates, antisocial personality pattern (e.g., "impulsive," "callous disregard for others"), and a history of antisocial behavior (Andrews and Bonta 2010, pp. 58–59). In what sense can a history of antisocial behavior be considered "dynamic"? The answer is that while a history cannot be changed, old antisocial repertoires can be replaced with new prosocial ones. This might include "building new noncriminal behaviors in high-risk situations and building self-efficacy beliefs supporting reform" (p. 58). Note that the Canadians are not attempting to construct a general theory of crime, which might involve a host of other factors (e.g., concentrated disadvantage). They are setting out a theory of recidivism, identifying the most promising targets for intervention: dynamic risk factors strongly related to reoffending.

The *responsivity principle* also is complex, because it involves both "general" and "specific" aspects. "General responsivity" involves, in parallel to medical terms, using the correct medicine for what ails the person (e.g., using antibiotics for an infection). For a treatment to work, it must target the true cause and be capable of addressing—that is, be "responsive" to—the problem in question. Given the content of the criminology component of their paradigm, the Canadians recommend use of cognitive-behavioral, social learning-based programs. Operant conditioning should be used to reinforce prosocial behaviors; modeling, shaping, and behavioral techniques should be employed to build prosocial skills, and cognitive restructuring should target distorted and antisocial cognitions.

"Specific responsivity" involves delivery of treatments in ways that take into account the characteristics of offenders. For example, some offenders might need to be motivated to participate in treatment. Others with low intelligence might respond better to formats that use concrete examples and do not require verbal engagement. Or consideration of gender might increase the capacity of a treatment to reach offenders (e.g., conducting an intervention in "women-only groups"; Andrews and Bonta 2010, pp. 507–10).

In summary, the RNR principles are legitimate precisely because they make sense. Thus, they recommend that correctional interventions focus on high-risk offenders, target empirically strong and malleable predictors of recidivism, and use treatments that are responsive to or capable of changing these dynamic risk factors. What, after all, would the alternative be? Focus on low-risk offenders? Target risk factors that are static or that are unrelated to recidivism? Use treatments that are unresponsive to the causes of reoffending? Of course, the principles will achieve reductions in recidivism only to the extent that the science underlying them is valid (e.g., the risk principle is true, the appropriate criminogenic needs have been identified, cognitive-behavioral programs are effective). Again, this appears to be the case (Gendreau, Smith, and French 2006; Smith, Gendreau, and Swartz 2009; Andrews and Bonta 2010; Smith 2013).

The RNR acronym has made the Canadians' model highly recognizable. One danger, however, is that observers often assume that the model consists only of three principles. This is not the case—and has not been for a long time (e.g., Andrews 1995; Gendreau 1996). In *The Psychology of Criminal Conduct*, Andrews and Bonta list 15 principles grouped into three categories: "overarching principles," "core RNR principles and key clinical issues," and "organizational principles, settings, staffing, and management" (2010, pp. 46–47). In evaluating the paradigm, commentators must move beyond the RNR principles and assess the full roster.

Two principles warrant special mention because they represent—in contrast to the more punitive goals of retribution/just deserts, deterrence, and incapacitation—the unique contribution that rehabilitation brings to corrections. Recall that the rehabilitative ideal mandates a focus not on the crime but on the criminal and that person's welfare. First, Andrews and Bonta instruct reformers to "introduce human service into the justice context. Do not rely on the sanction to bring about reduced offending" (2010, p. 46). Second, they instruct that services "should be delivered with respect to the person, including respect for personal autonomy, being humane, ethical, just, legal, decent, and being otherwise normative" (p. 46). It is this commitment to social welfare that provides the ethical context in which science should be used to treat offenders. In essence, the Canadians argue that interventions rooted in the combination of social welfare and science will do more to reduce recidivism than punitive sanctions that seek to scare offenders straight and otherwise care little about them.

Finally, the third dimension of the Canadians' paradigm is the *technology component*. Andrews, Bonta, and Gendreau understood that implementation of their model would be facilitated if practitioners were equipped with the needed treatment tools. They did several things to make this possible. First, they developed an inventory, the Level of Service Inventory, to assess offenders' risk levels. Now in its revised form, it is usually referred to by the acronym of "LSI-R." As described by Andrews and Bonta, the "LSI-R samples 54 risk and needs items, each scored on a zero-one format and distributed across 10 subcomponents (e.g., Criminal History, Education/Employment, Leisure)" (2010, p. 324). The items in the LSI-R "are those that the research shows to be associated with criminal conduct and that are theoretically relevant" (p. 325). Research reveals that the LSI-R has predictive validity (Vose, Cullen, and Smith 2008; Smith, Cullen, and Latessa 2009; Andrews and Bonta 2010).

Second, the Canadians also developed the Correctional Program Assessment Inventory—the "CPAI"—which is a measure of an agency's adherence to therapeutic integrity in light of the principles of effective treatment. As Andrews and Bonta note, many agencies "do what they do because that is what they have always done, or because that was what they were told to do. It may have nothing to do with outcomes, and they may have no idea what outcomes are of interest anyway" (2010, p. 405). The CPAI, which is administered on-site by trained external evaluators, is thus meant to help agencies institute effective practices that are consistent with their treatment paradigm. Evaluators use a 141-item instrument divided into eight surveys: organizational culture, program implementation/maintenance, management/staff characteristics, client risk/need practices, program characteristics, core correctional practice, interagency communication, and evaluation. Notably, scores on the CPAI are predictive of offender recidivism (Lowenkamp, Latessa, and Smith 2006; Andrews and Bonta 2010; Cullen and Smith 2011).

It is clear that the Canadians' paradigm is now the "dominant model" in offender rehabilitation (Polaschek 2012; see also Ogloff and Davis 2004). Virtually everyone in the treatment community knows the meaning of RNR and of the principles of effective correctional treatment. The CPAI has been applied to hundreds of programs across North America, including at least 40 American states (Cullen and Smith 2011; Edward J. Latessa, personal communication, April 23, 2012). The LSI-R has been used in over half of the states and in places as disparate as Australia, Bermuda, the Cayman Islands, Croatia, Hong Kong, Iceland, Mexico, Portugal, Scotland, Singapore, Sweden, Taiwan, and Trinidad Tobago. MHS, the company that markets the LSI-R, estimates that "over 11 million LS assessments have been delivered," including "more than a million" in the last year (Tammy M. Holwell, personal communication, April 20, 2012). In short, the Canadians' paradigm has helped restore rehabilitation's legitimacy by providing practitioners with the tools they need to implement treatment programs: The principles tell them what to do and the technology helps them do it. In short, Andrews and his colleagues have created a conduit through which broad empirical data showing rehabilitation's effectiveness can be translated into practical interventions in real-world correctional settings.

C. Evidence-Based Corrections

Rehabilitation received an additional boost from the infusion into corrections of evidence-based ideology. Over the past two decades, there has been a growing movement to use evidence as the basis of decision making in many fields, including medicine, education, and baseball (Lewis 2003; Timmermans and Berg 2003; Ayres 2007; Cullen, Myer, and Latessa 2009). Explicit calls also have been made to make criminal justice policy and practice, including corrections, evidence-based (Sherman 1998; Cullen and Gendreau 2000; MacKenzie 2000, 2006; Cullen, Myer, and Latessa 2009). This development has supported rehabilitation because it gained force in the correctional community precisely when published studies were beginning to show the effectiveness of treatment and the ineffectiveness of deterrence programs and harsh criminal sanctions (Cullen 2005).

At issue is legitimacy. The norm that interventions should be based on evidence is now widely shared, even if its use in agencies remains spotty. For two decades, the International Community Corrections Association has convened conferences and published articles with a "What Works?" theme (e.g., Harland 1996). Further, a growing effort is afoot to evaluate programs and to dismantle those that do not work (D.A.R.E. is one example). The federal Office of Justice Programs, to guide policy makers and practitioners, has developed a website—CrimeSolutions.gov—that lists programs according to whether the evaluation evidence shows that they are "effective," "promising," or have "no effects." The last category describes programs as having "strong evidence indicating that they had no effects or had harmful effects when implemented with fidelity." In this empirical contest, quality rehabilitation programs disproportionately are rated as falling into the top categories. It is becoming virtually impossible to claim that nothing works. The Martinson era is over.

IV. The Future of Rehabilitation

For most of my career, the United States has been in the grip of what Clear (1994) calls "the penal harm movement." In the past decade, however, cracks in this movement have appeared and widened (Listwan et al. 2008). Most recently, the financial crisis and strained state treasuries have fostered the view that mass incarceration, at least at current levels, is "not sustainable." State prison populations have declined for the first time in four decades (Pew Center on the States 2010). The punitive paradigm appears to have exhausted itself. As crime has receded as a political issue, officials have little to gain from looking tougher than their electoral opponents.

This has created an opportunity for another "new penology." Advocates of rehabilitation have an opportunity to design an agenda that specifies how best to conduct the correctional enterprise. Eight developments are likely to make up that agenda. It is unlikely that any of them will produce a major transformation of the correctional system, such as changing its basic organizational structure or the sentencing system. Taken together, however, they may operate to advance treatment goals, making the corrections process less gratuitously punitive and more attentive to offenders' welfare.

A. Policy Appeal of Rehabilitation

Three reasons exist why rehabilitation may have appeal to policy makers. First, with the growth of accountability in government, there is mounting pressure to use programs that can be justified as evidence-based. As noted, correctional interventions with empirical support are decidedly treatment oriented. Second, there is an increasing desire to limit prison populations. If officials are going to place offenders into the community, they will have to "do something with them." Routine parole or probation is not enough. To seem responsible—to be responsible—they will need to provide offenders with treatment programs. Third, the American public strongly supports the rehabilitation of offenders. Thus, there is substantial ideological space to implement treatment-related policies and practices. Phrased differently, no politician is likely to lose a reelection campaign for supporting correctional rehabilitation (Jonson, Cullen, and Lux 2013).

I am particularly interested in this latter issue because I conducted my first survey on the public's correctional orientation in 1979; it was reported in *Reaffirming Rehabilitation* (Cullen and Gilbert 1982, p. 258). Surveying residents of Springfield, Illinois, when "nothing works" enthusiasm was at a fever pitch, I expected to find little support for offender treatment. The data revealed a surprising pattern—one found in nearly every survey I have administered or read about in the past 30-plus years: The public supports not only the punishment but also the rehabilitation of offenders (Cullen, Fisher, and Applegate 2000; Jonson, Cullen, and Lux 2013). Thus, in that 1979 study, the respondents agreed that "criminals deserve to be punished" (87.9 percent) and might be deterred by "stiffer jail sentences" (62.9 percent). But 75.6 percent also agreed that "rehabilitating a criminal is just as important as making a criminal pay for his or her crime," and fully 90.4 percent agreed that although "criminals deserve to be punished," they "should be given the chance to be rehabilitated."

More recent surveys show the same level of support for rehabilitation, with especially favorable sentiments toward juvenile treatment and early intervention programs (Nagin et al. 2006; Cullen et al. 2007; Mears et al. 2007; Piquero et al. 2010). To cite just a few examples based on national samples of adults:

- A 2001 poll found that 92 percent of the respondents agreed that "it is a good idea to provide treatment for offenders who are in prison." When asked what the main emphasis of prison should be, 55 percent chose "rehabilitation" instead of "protect society" (25 percent), "punishment" (14 percent), and "not sure" (6 percent) (Cullen, Pealer, et al. 2002, pp. 136–37). Similar results were reported in a 2010 statewide poll in Oregon—rehabilitation (53 percent), protect society (38 percent), and punishment (9 percent) (Sundt et al. 2012).
- A 2006 survey found that 70 percent of the sample favored making "state-funded rehabilitation services available" to inmates both during and after incarceration; only 11 percent preferred to "treat prison as a punishment and to not offer rehabilitation services to people either during their time in prison or after their release" (Krisberg 2006, p. 3).
- Another 2006 survey showed that 79 percent of the public believed that "under the right conditions, many offenders can turn their lives around" (Princeton Survey Research Associates International 2006, p. 22).
- A 2010 poll reported that 78 percent of Americans agreed that "I think trying to rehabilitate people who have committed crimes is an important part of preventing crime" (Roberts and Hastings 2012, p. 492).
- The 2010 Oregon study, noted above, found that "the public voiced nearly unanimous support for providing inmates with services to help prepare them for release. More than 9 out of 10 Oregonians favored providing inmates with job training, mental health services, educational services, and drug treatment" (Sundt et al. 2012, p. 2). The embrace of "rehabilitative services" extended "to those already released from prison. Eighty percent or more of those polled favored providing housing assistance, mental health services, drug treatment, education, and job training to help prevent reoffending" (Sundt et al. 2012, p. 2)
- Similarly, a 2012 study found that 87 percent of Americans, including 82 percent of Republicans, agreed with this statement: "Ninety-

five percent of people in prison will be released. If we are serious about public safety, we must increase access to treatment and job training programs so they can become productive citizens once they are back in the community" (Public Opinion Strategies and the Mellman Group 2012, p. 12).

Recall that this level of support for rehabilitation has persisted after four decades of "nothing works" thinking, punitive rhetoric and policies, and a powerful mass imprisonment movement (Cullen 2006). The public's embrace of offender reformation is thus not fleeting or context specific but has endured across time and space. It is best seen as a "habit of the heart"—a term that Alexis de Tocqueville (1969, p. 287) used to describe fundamental cultural beliefs that constitute the core of the American character (see also Bellah et al. 1985; Cullen et al. 2007). From a practical standpoint, this means that the rehabilitative ideal is a form of cultural capital that can be used—now and for the foreseeable future—to justify correctional treatment policies and programs. Again, a reservoir of punitive sentiments exists and can be exploited to serve expressive political purposes—especially when a heinous crime occurs. Still, policy makers who argue that corrections should reaffirm rehabilitation and employ evidence-based programs are unlikely to face any opposition. In fact, they may even be seen as forward-looking and attract some added votes.

B. Power of the RNR Paradigm

I do not want to overstate the utility of the Canadians' RNR paradigm. It is not sacrosanct but is one possible approach to be improved upon (Porporino 2010; Polaschek 2012). However, the paradigm is powerful for the reasons previously articulated: It is firmly rooted in criminology, is evidenced based, has the technology to be delivered, and—perhaps most important—tells practitioners what to do to reduce recidivism (i.e., use appropriate treatment based on the RNR principles of effective intervention; Cullen 2012). For competing approaches to challenge—or match—the Canadians' paradigm, their advocates will have to undertake sustained scientific work, including conducting relevant meta-analyses and program evaluations. I have called this the task of "taking rehabilitation seriously" (Cullen 2012). Until this occurs, the RNR model will be "the only empirically validated guide for criminal justice interventions that aim to help offenders to depart from that system" (Polaschek 2012, p. 1) and will exert a disproportionately large influence. My view is not idiosyncratic. As Polaschek notes, the "RNR model of rehabilitation seems set to remain the 'premier rehabilitation theory.' . . . The achievements of the RNR model are quite remarkable" (2012, p. 12).

In addition, the RNR paradigm is being extended into office interactions between offenders and their probation or parole officers. Given that nearly 4.9 million offenders are under community supervision—about one in every 48 adults in the United States—this extension of the treatment model could prove quite consequential (Glaze and Bonczar 2011). Until now, officers have not been equipped with a "tool kit" on how to use office visits in an evidence-based, productive way (Gleicher, Manchak, and Cullen 2013).

However, three different models are being developed that outline strategies for training officers to apply RNR principles when meeting with offenders: Effective Practices in Community Supervision Training, Staff Training Aimed at Reducing Re-arrest, and Strategic Training Initiative in Community Supervision. Although still in their early days, evidence is emerging that these interactions can reduce recidivism (see, e.g., Andrews and Bonta 2010; Bonta et al. 2011; Robinson et al. 2012; Smith et al. 2012). To the extent that the RNR model shows its applicability in diverse correctional settings, it is likely to gain further influence.

C. Popularity of Desistance-Based Models

The RNR model emphasizes the importance of treating "criminogenic needs"—risk factors or deficits that lead to reoffending (e.g., antisocial attitudes, impulsivity). It favors interventions such as cognitive-behavioral therapies that are "responsive" to these problems. Many criminologists react negatively to this approach because they do not want to define offenders as different and, in particular, as somehow pathological. They do not want to objectify criminals as "the other"— as people to be set apart. By contrast, the Canadians are psychologists who believe in individual differences and believe that, unless the differences that make offenders high risk are addressed, offenders will recidivate because they are, alas, high risk! I am persuaded that the Canadians have criminological knowledge on their side (Cullen 2012).

How can scholars who wish to deny offender pathology nonetheless develop a credible rehabilitation model—one that might rival the RNR paradigm? The solution presented itself in the findings of desistance research, which reported that offenders move out of crime in natural settings through positive experiences. This might involve offenders' acquiring social bonds (Sampson and Laub 1993) or experiencing a cognitive transformation in which a redemption script is embraced (Maruna 2001). There is now a movement afoot—sometimes called "creative corrections"—to use desistance research as the basis for treatments that attempt to build on offenders' strengths as opposed to their weaknesses (Veysey, Christian, and Martinez 2009; Brayford, Cowe, and Deering 2010). Drawing also from positive psychology, the most developed of these approaches is the Good Lives Model set forth by Tony Ward and his colleagues (see, e.g., Ward, Mann, and Gannon 2007; Ward and Marshall 2007; Ward and Maruna 2007; Whitehead, Ward, and Collie 2007). It remains to be seen whether these approaches are sufficiently theoretically sound and effective to reduce recidivism and to outperform the RNR model (Andrews, Bonta, and Wormith 2011; Cullen 2012; see also Porporino 2010). In particular, the criminology of desistance—understanding how positive external and internal experiences trigger behavioral change—is in its beginning stages (Sullivan 2013). Basing an intervention on a developing body of evidence is a special challenge to be surmounted. Regardless, programs grounded in desistance research can be expected to grow in the time ahead (Raynor and Robinson 2009; Porporino 2010).

D. Reentry as a Conduit for Rehabilitation

Each year, more than 700,000 offenders are released from state and federal prisons—a number that does not include the hundreds of thousands who cycle annually through jails (West, Sabol, and Greenman 2010). Strangely, it had become common practice for returning offenders, most of whom had not received effective treatment services, to be "given a bus ticket, between $20 and $200, and told to report to their designated parole field office within a few days of release" (Petersilia 2011, p. 936). On its face, such a system seems designed to fail—at minimum a form of malign neglect that would foreseeably produce high rates of recidivism and endanger public safety. Yet nobody seemed to care very much or to be in a position to do much about it. In the past decade, however, a reentry movement has emerged that has illuminated the problem of returning offenders and catalyzed funding and development of hundreds of programs (Petersilia 2003, 2011; Travis 2005; Rhine and Thompson 2011; American Bar Association

Criminal Justice Section 2012). Most of these interventions focus on reintegrating offenders by assisting them with housing, education, employment, family reunification, and medical treatment.

According to the National Research Council, "'nothing works' is no longer a defensible conclusion from assessments of program effects on reentry outcomes" (2008, p. 82). Still, program evaluations have produced modest results, especially when the outcome is reducing recidivism (Lattimore and Visher 2009; Rhine and Thompson 2011). Part of the problem is that these programs focus primarily on offenders' immediate needs for a place to live, gainful employment, and reestablished contact with family members. In so doing, however, it is likely that the "academic 'what works' literature . . . barely touches these programs" (Petersilia 2011, p. 945; see also Listwan, Cullen, and Latessa 2006). But this need not be the case. Thus, Petersilia has offered seven principles, drawn largely from the RNR paradigm, that could be used to integrate evidence-based treatment into reentry programs (e.g., "treatment services should be behavioral in nature"; "treatment interventions should be used primarily with higher-risk offenders, targeting their criminogenic needs"; 2011, pp. 944–45).

Given the push to downsize prison populations, reentry is likely to remain in the policy limelight and to receive sustained support. If so, then reentry programs, which can begin in prison and extend into the community, offer a heretofore unexploited conduit to deliver evidence-based treatment services. A multimodal approach is required that addresses both offenders' reintegration needs and their criminogenic needs (Listwan, Cullen, and Latessa 2006). Such a dual-focused intervention promises to stabilize offenders' lives and to address the risk factors underlying their criminality. In turn, reentry programs should have a greater impact on recidivism and become even more cost-effective—two outcomes that would justify their expansion.

E. Integration of Early Intervention and Correctional Programs

Life-course research has demonstrated two findings with important implications for the correctional enterprise. First, for career or life-course-persistent offenders, entry into antisocial behavior typically occurs early in life (Wright, Tibbetts, and Daigle 2008). This means that continuity between childhood antisocial behavior and juvenile and adult crime often is seamless. Second, most high-risk youths destined for correctional supervision receive few, if any, interventions prior to entering the justice system (Stouthamer-Loeber, Loeber, and Thomas 1992; Stouthamer-Loeber et al. 1995). These two facts point to the irrationality of continuing to ignore the criminogenic development of wayward youngsters until they have victimized others and compromised their own healthy development. For these reasons, there is a growing call to implement evidence-based early intervention programs (Greenwood 2006; Farrington and Welsh 2007; Welsh et al. 2011; Welsh and Farrington 2012).

The more difficult challenge is to envision early intervention and corrections not as separate spheres of treatment with separate missions (Lösel 2007; Howell 2009). Integrating these missions makes sense because both systems are, or will be, rehabilitating many of the same high-risk youths. Still, the stubborn reality is that bureaucratic barriers exist between correctional and other human service agencies. Notably, Communities That Care (CTC) provides one example of how to overcome this lack of coordination.

Developed by J. David Hawkins, Richard Catalano, and their collaborators, CTC supplies a blueprint for implementing community-wide, evidence-based programs that seek to diminish risk factors and heighten protective factors. A key element is the development of a CTC coalition that is "structured, ideally with chairs, co-chairs, and workgroups" and that involves "representation from law enforcement, health and human service agencies, schools, youth-service groups, local or state government, business, religious groups, youth, and parents" (Fagan and Hawkins 2012, p. 262). The CTC model has shown the capacity to reduce delinquency and substance use (Hawkins et al. 2012). Thus, at least at the local level, it should be possible for juvenile correctional officials to work closely with other agencies to bring intensive resources to bear on antisocial youths who are in the beginning stages of their criminal careers.

F. Using Financial Incentives to Achieve Effectiveness

It is possible that a nascent initiative—"social impact bonds"—might create a financial incentive for the development and delivery of effective programs. This approach involves an investment model in which people invest in an intervention program that pays returns if the intervention is effective—that is, if it reduces the targeted behavior. Let's say, for example, that the government wished to reduce recidivism among inmates. It would then allow an investor to enroll inmates in treatment services during and after incarceration. The money to pay for these services would be raised by a "social impact bond issuing organization" (SIBIO). The SIBIO would secure financing from investors. The SIBIO would then use this money to contract with a provider for the treatment services. Now here is the key: The SIBIO would receive payment only if an agreed-upon reduction in recidivism was achieved. No reduction in recidivism, the government pays nothing (a reason these are sometimes called "pay-for-success bonds"). But if a lower rate of reoffending is realized, then the government pays the SIBIO an amount that would ensure profits for investors (Liebman 2011; Kohli, Besharov, and Costs 2012).

Experimentation with social impact bonds is now ongoing, including at Petersborough Prison in England and at Rikers Island in New York City, which has initiated the Adolescent Behavioral Learning Experience aimed at reducing recidivism among 16–19-year-olds (Office of the Mayor 2012). Should such efforts prove successful, it is possible that companies will arise that specialize in making profits through effective interventions. In turn, private financial incentives might exist to expand rehabilitation programs and, in particular, to fund research on effective treatment strategies—much as pharmaceutical companies do with drug treatment. Maximizing the effectiveness of interventions would be crucial to the companies' ability to maximizing profits. By contrast, correctional officials now have few incentives to support treatment experimentation because they are not paid to reduce recidivism (Cullen, Jonson, and Eck 2012). With social impact bonds, developing and implementing effective interventions would not be an academic calling but a means to making money for private investors.

Although not focusing on crime-related interventions, J. P. Morgan has assessed the potential profitability of global impact investing in populations now making under $3,000 annually across housing, rural water delivery, maternal health, primary education, and financial services. They estimate that "this segment of the market offers the potential over the next 10 years for invested capital of $400bn-$1 trillion and profits of $183-$667bn. . . . Market initiatives are in place to build third party systems to facilitate these efforts" (J. P. Morgan 2010, p. 7). To be sure, earning profits through offender treatment might prove more daunting than in other social areas (Aylott and Shelupanov 2011). Still, as the profitability of social impact bonds is demonstrated across outcomes and nations, their utility may become more apparent. Corrections should emerge as an inviting investment opportunity because of large budgets, the pressing demand to reduce spiraling costs, and high recidivism rates ripe for reduction. Already a technical guide exists for developing social impact bonds for the criminal justice system (Bolton and Palumbo 2011).

G. Rehabilitation Ceremonies

As we have seen, reentry has moved to the front burner in corrections. Initiatives have flourished, in part due to federal financial support to state and local jurisdictions through The Second Chance Act (Listwan et al. 2008). One concern is the extent to which reentry programs will prove effective in reducing recidivism. This is not my interest here. Rather, the focus is on a parallel development—one asserting that inmates should not only be rehabilitated but also *be seen as rehabilitated*.

Barriers to such a development certainly exist. Thus, Alexander's (2010) *The New Jim Crow* illuminates the array of collateral consequences that now accompany a felony conviction (i.e., rights denied by statute to convicted offenders). Such "invisible punishments," as they are sometimes called (Mauer and Chesney-Lind 2002), are not new (Burton, Cullen, and Travis 1987). Even so, during the "get tough" era, these restrictions were expanded dramatically and appear to have had a disquieting racially disparate impact (Alexander 2010).

But the pendulum may be swinging in the other direction. More intense public discussion of collateral consequences has challenged the prudence of permanently stigmatizing offenders and creating often gratuitous barriers to their successful reentry. Some states, such as Ohio and Colorado, are actively exploring ways to reduce and provide relief from collateral consequences (Mohr 2012; State of Colorado 2012). A number of states limit the effects of criminal convictions through judicial expungement of records or, after a certain passage of time without any reoffending, by creating a "presumption of rehabilitation" that limits when a conviction can be used to deny employment (Love and Frazier 2006). A few jurisdictions, most notably New York, offer "certificates of good conduct" or "certificates of rehabilitation" that restore "some or all of the legal rights and privileges lost as a result of conviction" (Love and Frazier 2006, p. 6).

In this context, the possibility exists to develop a process in which offenders are publicly and legally granted redemption—that is, are declared rehabilitated. Two lines of scholarship are laying the groundwork for this policy agenda: First, longitudinal studies are demonstrating empirically how long an offender must abstain from offending before the risk of recidivism is eliminated (or falls below the average level of the general public; see, e.g., Blumstein and Nakamura 2009; Bushway, Nieuwbeerta, and Blokland 2011). The point at which offenders might be declared crime free—truly rehabilitated—appears to vary by age, offense, and prior record. Still, the studies show that many offenders permanently desist if crime-free for a decade. This time to cure might well be shortened if offenders participated in evidence-based rehabilitation programs during their correctional supervision.

Second, Maruna (2011a, 2011b) has written eloquently on how we might create a process that would allow offenders to "wipe the slate clean." He has in mind more than expunging a criminal conviction. In his approach, he has called for "redemption rituals" that might be conducted in the community (similar to First Communion) or in court (Maruna 2011b). He has proposed a process of "judicial rehabilitation" (2011a). This process would involve not annulling and hiding the past (as occurs when criminal records are expunged) but a public affirmation that the offender is cured and thus deserves a clean bill of health.

For rehabilitation ceremonies to be effective, they should be universally available. At present, many offenders lack the eligibility (due to the seriousness of the crime committed), knowledge, access to legal representation, or cultural capital to take the steps needed to have their criminal records expunged. By contrast, such ceremonies should be widely publicized and held up as a goal to which all convicted criminals should aspire. If we wish offenders to graduate from crime to conformity, we should make a big deal of this event—just as we do when students graduate from high school or college.

Maruna (2011b) contends that the focus of these rituals should not be on offenders' appearing risk free based on their having avoided crime for a certain time period. Rather, similar to how merit badges are a precondition to becoming an Eagle Scout, earning the status of being rehabilitated should involve active or purposive efforts to improve oneself and the lives of others. According to Maruna, "Instead, rituals could be designed to recognize a person's efforts to 'make good' after committing an offense. These might include immediate efforts to apologize or make amends to one's victims, a period of 'good behavior' on the outside, and efforts to recover from addiction, find productive work, 'give something back' to one's community, or contribute to one's family responsibilities" (2011*b*, p. 19). We might even envision, I would add, the creation of "rehabilitation academies" in which offenders enroll and, over a 4-year period, engage in a structured curriculum of activities that could result in a successful rehabilitation ceremony.

These ideas might appear utopian, but on closer inspection they are far more practical than a system that stigmatizes, socially excludes, and produces high rates of recidivism. What we do currently cannot be defended on any grounds. Fresh ideas, even those that seem a touch idealistic, are needed to reinvent methods for how we integrate offenders back into the community.

H. Growth of Specialty Courts

Recent years have witnessed the growth of specialty courts—especially drug courts, which now exceed 2,100 (Mitchell 2011), and mental health courts, which now exceed 150 (Sarteschi 2009). These courts have diverted offenders from the justice system and provided treatment opportunities, albeit backed up with threats of graduated sanctions for noncompliance with specified conditions. Initial results suggest that they are at least modestly successful in reducing recidivism (see, e.g., Wilson, Mitchell, and MacKenzie 2006; Sarteschi 2009; Cross 2011; Mitchell 2011; Shaffer 2011). Their effectiveness, however, is less important than their very existence, although claims that they "work" have certainly enhanced their legitimacy.

The first drug courts were invented in the 1990s as a cost-effective, practical way to handle the influx of drug offenders into the criminal justice system (Mitchell 2011). They also grew because of a large infusion of federal funds. The courts were politically viable because they retained a criminal justice face, balancing compassion with the promise to supervise offenders closely and to hold them accountable for meeting "rigorous programming demands" (Mitchell 2011, p. 849). Still, drug and mental health courts both involve, in Mitchell's words, "the revitalization of individualized treatment" (p. 848). They have been called "problem-solving courts" because of their focus on using treatment to address the troubles—addiction, mental illness—underlying lawbreaking (National Research Council 2008). In short, there was a core recognition that exclusively punitive sanctions were ineffective; the delivery of human services was needed to respond to offenders' needs and diminish their recidivism.

It now appears that other categories of offenders will be identified as warranting special treatment. Domestic violence and DWI (driving while intoxicated) courts are spreading, as are special courts for the homeless and for military veterans. Taken together, these courts show the continuing tenacity of the rehabilitative ideal and offer yet another avenue for expanding the delivery of treatment services to offenders in the time ahead.

V. Conclusion: Beyond Nothing Works

When I left Columbia University for the cornfields of Illinois in 1976, I thought I would spend my career as a theoretical criminologist. Little did I know that I would be drawn into a multiple-decade defense of rehabilitation—hanging out with Canadians, psychologists, and assorted other scholars not found within the typical network of a sociologist! It was a road less traveled by fellow criminologists but one that has contributed to my having had a wonderful academic life (Cullen 2002).

As an early critic of so-called enforced treatment, I was intimately familiar with the limitations and dangers that inhered in the curing enterprise. In particular, unfettered discretion, exercised with few guidelines and little demonstrated expertise, is pregnant with the possibility of abuse. But as I have recounted, I became persuaded that the turn away from rehabilitation was a tragic mistake. The rehabilitative ideal—and note that no one speaks of the "punishment ideal"—functions as a reminder that corrections should serve higher social purposes (Allen 1981). Rehabilitation provides a rationale for saving, rather than demeaning and warehousing, offenders—a population whose harms are easily recalled and whose humanity is easily overlooked. It calls us to seek our better selves and, writ large, to fashion a better society.

But we would do well to recognize that rehabilitation's appeal is fundamentally rooted in its claim of utility. Correctional treatment comes with the promise that a human services response will not only improve offenders' lives but also enhance public safety. For this reason, it is essential that treatment programs work—that they reduce recidivism. Much as in medicine, interventions that provide comfort but not cure—and that cost a fair amount—will lose their legitimacy. And in corrections, the alternative to effective treatment has been the embrace of harsh punishment, including the fallback position that incapacitating the wicked will at least keep them off the streets for a while. Much is at stake.

For the rehabilitative ideal to be sustainable as a guiding correctional theory—for us to truly move beyond "nothing works" corrections—it must be grounded in a strong science of offender change (Cullen 2005). Martinson's (1974*b*) critique may have been too sweeping and too hyperbolic, but he was right to demand that correctional officials design and use effective interventions. For this goal to be achieved, two important challenges will have to be surmounted.

First, although important strides have been taken in the past decade, corrections must meet the challenge of becoming a fully evidence-based field. With support from policy makers, practitioners should be an outspoken constituency in demanding that they receive the "medicines" needed to reform offenders. This might involve lobbying for government funding to support treatment experimentation, the dissemination of knowledge, and training. Similar to innovations in problem-oriented policing, it might also be time to hold correctional officials accountable for reducing recidivism—a standard that should spark unprecedented interest in effective programming (Cullen, Jonson, and Eck 2012). Most important, corrections should be elevated to the status of a profession, with its hallmarks of scientific expertise and a code of ethics (Latessa, Cullen, and Gendreau 2002).

As I have argued elsewhere, I favor a "Correctional Hippocratic Oath" (Cullen 2011*b*). The Hippocratic Oath stands at the core of medicine's claim to be a profession, mandating that the physician always prescribe "regimens for the good of my patients according to my ability and my judgment and never do harm to anyone." Applied to corrections, it would mean that officials and practitioners would be obligated to develop the expertise to employ effective interventions and to treat offenders with an ethic of care. They would also be mandated to ensure that correctional programs do not needlessly endanger the public. To be a professional is thus to be responsible—to create a corrections that takes seriously its obligation to use best practices to rehabilitate in an ethical way. Such an oath would provide a strong rationale for opposing the use of unproven, punitive interventions such as boot camps that have little basis in science and have the potential to harm offenders.

Second, crime science is a branch of criminology whose mission is to prevent or lower crime, typically through strategies that focus on crime events and that block access to criminal opportunities (see, e.g., Clarke 2010). In a similar way, criminologists must take up the challenge to create a specialization in "correctional science" whose explicit raison d'être is to reduce recidivism. Again, Andrews, Bonta, Gendreau, and their Canadian colleagues provide a powerful example of what this might entail (Cullen 2012). Their RNR paradigm thus should be the first step in developing more effective treatment interventions in prison and in the community.

The difficulty, however, is that criminologists have complained a great deal about corrections but have done relatively little to help offenders under supervision escape their criminal careers. We have been high on empathy but low on action (see also Currie 2007; Matthews 2009). In fact, with only a few exceptions, our graduate programs teach students how to criticize but not how to apply knowledge to improve the world. This need not be the case. Sherman (2011) has urged criminologists to see themselves as "inventors." By bringing our best research to bear, it should be possible for more scholars to engage in applied projects that build treatment knowledge. As Sherman observes, criminology arose as "a new way of reducing human suffering. If an invention is a 'new design for doing something,' the something that criminology was designed for was less crime and injustice" (2011, p. 423).

Such a call to action might seem, if not be, a touch naive. An anonymous, fair-minded reviewer of this essay lamented that "when it comes to reforming correctional policy and practice, . . . anything we do will be swamped by the size and scope of the penal beast." Accordingly, promoting "the return of the rehabilitative ethic" might be "both a very good thing and also largely irrelevant to the main difficulty with today's prison policy." When I am alone and in a more despairing mood, I confess to sharing these reservations. How could I not? Mass imprisonment is the elephant in the room and cannot be ignored.

Still, my willingness to advocate for the rehabilitative ideal comes from my rejection of the view that no correctional goodness can be created until the larger problem of system scale is solved. To be honest, I can only speculate on how to harness the complex forces that have produced the "penal beast" that is of concern to all responsible policy commentators (Jonson, Eck, and Cullen 2014). But I also am not certain that most other criminologists can do any better, or I suspect that they would have done so already. In the absence of the easy fix, we must see corrections for what it is: a long-term struggle between those who wish to make corrections, and especially prisons, an instrument of pain, and those who wish to use offender intervention as a conduit to improve lives. For four decades, the prominence and legitimacy of the pain paradigm has had the cumulative effect of fostering not only mass imprisonment but also a mean season in corrections. We now need four decades of incremental change in the opposite, human services direction. In my view, the rehabilitative ideal provides the only culturally legitimate vision for why doing good should be embraced over doing harm. Offender treatment is no panacea for what ails corrections, but it is, as I have long believed, the best option available (Cullen and Gilbert 1982, 2013).

Indeed, as I look to the past and now toward the future, I am heartened by what might be achieved. Rehabilitation has weathered a sustained attack and is now increasingly guiding correctional policy and practice. Again, this is a time to avoid hubris and to be sober about what it will take to move beyond the "nothing works" era. It is not sufficient to decry the wastefulness of mass incarceration or to show that punitively oriented programs do not work. The special challenge is to create evidence-based treatment programs on a wide basis and to implement them with integrity. In short, it is time to take the task of rehabilitating offenders seriously.

REFERENCES

Adams, Stuart. 1976. "Evaluation: A Way Out of Rhetoric." In *Rehabilitation, Recidivism, and Research*, edited by Robert Martinson, Ted Palmer, and Stuart Adams. Hackensack, NJ: National Council on Crime and Delinquency.

Alexander, James, Christie Pugh, and Bruce Parsons. 1998. *Functional Family Therapy: Blueprints in Violence Prevention—Book 3*. Boulder: Institute of Behavioral Science, University of Colorado at Boulder.

Alexander, Michelle. 2010. *The New Jim Crow: Mass Incarceration in the Age of Colorblindness*. New York: New Press.

Allen, Francis A. 1964. *The Borderland of Criminal Justice: Essays in Law and Criminology*. Chicago: University of Chicago Press.

———. 1981. *The Decline of the Rehabilitative Ideal: Penal Policy and Social Purpose*. New Haven, CT: Yale University Press.

American Bar Association Criminal Justice Section. 2012. *Survey on Reentry*. Washington, DC: American Bar Association.

American Friends Service Committee Working Party. 1971. *Struggle for Justice: A Report on Crime and Punishment in America*. New York: Hill & Wang.

Andrews, D. A. 1980. "Some Experimental Investigations of the Principles of Differential Association through Deliberate Manipulations of the Structure of Service Systems." *American Sociological Review* 45:448–62.

———. 1995. "The Psychology of Criminal Conduct and Effective Treatment." In *What Works: Reducing Reoffending*, edited by James McGuire. West Sussex, UK: Wiley.

Andrews, D. A., and James Bonta. 2006. *The Psychology of Criminal Conduct*. 4th ed. New Providence, NJ: LexisNexis.

———. 2010. *The Psychology of Criminal Conduct*. 5th ed. New Providence, NJ: LexisNexis.

Andrews, D. A., James Bonta, and Robert D. Hoge. 1990. "Classification for Effective Rehabilitation: Rediscovering Psychology." *Criminal Justice and Behavior* 17:19–52.

Andrews, D. A., James Bonta, and J. Stephen Wormith. 2011. "The Risk-Need-Responsivity (RNR) Model: Does Adding the Good Lives Model Contribute to Effective Crime Prevention?" *Criminal Justice and Behavior* 38:735–55.

Andrews, D. A., Ivan Zinger, Robert D. Hoge, James Bonta, Paul Gendreau, and Francis T. Cullen. 1990. "Does Correctional Treatment Work? A Clinically Relevant and Psychologically Informed Meta-Analysis." *Criminology* 28:369–404.

Aylott, Mhairi, and Anton Shelupanov. 2011. "Social Impact Bonds in Criminal Justice: From Interesting Idea to Business as Usual." *Prison Service Journal* 195:3–8.

Ayres, Ian. 2007. *Super Crunchers: Why Thinking-by-Numbers Is the New Way to Be Smart*. New York: Bantam.

Beckett, Katherine. 1997. *Making Crime Pay: Law and Order in Contemporary American Politics*. New York: Oxford University Press.

Bellah, Robert N., Richard Madsen, William M. Sullivan, Ann Swidler, and Steven M. Tipton. 1985. *Habits of the Heart: Individualism and Commitment in American Life*. Berkeley: University of California Press.

Bennett, William J., John J. DiIulio Jr., and John P. Walters. 1996. *Body Count: Moral Poverty and How to Win America's War against Crime and Drugs*. New York: Simon & Shuster.

Binder, Arnold, and Gilbert Geis. 1984. "*Ad Populum* Argumentation in Criminology: Juvenile Diversion and Rhetoric." *Crime and Delinquency* 30:624–47.

Blumstein, Alfred, and Kiminori Nakamura. 2009. "Redemption in the Presence of Widespread Criminal Background Checks." *Criminology* 47:327–59.

Bolton, Emily, and Jenna Palumbo. 2011. *A Technical Guide to Developing a Social Impact Bond: Criminal Justice*. London: Social Finance.

Bonta, James, Guy Bourgon, Tanya Rugge, Terri-Lynne Scott, Annie K. Yessine, Leticia Gutierrez, and Jobina Li. 2011. "An Experimental Demonstration of Training Probation Officers in Evidence-Based Community Super-vision." *Criminal Justice and Behavior* 11:1127–48.

Brayford, Jo, Francis Cowe, and John Deering, eds. 2010 *What Else Works? Creative Work with Offenders*. Cullompton, UK: Willan.

Breckinridge, Sophonisba P., and Edith Abbott. 1912. *The Delinquent Child and the Home*. New York: Charities Publication Committee.

Brokaw, Tom. 2007. *Boom! Voices of the Sixties*. New York: Random House.

Burton, Velmer S., Jr., Francis T. Cullen, and Lawrence F. Travis III. 1987. "The Collateral Consequences of Felony Conviction: A National Study of State Statutes." *Federal Probation* 51(3):52–60.

Bushway, Shawn D., Paul Nieuwbeerta, and Arjan Blokland. 2011. "The Pre-dictive Value of Criminal Background Checks: Do Age and Criminal History Affect Time to Redemption?" *Criminology* 49:27–60.

Canby, Vincent. 1967. "The Screen: 'Titicut Follies' Observes Life in a Mod-ern Bedlam." *New York Times*, October 4. http://www.nytimes.com/1992/03/05/movies/the-tragedies-of-bedlam-in-titicut-follies-of-1967.html.

CBS Television Network. 1975. "It Doesn't Work." *60 Minutes* 7(32):1–9

Clarke, Ronald V. 2010. "Crime Science." In *The Sage Handbook of Crimino-logical Theory*, edited by Eugene McLaughlin and Tim Newburn. London: Sage.

Clarke, Ronald V., and Marcus Felson. 2011. "The Origins of the Routine Activity Approach and Situational Crime Prevention." In *The Origins of American Criminology: Advances in Criminological Theory*, vol. 16, edited by Francis T. Cullen, Cheryl Lero Jonson, Andrew J. Myer, and Freda Adler. New Brunswick, NJ: Transaction.

Clear, Todd R. 1994. *Harm in American Penology: Offenders, Victims, and Their Communities*. Albany: State University of New York Press.

Cloward, Richard A., and Lloyd E. Ohlin. 1960. *Delinquency and Opportunity: A Theory of Delinquent Gangs*. New York: Free Press.

Cole, Stephen. 1975. "The Growth of Scientific Knowledge: Theories of De-viance as a Case Study." In *The Idea of Social Structure: Papers in Honor of Robert K. Merton*, edited by Lewis A. Coser. New York: Harcourt Brace Jovanovich.

Collins, Gail. 2009. *When Everything Changed: The Amazing Journey of Amer-ican Women from 1960 to the Present*. New York: Little, Brown.

Conrad, John. 1973. "Corrections and Simple Justice." *Journal of Criminal Law and Criminology* 64:208–17.

Cressey, Donald R. 1958. "The Nature and Effectiveness of Correctional Tech-niques." In *Prison within Society: A Reader in Penology*, edited by Lawrence E. Hazelrigg. New York: Anchor.

Cross, Brittany. 2011. "Mental Health Courts Effectiveness in Reducing Re-cidivism and Improving Clinical Outcomes: A Meta-Analysis." PhD disser-tation, University of South Florida, Department of Criminology.

Cullen, Francis T. 1984. *Rethinking Crime and Deviance Theory: The Emergence of a Structuring Tradition*. Totowa, NJ: Rowman & Allanheld.

———. 2002. "It's a Wonderful Life: Reflections on a Career in Progress." In

The Lessons of Criminology, edited by Gilbert Geis and Mary Dodge. Cincinnati: Anderson.

———. 2005. "The Twelve People Who Saved Rehabilitation: How the Science of Criminology Made a Difference—the American Society of Criminology 2004 Presidential Address." *Criminology* 43:1–42.

———. 2006. "It's Time to Reaffirm Rehabilitation." *Criminology and Public Policy* 5:665–72.

———. 2011a. "Beyond Adolescence-Limited Criminology: Choosing Our Future—the American Society of Criminology 2010 Sutherland Address." *Criminology* 49:287–330.

———. 2011b. "Making Corrections Work: It's Time for a New Penology." *Journal of Community Corrections* 21(1):5–6, 15–18.

———. 2012. "Taking Rehabilitation Seriously: Creativity, Science, and the Challenge of Offender Change." *Punishment and Society* 14:94–114.

Cullen, Francis T., Kristie R. Blevins, Jennifer S. Trager, and Paul Gendreau. 2005. "The Rise and Fall of Boot Camps: A Case Study in Common-Sense Corrections." *Journal of Offender Rehabilitation* 40(3–4):53–70.

Cullen, Francis T., and John B. Cullen. 1978. *Toward a Paradigm of Labeling Theory*. Lincoln: University of Nebraska Studies.

Cullen, Francis T., Bonnie S. Fisher, and Brandon K. Applegate. 2000. "Public Opinion about Punishment and Corrections." In *Crime and Justice: A Review of Research*, vol. 27, edited by Michael Tonry. Chicago: University of Chicago Press.

Cullen, Francis T., and Paul Gendreau. 2000. "Assessing Correctional Rehabilitation: Policy, Practice, and Prospects." In *Policies, Processes, and Decisions of the Criminal Justice System*, edited by Julie Horney. Vol. 3 of *Criminal Justice 2000*. Washington, DC: US Department of Justice, National Institute of Justice.

———. 2001. "From Nothing Works to What Works: Changing Professional Ideology in the 21st Century." *Prison Journal* 81:313–38.

Cullen, Francis T., and Karen E. Gilbert. 1982. *Reaffirming Rehabilitation*. Cincinnati: Anderson.

———. 2013. *Reaffirming Rehabilitation*. 30th anniversary ed. Waltham, MA: Anderson.

Cullen, Francis T., and Cheryl Lero Jonson. 2011. "Rehabilitation and Treatment Programs." In *Crime and Public Policy*, edited by James Q. Wilson and Joan Petersilia. New York: Oxford University Press.

———. 2012. *Correctional Theory: Context and Consequences*. Thousand Oaks, CA: Sage.

Cullen, Francis T., Cheryl Lero Jonson, and John E. Eck. 2012. "The Accountable Prison." *Journal of Contemporary Criminal Justice* 28:77–95.

Cullen, Francis T., Cheryl Lero Jonson, and Daniel S. Nagin. 2011. "Prisons Do Not Reduce Recidivism: The High Cost of Ignoring Science." *Prison Journal* 91:48S–65S.

Cullen, Francis T., Edward J. Latessa, Velmer S. Burton Jr., and Lucien X.

Lombardo. 1993. "The Correctional Orientation of Prison Wardens: Is the Rehabilitative Ideal Supported?" *Criminology* 31:69–92.

Cullen, Francis T., Faith E. Lutze, Bruce G. Link, and Nancy T. Wolfe. 1989. "The Correctional Orientation of Prison Guards: Do Officers Support Rehabilitation?" *Federal Probation* 53(1):33–42.

Cullen, Francis T., Andrew J. Myer, and Edward J. Latessa. 2009. "Eight Lessons from *Moneyball*: The High Cost of Ignoring Evidence-Based Corrections." *Victims and Offenders* 4:197–213.

Cullen, Francis T., Jennifer A. Pealer, Bonnie S. Fisher, Brandon K. Applegate, and Shannon A. Santana. 2002. "Public Support for Correctional Rehabilitation in America: Change or Consistency?" In *Changing Attitudes to Punishment: Public Opinion, Crime and Justice*, edited by Julian V. Roberts and Michael Hough. Devon, UK: Willan.

Cullen, Francis T., Travis C. Pratt, Sharon Levrant Miceli, and Melissa M. Moon. 2002. "Dangerous Liaison? Rational Choice Theory as the Basis for Correctional Intervention." In *Rational Choice and Criminal Behavior: Recent Research and Future Challenge*, edited by Alex R. Piquero and Stephen G. Tibbetts. New York: Routledge.

Cullen, Francis T, and Paula Smith. 2011. "Treatment and Rehabilitation." In *The Oxford Handbook of Crime and Criminal Justice*, edited by Michael Tonry. New York: Oxford University Press.

Cullen, Francis T., Brenda A. Vose, Cheryl Lero Jonson, and James D. Unnever. 2007. "Public Support for Early Intervention: Is Child Saving a 'Habit of the Heart'?" *Victims and Offenders* 2:109–24.

Cullen, Francis T., John Paul Wright, and Brandon K. Applegate. 1996. "Control in the Community: The Limits of Reform?" In *Choosing Correctional Interventions That Work: Defining the Demand and Evaluating the Supply*, edited by Alan Harland. Thousand Oaks, CA: Sage.

Currie, Elliott. 1985. *Confronting Crime: An American Challenge*. New York: Pantheon.

———. 2007. "Against Marginality: Arguments for a Public Criminology." *Theoretical Criminology* 11:175–90.

Eriksson, Torsten. 1976. *The Reformers: An Historical Survey of Pioneer Experiments in the Treatment of Criminals*. New York: Oxford University Press.

Fagan, Abigail A., and J. David Hawkins. 2012. "Community-Based Substance Use Prevention." In *The Oxford Handbook of Crime Prevention*, edited by Brandon C. Welsh and David P. Farrington. New York: Oxford University Press.

Farrington, David P., Rolf Loeber, and Maria M. Ttofi. 2012. "Risk and Protective Factors for Offending." In *The Oxford Handbook of Crime Prevention*, edited by Brandon C. Welsh and David P. Farrington. New York: Oxford University Press.

Farrington, David. P., and Brandon C. Welsh. 2007. *Saving Children from a Life in Crime: Early Risk Factors and Effective Interventions*. New York: Oxford University Press.

Feld, Barry C. 1999. *Bad Kids: Race and the Transformation of the Juvenile Court.* New York: Oxford University Press.

Finn, Peter. 1996. "No Frills Prisons and Jails: A Movement in Flux." *Federal Probation* 60(3):35–44.

Fogel, David. 1979. *"We Are the Living Proof": The Justice Model for Corrections.* 2nd ed. Cincinnati: Anderson.

Foucault, Michel. 1977. *Discipline and Punish: The Birth of the Prison.* New York: Pantheon.

Frankel, Marvin E. 1972. *Criminal Sentences: Law without Order.* New York: Hill & Wang.

Frase, Richard S. 2005. "Sentencing Guidelines in Minnesota, 1978–2003." In *Crime and Justice: A Review of Research*, vol. 32, edited by Michael Tonry. Chicago: University of Chicago Press.

Garland, David. 2001. *The Culture of Control: Crime and Social Order in Contemporary Society.* Chicago: University of Chicago Press.

Gaylin, Willard. 1974. *Partial Justice: A Study of Bias in Sentencing.* New York: Vintage.

———. 1978. "Prisoners of Benevolence: Power versus Liberty in the Welfare State." In *Doing Good: The Limits of Benevolence*, edited by Willard Gaylin, Ira Glasser, Steven Marcus, and David J. Rothman. New York: Pantheon.

Gaylin, Willard, Ira Glasser, Steven Marcus, and David J. Rothman, eds. 1978. *Doing Good: The Limits of Benevolence.* New York: Pantheon.

Gendreau, Paul. 1996. "The Principles of Effective Intervention with Offenders." In *Choosing Correctional Interventions That Work: Defining the Demand and Evaluating the Supply*, edited by Alan T. Harland. Thousand Oaks, CA: Sage.

Gendreau, Paul, Tracy Little, and Claire Goggin. 1996. "A Meta-Analysis of the Predictors of Adult Offender Recidivism: What Works!" *Criminology* 34: 575–607.

Gendreau, Paul, and Robert R. Ross. 1979. "Effective Correctional Treatment: Bibliotherapy for Cynics." *Crime and Delinquency* 25:463–89.

———. 1987. "Revivification of Rehabilitation: Evidence from the 1980s." *Justice Quarterly* 4:349–407.

Gendreau, Paul, Paula Smith, and Sheila French. 2006. "The Theory of Effective Correctional Intervention: Empirical Status and Future Directions." In *Taking Stock: The Status of Criminological Theory*, edited by Francis T. Cullen, John Paul Wright, and Kristie R. Blevins. Vol. 15 of *Advances in Criminological Theory*, edited by Freda Adler and William Laufer. New Brunswick, NJ: Transaction.

Gibbons, Don C. 1999. "Review Essay: Changing Lawbreakers—What Have We Learned since the 1950s?" *Crime and Delinquency* 45:272–93.

Gitlin, Todd. 1987. *The Sixties: Years of Hope, Days of Rage.* New York: Bantam.

Glasser, Ira. 1978. "Prisoners of Benevolence: Power versus Liberty in the Welfare State." In *Doing Good: The Limits of Benevolence*, edited by Willard Gaylin, Ira Glasser, Steven Marcus, and David J. Rothman. New York: Pantheon.

Glaze, Lauren E., and Thomas P. Bonczar. 2011. *Probation and Parole in the United States, 2010.* Washington, DC: Bureau of Justice Statistics, US Department of Justice.

Gleicher, Lily, Sarah M. Manchak, and Francis T. Cullen. 2013. "Creating a Supervision Tool Kit: How to Improve Probation and Parole." *Federal Probation* 77(2):22–27.

Goffman, Erving. 1961. *Asylums.* Garden City, NY: Doubleday.

Gottfredson, Michael R. 1979. "Treatment Destruction Techniques." *Journal of Research in Crime and Delinquency* 16:39–54.

Gould, Stephen Jay. 1981. *The Mismeasure of Man.* New York: Norton.

Greenwood, Peter W. 2006. *Changing Lives: Delinquency Prevention as Crime-Control Policy.* Chicago: University of Chicago Press.

Griset, Pamela L. 1991. *Determinate Sentencing: The Promise and the Reality of Retributive Justice.* Albany: State University of New York Press.

Hagan, John. 1973. "Labeling and Deviance: A Case Study in the 'Sociology of the Interesting.'" *Social Problems* 20:447–58.

Halleck, Seymour J., and Ann D. Witte. 1977. "Is Rehabilitation Dead?" *Crime and Delinquency* 23:372–82.

Harland, Alan T., ed. 1996. *Choosing Correctional Options That Work: Defining the Demand and Evaluating the Supply.* Thousand Oaks, CA: Sage.

Hawkins, J. David, Sabrina Oesterle, Eric C. Brown, Kathryn C. Monahan, Robert D. Abbott, Michael W. Arthur, and Richard F. Catalano. "Sustained Decreases in Risk Exposure and Youth Problem Behaviors after Installation of the Communities That Care Prevention System in a Randomized Trial." *Archives of Pediatrics and Adolescent Medicine* 166:141–48.

Healy, William. 1915. *The Individual Delinquent.* Boston: Little, Brown.

Henggeler, Scott W. 1999. "Multisystemic Therapy: An Overview of Clinical Procedures, Outcomes, and Policy Implications." *Child Psychology and Psychiatry* 4:2–10.

Hofstadter, Richard. 1955. *The Age of Reform.* New York: Knopf.

Howell, James C. 2009. *Preventing and Reducing Juvenile Delinquency: A Comprehensive Framework.* 2nd ed. Thousand Oaks, CA: Sage.

Ignatieff, Michael. 1978. *A Just Measure of Pain: The Penitentiary in the Industrial Revolution, 1750–1850.* New York: Pantheon.

———. 1981. "State, Civil Society, and Total Institutions: A Critique of Recent Social Histories of Punishment." In *Crime and Justice: An Annual Review of Research,* vol. 3, edited by Michael Tonry and Norval Morris. Chicago: University of Chicago Press.

J. P. Morgan. 2010. *Impact Investments: An Emerging Class of Assets.* London: J. P. Morgan.

Jackson, George. 1970. *Soledad Brother: The Prison Letters of George Jackson.* New York: Bantam.

Johnson, Brian D. 2011. "Sentencing." In *The Oxford Handbook of Crime and Criminal Justice,* edited by Michael Tonry. New York: Oxford University Press.

Jonson, Cheryl Lero. 2010. "The Impact of Imprisonment on Reoffending: A

Meta-Analysis." PhD dissertation, University of Cincinnati, School of Criminal Justice.

Jonson, Cheryl Lero, Francis T. Cullen, and Jennifer L. Lux. 2013. "Creating Ideological Space: Why Public Support for Rehabilitation Matters." In *What Works in Offender Rehabilitation: An Evidence Based Approach to Assessment and Treatment*, edited by Leam Craig, Louise Dixon, and Theresa Gannon. London: Wiley-Blackwell.

Jonson, Cheryl Lero, John E. Eck, and Francis T. Cullen. 2014. "The Small Prison." In *The American Prison: Imagining a Different Future*, edited by Francis T. Cullen, Cheryl Lero Jonson, and Mary K. Stohr. Thousand Oaks, CA: Sage.

Kahneman, Daniel. 2011. *Thinking, Fast and Slow*. New York: Farrar, Straus & Giroux.

Kesey, Ken. 1962. *One Flew over the Cuckoo's Nest*. New York: Signet.

Kittrie, Nicholas N. 1971. *The Right to Be Different: Deviance and Enforced Therapy*. Baltimore: Penguin.

Kohli, Jitinder, Douglas J. Besharov, and Kristina Costs. 2012. *What Are Social Impact Bonds? An Innovative New Financing Tool for Social Programs*. Washington, DC: Center for American Progress.

Krisberg, Barry. 2006. *Focus: Attitudes of US Voters toward Prisoner Rehabilitation and Reentry Programs*. Oakland, CA: National Council on Crime and Delinquency.

Kruttschnitt, Candace, and Rosemary Gartner. 2005. *Marking Time in the Golden State: Women's Imprisonment in California*. New York: Cambridge University Press.

Kuhn, Thomas S. 1970. *The Structure of Scientific Revolutions*. 2nd ed. Chicago: University of Chicago Press.

Latessa, Edward J., Francis T. Cullen, and Paul Gendreau. 2002. "Beyond Correctional Quackery: Professionalism and the Possibility of Effective Treatment." *Federal Probation* 66(2):43–49.

Lattimore, Pamela K., and Christy A. Visher. 2009. *The Multi-site Evaluation of SVORI: Summary and Synthesis*. Final Report to the National Institute of Justice. Washington, DC: US Department of Justice.

Lewis, Jason E., David DeGusta, Marc R. Meyer, Janet M. Monge, Alan E. Mann, and Ralph L. Holloway. 2011. "The Mismeasure of Science: Stephen Jay Gould versus Samuel George Morton on Skulls and Bias." *PLoS Biology* 9(6):1–6.

Lewis, Michael. 2003. *Moneyball: The Art of Winning an Unfair Game*. New York: Norton.

Liebman, Jeffrey B. 2011. *Social Impact Bonds: A Promising New Financing Model to Accelerate Social Innovation and Improve Government Performance*. Washington, DC: Center for American Progress.

Lipset, Seymour Martin, and William Schneider. 1983. *The Confidence Gap: Business, Labor, and Government in the Public Mind*. New York: Free Press.

Lipsey, Mark W. 1992. "Juvenile Delinquent Treatment: A Meta-Analytic Treatment Inquiry into the Variability of Effects." In *Meta-Analysis for Ex-*

planation: A Casebook, edited by Thomas D. Cook, Harris Cooper, David S. Cordray, Heidi Hartmann, Larry V. Hedges, Richard J. Light, Thomas A. Lewis, and Frederick Mosteller. New York: Russell Sage Foundation.

———. 1995. "What Do We Learn from 400 Research Studies on the Effectiveness of Treatment with Juvenile Delinquency?" In *What Works: Reducing Reoffending*, edited by James McGuire. West Sussex, UK: Wiley.

———. 1999. "Can Rehabilitative Programs Reduce the Recidivism of Juvenile Offenders? An Inquiry into the Effectiveness of Practical Programs." *Virginia Journal of Social Policy and Law* 6:611–41.

———. 2009. "The Primary Factors That Characterize Effective Interventions with Juvenile Offenders: A Meta-Analytic Overview." *Victims and Offenders* 4:124–47.

Lipsey, Mark W., Gabrielle L. Chapman, and Nana A. Landenberger. 2001. "Cognitive Behavioral Programs for Offenders." *Annals of the American Academy of Political and Social Science* 578(November):144–57.

Lipsey, Mark W., and Francis T. Cullen. 2007. "The Effectiveness of Correctional Rehabilitation: A Review of Systematic Reviews." *Annual Review of Law and Social Science* 3:297–320.

Lipsey, Mark W., and David B. Wilson. 1993. "The Efficacy of Psychological, Educational, and Behavioral Treatment." *American Psychologist* 48:1181–1209.

———. 1998. "Effective Interventions for Serious Juvenile Offenders: A Synthesis of Research." In *Serious and Violent Juvenile Offenders: Risk Factors and Successful Interventions*, edited by Rolf Loeber and David P. Farrington. Thousand Oaks, CA: Sage.

Lipsey, Mark W., David B. Wilson, and Lynn Cothern. 2000. *Effective Intervention with Serious Offenders*. Washington, DC: Office of Juvenile Justice and Delinquency Prevention, US Department of Justice.

Lipton, Douglas, Robert Martinson, and Judith Wilks. 1975. *The Effectiveness of Correctional Treatment: A Survey of Treatment Evaluation Studies*. New York: Praeger.

Listwan, Shelley Johnson, Francis T. Cullen, and Edward J. Latessa. 2006. "How to Prevent Prisoner Re-entry Programs from Failing: Insights from Evidence-Based Corrections." *Federal Probation* 70(3):19–25.

Listwan, Shelley Johnson, Cheryl Lero Jonson, Francis T. Cullen, and Edward J. Latessa. 2008. "Cracks in the Penal Harm Movement: Evidence from the Field." *Criminology and Public Policy* 7:423–65.

Listwan, Shelley J., Christopher J. Sullivan, Robert Agnew, Francis T. Cullen, and Mark Colvin. 2013. "The Pains of Imprisonment Revisited: The Impact of Strain on Inmate Recidivism." *Justice Quarterly* 30:144–68.

Logan, Charles H., and Gerald D. Gaes. 1993. "Meta-Analysis and the Rehabilitation of Punishment." *Justice Quarterly* 10:245–63.

Lösel, Friedrich. 1995. "The Efficacy of Correctional Treatment: A Review and Synthesis of Meta-Evaluations." In *What Works: Reducing Reoffending*, edited by James McGuire. West Sussex, UK: Wiley.

———. 2007. "It's Never Too Early and Never Too Late: Towards an Integrated Science of Developmental Intervention in Criminology." *Criminologist* 32(5):1, 3–8.

Love, Margaret, and April Frazier. 2006. *Certificates of Rehabilitation and Other Forms of Relief from the Collateral Consequences of Conviction: A Survey of State Laws*. Washington, DC: American Bar Association.

Lowenkamp, Christopher T., Edward J. Latessa, and Paula Smith. 2006. "Does Correctional Program Quality Really Matter? The Importance of Adhering to the Principles of Effective Intervention." *Criminology and Public Policy* 5: 201–20.

MacKenzie, Doris Layton. 2000. "Evidence-Based Corrections: Identifying What Works." *Crime and Delinquency* 46:457–71.

———. 2006. *What Works in Corrections: Reducing the Criminal Activities of Offenders and Delinquents*. New York: Cambridge University Press.

Martin, Susan E., Lee B. Sechrest, and Robin Redner, eds. 1981. *New Directions in the Rehabilitation of Criminal Offenders*. Washington, DC: National Academy Press.

Martinson, Robert. 1974*a*. "Viewpoint." *Criminal Justice Newsletter* 5(21):4–5.

———. 1974*b*. "What Works?—Questions and Answers about Prison Reform." *Public Interest* 35(Spring):22–54.

———. 1979. "New Findings, New Views: A Note of Caution Regarding Sentencing Reform." *Hofstra Law Review* 7:243–58.

Maruna, Shadd. 2001. *Making Good: How Ex-Convicts Reform and Rebuild Their Lives*. Washington, DC: American Psychological Association.

———. 2011*a*. "Judicial Rehabilitation and the 'Clean Bill of Health' in Criminal Justice." *European Journal of Probation* 3:97–117.

———. 2011*b*. "Reentry as a Rite of Passage." *Punishment and Society* 13:3–28.

Matthews, Roger. 2009. "Beyond 'So What' Criminology: Rediscovering Realism." *Theoretical Criminology* 13:341–62.

Mauer, Marc, and Meda Chesney-Lind, eds. 2002. *Invisible Punishment: The Collateral Consequences of Mass Imprisonment*. New York: New Press.

McKelvey, Blake. 1977. *American Prisons: A History of Good Intentions*. Montclair, NJ: Patterson-Smith.

Mears, Daniel P., Carter Hay, Marc Gertz, and Christina Mancini. 2007. "Public Opinion and the Foundation of the Juvenile Court." *Criminology* 45:223–57.

Menninger, Karl. 1968. *The Crime of Punishment*. New York: Penguin.

Merton, Robert K. 1973. *The Sociology of Science: Theoretical and Empirical Investigations*. Edited by Norman K. Storer. Chicago: University of Chicago Press.

———. 1995. "Opportunity Structure: The Emergence, Diffusion, and Differentiation of a Sociological Concept, 1930s–1950s." In *The Legacy of Anomie Theory: Advances in Criminological Theory*, vol. 6, edited by Freda Adler and William Laufer. New Brunswick, NJ: Transaction.

Mitchell, Ojmarrh. 2011. "Drug and Other Specialty Courts." In *The Oxford Handbook of Crime and Criminal Justice*, edited by Michael Tonry. New York: Oxford University Press.

Mitford, Jessica. 1973. *Kind and Usual Punishment: The Prison Business*. New York: Vintage.

Mohr, Gary C. 2012. *Addressing Collateral Consequences in Ohio*. Columbus: Ohio Department of Rehabilitation and Correction.

Morris, Norval. 1974. *The Future of Imprisonment*. Chicago: University of Chicago Press.

Murphy, Patrick T. 1974. *Our Kindly Parent the State: The Juvenile Justice System and How It Works*. New York: Penguin.

Murray, Charles. 1984. *Losing Ground: American Social Policy, 1950–1980*. New York: Basic.

Nagin, Daniel S., Francis T. Cullen, and Cheryl Lero Jonson. 2009. "Imprisonment and Reoffending." In *Crime and Justice: A Review of Research*, vol. 38, edited by Michael Tonry. Chicago: University of Chicago Press.

Nagin, Daniel S., Alex R. Piquero, Elizabeth S. Scott, and Laurence Steinberg. 2006. "Public Preferences for Rehabilitation versus Incarceration of Juvenile Offenders: Evidence from a Contingent Valuation Survey." *Criminology and Public Policy* 5:627–52.

National Research Council. 2008. *Parole, Desistance from Crime, and Community Integration*. Washington, DC: National Academy Press.

Office of the Mayor. 2012. *Fact Sheet: The NYC ABLE Project for Incarcerated Youth—America's First Social Impact Bond*. New York: Office of the Mayor, City of New York.

Ogloff, James R. P., and Michael R. Davis. 2004. "Advances in Offender Assessment and Rehabilitation: Contributions of the Risk-Needs-Responsivity Approach." *Psychology, Crime, and Law* 10:229–42.

Olds, David L. 2007. "Preventing Crime with Prenatal and Infancy Support of Parents: The Nurse-Family Partnership." *Victims and Offenders* 2:205–25.

Page, Joshua. 2011. *The Toughest Beat: Politics, Punishment, and the Prison Officers in California*. New York: Oxford University Press.

Palmer, Ted. 1975. "Martinson Revisited." *Journal of Research in Crime and Delinquency* 12:133–52.

———. 1978. *Correctional Intervention and Research*. Lexington, MA: Lexington.

———. 1992. *The Re-emergence of Correctional Intervention*. Newbury Park, CA: Sage.

Patterson, James T. 1996. *Grand Expectations: The United States, 1945–1974*. New York: Oxford University Press.

Peter D. Hart Research Associates. 2002. *The New Politics of Criminal Justice: A Research and Messaging Report for the Open Society Institute*. Washington, DC: Peter D. Hart Research Associates.

Petersilia, Joan. 2003. *When Prisoners Come Home: Parole and Prisoner Reentry*. New York: Oxford University Press.

———. 2008. "California's Correctional Paradox of Excess and Deprivation." In *Crime and Justice: A Review of Research*, vol. 37, edited by Michael Tonry. Chicago: University of Chicago Press.

———. 2011. "Parole and Prisoner Re-entry." In *The Oxford Handbook of Crime and Criminal Justice*, edited by Michael Tonry. New York: Oxford University Press.

Pew Center on the States. 2009. *One in 31: The Long Reach of American Corrections*. Washington, DC: Pew Charitable Trusts.

———. 2010. *Prison Count 2010: State Population Declines for the First Time in 38 Years*. Washington, DC: Pew Charitable Trusts.

Pew Research Center for the People and the Press. 2010. *The People and Their Government: Distrust, Discontent, Anger, and Partisan Rancor*. Washington, DC: Pew Research Center for the People and the Press.

Piquero, Alex R., Francis T. Cullen, James D. Unnever, Nicole Leeper Piquero, and Jill Gordon. 2010. "Never Too Late: Public Opinion about Juvenile Rehabilitation." *Punishment and Society* 12:187–207.

Piven, Frances Fox, and Richard A. Cloward. 1977. *Poor People's Movements: Why They Succeed, How They Fail*. New York: Pantheon.

Platt, Anthony M. 1969. *The Child Savers: The Invention of Delinquency*. Chicago: University of Chicago Press.

Polaschek, Devon L. 2012. "An Appraisal of the Risk-Need-Responsivity (RNR) Model of Offender Rehabilitation and Its Application in Correctional Treatment." *Legal and Criminological Psychology* 17:1–17.

Porporino, Frank J. 2010. "Bringing Sense and Sensitivity to Corrections: From Programmes to 'Fix' Offenders to Services to Support Desistance." In *What Else Works? Creative Work with Offenders*, edited by Jo Brayford, Francis Cowe, and John Deering. Cullompton, UK: Willan.

Princeton Survey Research Associates International. 2006. *The NCSC Sentencing Attitudes Survey: A Report on the Findings*. Princeton, NJ: Princeton Survey Research Associates International.

Public Opinion Strategies and the Mellman Group. 2012. *Public Opinion on Sentencing and Corrections Policy in America*. Washington, DC: Pew Center on the States.

Raynor, Peter, and Gwen Robinson. 2009. *Rehabilitation, Crime and Justice*. Rev. and updated ed. Hampshire, UK: Palgrave Macmillan.

Rhine, Edward E., and Anthony C. Thompson. 2011. "The Reentry Movement in Corrections: Resiliency, Fragility, and Prospects." *Criminal Law Bulletin* 47:177–209.

Roberts, Julian V., and Ross Hastings. 2012. "Public Opinion and Crime Prevention: A Review of International Trends." In *The Oxford Handbook of Crime Prevention*, edited by Brandon Welsh and David P. Farrington. New York: Oxford University Press.

Robinson, Charles R., Christopher T. Lowenkamp, Alexander M. Holsinger, Scott Van Benshoten, Melissa Alexander, and J. C. Oleson. 2012. "A Random Model of Staff Training Aimed at Reducing Re-arrest (STARR): Using Core Correctional Practices in Probation Interaction." *Journal of Crime and Justice* 35:167–88.

Robinson, Ray. 2001. "Louis Gehrig: Columbia Legend and American Hero." *Columbia: The Magazine of Columbia University* (Fall), 28–35.

Rothman, David J. 1971. *The Discovery of the Asylum: Social Order and Disorder in the New Republic*. Boston: Little, Brown.

————. 1978. "The State as Parent: Social Policy in the Progressive Era." In *Doing Good: The Limits of Benevolence*, edited by Willard Gaylin, Ira Glasser, Steven Marcus, and David J. Rothman. New York: Pantheon.

————. 1980. *Conscience and Convenience: The Asylum and Its Alternatives in Progressive America*. Boston: Little, Brown.

————. 2002. *Conscience and Convenience: The Asylum and Its Alternatives in Progressive America*. Rev. ed. New York: Aldine de Gruyter.

Rotman, Edgardo. 1990. *Beyond Punishment: A New View on the Rehabilitation of Criminal Offenders*. Westport, CT: Greenwood.

Ryerson, Ellen. 1978. *The Best-Laid Plans: America's Juvenile Court Experiment*. New York: Hill & Wang.

Sampson, Robert J., and John H. Laub. 1993. *Crime in the Making: Pathways and Turning Points through Life*. Cambridge, MA: Harvard University Press.

Sarteschi, Christine Marie. 2009. "Assessing the Effectiveness of Mental Health Courts: A Meta-Analysis of Clinical and Recidivism Outcomes." PhD dissertation, University of Pittsburgh, School of Social Work.

Schur, Edwin M. 1973. *Radical Non-intervention: Rethinking the Delinquency Problem*. Englewood Cliffs, NJ: Prentice-Hall.

Serrill, Michael S. 1975. "Is Rehabilitation Dead?" *Corrections Magazine* 1(May–June):21–32.

Shaffer, Deborah Koetzle. 2011. "Looking Inside the Black Box of Drug Courts: A Meta-Analytic Review." *Justice Quarterly* 28:493–521.

Sherman, Lawrence W. 1993. "Why Crime Control Is Not Reactionary." In *Police Innovation and Control of the Police*, edited by David Weisburd and Craig Uchida. New York: Springer.

————. 1998. *Evidence-Based Policing*. Washington, DC: Police Foundation.

————. 2011. "Criminology as Invention." In *What Is Criminology?*, edited by Mary Bosworth and Carolyn Hoyle. Oxford: Oxford University Press.

Simon, Jonathan. 2007. *Governing through Crime: How the War on Crime Transformed American Democracy and Created a Culture of Fear*. New York: Oxford University Press.

Singer, Richard G. 1979. *Just Deserts: Sentencing Based on Equality and Desert*. Cambridge, MA: Ballinger.

Smith, Paula. 2013. "The Psychology of Criminal Conduct." In *The Oxford Handbook of Criminological Theory*, edited by Francis T. Cullen and Pamela Wilcox. New York: Oxford University Press.

Smith, Paula, Francis T. Cullen, and Edward J. Latessa. 2009. "Can 14,737 Women Be Wrong? A Meta-Analysis of the LSI-R and Recidivism for Female Offenders." *Criminology and Public Policy* 8:183–208.

Smith, Paula, Paul Gendreau, and Kristin Swartz. 2009. "Validating the Principles of Effective Intervention: A Systematic Review of the Contributions of Meta-Analysis in the Field of Corrections." *Victims and Offenders* 4:148–69.

Smith, Paula, Myrinda Schweitzer, Ryan M. Lebreque, and Edward J. Latessa.

2012. "Improving Probation Officers' Supervision Skills: An Evaluation of the EPIC'S Model." *Journal of Crime and Justice* 35:189–199.

State of Colorado. 2012. *Senate Bill 12–105: Concerning Provisions That Improve the Reintegration Opportunities for Persons Involved in the Criminal Justice System.* Denver: Sixty-Eighth General Assembly.

Stouthamer-Loeber, Magda, Rolf Loeber, and Christopher Thomas. 1992. "Caretakers Seeking Help for Boys with Disruptive and Delinquent Behavior." *Comprehensive Mental Health Care* 2:159–78.

Stouthamer-Loeber, Magda, Rolf Loeber, Welmoet van Kammen, and Quanwu Zhang. 1995. "Uninterrupted Delinquent Careers: The Timing of Parental Help-Seeking and Juvenile Court Contact." *Studies on Crime and Crime Prevention* 4:236–51.

Sullivan, Christopher J. 2013. "Change in Offending across the Life Course." In *The Oxford Handbook of Criminological Theory*, edited by Francis T. Cullen and Pamela Wilcox. New York: Oxford University Press.

Sundt, Jody, Renee Vanderhoff, Laura Shaver, and Sarah Lazzeroni. 2012. *Oregonians Nearly Unanimous in Support of Reentry Services for Former Prisoners: Research in Brief.* Portland, OR: Criminal Justice Policy Research Institute, Portland State University.

Sykes, Gresham M. 1958. *The Society of Captives: A Study of a Maximum Security Prison.* Princeton, NJ: Princeton University Press.

———. 1978. *Criminology.* New York: Harcourt, Brace, Jovanovich.

Szasz, Thomas S. 1970. *The Manufacture of Madness.* New York: Dell.

Tanner-Smith, Emily E., Sandra Jo Wilson, and Mark W. Lipsey. 2013. "Risk Factors and Crime." In *The Oxford Handbook of Criminological Theory*, edited by Francis T. Cullen and Pamela Wilcox. New York: Oxford University Press.

Timmermans, Stefan, and Marc Berg. 2003. *The Gold Standard: The Challenge of Evidence-Based Medicine and Standardization in Health Care.* Philadelphia: Temple University Press.

Toby, Jackson. 1964. "Is Punishment Necessary?" *Journal of Criminal Law, Criminology, and Police Science* 55:332–37.

Tocqueville, Alexis de. 1969. *Democracy in America.* Edited by J. P. Meyer and translated by George Lawrence. New York: Harper & Row. (Originally published in 1835 and 1840. London: Saunders and Otley.)

Tonry, Michael. 1996. *Sentencing Matters.* New York: Oxford University Press.

———. 2004. *Thinking about Crime: Sense and Sensibility in American Penal Culture.* New York: Oxford University Press.

———. 2007. "Determinants of Penal Policies." In *Crime, Punishment, and Politics in Comparative Perspective*, edited by Michael Tonry. Vol. 36 of *Crime and Justice: A Review of Research*, edited by Michael Tonry. Chicago: University of Chicago Press.

———. 2009. "The Mostly Unintended Effects of Mandatory Penalties: Two Centuries of Consistent Findings." In *Crime and Justice: A Review of Research*, vol. 38, edited by Michael Tonry. Chicago: University of Chicago Press.

Travis, Jeremy. 2005. *But They All Come Back: Facing the Challenges of Prisoner Reentry.* Washington, DC: Urban Institute.

Unnever, James D., John K. Cochran, Francis T. Cullen, and Brandon K. Applegate. 2010. "The Pragmatic American: Attributions of Crime and the Hydraulic Relation Hypothesis." *Justice Quarterly* 27:431–57.

Veysey, Bonita M., Johnna Christian, and Damian J. Martinez, eds. 2009. *How Offenders Transform Their Lives.* Cullompton, UK: Willan

von Hirsch, Andrew. 1976. *Doing Justice: The Choice of Punishments.* New York: Hill & Wang.

Vose, Brenda, Francis T. Cullen, and Paula Smith. 2008. "The Empirical Status of the Level of Service Inventory." *Federal Probation* 72(3):22–29.

Wacquant, Loïc. 2001. "Deadly Symbiosis: When Ghetto and Prison Meet and Mesh." *Punishment and Society* 3:95–134.

Ward, Tony, Ruth E. Mann, and Theresa A. Gannon. 2007. "The Good Lives Model of Offender Rehabilitation: Clinical Implications." *Aggression and Violent Behavior* 12:87–107.

Ward, Tony, and Bill Marshall. 2007. "Narrative Identity and Offender Rehabilitation." *International Journal of Offender Therapy and Comparative Criminology* 51:279–97.

Ward, Tony, and Shaad Maruna. 2007. *Rehabilitation: Beyond the Risk Paradigm.* London: Routledge.

Welsh, Brandon C., and David P. Farrington, eds. 2012. *The Oxford Handbook of Crime Prevention.* New York: Oxford University Press.

Welsh, Brandon C., Rolf Loeber, Bradley R. Stevens, Magda Stouthamer-Loeber, Mark A. Cohen, and David P. Farrington. 2011. "Costs of Juvenile Crime in Urban Areas: A Longitudinal Perspective." *Youth Violence and Juvenile Justice* 6:3–27.

Werth, Barry. 2009. *Banquet at Delmonico's: Great Minds, the Gilded Age, and the Triumph of Evolution in America.* New York: Random House.

West, Heather C., William J. Sabol, and Sarah J. Greenman. 2010. *Prisoners in 2009.* Washington, DC: Bureau of Justice Statistics, US Department of Justice.

Whitehead, Paul R., Tony Ward, and Rachael M. Collie. 2007. "Time for a Change: Applying the Good Lives Model of Rehabilitation to a High-Risk Offender." *International Journal of Offender Therapy and Comparative Criminology* 51:578–98.

Wicker, Tom. 1975. *A Time to Die.* New York: Ballantine.

Wilks, Judith, and Robert Martinson. 1976. "Is the Treatment of Criminal Offenders Really Necessary?" *Federal Probation* 40(1):3–9.

Wilson, David B., Ojmarrh Mitchell, and Doris L. MacKenzie. 2006. "A Systematic Review of Drug Court Effects on Recidivism." *Journal of Experimental Criminology* 2:459–87.

Wilson, James Q. 1975. *Thinking about Crime.* New York: Vintage.

Wines, E. C. 1910. "Declaration of Principles Promulgated at Cincinnati, Ohio, 1870." In *Prison Reform: Correction and Prevention*, edited by Charles

Richmond Henderson. New York: Russell Sage Foundation. (Originally published in 1870.)

Wooden, Kenneth. 1976. *Weeping in the Playtime of Others: America's Incarcerated Children*. New York: McGraw-Hill.

Wright, John Paul, Stephen G. Tibbetts, and Leah E. Daigle. 2008. *Criminals in the Making: Criminality across the Life Course*. Thousand Oaks, CA: Sage.

Zimbardo, Philip G. 2007. *The Lucifer Effect: Understanding How Good People Turn Evil*. New York: Random House.

Zimbardo, Philip G., W. Curtis Banks, Craig Haney, and David Jaffe. 1973. "A Pirandellian Prison: The Mind Is a Formidable Jailer." *New York Times Magazine* (April 8), 38–60.

Zimring, Franklin E., Gordon Hawkins, and Sam Kamin. 2001. *Punishment and Democracy: Three Strikes and You're Out in California*. New York: Oxford University Press.

Lawrence W. Sherman

The Rise of Evidence-Based Policing: Targeting, Testing, and Tracking

ABSTRACT

Evidence-based policing is a method of making decisions about "what works" in policing: which practices and strategies accomplish police missions most cost-effectively. In contrast to basing decisions on theory, assumptions, tradition, or convention, an evidence-based approach continuously tests hypotheses with empirical research findings. While research on all aspects of policing grew substantially in the late twentieth century, the application of research to police practice intensified in the early twenty-first century, especially for three tasks that make up the "triple-T" strategy of policing: targeting, testing, and tracking. Evidence-based targeting requires systematic ranking and comparison of levels of harm associated with various places, times, people, and situations that policing can lawfully address. Evidence-based testing helps assure that police neither increase crime nor waste money. Tracking whether police are doing what police leaders decide should be done may grow most rapidly in coming years by the use of GPS records of where police go and body-worn video records of what happens in encounters with citizens.

Can research help improve democratic policing? For over four decades, numerous colleagues and I have struggled to answer that question. When we began, policing was done very differently from how it is

Lawrence W. Sherman is Wolfson Professor of Criminology at Cambridge University, a director of the College of Policing (UK), Distinguished University Professor at the University of Maryland, and director of the Cambridge Police Executive Programme. He is grateful for comments on earlier drafts by Heather Strang, Peter Neyroud, Daniel Nagin, Stephen Mastrofski, John Eck, Alex Piquero, David Weisburd, Lorraine Mazerolle, Cynthia Lum, and Michael Tonry.

377

done now. In the years to come, it will be done even more differently. Yet the trajectory of change is likely to remain consistent: from less research evidence to more and from lesser to greater use of the evidence available. The 50 years covered in this volume bear witness to the rise of evidence-based policing in both the quantity of evidence and its influence on police practices. This essay reports on my ongoing participant-observation study of these changes, for which I have tried to be a primary instigator.

Policing in 1975 was largely delivered in a one-size-fits-all strategy, sometimes described as the "three Rs": random patrol, rapid response, and reactive investigations (Berkow 2011). After World War II, random patrols in police cars were promoted on the theory that police "omnipresence" would deter crime (Wilson 1950). In the 1960s, the advent of three-digit emergency phone numbers turned random patrol into an airport-style "holding pattern" for rapid response, also based on a theory of deterrence, but producing a new theory of organizational action: Albert J. Reiss's (1971) distinction between reactive and proactive actions. What police did when they reacted to a citizen call was not subject to much police agency direction or analysis. The main organizational requirement was to arrive, do something, and leave as quickly as possible. As Reiss reported, his 1966 Chicago study found patrol officers spending 14 percent of their time "reactively" answering such calls and investigating crime, about 1 percent of their time "proactively" stopping people at their own initiative, and 85 percent of their time in unstructured random patrolling. Reactive investigations, when required, were taken over by detectives, who in theory investigated all reported crimes but in practice closed most cases as unsolvable. Cases that were solved relied primarily on the evidence presented to them by crime victims and the patrol officers who arrived first on the scene (Greenwood and Petersilia 1975).

By 1975, the three Rs had become the standard model of urban policing (Skogan and Frdyl 2004, p. 223) across the United States as well as in the United Kingdom and other predominantly Anglo-Celtic cultures (e.g., Canada, Australia, New Zealand). There was almost no targeting of patterns or predictions of crime or disorder, no testing of what worked best to prevent or solve crimes and problems, or much tracking and managing of what police were doing, where, when, and how, in relation to any specific objectives. Most police agencies lacked computers. The few computers in use in 1975 were mainframes designed for dispatching police cars, not analyzing crime data. Police leaders rarely discussed crime at all unless a particularly gruesome crime received substantial publicity.

By 2012, the three Rs were changing into what I describe in this essay as the "triple-T" of targeting, testing, and tracking. While the standard model is far from gone, its resources are increasingly guided by statistical evidence. In the emerging triple-T strategy, both patrol and detective managers had moved toward far greater proactive management of police resources. Although these changes are far more evident in some police agencies than in others, Anglo-Celtic policing is increasingly targeting scarce resources on evidence of large, predictable, and harmful statistical patterns rather than on isolated cases (Spelman and Eck 1989). Compared to 1975, these focused police strategies are far more elaborate and differentiated, choosing from a wider range of priorities and objectives on the basis of extensive data analysis. Police methods have also become far more subject to testing, with evaluation and debate over "what works," the core idea of evidence-based policing (Sherman 1984, 1998). Yet the most evident use of new statistical evidence is the growth of tracking and managing what police were or were not doing in relation to the dynamic patterns of crime and public safety problems.

Examples of the growth of evidence-based policing abound. They include the US Supreme Court's citation of research on tests of restrictions on police shootings (Fyfe 1980, 1982; Sherman 1983), *Tennessee v. Garner* (471 U.S. 1 [1985]), a decision that fostered a major reduction in police killings of citizens in the United States (Tennenbaum 1994). Overall reductions in homicide have been associated with an increased targeting of US police work toward micro-level crime "hot spots" (Weisburd and Lum 2005; Police Executive Research Forum 2008; Braga and Weisburd 2010), where research showed that crime is heavily concentrated (Sherman, Gartin, and Buerger 1989). By 2012, evidence-based targeting for problem-oriented policing (POP) has, since Goldstein (1979) first proposed it, gradually become respected as real police work, not "social work," supported in some agencies with new case management systems. Crime analysts are more likely to identify repeat crime places, victims, suspects, situations, and other patterns to support targeting decisions for patrol, POP, and detectives. Even reactive detective work is more proactive, police-initiated, in gathering new evidence at crime scenes, using scientific methods to identify suspects and prove cases (Roman et al. 2009). What patrol officers do when responding to crime scenes has become more likely to be a method that has been tested. Where officers are at any moment is more likely to be tracked by global positioning satellite (GPS) systems generating weekly management analysis reports.

The best test of evidence-based policing is whether it has improved public safety and police legitimacy. There is certainly a correlation over time between the rise of evidence and a decline in serious crime, in both the United States and the United Kingdom. Proof that serious crime dropped because of evidence-based policing, however, is more elusive. There is some micro-level analysis of the New York City crime drop that offers a greater basis for causal inference than national trends (Zimring 2012), but it is impossible to rule out other plausible causes that also match the timing of the crime drop. There is also a danger that a sharper focus on crime can undermine police legitimacy, especially since proactive policing is structurally less legitimate than reactive policing with a personal victim's endorsement (Reiss 1971, p. 11). Yet there is no evidence that the rise of evidence in policing has caused reductions in police legitimacy. Indeed, more data about legitimacy have been incorporated into police management as part of evidence-based tracking than ever before. Overall, the vast scale of the rise of evidence in policing leaves it without a fair comparison group, just as it does in medicine (Sagan 1987), leaving causation unknowable. Still, the macro trends in reduced mortality suggest that we should celebrate the rise of evidence in both medicine and policing.

The changes from 1975 to 2012 raise the further question of what Anglo-Celtic policing will look like by 2025. The answers cannot be predicted just by extrapolating the trends of four decades, or even— ideally—by a causal model for prediction (Silver 2012). But by explaining why policing changed as it did from 1975 to 2012, a forecast using the same causal model can identify a range of possible scenarios for policing in 2025. Chief among these will be the possible global influence of the 2012 creation of the first professional body ever charged by a national government with recommending police practices on the basis of continuous review of new research evidence on what works: the United Kingdom's College of Policing (http://www.college.police .uk). This body has tremendous potential to follow the pathway to innovation Johnson (2010) associates with such major advances as the printing press, which was inspired by the wine press: a lateral-thinking style of adaptation of an idea used in one setting (such as evidence-based medicine) to another (such as evidence-based policing).

The Rise of Evidence. The causal model this essay suggests for these changes is a dynamic system that links external demands on police (to cut crime, cut costs, or build legitimacy) to research evidence on how to meet those demands, supported by the increasing availability of innovative technologies. While external factors drive the availability of both research evidence and technology, how policing responds depends on a fourth factor: the governmentally generated human capital of education and police professionalism. The role of government policies is crucial in setting salaries and recruitment standards that shape the quality of police skills and creativity in general and of police leaders in particular. Those human resources are so influential that the entire causal model can reasonably be said to call for evidence-based professionalism.

Inside this abstract causal model are many human beings struggling hard for change: influential leaders of policing, research, and efforts to combine the two. These include UK Home Secretary R. A. Butler creating a research unit in 1958; future FBI Director Clarence Kelly supporting the Kansas City Patrol Experiment in 1971 (Kelling et al. 1974); Minneapolis Police Chief Anthony V. Bouza supporting the first random assignment of arrest in 1981 (Sherman and Berk 1984); criminologist David Weisburd and his colleagues (Weisburd et al. 2004, 2006; Weisburd, Groff, and Yang 2012) analyzing criminal careers of places in Seattle and Jersey City; New York Police Department (NYPD) Commissioner William Bratton creating COMPSTAT in the 1990s; Assistant US Attorney General Laurie Robinson making evidence from police testing readily accessible at http://www.crime solutions.gov in 2010; and UK Chief Constable Peter Neyroud's proposal for the evidence-based College of Policing in 2011. What these leaders generally shared—with, most notably, NYPD Commissioner and US Police Foundation President Patrick V. Murphy—was a loosely articulated but deeply held belief that greater use of research could help transform policing into a more legitimate and respected profession.

A profession is widely defined as a public-interest occupation that restricts entry to those who have mastered knowledge and skills needed to provide a particular set of complex services. In the past century, the level of knowledge deemed necessary for a profession has become linked to requirements for university-based education. It is only a century, for example, since the radical proposal to force doctors to attend university was presented to the United Kingdom's Haldane Commission (Sherman 2011*b*). Similarly, proposals in repeated US commission reports in the 1960s and 1970s recommended that a university degree be a requirement for appointment as a police officer (Sherman and National Advisory Commission on Higher Education for Police Officers 1978). That idea remains controversial and widely unacceptable on both sides of the Atlantic. By conventional definition, then, policing has yet to become a profession.

Yet by the same definition, policing has made great strides toward professionalism. The past 40 years have seen a huge increase in the educational levels of police leaders. Almost half of English chief constables in 2010 had been educated at the Cambridge University Police Executive Program, and three decades of major city chiefs in the United States attended the nondegree Harvard Police Executive Sessions. The role of universities in disseminating police research has been a remarkably successful top-down change process.

Rising levels of police chief education have also fostered more support for research. First led by external scholars, and now increasingly led by police leaders in partnership with universities, the production of new research evidence has helped police respond to external demands for improvement. At minimum, research is perceived to be helpful with such demands. That is especially true when there is internal or external controversy about which police methods are best and whether new technologies are cost-effective.

Even a radical change in structures of police accountability can enhance the value of police research evidence. The 2012 devolution of control over chief constables in England and Wales to locally elected "police and crime commissioners," for example, created a potential for disputes between elected officials and professional police leaders. One possible solution is the professional College of Policing setting independent, evidence-based standards of police practice. Whether this institution, or its cognates in other countries, can create a global demand for more production and use of evidence is a crucial question for the next decade.

Targeting, Testing, and Tracking.   Both the demand for, and uses of, research evidence have become clustered around three strategic principles:

1. Police should conduct and apply good research to target scarce resources on predictable concentrations of harm from crime and disorder.
2. Once police choose their high-priority targets, they should review or conduct tests of police methods to help choose what works best to reduce harm.
3. Once police agencies use research to target their tested practices, they should generate and use internal evidence to track the daily delivery and effects of those practices, including public perceptions of police legitimacy.

The growing adoption of those three principles has given shape to what is increasingly called evidence-based policing (EBP). Broadly defined as the use of best research evidence on "what works" as a guide to police decisions (Sherman 1998), the EBP framework was meant to be only a method of making decisions rather than a substantive strategy for police operations. In the 15 years from 1997 to 2012, however, police have shaped their own emergent definition of EBP as a substantive strategy for managing large police agencies on the basis of these three principles.

The rise of the triple-T strategy did not emerge from any theoretical plan to use evidence in such a coherent strategy. The clustering of evidence around three key strategic tasks was driven as much by innovative police leadership as by police scholarship. Its success resulted from the surprisingly rational convergence of police reform with a flood of new research in criminology.

This essay has four sections. Section I discusses the key social trends, institutions, and people who helped shape research aiming to improve policing. The triple-T strategy emerged from the users of that evidence. Section II offers major examples of how much the evidence has grown since 1975 and how widely police have applied that knowledge. These examples address all three triple-T principles, including instances in which evidence and practice have sharply diverged. They are selected to highlight the wide range of what has already been accomplished, even as so much still remains to be done.

Section III analyzes conceptual issues and confusion that hold back progress in targeting, testing, and tracking. The issues are arguably little different from those arising in the development of evidence-based practices in professional baseball, election campaigns, or marketing. They reflect the current struggle between "system I" and "system II" thinking (Kahneman 2011) in a wide range of endeavors, all of which face the same challenge policing faces—to get much better at what they do in the next decade. In the conclusion I suggest 10 things institutions can do to institutionalize research evidence in ways that foster more fairness and effectiveness in democratic policing.

These are the most important points I make in this essay:

1. The evidence base for police decisions has grown enormously since 1975.
2. Use of that evidence lags behind the knowledge, but use has also grown.
3. Most police practices, despite their enormous cost, are still untested.
4. Targeting and testing require highly reliable measures of crime and harm.
5. Crime rates and counts are by themselves misleading; a crime harm index offers far better evidence to guide police decisions.
6. Police in 2012 used evidence on targeting much more widely than evidence from testing.
7. Research on tracking police outputs remains largely descriptive and incomplete, with great room for using new technologies to improve the quality of evidence.
8. More use of evidence can increase police legitimacy, both internal and external.
9. The State Boards of Police Officer Standards and Training in the United States and the College of Policing in the United Kingdom will be key institutions in making policing more effective, along with the practitioner-led Society for Evidence-Based Policing.

I. The Rise of Evidence for Police Decision Making

The rise of evidence in policing is mostly an Anglo-American story, with events on each side of the Atlantic influencing the other. Both sides began with parallel social trends in the 1960s that challenged police legitimacy. Both the United Kingdom and the United States faced rising crime rates and increasing racial tensions. Authoritative commissions in both set out ambitious agendas for "upgrading" the police, as one think tank put it (Saunders 1970). Both saw policing become a matter of national politics in unprecedented ways. The different responses of police in each country helped build a special intellectual relationship that was conceptually far deeper than the military collaboration of World War II. One continuing theme on both sides of the Atlantic has been that "they do policing better" on the other side.

A. Setting the Stage

By the early 1970s, Anglo-American policing faced a kind of Christmas tree of ideas for police reform, each idea an ornament unconnected to the others. One idea was that police needed more research, including experiments and demonstration projects, with criminologists and other social scientists becoming part of the police agency workforce focusing on crime prevention (President's Commission 1967, pp. 25–27). There was no consensus about the questions research should answer. There was no particular vision of a new policing strategy to which research could contribute. Yet belief in innovation and evaluation as a strategy in itself became a major force in police reform (Reiss 1992).

That belief led to public and charitable investments in new institutions for police research. The growing role of the British Home Office in police research helped inspire the creation of a similar function in the US Department of Justice. Yet neither government agency's efforts had much impact until after the Ford Foundation in 1970 funded the Police Foundation in Washington to "foster innovation and improvement in American policing." The bold experiments the foundation conducted led government funders to test policing more deeply. In less than a decade, the Police Foundation's and government-supported research discredited the intellectual basis for the three-Rs strategy of random patrol, rapid response, and reactive investigations.

What replaced that strategy was not a coherent new theory. Only in retrospect can we use the triple-T framework of targeting, testing, and tracking to make sense of what emerged. The multicentered work of examining current practices, designing innovations, and evaluating new programs produced something that scholars now call "emergence," the confluence of properties arising from a combination of elements not found in any one of the elements (Johnson 2001). The essential new property is the capacity to lead police organizations with dynamic evidence rather than static doctrine. This property arose initially from the destruction of the prevailing three-Rs model. That, in turn, opened the door to considering the implications of basic research provided by an earlier generation of thinkers.

The most important basic research had documented the existence of police discretion to choose different strategies rather than being handcuffed by the three Rs. Most notably, Reiss's (1971) conception of police work as divided between proactive and reactive discretion stimulated much creative thinking. At the same time, Banton's (1964) research in Britain and Wilson's (1968) research in the United States showed how the discretionary choices of police organizations differ on the basis of their political and cultural environments, despite their sharing a common legal system. These insights expanded the concept of police discretion from the level of case-by-case to agency-by-agency decision making and helped to set the stage for the emergence of triple-T. But that new, evidence-based strategy took almost four decades to emerge from the accumulation of new research evidence. What happened was a process of "prosumption" (Tapscott and Williams 2006) in which the producers of elements of the triple-T strategy were simultaneously its consumers.

B. Testing

The three-Rs strategy was intellectually discredited after three major efforts were made to assess the effects of key elements. These studies did not adequately support the conclusions attributed to them. They did not show that random patrol had no effect on crime, that rapid police response had no deterrent effect, or that detectives made no contribution to detection, prosecution, and general deterrence of crime. Regardless of what the research evidence really did show, those conclusions became widely accepted by police leaders and police scholars, then and now.

1. *Random Patrol.*   The Police Foundation's Kansas City Preventive Patrol Experiment (Kelling et al. 1974) launched the rise of evidence-based policing. The first attempt to undertake a scientifically controlled test of the effects of patrol staffing levels, it proved that bold experiments were possible in policing. The experimental design of withdrawing patrols from five patrol beats (and doubling it in five others) was stunning and unprecedented. That the "sky did not fall" made the world safe for further bold experiments. The reported conclusion—that frequency of police patrols did not affect crime—opened many minds to think more critically about police strategy. The experiment's

leadership by a police chief who was subsequently appointed FBI director also suggested that research, even with negative results, could be good for police career advancement.

It is unfortunate that the Kansas City experiment did not actually support its conclusion. The limitations of the experiment's research design have been extensively reviewed elsewhere (Sherman 1986, 1992*b*; Sherman and Weisburd 1995). The main problem is that the actual frequency of patrols was unmeasured and may well have been identical in all beats because of reactive responses to calls (Larson 1976). Moreover, there were large differences across treatment groups in certain crime rates but too few beats to call the differences "statistically significant." But the most important critique has never been published before: that random patrol was not compared to any other pattern of patrol, so there was no evidence showing that random patrol did not "work" relative to other patterns of patrol, such as concentration on crime hot spots. Policing still needs a strong randomized trial comparing random patrol to hot spots patrol.

Nonetheless, the conclusion that random patrol did not work was widely accepted. Tens of thousands of police officers lost their jobs in the aftermath of the study, which came coincidentally just before a financial crisis in many US cities. None of that stopped the widespread use of random patrol. But it did help drive a research agenda seeking alternative police strategies.

2. *Rapid Response.* The theory that marginally faster response times would catch and deter more criminals was effectively falsified by a National Institute of Justice–funded research project led by staff of the Kansas City Police Department (1977). The study reported that it was necessary to divide crimes into victim-offender "involvement" crimes (e.g., robbery, assault, rape) and after-the-crime "discovery" crimes (e.g., burglary, car theft). It then focused response time analysis on involvement crimes, with "response time" including three time periods: crime occurrence to calling the police ("reporting time"), police receipt of call to dispatch ("dispatch time"), and "travel time" of police from receipt of dispatch to arrival at the scene. Using systematic observation methods and interviews of victims, the Kansas City study found that there was no correlation between response-related arrest probability and reporting time once the reporting time exceeded 9 minutes. The average reporting time for involvement crimes was 41 minutes (Kansas City Police Department 1977, vol. 2, pp. 23, 39). Replications of the

reporting time segment in other US cities found similar results (Spelman and Brown 1981).

What the research did not show is that a capacity for rapid response had no effect on crime. The Kansas City study was not an experiment comparing police agencies or areas with very rapid responses to similar agencies or areas with slower responses, or even no response. Much remains to be learned about the effect of any rapid response capacity compared to none, the latter being the state of police services in much of the world, from India to parts of rural America.

What mattered historically was the growing recognition that there were better things police could do with their time than just wait for calls. While the research did not prove that point, it helped open the minds of police leaders and scholars about what those other things might be.

3. *Reactive Investigations.* The view that detectives "solve" crimes that are reported to them was strongly rejected by another National Institute of Justice (NIJ) project, this one conducted by the RAND Corporation (Greenwood and Petersilia 1975). This report examined the value detectives add to the information that was in the record at the end of a preliminary investigation by the first responders to a crime, usually uniformed patrol officers. The conclusion was that detectives rarely uncovered new evidence that made a difference in solving the crime—contrary to a century of detective fiction.

Here again, the evidence is thin in relation to the conclusion. An experiment comparing cases prosecuted without detective work to cases prosecuted after detective work would be a strong test of the "no-effect" hypothesis. But what mattered was that yet another sacred cow was wounded. For many police leaders, this completed the well-justified execution of the three-Rs strategy, which legitimated trying alternatives.

These three studies created a strong appetite for more experiments and support for funding them from influential scholars. Franklin E. Zimring, James Q. Wilson, Albert J. Reiss Jr., and others shaped several National Academy of Science reports recommending more NIJ funding for randomized experiments (Zimring 1976; White and Krislov 1977). These reports led to NIJ funding streams for most of the more than 100 tests of police practices listed online by Lum, Koper, and Telep (2010), many of which were funded in 1983–89 by James K.

Stewart, the only NIJ director to have served as an operational police officer and leader.

C. Targeting

Important as these tests were, they could not answer the more fundamental question: how can police resources be allocated more effectively? Once the idea of proactive policing became widely understood, it sparked a revolutionary insight in targeting that Goldstein (1979) called problem-oriented policing (POP). For reactive investigations, the RAND report also led to a revolutionary question: can detectives target which cases they can solve by predicting the likely outcome before they begin working on each case?

1. *Problem-Oriented Policing.* After decades of observing police operations for a major study of police discretion (LaFave 1965) and assisting one of the first university graduate police executives in history (O. W. Wilson) as police superintendent of Chicago, Herman Goldstein offered a revolutionary new targeting strategy for policing. Describing a case-by-case response to events as a myopic failure to see larger patterns, Goldstein (1979, 1990) recommended that police invest more time in treating the causes of those patterns rather than their symptoms. POP is more than a targeting strategy, however, since it also develops ideas for the content of police actions to deal with targeted problems. Yet the tactical content of POP is appropriately broad and highly dependent on good diagnosis and good research on what action would work best. The major breakthrough of the strategy is the injunction to first look for patterns—proactively.

2. *Crime and Harm Concentrations.* It was therefore no accident that Reiss, the person who first used the term "proactive" in a policing context, suggested that I study the distribution of all reactive police responses to reported crimes and disorder by each and every address in a major city. The result was our discovery of tiny, micro-level crime hot spots (Sherman 1987; Sherman, Gartin, and Buerger 1989), in contrast to conventional concepts of much larger high-crime areas. The city of Minneapolis provided the first, but by no means the last, evidence of far greater concentrations of repeat problems at individual street addresses than among individual offenders. Only 3 percent of all street addresses in Minneapolis generated over half of all police rapid responses. This addition to the existing research on crime concentrations showed how police scholars could identify important new targets

for proactive policing on both sides of the Atlantic. While Goldstein's examples were richly qualitative, the research on crime and harm concentrations was intensely quantitative. American scholars found hot spots of crime. British scholars found patterns of repeat victimization (Farrell 1995). In both cases, the numbers of potential patterns were unlimited. Only newly available computers could say how many addresses or people had more than 10, or 20, or 200 crimes over any given time period. Only the computer could rank every known offender, victim, location, neighborhood, weapon, modus operandi, or crime recruiter by the number of repeat events in a year (Reiss 1988). What these studies showed were highly concentrated distributions of crime in a small proportion of any of the units at risk, from people to places to times and situations.

3. *Investigative Solvability Factors.* News reports intermittently "reveal" that only a small proportion of crimes lead to arrests or convictions, as if they had discovered something new. There is, however, no evidence to suggest that it was ever otherwise, at any time in the last two centuries (see, e.g., Monkkonen 1992). At the same time the RAND report on detectives was under way, scholars at Stanford University asked whether they could target solvable crimes for priority investment, allocating resources that might otherwise be wasted on pursuing unsolvable crimes.

This idea of "triage" was at least as old as the US Civil War, when doctors worked first on people who would die without immediate assistance. They postponed work on two other groups (hence the term "tri-age"): those who would die even with treatment and those who would live without immediate treatment. The strategy was intended to optimize the number of lives. For policing, it offered a way to make policing far more effective.

As Greenberg and Lang (1973) suggested, the likely "solvability" of each case can be reliably, but not perfectly, identified at the time an initial investigation is completed. By using a checklist of available forensic evidence in each case when it arrives on a detective's desk, the detective can decide whether to close the case or start working on it. The checklist that Stanford developed included such items as fingerprints, witnesses, footprints, names of likely suspects, and other facts. A test of one such solvability model on over 12,000 burglary cases found that it correctly predicted in 85 percent of the cases whether the case would be solved or not (Eck 1979), suggesting that nonsolvable cases could be filed immediately with little difference in result. The next question, however, is still unanswered, as with the untested conclusions about response time and random patrols: how would a "checklist of solvability factors" regime compare to an "investigate every case" regime in terms of overall detection rates—or even to a "discretionary, nonchecklist decision about solvability" regime?

D. *Tracking*

No matter what targets are selected for police resources, no matter how well the police methods are tested, the central management question will always be, "what are police doing to accomplish our objectives, when, where, and with what apparent result?" In my first year at the NYPD in 1971, few police leaders ever discussed that question. By 1991, the question was asked all over the New York subways by then–Transit Police Chief William Bratton, and by 1995, he was grilling NYPD commanders on the question in front of 200 people at Police Headquarters. Yet long before New York reached that point, the British police were being driven hard by the numbers. Only the numbers, and the conversations, were very different.

1. *Performance Management, UK Style.* From the dawn of the Thatcher government, UK policing was dominated by two themes: huge pay increases and an explosion of statistical management. Key Performance Indicators were tabulated annually on a national level and monthly on a local level (Parkinson 2013). Eventually, police agencies were not only assessed on whether they had met specific goals set by central government but also compared to all other police agencies in a kind of "class rank," or football league table. One police agency would be ranked first, one ranked last.

These rankings created enormous pressure on police leadership to track what their officers were doing. Yet the pressure was not matched by any new tools, either hardware or managerial, for monitoring police activity. Only the numbers of police car dispatches, crime reports, or arrests were easily measurable. It was no surprise that these numbers were sometimes manipulated, including a "flexible" definition of crime types and other crimes "taken into consideration" when confessed by offenders caught red-handed. Even police response time was used in some years, despite its discredited status in the United States.

By 2012, these interagency competitions were mostly rejected in UK police culture. Yet the precedent they set for tracking in general is still widely accepted. What police now understand is that the number of actions tracked should be relatively small, and each one should have a direct connection to something that is well researched and found useful. What US police learned from the British experience is that timely data could help drive a police agency.

2. *COMPSTAT.* No one put that lesson to better use than William Bratton (1998), who served as the chief executive of the Boston, New York, and Los Angeles Police Departments. With his colleague Jack Maple (1999), he developed a more focused process of tracking police activity. Using area commanders as the conduit for strategic initiatives, Bratton and Maple developed the COMPSTAT (computerized statistics) meetings as a means of pushing for better policing and less crime. Local commanders were arrested from time to time and charged with manipulating crime statistics, but for the most part, the system has been seen as operating with integrity. By 2012 the NYPD system was 18 years old and was still in operation, despite turnover in mayors and police commissioners. There is enormous potential to expand it to better indicators and performance.

3. *Auditing for Evidence.* In late 2012 the Metropolitan Police at New Scotland Yard launched a top-to-bottom effort to push evidence into every aspect of police operations, training, and promotions (Stanko 2013). This decision included a plan to appoint a Commissioner's Professor of Policing in a major university, a position that would entail 50 percent time doing research for a 50,000-employee police agency. This research could include comprehensive reviews of police practices against what the research evidence—especially testing—says about those practices. It would also likely entail new randomized controlled trials to be conducted in London. This plan for evidence-based policing was premised on the recognition of a vast body of research that had not yet been fully applied to police operations. This decision of Police Commissioner Sir Bernard Hogan-Howe provides perhaps the clearest indication of the Anglo-American rise of evidence for police decisions.

E. Explaining the Rise

How policing learned so much, and put so much of it to work, cannot be easily explained by any current theory of knowledge. Even the history of medicine offers thin explanations of why doctors do research, and why, if ever, they decide to use it (Millenson 1997) or not, as in their continued failure to wash their hands after touching each patient (Pittet and Boyce 2001). What follows is my insider's hunch about a theory of police knowledge. This hunch is by no means a general theory of developing and using professional knowledge. My explanation is deeply, if not widely, "grounded" (Glaser and Straus 1967) in my continuous participant-observation study of Anglo-Celtic policing since 1968.

The theory has a major premise: that democratic policing is an extremely open system. Far more than any publicly held stockholder corporation, and probably more than any other government agency, policing is always vulnerable to the demands of any vocal constituency. No matter how small the group of demanders or how justified their complaints, police leaders must listen to them and give due consideration to them in providing better (or different) police practices. This pattern of organizational behavior has been observed in general since at least Thompson (1967, pp. 30, 37). Wilson (1968, p. 78) described a subset of this pattern in his discussion of "critical events" in policing, such as scandals, riots, police killings of citizens, and police strikes. The key question for evidence is what happens next: how critical events may shape evidence, and how evidence may then shape policy.

Figure 1 presents a causal model in which external demands for different policing are the major driving force. The theory claims that these demands are transformed by the human capital of the police institution, at both its core (police leaders) and its periphery (police scholars and research funders). In turn, human capital is shaped by the broader government policies that are also a target of public demands. The presence or absence of talented police leaders and scholars often reflects a 20- or 30-year lag in recruitment conditions and is highly dependent on national policies affecting police salaries, research funding, and other aspects of the capacity to generate and use research evidence. The people in a position to influence policy, if they are skilled enough, can then identify critical research questions and complete research projects, which are then communicated to police practitioners. Police managers and officers will then decide—immediately, somewhat later, or many years later—to apply the conclusions of the research evidence in their police practices. Sometimes this happens without their even knowing that the practice was shaped by research evidence (see, e.g., Police Executive Research Forum 2008).

These practices, and the ongoing critical events associated with

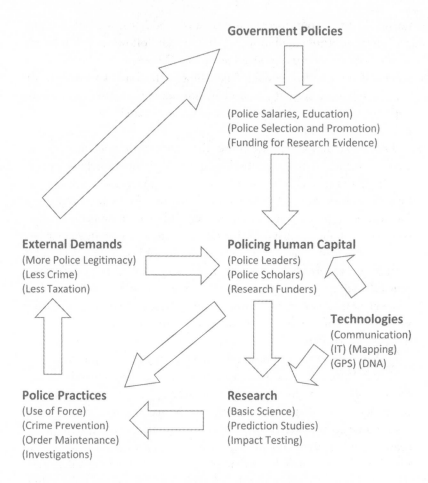

FIG. 1.—A theoretical model of the rise of evidence-based policing

them, continue to shape external demands on police. This happens only in part on the basis of police success or failure in meeting those demands. Many other things shape those demands, of course, and may be far more important than what police actually do. These other factors include economic ups and downs, emigration and immigration, ethnic and racial conflict, baby booms and busts, and possibly even a lag time from policies on leaded gasoline (Nevin 2000). Thus external demands on police are largely exogenous to the model, even though police can try to shape them to some degree. This makes the external demands fairly insensitive to how well police are performing in any objective sense. Yet the model leaves room for improvements in police practice at least to mitigate criticism and possibly even to increase legitimacy of the police and trust and confidence in them.

The role of technology is also exogenous to the model and may be even more important than citizen demands (Manning 1992). Both police and societies adopt new technologies rapidly when their advantages are obvious and their cost declines. Many technologies, such as the automobile and the computer, are sold initially at high cost and then become much cheaper. By the time most US households owned an auto, for example, most police patrols were also performed in cars. The adoption of personal computers also lagged but was much faster. The desktop computer that analyzed police mainframe data to identify hot spots of crime (Sherman 1987) was unavailable in the Minneapolis Police Department in the 1980s, but later, faster, cheaper laptop models were widely available in policing by the 1990s. The rise of DNA testing still hinges on reducing the cost of speedy results (Roman et al. 2009). The spread and impact of body-worn video may also hinge on reliability and the cost of data storage.

The model does not suggest that there is a direct pathway between demands for specific improvements in policing, such as more legitimate rape investigations, and research on how this demand can be met. To the contrary: demands for immediate solutions send governments and police in a frantic search for research that has already been done. If none exists, that merely provides evidence that policing lacks an evidence base. For example, the death of a bystander hit by a constable in a 2009 London protest was associated with a controversial police tactic called "kettling," or restraining people for hours in a cordoned-off area. The UK government launched a rapid evidence assessment on kettling but found that little research had been done. Rather than investing in such research over a longer time frame, the government chose to report the knowledge gap and then ignore it.

The direct pathway from specific demands for police innovations usually travels to police leaders through theory and precedent from other jurisdictions, but not through new research. The way research can affect policy is to anticipate the chronically recurring issues and have research evidence ready for the next critical event. As a member of Parliament for Cambridge once said, research findings are "money in the bank" (Howarth 2010). They do not have to be used immediately and can go unused for years until there is a demand for them. That is why the line from research goes directly to police practices, since research can be kept in readiness to shape the decisions on police practices when "critical events" press police leaders to meet external demands to change them.

This theory explains the past but need not predict the future. A more rational model of using evidence to improve policing would be proactively led by the police profession, not reactively driven by the political environment. That model might even reduce the number of critical events that threaten police legitimacy. It is one that, as applied to health care, has helped to keep down medical costs in the United Kingdom to less than half the percentage of gross domestic product as in the United States, where there is no system to target resources on the basis of professional research evidence (Sherman 2011*b*). It is also the plan for what the College of Policing might do as a champion and arbiter of evidence-based practice.

II. What We Know and What Police Do

The clearest test of my claims about evidence is whether police decisions are more consistent with the evidence now than in 1975. As of 2012 the record on that test was mixed but encouraging. There are many areas of triple-T in which the evidence is useful and police are using it. There are others in which the evidence is useful but is not used. The adoption of evidence-based decision making has been stronger for targeting and tracking than for testing, but all three areas have seen a substantial impact of research on practice. This section supports those conclusions with a series of short summaries of good evidence on many aspects of policing, followed by even shorter summaries of whether that evidence is used.

There are many other strategies that can use EBP besides triple-T. Evidence can be useful, for example, in the recruitment and promotion of more women police leaders, in developing better ways to train police, or in finding lighter-weight body armor with greater protection. This essay focuses on triple-T because it can shape the core of policing and holds the greatest potential for the direct reduction of harm in society.

The most accessible evidence of the large quantity of the testing police have done can be found by Googling the Evidence-Based Policing Matrix at George Mason University's Center for Evidence-Based Crime Policy (Lum, Koper, and Telep 2010). This website lists over 100 controlled tests of police practices, in both randomized experiments and quasi experiments. The matrix is designed by a former Baltimore detective to increase the use of research evidence in daily police operations. Other easily accessible sources, such as http://www.crime solutions.gov (at the US Department of Justice) and http://www .campbellcollaboration.org (operated by the Norwegian government), provide additional evidence on tests of police effectiveness.

Evidence on targeting and tracking resources is more scattered and inaccessible than it is for testing. The likely solution to that problem is for George Mason, the College of Policing, and other knowledge centers to broaden their knowledge repositories to include evidence on all areas of triple-T.

The evidence on the use of research in policing is much harder to come by and is badly in need of more evidence of its own. This section draws heavily on qualitative evidence gathered in over 54 weeks of discussions at Cambridge University with police executives from around the world in 2007–12 (primarily reporting on the United Kingdom, United States, and Australia). That evidence may be the least reliable of any reviewed here, but it is a consistent source applied equally to all the different topics addressed below.

A. Targeting Police Resources

In this subsection, I consider a range of evidence about ways police agencies can set priorities for investing their personnel with the greatest return on investment. It includes studies of how police use their time and of how they could focus their time on concentrations of high-priority events. It includes tests of targeting strategies as well as tests of predictions about high-priority targets, which must be distinguished from the tests of police impact on public safety discussed below.

1. Differential Police Response.

The Evidence.   There is good evidence that police can greatly limit their use of rapid response by car without offending citizens or putting them at risk. Callers will accept police decisions not to dispatch a police car for nonemergencies if the policy is explained to them by the person who answers the telephone. In randomized experiments in three US cities (McEwen, Connors, and Cohen 1986), citizens calling about matters that were not emergencies were given one of two responses: that police will come "as soon as they can" (standard policy at the time) or that no response is necessary since the matter can be handled by telephone or other methods. Citizens were equally satisfied with both responses. The benefit was that call takers performed the same work as patrol officers in about one-third of the work time, with no transportation costs or air pollution. In some agencies, rapid police responses could be reduced by 50 percent or more with substantial savings—or more resources preventing serious crime.

What Police Do. The use of "differential police response" (DPR) remains very mixed. Even when DPR is used, it is rarely evidence-based. The 1986 evaluation is generally unknown to contemporary police professionals, yet it is freely available online and could save millions annually in any large police agency. Every police agency could easily conduct its own randomized trial of different kinds of incidents for which callers would receive a nondispatch response. At a time when police resources are declining in the United States and the United Kingdom (Sherman 2011*b*), an evidence-based approach to targeting resources where they are needed most is now needed more than ever.

2. *Hot Spots of Crime.*

The Evidence. There is good descriptive evidence that police can target resources on most crimes by identifying the small fraction of small places in any city where crime happens repeatedly (Sherman, Gartin, and Buerger 1989; Weisburd, Groff, and Yang 2012). These hot spot concentrations are clearest at a very micro level, such as a single address, a cluster of addresses, or a "block-face" street segment from one corner to the next on a single street. While some hot spots may wax and wane from year to year or month to month, many are stable for 15 years or more (Weisburd et al. 2004). Hot spots can be mapped, ranked, classified by offense type, and analyzed in many ways relevant to police operations.

What Police Do. Crime mapping is widespread, with many police agencies using it to identify hot spots. By the 2007 US Law Enforcement Management and Administrative Statistics Survey, over half of all cities of 50,000 or more residents used computers to generate crime hot spots, including almost all cities of over 500,000 people (Reaves 2010, p. 22). But the definition of hot spots varies widely. In many UK agencies, these locations are usually much larger than what the original research evidence analyzed. Entire patrol beats, rather than street corners or face blocks, are the United Kingdom's more common unit of analysis, while the opposite tendency is found in the United States. A sample of 192 big US cities showed slightly higher use of intersections (63 percent) than of neighborhoods (57 percent) as the definition of hot spots (Police Executive Research Forum 2008, p. 3). UK police in 2012 were at a special disadvantage because of their dispatch systems, which often failed to pinpoint the locations where crimes occur; some audits have shown the mapped locations of crimes to be great distances from the actual locations. Any police agency that is serious about reducing crime must, arguably, invest in correcting crime location errors, ideally by using GPS devices to include the exact latitude and longitude of every crime reported. In Andhra Pradesh, India, some police stations had incorporated GPS data into all crime reports by early 2011, and Trinidad and Tobago adopted it nationally in 2012, when no UK agency had yet done so. GPS measures would also improve the accuracy of targeting analysis for directed patrol and problem solving.

3. *Hot Spots of Distrust.*

The Evidence.   There is good evidence that distrust of police is concentrated in a small proportion of urban neighborhoods. Police legitimacy is defined as a public (or police) perception of the moral right to exercise legal powers. This means that policing can be legal but illegitimate in the eyes of some (or most) beholders (Tankebe 2009; Bottoms and Tankebe 2012). The legitimacy of policing is highly correlated with minority or majority status in many populations (Sherman 2002), with majority populations attributing much greater legitimacy to police than minorities. Riots in US cities were concentrated in such hot spots (Rossi, Berk, and Eidson 1974). One recent study of public trust in a UK police jurisdiction showed very high levels of distrust in certain minority areas (Murray 2009). Yet not all majority-minority areas have highly negative views of police; some (as in Chicago) have more positive views (Skogan 1990; Skogan and Hartnett 1997; Sampson and Bartusch 1998).

What Police Do.   Very few police agencies take annual surveys of public attitudes toward police. The US agencies that pay for such evidence tend to focus on citywide ratings rather than neighborhood-level differences. Some UK agencies have paid for neighborhood-level breakdowns with samples as large as 30,000 responses agencywide. Targeting strategies for increasing police legitimacy cannot be accomplished on a geographic basis unless such evidence is generated annually, so that deterioration or progress can be identified.

4. *Hot Times and Days.*

The Evidence.   Crime risks vary enormously by time of day and day of week (Sherman 1992*a*), as well as season by season and holiday by holiday. Weather also has a strong effect on police workload (Cohn 1993), and in some regions it can be predicted days in advance with high reliability.

What Police Do.   This issue remains the major failure of evidence-based targeting (Sherman 1992*a*). More money is wasted by ignoring "hot times" targeting than by any other police management practice. As one UK inspection report observed (Her Majesty's Inspectorate of Constabulary 2010, p. 3), more police officers were on patrol on Monday mornings than on Friday nights. The failure to schedule a work-force based on high-crime times and days is largely due to police labor contracts. These agreements serve the reasonable interests of police officers in a predictable work schedule. What is unreasonable to tax-payers is chronic and predictable understaffing during the peak crime times and overstaffing during "cool" times.

5. *Repeat Offenders.*

The Evidence.   A small number of all offenders commit a high proportion of all crimes (Blumstein et al. 1986). Few specialize in any particular crime, and most of the crimes they commit are offenses against property. Controlling crime rates, and even the aggregated crime harm, may depend on police identifying, managing, or arresting prolific offenders.

What Police Do.   Some police agencies target high-volume offenders who are not in jail (Spelman 1990). Yet almost no police agency has an instant query capacity to determine whether a particular known offender is in prison or at large. No agency appears to develop objectives for reducing recidivism of high-rate offenders, or even tracking the proportion of known repeat offenders they have put behind bars or under correctional supervision at any given time. Since the population of such offenders at large changes daily, a substantial investment in evidence gathering would be needed to target repeat offenders day by day. Nonetheless, most agencies would report that "we do that already," without actually investing in what is required to target repeat offenders in an evidence-based way.

6. *Dangerous versus "Supersafe" Offenders.*

The Evidence. More important than repeat offenders, and far fewer in number, are the most dangerous offenders. People who are most likely to kill, rape, rob, or commit sex crimes against children can be identified and forecasted from large databases (Berk et al. 2009). While the error rates in forecasting dangerousness can be substantial, the errors in forecasting "supersafe" conduct are minimal. A UK analysis of 100,000 convicted offenders found 96 percent accuracy in classifying offenders as not dangerous if somewhat lower accuracy (84 percent) in forecasting zero recidivism over a 2-year period (Sherman, Cosma, and Neyroud 2012).

What Police Do. The techniques used to classify known offenders as very dangerous, supersafe, or in between are new to both criminology and policing. From around 2000, UK police chiefs tried hard to identify the most dangerous offenders, but with highly subjective "clinical" methods that have failed to pass basic statistical tests (Thornton 2011). UK chiefs have recently expressed great interest in applying statistical forecasting methods to their local offender populations, requesting the statistical models as soon as they could be made available (Peter Neyroud, personal communication). Meanwhile, the few police agencies employing their own statisticians are free to replicate the published models.

7. *Crime Recruiters.*

The Evidence. A small proportion of repeat offenders have a high propensity for being arrested with, and apparently "recruiting," many different co-offenders (Reiss 1988; Reiss and Farrington 1991; Sherman 1992*a*). Where these co-offenders are almost always younger than the more experienced offender, the pattern suggests that the frequent co-offender may be recruiting novices into crime or certain types of crime. The hypothesis is even more compelling if the younger offenders have no prior record. That is exactly what an analysis of all arrestees in Sacramento, California, found over a multiyear period (Englefield 2013).

What Police Do. Only one police agency so far is known to generate lists of high-volume crime recruiters (Sacramento), but others may follow suit. The fact that the strongest evidence was generated not by an academic but by a police officer writing a master's thesis (as a self-funded student at Cambridge) is a good indication of the rise of professionally driven research in policing (Weisburd and Neyroud 2011).

8. *Traumatized Victims.*

The Evidence.   Crime victims suffer great trauma from rape and rape attempts (Foa 1997). They also suffer lesser but high levels of trauma from noninjury crimes such as burglary and robbery, especially women (Angel 2005). While they are rarely diagnosed with post-traumatic stress disorder, they suffer elevated levels of post-traumatic stress symptoms.

What Police Do.   Anglo-Celtic police have become far more sensitive to rape-related trauma since 1975 and have developed elaborate protocols for rape investigations and related medical care. Police do not, however, generally target the victims of lesser trauma, largely because there has been little external pressure to do so. Yet well-tested methods exist that police could use to massively reduce the symptoms of post-traumatic stress.

9. *Repeat Victims.*

The Evidence.   High proportions of residential and personal crimes are committed against repeat victims (Pease 1998).

What Police Do.   Police programs on repeat victimization tend to target all victims rather than to identify repeat victims. Other than the Minneapolis RECAP program in the 1980s (Buerger 1993), few police agencies have even developed lists of repeat victims. This may be a missed opportunity for reducing both crime and harm.

10. *Near-Miss Victims.*

The Evidence.   One of the most predictable risks of a residential burglary is in the zone of a few buildings on either side, behind, and in front of a burglarized residence for the first 10–14 days after the burglary (Bowers, Johnson, and Pease 2004; Johnson and Bowers 2004).

What Police Do.   For a decade after these findings were published, almost no police agencies identified these "near-miss" areas for prevention programs. Then a few UK police agencies began doing so in 2011–12. The word-of-mouth interest in this approach came from presentations by University of London academics to practitioner audiences at Cambridge and Cardiff conferences of the Society of Evidence-Based Policing and was still spreading in 2012.

11. *"Solvability Factors."*

The Evidence.   There is good evidence, summarized above, that police investigations can be targeted on the cases most likely to be solved and that investigations are wasted on cases in which a detection is predicted to be highly unlikely.

What Police Do.   This is another major failure of getting research into practice, at least by 2012. It is hard to find a police agency that employs a statistical model of solvability factors to allocate the very scarce resource of investigators' time. Many police agencies still say they investigate all crimes. Others admit that they will close cases that are not solved after a certain period, but they do not use a statistical algorithm to decide which ones to abandon at the outset. Many confuse this research with closing cases on the basis of seriousness rather than solvability, such as when the value of property stolen is too low. It remains a prime opportunity for policing to save money and do more to help crime victims.

B. Testing Police Practices

The following subsections discuss a selection of major police practices that have been tested with at least a comparison group. Many have been tested with randomized controlled trials, and some have been tested repeatedly with up to 20 or more randomized trials. It is the most robust area of evidence supporting the triple-T strategy but also the area of biggest gaps between evidence and practice.

1. *Random Marked Car Patrol.*

The Evidence.   There is little direct evidence that random patrol of areas that have little crime can cause any less crime than having no patrol. The major exception is police strikes, which consistently cause crime to skyrocket (Sherman 1992*a*, pp. 192–93).

What Police Do.   Random patrol by "rapid response" cars is still widespread across Anglo-Celtic policing. Even when police are told to "concentrate" patrols in, or "give special attention to," certain areas, this can amount to only a few minutes per work shift. Random patrol predominates in practice if not in rhetoric; hot spot patrol is rising rapidly, at least in rhetoric if not yet in practice.

2. *Hot Spot Car Patrol.*

The Evidence.   Doubling the dosage of marked car patrols in high-crime hot spots at higher-crime times can measurably reduce crime and disorder in those hot spots (Sherman and Weisburd 1995). In the Minneapolis hot spots experiment, an average of 15 percent of at-risk time with police present produced moderately less crime, and half the disorder, than in a comparison group with police present for only 7 percent of at-risk time. Koper (1995) reported that the greatest residual deterrence in each hot spot (Sherman 1990) was associated with 15-

minute periods of patrol presence, compared to both shorter and longer periods of patrol. Various police strategies have been tested in other hot spots experiments (Braga, Papachristos, and Hureau 2012), but none has apparently replicated either the unit of analysis or the measured dosage levels of the initial Minneapolis experiment (Sherman and Weisburd 1995). Displacement was not measured in the initial experiment, but it has been falsified in a range of other hot spots patrol tests (Weisburd et al. 2006). No experiment, however, has compared hot spots to random patrol at the level of police districts. No test has yet made a direct comparison between, for example, 50 districts using random patrols and 50 districts concentrating patrols in crime hot spots. Until such a test is done, a huge gap remains in the evidence on hot spots policing.

What Police Do.   Directed patrols at crime hot spots in marked cars is a growing practice in the United States and the United Kingdom. Hot spots patrol has been identified by the NYPD as a major strategy to which it attributes a decline in homicide rates (Zimring 2012). Weisburd and Lum (2005) found that among the 92 US police departments responding to a survey of a random sample of 125 with 100 or more police officers, 62 percent had adopted computerized crime mapping by 2001. The most common reason these early adopters gave for their decision—43 percent—was to "facilitate hot spots policing." Thus by 2001, 27 percent of the responding agencies said that they had adopted computerized crime mapping to facilitate hot spots policing. By 2007, the Police Executive Research Forum survey of 192 large police agencies found that hot spots had become the most common police strategy for fighting violent crime since "nearly nine out of 10 agencies use hot spots enforcement efforts directed either at larger hot spot areas like neighborhoods (57 percent), smaller hot spot places like intersections (63 percent), or both" (2008, p. 3). In the United Kingdom, hot spots patrol is growing in tests as well as in practice, with three different police agencies testing such patrol in 2012–13.

3. *Random Foot Patrol.*

The Evidence.   Two quasi-experimental tests of random foot patrol found no effect on crime (Kelling et al. 1981; Trojanowicz and Baldwin 1982). The Newark Foot Patrol Experiment, however, found reduced public perceptions of crime and disorder in areas with foot patrols compared with control areas (Kelling et al. 1981).

What Police Do.   Random foot patrol has almost disappeared in

Anglo-Celtic policing. Its use is limited to the highest-density areas of the largest cities, such as New York and London. Hot spot foot patrol is far more common.

4. *Hot Spot Foot Patrol.*

The Evidence.   A brief but randomized controlled test of foot patrol in high-crime areas of Philadelphia found that foot patrol caused significant reductions in violent crime with only modest local displacement effects (Ratcliffe et al. 2011). The areas were much larger than the Minneapolis hot spot street corners but still smaller than a typical police district.

What Police Do.   In the United States, foot patrol in high-crime hot spots is most likely to be used in densely populated cities. In the United Kingdom, Police Community Support Officers, whose uniforms look much like those of police constables with full arrest powers, are often used for foot patrols in town centers and suburban shopping strips.

5. *Rapid Response Policing.*

The Evidence.   There is no direct evidence that rapid response can make any difference in detection or crime rates and some indirect evidence that it cannot. It is very rare that rapid response can catch an offender. Rarer still does rapid response save a crime victim from serious injury. The capacity to do so may be a core feature of police legitimacy, an aspect of this issue on which there is no evidence.

What Police Do.   Police agencies still spend substantial funds ensuring the capacity to respond very quickly. Some of them track average response times very closely and advertise the results by public announcements.

6. *Problem-Oriented Policing.*

The Evidence.   Both randomized experiments and quasi experiments have tested Goldstein's (1979, 1990) proposed strategy of attacking underlying causes, rather than just symptoms, of patterns of crime. Most reported studies have been before-after studies with no control group, most of which report substantial success. The largest randomized trial (Sherman, Gartin, and Buerger 1989) reported that POP caused a 15 percent reduction in calls over 6 months in a sample of some 250 residential locations, but not in a sample of 250 commercial locations. A systematic review of randomized trials of POP found, on average, that POP produces modest but clear reductions in the problems it targets (Weisburd et al. 2010).

What Police Do.   Thousands of US and UK police are enthusiastic about POP and often do it despite peer pressure not to. For many it is an unacknowledged addition to their random patrol work, which many police agencies have encouraged. What some, but still few, agencies have done is to create either specialized units of experts in POP (such as the Minneapolis RECAP Unit) or case management systems for identifying problems and assigning specific time periods for specific officers to undertake POP work and be held accountable for the results.

7. *Stop-and-Question.*

The Evidence.   There is highly consistent evidence that stop-and-question or stop-and-search causes reductions in weapons violence and homicide (Koper and Mayo-Wilson 2006), based on seven out of seven quasi experiments reducing either homicide or gunshot wounds. Repeated cross-sectional analyses across US cities show lower levels of robberies and other crimes where police proactively issue more traffic violations or make arrests for disorderly conduct (e.g., Kubrin et al. 2010). No evidence exists on the life course effects of police stops on those who are stopped, especially whether a contact with police that is seen as hostile can engender defiance that increases future offending (Sherman 1993). One survey of a residential area with high levels of gun violence found substantial support for this practice among residents (Shaw 1995), but no surveys were done of those stopped.

What Police Do.   For many police agencies, stop-and-question is an embedded part of patrol practice in high-crime areas. Its use in crime hot spots in New York and London is highly visible and highly controversial. Few debates distinguish between the questions of how stops should be done and whether they should be done at all. Many police agencies track the occurrence of stops, but not their qualities of procedural fairness. As Reiss (1971) suggested, all citizen encounters could end with police giving citizens a receipt with the officer's identifying details and the date and time. Such a system could lead to measures of quality.

8. *Covert Surveillance.*

The Evidence.   The use of covert surveillance on repeat offenders alleged to be committing serious crimes was tested in a Washington, DC, experiment (Martin and Sherman 1986). Random assignment of surveillance, compared to a control group, substantially increased the likelihood of a suspect being arrested as well as convicted and sentenced to prison.

What Police Do.   Police rarely use covert surveillance against ongoing street crime. UK police use it sparingly for very serious sex offenders who have been released from prison.

9. *Arrests for Domestic Assault.*

The Evidence. There is consistent evidence that arresting unemployed domestic abusers causes more violence but no consistent evidence that arrest reduces domestic violence. Three randomized controlled trials of arrests for domestic assault have examined the interaction between employment and arrest on repeat violence (Pate and Hamilton 1992; Sherman 1992*b*); a fourth examined the same interaction on repeat domestic calls including arguments as well as violent crime (Berk et al. 1992). All four tests showed that arrest had different effects on employed suspects than on unemployed suspects. The three studies of assault found that arrest reduced repeat crimes for employed suspects but substantially increased repeat crimes for unemployed suspects. Two of the five randomized trials of the main effect of arrest for assaults did not report tests for an interaction effect with suspect employment. But the Milwaukee experiment found that arrests for common assault caused significantly more domestic violence repeat offending than an on-site warning even after 24 years (Sherman and Harris 2012).

What Police Do. Elected legislators have prevented police from using evidence-based practice on domestic violence in over half of US states and all across England and Wales. Either a legal or a policy mandate requires police to make arrests whenever there is sufficient legal evidence to do so. Police in some US agencies have widely ignored this mandate for decades (Ferraro 1989). Others in the United States and most of the UK agencies have been more compliant, but with frequent sensitivity to victims' preferences. New experiments in policing domestic violence were launched in Hampshire (UK) in 2012, when evidence-based changes in policy were widely discussed across the United Kingdom.

10. *Warrants for Domestic Assault.*

The Evidence. There is good evidence that issuing an arrest warrant for an absent domestic violence suspect has a "sword of Damocles" effect in suppressing repeat assaults. A randomized controlled trial in Omaha, Nebraska, enrolled cases in which suspects had already left the scene before police arrived. The police then randomly assigned either the standard police policy of advising the victim how to pay for an arrest warrant to be issued in court or went to the court to arrange issuance of a warrant free of any charge to the victim. In the cases assigned to police-initiated warrants, there was significantly less repeat violence reported by the victims of abuse to the university interviewers. There were also substantially fewer police reports of repeat offending (Dunford 1990).

What Police Do. Police rarely issue warrants for simple assault. Some English police go looking for an absent suspect when there is evidence of an assault and "hand over" the case to the next shift if the absent suspect has not been found. No evidence exists on the rate at which absent offenders are found or the rates of those not found being subjected to a police-initiated warrant, but these rates could be part of tracking.

11. *"Second Responder" Follow-ups after Domestic Incidents.*

The Evidence. Several randomized controlled trials have tested follow-up visits by "second responder" police or social workers, or both, some days after police have responded to a domestic violence call or made an arrest. A systematic review of these experiments included both repeat calls to police and interviews with the victims (Davis, Wiesburd, and Taylor 2008). The review found no difference between the self-reported victimizations of those victims who had been visited and those who had not, but there were more calls to the police about new violence by those who had been visited than among those left alone. While the evidence is ambiguous, second response cannot be considered beneficial. Increased reporting might be of some benefit, but it may also just indicate more violence.

What Police Do. Few police agencies deploy second responders, yet some UK agencies "invented" the idea in 2010–12 without knowledge of the results of the Davis, Weisburd, and Taylor (2008) systematic review.

12. *Police-Led Restorative Justice Conferences.*

The Evidence. Eight randomized controlled trials have tested police-led restorative justice conferences (RJCs) with crime victims, their offenders, and their respective friends or family in Australia (two), the United Kingdom (five), and the United States (one). Seven of these eight tests found a reduction in repeat offending among offenders assigned to restorative justice (Sherman and Strang 2012). The one failure had a high proportion of Aboriginal offenders, for whom restorative justice badly backfired (Sherman et al. 2006). A systematic review and meta-analysis of these experiments, combined with two others in which nonpolice led the conference, found an average effect that was small but statistically significant among robbers, burglars, violent offenders, and property offenders (Strang et al. 2013).

What Police Do. Few Anglo-Celtic police officers were leading RJCs in 2012, although other kinds of people led them frequently in New Zealand and Northern Ireland. Police in England and Wales have been trained to use a "mini" version of these conferences in street settings, immediately after responding, which are often called "restorative disposals" or "community resolutions." This version of RJCs has not been tested.

13. *Prosecution of Juveniles.*

The Evidence. There is good evidence that when police prosecute most juvenile offenders, they cause more crime than they prevent—at least among those offenders. In 29 randomized controlled trials over four decades, in studies enrolling a total of 7,304 juvenile offenders, those who were prosecuted after arrest had more repeat offending than those who were diverted or cautioned (Petrosino, Turpin-Petrosino, and Guckenburg 2010). All tests were conducted in the United States except two of the restorative justice experiments in Australia. The offenders had committed a range of property and less serious violent crimes. Those who were diverted from prosecution had lower offending rates when the disposition required them to do less follow-up work, and the best success was found with no conditions at all.

What Police Do. Police practices with juvenile offenders remain mixed and largely unmeasured. In the United Kingdom, there has been a substantial increase in formal prosecution since 1975, but this trend may have reversed since 2010.

14. *Neighborhood Watch.*

The Evidence. Neighborhood watch appears to cause a small but consistent reduction in rates of burglary and other crimes. A systematic review examined 18 quasi-experimental controlled tests of neighborhood watch programs, either alone or in combination with other situational prevention strategies, such as property marking and home security surveys (Bennett, Holloway, and Farrington 2006). Crime was measured by both police-recorded crime and victimization surveys. The review found, on average, statistically significant crime reductions of 16–26 percent. Given the low levels of crime in many of the middle-class neighborhoods in which the tests were done, it remains unclear whether the crime reductions were cost-effective. Yet that issue can be raised about any evidence of a positive effect of a police strategy relative to a control group.

What Police Do. There is no good evidence about what police do in neighborhood watch programs after a local group has held its first meeting. There appears to be no tracking evidence on how much time police invest in starting or maintaining neighborhood volunteer interest in preventing crime. Signs warning would-be offenders that "this area is protected by neighborhood watch" are ubiquitous in many US suburbs, but whether there have been any neighborhood meetings to discuss crime in months or years is impossible to say.

15. *Drug Abuse Resistance Education (DARE).*

The Evidence. Repeated quasi experiments (Sherman et al. 1998) and a major randomized controlled trial (Perry et al. 2003) have failed to show that the standard DARE program reduces drug use or delinquency. The Perry et al. trial of 24 schools in Minneapolis did find that a greatly enhanced program called DARE Plus reduced multidrug use (but not marijuana use) among boys, with no effect on girls. But Dare Plus involved much greater use of parents than the standard DARE program, which relies heavily on police visits to classrooms for its delivery.

What Police Do. According to the DARE America home page, 220 US communities started DARE programs over the preceding 3 years—more than one per week. These new startups are in addition to the website's claim that 75 percent of the more than 14,000 US school districts offer DARE programs. Despite the example of former Mayor Rocky Anderson of Salt Lake City, Utah (population 190,000), ordering his police department in 2000 to stop wasting money on DARE (which he called a "fraud"; Eyle 2001–2), most US police agencies still appear to be sending police officers into classrooms to talk about drugs—with no demonstrated return on the taxpayers' cost.

16. *"Pulling Levers": Focused Deterrence.*

The Evidence. The use of directed sanction threats to specific individuals and groups gained worldwide attention when it preceded a complete cessation of youth homicide in Boston in the 1990s. A systematic review of 10 quasi-experimental evaluations of this approach, seven of which used nonequivalent (unmatched) control groups, examined the effect of this strategy on such crimes as homicide and gang violence, mostly at the citywide level (Braga and Weisburd 2012). The review found that nine out of 10 evaluations showed statistically significant reductions in crime. Given the many threats to the internal validity of these evaluations, the review authors described the evidence as "promising."

What Police Do. Police in communities with high homicide rates, from Trinidad to Scotland, often try to replicate the "Boston miracle," which has received further attention from David Kennedy's (2008, 2011) books on his experiences in Boston and elsewhere.

C. Tracking Outputs and Outcomes

1. Police Killings of Citizens.

The Evidence. Fifty years ago, criminologist Gerald Robin (1963) published the first cross-city comparison of the rates at which police committed justifiable homicide against the citizens of their communities. This study helped to spark two decades of research on the issue (e.g., Sherman and Langworthy 1979; Fyfe 1980, 1982; Sherman 1980, 1983) that supported an appeal of a police killing case to the US Supreme Court (*Tennessee v. Garner*, 471 U.S. 1 [1985]). The later research showed that limiting police killings to defense-of-life situations had reduced deaths, without any increases in crime or violence against police. The *Garner* decision, which cited the research evidence, ruled that common law powers to kill unarmed fleeing felons were an unconstitutional seizure without due process. The decision restricted police powers to kill in over half of the 50 US states.

What Police Do. Tennenbaum (1994) reports that killings by US police, which had already been dropping prior to the 1985 *Garner* decision, dropped by 16 percent in its immediate aftermath. He also showed that police shootings for all reasons, not just to catch fleeing felons, declined. Most US police shootings are now tracked very closely, and police gun use is regulated by agency managers far more intensely than in 1975. Police killings in the United States have risen and fallen since then, but shootings of unarmed fleeing felons have virtually disappeared.

2. Police Use of Force.

The Evidence. In the mid-1970s, city manager–run police agencies began to require police to file a use-of-force report each time they used weapons, handcuffs, or physical restraint against a citizen (Croft 1985). This paper file tracking system enabled police managers to identify statistical outliers in the frequency of use-of-force reports, as well as to justify in court or arbitration hearings any dismissal of overly frequent users of force from police service. An independent commission led by Warren Christopher (1991) in the aftermath of the Los Angeles Police Department's Rodney King case documented extreme concentrations of use of force among a small percentage of police officers.

What Police Do.   Use-of-force reports are now widely used in the United States, usually with stand-alone digital databases that allow frequent in-house tracking analysis of the evidence. Litigation over police use of force is defended with this evidence and possibly even prevented by managerial application of these analyses to personnel and assignment decisions.

3. *Complaints against Police.*

The Evidence.   In 1975, systems for receiving, recording, investigating, and resolving citizen complaints against the police were very scarce. Cities as big as Louisville, Kentucky, made it almost impossible for citizens to complain against police (Sherman 1976). By the mid-1980s, most US cities over 100,000 recorded and investigated complaints against police. By 2012 most US and UK forces had computerized systems for tracking complaints by officer characteristics, complainant characteristics, area demographics, type of encounters, and other factors of managerial interest.

What Police Do.   Most large police agencies in 2012 had "professional standards" units reporting to the police executive on trends and patterns in complaints against police. Few of these, however, appear to be adjusting the analyses for such crucial risk factors as how many encounters each officer had with citizens each year, in each unit, or in each area. As in tracking evidence generally, police managers often look at raw data that are not meaningful unless they are standardized by relevant denominators (Kahneman 2011). High levels of complaints may indicate high levels of misconduct. But unless complaints are divided by contacts, they could also indicate a high level of professional commitment to making as many appropriate contacts (and arrests) as possible. Fairness alone requires the use of a standardizing denominator, as well as good tracking measurement.

4. *Trust and Confidence in Police.*

The Evidence.   There is now abundant research tracking trust and confidence in policing. A recent government in the United Kingdom made public confidence the single performance measure it said would be used to judge police performance. Yet no governmental data supplement raw data with risk-adjusted data, the latter taking into account factors affecting public confidence that are irrelevant to police performance. Risk factors for public confidence may include population demographics, structural inequality, lack of collective efficacy (Sampson and Bartusch 1998), cultural backgrounds of populations, and other factors (e.g., Jackson and Bradford 2009). There is a great need for better risk-adjusted models of "expected" levels of trust and confidence in police.

What Police Do.   Many police agencies fail to track trust and confidence at all. Some track raw levels citywide, and a few track it by neighborhoods. There appears to be no use of risk-adjusted confidence measures in any of the police agencies from 10 countries whose representatives were asked about this in recent classes of the Cambridge Police Executive Programme.

5. *COMPSTAT.*

The Evidence.   Since 1975, nothing has done more than the COMPSTAT idea to increase the availability of evidence for tracking police performance at micro levels of activity. At highly structured and periodic meetings of senior police officials, operational commanders report the tracking data on their crime patterns and (less often) on their anticrime strategies. Pioneered by Bratton (1998) and Maple (1999), the COMPSTAT program was probably the first police "interaction ritual" (Collins 2004) to make a "sacred" meaning. By reporting the crime trends within days rather than months at very local levels, the institutional meaning and police legitimacy associated with crime control became far more intense than they had ever been before (Willis, Mastrofski, and Weisburd 2007). My own observations in the NYPD in 1972 and in 1995 revealed an enormous increase under COMPSTAT in the extent to which specific evidence about crime and police practices was portrayed in statistical and graphical visualizations. My own attempt to introduce something similar for the mayor of Indianapolis in 1994–95 had failed to mobilize the same kind of intensity, largely because the New York version engaged almost 200 people in the room listening very closely (compared to six or seven in Indianapolis). New York also used COMPSTAT with its unusually great legal authority to press unambitious area commanders to retire and to reward successful commanders with promotions—something few other agencies are able to do. NYPD officials who had used COMPSTAT moved to other large cities, where they also used COMPSTAT for citywide reviews of specific issues, from domestic violence to police corruption (Sherman 1978). No other system of tracking evidence on outcomes or outputs has been so influential or comprehensive.

What Police Do. In 1999, some 5 years after New York's COMPSTAT had become highly publicized, the Police Foundation conducted a national survey of US police agencies in cities over 100,000 residents (Weisburd et al. 2004). The survey found that over half of those agencies (with an 85 percent response rate) either had adopted a COMPSTAT-like program or were planning to do so. In the early twenty-first century, COMPSTAT-like meetings were held regularly in many UK police agencies. Few such meetings, however, track the key question under discussion: where are the police doing what, and for how much of their time on duty? That is a question that two major advances in technology will soon make it easier to answer.

6. *GPS Tracking of Officer Locations.*

The Evidence. Police agencies have been able to track the locations of police cars since at least the 1980s but have rarely done so. Police unions once resisted the idea, especially in the 1970s, when some US officers regularly slept in their cars on the midnight shift. The rise of GPS devices in police radios and "smart" phones now makes it possible to track the whereabouts of each officer every few minutes or seconds. Police officers also seem more willing to allow this, if only as a safety device that could enable a rapid response of other police to help them. An experiment in providing police supervisors with data on how much time each patrol officer spent at directed patrols in crime hot spots has been completed in Dallas, with encouraging results (Weisburd 2012). Other experiments testing the use of tracking evidence for effects on police performance are needed to determine whether tracking at this level of detail is cost-effective or not.

What Police Do. From the limited evidence available, it appears that as of 2012, no major police agency has made statistical use of GPS data about locations of police outputs as a standard part of tracking or COMPSTAT. For reasons discussed in the first section of this essay, however, it seems likely that such tracking will be widespread by 2025.

7. *Body-Worn Video.*

The Evidence. Inexpensive body-worn video (BWV) cameras with long-running batteries came on the market around 2010. As a student in the Cambridge Police Executive Program, Police Chief Tony Farrar of Rialto, California, decided to test the hypothesis that police officers wearing BWV would generate fewer complaints from encounters with citizens. One theory is that officers would be more polite and compliant with rules knowing that every word and action was on digital record. The other theory states exactly the same for citizens encountering police. In a randomized controlled trial of police shifts in which all patrol officers either did or did not wear the cameras, Farrar (2013) found initial evidence of fewer complaints on shifts when officers wore their BWV devices. Given spillover diffusion effects to shifts when officers did not wear cameras, it was no surprise that total complaints against police dropped sharply. Related hypotheses can be tested in this design for the rates at which arrestees plead guilty as charged or the rates at which either citizens or police are injured in their encounters. Note that this evidence is a prime example of testing a means of tracking police performance as distinct from testing the effects of performance itself. It asks whether tracking has benefits regardless of what police do and whether tracking improves police quality.

What Police Do. BWV is at a very early stage of development in policing. One UK agency tried to incorporate it into stop-and-question procedures, but citizens who were stopped refused to answer questions while police had their cameras on. A large Australian police agency has had problems with equipment failures. What no agency appears to have tried is the use of BWV to replace typing, with video-recorded crime reports, victim and investigative interviews, and other work. Such use of videos could keep police out of stations typing up text for many hours when they could be on patrol taking video statements as well as increasing patrol visibility. In the United Kingdom's ongoing effort to "cut red tape" and reduce reports, no solution could be easier or more elegant than downloading police video and audio as a digital logbook. If text reports need to be created for any reason, including prosecution, then civilian video specialists can do that rather than police trained to patrol, prevent, and investigate.

D. Summary: Knowledge and Its Use

The examples offered above support a key conclusion: there has been a massive growth of policing knowledge over the levels in 1975. Equally important is a second conclusion: there has been less progress in using knowledge than in generating it. But the crude (and perhaps inaccurate) measures of evidence in practice fail to suggest what may be the most important point: that police interest in using evidence grew most rapidly in the last decade before 2012. Even though the 1980s was the most intense period for producing police research, the 2000s and 2010s were the most intense periods for consuming it. If the demand for evidence continues to grow, so may the future production of evidence.

III. Improving Triple-T: Targeting, Testing, and Tracking

This section highlights the major conceptual issues that must be addressed for policing to use evidence in a fully professional way. These issues all relate to the way in which the concept of evidence is defined. The greatest threat to police professionalism is that the word "evidence" will be hijacked to mean what it is intended to replace: intuition, anecdote, and opinion. Just because a word is fashionable does not mean that people who use it will understand it, let alone accept it and agree with its message. Even with the best of intentions, the word "evidence" is often applied incorrectly by people who lack adequate training in how evidence should be used. This risk requires that police leaders and scholars pay close attention to the integrity of the concept and relentlessly challenge any claims that "the evidence shows" when no such evidence exists.

This threat has major implications for how police training and promotion processes teach and communicate about evidence-based practices. Simple lists of "best practices" may have great value in some contexts. But for people sitting at conference tables deciding on what best practices they should adopt, simplicity is not good enough. Policing is a complex enterprise, and so is drawing conclusions from evidence. People analyzing evidence need to be qualified to do so, one way or another. At minimum, they should understand the concepts presented in this section.

It is reassuring that these same conceptual issues bedevil other complex enterprises as well. There is nothing wrong with police thinking about evidence that is not also wrong with the thinking of highly seasoned politicians (Issenberg 2012), baseball managers (Lewis 2003), and nuclear power plant engineers (Silver 2012, chap. 5). As Kahneman (2011) demonstrates, it is very hard for humans to discipline their thinking away from intuitive snap judgments ("system I") to accept more systematic analyses that follow strict rules of evidence ("system II"). Fortunately, he concludes that it is at least possible for humans to achieve that discipline, but only if we work pretty hard at it.

This section considers four questions. Most important is the question of what good evidence is, and what it means to make policing "evidence-based." The other three questions cover related issues in targeting, testing, and tracking. The targeting subsection introduces the concept of a crime harm index as the best way to measure what matters in valuing police effectiveness. The testing subsection shows how testing is increasingly done by "pracademics," not just academics. The tracking subsection discusses how to use evidence for ensuring better implementation of evidence-based policies.

A. What Is Good Evidence?

What is "good evidence"? This question must be addressed almost daily if policing is to raise its level of professionalism. Even among those strongly committed to using good evidence, it is easy to lose the core principles of testing.

At an early meeting of the Society of Evidence-Based Policing, for example, a presentation led a session chair to endorse an innovation in taking witness statements that had just been described by two presenters. One speaker described laboratory tests of the new procedure, while the other speaker described its use in (just) three cases in the field. No controlled field test had been conducted, nor any test measuring the key outcome of conviction rates. Yet on the basis of the strong results of the lab experiments, the session chair enthusiastically described the research as "really strong" evidence and suggested that it was unethical for police at the conference not to adopt the innovation. I felt compelled to challenge that claim by pointing out the major difference between laboratory and field tests. I noted that "evidence-based medicine" limits its definition of evidence to field tests only, viewing lab tests as a necessary precursor to testing treatments on real people. In this police context, this means that the proper channel for the enthusiasm we all felt for the innovation would be to conduct a randomized field experiment, which had not yet been done. The session chair readily accepted this amendment to his initial conclusion. Yet few advocates of new ideas would be so open-minded as the session chair, who is widely seen as one of the most promising police leaders in Britain. It is people like him who will make a key difference in how well evidence is understood, used, and defined.

In science, as in law, "evidence" is an objective finding that can be confirmed by repeated observations of independent observers and that can help to support a conclusion. Most people, as philosopher David Hume (1748) observed, find great difficulty in accepting that their own subjective impressions, hunches, prejudices, theories, or opinions are not objective evidence. As the late Senator Daniel P. Moynihan observed, "the plural of anecdote is not data." The rules of science and statistics require many complex procedures and conceptual tests in order to establish that evidence is reliable, including probability sampling, causal inference, selection bias, statistical power, confidence intervals, and many other challenges to deciding what is a "fact"—let alone whether the known facts can support a conclusion. The US Supreme Court in *Daubert v. Merrell Dow* (509 U.S. 579 [1993]) codified these principles into federal court procedures for admitting scientific evidence of all kinds.

At a more advanced level of understanding, the challenge is grasping the full breadth of decision-making processes for which good evidence is essential—including but not limited to targeting, testing, or tracking. To some critics, "evidence" is only about testing, or even just about randomized controlled trials. To baseball fans familiar with the *Moneyball* story of the Oakland Athletics team (Lewis 2003), it is all about targeting: hiring the most cost-effective baseball players by replacing experienced baseball scouts with computer geeks. To some observers of President Obama's "victory lab" (Issenberg 2012), better evidence means replacing intuitive political "gurus" with computerized "geeks" for tracking the delivery of more favorable voters to the polls.

These partial understandings of evidence-based practice converge on a single "straw man" caricature: that quantitative thinking beats—and should replace—qualitative judgment. Nothing could be further from the truth. As the doctors who helped develop evidence-based medicine argued, the best evidence is a blend of individual clinical experience with the best quantitative and qualitative "external" evidence: research findings and experience about similar cases or problems (Sackett et al. 1996). As baseball statistician Nate Silver (2012, p. 100) observed, two baseball players could have identical statistics, but one could spend his evenings volunteering at a homeless shelter while the other is snorting cocaine in nightclubs. He writes that "there is probably no way to *quantify* this distinction. But you'd sure as hell want to take it into account."

Similarly, if a police commander knows that a robbery hot spot has developed in a racially tense minority area (targeting) and that the average effect of doubling police patrols in robbery hot spots is to cut robbery 50 percent (testing), that is not enough evidence for a good decision. The commander would also think of many other qualitative factors, such as the recent or long history of police-community relations in that area, the extent to which stop-and-frisk would be used, the likely weather or school vacations, the availability of minority group officers to work in the area, and the track record or personality of a sergeant who would directly supervise any effort to double patrols. The commander might also wish to consult with neighborhood leaders on how best to bring in more patrols, perhaps with a handout flyer for police to give everyone they encounter on the streets—a practice for which there is experimental evidence from Australia (Mazerolle et al. 2013).

Evidence-based practice does not and cannot replace judgment based on experience. It can only inform such judgment, and usually improve it. Attempts to portray EBP as trying to replace rather than supplement experience (Sparrow 2011) are merely "noise" in relation to the signal. Not even baseball teams, as Silver (2012, pp. 105–6) points out, replaced qualitative scouts with quantitative geeks after the events depicted in *Moneyball* (Lewis 2003). Instead, baseball teams increased their investments in both, integrating qualitative and quantitative information supported by a profession-led science (see Weisburd and Neyroud 2011).

The body of knowledge supporting EBP embraces and incorporates police experience and craft skills. It does not replace traditional thinking about legality, legitimacy, and common sense. Nor does it replace the wisdom and experience of police professionals. What it adds to these assets is the crucial step of an objectivity check about questions that have often been answered on the basis of subjective opinions (Sherman 1998): is there any systematic, scientifically generated evidence that bears on the decisions we are about to make? Moreover, is the evidence the right kind of evidence for the decision?

While the meaning of the phrase "what works in policing" may seem obvious, it is not. Whether a prediction model "works" simply means whether its predictions are accurate; no randomized controlled experiment is needed. Whether GPS works to track police locations accurately is simply a matter of auditing by physical tests: there is no cause and effect relationship, just measurement reliability. Whether arrest for domestic violence works, however, is a matter of testing for cause and

effect. This means that in a controlled experiment, cases in which police made arrests would have to have had less repeat offending than in
cases in which police did not make arrests. That is why the Maryland
Scale of Scientific Methods, levels 1–5 (Sherman et al. 1998), is relevant
to testing police actions in triple-T but not to assessing the accuracy
of predictions for police targeting decisions. The Maryland scale is also
irrelevant for audits, measures, and descriptions intended for tracking
police performance. The best evidence for answering any question of
"what works" thus depends on "which T?"

Table 1 summarizes the different standards for good evidence of
"what works" for the three different Ts. The left-hand column shows
three different levels of strength of evidence, combining several key
dimensions: replications of evidence collection (for measurement reliability), consistency of findings (for content reliability), and—only in
the case of testing—the capacity of the research design to rule out
other causes besides the police practice being tested. These standards
are certainly subject to debate. But perhaps the bare minimum, rock-
bottom standard for EBP is this: a comparison group is essential to
every test to be included as "evidence" that a police decision causes a
certain result. That was the standard used for reporting on evidence
to the US Congress (Sherman 1998), and the global police profession
should arguably have standards that are at least as high or higher.

These distinctions illustrate the need for police professionals to raise
their game in mastering the (scientific) rules of evidence. What follows
is an overview of some of the key issues and of my ideas for addressing
them. Further readings of the sources cited would be useful for anyone
who proposes to use or, especially, produce evidence for policing.

B. Issues in Targeting Resources

The targeting of scarce resources can be compared to an investment
portfolio. Like police agencies, investors have a variety of objectives,
such as growth, income, and security. Like police, investors make a
variety of investments to accomplish different objectives. Like police,
investors face an endless array of choices about how to invest scarce
resources. But investors have one great advantage over police that
makes the investors' job much easier: a common currency. Police can
have a common currency as well, but only if they create it.

This subsection starts by describing a way in which police can guide
targeting decisions with a common currency of return on investment.

TABLE 1

"Good Evidence" Scales for Different Kinds of Police Decisions: Criteria for Strength of Evidence

Strength of Evidence	Kinds of Decisions		
	Targeting	Testing	Tracking
Strong	85% or greater accuracy of predictions in over 5,000 cases	Multiple random control trials producing similar findings in field settings	Monthly audits of measurement systems; less than 5% magnitude of error
Medium	60% or greater accuracy of predictions in over 1,000 cases	One random control trial, or 5–10 controlled quasi experiments with similar findings, in field settings	Annual audits of measurement systems; less than 5% magnitudes of error
Suggestive	Correlations without prospective tests of prediction accuracy	One or two before-after field tests with large effect sizes	Audit within past 3–5 years; less than 5% magnitude of error

It then shows how different methods of predicting returns of investment in that currency will produce much higher or lower rates of error
in making targeting decisions, including the new decision tool called
"predictive policing," as well as the neglected tool called "solvability
factors."

1. *A Crime Harm Index.* The biggest obstacle to reducing crime
may be the misleading way in which it is counted: as a raw summation
of all crimes, regardless of any differences in public views of the
seriousness of harm across crime categories (Rossi et al. 1974). From
Washington to London to Delhi, governments earnestly report
whether there were more "crimes" this year than last. This count of
the crime total treats every crime as equal.

All crimes are not created equal. Some crimes cause horrible injuries
and deaths. Others cause scant meaningful harm to anyone, such as
possessing a 1-inch joint of marijuana. Crime counts are dominated by
such high-volume but minor crimes as shoplifting from large chain
stores. In England and Wales, only 10 percent of reported crimes in
the 12 months to October 2012 included injury or a sex offense. Yet
public officials are pleased to report "success" when total crime drops
and displeased when total crime counts rise—even if murders, rapes,
and serious woundings stay constant. If EBP accepts this "fungibility
fallacy" that all crimes are equal, its value will be greatly restricted.

Police professionals are acutely sensitive to the idea that the weight
of harm from crime matters more than a raw count of incidents (Sherman 2011*a*). They know that a car theft is less harmful than a rape,
that a £5,000 fraud is less harmful than a stabbing. What they lack is
a way to account for these differences in combination across all crimes.
This would allow police to know whether total harm from crime in
one city is higher this year than last, higher in this part of town than
that, or with this offender's record compared to that one's.

The best way to compile meaningful "evidence" about reported
crime is to give each type of crime a weight that represents how harmful each type of crime is. Combining crime in this way would create
what statisticians call an "index," yielding a single bottom line. The
weight can be based on a variety of metrics. The simplest metric would
be taken from any sentencing guideline recommendations of the number of days in prison for a first offender convicted of that offense. This
would give an approximation of the "pure" weight of harm of the offense itself in contrast to the actual sentence length an offender may

receive—the latter being influenced by the number of prior convictions of the offender.

Summing the total weight for each type of any indicator (such as crime types), then adding the subtotal weights together, is the basis for a commonly used method of constructing an "index" of multiple indicators. A consumer price index (CPI), for example, takes the cost of consumer goods in different categories (food, housing, transportation) and then assigns a weight to those costs based on the average household's budget proportions for each category. If housing costs rise 10 percent but housing is only 33 percent of the family's budget, then the housing increase of 10 percent becomes a 3.3 percent increase in the total CPI. Similarly, a crime harm index (CHI) is a tool for creating just such a bottom line for the harm caused by crime (Sherman 2007, 2010, 2011*a*).

Weighting crimes on the basis of sentencing guidelines can be justified on good democratic grounds as reflecting the will of the people. Almost every sentencing guideline process in the United States and United Kingdom has reflected awareness of opinion polls, debates, and scrutiny by elected officials and news media. The scrutiny may not have been perfect. Yet it remains far closer to the will of the people than any theoretical or even empirical system of weighting that academics might develop. Most important, it is readily available to be applied to any set of crimes, whether for an individual, a community, or a nation.

Any police agency or government can construct its own index with the following seven steps:

1. counting up the number of crimes of each type in an area (or for one offender);
2. multiplying the count for each type by the median number of prison days recommended for crimes of that type by first offenders;
3. calling the product of that multiplication (crime count for a crime type × median days in prison) the HST for the crime type (for harm subtotal of days of prison for that offense type);
4. repeating steps 1, 2, and 3 for every type of crime recorded for the area or person;
5. summing up all HSTs to yield the total crime harm (TCH);
6. creating a standardized CHI for any *area or population* by dividing the estimated population size into the TCH to yield the

CHI in that time period for that area (where population size estimates should ideally include the average daily transient counts, such as [adjusted] arrivals minus departures by train and bus);

7. creating a standardized CHI for any *individual offender* by dividing the person's TCH by the number of years the person has been at risk of committing crime as an adult (usually since age 18), either removing days in prison or not, depending on data availability.

As an example of how a CHI works, consider a community (or an offender) with 100 crimes in the record. Assume that the recommended sentence for a shoplifting crime is 1 day in prison and that the recommended sentence for a first manslaughter is 10 years in prison, or 3,650 days. If all 100 crimes are shoplifting cases, the CHI value of those 100 crimes would be 100 days. If all 100 crimes are manslaughter cases, then the CHI value would be $10 \times 3,650 = 36,500$. In both cases the crime count is 100, but the range of CHI varies from 100 in the first example to 36,500 in the second. Which would tell voters more about how safe or dangerous their community is? By creating a more sensitive bottom line, a CHI can show much more transparently whether the harm from crime is higher or lower depending on the exact nature of the crimes.

To translate a CHI into an overall targeting plan, police leaders can simply use a checklist of possible targets to pick one or more ways of organizing a resource targeting strategy. Such a strategy can be based on hot spot places, convicted offenders, repeat victims, crime "recruiters" (see below), criminal networks, predicted crime patterns, times of day, days of the week, situations, or crime types. Any of these will do, as long as the analysis is comprehensive. That is, a CHI analysis of all of these units should encompass 100 percent of the CHI for the entire jurisdiction.

Perhaps the greatest value of a CHI would be in using it to forecast how much harm an individual offender, suspect, or defendant is likely to cause in the next 2 years. Such forecasts can help guide the massive use of police discretion to divert cases from prosecution into out-of-court penalties—constituting some 50 percent of all nontraffic penalties in England and Wales (Judge 2010). The legitimacy of policing could be enhanced by using these forecasts to reduce the risk of releasing a very dangerous offender who may, for example, soon murder someone. Such forecasting can provide missing evidence for the exist-ing system of "triage" in allocating scarce tax revenues for maximum public benefit.

The triage of targeting police resources embraces all police services. Better evidence can make the likely consequences of these hard choices clearer to those who must make them. A standard metric, such as a CHI, for predicting the benefit of one choice over another can make such evidence much easier to apply in practice.

2. *Good and Bad Predictions—or Forecasts.*   No matter what currency police use to target police resources, the evidence they need to make good decisions is a reliable forecast of future events. They may prefer to have a prediction, but predictions are far less reliable than forecasts. The difference between a forecast and a prediction is crucial, as the scientists who study earthquakes know to their cost. Silver (2012, p. 149) reports that in seismology,

1. a prediction is a definitive and specific statement about when and where an earthquake will strike: *a major earthquake will hit Kyoto, Japan on June 28.*
2. a forecast is a probabilistic statement, usually over a longer time scale: *there is a 60 percent chance of an earthquake in Southern California over the next thirty years.*

Silver notes that the official position of the US Geological Survey (USGS) is that earthquakes can be forecasted, but they cannot be pre-dicted.

Much the same can be said about evidence-based police targeting: it employs forecasting, not precise predictions, about when and where crimes are likely to occur. In the first published analysis of crime across every address in an entire city, for example, there were many instances in which there was a 100 percent chance of crime at a specific address every 10 days (Sherman, Gartin, and Buerger 1989). What the analysis did not do is to name a time and date when the next robbery would occur at a specific place—nor the name of the robber(s) or the vic-tim(s). This same approach allowed Weisburd, Groff, and Yang (2012) to undertake their remarkable forecasting of crimes over every street segment in Seattle for a 16-year period. This work, for the first time, identified different trajectories of crime by place, showing most kinds of places to have highly stable levels of crime (high, medium, or low), while others were highly variable.

Most crime forecasting takes the form of projecting the future on the basis of the past, or what might be called "post-casting" based on long time periods with stable estimates of risk. The time periods used to make a forecast this way can be 1–15 years; the future time window in which the forecast applies could be 6 months or a year. These forecasts have high levels of accuracy but low levels of precision: they cannot tell police exactly where and when the next crime will occur.

A newer approach may offer both precision and accuracy, at least for high-volume crime types. It uses more short-term analysis of changing crime patterns to make short-term forecasts about where crime concentrations will soon pop up. The originators of this approach, Bowers, Johnson, and Pease (2004), developed ways to forecast the location of burglary hot spots before they had even developed. Yet the method remained within the definition of a forecast rather than claiming to predict the exact date, time, and location of each crime.

By 2010, a new tool for targeting claimed to offer far more exact predictions. PredPol, the predictive policing company, sells police agencies proprietary software that identifies extremely tight bounding of time and place in which crime is predicted to occur. A *New York Times* story on the Santa Cruz field test reported the following: "Based on models for predicting aftershocks from earthquakes, [our equation] generates projections about which areas and windows of time are at highest risk for future crimes by analyzing and detecting patterns in years of past crime data. The projections are recalibrated daily, as new crimes occur and updated data is fed into the program" (Goode 2011). The fact that the USGS says that accurate earthquake prediction is not even possible provides little comfort for PredPol's reliance on earthquake models. At this writing no evidence is available for the accuracy of the forecasts or the crime reduction benefits of using them. But if such predictions do prove to have high reliability, they could make the targeting of police resources more valuable than ever.

What all these approaches offer, at least in principle, are empirical tests of the accuracy of the forecasts. The evolution of evidence-based policing will draw increasing attention to the results of those tests and no doubt compare crime predictions in ways similar to Silver's (2012) own comparisons of election forecasting by different polling companies. The bright line for evidence-based targeting lies not between forecasting and prediction but between quantitative methods and subjective judgments—also known as informed "guessing."

a. Three Methods of Targeting. There are three basic ways to make statements about future harm, whether predictions or forecasts: subjective or "clinical" methods, a checklist of tested factors, and "supercomputer" data mining based on large sample sizes.

By far the most common method is the subjective, intuitive, system I approach based on experience with similar situations (Kahneman 2011). The second method is a "checklist" approach that moves past experience from qualitative to quantitative analysis. It translates prior experience into a more systematic "algorithm" (the word statisticians prefer for a formula or equation) based on a few consistent criteria, forcing the forecaster to answer a checklist of weighted questions to make decisions about predictive factors found in large samples of previous cases. Crime solvability factors (Eck 1979) provide an example of the checklist approach. The third method requires the use of a supercomputer performing massive calculations about each individual case in relation to tens of thousands of similar but slightly different cases. Developed initially by meteorologists, such "data-mining" predictions use massive amounts of data on previous events to predict future events. It is especially useful in forecasting very rare events, such as hurricanes or homicides.

The primary published example of data mining in crime forecasting is the classification of likely murderers with huge samples of previous cases: over 30,000 in Philadelphia (Berk et al. 2009) and 100,000 in England and Wales (Sherman, Cosma, and Neyroud 2012). Like weather forecasting, individual forecasting of crime risks uses the recent growth in supercomputers to find highly specific combinations of predictors that raise the odds of fairly rare events occurring. The Philadelphia forecast identifies the offenders on probation who are most likely to be among the 2 percent of offenders on probation who are charged with murder 75 times more often than the 60 percent of probationers who are classified as low risk. The England and Wales models can correctly classify low-risk offenders with 96 percent accuracy, or 4 percent error in forecasting that they will not be convicted of a serious crime (Sherman, Cosma, and Neyroud 2012).

b. Clinical versus Statistical Predictions. Since at least the advent of Freudian theory, professionals such as psychiatrists have been paid well to make predictions about human behavior. These predictions have been based on detailed analysis of an individual's personality and previous behavior. The method has been highly respected. It is still used widely to decide whether violent people are insane or criminally responsible for their conduct. Many police agencies also use it to screen police recruits for mental health.

Since the advent of mechanical calculators, a far less expensive approach to prediction has been used by institutions dealing with large volumes of decisions. From insurance companies to university admissions offices, decisions have been made on the basis of classifying people by their numbers: how many accidents, how high a test score, what average grades, how many speeding violations, and so on. These characteristics can be recorded at much lower expense than the cost of having a professional personality assessment, while making exactly the same kind of predictions.

Until Meehl's (1954) comparison of these inexpensive statistical methods to the expensive clinical methods, no one had ever shown which method is more accurate. Since then, no research has ever contradicted his central conclusion. What Meehl found was that statistically validated predictions were always either more accurate than clinical prediction or—at worst—just as good, at a much lower cost. His book reviewed over 20 studies comparing subjective judgments of trained professionals to rather modest combinations of numerical information about the same people, organized according to a rule. Such rules are called algorithms. The statistical predictions based on algorithms in Meehl's comparison were very simple by modern standards, without extensive analysis. Nonetheless, they usually did better than predictions made on the same cases based only on open-ended interviews. Over 200 comparisons have now tested Meehl's conclusions on a wide range of behaviors and phenomena. In some 60 percent of comparisons, statistical forecasting does much better than clinical. In the rest, there is little difference, but statistics remain cheaper than qualitative data for the same accuracy rate (Kahneman 2011, p. 223). There is no convincing case in which clinical forecasting has beaten statistical forecasts.

Until recently this debate had no relevance to policing since police made little use of either kind of prediction in targeting their resources. Yet by the early twenty-first century, police on both sides of the Atlantic had invested in clinical prediction rather than in statistical forecasting. UK police developed national policies for clinical prediction of serious domestic violence cases, as well as risk assessments for sex offenders and other serious criminals. In the United States, problem-oriented policing picked targets more subjectively than systematically (Goldstein 1990). UK police employed entirely subjective criteria for determining which people released from prison were dangerous enough to justify an expensive Multi-Agency Public Protection Agreement for preventing serious crime.

The cost of subjective methods of crime forecasting often becomes apparent when they are audited against what really happens. An analysis of cases of domestic murder or attempted murder in one major UK police force did not find one case of serious injury committed by someone who was on the list of dangerous people; the lists of thousands of "dangerous" people had excluded all of the fewer than 100 actual attackers (Thornton 2011). Some might say that proves the success of the monitoring program; other might see it as evidence of vast overprediction. Most important, there had been no investment in preventing the attacks that ultimately occurred.

3. *Solvability Factors.* In principle, evidence-based solvability factors could substantially increase detection rates (Eck 1979). At minimum, their use could achieve the same detection rates but at much lower cost. This approach offers a major opportunity for evidence-based targeting. Yet it lacks a crucial piece of evidence that is needed to recommend their widespread adoption.

The most important new evidence about statistical solvability factors would be a randomized trial comparing the overall detection rates of a team of detectives using tested solvability factors to target cases for investigation to those of a team using unstructured discretion to target cases. By randomly assigning all incoming cases to one or the other of the two teams, the experiment would yield a valid estimate of using one system or the other. Even better, such an experiment could use a CHI to weight the value of the cases in the two teams resulting in prosecution. This would create an incentive for the investigators to use harm weightings in combination with solvability factors to decide which cases to investigate. The investigative results could then be compared by both the CHI weight of the crimes solved and the criminal record of the criminals accused.

C. Issues in Testing for Outcomes

Evidence-based policing requires a clear understanding of the difference between "trying" and "testing." Many police agencies say they have "evidence" that a police practice "works" because they have "tried" it. Yet in most cases, there is no good evidence gained from "piloting" a new practice or "trying it out." The minimal standards of evidence from the kind of test that should be used to guide policy require direct measurement of outputs and outcomes and direct comparison of those outcomes with a control group's outcomes. There is no better example than the case of the free chocolate.

1. *Trying versus Testing: The Chocolate Case.*   The Dorset (UK) police tried a very interesting idea in Bournemouth in the early twenty-first century, when all pubs still closed at 11:00 p.m. sharp. What happened between 11:00 and midnight each evening was reportedly a big spike in the hourly number of fights. Many fights happened while people were waiting in line at fish and chips shops, hungry for their first food after drinking beer for 5 or 6 hours. A creative police leader reasoned that this pattern—or problem, as Goldstein (1979) defined it—was caused by low blood sugar, making people more irritable. The Dorset police then tried handing out free chocolates to people waiting in line for their takeaway food. Media reports at the time quoted police saying the idea "worked."

This brilliant idea appears, however, never to have been tested at the standard required by evidence-based policing. I found no report of any counts of fights between 11:00 and midnight, either before or after the free chocolate policy. The first standard of a scientific test is that there be consistently defined and reliable measurement of both the problem to be solved—fights, in this case—and the solution itself—in this case, chocolate. As a public health doctor might ask, what was the dosage of chocolate handed out? How many individuals took the chocolate? How many ate it? How many nights a week was the chocolate handed out? Was it handed out equally at every fish and chips shop? If not, were there fewer fights where there was more chocolate? Over a long enough time period to constitute a statistically "powerful" test, by what percentage did the average number of fights in Bournemouth between 11:00 and midnight go down?

Even if all those questions of measurement were answered, however, there would still be no assurance that the chocolates had "worked" unless the second standard of a test were to be met: a fair comparison to a control group that did not receive the free chocolates. A control group could be selected from the central entertainment area of a similar city nearby, which would constitute a "level 3" test on the Maryland Scale of Scientific Methods (Sherman et al. 1998), the minimum level recommended for evidence on which to base policy. Even better would have been the identification of 100 fish and chips shops in Dorset's entertainment areas in multiple cities and towns, with 50 of them selected at random for the free chocolate treatment.

The distinction between "trying" and "testing" has become increasingly clear to police leaders, if not the rank and file, in the United States and United Kingdom over the past four decades. Yet the absolute comprehension level remains low. It is hard to teach these concepts to senior police leaders in a short conversation, even though they now feel obliged to discuss them as if they understand them perfectly. The concept of testing has not, until recently, been a part of police training, for leaders or street officers. But since 1996, the Cambridge University Institute of Criminology has been teaching these ideas to a large proportion of all the leaders who became chief constables. The success of that teaching has been far from perfect. But it is no accident that the UK police leadership spends far more time talking about the evidence for policies than US police leaders do.

What may work better than training is to have a much greater volume of experiments going on in police agencies than ever before. Since 2010, this has been happening in the United Kingdom if not in the United States. The downside of this development may be less rigor and care in the conduct of experiments, for reasons discussed below. These problems may be outweighed, however, by the increased awareness they promote of the difference between trying and testing: between evidence-free and evidence-based policing.

2. *What Works: Testing Practices, Using Tests.* There are two ways for police to find out whether a specific police practice is effective. One is to have someone look for relevant evidence in the growing police research repositories (see the Appendix). The other is for police to conduct tests in their own agencies.

In an ideal world, there would be so many tests of police services (as there are of medical services) that EBP would operate primarily by "looking up" tests rather than doing them. The EBP Matrix (Lum, Koper, and Telep 2010) and other tools already make it easy to do this. Other tools for easy "lookups" are under development, some of them designed for access via smart phones. The College of Policing may even develop the ideas of computerized medicine for instant access to relevant evidence (Hafner 2012).

In the foreseeable future, however, many expensive police services will remain untested. The costs of conducting tests are minimal in comparison to the costs of delivering untested services. And every time a police agency contributes a high-quality cost-effectiveness test to the global police literature, the entire world will gain.

Unlike such agencies as the UK National Health Service, police are not yet required to have randomized trials justify large portions of the police budget. But it would be major progress if at least 10 or 20 percent of a police operating budget could be based on good evidence. The most relevant question for any police leader is, "which of our services is so expensive and of such doubtful value that it is worthwhile to do our own local randomized controlled trial?"

a. Generalizability of Evidence.   There is also a scientific question of how reliably research in one police agency (or more) will predict effectiveness in any other agency. The present state of science cannot say whether one, 10, or even 20 strong tests are enough to generalize to all democracies, or even across the country where the tests were done. This problem is confounded by the wide range of results reported in such systematic reviews as the meta-analysis of the effects of hot spot policing (Braga, Papachristos, and Hureau 2012). While the average effect is beneficial, the range of effects is very great. Whether another agency implementing some form of hot spot policing will achieve a large or small effect remains highly uncertain from the available research.

The external validity of results is also challenged by the wide variety of practices tested, even under a common rubric like "hot spots policing." The range of specific police methods of policing included in that review is almost as great as the range of effect sizes (Braga, Papachristos, and Hureau 2012). While the review is nonetheless a major contribution to the literature, the wide range of research designs unavoidably strains the scientific definition of "replication" on which the statistical procedures are premised. For example, while the hot spot review found 11 randomized trials of hot spot policing (and more have been finished since), only one of them tested a substantial increase in marked car patrols in street corner hot spots. Other designs are of interest. But for a police leader considering a 100 percent increase in hot spot patrols at street corners, any other design is a different research question.

For the foreseeable future, the best evidence on outcomes police agencies can get will come from conducting their own experiments.

Most readers may wonder whether that idea is feasible or is a fantasy. The answer depends entirely on who does the experiments: who designs them, leads them, and analyzes them. Those tasks have been the traditional domain of police scholars, with police practitioners as their partners. Yet a rapidly growing appetite for good evidence will soon swamp the available numbers of experimental criminologists unless they reinvent their partnerships with policing.

b. Who Shall Test: The Police Themselves? From 1970 until 2010, police testing was largely orchestrated by academics in universities who had found police chiefs to partner with them. The experiments typically involved large grants from foundations or national governments' research agencies (US National Institute of Justice, UK Home Office, Australian Research Council). These grants usually provided for well-trained and closely supervised doctoral students to work with police in the delivery and measurement of the experimental variables, ensuring independent quality control and monitoring of the data collection. Senior academics would then analyze the data and write the report. Since the number of academics interested in doing all this work was limited, the maximum number of experiments was limited by human resources as much as by the tiny overall funding stream for such experiments.

Since around 2010, both funding and leadership barriers have started to fall. Funding has been increasingly provided by police agencies, subsidized by universities teaching police executives. The leadership of police experiments has been moving from professors to "pracademics," as police practitioner-academics increasingly describe themselves (e.g., Mitchell 2012). While professional research scientists still play a strong role in designing and analyzing police experiments, more of the massive labor of organizing people to deliver good experiments is being shouldered by experienced police (e.g., Telep, Mitchell, and Weisburd 2012). Many pracademics are launched on a path to earn a doctoral degree, some in midcareer and some retired after 30 years in policing. Whatever their background, they are rapidly increasing the numbers of people who can produce good evidence on policing.

This change is especially visible in the United Kingdom, where Cambridge graduates form a critical mass to pioneer the new model for testing police practices. This model has made possible a far greater volume of experimentation because police officers from sergeant to police chief have designed and delivered their own experiments. This benefit must be weighed against important issues of quality control in the integrity of the random assignment, the measures of outcomes, and other important issues. Even innovative solutions like an online "randomizer" (Ariel, Vila, and Sherman 2012) may pose surprising errors unless the experiment is closely monitored by a site manager (Neyroud and Slothower 2013).

D. Issues in Tracking Police Outputs and Outcomes

Three key issues shape the growth of tracking police outputs and outcomes. One is how police leaders measure what police officers do. A second is how they compare measures of performance across officers and units. The third is how they use tracking data to deliver better policing by evidence-based management.

1. *Measuring What Police Do.*   For all the progress that COMPSTAT has brought policing, it is striking how little measurement it has used of what police do. In 1999–2005, for example, the Philadelphia Police Department's COMPSTAT never reviewed data on where police patrolled, where they made arrests, where they conducted stop-and-frisks, or even how many police were scheduled to work by time or day in relation to the hourly frequency of crime in any police district. In social science terms, COMPSTAT was a discussion of dependent variables without any review of independent variables. They discussed crime patterns endlessly each week, with rarely any evidence on policing.

Since then, technologies such as GPS have made such measurement even easier. All that is required is a commitment to tracking policing along with crime and an investment in information technology to produce the data and graphics. Mapping police presence in relation to crime harm, for example, would produce an algorithm that could identify outliers. Wherever a patrol district deployed its patrols (or arrests) in too great a departure from the occurrence of crime, a list of such "exceptions" can be generated for police managers. If they fail to correct the discrepancies, the lists can be reviewed in aggregate at COMPSTAT meetings.

2. *Comparing Police Performance.*   One reason police activity is undermeasured may be the risk of making inappropriate comparisons with disciplinary implications. The number of arrests per officer, for example, is likely to be much higher in certain areas than in others, if only because there is more crime per square foot in some areas. Yet

there are many ways to adjust for these differences in order to create fair comparisons across officers and units.

The critical tool for fair comparisons is a *risk model for each policing area*. Such a model can be computed on the basis of any large sample, such as the hundreds of local policing areas in England and Wales. The models can address both police outputs and outcomes. Using social, economic, and demographic data, the models can forecast how much work police will be asked to do reactively by citizens and how much work they may choose to initiate proactively in relation to social conditions. The models can estimate how many calls will be dispatched, how many arrests may be made, and even how much force police will use with how much injury to citizens and police.

Once a risk model is found to be reliable in forecasting outputs or outcomes, it can detect major changes in delivery of those measures over what was predicted. If police produce more proactive work than predicted or less, the model can say so. This could be done in a way that could confirm or disprove the success of an area commander in delivering specific changes in police patrols, arrests, problems solved, or any objective for police outputs.

The greatest benefit of a fair comparisons model would be to link changes in outputs to changes in crime harm (CHI). Within a range of error, these models can forecast the likely CHI (or CHI per capita) in each area for each year. If a change in outputs appears linked to changes in CHI outcomes, then police leaders can begin to develop skill in relating these two tools at a strategic level. In contrast, if there is no change in outputs but the CHI gets worse, that can be taken as evidence of sudden changes in social conditions rather than as a failure of policing. If police outputs worsen and the CHI rises, that can be taken as evidence that police failures actually caused an increase in harm.

This kind of macro-level strategic management is already the substance of discussion in many COMPSTAT meetings. What it lacks is any kind of evidence base. There are a few published studies, for example, of the effect of the ratio of arrests to crime (output) on crime rates (outcome) themselves (Tittle and Rowe 1974; Brown 1978; Chamlin 1991), but they would quickly be replaced by current studies within large police agencies. Better evidence could lead to better strategic decisions, with less crime harm as a result.

3. *Delivering Policing with Evidence-Based Management.* The great-

est value of measuring police performance comes from leaders taking immediate corrective action. All too often, police leaders are flying blind about whether policies or operations are being implemented. Tracking evidence provides independent audits on a timely basis about whether the plans are being delivered. If they are not, then commanders can be transferred and tighter control can be imposed. If they are, then rewards can be given and medals can be pinned.

The use of tracking to focus on implementation can have major consequences. For example, there is much controversy about whether stop-and-questioning in minority areas reduces crime. By using tracking evidence for deciding whether stop-and-question has been reducing robberies in minority group areas, a police leader can ask to have stop-and-question encounters plotted against robberies. If the answer is that very few stops have actually been done, the leader can take stronger action to ensure that the policy is carried out. If the policy has been delivered, the leader can ask what level of crime reduction is needed to be cost-effective. At the same time, tracking may raise the question of police legitimacy. Are complaints up since stops have increased? Are public surveys needed? Should people who have been stopped be interviewed to assess their reactions? Should training be refreshed on how to speak to suspects? Tracking can often raise questions that would otherwise never be asked. Asking them could, in turn, substantially improve service delivery.

Tracking methods can even be subjected to testing for outcomes. In a Dallas experiment, for example, Weisburd, Groff, and Yang (2012) randomly assigned GPS information to some middle managers (and not others) showing how much time officers were spending in their assigned hot spots. The experiment suggested that the assignment of that information led to less crime in the high-crime hot spots. Other experiments with tracking systems could profitably use similar designs across police districts, across patrol beats, or even (in large police agencies such as India's or Chile's with hundreds of police stations) across police districts themselves.

E. Connecting the Three Ts

Thinking of triple-T as a triangle may allow police leaders to think about evidence in a more integrated way. Agencies can use the triangle to design checklists of all the numbers that must be examined simultaneously in EBP. Like the pilots who look at all the dials on the

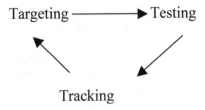

Targeting ⟶ Testing

Tracking

FIG. 2.—The dynamic process of triple-T

dashboard of a B-747 cockpit, police leaders must be aware of multiple sources of threat to smooth performance. When all three Ts are able to be seen at once, the combined triple-T can become a dynamic process: targets can be adjusted as crime goes down on some targets and rises on others, tested treatments can change as the types of targets shift, and tracking may look at different delivery indicators as both targets and practices shift (fig. 2). No police agency stands still for a day, let alone for a 3-year plan. Triple-T is a *plan for a plan*, for a constantly updated plan, one that keeps changing as the facts change (O'Connor 2012).

Connecting the Ts may be the best response to a major challenge to EBP: quantitatively derived conclusions are often hard to sell. When the conclusion directly challenges conventional thinking, acceptance of evidence requires nothing less than a culture change. This phenomenon has been observed repeatedly in medicine (Giluk and Rynes-Weller 2012), baseball (Lewis 2003), and politics (Issenberg 2012). Yet these cases also offer much hope that experience and evidence can work together (Silver 2012, chap. 3). That is what can happen to make culture change more likely to succeed. The open window may be a need to cut budgets and to do more with less.

By connecting policy decisions on tested services with policy decisions on what to target, police leaders can develop a clear dialogue about hard choices. Operational police may accuse them of "robbing Peter to pay Paul," as if all priorities are of equal importance. But the use of evidence to make those decisions can disprove that claim. By combining the seriousness of the harm being targeted with the effectiveness of the police practice being considered for a target, police leaders can compare two different choices for their likely cost-benefit ratios. If spending $10,000 can yield a 25 percent reduction in the harm of a robbery pattern but only a 10 percent reduction in the harm of a burglary pattern, the better choice may seem obvious. It is not. The key evidence in such a choice would be the absolute levels of harm associated with the burglary pattern and the robbery pattern. Creating or using such a metric is not routinely done in EBP—yet. But it could be the key to pulling triple-T into a viable operating system. That key is the idea of a crime harm index, which may ultimately be the key to sustaining EBP.

IV. Future Prospects for Evidence in Policing

> The best way to predict your future is to create it.
> (Attributed to Abraham Lincoln)

By 2013, more people than ever before were trying to create the future of evidence-based policing. The Society of Evidence-Based Policing had over 600 members. The new professional College of Policing had a mandate from the UK government to develop and share "evidence on what works in policing." The George Mason University Center for Evidence-Based Crime Policy joined with the Scottish Institute of Police Research to communicate EBP to policy makers in Washington. Newly elected police and crime commissioners in England and Wales organized an all-day seminar at Cambridge University to gain an introduction to the evidence on policing. Over 75 percent of senior leaders at Scotland Yard said they had at least heard of EBP (Stanko 2013).

Yet the same study at Scotland Yard found that 20 percent of its leaders said they would not change a policy if the evidence showed it did not work (Stanko 2013). Many, if not most, operational police officers remained skeptical that research could help improve policing. Laws in the majority of US states, as of 2013, still required police to make arrests when evidence shows that they would only increase crime rather than prevent it (Sherman 1992a). Evidence-based policing in 2013 still had a long way to go. As Kahneman (2011) and others have documented, our intuitive preference for "fast thinking" with an emotional system I will always cause resistance to conclusions based on more comprehensive "slow thinking" by our system II reasoning. Which system will win depends on a larger cultural struggle for the "branding" of policing as a complex profession.

For those who take Lincoln's advice seriously, it may be useful to suggest 10 ways to create a stronger future for using evidence in policing. The suggestions are speculations, informed by a deep engagement in the context: the kind of experience that is essential for making the best use of evidence. The suggestions aim at institutional decisions as the outcomes. But they are also aimed at the individuals whose actions can make institutions change their policies.

The key institutions are the College of Policing in the United Kingdom, the state Police Officer Standards and Training Boards in the United States, the Australian Institute for Police Management, and the Australia New Zealand Policing Advisory Agency. These are all professionally driven institutions with governmental funding capable of making substantial changes in the incentives and organizational culture for better use of research evidence. Until recently they were largely unconnected to the academic community. But the invention of a new professional body in the cradle of Anglo-Celtic policing is committed to forging that connection, with a working agenda for police-university relationships. It is not impossible that professional bodies in other countries may follow suit. Unless otherwise indicated, each suggestion below is aimed at the institutions named above.

1. *A graduate-level education in evidence-based policing should be required for all chief police executives.* Starting at the top is a path of least resistance from police labor organizations and an ideal first step toward a "total evidence" strategy of the kind Scotland Yard has adopted. Police Commissioner Sir Bernard Hogan-Howe, who approved that plan, not only has a master of business administration and a law degree but also completed the graduate-level Cambridge Police Executive Programme that teaches evidence in policing.

2. *A graduate-level knowledge of evidence-based policing should be required for all police managers at ranks equivalent to chief inspectors in UK policing and captains in the New York or Los Angeles police.* An early second step toward a culture of evidence in policing would be to focus ambitious officers on the first major step to police command. Knowing that research evidence is constantly growing could foster a habit of keeping up, a habit that may continue even after completing a degree or taking an exam, or doing whatever is established as the requirement for promotion to that level. Most important may be the substantial impact this requirement would have on the demand for graduate education.

3. *Promotion to first-line supervision (e.g., sergeant) should be based in equal parts on knowledge of the law and of the evidence on what works in*

policing. Perhaps some time after the first two suggestions are adopted, a cultural familiarity with EBP will ease a transition to changing the content of promotional examinations. Once knowledge of evidence becomes essential for any promotion at all in policing, it will greatly broaden the incentive to study evidence and use it in police operational decisions. Research could even be cited in arrest reports and court testimony, thereby promoting a stronger public image of the complex knowledge police must master.

4. *Completion of probation at the end of police recruit training should be based on an examination that includes equal parts on knowledge of the law and of the evidence on what works in policing.* Once EBP becomes an expected part of promotional examinations, it will be less difficult to add it to the final requirement for permanent police officer status (if that concept itself survives). It will also enhance the use of evidence in police operations since officers at all rank levels would then be tested on their knowledge. It would also mean that research evidence would have to be taught in police recruit schools.

5. *Police professionals at all ranks should be able to achieve international certification of advanced knowledge by an exam-based Fellowship of the College of Policing (to be designated an FCP).* The practice of advanced testing of highly skilled practitioners is well established in medicine and other professions; US doctors have an equivalent process of becoming board certified. Since the sixteenth century, British professional colleges have been administering such examinations and certifying knowledge for people from all over the world. Online educational preparation will make such examinations even easier to pass, providing free access to knowledge worldwide.

6. *Universities should create faculties of policing that would eventually operate like medical schools.* The growth of demand for police evidence requires far greater commitment by universities to this kind of public service. The rise of "pracademics" makes it even more important since the technical support they need to do experiments at a high standard will grow rapidly.

7. *Academic positions in faculties of policing should include "clinical" lectureships and professorships modeled on those in medical schools, in which academics split their time equally between working on police operational matters and teaching-research activity in the university.* By investing in partial funding of clinical professorships, police agencies or the institutions

named above could speed up the process of creating more police faculties.

8. *Promotion to senior police posts, as with senior medical positions, should require demonstrated achievements in research and teaching within the profession.* This suggestion builds on the recommendations of the UK Home Secretary (May 2012). It could be achieved with evidence of publications in peer-reviewed journals or teaching in university faculties or police training institutions.

9. *The College of Policing (UK) should create a global example of a process for approving and recommending evidence-based police practices, engaging police leaders at all ranks with researchers, victims, and others affected by police policies in deciding what works, when, and for whom.* The transparency of evidence is a hallmark of science, just as openness to public demands is a hallmark of policing. The model of the process used by the United Kingdom's National Institute for Health and Clinical Evidence is one that can be widely adopted (Sherman 2009).

10. *Every nation should develop its own inventory of evidence-based practices, based on its own domestic police research, international research, approved practices of the College of Policing, and a list of similar institutions in other nations.* Once a process is adopted to review evidence for policy decisions, the dearth of such evidence in most countries will become clear. There is no point in American police research providing the only evidence for policing in New Zealand, India, or Hong Kong. Each and every country may have its own social and cultural context that affects the transportability of evidence of what works. The only way to be certain of how police practices work in each country is to test those practices in that country.

Since the twenty-first century began, the pace at which police use evidence has grown geometrically. That pace could still slow, reverse, or be crippled by a hijacking of the meaning of "evidence" in police practice. But if even half the suggestions offered here are adopted, evidence-based policing will continue to grow. That trend may ultimately provide many tangible benefits to police officers, making their work more legitimate and meaningful. A majority of neither police nor the public may ever accept or even understand the benefits of evidence, but popularity is not the right test for the success of EBP. The sole test is whether it benefits the public. All the evidence suggests that it will.

APPENDIX

The resources for locating external tests of police services are growing rapidly. In the past decade, the Campbell Collaboration (hosted by the Norwegian government) has completed over 20 systematic reviews of multiple tests of practices relevant to crime and policing. A "systematic review" in this context is a comprehensive inventory of all possible tests of a specific practice, which then examines the pattern of results to conclude whether the program is effective where it has already been tested. The results in other countries do not necessarily predict results in all countries. But the information in these reviews is highly detailed, reporting exactly where the tests were done and how. Reviews are in PDF files that can be downloaded for free from http://www .campbellcollaboration.org. As of late 2012, the reviews included such police services or issues as problem-oriented policing, hot spots policing, focused deterrence, second responders to domestic violence cases, gun crime prevention patrols, effects of DNA testing on detection rates, community-oriented policing, legitimacy in policing, "broken windows" policing, and crime displacement from place-targeted crime prevention programs.

A second resource is less rigorous and comprehensive within subjects but has broader coverage of topics and tested police services: the US Department of Justice website at http://www.crimesolutions.gov. This site provides an accessible, test-by-test summary of what was tested and how.

A bolder model of retrieving police field tests is the EBP Matrix posted at George Mason University in Virginia, with over 100 tests that can be retrieved by a point-and-click scan of the study summaries represented as dots on the matrix (Lum, Koper, and Telep 2010). This matrix can be found at http:// gemini.gmu.edu/cebcp/matrix.html. It is accessible on three dimensions: scope of target (individuals to nation), specificity of police service (general to specific), and proactivity of police service (from citizen-initiated to police-initiated).

REFERENCES

Angel, Caroline M. 2005. "Crime Victims Meet Their Offenders: Testing the Impact of Restorative Justice Conferences on Victims' Post-traumatic Stress Symptoms." PhD dissertation, University of Pennsylvania, Department of Criminology and School of Nursing.

Ariel, B., J. Vila, and L. Sherman. 2012. "Random Assignment without Tears: How to Stop Worrying and Love the Cambridge Randomizer." *Journal of Experimental Criminology* 8(2):1–16. DOI: 10.1007/s11292-012-9141-4.

Banton, Michael. 1964. *The Policeman in the Community*. London: Tavistock.

Bennett, Trevor, Katy Holloway, and David P. Farrington. 2006. "Does Neighborhood Watch Reduce Crime? A Systematic Review and Meta-Analysis." *Journal of Experimental Criminology* 2:437–58.

Berk, Richard A., Alec Campbell, Ruth Klap, and Bruce Western. 1992. "The Deterrent Effect of Arrest in Incidents of Domestic Violence: A Bayesian Analysis of Four Field Experiments." *American Sociological Review* 57:698–708.

Berk, Richard A., Lawrence W. Sherman, G. Barnes, E. Kurtz, and L. Ahlman. 2009. "Forecasting Murder within a Population of Probationers and Parolees: A High Stakes Application of Statistical Learning." *Journal of the Royal Statistical Society: Series A, Statistics in Society* 172:191–211.

Berkow, Michael. 2011. Lecture to the National Police Academy, Hyderabad, India, June 10.

Blumstein, Alfred, Jacqueline Cohen, Jeffrey A. Roth, and Daniel Nagin. 1986. *Criminal Careers and "Career Criminals."* Washington, DC: National Academies Press.

Bottoms, Anthony, and Justice Tankebe. 2012. "Beyond Procedural Justice: A Dialogic Approach to Legitimacy in Criminal Justice." *Journal of Criminal Law and Criminology* 102:119–253.

Bowers, Kate, Shane Johnson, and Ken Pease. 2004. "Prospective Hot-Spotting: The Future of Crime Mapping?" *British Journal of Criminology* 44(5): 641–58.

Braga, Anthony A., Andrew V. Papachristos, and David M. Hureau. 2012. "The Effects of Hot Spots Policing on Crime: An Updated Systematic Review and Meta-Analysis." Campbell Systematic Reviews 2012:8. DOI: 10.4073/csr .2012.8.

Braga, Anthony A., and David L. Weisburd. 2010. *Policing Problem Places.* New York: Oxford University Press.

———. 2012. "The Effects of Focused Deterrence Strategies on Crime: A Systematic Review and Meta-Analysis of the Empirical Evidence." *Journal of Research in Crime and Delinquency* 49(3):323–58.

Bratton, William J. 1998. *Turnaround: How America's Top Cop Reversed the Crime Epidemic.* New York: Random House.

Brown, Don W. 1978. "Arrest Rates and Crime Rates: When Does a Tipping Effect Occur?" *Social Forces* 57:671–82.

Buerger, Michael E. 1993. "Convincing the Recalcitrant: An Examination of the Minneapolis RECAP Experiment." PhD dissertation, Rutgers University, School of Criminal Justice.

Chamlin, Mitchell B. 1991. "A Longitudinal Analysis of the Arrest-Crime Relationship: A Further Examination of the Tipping Effect." *Justice Quarterly* 8:187–99.

Christopher, Warren, ed. 1991. *Report of the Independent Commission on the Los Angeles Police Department.* Los Angeles: Diane Publishing.

Cohn, Ellen G. 1993. "The Prediction of Police Calls for Service: The Influence of Weather and Temporal Variables on Rape and Domestic Violence." *Journal of Environmental Psychology* 13:71–83.

Collins, Randall. 2004. *Interaction Ritual Chains.* Princeton, NJ: Princeton University Press.

Croft, Elizabeth B. 1985. "Police Use of Force: An Empirical Analysis." PhD dissertation, State University of New York at Albany, School of Criminal Justice.

Davis, Robert C., David Weisburd, and Bruce Taylor. 2008. "Effects of Second Responder Programs on Repeat Incidents of Family Abuse." Campbell Systematic Reviews 2008:15. DOI: 10.4073/csr.2008.15.

Dunford, Franklyn W. 1990. "System-Initiated Warrants for Suspects of Misdemeanor Domestic Assault: A Pilot Study." *Justice Quarterly* 7(4):631–53.

Eck, John E. 1979. *Managing Case Assignments: The Burglary Investigation Decision Model Replication.* Washington, DC: Police Executive Research Forum.

Englefield, Ashley E. 2013. M.St. thesis, Cambridge University, Institute of Criminology.

Eyle, Alexandra. 2001–2. "Mayor Rocky Anderson Talks about What It's Like to . . . Drop the D.A.R.E. Program." *Reconsider Quarterly* 1(4):12–13.

Farrar, Tony. 2013. M.St. Thesis, Cambridge University, Institute of Criminology.

Farrell, Graham. 1995. "Preventing Repeat Victimization." In *Building a Safer Society: Strategic Approaches to Crime Prevention*, edited by Michael Tonry and David P. Farrington. Vol. 19 of *Crime and Justice: A Review of Research*, edited by Michael Tonry. Chicago: University of Chicago Press.

Ferraro, Kathleen J. 1989. "Policing Woman Battering." *Social Problems* 36:61–74.

Foa, Edna. 1997. "Trauma and Women: Course, Predictors, and Treatment." *Journal of Clinical Psychiatry* 58:25–28.

Fyfe, James J. 1980. "Administrative Interventions on Police Shooting Discretion: An Empirical Examination." *Journal of Criminal Justice* 7(4):309–23.

———. 1982. "Blind Justice: Police Shootings in Memphis." *Journal of Criminal Law and Criminology* 73(2):707–22.

Giluk, Tamara L., and Sara Rynes-Weller. 2012. "Research Findings Practitioners Resist: Lessons for Management Academics from Evidence-Based Medicine." In *The Oxford Handbook of Evidence-Based Management*, edited by Denise M. Rousseau. New York: Oxford University Press.

Glaser, Barney, and Anselm Straus. 1967. *The Discovery of Grounded Theory.* New York: Aldine.

Goldstein, Herman. 1979. "Improving Policing: A Problem-Oriented Approach." *Crime and Delinquency* 25:236–58.

———. 1990. *Problem-Oriented Policing.* New York: McGraw-Hill.

Goode, Erica. 2011. "Sending the Police before There's a Crime." *New York Times*, August 15. http://www.nytimes.com/2011/08/16/us/16police.html?_r=0.

Greenberg, Bernard, and Karen Lang. 1973. *Enhancement of the Investigative Function.* Vol. 4, *Burglary Investigative Checklist and Handbook.* Stanford, CA: Stanford Research Institute.

Greenwood, Peter, and Joan Petersilia. 1975. *The Criminal Investigation Process.* Santa Monica, CA: RAND.

Hafner, Katie. 2012. "For Second Opinion, Consult a Computer?" *New York*

Times, December 3. http://www.nytimes.com/2012/12/04/health/quest-to-eliminate-diagnostic-lapses.html?pagewanted = all&_r = 0.

Her Majesty's Inspectorate of Constabulary. 2010. *Valuing the Police: Policing in an Age of Austerity*. London: Her Majesty's Inspectorate of Constabulary.

Howarth, David M. P. 2010. Address to the Third Cambridge-NPIA International Conference on Evidence-Based Policing. Cambridge University, July 4.

Hume, David. 1748. *An Enquiry Concerning Human Understanding*. http://www.gutenberg.org/.

Issenberg, Sasha. 2012. *The Victory Lab: The Secret Science of Winning Campaigns*. New York: Crown.

Jackson, Jonathan, and Ben Bradford. 2009. "Crime, Policing and Social Order: On the Expressive Nature of Public Confidence in Policing." *British Journal of Sociology* 60(3):493–521.

Johnson, Shane D., and Kate J. Bowers. 2004. "The Burglary as Clue to the Future: The Beginnings of Prospective Hot-Spotting." *European Journal of Criminology* 1:237–55.

Johnson, Steven Berlin. 2001. *Emergence: The Connected Lives of Ants, Brains, Cities, and Software*. New York: Scribners.

———. 2010. *Where Good Ideas Come From: The Natural History of Innovation*. New York: Riverside.

Judge, Igor. 2010. "Summary Justice In and Out of Court: The Police Foundation's John Harris Memorial Lecture." Lecture presented at Draper's Hall, London, July 7. http://www.judiciary.gov.uk/Resources/JCO/Documents/Speeches/lcj-speech-john-harris-lecture.pdf.

Kahneman, D. 2011. *Thinking, Fast and Slow*. New York: Farrar, Straus & Giroux.

Kansas City Police Department. 1977. *Response Time Analysis: Executive Summary*. Kansas City: Kansas City Police Department.

Kelling, George L., Antony Pate, Duane Dieckman, and Charles E. Brown. 1974. *The Kansas City Preventive Patrol Experiment: A Summary Report*. Washington, DC: Police Foundation.

Kelling, George L., Antony Pate, Amy Ferrara, Mary Utne, and Charles E. Brown. 1981. *The Newark Foot Patrol Experiment*. Washington, DC: Police Foundation.

Kennedy, David M. 2008. *Deterrence and Crime Prevention*. London: Routledge.

———. 2011. *Don't Shoot: One Man, a Street Fellowship, and the End of Violence in Inner-City America*. New York: Bloomsbury.

Koper, Christopher S. 1995. "Just Enough Police Presence: Reducing Crime and Disorderly Behavior by Optimizing Patrol Time in Crime Hot Spots." *Justice Quarterly* 12:649–72.

Koper, Christopher S., and Evan Mayo-Wilson. 2006. "Police Crackdowns on Illegal Gun Carrying: A Systematic Review of Their Impact on Gun Crime." *Journal of Experimental Criminology* 2:227–61.

Kubrin, Charis E., Steven F. Messner, Glenn Deane, Kelly McGeever, and

Thomas D. Stucky. 2010. "Proactive Policing and Robbery Rates across US Cities." *Criminology* 48:57–97.

LaFave, Wayne. 1965. *Arrest: The Decision to Take a Suspect into Custody.* Boston: Little, Brown.

Larson, Richard C. 1976. "What Happened to Patrol Operations in Kansas City? A Review of the Kansas City Preventive Patrol Experiment." *Journal of Criminal Justice* 3:267–97.

Lewis, Michael. 2003. *Moneyball: The Art of Winning an Unfair Game.* New York: Norton.

Lum, Cynthia, Christopher S. Koper, and Cody D. Telep. 2010. "The Evidence-Based Policing Matrix." *Journal of Experimental Criminology* 7:3–26.

Manning, Peter K. 1992. "Information Technologies and the Police." In *Modern Policing*, edited by Michael Tonry and Norval Morris. Vol. 15 of *Crime and Justice: A Review of Research*, edited by Michael Tonry. Chicago: University of Chicago Press.

Maple, Jack. 1999. *The Crime Fighter: How You Can Make Our Community Crime-Free.* New York: Doubleday.

Martin, Susan E., and Lawrence W. Sherman. 1986. "Selective Apprehension: A Police Strategy for Repeat Offenders." *Criminology* 24:155–73.

May, T. 2012. Speech by the Home Secretary to the Police Superintendents' Association Conference, September 11. http://www.homeoffice.gov.uk /media-centre/speeches/supers2012?version=2.

Mazerolle, Lorraine, Emma Antrobus, Sarah Bennett, and Tom R. Tyler. 2013. "Shaping Citizen Perceptions of Police Legitimacy: A Randomized Field Trial of Procedural Justice." *Criminology* 51:33–63.

McEwen, Thomas, Edward F. Connors, and Marcia Cohen. 1986. *Evaluation of the Differential Police Response Field Test.* Washington, DC: National Institute of Justice.

Meehl, Paul E. 1954. *Clinical vs. Statistical Prediction: A Theoretical Analysis and a Review of the Evidence.* Minneapolis: University of Minnesota Press.

Millenson, M. 1997. *Demanding Medical Excellence: Doctors and Accountability in the Information Age.* Chicago: University of Chicago Press.

Mitchell, Renee. 2012. Presentation to the Cambridge Police Executive Programme, April 17.

Monkkonen, Eric H. 1992. "History of Urban Police." In *Modern Policing*, edited by Michael Tonry and Norval Morris. Vol. 15 of *Crime and Justice: A Review of Research*, edited by Michael Tonry. Chicago: University of Chicago Press.

Murray, Alexander. 2009. M.St. thesis, University of Cambridge, Institute of Criminology.

Nevin, Rick. 2000. "How Lead Exposure Relates to Temporal Changes in IQ, Violent Crime, and Unwed Pregnancy." *Environmental Research* 83:1–22.

Neyroud, Peter, and Molly Slothower. 2013. *Operation Turning Point: Progress Report.* Cambridge: Jerry Lee Centre of Experimental Criminology, Institute of Criminology, University of Cambridge.

O'Connor, Denis. 2012. Lecture to the Cambridge Police Executive Programme, Institute of Criminology, University of Cambridge, September.

Parkinson, John. 2013. M.St. thesis, University of Cambridge, Institute of Criminology.

Pate, Antony M., and Edwin E. Hamilton. 1992. "Formal and Informal Deterrents to Domestic Violence: The Dade County Spouse Assault Experiment." *American Sociological Review* 57:691–97.

Pease, Ken. 1998. "Repeat Victimisation: Taking Stock." Crime Detection and Prevention Series Paper 90. London: Home Office.

Perry, Cheryl L., Kelli A. Komro, Sara Veblen-Mortenson, Linda M. Bosma, Kian Farbakhsh, Karen A. Munson, Melissa H. Stigler, and Leslie A. Lytle. 2003. "A Randomized Controlled Trial of the Middle and Junior High School DARE and DARE Plus Programs." *Archives of Pediatrics and Adolescent Medicine* 157:178–84.

Petrosino, Anthony, Carolyn Turpin-Petrosino, and Sarah Guckenburg. 2010. "Formal System Processing of Juveniles: Effects on Delinquency." Campbell Systematic Reviews 2010:1. DOI: 10.4073/csr.2010.1.

Pittet, Didier, and John M. Boyce. 2001. "Hand Hygiene and Patient Care: Pursuing the Semmelweis Legacy." *Lancet Infectious Diseases* 1:9–20.

Police Executive Research Forum. 2008. *Violent Crime in America: What We Know about Hot Spots Enforcement*. Washington, DC: Police Executive Research Forum.

President's Commission on Law Enforcement and Administration of Justice. 1967. *Task Force Report: The Police*. Washington, DC: US Government Printing Office.

Ratcliffe, Jerry H., Travis Taniguchi, Elizabeth R. Groff, and Jennifer D. Wood. 2011. "The Philadelphia Foot Patrol Experiment: A Randomized Controlled Trial of Police Patrol Effectiveness in Violent Crime Hotspots." *Criminology* 49:795–831.

Reaves, Brian. 2010. *Local Police Departments, 2007*. Washington, DC: Bureau of Justice Statistics, Office of Justice Programs, US Department of Justice.

Reiss, Albert J., Jr. 1971. *The Police and the Public*. New Haven, CT: Yale University Press.

———. 1988. "Co-offending and Criminal Careers." In *Crime and Justice: A Review of Research*, vol. 10, edited by Michael Tonry and Norval Morris. Chicago: University of Chicago Press.

———. 1992. "Police Organization in the Twentieth Century." In *Modern Policing*, edited by Michael Tonry and Norval Morris. Vol. 15 of *Crime and Justice: A Review of Research*, edited by Michael Tonry. Chicago: University of Chicago Press.

Reiss, Albert J., Jr., and David P. Farrington. 1991. "Advancing Knowledge about Co-offending: Results from a Prospective Longitudinal Survey of London Males." *Journal of Criminal Law and Criminology* 82:360-95.

Robin, Gerald D. 1963. "Justifiable Homicide by Police Officers." *Journal of Criminal Law, Criminology and Police Science* 54:225–31.

Roman, John, Shannon E. Reid, Aaron J. Chalfin, and Carly R. Knight. 2009.

"The DNA Field Experiment: A Randomized Trial of the Cost-Effectiveness of Using DNA to Solve Property Crimes." *Journal of Experimental Criminology* 5:345–69.

Rossi, Peter H., Richard E. Berk, and Bettye Eidson. 1974. *The Roots of Urban Discontent*. New York: Wiley.

Rossi, Peter H., Emily Waite, Christine E. Bose, and Richard E. Berk. 1974. "The Seriousness of Crimes: Normative Structure and Individual Differences." *American Sociological Review* 39:224–37.

Sackett, David L., William M. Rosenberg, J. A. Gray, R. Brian Haynes, and W. Scott Richardson. 1996. "Evidence Based Medicine: What It Is and What It Isn't." *British Medical Journal* 312:71–72.

Sagan, Leonard. 1987. *The Health of Nations*. New York: Basic Books.

Sampson, Robert J., and Dawn Jeglum Bartusch. 1998. "Legal Cynicism and Subcultural Tolerance of Deviance: The Neighborhood Context of Racial Difference." *Law and Society Review* 32:777–804.

Saunders, Charles. 1970. *Upgrading the American Police: Education and Training for Better Law Enforcement*. Washington, DC: Brookings Institution.

Shaw, James W. 1995. "Community Policing against Guns: Public Opinion of the Kansas City Gun Experiment." *Justice Quarterly* 12:695–710.

Skogan, Wesley. 1990. *Disorder and Decline: Crime and the Spiral of Decay in American Neighborhoods*. New York: Free Press.

Skogan, Wesley, and Kathleen Frdyl, eds. 2004. *Fairness and Effectiveness in Policing: The Evidence*. National Research Council, Committee to Review Research on Police Policy and Practice. Washington, DC: National Academies Press.

Skogan, Wesley, and Susan Hartnett. 1997. *Community Policing, Chicago Style*. New York: Oxford University Press.

Sherman, Lawrence W. 1976. *The Control of Police Misconduct in Louisville, Kentucky*. Louisville: Office of the Public Safety Commissioner.

———. 1978. *Scandal and Reform: Controlling Police Corruption*. Berkeley: University of California Press.

———. 1980. "Execution without Trial: Police Homicide and the Constitution." *Vanderbilt Law Review* 33:71–100.

———. 1983. "Reducing Police Gun Use: Critical Events, Administrative Policy, and Organizational Change." In *Control in the Police Organization*, edited by Maurice Punch. Cambridge, MA: MIT Press.

———. 1984. "Experiments in Police Discretion: Scientific Boon or Dangerous Knowledge?" *Law and Contemporary Problems* 47:61–81.

———. 1986. "Policing Communities: What Works?" In *Communities and Crime*, edited by Albert J. Reiss Jr. and Michael Tonry. Vol. 8 of *Crime and Justice: A Review of Research*, edited by Michael Tonry and Norval Morris. Chicago: University of Chicago Press.

———. 1987. *Repeat Calls to Police in Minneapolis*. Crime Control Reports 4. Washington, DC: Crime Control Institute.

———. 1990. "Police Crackdowns: Initial and Residual Deterrence." In *Crime and Justice: A Review of Research*, vol. 12, edited by Michael Tonry and Norval Morris. Chicago: University of Chicago Press.

———. 1992*a*. "Attacking Crime: Police and Crime Control." In *Modern Policing*, edited by Michael Tonry and Norval Morris. Vol. 15 of *Crime and Justice: A Review of Research*, edited by Michael Tonry. Chicago: University of Chicago Press.

———. 1992*b*. *Policing Domestic Violence: Experiments and Dilemmas*. With Janell D. Schmidt and Dennis P. Rogan. New York: Free Press.

———. 1993. "Defiance, Deterrence, and Irrelevance: A Theory of the Criminal Sanction." *Journal of Research in Crime and Delinquency* 30:445–73.

———. 1998. *Evidence-Based Policing*. Ideas in American Policing Series. Washington, DC: Police Foundation. http://www.policefoundation.org.

———. 2002. "Trust and Confidence in Criminal Justice." *National Institute of Justice Journal* 248:23–31.

———. 2007. "The Power Few Hypothesis: Experimental Criminology and the Reduction of Harm." *Journal of Experimental Criminology* 3:299–321.

———. 2009. "Evidence and Liberty: The Promise of Experimental Criminology." *Criminology and Criminal Justice* 9(1):5–28.

———. 2010. "Less Prison, More Police, Less Crime: How Criminology Can Save the States from Bankruptcy." Lecture presented to the National Institute of Justice, April 21. http://www.nij.gov/multimedia/presenter/presenter-sherman/data/resources/presenter-sherman-transcript.htm.

———. 2011*a*. "Al Capone, the Sword of Damocles, and the Police-Corrections Budget Ratio." *Criminology and Public Policy* 10:195–206.

———. 2011*b*. "Professional Policing and Liberal Democracy." Benjamin Franklin Medal Lecture delivered to the Royal Society for the Encouragement of Arts, Manufactures, and Commerce, London, November 1. http://www.thersa.org/events/audio-and-past-events/2011/professional-policing-and-liberal-democracy.

Sherman, Lawrence W., and Richard A. Berk. 1984. "The Specific Deterrent Effects of Arrest for Domestic Assault." *American Sociological Review* 49(2): 261–71.

Sherman, Lawrence W., Ioana Cosma, and Peter Neyroud. 2012. "Forecasting Serious Crime among Convicted Offenders in England and Wales: A Random Forests Approach." Paper presented to the American Society of Criminology, Chicago, November.

Sherman, Lawrence W., Patrick R. Gartin, and Michael E. Buerger. 1989. "Hot Spots of Predatory Crime: Routine Activities and the Criminology of Place." *Criminology* 27:27–55.

Sherman, Lawrence W., Denise Gottfredson, Doris MacKenzie, John E. Eck, Peter Reuter, and Shawn D. Bushway. 1998. *Preventing Crime: What Works, What Doesn't, What's Promising*. Research in Brief. Washington, DC: National Institute of Justice.

Sherman, Lawrence W., and Heather Harris. 2012. "Life-Course Effects of Arrest for Domestic Violence: Informal and Formal Control over 24 Years."

Paper presented to the American Society of Criminology, Chicago, November.

Sherman, Lawrence W., and Robert H. Langworthy. 1979. "Measuring Homicide by Police Officers." *Journal of Criminal Law and Criminology* 70:546–60.

Sherman, Lawrence W., and the National Advisory Commission on Higher Education for Police Officers. 1978. *The Quality of Police Education.* San Francisco: Jossey-Bass.

Sherman, Lawrence W., and Heather Strang. 2012. "Restorative Justice as Evidence-Based Sentencing." In *The Oxford Handbook of Sentencing and Corrections,* edited by Joan Petersilia and Kevin Reitz. New York: Oxford University Press.

Sherman, Lawrence W., Heather Strang, Geoffrey C. Barnes, and Daniel J. Woods. 2006. "Race and Restorative Justice." Paper presented to the American Society of Criminology, Los Angeles, November.

Sherman, Lawrence W., and David Weisburd. 1995. "General Deterrent Effects of Police Patrol in Crime Hot Spots: A Randomized, Controlled Trial." *Justice Quarterly* 12:635–48.

Silver, Nate. 2012. *The Signal and the Noise: Why So Many Predictions Fail—but Some Don't.* New York: Penguin.

Sparrow, M. 2011. *Governing Science.* Cambridge, MA: Harvard University. http://www.nij.gov/pubs-sum/232179.htm.

Spelman, William. 1990. *Repeat Offender Programs for Law Enforcement.* Washington, DC: Police Executive Research Forum.

Spelman, William, and Dale K. Brown. 1981. *Calling the Police: Citizen Reporting of Serious Crime.* Washington, DC: Police Executive Research Forum.

Spelman, William, and John E. Eck. 1989. *Sitting Ducks, Ravenous Wolves and Helping Hands: New Approaches to Urban Policing.* Austin, TX: Lyndon B. Johnson School of Public Affairs, University of Texas.

Stanko, Betsy. 2013. Paper presented to the Society of Evidence-Based Policing, University of Edinburgh, February 12.

Strang, Heather, Lawrence Sherman, Evan Mayo-Wilson, Daniel J. Woods, and Barak Ariel. 2013. "Restorative Justice Conferencing (RJC) Using Face-to-Face Meetings of Offenders and Victims: Effects on Offender Recidivism and Victim Satisfaction." Campbell Systematic Reviews, forthcoming.

Tankebe, Justice. 2009. "Public Cooperation with the Police in Ghana: Does Procedural Fairness Matter?" *Criminology* 47:1265–93.

Tapscott, Don, and Anthony D. Williams. 2006. *Wikinomics: How Mass Collaboration Changes Everything.* London: Portfolio.

Telep, Cody W., Renée J. Mitchell, and David Weisburd. 2012. "How Much Time Should the Police Spend at Crime Hot Spots? Answers from a Police Agency Directed Randomized Field Trial in Sacramento, California." *Justice Quarterly* 2012:1–29.

Tennenbaum, Abraham N. 1994. "The Influence of the 'Garner' Decision on Police Use of Deadly Force." *Journal of Criminal Law and Criminology* 85(1): 241–60.

Thompson, James D. 1967. *Organizations in Action*. New York: McGraw-Hill.

Thornton, Sara D. 2011. M.St. thesis, University of Cambridge, Institute of Criminology.

Tittle, Charles R., and Allan R. Rowe. 1974. "Certainty of Arrest and Crime Rates: A Further Test of the Deterrence Hypothesis." *Social Forces* 52:455–62.

Trojanowicz, Robert C., and Robert Baldwin. 1982. *An Evaluation of the Neighborhood Foot Patrol Program in Flint, Michigan*. East Lansing: Michigan State University.

Weisburd, David. 2012. "Can Automobile Vehicle Locator Systems Be Used to Manage Police Presence and Reduce Crime? The Dallas, TX AVL Experiment." Paper Presented to the Fifth Cambridge University International Conference on Evidence-Based Policing, July 10. http://sms.cam.ac.uk/media/1277185.

Weisburd, David, Elizabeth R. Groff, and Sue-Ming Yang. 2012. *The Criminology of Place: Street Segments and Our Understanding of the Crime Problem*. Oxford: Oxford University Press.

Weisburd, David, and Cynthia Lum. 2005. "The Diffusion of Computerized Crime Mapping in Policing: Linking Research and Practice." *Police Practice and Research* 6:419–34.

Weisburd, David, Stephen D. Mastrofski, Rosann Greenspan, and James J. Willis. 2004. *The Growth of Comp-Stat in American Policing*. Police Foundation reports. Washington, DC: Police Foundation.

Weisburd, David, and Peter Neyroud. 2011. *Police Science: Toward a New Paradigm*. Cambridge, MA: Harvard University. https://www.ncjrs.gov/pdffiles1/nij/228922.pdf.

Weisburd, David, Cody W. Telep, Joshua C. Hinkle, and John E. Eck. 2010. "Is Problem-Oriented Policing Effective in Reducing Crime and Disorder?" *Criminology and Public Policy* 9:139–72.

Weisburd, David, Laura A. Wyckoff, Justin Ready, John E. Eck, Joshua C. Hinkle, and Frank Gajewski. 2006. "Does Crime Just Move around the Corner? A Controlled Study of Spatial Displacement and Diffusion of Crime Control Benefits." *Criminology* 44:549–92.

White, Susan O., and Samuel Krislov. 1977. *Understanding Crime: An Evaluation of the National Institute of Law Enforcement and Criminal Justice*. Washington, DC: National Academy of Sciences.

Willis, J. J., Stephen D. Mastrofski, and David Weisburd. 2007. "Making Sense of COMPSTAT: A Theory-Based Analysis of Organizational Change in Three Police Departments." *Law and Society Review* 41:147–88.

Wilson, James Q. 1968. *Varieties of Police Behavior*. Cambridge, MA: Harvard University Press.

Wilson, Orlando W. 1950. *Police Administration*. New York: McGraw-Hill.

Zimring, Franklin E. 1976. "Field Experiments in General Deterrence: Preferring the Tortoise to the Hare." *Evaluation* 3:132–35.

———. 2012. *The City That Became Safe: New York's Lessons for Urban Crime and Its Control*. New York: Oxford University Press.

David P. Farrington

Longitudinal and Experimental Research in Criminology

ABSTRACT

Longitudinal and experimental studies in criminology have advanced substantially since publication of my *Crime and Justice* reviews of longitudinal studies (in 1979) and randomized experiments (in 1983). Longitudinal surveys have become larger and longer-lasting; have focused more on self-reported offending; have made increasing efforts to study biological, neighborhood, and protective factors; and have increasingly investigated intergenerational transmission and desistance. Randomized experiments have become much more common in the United States but not elsewhere, and there have been more large-scale, replicated, and multisite experiments. Experiments have demonstrated that many types of interventions are effective, including nurse home visiting, cognitive-behavioral skills training, parent management training, preschool intellectual enrichment programs, multisystemic therapy, mentoring, hot spots policing, and drug courts. Experiments are needed on the effectiveness of major sentences such as prison and probation and on intervening processes between interventions and outcomes. A multiple cohort longitudinal-experimental study should be mounted to simultaneously advance knowledge about the development, explanation, prevention, and treatment of offending.

David P. Farrington is emeritus professor of psychological criminology and Leverhulme Trust emeritus fellow at the Institute of Criminology, Cambridge University. For providing helpful information and articles for this essay, he is grateful to Deborah Capaldi, Jane Costello, Manuel Eisner, David Fergusson, Sheryl Hemphill, David Henry, David Huizinga, Marc LeBlanc, Friedrich Lösel, Tara McGee, Barbara Maughan, Terrie Moffitt, Lawrence Sherman, Heather Strang, Terence Thornberry, Richard Tremblay, Maria Ttofi, Suzanne Vassallo, Pat Van Voorhis, David Weisburd, and Helene White.

453

The causes of offending can be established most convincingly in longitudinal and experimental studies. For example, consider the proposition that unemployment causes offending. The main problem in testing this hypothesis is to disentangle the effects of unemployment from the effects of numerous other variables that might influence offending. This can be achieved in a longitudinal study in which individual rates of offending during periods of unemployment are compared with individual rates of offending during periods of employment of the same people. Each person would act as his or her own control, because most individual variables (e.g., gender, education, intelligence) are the same during unemployment periods and during employment periods. Similarly, the effects on offending of a life event such as getting married could be established convincingly in a longitudinal study in which the same people are followed up before and after marriage.

The causes of offending can also be established convincingly in randomized experiments. For example, it might be demonstrated that improving the employment of an experimental group (compared to a control group) led to a decrease in offending by the experimental group (compared to the control group). Because of the random assignment of persons to conditions, the average person in the experimental group will be equivalent to the average person in the control group on all possible measured and unmeasured variables. Therefore, we can be sure that the change in employment caused the change in offending.

The main argument in this essay is that the most important and convincing information about the development, explanation, prevention, and treatment of offending has been and can be obtained in longitudinal and experimental studies. In the first volume of *Crime and Justice*, I reviewed knowledge about longitudinal studies in criminology (Farrington 1979c), and in the fourth volume I reviewed knowledge about randomized experiments in criminology (Farrington 1983). In this essay, I review what we knew then from these methods, what we know now from research in the intervening 30 years, what we need to know in the future, and how we can learn those things.

At the time of my earlier review of prospective longitudinal surveys, relatively few had been carried out in the United States, notwithstanding the classic studies of the Gluecks, the McCords, and Robins. In contrast, the 1980s were a "golden age" for the initiation of high-quality American longitudinal surveys. In the rest of the Western world, there were a number of excellent surveys before the 1970s and there have been a number since, but there have not been comparably large investments in longitudinal surveys in other countries. The early surveys aimed to advance knowledge about official criminal careers and tended to focus on individual, family, peer, and school risk factors. As time has gone by, there has been more emphasis on self-reported offending, adult offending, desistance, protective factors, the influence of adult life events, different offending trajectories, biological and neighborhood influences, developmental and life course theories, and the intergenerational transmission of offending.

At the time of my earlier review of randomized experiments, a number had been carried out in the United States and elsewhere (especially in the United Kingdom). These demonstrated that such experiments were feasible. Beginning in the 1980s, there was an enormous increase in American experiments and a great decrease in British experiments. The earlier experiments, especially those focused on counseling or more intensive supervision, suggested that interventions were generally not very effective in reducing offending. In contrast, the later experiments indicated that many interventions were effective, including nurse home visiting, parent training, preschool programs, cognitive-behavioral skills training, hot spots policing, and drug courts. The later experiments are often bigger and better, with larger samples, several sites, and a focus on replication.

There have also been a number of longitudinal-experimental studies in which participants have been followed up for many years after an intervention. These have often shown that conclusions change as the follow-up progresses. For example, the damaging effects of the Cambridge-Somerville Youth Study and the beneficial effects of the Perry Preschool and Nurse Home Visiting programs gradually became clearer. In some studies, desirable effects increased over time, while in other studies these effects decreased.

Here is how this essay is organized. Section I reviews advantages and problems of prospective longitudinal surveys, key longitudinal studies that have been conducted before and since the *Crime and Justice* review, and what we have learned from these surveys. Section II reviews advantages and problems of randomized experiments, key experiments that have been conducted before and since the *Crime and Justice* review, and what we have learned from these experiments. Section III reviews advantages and problems of combined longitudinal-experimental surveys and what we have learned from them. In order to avoid repetition, longitudinal-experimental surveys (with a follow-up of at least 10 years) are discussed only in Section III and not in Section I or II. Sections IV and V summarize what we know and discuss what we need to know and how we can find out using longitudinal and experimental research.

I. Prospective Longitudinal Surveys

Prospective longitudinal surveys involve repeated measures of the same people. Therefore, they involve at least two data collection points. The word "prospective" implies that risk and protective factors are measured before outcomes. Risk factors predict a high probability of an undesirable outcome such as offending, whereas protective factors predict a low probability of offending in the presence of risk.

The most important prospective longitudinal surveys focus on community samples of hundreds of people, with repeated personal interviews spanning a period of at least 5 years (Farrington 1979c; Farrington and Welsh 2007). I focus on community surveys (as opposed to surveys of offenders) because they are needed to study the natural history of offending and the effects of risk or protective factors and life events. In order to avoid retrospective bias, it is important to measure risk and protective factors before the development of offending and to calculate prospective probabilities. Therefore, I focus on prospectively chosen samples rather than retrospectively chosen ones. I require follow-up interview or questionnaire data because I believe that official record data cannot provide adequate information on offending, risk and protective factors, and life events. The best surveys collect data from several different sources, such as the participants, their parents, teachers, peers, and records. I set a minimum of a 5-year follow-up period because I think that at least this period is required to provide minimally adequate information about the natural history of development of offending. Of course, many prospective longitudinal surveys of offending extend for much longer, for 30–40 years or more (see, e.g., Laub and Sampson 2003; Farrington and Pulkkinen 2009).

In criminology, the main advantage of these longitudinal surveys is that they provide information about the development of offending over time, including data on ages of onset and desistance, frequency and seriousness of offending, duration of criminal careers, continuity or discontinuity of offending, and specialization and escalation. They also provide information about developmental sequences, within-individual change, effects of life events, and effects of risk and protective factors at different ages on offending at different ages (Loeber and Farrington 1994; Farrington 2003*b*). A great advantage of longitudinal compared with cross-sectional surveys is that longitudinal surveys provide information about time ordering, which is needed in trying to draw conclusions about causes.

While prospective longitudinal surveys have many advantages, they also have problems. The main challenge is to draw convincing conclusions about causal effects (see Murray, Farrington, and Eisner 2009). Because of their focus on naturalistic observation, it is difficult in longitudinal surveys to disentangle the effects of any particular variable from the effects of numerous others. It is particularly difficult to rule out selection effects; for example, child abuse may predict delinquency because antisocial parents tend to abuse their children and also tend to have delinquent children, without there being any causal effect of child abuse on delinquency. Few researchers have tried to study the effects of life events by following up people before and after them in within-individual analyses.

Other problems can be overcome more easily. Attrition is a problem in some longitudinal surveys, but others have very high response rates (Farrington 2003*c*; Farrington et al. 2006). The infrequency of data collection often makes it difficult to pinpoint causal order, although some studies (e.g., the Pittsburgh Youth Study; see Loeber et al. 2008) have many years of repeated assessments. Testing effects can also be problematic; these refer to the effect of completing one assessment (e.g., a questionnaire or an interview) on a subsequent assessment. For example, it is commonly found that self-reported delinquency admissions are greater in a first assessment than subsequently, especially if participants realize that each admission triggers further questions and therefore prolongs the interview. The importance of testing effects can often be estimated (Thornberry 1989). It is sometimes difficult to determine if changes (e.g., in offending) over time are attributable to aging, changing time periods, or changing birth cohorts, and the length of time before key results are available is sometimes a problem. These difficulties can be overcome by following up multiple cohorts in an accelerated longitudinal design.

As an example of such a design, Tonry, Ohlin, and Farrington (1991) proposed that seven cohorts, beginning at birth and at ages 3, 6, 9, 12, 15, and 18, should be followed up by annual assessments for 8 years.

These seven cohorts were indeed followed up in the Project on Human Development in Chicago Neighborhoods, but only three waves of data were collected (in 1994–97, 1997–99, and 2000–2001), with an average interval between interviews of 2.5 years (see, e.g., Kirk 2006; Gibson, Morris, and Beaver 2009; Sampson 2012).

A. What Did We Know?

In my first *Crime and Justice* essay on longitudinal studies (Farrington 1979*c*), I focused on prospective community surveys of at least several hundred people, with measures of offending, and with a follow-up of at least 5 years involving interviews or questionnaires. Tables 1 and 2 summarize the most important early American and non-American longitudinal surveys (respectively) of this kind. The most important surveys are those with large numbers of participants, a long-term follow-up, frequent assessments from different sources, and a great deal of information about offending. In general, large omnibus national surveys such as the UK National Child Development Study (Bowles and Florackis 2012) have provided little information on offending, whereas smaller focused city-based surveys such as the Cambridge Study in Delinquent Development (Farrington, Piquero, and Jennings 2013) have produced hundreds of articles on offending. Because of their historical importance, three retrospective longitudinal surveys are shown in the tables.[1] The study by Howard Kaplan was not reviewed in 1979 because it focused primarily on drug use.

While all of these projects had begun before 1979, not all of them had produced results on offending by the time of the first *Crime and Justice* essay. Many have now been followed up to the present. Nine surveys have followed a community sample of children at least to age 40, with repeated assessments including measures of offending (Werner, Eron/Huesmann, Elliott/Huizinga, West/Farrington, Magnusson/Stattin, Pulkkinen, Venables/Raine, LeBlanc, plus the longitudinal-experimental study of McCord [1978]).

The early longitudinal surveys advanced knowledge especially about criminal careers. In particular, the high prevalence of arrests or convictions of males that was discovered in these surveys was shocking to many. For example, in Philadelphia, Wolfgang, Figlio, and Sellin (1972) found that 35 percent of males were arrested before their 18th

---

[1] These tables are not exhaustive; see Farrington (1979*c*) for more exhaustive tables.

TABLE 1

Early American Longitudinal Surveys

Investigator and Title	Initial Sample	Follow-ups
Glueck and Glueck, Unraveling Juvenile Delinquency	500 male delinquents and 500 matched male non-delinquents aged 14 in 1939–44 (Boston, MA)	Interviews at ages 25 and 31–32 (Glueck and Glueck 1968); delinquents followed up by Laub and Sampson (2003)
Hathaway, MMPI study	1,958 boys (ave. age 15) tested in 1947–48 (Minneapolis, MN)	Samples contacted 4 and 8 years later (Hathaway, Reynolds, and Monachesi 1969)
Werner, Kauai Longitudinal Study	698 children, born 1955 (Kauai, HI)	Five assessments and records up to age 40 (Werner and Smith 2001)
Eron and Huesmann, Columbia County Study	876 children, aged 8 in 1959–60 (New York State)	Three interviews and records up to age 48 (Huesmann, Dubow, and Boxer 2009)
Wolfgang, Philadelphia Birth Cohort Study*	9,945 boys born in Philadelphia in 1945 and living there up to the 18th birthday in 1963 (Philadelphia, PA)	974 boys interviewed at age 26 and followed in records to age 30 (Wolfgang, Thornberry, and Figlio 1987)
Polk, Marion County Youth Study	1,227 high school boys completing questionnaire age 16 in 1964 (Marion County, OR)	Postal questionnaires up to age 30 (Polk et al. 1981)
Robins*	235 African American males born 1930–34 (St. Louis, MO)	Interview in 1965–66 (Robins, West, and Herjanic 1975)
Kaplan	7,618 adolescents aged 12–13 in 1971 (Houston, TX)	Five interviews up to ages 35–39 (Kaplan 2003)
Kellam and Ensminger, Woodlawn Project	1,242 African American children aged 6 in 1966 (Chicago, IL)	Interview at age 32 (McCord and Ensminger 1997)
Elliott and Huizinga, National Youth Survey—Family Study	1,725 adolescents aged 11–17 in 1976 (national sample)	Interview up to 2002–3 (ages 38–44) and arrest records collected (Elliott 1994)

* Retrospectively identified sample.

TABLE 2
Early Non-American Longitudinal Surveys

Investigator and Title	Initial Sample	Follow-ups
Douglas and Wadsworth, National Survey of Health and Development	5,362 children born 1946 (national UK sample)	Interviews up to age 53, criminal records up to 21st birthday (Wadsworth 1979)
Miller and Kolvin, Newcastle Thousand Family Study	1,142 children born 1947 (Newcastle, UK)	Interviews up to age 50, criminal records up to age 33 (Kolvin et al. 1990)
Butler and Davie, National Child Development Study	17,416 children born 1958 (national UK sample)	Eight interviews up to ages 50–51, self-reported convictions at ages 41–42 (Bowles and Florackis 2012)
West and Farrington, Cambridge Study in Delinquent Development	411 boys aged 8–9 in 1961–62 (London, UK)	Nine interviews up to age 48, records up to age 56 (Farrington, Piquero, and Jennings 2013)
Magnusson and Stattin, Individual Development and Adaptation	1,027 children aged 10 in 1965 (Orebro, Swed.)	Questionnaire and record data up to ages 43–45 (Bergman and Andershed 2009)
Pulkkinen, Jyvaskyla Longitudinal Study	369 children aged 8–9 in 1968 (Jyvaskyla, Fin.)	Five follow-ups to age 42, with interviews, questionnaires, records (Pulkkinen, Lyyra, and Kokko 2009)
Mednick*	1,944 boys born 1936–38 (Copenhagen, Den.)	Interviews with selected samples 30+ years later? (Mednick and Hutchings 1978)
Mednick and Witkin*	4,591 males born 1944–47 and over 6 feet tall (Copenhagen, Den.)	Interview at age 26 (Witkin et al. 1976)
Venables and Raine, Mauritius Child Health Project	1,795 children aged 3 in 1972 (Mauritius)	Seven interviews up to age 40 (Raine et al. 2010)
LeBlanc, Montreal Two Samples Longitudinal Study	3,070 adolescents aged 12–16 in 1974 (Montreal, Can.)	Seven interviews and records up to age 50 (LeBlanc and Frechette 1989)

* Retrospectively identified sample.

birthday, and 43 percent were arrested before their 27th birthday; half of the nonwhites and 29 percent of the whites were arrested before age 18. In the Cambridge Study in London, 21 percent of males were convicted by age 16 and 41 percent by age 50 (Farrington et al. 2006).

The early surveys revealed considerable continuity in criminal careers. In London, 61 percent of juvenile delinquents (convicted up to age 16) were reconvicted before age 21 (Farrington and West 1981), while in Philadelphia 44 percent of juvenile delinquents (arrested up to age 17) were rearrested before age 27 (Wolfgang 1973). Offenders were also versatile, both in the variety of crimes they committed and also in their antisocial behavior. In London, boys convicted up to age 18 tended to be heavy drinkers, heavy smokers, drug users, heavy gamblers, and very aggressive and reckless drivers; to be sexually promiscuous; and to have unstable, low-status job histories.

In St. Louis, Robins (1966, 1978) was one of the first researchers to highlight the versatility of antisocial behavior and its continuity from childhood to adulthood. In her 30-year follow-up of children referred to a child guidance clinic in St. Louis (not shown in table 1 because it was not a community study), she found that the children tended to steal, skip school, and run away from home; to be aggressive and enuretic; to have disciplinary problems in school; and to be pathological liars. As adults, they tended to be arrested, divorced, and placed in mental hospitals; to be alcoholics, vagrants, bad debtors, and poor workers; and to be sexually promiscuous.

Numerous risk factors for delinquency were identified by Glueck and Glueck (1950), including parental discipline, parental supervision, parental affection, and family cohesiveness, although they did not predict delinquency prospectively. The Cambridge Study found that many factors measured before age 10 predicted future convictions, particularly low family income, large family size, a convicted parent, poor child rearing, and low IQ (West and Farrington 1973). These factors were additive in the sense that the more adversities a boy possessed, the more likely he was to be convicted. The Cambridge Study also found that the predictors of high self-reported delinquency were similar to the predictors of convictions (Farrington 1979a).

Glueck and Glueck (1968) also pioneered the prediction of recidivism and the future course of criminal careers. The very long-term follow-up studies of Soothill and Gibbens (1978) in the United Kingdom (not shown in table 2 because of the lack of follow-up interviews) were particularly interesting in showing that reconvictions could be long delayed. They followed 184 male sex offenders for up to 22 years after their offenses. The proportion (48 percent) who were reconvicted up to 22 years later was much greater than the proportion (33 percent) of those who had been reconvicted up to 10 years later. There was a widespread belief (see, e.g., Brody 1976) that almost all offenders who are ever going to be reconvicted will be reconvicted within 5 years, and mostly within 2 years, but the research of Soothill and Gibbens showed that this was not necessarily true. The benefits of long-term follow-ups are discussed in Section III.

Several longitudinal studies investigated the effects of life events on the course of development of offending. In agreement with labeling theory, the Cambridge Study showed that self-reported offending increased after a first conviction (Farrington 1977). Also, boys who went to high–delinquency rate secondary schools at age 11 were more likely to be convicted than those who went to low–delinquency rate secondary schools, after controlling for their prior troublesomeness (Farrington 1972). However, there was no effect of early marriage between ages 18 and 21 on official or self-reported delinquency (Knight, Osborn, and West 1977).

In their follow-up of African American males in St. Louis, Robins, West, and Herjanic (1975) found that convicted parents tended to have convicted children. Furthermore, a comparison between the juvenile records of parents and children showed that they had similar rates and types of crimes. Several longitudinal surveys were carried out in the Scandinavian countries to investigate biological factors, and especially the importance of genetic factors. Hutchings and Mednick (1975) followed up all males who were born in Copenhagen in 1927–41 and adopted by someone outside the biological family. They compared the conviction records of the adoptees with the conviction records of their biological and adoptive fathers and found close relationships in both cases. Since there was generally little contact between the son and his biological father, these results suggested that both genetic and environmental factors influenced convictions.

One specific biological factor that was investigated was the XYY chromosome abnormality. Witkin et al. (1976) followed up all males born in Copenhagen in 1944–47 and obtained information about their heights at age 26 from the draft boards (to which all men were required to report). Since it was known that the XYY abnormality was more common among tall men, they identified 4,591 males with heights exceeding 6 feet (184 centimeters or more). They obtained current addresses from the Danish National Register and managed to contact 91 percent of these males and obtain buccal smears and blood samples. Only 12 XYY males were found, but they were disproportionately likely to have been convicted (five out of 12, compared with the base rate of 9 percent).

B. What Have We Found Out Since?

Some of the longitudinal research on offending since 1979 has continued to advance knowledge about the topics studied before, but other research has focused on new topics. Tables 3 and 4 summarize important later American and non-American longitudinal surveys (respectively) that have come to fruition since 1979. These are again chosen according to the criteria listed above. Most of these are much larger than the earlier surveys, with initial samples of at least 1,000 children.[2]

Later research has continued to study criminal careers, especially using self-report information. For example, Elliott (1994) used his presidential address to the American Society of Criminology to review results obtained in the US National Youth Survey on the prevalence, onset, and continuity of serious violent offending (according to self-reports). In the Pittsburgh Youth Study, Loeber et al. (2008) compared prospective age-crime curves based on reported offending (by boys, mothers, and teachers) with similar curves based on arrests and convictions. They found that the prevalence, frequency, and duration of criminal careers were all greater for reported offending than for arrests and that the escalation from minor to more serious crimes was greater for reported offending than for arrests. Also, there were differences in offending between different birth cohorts: boys who became teenagers during a period of high societal violence tended to be more violent themselves than boys who became teenagers when societal violence was lower (Fabio et al. 2006).

In the 1980s, US governmental and funding agencies began to appreciate the enormous importance of criminal career research and longitudinal studies. Major bodies such as the US National Institute of Justice, the US Office of Juvenile Justice and Delinquency Prevention,

---

[2] These tables are not exhaustive; for lists of longitudinal surveys in criminology, see Farrington and Welsh (2007, chap. 2) and Liberman (2008, app.).

TABLE 3

Later American Longitudinal Surveys

Investigator and Title	Initial Sample	Follow-ups
Cohen and Brook, New York State Longitudinal Study	976 children aged 1–10 in 1975 (New York State)	Six interviews up to age 37 (Johnson et al. 2004)
White, Rutgers Health and Human Development Project	1,380 adolescents aged 12–18 in 1979–81 (NJ)	Five interviews up to ages 30–31 in 2000 (Barker et al. 2007)
Hawkins and Catalano, Seattle Social Development Project	808 children aged 10 in 1985 (original intervention study in 1981) (Seattle, WA)	Interviews and records up to age 33 (Hawkins et al. 2003)
Patterson and Capaldi, Oregon Youth Study	206 boys aged 10 in 1983–85 (Eugene/Springfield, OR)	Interviews and records up to ages 37–38 (Capaldi and Patterson 1996)
Loeber and Stouthamer-Loeber, Pittsburgh Youth Study	1,513 boys aged 7–13 in 1987–88 (Pittsburgh, PA)	Interviews and records up to age 35 (Loeber et al. 2003)
Huizinga, Denver Youth Study	1,528 children aged 7–15 in 1988 (Denver, CO)	Interviews up to ages 22–26 in 2003, arrest records up to 2011 (Huizinga et al. 2003)
Thornberry, Rochester Youth Development Study	1,000 adolescents aged 13–14 in 1988 (Rochester, NY)	Interviews and records up to age 32 (Thornberry et al. 2003)
Tolan, Chicago Youth Development Study	341 males aged 11–13 in 1990 (Chicago, IL)	Six interviews up to age 22 (Tolan, Gorman-Smith, and Henry 2003)
Resnick, National Longitudinal Study of Adolescent Health	20,745 adolescents aged 13–18 in 1994–95 (national sample)	Four interviews up to ages 24–32 in 2007–8 (Bernat et al. 2012)
Earls and Sampson, Project on Human Development in Chicago Neighborhoods	About 6,400 children from birth to age 18 (seven cohorts) in 1994–97 (Chicago, IL)	Three interviews up to 2000–2001 (Kirk 2006)

TABLE 4
Later Non-American Longitudinal Surveys

Investigator and Title	Initial Sample	Follow-ups
Butler and Golding, British Cohort Study	17,287 children born 1970 (national UK sample)	Interviews up to age 34 (Murray et al. 2010)
Silva and Moffitt, Dunedin Multidisciplinary Health and Development Study	1,037 children aged 3 in 1975–76 (Dunedin, NZ)	Interviews up to age 38 and records (Moffitt et al. 2001)
Fergusson, Christchurch Health and Development Study	1,365 children born 1977 (Christchurch, NZ)	Interviews and records up to age 35 (Fergusson, Swain-Campbell, and Horwood 2004)
Bor and Najman, Mater University Study of Pregnancy	7,233 children born 1981 (Brisbane, Aust.)	Interviews up to age 30 (McGee et al. 2011)
Prior and Sanson, Australian Temperament Project	2,443 children born 1982–83 (Victoria, Aust.)	Interviews up to age 28 (Prior et al. 2000)
Golding, Avon Longitudinal Study of Children and Parents	14,062 children born 1991–92 (Avon, UK)	Interviews up to age 21 (Barker et al. 2008)
McAra and McVie, Edinburgh Study of Youth Transitions and Crime	About 4,300 children aged 11 in 1998 (Edinburgh, UK)	Six interviews up to age 17, records up to age 22 (McAra and McVie 2010)
Hemphill and Catalano, International Youth Development Study	5,769 students aged 10–15 in 2002 (Victoria, Aust., and WA)	Interviews up to 2012–13 (McMorris et al. 2007)
Wikström, Peterborough Adolescent Development Study	716 children aged 12–13 in 2004 (Peterborough, UK)	Seven interviews up to ages 20–21 in 2012 (Wikström et al. 2012)

465

the US National Institute of Mental Health, and the MacArthur Foundation started devoting significant funding to criminal career and longitudinal research and consequently reduced their funding of the more traditional cross-sectional theory-testing sociological research such as that carried out by Hirschi (1969).

It was perhaps no coincidence, then, that Travis Hirschi and his colleague Michael Gottfredson launched a series of attacks on criminal career and longitudinal research in the 1980s, including the provocatively titled paper "The True Value of Lambda Would Appear to Be Zero" (Gottfredson and Hirschi 1986). They explicitly complained that "the criminal career notion . . . dominates discussion of criminal justice policy and . . . controls expenditure of federal research funds" (p. 213). Their main substantive argument was that individual age-crime curves were the same as the aggregate age-crime curve. Therefore, it was unnecessary to distinguish prevalence and frequency because both varied similarly with age. Between-individual differences in offending depended on a single underlying theoretical construct of self-control (Gottfredson and Hirschi 1990) that persisted from childhood to adulthood. Persons with low self-control had a high prevalence, frequency, and seriousness of offending, an early onset, a late termination, and a long criminal career, so the predictors and correlates of any one of these criminal career features were the same as the predictors and correlates of any other. Gottfredson and Hirschi (1987) also argued that longitudinal research was unnecessary because the causes and correlates of offending (which depended on the stable underlying construct of self-control) were the same at all ages.

Blumstein, Cohen, and Farrington (1988a, 1988b) responded to the main criticisms. First, they argued that the predictors and correlates of one criminal career feature (e.g., prevalence or onset) were different from the predictors of another (e.g., frequency or desistance). Second, they pointed out that individual age-crime curves for frequency (which was constant over time for active offenders) were very different from the aggregate age-crime curve. Third, they contended that longitudinal research was needed to test many of Gottfredson and Hirschi's key hypotheses, such as the stability of self-control from childhood to adulthood. Fourth, they argued that, because of their emphasis on and experience of cross-sectional research, Gottfredson and Hirschi tried to draw conclusions about causes from between-individual differences, but the idea of cause required within-individual change over time, which could be studied only in longitudinal research (Farrington 1988).

Several researchers have tried to estimate the "scaling-up" factor from official to self-reported offending. This is important, for example, in evaluating the effectiveness of intervention programs, and especially for cost-benefit analyses. Most intervention programs are evaluated using official offending measures, but it is necessary to scale these up to the "true" number of offenses in order to get a more accurate estimate of the number and cost of crimes prevented by the program. In the Pittsburgh Youth Study, there were 80 self-reported crimes per juvenile court petition (Farrington et al. 2007). The ratio was 15 for property crimes, 154 for violent crimes, and 424 for drug crimes. In the Seattle Social Development Project, there were 29 self-reported crimes per juvenile court referral (Farrington et al. 2003). The ratio was 14 for property crimes, 25 for violent crimes, and 250 for drug crimes. With scaling-up factors greater than 10, the financial benefits would exceed the financial costs for almost all interventions that caused a decrease in official offending. Generally, the scaling-up factor decreased with age, showing that the probability of a self-reported crime leading to an official record increased with age.

As longitudinal surveys have followed up participants to older ages, the interest has tended to shift from onset to desistance and from early onset to later adult onset. The burgeoning knowledge about desistance has been reviewed by Kazemian and Farrington (2010) and by Bushway and Paternoster (2013). In general, the most important influences on desistance are getting married, becoming employed, joining the military, and breaking up with delinquent peers (see, e.g., Sampson and Laub 1993). Krohn, Gibson, and Thornberry (2013) reviewed knowledge about adult-onset offenders. Their offending is often different from that of earlier-onset offenders; in the Cambridge Study, late-onset offenders tended to commit sex crimes, theft from work, vandalism, and fraud, whereas juvenile-onset offenders were most likely to commit burglary and vehicle theft (McGee and Farrington 2010). In the same project, Zara and Farrington (2009) found that the best predictors of late-onset offenders were high nervousness and few friends, which may perhaps have protected boys from offending in adolescence.

There has also been more interest in intergenerational transmission, and several longitudinal studies have followed up the children of the original participants.[3] Many researchers have been interested in factors that might intervene between parental offending and child offending. For example, in the Rochester Youth Development Study, Thornberry, Freeman-Gallant, and Lovegrove (2009) found that the continuity from parental self-reported delinquency to child antisocial behavior was primarily mediated by parental stress and ineffective parenting. Similarly, in the Cambridge Study, the intergenerational transmission of convictions decreased in strength after controlling for intervening family and socioeconomic risk factors (Farrington, Coid, and Murray 2009).

Trajectory analysis, pioneered in criminology by Nagin (2005), has become extremely popular in the last 20 years. The reason is that researchers realized that the aggregate age-crime curve, typically rising to a peak in the teenage years and then decreasing, may not apply to all individuals. Indeed, trajectory analysis typically reveals different categories of offenders, such as high-rate chronics, low-rate chronics, and adolescence-limited offenders (Piquero 2008). For example, in the Dunedin project, Odgers et al. (2008) identified four antisocial trajectories (life course–persistent, adolescent-onset, childhood-limited, and low antisocial behavior) and found that, at age 32, women and men on the life course–persistent pathway were engaging in serious violence and had significant mental and physical health problems. The value of trajectory analysis is quite controversial, as shown by the exchange between Skardhamar (2010) and Brame, Paternoster, and Piquero (2012). Skardhamar argued that, even when no groups exist in reality and the data are truly continuous, trajectory analysis will yield several categories of offenders. In response, Brame and his colleagues did not disagree with this argument but contended that trajectory analysis was useful for description and visualization of criminal career data and for testing theories.

In recent years, there has been a great deal of research on continuity and change in offending. Researchers now realize that relative stability is perfectly compatible with absolute change (Farrington 1990). Nagin and Paternoster (1991, 2000) proposed that the continuity between juvenile and adult offending may reflect persistent or population heterogeneity (the persistence of an underlying construct such as an an-

---

[3] Special sections of journals on this topic have been edited by Capaldi et al. (2003) and by Bijleveld and Farrington (2009).

tisocial personality or low self-control) or state dependence (the fact that the occurrence of an early crime increases the probability of a later crime, e.g., because of labeling or stigmatization) or both. In the Cambridge Study, persistent heterogeneity was more important (Paternoster, Brame, and Farrington 2001). The same was true in the Dunedin study, but additionally, Piquero, Brame, and Moffitt (2005) found that continuity was similar for males and females. In related research, Gordon et al. (2004) found that boys who joined a gang were worse beforehand, but they became even more delinquent after joining a gang.

The conclusions reached (retrospectively) by Robins (1966) about the continuity and versatility of antisocial behavior throughout life were confirmed (prospectively) in the UK National Survey of Health and Development. Colman et al. (2009) followed 3,652 participants up to age 53 and found that those who were the most antisocial at ages 13–15 tended to have the most adverse outcomes later in life (in mental health, family life, and educational and economic problems). Similarly, in the Cambridge Study, persistent offenders tended to be leading unsuccessful lives at ages 32 and 48 (in accommodation, cohabitation, employment, and alcohol and drug use) and were predicted by troublesome behavior at ages 8–10 (Farrington, Ttofi, and Coid 2009).

The language of risk and protective factors has taken over criminology (Hawkins and Catalano 1992; Farrington 2000). The key risk factors for offending that were identified in early longitudinal surveys have generally been confirmed in later surveys: high impulsiveness or low self-control, low IQ, low school attainment, poor child rearing, poor parental supervision, young mothers, child abuse, parental conflict, disrupted families, low socioeconomic status, delinquent peers, and bad neighborhoods (Leschied et al. 2008; Derzon 2009; Jolliffe and Farrington 2009; Farrington, Loeber, and Ttofi 2012).

However, there have been some new developments. For example, researchers have tested alternative hypotheses about intervening mechanisms between risk factors and offending (e.g., Juby and Farrington 2002). In the British Cohort Study, Murray et al. (2010) investigated the extent to which very early risk factors (measured up to age 5) predicted self-reported convictions at ages 30 and 34. Most of the early longitudinal studies did not start until age 6 or later. Murray et al. found that the strongest early predictors were a single mother, a teenage mother, maternal smoking during pregnancy, loss of a biological parent, and family deprivation (low social class, low parental education, poverty, and household overcrowding). The likelihood of a conviction increased with the early risk score, from 17 percent to 44 percent for boys and from 3 percent to 11 percent for girls.

Another new development was the prediction of homicide offenders and victims in the Pittsburgh Youth Study. Previously, it was thought that risk factors for homicide could be studied only in retrospective case-control comparisons because of the rarity of homicide offending. In the Pittsburgh Youth Study, however, there were 37 convicted homicide offenders, an additional 33 males who were arrested for homicide but not convicted (often because witnesses were too terrified to testify), and 39 homicide victims out of 1,512 males at risk. Loeber and Farrington (2011) found that the strongest early predictors of convicted homicide offenders were sociodemographic (a broken home, a young or unemployed mother, a bad neighborhood, the family on welfare), whereas homicide victims tended to be predicted more by individual factors (hyperactivity, low achievement, lack of guilt). Thus, victims tended to be individually deviant while offenders tended to be socially deprived. There has been more interest in research on victims as well as offenders in recent longitudinal studies (see, e.g., Jennings et al. 2010).

Another recent development has been the focus on protective factors and resilience in addition to risk factors (Farrington, Loeber, and Ttofi 2012; Lösel and Farrington 2012). For example, in the Avon Longitudinal Study, Bowen, El Komy, and Steer (2008) identified resilient children who were at risk because of family adversity but who were nevertheless not antisocial at age 8. They reported that the resilient children tended to have high IQ, high self-esteem, and greater school enjoyment, and their mothers had better parenting skills. In the Cambridge Study, Farrington and Ttofi (2012) found that, among boys at risk because they were living in very poor housing at ages 8–10, the most important protective factors against later convictions were good maternal discipline, parental interest in education, and low impulsiveness. These studies of protective factors and resilience have important policy implications in identifying targets for early intervention.

Most early longitudinal studies focused on individual, family, peer, and school factors, but in recent years there has been increased research on biological influences on offending. For example, in the US National Longitudinal Study of Adolescent Health, many participants submitted buccal cells (from buccal swabs in the mouth) for genetic assessments. Beaver et al. (2010) found a genetic influence on gang membership and weapon use for males but not for females: males with the low monoamine oxidase A genotype tended to become gang members and to use weapons in a fight. In the same project, Vaughn, Beaver, and DeLisi (2009) discovered that dopamine transporter and receptor genes influenced neurocognitive skills (in males), which in turn influenced ADHD (attention deficit hyperactivity disorder) and antisocial behavior. As another example of a biological finding, in the Mater University Study of Pregnancy, early pubertal development predicted drug use up to age 21 (Hayatbakhsh et al. 2009).

Just as there has been increased interest in biological factors, there also has been increased research in longitudinal studies in recent years on neighborhood and community factors. Most studies (e.g., Larzelere and Patterson 1990; Gottfredson, McNeil, and Gottfredson 1991) have reported that neighborhood and community factors have only indirect influences on offending through their influence on family factors. For example, in the Chicago Youth Development Study, Tolan, Gorman-Smith, and Henry (2003) found that community structural characteristics (concentrated poverty, ethnic heterogeneity, economic resources, violent crime rate) influenced parenting practices (parental discipline, parental involvement, parental reinforcement), which in turn influenced self-reported violence at ages 18–22. Other projects have focused on interactive effects. For example, in the Pittsburgh Youth Study, Lynam et al. (2000) concluded that the effects of impulsiveness on juvenile offending were stronger in poorer neighborhoods. Sampson, Raudenbush, and Earls (1997) emphasized the importance of the "collective efficacy" of a neighborhood (reflecting community cohesiveness and the willingness of residents to intervene to prevent antisocial behavior) in preventing crime.

Surprisingly, there have been relatively few attempts in longitudinal studies to carry out within-individual analyses to study the effects of life events on the course of development of offending. Some researchers have retrospectively used life history calendars to study this. For example, Horney, Osgood, and Marshall (1995) obtained monthly data from incarcerated felons on life circumstances such as living with a wife and drinking heavily on crimes committed and showed that life circumstances influenced offending.

The life event that has been investigated most in prospective longitudinal studies is getting married. In the Cambridge Study, Theobald and Farrington (2009) found that convictions decreased after a man got married. They matched married and unmarried men on their prior number of convictions and on a propensity score measuring their likelihood of getting married. In follow-up research, Theobald and Farrington (2011) reported that getting married at older ages had little effect on offending because the later-married men tended to be drug users and binge drinkers and because they maintained their aggressive attitudes and continued to go out with their male friends after marriage.

There has been a dramatic increase in recent years in the formulation and testing of developmental and life course (DLC) theories of offending (see Farrington 2005). Several longitudinal studies, including the Seattle Social Development Project (Hawkins et al. 2003) and the Peterborough Adolescent Development Study (Wikström et al. 2012), have been primarily designed to test the principal investigator's theory. There have been relatively few independent tests of DLC theories, but Moffitt's (1993) theory has been independently tested the most and indeed has been revised and extended as a result of these tests (see Moffitt 2006). For example, in the Individual Development and Adaptation (Orebro) project, Stattin, Kerr, and Bergman (2010) found that there were adolescence-limited and life course–persistent offenders, as predicted by the theory, but that there was also a large group of "childhood-onset-desister" males who were aggressive up to age 13 but not afterward.

There have also been increased efforts to carry out cross-national comparisons of results in longitudinal studies. For example, Pulkkinen and Tremblay (1992) found similar clusters of boys in the Jyvaskyla and Montreal studies, Farrington and Wikström (1994) compared criminal careers in the Cambridge and Project Metropolitan studies, and Broidy et al. (2003) compared developmental trajectories in six sites in three countries. The International Youth Development Study was designed as a comparable longitudinal study in Victoria, Australia, and Washington State (McMorris et al. 2007), and many of the predictors of youth violence were similar in the two places (Hemphill et al. 2009). Cross-national comparisons are important to establish to what extent results are replicated in different settings and conversely to what extent findings might be influenced by environmental and cultural differences. Farrington and Loeber (1999) compared risk factors for delinquency in London and Pittsburgh and found that they were generally similar. However, physical punishment by parents was a more important risk factor in London, possibly because the London boys were almost all Caucasian whereas over half of the Pittsburgh boys were African American.

There have been a number of studies of race and gender differences in risk factors. For example, in the Pittsburgh Youth Study, physical punishment, young mothers, and low socioeconomic status predicted violence more strongly for Caucasian boys than for African American boys (Farrington, Loeber, and Stouthamer-Loeber 2003). All three risk factors were more prevalent among African American boys. There have also been studies of gender differences in risk and protective factors (e.g., Moffitt et al. 2001; Fagan et al. 2007) and the first large-scale longitudinal study of the development of antisocial behavior in girls (Keenan et al. 2010). In the Cambridge Study, risk factors for brothers and sisters were generally similar, but socioeconomic and child rearing factors (such as low family income and poor parental supervision) were more important for sisters, whereas parental characteristics (such as nervous fathers and mothers) were more strongly predictive of offending for brothers (Farrington and Painter 2004). It is usually concluded that race and gender differences in offending are attributable to race and gender differences in the prevalence or level of risk factors rather than to race and gender differences in the developmental processes or relationships between risk factors and offending (see, e.g., Rowe, Vaszonyi, and Flannery 1994, 1995).

Finally, it is undoubtedly true that the statistical methods used in longitudinal studies have become more advanced and complex over time. In addition to newly available trajectory analysis and propensity score matching, it is common to use structural equation modeling, negative binomial regression, survival analysis, multilevel modeling, latent transition analysis, latent growth curve analysis, event history analysis, hierarchical linear modeling, and a host of other techniques. For example, Wiesner, Capaldi, and Kim (2010) used event history analysis to show that arrests, getting married, and drug use influenced job losses in the Oregon Youth Study. My own view is that, before carrying out sophisticated analyses, it is important to report basic information about prevalence, frequency, and cross-tabulations in order to understand later results fully.

II. Randomized Experiments

An experiment is a systematic attempt to investigate the effect of variations in one factor (the independent or explanatory variable) on another (the dependent or outcome variable). In criminology, the independent variable is often some kind of intervention and the dependent variable is some measure of offending. Most criminological experiments are pragmatic trials designed to test the effectiveness of an intervention rather than explanatory trials designed to test causal hypotheses (Schwartz, Flamant, and Lelouch 1980). The independent variable is under the control of the experimenter; in other words, the experimenter decides which people receive which treatment (using the word "treatment" very widely to include all kinds of interventions).

The focus here is on randomized experiments, where people are randomly assigned to different treatments. The unique advantage of randomized experiments is their high internal validity (Cook and Campbell 1979; Farrington 2003d). Provided that a large enough number of people are assigned, randomization ensures that the average person receiving one treatment is equivalent (on all possible measured and unmeasured extraneous variables) to the average person receiving another treatment, within the limits of small statistical fluctuations. Therefore, it is possible to isolate and disentangle the effect of the independent variable (the intervention) from the effects of all other extraneous variables (Farrington 1983; Farrington and Welsh 2005, 2006). However, it is also desirable to investigate intervening mechanisms or mediators (e.g., Harachi et al. 1999).

Because of the concern with internal validity, I focus on relatively large-scale experiments in which at least 100 persons or other units are randomly assigned to experimental or control conditions. This excludes the vast majority of experiments in which schools are randomly assigned (e.g., Metropolitan Area Child Study Research Group 2002; Brown et al. 2005; Petras et al. 2008), although below I will discuss two large studies (Fast Track and Z-Proso) in which over 50 schools were randomly assigned to conditions. A power analysis should be carried out before embarking on any longitudinal or experimental study to assess whether the likely relationships or effects can be statistically detected, bearing in mind the sample size (Weisburd, Petrosino, and Mason 1993). Smaller numbers of schools (or other larger units) would have the same statistical power as a larger number of individuals (Weisburd and Gill 2013).

Many problems arise in randomized experiments on offending. For example, it is difficult to ensure that all those in an experimental group actually receive the treatment while all those in a control group do not. Manipulation checks and studies of implementation are desirable. Also, differential attrition from experimental and control groups can produce noncomparable groups and lead to low internal validity (Farrington and Welsh 2005). There is often some blurring of the distinction between experimental and control groups (treatment crossovers), leading to an underestimation of the effect of the treatment. Angrist (2006) has described a method of correcting for this. Another difficulty is that participants and treatment professionals can rarely be kept blind to the experiment, and knowledge about participation in the experiment may bias outcomes or outcome measurement.

Typically, it is possible in an experiment to study the effect of only one or two independent variables at two or three different levels (different experimental conditions). Few of the possible causes of offending could in practice be studied experimentally because few of the important variables could be experimentally manipulated (but see Farrington [1979b, 2008] for experiments on causes of offending). Experiments are usually designed to investigate only immediate or short-term causal effects. However, some interventions may have long-term rather than short-term effects, and in some cases the long-term effects may differ from the short-term ones. More fundamentally, researchers rarely know the likely time delay between cause and effect, suggesting that follow-up measurements at several different time intervals are desirable. A longitudinal-experimental study can deal with many of these problems (see Sec. III).

Many ethical, legal, and practical issues arise in randomized experiments (Short, Zahn, and Farrington 2000). For example, Farrington and Jolliffe (2002) carried out a study of the feasibility of evaluating the treatment of dangerous, severely personality-disordered offenders using a randomized controlled trial. They found that all the clinicians were opposed to such a trial because they thought that everyone should be treated and that no one should be denied treatment. In the Netherlands, Asscher et al. (2007) also reported resistance from agencies. However, where the number of persons who need or want treatment exceeds the number who can be treated (in light of available resources), random assignment may be the fairest way to select people for treatment (Wortman and Rabinowitz 1979). Cook and Payne (2002) have set out and answered many objections to randomized experiments, while Boruch (1997) has provided detailed practical advice about how to mount such experiments successfully.

A. What Did We Know?

In my first *Crime and Justice* essay on randomized experiments in criminology (Farrington 1983), I focused on real-life experiments with at least 50 (or so) persons or other units per condition. Additionally, in this essay I focus on experiments with outcome measures of offending. Tables 5 and 6 summarize the most important early American and non-American randomized experiments in criminology. These are generally the largest experiments with the most interesting findings.[4]

The overwhelming conclusion from tables 5 and 6 is that most interventions did not succeed in reducing offending. In most cases, the intervention group did not have significantly lower offending than the control group in the follow-up period. Most interventions involved group or individual counseling or some kind of more intensive treatment than usual.

It is worrisome that, even where the intervention was effective in a small-scale demonstration project (e.g., LIFE or Living Insurance for Ex-Prisoners), it was not effective in two replication experiments (TARP, or Transitional Aid Research Project; Rossi, Berk, and Lenihan 1980). However, the effect was quite weak in the original LIFE experiment: barely statistically significant at $p = .05$ on a one-tailed test. In recent years, researchers have come to realize that it is at least as important to measure effect size as statistical significance. The early experiments focused on statistical significance, but a significant result may signify a large effect in a small sample or a small effect in a large sample (or some intermediate result). Farrington and Welsh (2006) estimated the effect in the LIFE experiment as corresponding to 57 percent rearrested for controls versus 50 percent rearrested for the intervention group, which was not significant either on a chi-squared test (2.09) or as an odds ratio (1.35). It is desirable to carry out a power analysis before conducting an experiment to estimate what sample sizes are needed to detect the likely effect size, but only Baker and Sadd (1981) did this.

---

[4] These tables are not exhaustive; see Farrington (1983) and Farrington and Welsh (2006) for more exhaustive tables.

Most outcomes were official measures of rearrest, reconviction, or revocation. Only Empey and Lubeck (1971) and Empey and Erickson (1972) had before and after measures of offending, and only Reckless and Dinitz (1972) and Waldo and Chiricos (1977) had self-report as well as official measures of offending. The problem with parole revocation in particular is that it reflects the behavior of parole officers as well as that of offenders. Palmer's (1974) desirable results in the Community Treatment Project may be influenced by this. According to Lerman (1975), the community treatment and institutional groups had equal rearrest rates but different probabilities of having their parole revoked after an arrest.

Differential attrition from experimental and control conditions is a great problem and can create illusory differences between conditions. This would be true, for example, if only those who successfully completed a treatment were analyzed. Williams (1970, 1975) found that males who were treated in a casework borstal were significantly less likely to be reconvicted than those who were treated in group counseling or traditional institutions. However, only inmates who were not transferred out of the borstals were followed up for recidivism. Since more of the casework inmates were transferred out (in some cases because of disciplinary infractions), it was possible that the followed-up casework inmates were a better group to start with than the other followed-up inmates. Thus, the random assignment may not have ensured comparable groups in the analysis because of the differential attrition.

Subgroup analyses were sometimes carried out but were often doubtful. For example, O'Donnell, Lydgate, and Fo (1979) reported that their "buddy" group had a lower rearrest rate if they had previous major arrests but a higher rearrest rate if they had no previous arrests. Both of these effects were significant only at $p = .05$ on one-tailed tests, which seem illegitimate in the absence of prior directional hypotheses. To test these hypotheses, the researchers should have stratified their sample on previous arrest records before randomization, but there is no evidence that they did this. The same objection does not apply to the PICO project because Adams (1970) specified that he classified offenders as "amenable" or "nonamenable" before the random assignment. Adams found that the treated amenable inmates had significantly lower recidivism rates than the controls, whereas the treated nonamenable inmates had nonsignificantly higher recidivism

TABLE 5
Early American Randomized Experiments

Investigator and Title	Initial Sample	Intervention Conditions	Results
Reimer and Warren, Special Intensive Parole Unit	3,793 male parolees (CA)	Low vs. regular caseload	NSD major arrests in 23 months (Reimer and Warren 1957)
Meyer	381 schoolgirls (New York City)	Counseling vs. control	NSD court appearances in 3 years (Meyer, Borgatta, and Jones 1965)
Ditman	301 drunk offenders (San Diego, CA)	Alcohol treatment vs. control	Rearrests in 1 year lower if treated (Ditman et al. 1967)
Adams, PICO Project	400 delinquents (CA)	Counseling vs. control	Return to custody in 33 months: counseling lower if amenable (Adams 1970)
Kassebaum and Ward	512 male prisoners (CA)	Small-group counseling vs. large-group counseling vs. control	NSD rearrests in 3 years (Kassebaum, Ward, and Wilmer 1971)
Empey and Lubeck, Silverlake Experiment	261 male recidivists (CA)	Community (GGI) vs. institution	NSD recidivism in 1 year (Empey and Lubeck 1971)
Jesness	281 male delinquents (CA)	20-bed unit vs. 50-bed unit	NSD revocations in 5 years (Jesness 1971a)
Jesness, Preston Typology Study	1,173 male delinquents (CA)	Treated according to interpersonal maturity level vs. control	NSD revocations in 2 years (Jesness 1971b)
Empey and Erickson, Provo Experiment	150 male recidivists (Provo, UT)	Community (GGI) vs. probation	NSD rearrests in 4 years (Empey and Erickson 1972)
Venezia	123 delinquents (Woodland, CA)	Unofficial probation vs. counsel/release	NSD referral to probation in 6 months (Venezia 1972)
Reckless and Dinitz	1,094 schoolboys (Columbus, OH)	Self-concept classes vs. control	NSD police contacts and SRD in 3 years (Reckless and Dinitz 1972)

478

Study	Sample	Comparison	Result
Berecochea	1,009 prisoners (CA)	6-month reduction in time served vs. control	NSD return to prison in 1 year (Berecochea, Jaman, and Jones 1973)
Palmer, Community Treatment Project	802 male delinquents (CA)	Community vs. institution	Community lower revocations in 2 years (Palmer 1974)
Lamb and Goertzel, Ellsworth House	110 males sentenced to jail (San Mateo, CA)	Community vs. jail	NSD parole revocations in 6 months (Lamb and Goertzel 1974)
Jesness	913 male delinquents (CA)	Psychodynamic vs. behavioral institution	NSD violations in 2 years (Jesness 1975)
Quay and Love	568 referred juveniles (Pinellas County, FL)	Counseling vs. control	Counseled lower rearrests in 1 year (Quay and Love 1977)
Waldo and Chiricos	281 prisoners (FL)	Work release vs. control	NSD in self-reported and official arrests in 46 months (Waldo and Chiricos 1977)
Fo and O'Donnell, Buddy System	553 referred youths (HI)	Buddy vs. control	NSD rearrests in 3 years (O'Donnell, Lydgate, and Fo 1979)
Maynard	1,252 unemployed high school dropouts (five US sites)	Supported work vs. control	Arrests in 27 months lower for supported work (Maynard 1980)
Rossi and Berk, LIFE	432 male prisoners (Baltimore, MD)	Job placement vs. financial aid vs. both vs. control	Rearrests in 1 year lower for unemployment benefit (Rossi, Berk, and Lenihan 1980)
Rossi and Berk, TARP	3,982 prisoners (GA, TX)	Job counseling vs. unemployment benefit vs. control	NSD rearrests in 1 year (Rossi, Berk, and Lenihan 1980)
Baker and Sadd, Court Employment Project	666 male defendants in felony cases (New York City)	Job counseling and help in court vs. control	NSD rearrests in 1 year (Baker and Sadd 1981)
Lichtman and Smock	503 male probationers (Wayne County, MI)	Intensive vs. regular probation	NSD reconvictions in 2–3 years (Lichtman and Smock 1981)

NOTE.—GGI = guided group interaction; NSD = not significantly different; SRD = self-reported delinquency.

TABLE 6
Early Non-American Randomized Experiments

Investigator and Title	Initial Sample	Intervention Conditions	Results
Berntsen and Christiansen	252 prisoners (Copenhagen, Den.)	Counseling vs. control	Counseled lower reconvictions in 6 years (Berntsen and Christiansen 1965)
Rose and Hamilton	394 male arrested juveniles (Blackburn, UK)	Cautioned and supervised vs. cautioned	NSD recidivism in 2 years (Rose and Hamilton 1970)
Williams, Borstal Allocation Project	610 male institutionalized youths (UK)	Casework vs. group counseling vs. traditional institution	Lower reconvictions in 2 years in casework institution (Williams 1970)
Shaw	176 male prisoners (UK)	Counseling vs. control	Counseled lower reconvictions in 2 years (Shaw 1974)
Cornish and Clarke	173 male institutionalized delinquents (Bristol, UK)	Therapeutic community vs. traditional training	NSD reconvictions in 2 years (Cornish and Clarke 1975)
Folkard, IMPACT	900 probationers (four sites in UK)	Intensive vs. regular probation	NSD reconvictions in 2 years (Folkard, Smith, and Smith 1976)
Berg	96 truants (Leeds, UK)	Adjourned vs. supervised	Adjourned lower reoffending in 6 months (Berg et al. 1978)
Fowles	290 male prisoners (Liverpool, UK)	Counseling vs. control	NSD reconvictions in 1 year (Fowles 1978)
Byles and Maurice, Juvenile Services Project	305 arrested juveniles (Hamilton, Can.)	Family therapy vs. traditional	NSD recidivism in 2 years (Byles and Maurice 1979)
Annis	150 male prisoners (Ontario, Can.)	Group therapy vs. control	NSD reconvictions in 1 year (Annis 1979)

NOTE.—NSD = not significantly different.

rates than the controls. Thus, assessment before treatment seemed to be essential.

A common problem was that the degree to which the treatment was implemented, and its intensity, were often unclear. Where implementation was studied, this was often illuminating. For example, Kassebaum, Ward, and Wilner (1971) gave extensive details about their "group counseling" in prison (which lasted 1–2 hours per week), leading Quay (1977) to argue that it was inadequately delivered by minimally trained and inexpert personnel. In the IMPACT (Intensive Matched Probation and After-Care Treatment) project, offenders were randomly assigned either to regular probation (where officers had an average caseload of 40–45 offenders) or to "intensive" probation (where officers had a maximum caseload of 20 offenders and no court work or social inquiry reports). However, the average number of contacts per month of offenders with their probation officers was three in the "intensive" condition versus 1.5 in the regular condition (Folkard, Smith, and Smith 1976). It is perhaps not surprising that increasing the number of contacts from 1.5 to three per month had no effect on reconvictions. It would be desirable, ideally, to plot a dose-response curve relating treatment intensity to effect size.

It is also highly desirable to replicate experiments. Shaw (1974) found that special casework assistance from welfare officers during the last 6 months of prison sentences was successful in decreasing recidivism. Unfortunately, when this experiment was replicated by Fowles (1978), there was no effect on recidivism. The reason for the difference in results is not entirely clear, but the Shaw experiment was carried out with long-term prisoners while the Fowles experiment was carried out with short-term prisoners. Possibly the long-term prisoners may have been older and more highly motivated to try to desist from offending.

There were various other difficulties with these early experiments, including case flow problems. Clarke and Cornish (1972) reported that the number of juveniles who were sent to their institution decreased steadily over time because the classifying center became concerned that the inmates might not receive the most suitable treatment (because of the randomization). Also, there was some contamination of one treatment by another in this experiment because the inmates received two different treatments in two different living units but shared many facilities (Cornish and Clarke 1975). In addition, it was often difficult to manipulate only one factor because changes in one factor often led to changes in others. For example, Jesness (1971*a*) was interested in comparing 20-bed and 50-bed living units in an institution, but the inmate-staff ratio was much greater in the larger unit. Perhaps because of this, the regime in the 50-bed unit was more controlling and punitive, whereas the regime in the 20-bed unit was more informal, allowing greater willingness of the staff to involve themselves in the boys' problems. Nevertheless, there was no difference between the units in parole revocation rates.

These early experiments were encouraging in some respects but discouraging in others. They were encouraging because they demonstrated that many different types of randomized experiments in criminology could be successfully mounted and carried through to completion. However, they were discouraging because in most cases the interventions had no significant effects on offending (compared to control conditions). Even worse, where significant effects were found, there were often problems that cast doubt on the validity of the desirable results.

B. What Have We Found Out Since?

Since 1983, there has been an enormous increase in American randomized experiments in criminology. Seventy-six experiments (with at least 50 or other units per condition) were identified by Farrington and Welsh (2006) in five categories: policing, prevention, corrections, court, and community treatment. More American experiments have been published since 2006, of course (e.g., Blais and Bacher 2007; Green and Winik 2010). There has been no comparable increase in non-American randomized experiments since 1983, and only nine were identified by Farrington and Welsh (2006). In contrast to these experiments before 1983, when seven out of 10 were carried out in the United Kingdom, none of the nine later experiments was carried out in the United Kingdom (although there has recently been a series of UK experiments on restorative justice that I discuss below).

British randomized experiments were stopped as a result of objections to them raised by Clarke and Cornish (1972). They argued that randomized experiments raised ethical and practical problems, could not easily be generalized, and often studied heterogeneous interventions where the active ingredients were unclear. I have discussed and tried to answer these objections in my review of British experiments (Farrington 2003*a*). Clarke and Cornish recommended studies of a number of institutions, with measures of effectiveness of each institution correlated with treatment variables and statistical controls for noncomparability. However, internal validity is inevitably lower in such studies than in randomized experiments.

Because of the large number of American experiments carried out since 1983, there is not space to describe them all here. I have chosen to show four important experiments in each of the five categories in table 7, and I mention others on similar topics (e.g., domestic violence, boot camps, or drug courts) in the text. Table 8 shows all available non-American randomized experiments since 1983. Since 2000, there have been several systematic reviews of the effectiveness of specific criminological interventions; they have reviewed both randomized experiments and quasi-experimental evaluations, and I refer to their conclusions. Randomized experiments followed by interviews at least 10 years later are reviewed as longitudinal-experimental studies in Section III. Randomized experiments with a long follow-up in records or with a shorter follow-up by interviews are reviewed here.[5]

In contrast to the conclusions in 1983, when most interventions (primarily based on counseling) seemed to be ineffective, it can now be concluded that many types of interventions are effective in reducing offending: partly because of improvements in interventions (e.g., using cognitive-behavioral skills training rather than counseling) and partly because of improvements in methods of summarizing results (e.g., using meta-analysis of effect sizes rather than counting significant versus nonsignificant findings; see Lipsey and Wilson 2001). For consistency with earlier tables, I have focused on significant versus nonsignificant findings in table 8, but more information about effect sizes is given in Farrington and Welsh (2005, 2006).

In a comparison of later with earlier experiments, there have been three major methodological changes. First, there have been more outcome measures of self-reported offending as well as official offending. Second, researchers have often used survival analysis rather than reporting offending during a specific follow-up period. Third, researchers have reported effect sizes as well as statistical significance. In general, researchers have used "intent-to-treat" analyses and studied those

---

[5] For more information about criminological experiments since 1983, see Farrington and Welsh (2005, 2006).

TABLE 7
Later American Randomized Experiments

Investigator and Title	Initial Sample	Intervention Conditions	Results
Policing:			
Sherman and Berk, Minneapolis Domestic Violence Experiment	330 male domestic violence suspects (Minneapolis, MN)	Arrest vs. advise/separate	Rearrests in 6 months lower for those arrested (Sherman and Berk 1984)
Abrahamse, Phoenix Repeat Offender Program	480 repeat offenders (Phoenix, AZ)	Police targeting vs. no targeting	Arrests in 6 months higher for those targeted (Abrahamse et al. 1991)
Sherman, Milwaukee Domestic Violence Experiment	1,200 domestic violence suspects (Milwaukee, WI)	Arrest vs. warning	NSD rearrests in 7–9 months (Sherman et al. 1992)
Sherman and Weisburd	110 hot spots	Increased vs. normal patrolling	Crime calls in 12 months lower for increased patrolling (Sherman and Weisburd 1995)
Prevention:			
Grossman and Tierney, Big Brothers Big Sisters	1,138 youths (US)	Mentoring vs. no treatment	NSD self-reported violence in 12 months (Grossman and Tierney 1998)
Schochet, Job Corps	15,386 youths (US)	Job Corps vs. no treatment	Arrests in 40 months lower for Job Corps (Schochet, Burghardt, and Glazerman 2001)
Kling and Ludwig, Moving to Opportunity	3,079 persons (five sites in US)	Move to better area vs. no vouchers	NSD arrests in 5 years (Kling, Ludwig, and Katz 2005)
Borduin	176 delinquents (Columbia, MO)	MST vs. individual therapy	MST have fewer felony arrests up to 23 years later (Sawyer and Borduin 2011)
Corrections:			
Cook and Spirrison, Project Aware	176 male delinquents (MS)	Scared Straight vs. no treatment	NSD offenses in 12 months (Cook and Spirrison 1992)

Peters	About 1,200 male delinquents (AL, CO, OH)	Boot camp vs. confinement or probation	Convictions in 9 months higher for boot camp in OH, NSD in AL, CO (Peters, Thomas, and Zamberlan 1997)
Marques	484 male sex offenders (CA)	Cognitive behavioral treatment vs. no treatment	NSD reoffending in 8 years (Marques et al. 2005)
Gaes	561 prisoners (CA)	High-security vs. low-security prison	Return to prison in 6 years higher for high security (Gaes and Camp 2009)
Court:			
Klein	306 juvenile arrestees (US)	Release vs. court	Rearrests in 27 months lower if released (Klein 1986)
Schneider	1,047 adjudicated juveniles (DC, GA, ID, OK)	Restitution vs. probation or incarceration	NSD court referrals in 22–36 months (Schneider 1986)
Gottfredson	235 drug arrestees (Baltimore, MD)	Drug court vs. usual court	Arrests in 2 years lower for drug court (Gottfredson, Najaka, and Kearley 2003)
Jeong and McGarrell, Indianapolis Restorative Justice Experiment	782 juvenile offenders (Indianapolis, IN)	Restorative justice vs. court diversion	NSD arrests in 12 years (Jeong, McGarrell, and Hipple 2012)
Community:			
Petersilia and Turner	1,762 offenders (14 sites in US)	Intensive vs. usual supervision	Arrests in 12 months lower in one site (Petersilia and Turner 1993a)
Van Voorhis, Georgia Cognitive Skills Experiment	468 male parolees (GA)	Reasoning and Rehabilitation vs. control	NSD arrests in 9 months (Van Voorhis et al. 2004)
Barnes, Philadelphia Low Intensity Community Supervision Experiment	1,559 offenders (Philadelphia, PA)	Less intensive vs. usual supervision	NSD arrests in 1 year (Barnes et al. 2010)
Prendergast	812 offenders (four sites in US)	Case management vs. usual parole	NSD arrests in 9 months (Prendergast et al. 2011)

NOTE.—NSD = not significantly different; MST = multisystemic therapy.

TABLE 8
Later Non-American Randomized Experiments

Investigator and Title	Initial Sample	Intervention Conditions	Results
Robinson	4,072 male offenders (Can.)	Reasoning and Rehabilitation vs. other	NSD convictions in 12 months (Robinson 1995)
Ortmann	228 male prisoners (Ger.)	Social therapy prison vs. usual prison	NSD convictions in 5 years (Ortmann 2000)
Sherman and Strang, Reintegrative Shaming Experiments (RISE)	1,413 offenders of four types (Canberra, Aust.)	Restorative justice vs. court	Arrests in 12 months lower for violent offenders (Sherman, Strang, and Woods 2000)
Leschied and Cunningham	409 delinquents (London, Can.)	MST vs. probation	NSD convictions in 12 months (Leschied and Cunningham 2002)
Sherman and Strang	728 offenders (three sites in UK)	Restorative justice vs. control	Reconvictions in 2 years lower in one site, NSD in two others (Shapland et al. 2008)
Killias, Switzerland Sentencing Experiment	113 offenders (Switz.)	Community service vs. 2 weeks' imprisonment	NSD reconvictions in 11 years (Killias et al. 2010)
Eisner and Ribeaud, Zurich Project on the Social Development of Children (Z-Proso)	56 schools and 1,675 children aged 6 (Zurich, Switz.)	Child + parent training vs. child training vs. parent training vs. neither	Antisocial behavior in 2 years decreased after child training (Malti, Ribeaud, and Eisner 2011)
Lösel and Stemmler, Erlangen-Nuremberg Development and Prevention Study	675 children age 5 (Erlangen-Nuremberg, Ger.)	Child/parent training vs. child training vs. parent training vs. neither	Antisocial behavior in 4-5 years decreased (Lösel and Stemmler 2012)

NOTE.—NSD = not significantly different; MST = multisystemic therapy.

who were originally assigned to interventions rather than those who completed treatment.

1. *Policing.* Since 1983, there has been a marked increase in larger experiments and in multisite experiments. There has also been much more interest in replicating experiments. The classic example of replication is the Minneapolis Domestic Violence Experiment (Sherman and Berk 1984), which showed that arresting male perpetrators for misdemeanor domestic assaults was followed by fewer repeat incidents of this crime (against the same victim) than ordering the offender to leave the premises for 8 hours or offering advice and mediation. These results were welcomed by the US Department of Justice and used to encourage police forces to arrest male perpetrators of domestic violence rather than to deal with them in other ways (Sherman and Cohn 1989; Meeker and Binder 1990). According to Sherman (1992, p. 103), "the publicity helped to gain acceptance for the idea of randomized experiments."

The results of the original Minneapolis experiment encouraged the US National Institute of Justice to fund an ambitious program of research to see whether the findings could be replicated in different settings (Maxwell, Garner, and Fagan 2002). Unfortunately, they were not. Only arrests in Omaha when the offender had left the premises produced a similar reduction in rearrests to Minneapolis (Dunford 1990). In attempting to reconcile all these results, Sherman (1992) concluded that male offenders with a lower stake in conformity (e.g., unemployed or unmarried) tended to get worse after arrest, whereas those with a greater stake in conformity tended to improve (i.e., offend less). Offenders in the Milwaukee Domestic Violence Experiment (Sherman et al. 1992) have now been followed up in records for over 20 years, but no results have yet been published from this follow-up.[6]

Experiments on the deterrent effects of police activity in crime "hot spots" are more convincing. Sherman and Weisburd (1995) found that increased police patrolling in hot spots caused a significant (11 percent) decrease in crime calls for service, and similarly encouraging results were reported in smaller scale experiments by Weisburd and Green (1995), Braga et al. (1999), and Taylor, Koper, and Woods (2011). Braga's (2006) systematic review of the effectiveness of policing of hot

---

[6] For the latest review of experiments on violence against women, see Davis and Auchter (2010).

spots concluded that targeted police actions are effective in reducing crime and disorder in high-activity crime locations.

Targeting offenders is also effective. In the Phoenix Repeat Offender Program (Abrahamse et al. 1991), offenders were randomly assigned either to receive special attention (thoroughly documenting prior criminal records, devoting extra effort to obtaining and maintaining cooperation from victims and witnesses) or to receive no special treatment. The special attention was effective in increasing rearrests, reincarceration, and sentence length.

2. *Prevention.* Several famous prevention experiments with long follow-ups are described in Section III. Grossman and Tierney (1998) found that the Big Brothers Big Sisters mentoring program had some beneficial effects in decreasing drug and alcohol use, but it did not decrease self-reported violence. However, systematic reviews of mentoring programs suggest that they are effective in reducing offending (Jolliffe and Farrington 2008; Tolan et al. 2008). Similarly, the Job Corps program was effective in reducing arrests as well as increasing employment and earnings (Schochet, Burghardt, and Glazerman 2001). This program was designed to improve the employability of at-risk young people through vocational skills training, basic education, and health care.

Changing neighborhoods and environments seems to be less effective in reducing crime. Kling, Ludwig, and Katz (2005) evaluated the impact of the Moving to Opportunity program in five cities in the United States, in which low–socioeconomic status (often minority) families were given vouchers to enable them to move to better areas. The effects of this move on the offending of their children were investigated. There was little effect on the prevalence of arrests overall, but arrests of girls decreased while arrests of boys increased. The authors speculated that girls may have reacted to their more affluent classmates by behaving more conventionally and trying harder in school, while boys may have reacted more aggressively and by not making much effort in school.

A number of evaluations suggest that multisystematic therapy (MST) is effective in reducing offending. MST is a multimodal treatment that is chosen according to the needs of the young person, and it may include individual, family, peer, school, and community interventions. In the longest follow-up (up to 23 years), Sawyer and Borduin (2011) found that juvenile offenders who received MST had significantly fewer felony arrests (35 percent compared with 55 percent) than those who received individual therapy up to age 37, as well as fewer years of incarceration. However, the one large-scale independent evaluation of MST, by Leschied and Cunningham (2002) in London, Canada, discovered that it was not effective in reducing later convictions (compared with the usual probation supervision). Furthermore, two meta-analyses of the effectiveness of MST came to diametrically opposed conclusions. Curtis, Ronan, and Borduin (2004) found that MST was effective, but Littell (2005) concluded that it was not.

In an effort to include more non-American experiments in table 8, I listed the Erlangen-Nuremberg Development and Prevention Project (Lösel and Stemmler 2012) and the Zurich Project on the Social Development of Children (Malti, Ribeaud, and Eisner 2011). In the Zurich project, 56 schools (and 1,675 children) were randomly assigned to four conditions. Both are excellent experiments on the effectiveness of child and parent training, but neither has reported offending outcomes as yet (only results on childhood antisocial behavior). So far, the interventions in the Erlangen-Nuremberg project seem to be effective according to child reports, but only the child skills training seems to be effective in the Zurich project.

3. *Corrections.* "Scared Straight" has proved to be an ineffective and even damaging intervention. In this program, adult prisoners harangue young delinquents (or at-risk youth) about the terrors of imprisonment in an attempt to deter them from offending. Table 7 shows that in Mississippi, Cook and Spirrison (1992) found no effect of the program on offending (comparing 12 months before with 12 months after). Similar results were obtained in a randomized experiment by Lewis (1983) in California. In both experiments, delinquents who received the program were more likely to reoffend. These results are quite typical. A systematic review and meta-analysis by Petrosino et al. (2014) concluded that Scared Straight had damaging effects. Also, in agreement with the hypothesis that more deterrent interventions have damaging effects, Gaes and Camp (2009) found that offenders who were randomly assigned to a high-security (compared with a low-security) prison had higher recidivism rates.

Boot camps are also ineffective in reducing offending. These were introduced in the late 1980s as a way to deter and rehabilitate offenders by subjecting them to rigorous military-style training, often combined with treatment programs. Peters, Thomas, and Zamberlan (1997) carried out three experiments on boot camps in Alabama, Colorado, and Ohio. None of these found a significant desirable effect of a boot camp on offending, and in Cleveland the boot camp led to a significantly increased prevalence of offending compared with confinement in youth services facilities. A later follow-up by Bottcher and Ezell (2005) concluded that overall, these boot camps had no effect on rearrests. Again, these results are quite typical. In a systematic review and meta-analysis of boot camps, Wilson and MacKenzie (2006) concluded that, overall, they had no effect on reoffending. However, in a later randomized experiment, MacKenzie, Bierie, and Mitchell (2007) found that a boot camp for adults that included therapeutic programs was effective in reducing rearrests.

The results were similarly discouraging in randomized experiments on moral reconation therapy by Armstrong (2003) and on cognitive-behavioral treatment for sex offenders by Marques et al. (2005), which had a long follow-up averaging 8 years. Also, in Germany, Ortmann (2000) found that reconviction rates were not significantly lower for inmates who went to a special social therapy prison compared to a usual prison.

In a review by Farrington and Welsh (2006), only one out of 14 correctional experiments had a desirable result. In Delaware, Inciardi et al. (1997) found that therapeutic community treatment for drug-involved inmates was followed by a significant 20 percent decrease in reoffending. However, in a similar experiment in Washington State, Dugan and Everett (1998) reported that therapeutic community treatment for drug-involved inmates was followed by a (nonsignificant) 32 percent increase in reoffending. A systematic review and meta-analysis of 74 evaluations of prison-based drug treatment concluded that it was effective in reducing reoffending (Mitchell, Wilson, and MacKenzie 2012).

4. *Court.*   Labeling theory suggests that court appearances tend to have undesirable stigmatizing and delinquency-amplifying effects; reviews of the literature generally confirm this (e.g., Huizinga and Henry 2008; Petrosino, Turpin-Petrosino, and Guckenburg 2010). Klein (1986) carried out a randomized experiment to evaluate the effectiveness of diversion programs compared with court petitions for juveniles. In agreement with labeling theory, he found that the reoffending rate was significantly (33 percent) lower for the released cases. However,

Stickle et al. (2008) reported that a diversionary teen court was followed by higher self-reported offending and arrests.

Schneider (1986) carried out a multisite evaluation of restitution (compared with probation or incarceration) in four communities. In all four cases, restitution was followed by a nonsignificant decrease in reoffending. Similarly, in a long-term (12-year) follow-up of an experiment on restorative justice conferences (compared with court diversion), Jeong, McGarrell, and Hipple (2012) found that restorative justice had no effect on reoffending. McCold and Wachtel (1998) came to the same conclusion. The most ambitious and extensive experiments on restorative justice have been carried out by Sherman et al. (2005) in Australia and England. Table 8 shows that there were significantly desirable results in one experiment in Australia and in one experiment in England, but not in other cases. However, a systematic review and meta-analysis showed that, overall, restorative justice has encouraging results in reducing reoffending (Strang and Sherman 2006).

A systematic review and meta-analysis by Mitchell et al. (2012) showed that drug courts are also effective in reducing reoffending by drug offenders. In Baltimore, Gottfredson, Najaka, and Kearley (2003) found that the rearrest rate after drug court treatment was significantly lower than after the regular court treatment (66 percent compared to 81 percent). Furthermore, even when they reoffended, drug offenders who had been treated in the drug court took longer to reoffend (Banks and Gottfredson 2004).

5. *Community Treatment.* Most of the community treatment experiments have compared intensive supervision of offenders with the usual supervision. However, the results have not been encouraging. Possibly the largest ever experimental criminological evaluation was carried out by Petersilia and Turner (1993a, 1993b). In a nationwide 14-site evaluation of intensive supervision/probation/parole, desirable effects on recidivism were found in only one of the 14 sites. Similarly, the effects on recidivism were small or nonsignificant in the experiments of Barton and Butts (1990), Land, McCall, and Williams (1990), Greenwood, Deschenes, and Adams (1993), Sontheimer and Goodstein (1993), and most recently Lane et al. (2007).

Prendergast et al. (2011) evaluated a particular type of parole supervision, called strengths-based case management, that aimed to build on and enhance the strengths of offenders. However, compared with the more usual parole supervision, this had no effect on recidivism.

Similarly, Barnes et al. (2010) experimentally evaluated the effects of decreasing the frequency of probation supervision (from an average of 4.5 to 2.4 visits per year) and found that this had no effect on recidivism.

Reasoning and Rehabilitation is a program designed to improve the cognitive skills of offenders (Ross and Ross 1995). It was experimentally evaluated with parolees in Georgia by Van Voorhis et al. (2004) and with prisoners in Canada by Robinson (1995). The recidivism rate of the treated offenders was not significantly less than that of the control offenders in either case. However, systematic reviews and meta-analyses by Tong and Farrington (2006, 2008) concluded that, overall, Reasoning and Rehabilitation was effective in reducing offending, and Lipsey and Landenberger (2006) found that cognitive-behavioral interventions in general were effective.

III. Longitudinal-Experimental Research
Strictly speaking, every experiment is prospective and longitudinal in nature since it involves a minimum of two contacts or data collections with the participants: one consisting of the experimental intervention (the independent variable) and one consisting of the outcome measurement (the dependent variable). However, the time interval covered by the typical experiment is relatively short. Farrington, Ohlin, and Wilson (1986) argued that longitudinal-experimental studies were needed with three elements: several data collections, covering several years; the experimental intervention; and several more data collections, covering several years, afterward. No study of this kind has ever been carried out on offending using interview data. A few experiments collected official record data retrospectively for a few years before an intervention and prospectively for a few years after the intervention (e.g., Empey and Lubeck 1971; Empey and Erickson 1972), but these did not assess the effect of the intervention on criminal career trajectories or developmental sequences of offending. In the Montreal longitudinal-experimental study, Vitaro, Brendgen, and Tremblay (2001) and Lacourse et al. (2002) pioneered the method of studying the effects of the intervention on subsequent offending trajectories.

An important advantage of a combined longitudinal-experimental study in comparison with separate longitudinal and experimental projects is economy. It is cheaper to carry out both studies with the same individuals than with different individuals. For example, the effect of interventions and the effect of risk and protective factors can be compared on the same people. The number of individuals and separate data collections (e.g., interviews) is greater in two studies than in one (other things being equal).

More fundamentally, the two types of studies have complementary strengths and weaknesses, and a combined longitudinal-experimental study could build on the strengths of both. For example, the longitudinal survey could provide information about the natural history of development, while the experiment could yield knowledge about the impact of interventions on development. Even if the experimental part could not be carried through successfully (e.g., because of case flow problems or implementation failure), the longitudinal-experimental study would yield valuable knowledge about the natural history of development, and quasi-experimental research on the impact of risk or protective factors and life events would still be possible. Therefore, longitudinal-experimental research is arguably less risky than experimental research.

Experiments are designed to test hypotheses. In the combined project, causal hypotheses could be generated in the longitudinal study from risk and protective factors and life events and then tested on the same individuals in the experimental study. Experiments are the best method of testing the effects of variations (between individuals) in an independent variable on a dependent one, whereas the longitudinal study can investigate the effect of changes (within individuals) in an independent variable on a dependent one. The combined project can compare the impact of variation with the impact of change to see if the same results are obtained with the same individuals. This is an important issue because most findings on risk and protective factors for offending essentially concern variations between individuals, whereas most theories and interventions refer to changes within individuals (Farrington 1988; Farrington et al. 2002). The longitudinal and experimental elements are also complementary in that the experiment can demonstrate (with high internal validity) the effect of only one or two independent variables, whereas the longitudinal study can demonstrate (with somewhat lower internal validity in quasi-experimental analyses) the interactive, sequential, and relative effects of many independent variables.

The main advantages of longitudinal-experimental research have been summarized by Blumstein, Cohen, and Farrington (1988*b*). The impact of interventions can be better understood in the context of preexisting trends or developmental sequences, which would help in assessing maturation, instability, and regression effects in before and after comparisons. The prior information about participants would help to verify that comparison groups were equivalent, to set baseline measures, to investigate interactions between types of persons (and their risk and protective factors and prior histories) and types of treatments, to establish eligibility for inclusion in the experiment, and to estimate the impact of differential attrition from experimental conditions. The long-term follow-up information would show effects of the intervention that were not immediately apparent to facilitate the study of different age-appropriate outcomes over time, to make it possible to compare short-term and long-term effects, and to investigate the developmental sequences linking them. The experimental intervention could help to distinguish causal or developmental sequences from different age-appropriate behavioral manifestations of the same underlying construct.

A major problem centers on the extent to which the experiment might interfere with the goals of the longitudinal study. In a simple experiment, some of the sample will be ineligible, some will be in the experimental group, and the remainder will be in the control group. After the experimental intervention, it might be inadvisable to draw conclusions about the natural history of offending from the experimental group, since this would have been treated in an unusual way. The experiment may increase or decrease attrition (or cause differential attrition) from the longitudinal study. Therefore, in drawing conclusions about the whole sample, results obtained with the ineligibles, experimentals, and controls might have to be treated differently.

It is less obvious that experimental persons would have to be eliminated in investigations of impact questions using quasi-experimental analyses. If the experimental intervention could be viewed as just another independent variable impinging on them, investigations of the effect of nonmanipulated independent variables could be based on the whole sample. Of course, it might be interesting to investigate whether the impact of one independent variable was different at different levels of another independent variable (e.g., in experimental and control groups).

It could be argued that each person should receive only one experimental treatment because of the likely effect of the treatment in making the person different from a control or an ineligible. However, there may be good reasons to investigate the interactive effect of two consecutive treatments. The analysis of the data needs to mirror the factorial nature of the design. If the controls received a special treatment (e.g., being denied something that was usually available in the community), then it might even be argued that they also should not be included in a subsequent experiment.

The passage of time will inevitably cause problems. An experiment that was desirable and feasible at one time (e.g., at the start of a longitudinal study) may be less desirable and feasible some years later because of changes in theory or policy concerns, in methodology, or in practical constraints (e.g., a change in a "gatekeeper" such as a police chief). Also, the participants in a longitudinal study will move around, and it may be that an experiment can be conducted only in a specific location. Possibly only those who are residentially stable (at least in staying in the same metropolitan area) should be eligible to participate in the experiment. For a number of reasons, the eligibility of participants could change over time, as their personal circumstances changed.

Since it is likely that attrition will increase with the length of the follow-up, differential attrition could prove to be one of the greatest problems that need to be overcome in a longitudinal-experimental study (Farrington and Welsh 2005). It is important to use methods that minimize attrition and to carry out research on this topic. For example, successful methods of tracing and securing cooperation used in the Cambridge Study have been described (Farrington et al. 1990). Famous longitudinal researchers such as Robins (1966) and McCord (1979) were able to locate and interview high percentages of their samples over follow-up periods of 30 years or more.

What Have We Learned?   Table 9 lists all the large-scale randomized experiments in criminology that have a follow-up by interviews or questionnaires lasting at least 10 years.[7] Undoubtedly the best-known and most famous longitudinal-experimental studies in criminology are those by McCord (1978), Tremblay et al. (1996), Olds et al. (1998), and Schweinhart et al. (2005). All of these studies essentially added a long-term follow-up to a randomized experiment. McCord and Trem-

---

[7] For more detailed reviews, see Farrington (2006), Farrington, Loeber, and Welsh (2010), and Farrington and Welsh (2013).

TABLE 9
Longitudinal-Experimental Studies

Investigator and Title	Initial Sample	Intervention Conditions	Follow-ups
McCord, Cambridge-Somerville Study	325E, 325C, male, ave. age 10 in 1939 (Boston, MA)	5 years counseling vs. control	Ave. age 48 in 1975–79: interviews, questionnaires, records (McCord 1990)
Schweinhart, Perry Preschool Program	58E, 65E, African American, ages 3–4 in 1962–65 (Ypsilanti, MI)	1–2 years preschool vs. control	Last interviews at ages 19, 27, 40 (Schweinhart et al. 2005)
Campbell, Carolina Abecedarian Project	57E, 54C, most African American, born 1972–77 (Chapel Hill, NC)	5 years full-day child care vs. control	Interview at age 21 (Campbell et al. 2002)
Olds, Nurse-Family Partnership	100 E1 (pregnancy), 116 E2 (up to 2), 184C, unmarried low-socioeconomic status mothers, born 1978–80 (Elmira, NY)	1–3 years home visiting vs. control	Interviews at ages 15 and 19 (Eckenrode et al. 2010)
Brooks-Gunn, Infant Health and Development Program	377E, 608C, low birth weight, born 1984–85 (eight US sites)	3 years home visiting/day care educational intervention vs. control	Last interview at age18 (McCormick et al. 2006)
Mills, Washington Preschool Program	104E (DI), 101C (ML), special education children ave. age 5 in 1984–88 (Seattle, WA)	1–4 years direct instruction vs. mediated learning control (preschool)	Interview at age 15 (Mills et al. 2002)
Tremblay, Montreal Longitudinal-Experimental Study	69E, 181C, disruptive males age 7 in 1985–87 (Montreal, Can.)	2 years child skills and parent training vs. control	Questionnaires up to age 17, records at age 24 (Boisjoli et al. 2007)
Greenberg, Fast Track	445E, 446C, high risk, ages 6–7 in 54 schools in 1991–93 (four US sites)	5 years child skills and parent training vs. control	Interviews up to age 18, records up to age 19 (CPPRG 2010)

NOTE.—E = experimental group; C = control group; DI = direct instruction; ML = mediated learning; CPPRG = Conduct Problems Prevention Research Group.

blay have provided a great deal of information about both the effects of the intervention and the development of offending, while Schweinhart and Olds have focused more on the effects of the intervention. There are several other important longitudinal-experimental studies in which the participants were not strictly randomly assigned to interventions (e.g., Raine et al. 2003; Reynolds et al. 2007), but they are not reviewed here.

McCord (1978) carried out the most important pioneering longitudinal-experimental study. In the Cambridge-Somerville Study in Boston, the experimental boys received special counseling help between the average ages of 10 and 15, and over 500 boys in both experimental and control groups were then followed up for over 30 years afterward, in records and through questionnaires and interviews (McCord 1990). The treatment was ineffective in preventing offending since about a quarter of both groups were known to have committed crimes as juveniles, while about two-thirds of both groups had been convicted as adults. Significantly more of the experimental boys had two or more convictions. Other undesirable effects of this treatment were that more of the experimental group were alcoholics, they tended to die earlier, they were more likely to have high blood pressure or heart trouble, and they were less likely to have professional or white-collar jobs (McCord 2003).

The Montreal Longitudinal-Experimental Study (Tremblay et al. 1995) is also very well known. Initially, over 1,000 Montreal boys in 53 schools were rated by teachers on their disruptive behavior at age 6, and 250 scoring above the 70th percentile were randomly assigned to experimental or control groups. The experimental boys received child skills training and parent training between ages 7 and 9. The results of the intervention showed that the experimental boys committed less delinquency (according to self-reports) between ages 10 and 15. The experimental boys were less likely to be gang members, to get drunk, or to take drugs, but they were not significantly different from the controls in having sexual intercourse by age 15 (Tremblay et al. 1996). Interestingly, the differences in antisocial behavior between experimental and control boys increased as the follow-up progressed. A later follow-up showed that fewer experimental boys had a criminal record by age 24 (Boisjoli et al. 2007).

Another extremely influential experiment with a long-term follow-up is the Perry Preschool Project in Ypsilanti, Michigan (Schweinhart et al. 2005). This was essentially a Head Start program targeted to disadvantaged African American children. The experimental children attended a daily preschool program, backed up by weekly home visits, usually lasting 2 years, covering ages 3 and 4. The aim of the program was to provide intellectual stimulation, to increase cognitive (thinking and reasoning) abilities, and to increase later school achievement.

An important feature of this project is that its true significance became apparent only after long-term follow-ups to ages 15 (Schweinhart and Weikart 1980), 19 (Berrueta-Clement et al. 1984), 27 (Schweinhart, Barnes, and Weikart 1993), and 40 (Schweinhart et al. 2005). As demonstrated in several other Head Start projects, the experimental group initially showed higher intelligence at ages 4–5 but was no different from the control group by ages 8–9 (Schweinhart and Weikart 1980). This led to the argument that compensatory education was ineffective (Westinghouse Learning Corporation and Ohio University 1969). However, by age 27, the experimental group had accumulated only half as many arrests as the controls: an average of 2.3 compared with 4.6 arrests. Also, they had significantly higher earnings and were more likely to be homeowners. A cost-benefit analysis showed that, for every $1 spent on the program, $7 was saved in the long term (Barnett 1996). At age 40, 91 percent of the participants were interviewed (112 out of the original 123), and the average number of arrests was still significantly greater for the control group (9.4 compared with 5.6). The experimental group was more likely to be married and less likely to be off work sick. It was estimated that $17 was saved for every $1 spent on the program, and most of these savings were attributable to decreased offending (Schweinhart et al. 2005).

Another famous experiment was conducted by Olds et al. (1998) on the effects of home visiting. In Elmira, New York, 400 pregnant women were randomly assigned to receive home visits from nurses during pregnancy and for the first 2 years of their child's life, to receive visits only in pregnancy, or to receive no visits. The nurses visited every 2 weeks and gave advice about child rearing, infant nutrition, infant development, avoidance of substance use, and maternal life course development (family planning, educational achievement, and participation in the workforce). Fifteen years later, it was found that the women who had received visits in pregnancy and infancy had fewer substantiated reports of child abuse and neglect, and their children had fewer arrests and convictions, compared with the control group (Olds et al.

1997, 1998). In the latest follow-up to age 19 (Eckenrode et al. 2010), fewer of the experimental children were arrested, but the difference was mainly found for girls.

Several other experiments have been conducted with long follow-up periods but with few developmental analyses. In the Carolina Abecedarian Project, 111 children aged 3 were randomly assigned to receive either full-time preschool child care (concentrating on the development of cognitive and language skills) or none. At age 21, 104 were interviewed, and 36 percent fewer of the experimental participants reported being convicted or incarcerated (Campbell et al. 2002). Significantly fewer of the experimental participants were regular smokers or marijuana users, significantly more had attended college or university, and they had significantly higher-status jobs.

In another preschool experiment in Washington State, Mills et al. (2002) randomly assigned 205 children (average age 5) to either a cognitively oriented or a direct instruction preschool program. The cognitively oriented program emphasized the development of thinking and problem-solving processes and did not include formal instruction in reading, math, and language skills, unlike the direct instruction program. At age 15, 171 children were reinterviewed and their self-reported delinquency was measured. The researchers found that the experimental and control participants did not differ significantly in their delinquency.

In the Infant Health and Development Project, the effects of the intervention were greater for the children who were heavier at birth (2,000–2,499 grams) compared with those who were lighter (less than 2,000 grams). There were desirable effects on IQ at 24 and 36 months of age (Brooks-Gunn et al. 1993). At age 8, there were desirable effects on IQ and math scores, but only for the heavier babies (McCarton et al. 1997). Similar results were found at age 18 (McCormick et al. 2006). The effects of the program on child arrests at age 18 (reported by the child and parent) were desirable but small.

The Fast Track project also found subgroup differences. In this project, 54 schools (and 891 children) were randomly assigned to receive child skills training and parent training or neither. In the first evaluation in first grade, effect sizes were presented (CPPRG 1999). These were significant and quite substantial: $d = .53$ for teacher ratings of child behavior change and $d = .50$ for parent ratings of child behavior change. In the second evaluation in third grade (CPPRG 2002), the effect sizes were lower but still significant: $d = .27$ for teacher ratings of child behavior change and $d = .20$ for parent ratings of child behavior change. On the basis of conduct disorder, oppositional defiant disorder, special education diagnosis, and high conduct problems, 37 percent of experimental children were classified as problem-free, compared with 27 percent of control children.

The effects of the program continued to decrease by the fifth grade (CPPRG 2004). The effect size for home and community problems (based on self-reports and parent ratings) was $d = .15$ ($p < .02$), but the effect size for school behavioral and academic problems was not presented and was said to be nonsignificant. After this evaluation, effect sizes were not presented and results were given separately for high- and low-risk subgroups (based on behavior ratings by teachers and parents in the initial assessment). The high-risk children constituted the worst one-sixth of the sample.

In the sixth-grade evaluation (CPPRG 2007), the intervention had no overall effect on disruptive behavior disorders, but there was a significant desirable effect on ADHD in the high-risk subgroup. In the ninth-grade evaluation (CPPRG 2007), there was a significant desirable effect of the intervention on self-reported antisocial behavior. There was no overall effect on disruptive behavior disorders, but there was a significant desirable effect on conduct disorder and ADHD in the high-risk subgroup.

In the twelfth-grade follow-up (CPPRG 2010), there seemed little effect of the intervention on a severity-weighted juvenile arrest index, a similar adult arrest index, or a similar self-reported offending index. However, an ordered logit regression suggested that the intervention had a significantly desirable effect on the juvenile arrest index. As before, there was no overall effect of the intervention on disruptive behavior disorders but a significant desirable effect on conduct disorder and oppositional defiant disorder, rated by parents, in the high-risk subgroup (CPPRG 2011).

What has been learned from these long-term follow-ups of randomized experiments? First, the damaging effects of the Cambridge-Somerville intervention became much clearer as a wide variety of outcomes were measured at later ages. Second, the unexpected beneficial effects of programs such as Perry and Nurse-Family Partnership on offending and other later life outcomes became increasingly apparent. These programs were intended to influence only short-term outcomes such as IQ (Perry) and child abuse (Nurse-Family Partnership). Third, the Perry program was initially considered to be a failure because its immediate effects on IQ soon wore off, but the long-term follow-up showed that it was successful in many different ways.

Fourth, the benefit-cost ratio of the Perry program became more and more impressive as the follow-up period was extended. Fifth, the effects of the intervention persisted over a long time period in the Perry and Montreal studies. Sixth, the effects of the intervention decreased over time in Fast Track. Seventh, the effects of the intervention became apparent only for subgroups in some studies (Nurse-Family Partnership, Fast Track, Infant Health and Development Program). It can be concluded that the future course of development cannot necessarily be predicted from short-term follow-ups and that a great deal can be learned from long-term follow-ups.

IV. What Have We Learned?

In the last 30 years, prospective longitudinal surveys have become larger and longer-lasting. Several have followed up the children of the original participants to investigate mechanisms of intergenerational transmission. Well-known risk factors for offending, such as high impulsiveness, low school achievement, poor child rearing, and low family income, have proved to be highly replicable over time and place. However, there have been increased efforts to investigate biological neighborhood and community factors in longitudinal studies. There has also been increased emphasis on identifying protective factors against offending. It is disappointing that there have been few efforts to capitalize on the longitudinal data to study to what extent changes within individuals in risk and protective factors and life events are followed by changes within individuals in offending. Also, there have been relatively few cross-national comparisons. However, there has been an explosion of development and life course theories of offending.

Research on criminal careers has become more sophisticated. Trajectory analyses have revealed the existence of different types of offenders within the age-crime curve. Research on persistent heterogeneity versus state dependence has thrown new light on the continuity of offending. There has been a great increase in the study of criminal careers using self-report information but only a meager increase in knowledge about scaling-up factors from official to self-reported offending. Research on desistance has increased enormously, but there still has not been a great deal of research on adult-onset offending.

In the last 30 years, randomized experiments on criminological topics have greatly increased in the United States but not elsewhere. After a "golden age" in the 1960s and 1970s, randomized experiments in the United Kingdom have decreased considerably. In the United States, there have been many more large-scale experiments, more multisite experiments, and more attempts to replicate experimental findings.

On the basis of experimental research and systematic reviews, we now know that many types of interventions are effective, including nurse home visiting, cognitive-behavioral skills training, parent management training, preschool intellectual enrichment programs, multisystemic therapy, mentoring, hot spots policing, and drug courts. We also know that Scared Straight and convictions of juveniles are damaging and that boot camps, more intensive supervision, and many correctional treatments are ineffective.

Long-term longitudinal-experimental studies show that conclusions often change as participants in experiments are followed up. As mentioned above, the damaging effects of the Cambridge-Somerville Youth Study and the beneficial effects of the Perry Preschool and Nurse Home Visiting programs became clearer. Importantly, the benefit-cost ratios in the Perry program increased over time. In Fast Track, the desirable effects tended to decrease over time, while the effects persisted or even increased in the Montreal study. In short, the long-term follow-ups added greatly to knowledge.

V. What Do We Need to Know, and How Can We Find Out?

In future prospective longitudinal studies, there should be regular, repeated assessments that would permit within-individual analyses relating changes in risk and protective factors or life events to later changes in offending. This would enormously advance knowledge about the causes of offending. Also, it would be highly desirable to carry out such analyses in existing longitudinal surveys that have repeated assessments, such as the Pittsburgh Youth Study.

In the interests of drawing conclusions about development within a reasonably short time, there should be multiple-cohort accelerated longitudinal studies such as those recommended by Farrington, Ohlin, and Wilson (1986) and Tonry, Ohlin, and Farrington (1991).

More comparisons of self-reported and official offending at different ages are needed in order to obtain detailed, replicable information about scaling-up factors. This information is essential for cost-benefit analyses of the effectiveness of interventions. It is desirable to carry out coordinated longitudinal studies following both community and offender samples, as LeBlanc and Frechette (1989) did.

It is important to conduct research on biological, neighborhood, and community factors in longitudinal studies as well as on the more traditional individual, family, peer, and school factors. In order to investigate some biological (e.g., genetic) factors, special designs may be needed, such as following up monozygotic and dizygotic twins (as in the E-Risk study; see Bowes et al. 2009). It is particularly important to study situational factors in longitudinal studies, to explain both the development of offenders and the commission of offenses. For example, Fox and Farrington (2012) showed that particular types of burglars tended to commit particular types of burglaries: older white males tended to commit opportunistic crimes (with no tools used and no forced entry), whereas older African American males tended to commit interpersonal crimes (where dwellings were occupied and there was confrontation with the victim). It is important to design longitudinal studies not only to explain how offenders develop but also to explain how and why the potential offender commits the actual crime in the situation.

A major problem with developmental and life course theories (like other criminological theories) is that they do not make quantitative predictions. Because of this, it is rare for any criminological theory to be disproved. It would be desirable for theories to build on simple mathematical models that make and test quantitative predictions. For example, MacLeod, Grove, and Farrington (2012) were able to predict many features of criminal careers accurately by assuming that there were only three types of offenders: high-rate/high-risk, low-rate/high-risk, and low-rate/low-risk. A theory could start with these simple types of offenders and add postulates about the effects of risk and protective factors and life events in order to explain more and more findings.

It would be desirable to combine a longitudinal study of people with a longitudinal study of places (Weisburd, Groff, and Yang 2012) to try to explain how the individual and the environment interact to produce crimes. It would also be desirable to systematically observe offending as it happens in these places, as Buckle and Farrington (1984) did for shoplifting. More cross-national comparative studies are also needed in order to investigate the replicability of results over time and place and the importance of cultural context and environment.

It is particularly important in any new longitudinal studies to minimize attrition (Farrington et al. 1990). The people who are lost from longitudinal studies tend to be the most uncooperative, elusive, and antisocial. Therefore, I do not believe that multiple imputation (which essentially imposes more regularity on the data) is an adequate method of dealing with attrition. It is much better to expend more resources, time, and effort to try to interview the highest possible proportion of the target sample.

More large-scale randomized experiments are needed in criminology, especially outside the United States. Multisite evaluations and replication experiments are essential. More independent evaluations of interventions are needed because of the problem that, if a person evaluates his or her own program, there could be bias because of conflict of interest (Eisner and Humphreys 2012). More research is also needed on how to maintain effectiveness in going from a small-scale demonstration project to large-scale routine implementation (Welsh, Sullivan, and Olds 2010).

More experiments are needed that would advance knowledge about the causes of offending (Robins 1992; Farrington 2008). Experimenters are usually particularly concerned to have a successful program, and so they tend to use multimodal interventions, which are known to be more effective than single-modality interventions (Wasserman and Miller 1998). However, if a multimodal intervention works, it is difficult to know which are the "active ingredients." More research is needed in experiments on the intervening processes between the intervention and the outcome. And it would be highly desirable to have offending outcome measures both before and after the experimental intervention.

Most experiments investigate the effectiveness of a relatively minor change in the criminal justice system, such as cognitive-behavioral programs in prison or more intensive probation. More experiments are needed on the effectiveness of the major sentences such as prison and probation. Researchers should build on the brave experiments of Berecochea, Jaman, and Jones (1973), who randomly released prisoners 6 months early, and Killias et al. (2010), who randomly assigned offenders to prison or community service, to carry out new experiments on the effectiveness of major sentences. Also, the reporting of experiments should be improved in line with the Consolidated Standards of Reporting Trials (CONSORT) statement for medical research (Perry, Weisburd, and Hewitt 2010). The CONSORT statement consists of a 22-item checklist and flow diagram (see http://www.consort-statement.org). It specifies what information should be provided: introduction and background, methods (objectives, participants, sample size, randomization, interventions, outcomes, statistical methods), results (recruitment of participants, baseline data, numbers analyzed, outcome measures), interpretation, generalizability, and conclusions.

Finally, in order to investigate both the development of offenders and the effectiveness of interventions, longitudinal-experimental studies are needed with several years of interviews, then a randomized intervention, and then several more years of interviews. In such a study, hypotheses about the causes of offending could be generated in the longitudinal data and tested both in the experiment and quasi-experimentally by following up the same people before and after a naturally occurring event. For example, the effects of unemployment on offending could be tested both by experimentally evaluating an employment program and by studying the offending of individuals during their periods of employment and their periods of unemployment. To the extent that the findings were similar, this would greatly increase confidence that unemployment really was a cause of offending.

More than a quarter century ago, my colleagues and I proposed an accelerated longitudinal-experimental design that involved following up four cohorts in a large city, from birth to age 6, age 6 to age 12, age 12 to age 18, and age 18 to age 24, with yearly assessments (Farrington, Ohlin, and Wilson 1986; Tonry, Ohlin, and Farrington 1991). We suggested testing the effects of preschool and parent training interventions in infancy and childhood, peer and school programs at age 15, and employment and drug programs at age 21. I believe that some version of this design is still basically sound and would lead to significant advances in knowledge about the development, explanation, prevention, and treatment of offending and antisocial behavior. I hope very much that an accelerated longitudinal-experimental design might be funded and implemented before 2025.

REFERENCES

Abrahamse, Allan F., Patricia A. Ebener, Peter W. Greenwood, Nora Fitzgerald, and Thomas E. Kosin. 1991. "An Experimental Evaluation of the Phoenix Repeat Offender Program." *Justice Quarterly* 8:141–68.

Adams, Stuart. 1970. "The PICO Project." In *The Sociology of Punishment and Correction*, edited by Norman Johnston, Leonard Savitz, and Marvin E. Wolfgang. New York: Wiley.

Angrist, Joshua D. 2006. "Instrumental Variables Methods in Experimental Criminological Research: What, Why and How." *Journal of Experimental Criminology* 2:23–44.

Annis, Helen M. 1979. "Group Treatment of Incarcerated Offenders with Alcohol and Drug Problems: A Controlled Evaluation." *Canadian Journal of Criminology* 21:3–15.

Armstrong, Todd A. 2003. "The Effect of Moral Reconation Therapy on the Recidivism of Youthful Offenders: A Randomized Experiment." *Criminal Justice and Behavior* 30:668–87.

Asscher, Jessica, Maja Dekovic, Peter H. Van Der Laan, Pier J. M. Prins, and Sander Van Arum. 2007. "Implementing Randomized Experiments in Criminal Justice Settings: An Evaluation of Multisystemic Therapy in the Netherlands." *Journal of Experimental Criminology* 3:113–29.

Baker, Sally H., and Susan Sadd. 1981. *Diversion of Felony Arrests: An Experiment in Pretrial Intervention*. Washington, DC: US National Institute of Justice.

Banks, Duren, and Denise C. Gottfredson. 2004. "Participation in Drug Treatment Court and Time to Rearrest." *Justice Quarterly* 21:637–58.

Barker, Edward D., Louise Arseneault, Mara Brendgen, Nathalie Fontaine, and Barbara Maughan. 2008. "Joint Development of Bullying and Victimization in Adolescence: Relations to Delinquency and Self-Harm." *Journal of the American Academy of Child and Adolescent Psychiatry* 47:1030–38.

Barker, Edward D., Jean R. Seguin, Helene R. White, Marsha E. Bates, Eric Lacourse, Rene Carbonneau, and Richard E. Tremblay. 2007. "Developmental Trajectories of Male Physical Violence and Theft: Relations to Neurocognitive Performance." *Archives of General Psychiatry* 64:592–99.

Barnes, Geoffrey, Lindsay Ahlman, Charlotte Gill, Lawrence W. Sherman, Ellen Kurtz, and Robert Malvestuto. 2010. "Low-Intensity Community Supervision for Low-Risk Offenders: A Randomized Controlled Trial." *Journal of Experimental Criminology* 6:159–89.

Barnett, W. Stephen. 1996. *Lives in the Balance: Age 27 Benefit-Cost Analysis of the High/Scope Perry Preschool Program*. Ypsilanti, MI: High/Scope Press.

Barton, William H., and Jeffrey A. Butts. 1990. "Viable Options: Intensive Supervision Programs for Juvenile Delinquents." *Crime and Delinquency* 36:238–56.

Beaver, Kevin M., Matt DeLisi, Michael G. Vaughan, and J. C. Barnes. 2010. "Monoamine Oxidase A Genotype Is Associated with Gang Membership and Weapon Use." *Comprehensive Psychiatry* 51:130–34.

Berecochea, John E., Dorthy R. Jaman, and Welton A. Jones. 1973. *Time*

Served in Prison and Parole Outcome: An Experimental Study. Sacramento: State of California, Department of Corrections, Research Division.

Berg, Ian, Margaret Consterdine, Roy Hullin, Ralph McGuire, and Stephen Tyrer. 1978. "The Effect of Two Randomly Allocated Court Procedures on Truancy." *British Journal of Criminology* 18:232–44.

Bergman, Lars R., and Anna-Karin Andershed. 2009. "Predictors and Outcomes of Persistent or Age-Limited Registered Criminal Behavior: A 30-Year Longitudinal Study of a Swedish Urban Population." *Aggressive Behavior* 35:164–78.

Bernat, Debra H., J. Michael Oakes, Sandra L. Pettingell, and Michael Resnick. 2012. "Risk and Direct Protective Factors for Youth Violence: Results from the National Longitudinal Study of Adolescent Health." *American Journal of Preventive Medicine* 43(2S1):S67–S75.

Berntsen, Karen, and Karl O. Christiansen. 1965. "A Resocialization Experiment with Short-Term Offenders." In *Scandinavian Studies in Criminology*, vol. 1, edited by Karl O. Christiansen. London: Tavistock.

Berrueta-Clement, John R., Lawrence J. Schweinhart, W. Steven Barnett, Ann S. Epstein, and David P. Weikart. 1984. *Changed Lives: The Effects of the Perry Preschool Program on Youths through Age 19.* Ypsilanti, MI: High/Scope Press.

Bijleveld, Catrien C. J. H., and David P. Farrington. 2009. "Editorial: The Importance of Studies of Intergenerational Transmission of Antisocial Behaviour." *Criminal Behaviour and Mental Health* 19:77–79.

Blais, Etienne, and Jean-Luc Bacher. 2007. "Situational Deterrence and Claim Padding: Results from a Randomized Field Experiment." *Journal of Experimental Criminology* 3:337–52.

Blumstein, Alfred, Jacqueline Cohen, and David P. Farrington. 1988*a*. "Criminal Career Research: Its Value for Criminology." *Criminology* 26:1–35.

———. 1988*b*. "Longitudinal and Criminal Career Research: Further Clarifications." *Criminology* 26:57–74.

Boisjoli, Rachel, Frank Vitaro, Eric Lacourse, Edward D. Barker, and Richard E. Tremblay. 2007. "Impact and Clinical Significance of a Preventive Intervention for Disruptive Boys." *British Journal of Psychiatry* 191:415–19.

Boruch, Robert F. 1997. *Randomized Experiments for Planning and Evaluation: A Practical Guide.* Thousand Oaks, CA: Sage.

Bottcher, Jean, and Michael E. Ezell. 2005. "Examining the Effectiveness of Boot Camps: A Randomized Experiment with a Long-Term Follow-up." *Journal of Research in Crime and Delinquency* 42:309–32.

Bowen, Erica, May El Komy, and Colin Steer. 2008. *Characteristics Associated with Resilience in Children at High Risk of Involvement in Antisocial and Other Problem Behaviour.* Findings no. 283. London: Home Office.

Bowes, Lucy, Louise Arseneault, Barbara Maughan, Alan Taylor, Aveshalom Caspi, and Terrie E. Moffitt. 2009. "School, Neighborhood, and Family Factors Are Associated with Children's Bullying Involvement: A Nationally Representative Longitudinal Study." *Journal of the American Academy of Child and Adolescent Psychiatry* 48:545–53.

Bowles, Roger, and Chrisostomos Florackis. 2012. "Impatience, Reputation, and Offending." *Applied Economics* 44:177–87.

Braga, Anthony A. 2006. "Policing Crime Hot Spots." In *Preventing Crime: What Works for Children, Offenders, Victims, and Places*, edited by Brandon C. Welsh and David P. Farrington. Dordrecht, Neth.: Springer.

Braga, Anthony A., David L. Weisburd, Elin J. Waring, Lorraine G. Mazerolle, William Spelman, and Francis Gajewski. 1999. "Problem-Oriented Policing in Violent Crime Places: A Randomized Controlled Experiment." *Criminology* 37:541–80.

Brame, Robert, Raymond Paternoster, and Alex R. Piquero. 2012. "Thoughts on the Analysis of Group-Based Developmental Trajectories in Criminology." *Justice Quarterly* 29:469–90.

Brody, Stephen R. 1976. *The Effectiveness of Sentencing*. London: Her Majesty's Stationery Office.

Broidy, Lisa M., et al. 2003. "Developmental Trajectories of Childhood Disruptive Behaviors and Adolescent Delinquency: A Six-Site, Cross-National Study." *Developmental Psychology* 39:222–45.

Brooks-Gunn, Jeanne, P. K. Klebanov, F. Liaw, F. Spiker, and D. Spiker. 1993. "Enhancing the Development of Low Birthweight, Premature Infants: Changes in Cognition and Behavior over the First Three Years." *Child Development* 64:734–53.

Brown, Eric C., Richard F. Catalano, Charles B. Fleming, Kevin P. Haggerty, and Robert D. Abbott. 2005. "Adolescent Substance Use Outcomes in the Raising Healthy Children Project: A Two-Part Latent Growth Curve Analysis." *Journal of Consulting and Clinical Psychology* 73:699–710.

Buckle, Abigail, and David P. Farrington. 1984. "An Observational Study of Shoplifting." *British Journal of Criminology* 24:63–73.

Bushway, Shawn D., and Raymond Paternoster. 2013. "Desistance from Crime: A Review and Ideas for Moving Forward." In *Handbook of Life-Course Criminology*, edited by Chris L. Gibson and Marvin D. Krohn. New York: Springer.

Byles, John A., and Andrea Maurice. 1979. "The Juvenile Services Project: An Experiment in Delinquency Control." *Canadian Journal of Criminology* 21:155–65.

Campbell, Frances A., Craig T. Ramey, Elizabeth Pungello, Joseph Sparling, and Shari Miller-Johnson. 2002. "Early Childhood Education: Young Adult Outcomes from the Abecedarian Project." *Applied Developmental Science* 6:42–57.

Capaldi, Deborah M., Rand D. Conger, Hyman Hops, and Terence P. Thornberry. 2003. "Introduction to Special Section on Three-Generation Studies." *Journal of Abnormal Child Psychology* 31:123–25.

Capaldi, Deborah M., and Gerald R. Patterson. 1996. "Can Violent Offenders Be Distinguished from Frequent Offenders? Prediction from Childhood to Adolescence." *Journal of Research in Crime and Delinquency* 33:206–31.

Clarke, Ronald V. G., and Derek B. Cornish. 1972. *The Controlled Trial in Institutional Research*. London: Her Majesty's Stationery Office.

Colman, Ian, Joseph Murray, Rosemary A. Abbott, Barbara Maughan, Diana Kuh, Tim J. Croudace, and Peter B. Jones. 2009. "Outcomes of Conduct Problems in Adolescence: 40 Year Follow-up of National Cohort." *British Medical Journal* 338:208–15.

Cook, David D., and Charles L. Spirrison. 1992. "Effects of a Prisoner-Operated Delinquency Deterrence Program: Mississippi's Project Aware." *Journal of Offender Rehabilitation* 17:89–99.

Cook, Thomas D., and Donald T. Campbell. 1979. *Quasi-Experimentation: Design and Analysis Issues for Field Settings*. Chicago: Rand McNally.

Cook, Thomas D., and Monique R. Payne. 2002. "Objecting to the Objections to Using Random Assignment in Educational Research." In *Evidence Matters: Randomized Trials in Education Research*, edited by Frederick Mosteller and Robert F. Boruch. Washington, DC: Brookings Institution Press.

Cornish, Derek B., and Ronald V. G. Clarke. 1975. *Residential Treatment and Its Effects on Delinquency*. London: Her Majesty's Stationery Office.

CPPRG (Conduct Problems Prevention Research Group). 1999. "Initial Impact of the Fast Track Prevention Trial for Conduct Problems: I. The High-Risk Sample." *Journal of Consulting and Clinical Psychology* 67:631–47.

———. 2002. "Evaluation of the First 3 Years of the Fast Track Prevention Trial with Children at High Risk for Adolescent Conduct Problems." *Journal of Abnormal Child Psychology* 30:19–35.

———. 2004. "The Effects of the Fast Track Program on Serious Problem Outcomes at the End of Elementary School." *Journal of Clinical Child and Adolescent Psychology* 33:650–61.

———. 2007. "Fast Track Randomized Controlled Trial to Prevent Externalizing Psychiatric Disorders: Findings from Grades 3 to 9." *Journal of the American Academy of Child and Adolescent Psychiatry* 46:1250–62.

———. 2010. "Fast Track Intervention Effects on Youth Arrests and Delinquency." *Journal of Experimental Criminology* 6:131–57.

———. 2011. "The Effects of the Fast Track Preventive Intervention on the Development of Conduct Disorder across Childhood." *Child Development* 82: 331–45.

Curtis, Nicola M., Kevin R. Ronan, and Charles M. Borduin. 2004. "Multisystemic Treatment: A Meta-Analysis of Outcome Studies." *Journal of Family Psychology* 18:411–19.

Davis, Robert C., and Bernard Auchter. 2010. "National Institute of Justice Funding of Experimental Studies of Violence against Women: A Critical Look at Implementation Issues and Policy Implications." *Journal of Experimental Criminology* 6:377–95.

Derzon, James H. 2009. "The Correspondence of Family Features with Problem, Aggressive, Criminal, and Violent Behavior: A Meta-Analysis." *Journal of Experimental Criminology* 6:263–92.

Ditman, Keith S., George G. Crawford, Edward W. Forgy, Herbert Moskowitz, and Craig Macandrew. 1967. "A Controlled Experiment on the Use of Court Probation for Drunk Arrests." *American Journal of Psychiatry* 124:160–63.

Dugan, John R., and Ronald S. Everett. 1998. "An Experimental Test of Chemical Dependency Therapy for Jail Inmates." *International Journal of Offender Therapy and Comparative Criminology* 42:360–68.

Dunford, Franklyn W. 1990. "System-Initiated Warrants for Suspects of Misdemeanor Domestic Assault: A Pilot Study." *Justice Quarterly* 7:631–53.

Eckenrode, John, M. Campa, D. W. Luckey, Charles R. Henderson, R. Cole, Harriet Kitzman, A. Anson, Kimberley Sidora-Arcoleo, J. Powers, and David Olds. 2010. "Long-Term Effects of Prenatal and Infancy Nurse Home Visitation on the Life Course of Youths: 19-Year Follow-up of a Randomized Trial." *Archives of Pediatrics and Adolescent Medicine* 164:9–15.

Eisner, Manuel, and David Humphreys. 2012. "Measuring Conflict of Interest in Prevention and Intervention Research: A Feasibility Study." In *Antisocial Behavior and Crime: Contributions of Developmental and Evaluation Research to Prevention and Intervention*, edited by Thomas Bliesener, Andreas Beelman, and Mark Stemmler. Cambridge, MA: Hogrefe.

Elliott, Delbert S. 1994. "Serious Violent Offenders: Onset, Developmental Course, and Termination." *Criminology* 32:1–21.

Empey, LaMar T., and Maynard L. Erickson. 1972. *The Provo Experiment: Evaluating Community Control of Delinquency*. Lexington, MA: Heath.

Empey, LaMar T., and Steven G. Lubeck. 1971. *The Silverlake Experiment: Testing Delinquency Theory and Community Intervention*. Chicago: Aldine.

Fabio, Anthony, Rolf Loeber, G. K. Balasubramani, Jeffrey A. Roth, W. Fu, and David P. Farrington. 2006. "Why Some Generations Are More Violent than Others: Assessment of Age, Period, and Cohort Effects." *American Journal of Epidemiology* 164:151–60.

Fagan, Abigail A., M. Lee Van Horn, J. David Hawkins, and Michael W. Arthur. 2007. "Gender Similarities and Differences in the Association between Risk and Protective Factors and Self-Reported Serious Delinquency." *Prevention Science* 8:115–24.

Farrington, David P. 1972. "Delinquency Begins at Home." *New Society* 21:495–97.

———. 1977. "The Effects of Public Labelling." *British Journal of Criminology* 17:112–25.

———. 1979a. "Environmental Stress, Delinquent Behavior, and Convictions." In *Stress and Anxiety*, vol. 6, edited by I. G. Sarason and C. D. Spielberger. Washington, DC: Hemisphere.

———. 1979b. "Experiments on Deviance with Special Reference to Dishonesty." In *Advances in Experimental Social Psychology*, vol. 12, edited by Leonard Berkowitz. New York: Academic Press.

———. 1979c. "Longitudinal Research on Crime and Delinquency." In *Crime and Justice: An Annual Review of Research*, vol. 1, edited by Norval Morris and Michael Tonry. Chicago: University of Chicago Press.

———. 1983. "Randomized Experiments on Crime and Justice." In *Crime and Justice: An Annual Review of Research*, vol. 4, edited by Michael Tonry and Norval Morris. Chicago: University of Chicago Press.

———. 1988. "Studying Changes within Individuals: The Causes of Offending." In *Studies of Psychosocial Risk: The Power of Longitudinal Data*, edited by Michael Rutter. New York: Cambridge University Press.

———. 1990. "Age, Period, Cohort, and Offending." In *Policy and Theory in Criminal Justice: Contributions in Honour of Leslie T. Wilkins.* Aldershot, UK: Avebury.

———. 2000. "Explaining and Preventing Crime: The Globalization of Knowledge—the American Society of Criminology 1999 Presidential Address." *Criminology* 38:1–24.

———. 2003*a*. "British Randomized Experiments on Crime and Justice." *Annals of the American Academy of Political and Social Science* 589:150–67.

———. 2003*b*. "Developmental and Life-Course Criminology: Key Theoretical and Empirical Issues." *Criminology* 41:221–55.

———. 2003*c*. "Key Results from the First 40 Years of the Cambridge Study in Delinquent Development." In *Taking Stock of Delinquency: An Overview of Findings from Contemporary Longitudinal Studies*, edited by Terence P. Thornberry and Marvin D. Krohn. New York: Kluwer/Plenum.

———. 2003*d*. "Methodological Quality Standards for Evaluation Research." *Annals of the American Academy of Political and Social Science* 587:49–68.

———, ed. 2005. *Integrated Developmental and Life-Course Theories of Offending*. Advances in Criminological Theory, vol. 14. New Brunswick, NJ: Transaction.

———. 2006. "Key Longitudinal-Experimental Studies in Criminology." *Journal of Experimental Criminology* 2:121–41.

———. 2008. "Criminology as an Experimental Science." In *Experiments in Criminology and Law*, edited by Christine Horne and Michael Lovaglia. Lanham, MD: Rowman & Littlefield.

Farrington, David P., Jeremy W. Coid, Louise Harnett, Darrick Jolliffe, Nadine Soteriou, Richard Turner, and Donald J. West. 2006. *Criminal Careers Up to Age 50 and Life Success Up to Age 48: New Findings from the Cambridge Study in Delinquent Development.* Research Study no. 299. London: Home Office.

Farrington, David P., Jeremy W. Coid, and Joseph Murray. 2009. "Family Factors in the Intergenerational Transmission of Offending." *Criminal Behaviour and Mental Health* 19:109–24.

Farrington, David P., Bernard Gallagher, Lynda Morley, Raymond St. Ledger, and Donald J. West. 1990. "Minimizing Attrition in Longitudinal Research: Methods of Tracing and Securing Cooperation in a 24-Year Follow-up." In *Data Quality in Longitudinal Research*, edited by David Magnusson and Lars Bergman. Cambridge: Cambridge University Press.

Farrington, David P., and Darrick Jolliffe. 2002. *A Feasibility Study into Using a Randomized Controlled Trial to Evaluate Treatment Pilots at HMP Whitemoor.* Online Report no. 14/02. London: Home Office.

Farrington, David P., Darrick Jolliffe, J. David Hawkins, Richard F. Catalano, Karl G. Hill, and Rick Kosterman. 2003. "Comparing Delinquency Careers in Court Records and Self-Reports." *Criminology* 41:933–58.

Farrington, David P., Darrick Jolliffe, Rolf Loeber, and D. Lynn Homish.

2007. "How Many Offenses Are Really Committed per Juvenile Court Offender?" *Victims and Offenders* 2:227–49.

Farrington, David P., and Rolf Loeber. 1999. "Transatlantic Replicability of Risk Factors in the Development of Delinquency." In *Historical and Geographical Influences on Psychopathology*, edited by Patricia Cohen, Cheryl Slomkowski, and Lee N. Robins. Mahwah, NJ: Erlbaum.

Farrington, David P., Rolf Loeber, and Magda Stouthamer-Loeber. 2003. "How Can the Relationship between Race and Violence Be Explained?" In *Violent Crime: Assessing Race and Ethnic Differences*, edited by Darnell F. Hawkins. Cambridge: Cambridge University Press.

Farrington, David P., Rolf Loeber, and Maria M. Ttofi. 2012. "Risk and Protective Factors for Offending." In *The Oxford Handbook of Crime Prevention*, edited by Brandon C. Welsh and David P. Farrington. Oxford: Oxford University Press.

Farrington, David P., Rolf Loeber, and Brandon C. Welsh. 2010. "Longitudinal-Experimental Studies." In *Handbook of Quantitative Criminology*, edited by Alex R. Piquero and David Weisburd. New York: Springer.

Farrington, David P., Rolf Loeber, Yanming Yin, and Stewart Anderson. 2002. "Are Within-Individual Causes of Delinquency the Same as Between-Individual Causes?" *Criminal Behaviour and Mental Health* 12:53–68.

Farrington, David P., Lloyd E. Ohlin, and James Q. Wilson. 1986. *Understanding and Controlling Crime: Toward a New Research Strategy*. New York: Springer-Verlag.

Farrington, David P., and Kate A. Painter. 2004. *Gender Differences in Risk Factors for Offending*. Research Findings no. 196. London: Home Office.

Farrington, David P., Alex R. Piquero, and Wesley G. Jennings. 2013. *Offending from Childhood to Late Middle Age: Recent Results from the Cambridge Study in Delinquent Development*. New York: Springer.

Farrington, David P., and Lea Pulkkinen. 2009. "Introduction: The Unusualness and Contribution of Life Span Longitudinal Studies of Aggressive and Criminal Behavior." *Aggressive Behavior* 35:115–16.

Farrington, David P., and Maria M. Ttofi. 2012. "Protective and Promotive Factors in the Development of Offending." In *Antisocial Behavior and Crime: Contributions of Developmental and Evaluation Research to Prevention and Intervention*, edited by Thomas Bliesener, Andreas Beelman, and Mark Stemmler. Cambridge, MA: Hogrefe.

Farrington, David P., Maria M. Ttofi, and Jeremy W. Coid. 2009. "Development of Adolescence-Limited, Late-Onset, and Persistent Offenders from Age 8 to Age 48." *Aggressive Behavior* 35:150–63.

Farrington, David P., and Brandon C. Welsh. 2005. "Randomized Experiments in Criminology: What Have We Learned in the Last Two Decades?" *Journal of Experimental Criminology* 1:9–38.

———. 2006. "A Half Century of Randomized Experiments on Crime and Justice." In *Crime and Justice: A Review of Research*, vol. 34, edited by Michael Tonry. Chicago: University of Chicago Press.

————. 2007. *Saving Children from a Life of Crime: Early Risk Factors and Effective Interventions*. New York: Oxford University Press.

————. 2013. "Randomized Experiments in Criminology: What Has Been Learned from Long-Term Follow-ups?" In *Experimental Criminology: Prospects for Advancing Science and Public Policy*, edited by Brandon C. Welsh, Anthony A. Braga, and Gerben J. N. Bruinsma. Cambridge: Cambridge University Press.

Farrington, David P., and Donald J. West. 1981. "The Cambridge Study in Delinquent Development." In *Prospective Longitudinal Research: An Empirical Basis for the Primary Prevention of Psychosocial Disorders*, edited by Sarnoff A. Mednick and A. E. Baert. Oxford: Oxford University Press.

Farrington, David P., and Per-Olof H. Wikström. 1994. "Criminal Careers in London and Stockholm: A Cross-National Comparative Study." In *Cross-National Longitudinal Research on Human Development and Criminal Behavior*, edited by Elmar G. M. Weitekamp and Hans-Jurgen Kerner. Dordrecht, Neth.: Kluwer.

Fergusson, David M., Naomi Swain-Campbell, and L. John Horwood. 2004. "How Does Childhood Economic Disadvantage Lead to Crime?" *Journal of Child Psychology and Psychiatry* 45:956–66.

Folkard, M. Steven, David E. Smith, and David D. Smith. 1976. *IMPACT*. Vol. 2. London: Her Majesty's Stationery Office.

Fowles, Anthony J. 1978. *Prison Welfare*. London: Her Majesty's Stationery Office.

Fox, Bryanna H., and David P. Farrington. 2012. "Creating Burglary Profiles Using Latent Class Analysis: A New Approach to Offender Profiling." *Criminal Justice and Behavior* 39:1582–1611.

Gaes, Gerald G., and Scott D. Camp. 2009. "Unintended Consequences: Experimental Evidence for the Criminogenic Effect of Prison Security Level Placement on Post-release Recidivism." *Journal of Experimental Criminology* 5:139–62.

Gibson, Chris L., S. Z. Morris, and Kevin M. Beaver. 2009. "Secondary Exposure to Violence during Childhood and Adolescence: Does Neighborhood Context Matter?" *Justice Quarterly* 26:30–57.

Glueck, Sheldon E., and Eleanor T. Glueck. 1950. *Unraveling Juvenile Delinquency*. New York: Commonwealth Fund.

————. 1968. *Delinquents and Nondelinquents in Perspective*. Cambridge, MA: Harvard University Press.

Gordon, Rachel A., Benjamin B. Lahey, Eriko Kawai, Rolf Loeber, Magda Stouthamer-Loeber, and David P. Farrington. 2004. "Antisocial Behavior and Youth Gang Membership: Selection and Socialization." *Criminology* 42: 55–87.

Gottfredson, Denise C., Richard J. McNeil, and Gary D. Gottfredson. 1991. "Social Area Influences on Delinquency: A Multilevel Analysis." *Journal of Research in Crime and Delinquency* 28:197–226.

Gottfredson, Denise C., Stacy S. Najaka, and Brook Kearley. 2003. "Effectiveness of Drug Treatment Courts: Evidence from a Randomized Trial." *Criminology and Public Policy* 2:171–96.

Gottfredson, Michael R., and Travis Hirschi. 1986. "The True Value of Lambda Would Appear to Be Zero: An Essay on Career Criminals, Criminal Careers, Selective Incapacitation, Cohort Studies, and Related Topics." *Criminology* 24:213–34.

———. 1987. "The Methodological Adequacy of Longitudinal Research on Crime." *Criminology* 25:581–614.

———. 1990. *A General Theory of Crime*. Stanford, CA: Stanford University Press.

Green, Donald P., and Daniel Winik. 2010. "Using Random Judge Assignments to Estimate the Effects of Incarceration and Probation on Recidivism among Drug Offenders." *Criminology* 48:357–87.

Greenwood, Peter W., Elizabeth P. Deschenes, and John Adams. 1993. *Chronic Juvenile Offenders: Final Results from the Skillman Aftercare Experiment*. Santa Monica, CA: RAND.

Grossman, Jean B., and Joseph P. Tierney. 1998. "Does Mentoring Work? An Impact Study of the Big Brothers Big Sisters Program." *Evaluation Review* 22:403–26.

Harachi, Tracy W., Robert D. Abbott, Richard F. Catalano, Kevin P. Haggerty, and C. B. Fleming. 1999. "Opening the Black Box: Using Process Evaluation Measures to Assess Implementation and Theory Building." *American Journal of Community Psychology* 27:711–31.

Hathaway, Starke R., Phyllis C. Reynolds, and Elio D. Monachesi. 1969. "Follow-up of the Later Careers and Lives of 1,000 Boys Who Dropped Out of High School." *Journal of Consulting and Clinical Psychology* 33:370–80.

Hawkins, J. David, and Richard F. Catalano. 1992. *Communities That Care: Action for Drug Abuse Prevention*. San Francisco: Jossey-Bass.

Hawkins, J. David, Brian H. Smith, Karl G. Hill, Rick Kosterman, Richard F. Catalano, and Robert D. Abbott. 2003. "Understanding and Preventing Crime and Violence: Findings from the Seattle Social Development Project." In *Taking Stock of Delinquency: An Overview of Findings from Contemporary Longitudinal Studies*, edited by Terence P. Thornberry and Marvin D. Krohn. New York: Kluwer/Plenum.

Hayatbakhsh, Mohammad R., Jake M. Najman, Tara R. McGee, William Bor, and Michael J. O'Callaghan. 2009. "Early Pubertal Maturation in the Prediction of Early Adult Substance Use: A Prospective Study." *Addiction* 104:59–66.

Hemphill, Sheryl A., Rachel Smith, John W. Toumbourou, Todd I. Herrenkohl, Richard F. Catalano, Barbara J. McMorris, and Helena Romaniuk. 2009. "Multiple Determinants of Youth Violence in Australia and the United States: A Longitudinal Study." *Australian and New Zealand Journal of Criminology* 42:289–309.

Hirschi, Travis. 1969. *Causes of Delinquency*. Berkeley: University of California Press.

Horney, Julie D., Wayne Osgood, and Ineke H. Marshall. 1995. "Criminal

Careers in the Short-Term: Intra-individual Variability in Crime and Its Relation to Local Life Circumstances." *American Sociological Review* 60:655–73.

Huesmann, L. Rowell, Eric F. Dubow, and Paul Boxer. 2009. "Continuity of Aggression from Childhood to Early Adulthood as a Predictor of Life Outcomes: Implications for the Adolescent-Limited and Life-Course-Persistent Models." *Aggressive Behavior* 35:117–35.

Huizinga, David, and Kimberly L. Henry. 2008. "The Effect of Arrest and Justice System Sanctions on Subsequent Behavior: Findings from Longitudinal and Other Studies." In *The Long View of Crime: A Synthesis of Longitudinal Research*, edited by Akiva M. Liberman. New York: Springer.

Huizinga, David, Anne W. Weiher, Rachel Espiritu, and Finn Esbensen. 2003. "Delinquency and Crime: Some Highlights from the Denver Youth Survey." In *Taking Stock of Delinquency: An Overview of Findings from Contemporary Longitudinal Studies*, edited by Terence P. Thornberry and Marvin D. Krohn. New York: Kluwer/Plenum.

Hutchings, Barry, and Sarnoff A. Mednick. 1975. "Registered Criminality in the Adoptive and Biological Parents of Registered Male Criminal Adoptees." In *Genetic Research in Psychiatry*, edited by Ronald R. Fieve, David Rosenthal, and Henry Brill. Baltimore: Johns Hopkins University Press.

Inciardi, James A., Steven S. Martin, Clifford A. Butzin, Robert M. Hooper, and Lana D. Harrison. 1997. "An Effective Model of Prison-Based Treatment for Drug-Involved Offenders." *Journal of Drug Issues* 27:261–78.

Jennings, Wesley G., George E. Higgins, Richard Tewkesbury, Angela R. Gover, and Alex R. Piquero. 2010. "A Longitudinal Assessment of the Victim-Offender Overlap." *Journal of Interpersonal Violence* 25:2147–74.

Jeong, Seokjin, Edmund F. McGarrell, and Natalie K. Hipple. 2012. "Long-Term Impact of Family Group Conferences on Reoffending: The Indianapolis Restorative Justice Experiment." *Journal of Experimental Criminology* 8:369–85.

Jesness, Carl F. 1971a. "Comparative Effectiveness of Two Institutional Treatment Programs for Delinquents." *Child Care Quarterly* 1:119–30.

———. 1971b. "The Preston Typology Study." *Journal of Research in Crime and Delinquency* 8:38–52.

———. 1975. "Comparative Effectiveness of Behavior Modification and Transactional Analysis Programs for Delinquents." *Journal of Consulting and Clinical Psychology* 43:758–79.

Johnson, Jeffrey G., Elizabeth Smailes, Patricia Cohen, Stephanie Kasen, and Judith S. Brook. 2004. "Antisocial Parental Behavior, Problematic Parenting, and Aggressive Offspring Behavior during Adulthood." *British Journal of Criminology* 44:915–30.

Jolliffe, Darrick, and David P. Farrington. 2008. *The Influence of Mentoring on Reoffending*. Stockholm: National Council for Crime Prevention.

———. 2009. "A Systematic Review of the Relationship between Childhood Impulsiveness and Later Violence." In *Personality, Personality Disorder, and*

Violence, edited by Mary McMurran and Richard Howard. Chichester, UK: Wiley.

Juby, Heather, and David P. Farrington. 2002. "Disentangling the Link between Disrupted Families and Delinquency." *British Journal of Criminology* 41:22–40.

Kaplan, Howard B. 2003. "Testing an Integrative Theory of Deviant Behavior: Theory-Syntonic Findings from a Long-Term Multi-generation Study." In *Taking Stock of Delinquency: An Overview of Findings from Contemporary Longitudinal Studies*, edited by Terence P. Thornberry and Marvin D. Krohn. New York: Kluwer/Plenum.

Kassebaum, Gene, David Ward, and Daniel Wilner. 1971. *Prison Treatment and Parole Survival: An Empirical Assessment*. New York: Wiley.

Kazemian, Lila, and David P. Farrington. 2010. "The Developmental Evidence Base: Desistance." In *Forensic Psychology*, edited by Graham J. Towl and David A. Crighton. Oxford: Blackwell.

Keenan, Kate, Alison Hipwell, Tammy Chung, Stephanie Stepp, Magda Stouthamer-Loeber, Rolf Loeber, and K. McTigue. 2010. "The Pittsburgh Girls Study: Overview and Initial Findings." *Journal of the American Academy of Child and Adolescent Psychiatry* 39:506–21.

Killias, Martin, Gwladys Gillieron, Francoise Villard, and Clara Poglia. 2010. "How Damaging Is Imprisonment in the Long-Term? A Controlled Experiment Comparing Long-Term Effects of Community Service and Short Custodial Sentences on Reoffending and Social Integration." *Journal of Experimental Criminology* 6:115–30.

Kirk, David S. 2006. "Examining the Divergence across Self-Report and Official Data Sources on Inferences about the Adolescent Life-Course of Crime." *Journal of Quantitative Criminology* 22:107–29.

Klein, Malcolm W. 1986. "Labeling Theory and Delinquency Policy: An Experimental Test." *Criminal Justice and Behavior* 13:47–79.

Kling, Jeffrey R., Jens Ludwig, and Lawrence F. Katz. 2005. "Neighborhood Effects on Crime for Female and Male Youth: Evidence from a Randomized Housing Voucher Experiment." *Quarterly Journal of Economics* 120:87–130.

Knight, Barry J., Steven G. Osborn, and Donald J. West. 1977. "Early Marriage and Criminal Tendency in Males." *British Journal of Criminology* 17:348–60.

Kolvin, Israel, Frederick J. W. Miller, David M. Scott, S. R. M. Gatzanis, and Mary Fleeting. 1990. *Continuities of Deprivation? The Newcastle 1000 Family Study*. Aldershot, UK: Avebury.

Krohn, Marvin D., Chris L. Gibson, and Terence P. Thornberry. 2013. "Under the Protective Bud the Bloom Awaits: A Review of Theory and Research on Adult-Onset and Late-Blooming Offenders." In *Handbook of Life-Course Criminology*, edited by Chris L. Gibson and Marvin D. Krohn. New York: Springer.

Lacourse, Eric, Sylvana Cote, Daniel S. Nagin, Frank Vitaro, Mara Brendgen, and Richard E. Tremblay. 2002. "A Longitudinal-Experimental Approach to

Testing Theories of Antisocial Behavior Development." *Development and Psychopathology* 14:909–24.

Lamb, H. Richard, and Victor Goertzel. 1974. "Ellsworth House: A Community Alternative to Jail." *American Journal of Psychiatry* 131:64–68.

Land, Kenneth C., Patricia L. McCall, and Jay R. Williams. 1990. "Something That Works in Juvenile Justice: An Evaluation of the North Carolina Court Counselors' Intensive Protective Supervision Randomized Experimental Project, 1987–1989." *Evaluation Review* 14:574–606.

Lane, Jodi, Susan Turner, Terry Fain, and Amber Sehgal. 2007. "The Effects of an Experimental Intensive Juvenile Probation Program on Self-Reported Delinquency and Drug Use." *Journal of Experimental Criminology* 3:201–19.

Larzelere, Robert E., and Gerald R. Patterson. 1990. "Parental Management: Mediator of the Effect of Socioeconomic Status on Early Delinquency." *Criminology* 28:301–24.

Laub, John H., and Robert J. Sampson. 2003. *Shared Beginnings, Divergent Lives: Delinquent Boys to Age 70.* Cambridge, MA: Harvard University Press.

LeBlanc, Marc, and Marcel Frechette. 1989. *Male Criminal Activity from Childhood through Youth.* New York: Springer-Verlag.

Lerman, Paul. 1975. *Community Treatment and Social Control.* Chicago: University of Chicago Press.

Leschied, Alan, Debbie Chiodo, Elizabeth Nowicki, and Susan Rodger. 2008. "Childhood Predictors of Adult Criminality: A Meta-Analysis Drawn from the Prospective Longitudinal Literature." *Canadian Journal of Criminology and Criminal Justice* 50:435–67.

Leschied, Alan, and Alison Cunningham. 2002. *Seeking Effective Interventions for Serious Young Offenders: Interim Results of a Four-Year Randomized Study of Multisystemic Therapy in Ontario, Canada.* London, ON: London Family Court Clinic.

Lewis, Roy V. 1983. "Scared Straight—California Style: Evaluation of the San Quentin Squires Program." *Criminal Justice and Behavior* 10:209–26.

Liberman, Akiva M., ed. 2008. *The Long View of Crime: A Synthesis of Longitudinal Research.* New York: Springer.

Lichtman, Cary M., and Sue M. Smock. 1981. "The Effects of Social Services on Probationer Recidivism: A Field Experiment." *Journal of Research in Crime and Delinquency* 18:81–100.

Lipsey, Mark W., and Nana A. Landenberger. 2006. "Cognitive-Behavioral Interventions." In *Preventing Crime: What Works for Children, Offenders, Victims, and Places,* edited by Brandon C. Welsh and David P. Farrington. New York: Springer.

Lipsey, Mark W., and David B. Wilson. 2001. *Practical Meta-Analysis.* Thousand Oaks, CA: Sage.

Littell, Julia H. 2005. "Lessons from a Systematic Review of Effects of Multisystemic Therapy." *Children and Youth Services Review* 27:445–63.

Loeber, Rolf, and David P. Farrington. 1994. "Problems and Solutions in Longitudinal and Experimental Treatment Studies of Child Psychopathology and Delinquency." *Journal of Consulting and Clinical Psychology* 62:887–900.

———. 2011. *Young Homicide Offenders and Victims: Risk Factors, Prediction, and Prevention from Childhood.* New York: Springer.

Loeber, Rolf, David P. Farrington, Magda Stouthamer-Loeber, Terrie E. Moffitt, Avshalom Caspi, Helene R. White, Evelyn Wei, and Jennifer M. Beyers. 2003. "The Development of Male Offending: Key Findings from 14 Years of the Pittsburgh Youth Study." In *Taking Stock of Delinquency: An Overview of Findings from Contemporary Longitudinal Studies,* edited by Terence P. Thornberry and Marvin D. Krohn. New York: Kluwer/Plenum.

Loeber, Rolf, David P. Farrington, Magda Stouthamer-Loeber, and Helene R. White. 2008. *Violence and Serious Theft: Development and Prediction from Childhood to Adulthood.* New York: Routledge.

Lösel, Friedrich, and David P. Farrington. 2012. "Direct Protective and Buffering Protective Factors in the Development of Youth Violence." *American Journal of Preventive Medicine* 43(2S1):S8–S23.

Lösel, Friedrich, and Mark Stemmler. 2012. "Preventing Child Behavior Problems in the Erlangen-Nuremberg Development and Prevention Study: Results from Preschool to Secondary School Age." *International Journal of Conflict and Violence* 6:214–24.

Lynam, Donald R., Avshalom Caspi, Terrie E. Moffitt, Per-Olof H. Wikström, Rolf Loeber, and Scott Novak. 2000. "The Interaction between Impulsivity and Neighborhood Context on Offending: The Effects of Impulsivity Are Stronger in Poorer Neighborhoods." *Journal of Abnormal Psychology* 109:563–74.

MacKenzie, Doris L., David Bierie, and Ojmarrh Mitchell. 2007. "An Experimental Study of a Therapeutic Boot Camp: Impact on Impulses, Attitudes, and Recidivism." *Journal of Experimental Criminology* 3:221–46.

MacLeod, John F., Peter G. Grove, and David P. Farrington. 2012. *Explaining Criminal Careers: Implications for Justice Policy.* Oxford: Oxford University Press.

Malti, Tina, Denis Ribeaud, and Manuel P. Eisner. 2011. "The Effectiveness of Two Universal Preventive Interventions in Reducing Children's Externalizing Behavior: A Cluster Randomized Controlled Trial." *Journal of Clinical Child and Adolescent Psychology* 40:677–92.

Marques, Janice K., Mark Wiederanders, David M. Day, Craig Nelson, and Alice Van Ommeren. 2005. "Effects of a Relapse Prevention Program on Sexual Recidivism: Final Results from California's Sex Offender Treatment and Evaluation Project (SOTEP)." *Sexual Abuse: A Journal of Research and Treatment* 17:79–107.

Maxwell, Christopher D., Joel H. Garner, and Jeffrey A. Fagan. 2002. "The Preventive Effects of Arrest on Intimate Partner Violence: Research, Policy, and Theory." *Criminology and Public Policy* 2:51–79.

Maynard, Rebecca. 1980. *The Impact of Supported Work on Young School Dropouts.* New York: Manpower Demonstration Research Corp.

McAra, Lesley, and Susan McVie. 2010. "Youth Crime and Justice: Key Messages from the Edinburgh Study of Youth Transitions and Crime." *Criminology and Criminal Justice* 19:211–30.

McCarton, Cecelia M., et al. 1997. "Results at Age 8 Years of Early Intervention for Low-Birth-Weight Premature Infants: The Infant Health and Development Program." *Journal of the American Medical Association* 277:126–32.

McCold, Paul, and Benjamin Wachtel. 1998. *Restorative Policing Experiment: The Bethlehem Pennsylvania Police Family Group Conferencing Project*. Pipersville, PA: Community Service Foundation.

McCord, Joan. 1978. "A Thirty-Year Follow-up Report on the Cambridge-Somerville Youth Study." *American Psychologist* 33:284–89.

———. 1979. "Some Child-Rearing Antecedents of Criminal Behavior in Adult Men." *Journal of Personality and Social Psychology* 37:1477–86.

———. 1990. "Crime in Moral and Social Contexts—the American Society of Criminology 1989 Presidential Address." *Criminology* 28:1–26.

———. 2003. "Cures That Harm: Unanticipated Outcomes of Crime Prevention Programs." *Annals of the American Academy of Political and Social Science* 587:16–30.

McCord, Joan, and Margaret E. Ensminger. 1997. "Multiple Risks and Comorbidity in an African-American Population." *Criminal Behaviour and Mental Health* 7:339–52.

McCormick, Marie C., et al. 2006. "Early Intervention in Low Birth Weight Premature Infants: Results at 18 Years of Age for the Infant Health and Development Program." *Pediatrics* 117:771–80.

McGee, Tara R., and David P. Farrington. 2010. "Are There Any True Adult Onset Offenders?" *British Journal of Criminology* 50:530–49.

McGee, Tara R., Mohammad R. Hayatbakhsh, William Bor, Michael Cerruto, Angela Dean, Rosa Alati, Ryan Mills, Gail M. Williams, Michael O'Callaghan, and Jake M. Najman. 2011. "Antisocial Behaviour across the Life Course: An Examination of the Effects of Early Onset Desistance and Early Onset Persistent Antisocial Behaviour in Adulthood." *Australian Journal of Psychology* 63:44–55.

McMorris, Barbara J., Sheryl A. Hemphill, John W. Toumbourou, Richard F. Catalano, and George C. Patton. 2007. "Prevalence of Substance Use and Delinquent Behavior in Adolescents from Victoria, Australia, and Washington State, United States." *Health Education and Behavior* 34:634–50.

Mednick, Sarnoff, and Barry Hutchings. 1978. "Genetic and Psychophysiological Factors in Asocial Behavior." In *Psychopathic Behavior: Approaches to Research*, edited by Robert D. Hare and Daisy Schalling. New York: Wiley.

Meeker, James W., and Arnold Binder. 1990. "Experiments as Reforms: The Impact of the 'Minneapolis Experiment' on Police Policy." *Journal of Police Science and Administration* 17:147–53.

Metropolitan Area Child Study Research Group. 2002. "A Cognitive-Ecological Approach to Preventing Aggression in Urban Settings: Initial Outcomes for High-Risk Children." *Journal of Consulting and Clinical Psychology* 70:179–94.

Meyer, Henry J., Edgar F. Borgatta, and Wyatt C. Jones. 1965. *Girls at Vocational High: An Experiment in Social Work Intervention*. New York: Russell Sage Foundation.

Mills, Paulette E., Kevin N. Cole, Joseph R. Jenkins, and Philip S. Dale. 2002. "Early Exposure to Direct Instruction and Subsequent Juvenile Delinquency: A Prospective Examination." *Exceptional Children* 69:85–96.

Mitchell, Ojmarrh, David B. Wilson, Amy Eggers, and Doris L. MacKenzie. 2012. "Assessing the Effectiveness of Drug Courts on Recidivism: A Meta-Analytic Review of Traditional and Non-traditional Drug Courts." *Journal of Criminal Justice* 40:60–71.

Mitchell, Ojmarrh, David B. Wilson, and Doris L. MacKenzie. 2012. "The Effectiveness of Incarceration-Based Drug Treatment on Criminal Behavior: A Systematic Review." Campbell Systematic Reviews 2012:18. http://www.campbellcollaboration.org.

Moffitt, Terrie E. 1993. "Adolescence-Limited and Life-Course-Persistent Antisocial Behavior: A Developmental Taxonomy." *Psychological Review* 100: 674–701.

———. 2006. "A Review of Research on the Taxonomy of Life-Course Persistent versus Adolescence-Limited Antisocial Behavior." In *Taking Stock: The Status of Delinquency Theory*, edited by Francis T. Cullen, John P. Wright, and Kristie Blevins. New Brunswick, NJ: Transaction.

Moffitt, Terrie E., Avshalom Caspi, Michael Rutter, and Phil A. Silva. 2001. *Sex Differences in Antisocial Behaviour.* Cambridge: Cambridge University Press.

Murray, Joseph, David P. Farrington, and Manuel P. Eisner. 2009. "Drawing Conclusions about Causes from Systematic Reviews of Risk Factors: The Cambridge Quality Checklists." *Journal of Experimental Criminology* 5:1–23.

Murray, Joseph, Barrie Irving, David P. Farrington, Ian Colman, and Claire A. J. Bloxsom. 2010. "Very Early Predictors of Conduct Problems and Crime: Results from a National Cohort Study." *Journal of Child Psychology and Psychiatry* 51:1198–1207.

Nagin, Daniel S. 2005. *Group-Based Modeling of Development.* Cambridge, MA: Harvard University Press.

Nagin, Daniel S., and Raymond Paternoster. 1991. "On the Relationship of Past to Future Participation in Delinquency." *Criminology* 29:163–89.

———. 2000. "Population Heterogeneity and State Dependence: State of the Evidence and Directions for Future Research." *Journal of Quantitative Criminology* 16:117–44.

Odgers, Candice L., Terrie E. Moffitt, Jonathan M. Broadbent, Nigel Dickson, Robert J. Hancox, Honalee Harrington, Richie Poulton, Malcolm R. Sears, W. Murray Thomson, and Avshalom Caspi. 2008. "Female and Male Antisocial Trajectories: From Childhood Origins to Adult Outcomes." *Development and Psychopathology* 20:673–716.

O'Donnell, Clifford R., Tony Lydgate, and Walter S. O. Fo. 1979. "The Buddy System: Review and Follow-up." *Child Behavior Therapy* 1:161–69.

Olds, David L., John Eckenrode, Charles R. Henderson, Harriet Kitzman, Jane Powers, Robert Cole, Kimberly Sidora, Pamela Morris, Lisa M. Pettitt, and Dennis Luckey. 1997. "Long-Term Effects of Home Visitation on Maternal Life Course and Child Abuse and Neglect: Fifteen-Year Follow-up of a Randomized Trial." *Journal of the American Medical Association* 278:637–43.

Olds, David L., Charles R. Henderson, Robert Cole, John Eckenrode, Harriet Kitzman, Dennis Luckey, Lisa Pettitt, Kimberley Sidora, Pamela Morris, and Jane Powers. 1998. "Long-Term Effects of Nurse Home Visitation on Children's Criminal and Antisocial Behavior: 15-Year Follow-up of a Randomized Controlled Trial." *Journal of the American Medical Association* 280: 1238–44.

Ortmann, Rudiger. 2000. "The Effectiveness of Social Therapy in Prison: A Randomized Experiment." *Crime and Delinquency* 46:214–32.

Palmer, Ted B. 1974. "The Youth Authority's Community Treatment Project." *Federal Probation* 38(1):3–14.

Paternoster, Raymond, Robert Brame, and David P. Farrington. 2001. "On the Relationship between Adolescent and Adult Offending Frequencies." *Journal of Quantitative Criminology* 17:201–25.

Perry, Amanda E., David Weisburd, and Catherine Hewitt. 2010. "Are Criminologists Describing Randomized Controlled Trials in Ways That Allow Us to Assess Them? Findings from a Sample of Crime and Justice Trials." *Journal of Experimental Criminology* 6:245–62.

Peters, Michael, David Thomas, and Christopher Zamberlan. 1997. *Boot Camps for Juvenile Offenders*. Washington, DC: US Office of Juvenile Justice and Delinquency Prevention.

Petersilia, Joan, and Susan Turner. 1993*a*. *Evaluating Intensive Supervision Probation/Parole: Results of a Nationwide Experiment*. Research in Brief. Washington, DC: US National Institute of Justice.

———. 1993*b*. "Intensive Probation and Parole." In *Crime and Justice: A Review of Research*, vol. 17, edited by Michael Tonry. Chicago: University of Chicago Press.

Petras, Hanno, Sheppard G. Kellam, C. Henricks Brown, Bengt O. Muthen, Nicholas S. Ialongo, and J. M. Poduska. 2008. "Developmental Epidemiological Courses Leading to Antisocial Personality Disorder and Violent and Criminal Behavior: Effects by Young Adulthood of a Universal Preventive Intervention in First and Second Grade Classrooms." *Drug and Alcohol Dependence* 95S:S45–S59.

Petrosino, Anthony, Carolyn Petrosino, Megan Hollis-Peel, and Julia Lavenberg. 2014. "Effects of Scared Straight on Subsequent Delinquency." In *Encyclopedia of Criminology and Criminal Justice*, edited by Gerben J. N. Bruinsma and David Weisburd. New York: Springer-Verlag.

Petrosino, Anthony, Carolyn Turpin-Petrosino, and Sarah Guckenburg. 2010. "Formal System Processing of Juveniles: Effects on Delinquency." Campbell Systematic Reviews 2010:1. http://www.campbellcollaboration.org.

Piquero, Alex R. 2008. "Taking Stock of Developmental Trajectories of Criminal Activity over the Life Course." In *The Long View of Crime: A Synthesis of Longitudinal Research*, edited by Akiva M. Liberman. New York: Springer.

Piquero, Alex R., Robert Brame, and Terrie E. Moffitt. 2005. "Extending the Study of Continuity and Change: Gender Differences in the Linkage between Adolescent and Adult Offending." *Journal of Quantitative Criminology* 21:219–43.

Polk, Kenneth, Christine M. Alder, Gordon Bazemore, G. Blake, S. Cordray, G. Coventry, J. Galvin, and M. Temple. 1981. *Becoming Adult: An Analysis of Maturational Development from Age Sixteen to Thirty of a Cohort of Young Men.* Final report of the Marion County Youth Study. Eugene: University of Oregon, Department of Sociology.

Prendergast, Michael, Linda Frisman, JoAnn Y. Sacks, Michele Staton-Tindall, Lisa Greenwell, Hsiu-Ju Lin, and Jerry Cartier. 2011. "A Multisite, Randomized Study of Strengths-Based Case Management with Substance-Abusing Parolees." *Journal of Experimental Criminology* 7:225–53.

Prior, Margot, Ann Sanson, Diana Smart, and Frank Oberklaid. 2000. *Pathways from Infancy to Adolescence: Australian Temperament Project, 1983–2000.* Melbourne: Australian Institute of Family Studies.

Pulkkinen, Lea, Anna-Liisa Lyyra, and Katja Kokko. 2009. "Life Success of Males on Non-offender, Adolescence-Limited, Persistent, and Adult-Onset Antisocial Pathways: Follow-up from Age 8 to 42." *Aggressive Behavior* 35: 117–35.

Pulkkinen, Lea, and Richard E. Tremblay. 1992. "Patterns of Boys' Social Adjustment in Two Cultures and at Different Ages: A Longitudinal Perspective." *International Journal of Behavioral Development* 15:527–53.

Quay, Herbert C. 1977. "The Three Faces of Evaluation: What Can Be Expected to Work." *Criminal Justice and Behavior* 4:341–54.

Quay, Herbert C., and Craig T. Love. 1977. "The Effect of a Juvenile Diversion Program on Rearrests." *Criminal Justice and Behavior* 4:377–96.

Raine, Adrian, Jianghong Liu, Peter H. Venables, Sarnoff A. Mednick, and C. Dalais. 2010. "Cohort Profile: The Mauritius Child Health Project." *International Journal of Epidemiology* 39:1441–51.

Raine, Adrian, K. Mellingen, Jianghong Liu, Peter H. Venables, and Sarnoff A. Mednick. 2003. "Effects of Environmental Enrichment at Ages 3–5 Years on Schizotypal Personality and Antisocial Behavior at Ages 17 and 23 Years." *American Journal of Psychiatry* 160:1627–35.

Reckless, Walter C., and Simon Dinitz. 1972. *The Prevention of Juvenile Delinquency: An Experiment.* Columbus: Ohio State University Press.

Reimer, Ernest, and Martin Warren. 1957. "Special Intensive Parole Unit." *NPPA Journal* 3:222–29.

Reynolds, Arthur J., Judy A. Temple, Suh-Ruu Ou, Dylan L. Robertson, Joshua P. Mersky, James W. Topitzes, and Michael D. Niles. 2007. "Effects of a School-Based, Early Childhood Intervention on Adult Health and Well-Being." *Archives of Pediatrics and Adolescent Medicine* 161:730–39.

Robins, Lee N. 1966. *Deviant Children Grown Up.* Baltimore: Williams & Wilkins.

———. 1978. "Sturdy Childhood Predictors of Adult Outcomes: Replications from Longitudinal Studies." In *Stress and Mental Disorder,* edited by James E. Barrett, Robert M. Rose, and Gerald L. Klerman. New York: Raven Press.

————. 1992. "The Role of Prevention Experiments in Discovering Causes of Children's Antisocial Behavior." In *Preventing Antisocial Behavior: Interventions from Birth through Adolescence*, edited by Joan McCord and Richard E. Tremblay. New York: Guilford.

Robins, Lee N., Patricia A. West, and Barbara L. Herjanic. 1975. "Arrests and Delinquency in Two Generations: A Study of Black Urban Families and Their Children." *Journal of Child Psychology and Psychiatry* 16:125–40.

Robinson, David. 1995. *The Impact of Cognitive Skills Training on Post-release Recidivism among Canadian Federal Offenders*. Research Report no. R-41. Ottawa: Correctional Service of Canada.

Rose, Gordon, and R. A. Hamilton. 1970. "Effects of a Juvenile Liaison Scheme." *British Journal of Criminology* 10:2–20.

Ross, Robert R., and Rosslyn D. Ross, eds. 1995. *Thinking Straight: The Reasoning and Rehabilitation Program for Delinquency Prevention and Offender Rehabilitation*. Ottawa: Air Training and Publications.

Rossi, Peter H., Richard A. Berk, and Kenneth J. Lenihan. 1980. *Money, Work, and Crime: Experimental Evidence*. New York: Academic Press.

Rowe, David C., Alexander T. Vaszonyi, and Daniel J. Flannery. 1994. "No More than Skin Deep: Ethnic and Racial Similarity in Developmental Process." *Psychological Review* 101:396–413.

————. 1995. "Sex Differences in Crime: Do Means and Within-Sex Variation Have Similar Causes?" *Journal of Research in Crime and Delinquency* 32:84–100.

Sampson, Robert J. 2012. *Great American City: Chicago and the Enduring Neighborhood Effect*. Chicago: University of Chicago Press.

Sampson, Robert J, and John H. Laub. 1993. *Crime in the Making: Pathways and Turning Points through Life*. Cambridge, MA: Harvard University Press.

Sampson, Robert J., Stephen W. Raudenbush, and Felton Earls. 1997. "Neighborhoods and Violent Crime: A Multilevel Study of Collective Efficacy." *Science* 277:918–24.

Sawyer, Aaron M., and Charles M. Borduin. 2011. "Effects of Multisystemic Therapy through Midlife: A 21.9-Year Follow-up to a Randomized Clinical Trial with Serious and Violent Juvenile Offenders." *Journal of Consulting and Clinical Psychology* 79:643–52.

Schneider, Anne L. 1986. "Restitution and Recidivism Rates of Juvenile Offenders: Results from Four Experimental Studies." *Criminology* 24:533–52.

Schochet, Peter Z., John Burghardt, and Steven Glazerman. 2001. *National Job Corps Study: The Impacts of Job Corps on Participants' Employment and Related Outcomes*. Princeton, NJ: Mathematica Policy Research.

Schwartz, Daniel, Robert Flamant, and Joseph Lelouch. 1980. *Clinical Trials*. London: Academic Press.

Schweinhart, Lawrence J., Helen V. Barnes, and David P. Weikart. 1993. *Significant Benefits: The High/Scope Perry Preschool Study through Age 27*. Ypsilanti, MI: High/Scope Press.

Schweinhart, Lawrence J., Jeanne Montie, Xiang Zongping, W. Steven Barnett, Clive R. Belfield, and Milagros Nores. 2005. *Lifetime Effects: The High/Scope Perry Preschool Study through Age 40*. Ypsilanti, MI: High/Scope Press.

Schweinhart, Lawrence J., and David P. Weikart. 1980. *Young Children Grow Up: The Effects of the Perry Preschool Program on Youths through Age 15*. Ypsilanti, MI: High/Scope Press.

Shapland, Joanna, Anne Atkinson, Helen Atkinson, James Dignan, Lucy Edwards, Jeremy Hibbert, Marie Howes, Jennifer Johnstone, Gwen Robinson, and Angela Sorsby. 2008. *Does Restorative Justice Affect Reconviction? The Fourth Report from the Evaluation of Three Schemes*. Research Series 10/08. London: Ministry of Justice.

Shaw, Margaret. 1974. *Social Work in Prison*. London: Her Majesty's Stationery Office.

Sherman, Lawrence W. 1992. *Policing Domestic Violence: Experiments and Dilemmas*. New York: Free Press.

Sherman, Lawrence W., and Richard A. Berk. 1984. "The Specific Deterrent Effects of Arrest for Domestic Assault." *American Sociological Review* 49:261–72.

Sherman, Lawrence W., and Ellen G. Cohn. 1989. "The Impact of Research on Legal Policy: The Minneapolis Domestic Violence Experiment." *Law and Society Review* 23:117–44.

Sherman, Lawrence W., Janell D. Schmidt, Dennis P. Rogan, Douglas A. Smith, Patrick R. Gartin, Ellen G. Cohn, Dean J. Collins, and Anthony R. Bacich. 1992. "The Variable Effects of Arrest on Criminal Careers: The Milwaukee Domestic Violence Experiment." *Journal of Criminal Law and Criminology* 83:137–69.

Sherman, Lawrence W., Heather Strang, Caroline Angel, Daniel Woods, Geoffrey C. Barnes, Sarah Bennett, and Nova Inkpen. 2005. "Effects of Face-to-Face Restorative Justice on Victims of Crime in Four Randomized Controlled Trials." *Journal of Experimental Criminology* 1:367–95.

Sherman, Lawrence W., Heather Strang, and Daniel J. Woods. 2000. *Recidivism Patterns in the Canberra Reintegrative Shaming Experiments (RISE)*. Canberra: Centre for Restorative Justice, Australian National University.

Sherman, Lawrence W., and David Weisburd. 1995. "General Deterrent Effects of Police Patrol in Crime 'Hot Spots': A Randomized Controlled Trial." *Justice Quarterly* 12:625–48.

Short, James F., Margaret A. Zahn, and David P. Farrington. 2000. "Experimental Research in Criminal Justice Settings: Is There a Role for Scholarly Societies?" *Crime and Delinquency* 46:295–98.

Skardhamar, Torbjorn. 2010. "Distinguishing Facts and Artifacts in Group-Based Modeling." *Criminology* 48:295–320.

Sontheimer, Henry, and Lynne Goodstein. 1993. "An Evaluation of Juvenile Intensive Aftercare Probation: Aftercare versus System Response Effects." *Justice Quarterly* 10:197–227.

Soothill, Keith L., and Trevor C. N. Gibbens. 1978. "Recidivism of Sex Offenders: A Reappraisal." *British Journal of Criminology* 18:267–76.

Stattin, Hakan, Margaret Kerr, and Lars R. Bergman. 2010. "On the Utility of Moffitt's Typology: Trajectories in Long-Term Perspective." *European Journal of Criminology* 7:1–25.

Stickle, Wendy P., Nadine M. Connell, Denise M. Wilson, and Denise C. Gottfredson. 2008. "An Experimental Evaluation of Teen Courts." *Journal of Experimental Criminology* 4:137–63.

Strang, Heather, and Lawrence W. Sherman. 2006. "Restorative Justice to Reduce Victimization." In *Preventing Crime: What Works for Children, Offenders, Victims, and Places*, edited by Brandon C. Welsh and David P. Farrington. New York: Springer.

Taylor, Bruce, Christopher S. Koper, and Daniel J. Woods. 2011. "A Randomized Controlled Trial of Different Policing Strategies at Hot Spots of Violent Crime." *Journal of Experimental Criminology* 7:149–81.

Theobald, Delphine, and David P. Farrington. 2009. "Effects of Getting Married on Offending: Results from a Prospective Longitudinal Survey of Males." *European Journal of Criminology* 6:496–516.

———. 2011. "Why Do the Crime-Reducing Effects of Marriage Vary with Age?" *British Journal of Criminology* 51:136–58.

Thornberry, Terence P. 1989. "Panel Effects and the Use of Self-Reported Measures of Delinquency in Longitudinal Studies." In *Cross-National Research in Self-Reported Crime and Delinquency*, edited by Malcom W. Klein. Dordrecht, Neth.: Kluwer.

Thornberry, Terence P., Adrienne Freeman-Gallant, and Peter J. Lovegrove. 2009. "Intergenerational Linkages in Antisocial Behaviour." *Criminal Behaviour and Mental Health* 19:80–93.

Thornberry, Terence P., Alan J. Lizotte, Marvin D. Krohn, Carolyn A. Smith, and Pamela K. Porter. 2003. "Causes and Consequences of Delinquency: Findings from the Rochester Youth Development Study." In *Taking Stock of Delinquency: An Overview of Findings from Contemporary Longitudinal Studies*, edited by Terence P. Thornberry and Marvin D. Krohn. New York: Kluwer/ Plenum.

Tolan, Patrick H., Deborah Gorman-Smith, and David B. Henry. 2003. "The Developmental Ecology of Urban Males' Youth Violence." *Developmental Psychology* 39:274–91.

Tolan, Patrick, David Henry, Michael Schoeny, and Arin Bass. 2008. "Mentoring Interventions to Affect Juvenile Delinquency and Associated Problems." Campbell Systematic Reviews 2008:16. http://www.campbell collaboration.org.

Tong, L. S. Joy, and David P. Farrington. 2006. "How Effective Is the 'Reasoning and Rehabilitation' Program in Reducing Reoffending? A Meta-Analysis of Evaluations in Four Countries." *Psychology, Crime, and Law* 11: 3–24.

———. 2008. "Effectiveness of 'Reasoning and Rehabilitation' in Reducing Offending." *Psicothema* 20:20–28.

Tonry, Michael, Lloyd E. Ohlin, and David P. Farrington. 1991. *Human Development and Criminal Behavior: New Ways of Advancing Knowledge*. New York: Springer-Verlag.

Tremblay, Richard E., Louise C. Masse, Linda Pagani, and Frank Vitaro. 1996. "From Childhood Physical Aggression to Adolescent Maladjustment: The Montreal Prevention Experiment." In *Preventing Childhood Disorders, Substance Use, and Delinquency*, edited by Ray D. Peters and Robert J. McMahon. Thousand Oaks, CA: Sage.

Tremblay, Richard E., Linda Pagani-Kurtz, Louise C. Mâsse, Frank Vitaro, and Robert O. Pihl. 1995. "A Bimodal Preventive Intervention for Disruptive Kindergarten Boys: Its Impact through Mid-Adolescence." *Journal of Consulting and Clinical Psychology* 63:560–68.

Van Voorhis, Patricia, Lisa M. Spruance, Neal P. Ritchey, Shelley J. Listwan, and Renita Seabrook. 2004. "The Georgia Cognitive Skills Experiment: A Replication of Reasoning and Rehabilitation." *Criminal Justice and Behavior* 31:282–305.

Vaughn, Michael G., Kevin M. Beaver, and Matt DeLisi. 2009. "A General Biosocial Paradigm of Antisocial Behavior: A Preliminary Test in a Sample of Adolescents." *Youth Violence and Juvenile Justice* 7:279–98.

Venezia, Peter S. 1972. "Unofficial Probation: An Evaluation of Its Effectiveness." *Journal of Research in Crime and Delinquency* 9:149–70.

Vitaro, Frank, Mara Brendgen, and Richard E. Tremblay. 2001. "Preventive Intervention: Assessing Its Effects on the Trajectories of Delinquency and Testing for Mediational Processes." *Applied Developmental Science* 5:201–13.

Wadsworth, Michael. 1979. *Roots of Delinquency: Infancy, Adolescence, and Crime*. London: Martin Robertson.

Waldo, Gordon P., and Theodore G. Chiricos. 1977. "Work Release and Recidivism: An Empirical Evaluation of a Social Policy." *Evaluation Quarterly* 1:87–108.

Wasserman, Gail A., and Laurie S. Miller. 1998. "The Prevention of Serious and Violent Juvenile Offending." In *Serious and Violent Juvenile Offenders: Risk Factors and Successful Interventions*, edited by Rolf Loeber and David P. Farrington. Thousand Oaks, CA: Sage.

Weisburd, David, and Charlotte Gill. 2013. "Block Randomized Trials at Places: Rethinking the Limitations of Small N Experiments." *Journal of Quantitative Criminology*, forthcoming.

Weisburd, David, and Lorraine Green. 1995. "Policing Drug Hot Spots: The Jersey City Drug Market Analysis Experiment." *Justice Quarterly* 12:711–35.

Weisburd, David, Elizabeth R. Groff, and Sue-Ming Yang. 2012. *The Criminology of Place: Street Segments and Our Understanding of the Crime Problem*. Oxford: Oxford University Press.

Weisburd, David, Anthony Petrosino, and Gail Mason. 1993. "Design Sensitivity in Criminal Justice Experiments." In *Crime and Justice: A Review of Research*, vol. 17, edited by Michael Tonry. Chicago: University of Chicago Press.

Welsh, Brandon C., Christopher J. Sullivan, and David L. Olds. 2010. "When Early Crime Prevention Goes to Scale: A New Look at the Evidence." *Prevention Science* 11:115–25.

Werner, Emmy E., and Ruth S. Smith. 2001. *Journeys from Childhood to Midlife.* Ithaca, NY: Cornell University Press.

West, Donald J., and David P. Farrington. 1973. *Who Becomes Delinquent?* London: Heinemann.

Westinghouse Learning Corporation and Ohio University. 1969. *The Impact of Head Start Experience on Children's Cognitive and Affective Development.* PB 184328. Springfield, VA: US Department of Commerce Clearinghouse.

Wiesner, Margit, Deborah M. Capaldi, and Hyoun K. Kim. 2010. "Arrests, Recent Life Circumstances, and Recurrent Job Loss for At-Risk Young Men: An Event-History Analysis." *Journal of Vocational Behavior* 76:344–54.

Wikström, Per-Olof H., Dietrich Oberwittler, Kyle Treiber, and Beth Hardie. 2012. *Breaking Rules: The Social and Situational Dynamics of Young People's Urban Crime.* Oxford: Oxford University Press.

Williams, Mark. 1970. *A Study of Some Aspects of Borstal Allocation.* London: Home Office Prison Department, Office of the Chief Psychologist.

———. 1975. "Aspects of the Psychology of Imprisonment." In *The Use of Imprisonment,* edited by Sean McConville. London: Routledge.

Wilson, David B., and Doris L. MacKenzie. 2006. "Boot Camps." In *Preventing Crime: What Works for Children, Offenders, Victims, and Places,* edited by Brandon C. Welsh and David P. Farrington. Dordrecht, Neth.: Springer.

Witkin, Herman A., et al. 1976. "Criminality in XYY and XXY Men." *Science* 193:547–55.

Wolfgang, Marvin E. 1973. "Crime in a Birth Cohort." *Proceedings of the American Philosophical Society* 117:404–11.

Wolfgang, Marvin E., Robert M. Figlio, and Thorsten Sellin. 1972. *Delinquency in a Birth Cohort.* Chicago: University of Chicago Press.

Wolfgang, Marvin E., Terence P. Thornberry, and Robert M. Figlio. 1987. *From Boy to Man, from Delinquency to Crime.* Chicago: University of Chicago Press.

Wortman, Camille B., and Vita C. Rabinowitz. 1979. "Random Assignment: The Fairest of Them All." In *Evaluation Studies Review Annual,* vol. 4, edited by Lee N. Sechrest, Stephen G. West, Melinda A. Phillips, Robin Redner, and William Yeaton. Beverly Hills, CA: Sage.

Zara, Georgia, and David P. Farrington. 2009. "Childhood and Adolescent Predictors of Late Onset Criminal Careers." *Journal of Youth and Adolescence* 38:287–300.

Index

ACA. *See* Affordable Care Act
acquired immunodeficiency syndrome. *See* AIDS
ADHD. *See* attention deficit hyperactivity disorder
Affordable Care Act (ACA), 121
African Americans: Cincinnati incident, 235; DiIulio projections and, 275; drug offenses, 75, 91, 123; guns and, 29; longitudinal studies, 459t, 462, 473, 494t, 503; marijuana arrests and, 91; Obama and, 85; Perry Project and, 497–98; racial stereotyping, 318, 331; risk factors and, 473; war on drugs and, 121
age-crime curves, 182–83, 466, 501
AIDS, 98, 99, 101, 105, 106, 107, 108
alcohol, 79, 98; antisocial behavior and, 461, 469; Big Brothers Big Sisters program and, 488; drugs and, 78; drunk driving, 214, 247, 251; juvenile crime and, 497; marijuana and, 96, 98; prohibition, 79
Andenaes model, 234–35
Andrews, D. A., 234–35, 305, 337, 338, 339, 342, 345, 346, 360. *See also* risk-need-responsivity model
Anti–Drug Abuse Act (1986), 159, 161
antisocial behavior: ADHD and,

471; alcohol and, 461, 469; Anti-social Behaviour Orders initiative, 9; child abuse, 457; criminal behavior and, 306, 461, 489; longitudinal studies, 497, 500, 504, 505; origins of, 353, 457, 468, 470, 473; RNR model and, 341, 342, 343; trajectories of, 468, 469; U.K. National Survey, 469
Arizona, 155, 246, 250
assault: aggravated, 40, 268; assassinations, 7, 24t, 25, 29, 30, 321; crime categories, 387; domestic, 407–8; FBI reporting system, 40–41; frequency of, 29, 268, 268f; guns and (*see* guns); homicide (*see* homicide); on public figures, 29 (*see also* assassinations); resistance to, 58; robbery and, 32, 49, 57t, 179, 268; sexual, 212, 243; types of weapons, 30–31, 286 (*see also* guns); waiver trials, 168; youth and, 41, 263, 268, 270, 271, 271f, 290 (*see also* juveniles)
ATF. *See* Bureau of Alcohol, Tobacco, Firearms and Explosives
attention deficit hyperactivity disorder (ADHD), 471, 500

Barr, W., 162
Bayesian updating model, 248–49
Beccaria, C., 170, 205, 206, 207, 213, 225, 252